QUICK REFERENCE TABLE OF CONTENTS

PERSONAL FINANCE

PERSONAL FINANCE

Second Edition

JACK R. KAPOOR
College of DuPage

LES R. DLABAY
Lake Forest College

ROBERT J. HUGHES
Richland College

IRWIN

Homewood, IL 60430
Boston, MA 02116

© RICHARD D. IRWIN, INC., 1988 and 1991

Cover illustration: Bob Conge

Sponsoring editor: Michael W. Junior
Developmental editor: Ann Sass
Project editor: Paula M. Buschman
Production manager: Ann Cassady
Designer: Tara L. Bazata
Artist: Mark Swindle
Compositor: Carlisle Communications, Ltd.
Typeface: 10/12 New Caledonia
Printer: Von Hoffmann Press, Inc.

Library of Congress Cataloging-in-Publication Data
Kapoor, Jack R.
    Personal finance / Jack R. Kapoor, Les R. Dlabay, Robert J.
Hughes. — 2nd ed.
        p.   cm.
    Includes index.
    ISBN 0-256-07905-6
    1. Finance, Personal,   I. Dlabay, Les R.   II. Hughes, Robert
James, 1946–   .   III.   Title.
HG179.K37   1991
332.024 — dc20

                                                    90–4994
                                                     CIP

Printed in the United States of America
1 2 3 4 5 6 7 8 9 0 VH 7 6 5 4 3 2 1 0

To my parents, Ram and Sheila Kapoor; my wife, Theresa; and my children, Karen, Kathryn, and Dave

To my parents, Les and Mary Dlabay; my wife, Linda; and my children, Carissa and Kyle

To my mother, Barbara Y. Hughes; and my wife, Peggy

Preface

In recent years, significant economic and social developments have influenced the personal financial planning environment. Spending, saving, borrowing, and investing decisions are now frequently affected by the following:

- The changing structure of our economy, along with variable interest rates, consumer prices, and employment opportunities.
- Changes in the patterns of American families, with increases in the number of dual-income, single-parent, one-person, and mixed-generation households.
- Expanded financial services and investment opportunities as a result of deregulation of financial institutions and foreign business.
- Technological advances that have fostered new financial products, delivery systems, and access to information for improved personal financial decision making.

These developments form the basis for the selection and organization of the material contained in this edition of *Personal Finance*.

TEXT THEMES

In an effort to address the changing environment for financial planning, this edition emphasizes the following themes:

- *Decision making and opportunity costs.* Starting in Chapter 1, and continuing throughout the text, the evaluation of alternatives and trade-offs is highlighted.
- *Quantitative analysis of personal financial decisions.* Again starting in Chapter 1, emphasis is placed on the many analytic aspects of assessing financial choices. (See inside front cover for complete list.)
- *Personal financial planning needs for contemporary life situations.* The increasingly numerous single-parent, two-income, and mixed-generation households require a contemporary, flexible approach to financial planning. Moreover, the life situation emphasis in this text recognizes that even traditional households must adapt to such events as marriage, childbirth, career changes, health difficulties, retirement, and the death of household members.

NEW TO THIS EDITION

The second edition of *Personal Finance* has been thoroughly updated; it presents expanded coverage of important personal finance issues, focuses on differing personal lifestyles, and contains many pedagogical features.

To better serve the educational needs of students, the following additions and revisions are offered in this edition of *Personal Finance:*

- A completely revised Chapter 1 emphasizes decision making, opportunity costs, and the economic and social environment of financial planning. The basic explanations of future and present value calculations are presented to stress the financial aspects of opportunity cost and the personal economic trade-offs associated with a financial decision. Chapter 1 also provides an introduction to the financial planning process, the components of financial planning, and the development of a financial plan.
- Chapter 2 continues to address the needs of people in the process of establishing careers, while also emphasizing the needs of people who are interested in changing careers or advancing in their current field. Chapter 2 also includes techniques for assessing a compensation package and for comparing the value of employee benefits.
- New exhibits in Chapter 3 offer clear explanations of the processes involved in creating a personal balance sheet and cash flow statement. Chapter 3 also includes an expanded discussion of the budgeting process and possible budget allocations for different life situations.
- The tax chapter, now Chapter 4, contains five main areas: (1) the relationship of taxes to personal financial planning, (2) income tax fundamentals, (3) the process of completing Form 1040 and Schedule A, (4) tax information sources and the auditing process, and (5) tax planning strategies.
- Chapters 6 and 7 explore the financial and personal opportunity costs of using consumer credit including the debt payments-to-income ratio and debt-to-equity ratio to measure credit capacity. In addition, the appendix to Chapter 7 presents additional methods used to calculate interest by consumer credit providers. The key formulas in Chapters 7, 15, and 17 are summarized in tables at the end of those chapters.
- Because most people rent housing at some point in their lives, Chapter 9 includes expanded coverage of rental options, procedures, and agreements.

- Chapter 11 continues to stress the importance of financial trade-offs in choosing insurance coverages as well as the concept of self-insurance.
- In Chapter 13, rising health care costs, sources of disability insurance, and methods of determining disability income insurance needs are discussed.
- Several methods of determining life insurance needs—the easy method, the Dink (Dual Income No Kids) method, the nonworking spouse method, and the thorough method—are explored in Chapter 14. The chapter continues to expand on the theme of time value of money and the opportunity costs involved in determining the cost of insurance.
- A separate chapter on mutual funds provides expanded coverage of an investment vehicle that is frequently used for portfolio diversification.
- "Financial Planning in Action" features provide formats for the analysis of various decisions in relation to the "Financial Planning Process" flowchart discussed in Chapter 1.
- "Financial Planning Calculations" highlight specific analytical approaches to financial planning decisions.
- The *Personal Financial Planner,* provided at no cost to each student who purchases a book through Richard D. Irwin, is a 70-page planning tool for developing and implementing a comprehensive personal financial plan.

TEXT FEATURES

Everything in the second edition of *Personal Finance* is designed to help instructors be more effective and to help students do better in class. It all starts with learning objectives, which spell out what is expected of the student in each chapter. As students read material, the learning objectives are repeated at each major section. At the end of the chapter, the learning objectives appear again within the summary and next to the Discussion Questions and Problems and Activities sections.

Key Personal Financial Calculations and Decisions

The front inside cover presents a summary of the more than 70 analytic topics covered in the text. The back inside cover provides an easy reference for locating the text material on a specific personal financial decision.

Chapter Format

Each chapter has been designed to present its content in a clear and motivating manner. The major features of each chapter are

- A chapter overview and a list of the chapter's behavioral learning objectives.
- An opening case that introduces the content of the chapter through a real-world situation. Questions related to this case appear at the end of the chapter.
- Essay and financial analysis features that expand the content of the chapter. These features appear under the headings "Personal Finance Journal," "Financial Planning in Action," and "Financial Planning Calculations."
- A chapter summary that reviews the content for each of the chapter's learning objectives.
- A chapter glossary that defines the key terms in the chapter.
- Discussion questions that are tied to the learning objectives and review the chapter's key ideas and expand its main topic areas.
- Problems and activities that are tied to the learning objectives and provide opportunities to use chapter material in various types of settings.
- Life situation cases that allow students to apply their financial planning skills to real-world situations.
- A list of supplementary readings that expand upon the content of the chapter.

End-of-Part Cases

At the end of Chapters 4, 7, 10, 14, 19, and 21 are comprehensive cases. Each of the situations described in these cases encompasses a number of financial planning concepts and gives students a basis for practicing their decision-making skills.

Appendixes

These end-of-text appendixes supplement the main content: "Using a Financial Planner and Other Financial Planning Information Sources," "The Time Value of Money: Future Value and Present Value Calculations," "Using a Personal Computer for Personal Financial Planning," and "Consumer Agencies and Organizations." The practical information contained in these appendixes can enhance the personal financial decision-making process.

INSTRUCTIONAL SUPPLEMENTS

The integrated teaching-learning package for *Personal Finance* consists of the following materials:

- *Personal Financial Planner.* This publication, packaged free with every book purchased through Richard D. Irwin, is a 70-page planning tool for developing and implementing a personal financial plan.
- *Student Resource Manual.* This study guide is designed for the review and application of concepts developed in the text. Each chapter of the manual contains a chapter overview, a pretest, self-guided study questions, a post-test, problems, applications, and cases. The manual also includes recent articles on personal financial planning topics from *The Wall Street Journal;* each of these articles is accompanied by study questions.
- *Instructor's Manual with Lecture Guide.* The first section of this publication is the "Course Planning Guide," which offers suggestions for instructional strategies, course projects, supplementary readings, and teaching resources. The "Chapter Teaching Materials" section provides a chapter overview, a list of learning objectives with content summaries, introductory activities, detailed lecture outlines with teaching ideas, concluding activities, ready-to-duplicate quizzes, supplementary lecture materials and activities, and answers to end-of-chapter questions, problems, and cases.
- *Color Transparencies.* Forty ready-to-use color transparencies covering the major content of each text chapter are available. Each of these transparencies has a one-page teaching note that provides the text page reference, points to highlight, discussion questions, and a suggested supplementary exercise. These teaching notes are packaged with the transparency masters.

- *Transparency Masters.* Over 100 ready-to-duplicate transparency masters may be used for class presentations or as handouts for student note-taking.
- *Manual of Tests.* The testing program for *Personal Finance* consists of over 1,400 true-false, multiple-choice, and essay/case questions. These test items are organized by the learning objectives for each chapter. Answers, text page references, and difficulty level are provided.
- *CompuTest 3.* The test items are also available on disks for IBM-compatible and Apple personal computer systems to allow the easy creation of tests based on text chapter, type of question, and difficulty level. *CompuTest 3* makes it possible to combine your own questions with those created by the authors of *Personal Finance.* The system can be used to edit existing questions and create up to 99 versions of each test. It accepts graphics, allows password protection of saved tests and question databases, and is networkable.
- *Teletest.* By far the easiest way to generate an exam is to use Teletest. Teletest is a service that will create a master copy of an exam. All you have to do is call 1-800-331-5094. You can ask for specific questions, by number, on the exam or ask for questions covering various issues at different levels of learning to be randomly selected. You will get your exam within a few days.
- *Personal Finance Software.* Free master disks are available to adopters. The personal computer software (IBM compatible) that accompanies *Personal Finance* consists of two disks. The spreadsheet template disk, designed for use with Lotus 1-2-3®, contains worksheets for handling over 40 financial planning calculations. The self-contained tutorial disk, designed for use with MS-DOS or PC-DOS systems, offers over 30 financial planning routines and two interactive cases. The instructor's manual for *Personal Finance* presents detailed operating instructional activities, sample problems, and application exercises.
- *Personal Finance Videos.* The video supplement to *Personal Finance* offers presentations to enhance the teaching-learning process.

Each video segment is accompanied by a "Viewing Guide" that contains a synopsis of its content, discussion questions, and suggestions for follow-up activities.

ACKNOWLEDGMENTS

We would like to express our appreciation to the colleagues who provided extensive comments on this edition of *Personal Finance* and suggestions for its development.

Robert Moorman
Texas A & M University

David R. Pingree, Jr.
University of Utah

Vickie Hampton
University of Texas, Austin

Thomas Arcuri
Florida Community College at Jacksonville

Joan S. Ryan
Lane Community College

Peter M. Gladhart
Michigan State University

Jeannette R. Jesinger
University of Nevada, Las Vegas

Claudia M. Hyatt
Western Carolina University

S. E. Spence
Central Texas College

Anthony J. Campolo
Columbus State Community College

We would also like to express our appreciation to those who helped make the first edition a successful endeavor and to the many Personal Finance teachers who responded to surveys and correspondence.

Doris Ackerman
Western Montana College

Joyce Alman
Aquinas College

Richard Ammon
Mercer University

Thomas Arcuri
Florida Community College

Bill Bailey
Casper College

Paul Bates
Gannon University

Homer Benton
Pacific Christian College

Bettie Clemans
Central Arizona College

Mary Dickerson
San Diego State University

Chet Duckhorn
Fresno City College

Robert Ek
Seminole Community College

James Evans
Johnson County Community College

Carol Fethke
University of Iowa

Vicki Fitzsimmons
University of Illinois

Robert Flammang
Louisiana State University A & M

Aurelia Gomez
Glendale Community College

Jim Hagel
Grand Valley State College

Marcy Hall
College of the Sequoias

Paul Joice
Walla Walla College

Virginia Junk
University of Idaho

Robert Kegel
Cypress College

James Kopel
Black Hawk College

Jerry Leadham
Clackamas Community College

Tom Livingston
College of Charleston

William Marrs
Vincennes University

Gerri Miller
Joliet Junior College

W. Aubrey Morrow
University of California, San Diego

Larry Pagel
St. Cloud State University

John Palipchak
Penn State University

Barbara Pershing
University of Northern Iowa

Jeanne Peters
University of Nevada

David R. Pingree, Jr.
University of Utah

Pat Quinn
University of Wisconsin, Superior

Judy Ramaglia
Pacific Lutheran University

Shirley Reagan
Louisiana Tech University

Joan S. Ryan
Lane Community College

Daniel Schneid
Central Michigan University

Donna Selnick
California State University

Cindy Van Gelderen
Aquinas College

Rosemary Walker
Michigan State University

Jane Wiese
Valencia Community College

We are also indebted to the professionals who provided their expertise in the development of this book's content.

Gene Monterastelli
State Farm Insurance

George Wysocki
CenTrust Mortgage Company

Many talented editorial, production, and marketing professionals at Richard D. Irwin have contributed to the success of *Personal Finance*. We are especially grateful to Mike Junior, Sponsoring Editor, and Ann Sass, Developmental Editor, for their inspiration, patience, and friendship. We also express our appreciation to the individuals at Richard D. Irwin with whom we had frequent contact, including Paula Buschman, Tara Bazata, Randy Haubner, Tammy Szajerski, John Biernat, Herb Licon, Brian Murray, Bruce Powell, Jeff Shelstad, Kathy Sutherland, and Clark White. A special note of thanks to Mitch Meyer for his work on our financial planning spreadsheet templates. In addition, Jack Kapoor expresses his appreciation to his daughter, Kathryn, and son, Dave, for their typing, proofreading, and research assistance. Finally, we thank our wives and families for their patience, understanding, and encouragement throughout the project.

Jack R. Kapoor
Les R. Dlabay
Robert J. Hughes

A NOTE TO STUDENTS

Since many fundamentals of successful personal financial management remain constant, we are sure you will find this book a valuable reference for many years. Best wishes for a satisfying and fulfilling personal and financial existence.

Contents

• •

PART II

Managing Your Personal Finances

PART IV

Insuring Your Resources

• •

PART V

Investing Your Financial Resources

· ·

PART VI

Controlling Your Financial Future

PERSONAL FINANCE

I

Planning Your Personal Finances

Part I of *Personal Finance* provides the foundation for studying and applying personal financial planning techniques. In Chapter 1, we discuss financial decision making in relation to the personal, social, and economic factors that influence choices. We also offer

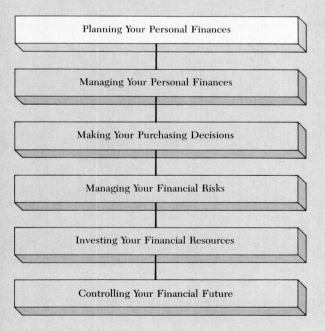

a complete overview of the financial planning environment and a framework for making personal financial decisions. Next, in Chapter 2, we present practical assistance for gaining financial independence and personal fulfillment through careful career planning. We also discuss the need for continuing education as the work environment evolves because of technological and social changes. In Chapter 3, we focus on financial recordkeeping and budgeting techniques. The guidelines given will help you develop a spending and savings plan that meets your unique needs and goals. The practical suggestions offered will help you improve your handling of financial records. Budgeting will not change the basic realities of income and expenses, but wise planning can assist you in maximizing your personal economic satisfaction. Finally, in Chapter 4, we provide an overview of taxes in relation to financial planning along with the fundamentals for preparing your federal income tax return. Part I consists of

Chapter 1   Personal Financial Planning: An Introduction
Chapter 2   Personal Career Strategies
Chapter 3   Money Management Strategy: Financial Statements and Budgeting
Chapter 4   Planning Your Tax Strategy

1 Personal Financial Planning
An Introduction

Financial decisions are an integral part of everyone's life. Most people want to handle their finances so that they can get as much satisfaction as possible from each available dollar. Typical financial goals include such things as a new car, a luxury apartment, advanced career training, extended travel, and the assurance of self-sufficiency during our working and retirement years. To achieve these and other goals, however, we need to identify and set priorities. Financial and personal satisfaction are the result of an organized process that is commonly referred to as personal money management or personal financial planning.

LEARNING OBJECTIVES
After studying this chapter, you will be able to

L.O.1 Analyze the process of making personal financial decisions.

L.O.2 Determine the personal and financial opportunity costs associated with personal financial decisions.

L.O.3 Assess the personal, social, and economic factors that influence the personal financial planning environment.

L.O.4 Identify the steps involved in personal financial planning.

L.O.5 Determine possible strategies for achieving personal financial goals for different life situations.

OPENING CASE

Winners Can Still Be Losers°

Poor personal financial management is the most important cause of bankruptcy and the greatest cause of anxiety in American households. Consider the case of Erika Earnhart of Lexington Park, Maryland, who won $1 million in the Maryland lottery. Erika says she is in debt, lives in a trailer park, and is unable to work because of a knee injury.

"I thought I'd be on easy street the rest of my life," said Erika. "Now I live from April to April. I admit I've had some fun, but it's not everything it's cracked up to be."

Each April, Erika receives her annual $50,000 check, a prize guaranteed for 20 years. Erika spent the first $50,000 on a four-bedroom house, gifts of money to her parents and sister, a Volkswagen, and some travel. She did not pay taxes on this money, so when her second check came, she had to pay $18,000 in taxes on the first year's winnings plus advance taxes for the second year. Consequently, the second annual windfall immediately plunged from $50,000 to about $20,000.

Now—after two divorces, a still unresolved child custody case, two knee operations without any health insurance to defray costs, and moves to Michigan, Colorado, California, and back to Maryland—Erika is broke. She sold her house and lives in a nearly new, extra-wide trailer. She visits her bank frequently. The bank vice president does not even ask Erika the purpose of her visit. He knows that Erika is borrowing against her next lottery check, and he just needs to know what amount she wants to withdraw.

"When I got this year's check, I already owed the bank $10,000," she said.

There are still several checks to come, but Erika said that if she had known what would happen after she won the million dollars, "I'd have torn up the ticket or put it in someone else's name." Still she continues to play the Maryland lottery periodically in the hope of winning again, "to pay off my debts."

Erika's financial woes demonstrate that using money effectively is one of the biggest problems in the lifetime of any individual or family. But personal financial planning and money management are skills that can be learned, developed, and enjoyed.

The job of managing your money is lifelong. Some people do it well and live smoothly and pleasantly, free from monetary cares and worries. They enjoy the pleasures and satisfactions of a full life. Others ineptly stumble from one financial mess to the next. They never seem to solve their personal financial problems. Some families can live comfortably and save money on an annual income of $30,000. Others, with annual incomes of more than $100,000, can't make ends meet. Most of us work hard for our money. We should make an additional effort to see that it is managed and used wisely.

°Adapted from "'I'm Broke,' Says Winner of Lottery," *Chicago Tribune*, October 11, 1984, sec. 1A, p. 32.

Personal financial planning is the process of managing your money to achieve personal economic satisfaction. This planning process allows you to take control of your financial situation. Every person or family has a unique financial position, and any financial activity must therefore also be unique—that is, carefully planned to meet specific needs and goals.

MAKING FINANCIAL DECISIONS

L.O.1
Analyze the process of making personal financial decisions.

Every day, we each make hundreds of decisions. Most of these decisions are quite simple and have few consequences, but others are complex and have long-term effects on your personal and financial existence. Making decisions is something that everyone does, but few people consider how to do it better. The decision-making process is a logical procedure (see Exhibit 1–1) with the following major elements:

1. Identification of the basic problem, or the need to make a decision.
2. Generation of alternative courses of action.
3. Consideration of the personal, social, and economic factors that influence the decision.

EXHIBIT 1–1   The Personal Decision-Making Process

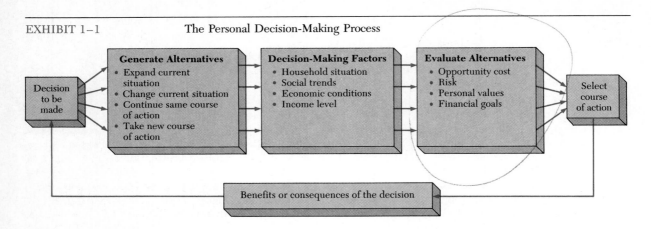

4. Evaluation of the alternative courses of action and selection of the most appropriate course.
5. Implementation and evaluation of the course selected along with other decisions.

Decision making is a circular, ongoing process in which your current decisions will influence your future choices. For example, your ability to meet your future need for larger housing may be influenced by your current decision regarding the purchase of a car. To save money for a house purchase, you may decide to buy a used car or a less expensive new car.

Creating and considering alternatives are crucial to making good decisions. Although many external factors influence the available alternatives, your possible courses of action usually fall into these categories:

- Expand the current situation.
- Change the current situation.
- Continue the same course of action.
- Take a new course of action.

These categories may not all apply to every decision situation, but possible causes of action are likely to fall within one or more of them. For example, if you want to stop working full-time to go to school, you must generate several alternatives under the category "Take a new course of action."

Creativity in decision making is vital to effective choices. Considering all of the possible alternatives will help you make more effective and satisfying decisions. Most people believe that they must have a car to get to work or school. But other alternatives—public transportation, car pool, renting, shared ownership, company car—should also be considered.

Consequences of Our Choices

Every decision closes off alternatives. For example, a decision to purchase stock as an investment may mean that you cannot take a vacation. Or a decision to go to school full-time may mean that you cannot work full-time. **Opportunity cost** is what a person gives up by making a choice. This cost, commonly referred to as the *trade-off* of a decision, sometimes cannot be measured in dollars. It may refer to the money you lose by attending school rather than working; but it may also

EXHIBIT 1–2
Types of Risk

Inflation Risk

Rising prices may result in lost buying power. You must decide whether to buy something now or later. If you buy it later, you may have to pay more for it.

Interest-Rate Risk

Changing interest rates affect your costs (when you borrow) and your benefits (when you save or invest). Borrowing at a low interest rate if higher interest rates follow can be to your advantage. But if you buy when interest rates are dropping, you will earn less interest if you buy a six-month savings certificate rather than a certificate with a longer maturity.

Economic Risk

You can lose your job as a result of such things as changes in consumer spending. Individuals who face the risk of unemployment need to save while employed or to acquire skills that they can use to obtain a different type of work.

Personal Risk

Various tangible and intangible factors may create a less than desirable situation. Purchasing a certain brand or from a certain store may entail the risk of having to obtain repairs at an inconvenient location. Personal risk may also be in the form of the health, safety, or additional costs associated with various purchases or financial decisions.

refer to the time you spend shopping around to compare brands for a major purchase. In either case, the resources you give up (money or time) have a value that is lost.

Decision making will be an ongoing part of your personal and financial existence. Thus, you will need to consider the lost opportunities that result from your decisions. Since decisions vary based on each person's situation and values, opportunity costs will be different for each person. Some people value their time too highly to do extensive comparison shopping. Satisfying personal decisions are based on the various opportunity costs associated with financial activities.

Evaluation of Risk

Uncertainty is a part of every decision. Selecting a college major and a career field involves a high degree of risk. What if you do not like working in this field or cannot obtain employment in it? Other types of decisions involve a very low degree of risk. Very little risk is associated with putting money in a savings account or with purchasing items that cost only a few dollars. Your chances of losing something of great value are low in these situations.

In many financial decisions, identifying (see Exhibit 1–2) and evaluating risk is a difficult task. The best way to consider risk in such decisions is to gather information based on your experiences and those of others and on the research of financial planning sources.

Financial Planning Information Sources

Relevant information is required at each stage of the decision-making process. This book provides the informational basis you need to make decisions in the area of personal financial planning. Due to changing personal, social, and economic conditions, you will need to continually supplement and update your knowledge.

EXHIBIT 1–3   Financial Planning Information Sources

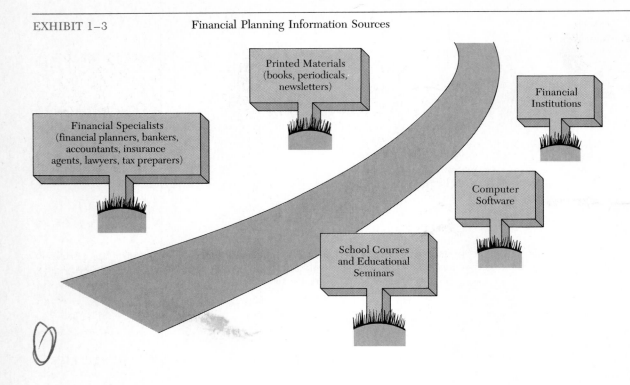

Exhibit 1–3 offers an overview of the informational resources available to assist you in making personal financial decisions. In addition, Appendix A, "Using a Financial Planner and Other Financial Planning Information Sources," provides supplementary details regarding this topic.

OPPORTUNITY COSTS AND THE TIME VALUE OF MONEY

L.O.2
Determine the personal and financial opportunity costs associated with personal financial decisions.

In every financial decision, you will sacrifice something in order to obtain something else that you consider more desirable. For example, you might forgo current consumption in order to invest funds for future purchases or long-term financial security. Or you might gain the use of an expensive item now by making credit payments from future earnings. In either case, you should carefully consider the trade-off between the alternatives. Opportunity costs may be viewed in terms of both personal and financial resources (see Exhibit 1–4).

Personal Opportunity Costs

The most common personal opportunity cost is time. Time spent in studying, working, or shopping cannot be used for other activities. You should analyze your use of such personal resources as time in light of your values and goals.

Financial Opportunity Costs

Like time, money used in one way cannot be used in other ways. Thus, you are constantly making choices among various financial decisions. In making those choices, you must consider the **time value of money**—the increases in an amount of money as a result of interest earned. Saving or investing a dollar instead

EXHIBIT 1–4
Opportunity Costs and
Financial Decision Making

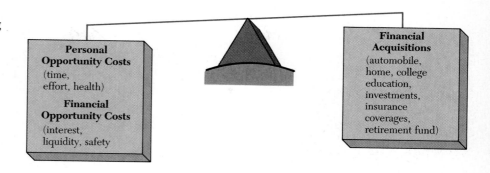

of spending it today would yield a future amount greater than a dollar. Every time you spend, save, invest, or borrow money, you need to consider the time value of that money as an opportunity cost. Spending money in your savings account means lost interest earnings, but what you buy with that money may have a higher priority than those earnings. Borrowing to make a purchase involves the opportunity cost of paying interest on the loan, but your current needs or desires may make this trade-off worthwhile.

The opportunity cost of the time value of money is also present in these financial decisions:

- The lower interest earned from a savings plan with little or no risk as compared with the potentially higher return from an investment with greater risk.
- The lost interest on your tax refund if too much money is withheld from your paycheck.
- The growth value of annual deposits in a retirement fund.
- The future savings on energy and maintenance when a new automobile or home appliance is purchased.

Three items are used to calculate the time value of money for savings in the form of interest earned:

- The amount of the savings.
- The annual interest rate.
- The length of time that the money is on deposit.

These three items are multiplied to obtain the amount of interest. The interest formula is as follows:

| Amount in savings | times | The annual interest rate | times | Time period | equals | Interest |

For example, $500 on deposit for six months at 6 percent would earn $15 ($500 × 0.06 × 6/12, or ½ year).

The increased value of your money from interest earned can be viewed in two ways. You can calculate the total amount that will be available in the future, or you can determine the current value of an amount desired in the future.

Future Value   Deposited money earns interest that will increase over time. **Future value,** also referred to as *compounding,* is the amount to which current savings will increase based on a certain interest rate and a certain time period. For example, $100 deposited in a 6 percent account for one year will grow to $106. This amount is computed as follows:

Future value = $100 + ($100 × 0.06 × 1 year) = $106

Original	Amount of
amount in	interest
savings	earned

The same process could be continued for a second, third, and fourth year, but the computations are time consuming. To simplify the process, future value tables are available (see Exhibit 1–5). To use a future value table, multiply the amount of savings by the factor for the desired interest rate and time period. For example, $650 at 8 percent for 12 years would have a future value of $1,636.70 ($650 × 2.518). The future value of an amount will always be greater than the original amount. As seen in Exhibit 1–5, the future value factors are all larger than one.

To determine the future value of equal yearly savings deposits, use Exhibit 1–6. For this table to be used, the deposits must earn a constant interest rate. A person who deposits $50 a year at 7 percent for six years, starting at the end of the first year, would have $357.65 at the end of that time ($50 × 7.153).

Present Value   Another aspect of the time value of money involves determining the current value of a desired amount for the future. **Present value** is the current value for a future sum based on a certain interest rate and a certain time period. Present value computations, referred to as *discounting,* allow you to determine how much to deposit now to obtain a desired total in the future. Present value tables (Exhibit 1–7) can be used in making the computations. If you want $1,000 three years from now and you earn 5 percent on your savings, you need to deposit $864 ($1,000 × 0.864). The present value of the amount you want in the future will always be less than the future value since all of the factors on Exhibit 1–7 are less than one and since interest earned will increase the present value amount to the desired future amount.

Present value computations can also be used to determine how much you need to deposit so that you can take a certain amount out of the account for a desired number of years. If you want to take $400 out of savings each year for nine years and your money is earning 8 percent, you can see from Exhibit 1–8 that you would need to make a current deposit of $2,498.80 ($400 × 6.247).

The formulas for calculating future and present values as well as tables covering a wider range of interest rates and time periods are presented in Appendix B.

EXHIBIT 1–5
Future Value of $1

			Percent		
Year	**5%**	**6%**	**7%**	**8%**	**9%**
1	1.050	1.060	1.070	1.080	1.090
2	1.103	1.124	1.145	1.166	1.188
3	1.158	1.191	1.225	1.260	1.295
4	1.216	1.262	1.311	1.360	1.412
5	1.276	1.338	1.403	1.469	1.539
6	1.340	1.419	1.501	1.587	1.677
7	1.407	1.504	1.606	1.714	1.828
8	1.477	1.594	1.718	1.851	1.993
9	1.551	1.689	1.838	1.999	2.172
10	1.629	1.791	1.967	2.159	2.367
11	1.710	1.898	2.105	2.332	2.580
12	1.796	2.012	2.252	2.518	2.813
13	1.886	2.133	2.410	2.720	3.066
14	1.980	2.261	2.579	2.937	3.342
15	2.079	2.397	2.759	3.172	3.642
16	2.183	2.540	2.952	3.426	3.970
17	2.292	2.693	3.159	3.700	4.328
18	2.407	2.854	3.380	3.996	4.717
19	2.527	3.026	3.617	4.316	5.142
20	2.653	3.207	3.870	4.661	5.604

EXHIBIT 1–6
Future Value of a
Series of Deposits

			Percent		
Year	**5%**	**6%**	**7%**	**8%**	**9%**
1	1.000	1.000	1.000	1.000	1.000
2	2.050	2.060	2.070	2.080	2.090
3	3.153	3.184	3.215	3.246	3.278
4	4.310	4.375	4.440	4.506	4.573
5	5.526	5.637	5.751	5.867	5.985
6	6.802	6.975	7.153	7.336	7.523
7	8.142	8.394	8.654	8.923	9.200
8	9.549	9.897	10.260	10.637	11.028
9	11.027	11.491	11.978	12.488	13.021
10	12.578	13.181	13.816	14.487	15.193
11	14.207	14.972	15.784	16.645	17.560
12	15.917	16.870	17.888	18.977	20.141
13	17.713	18.882	20.141	21.495	22.953
14	19.599	21.015	22.550	24.215	26.019
15	21.579	23.276	25.129	27.152	29.361
16	23.657	25.673	27.888	30.324	33.003
17	25.840	20.213	30.840	33.750	36.974
18	28.132	30.906	33.999	37.450	41.301
19	30.539	33.760	37.379	41.446	46.018
20	33.066	36.786	40.995	45.762	51.160

EXHIBIT 1–7
Present Value of $1

	Percent				
Year	5%	6%	7%	8%	9%
1	0.952	0.943	0.935	0.926	0.917
2	0.907	0.890	0.873	0.857	0.842
3	0.864	0.840	0.816	0.794	0.772
4	0.823	0.792	0.763	0.735	0.708
5	0.784	0.747	0.713	0.681	0.650
6	0.746	0.705	0.666	0.630	0.596
7	0.711	0.665	0.623	0.583	0.547
8	0.677	0.627	0.582	0.540	0.502
9	0.645	0.592	0.544	0.500	0.460
10	0.614	0.558	0.508	0.463	0.422
11	0.585	0.527	0.475	0.429	0.388
12	0.557	0.497	0.444	0.397	0.356
13	0.530	0.469	0.415	0.368	0.326
14	0.505	0.442	0.388	0.340	0.299
15	0.481	0.417	0.362	0.315	0.275
16	0.458	0.394	0.339	0.292	0.252
17	0.436	0.371	0.317	0.270	0.231
18	0.416	0.350	0.296	0.250	0.212
19	0.396	0.331	0.277	0.232	0.194
20	0.377	0.312	0.258	0.215	0.178

EXHIBIT 1–8
Present Value of a
Series of Deposits

	Percent				
Period	5%	6%	7%	8%	9%
1	0.952	0.943	0.935	0.926	0.917
2	1.859	1.833	1.808	1.783	1.759
3	2.723	2.673	2.624	2.577	2.531
4	3.546	3.465	3.387	3.312	3.240
5	4.329	4.212	4.100	3.993	3.890
6	5.076	4.917	4.767	4.623	4.486
7	5.786	5.582	5.389	5.206	5.033
8	6.463	6.210	5.971	5.747	5.535
9	7.108	6.802	6.515	6.247	5.995
10	7.722	7.360	7.024	6.710	6.418
11	8.306	7.887	7.499	7.139	6.805
12	8.863	8.384	7.943	7.536	7.161
13	9.394	8.853	8.358	7.904	7.487
14	9.899	9.295	8.745	8.244	7.786
15	10.380	9.712	9.108	8.559	8.061
16	10.838	10.106	9.447	8.851	8.313
17	11.274	10.477	9.763	9.122	8.544
18	11.690	10.828	10.059	9.372	8.756
19	12.085	11.158	10.336	9.604	8.950
20	12.462	11.470	10.594	9.818	9.129

THE FINANCIAL PLANNING ENVIRONMENT

L.O.3
Assess the personal, social, and economic factors that influence the personal financial planning environment.

Your daily financial decisions are influenced by many factors, ranging from age and household size to interest rates and inflation. The financial planning environment can be viewed as comprising three major types of factors: personal factors, social factors, and economic factors (see Exhibit 1–9).

The personal factors include your age, your income, the size of your household, and the attitudes and beliefs that influence your spending and saving patterns. Your *life situation* or *lifestyle* is created by the combination of many personal factors.

Your life situation is significantly affected not only by personal factors but also by such personal events as the following:

· Graduation (at all levels of education).
· Engagement and marriage.
· Birth or adoption of a child.
· Career change or a move to a new area.
· Changes in health condition.
· Divorce.
· Retirement.
· Death of a spouse, family member, or other dependent.

Financial planning decisions must adapt to changes in life situations and require ongoing communication among the household members and others affected by those decisions.

EXHIBIT 1–9
The Financial Planning Environment

Personal Factors
· Age, income
· Life situation
· Personal values and goals
· Values and goals of other household members
· Health condition

Social Factors
· Changing demographics
· Government actions

Economic Factors
· Changing economic conditions (supply and demand, consumer prices, interest rates)
· Economic institutions (business, labor, and government)

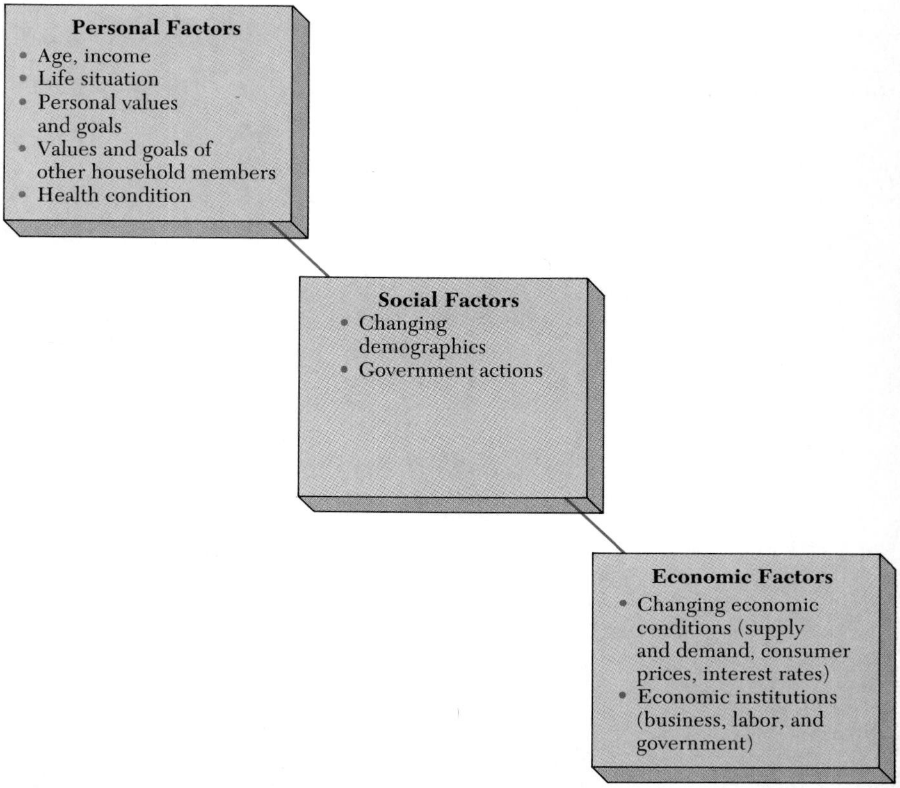

Social factors also affect financial planning. Changing demographic trends influence your working, investing, and spending opportunities. As the average age in our society increases, greater emphasis will be placed on health care and retirement living. Greater numbers of two-income and single-parent households mean increased demand for child care services.

Government influences the social environment of financial planning through changes in legislation. The deregulation of financial services has created many new savings, investing, and insurance options. Changing tax laws may influence the types of investments that a person selects.

Economic factors are the final component of the financial planning environment. In our society, the forces of supply and demand play an important role in setting prices for goods and services. The economic environment also includes various institutions, principally business, labor, and government, that must work together to satisfy the needs and wants of each of us.

ECONOMIC INFLUENCES ON FINANCIAL PLANNING

Economics is the study of how wealth is created and distributed. The many principles, institutions, and changing conditions of our economy influence your personal financial decisions.

Market Forces

The price of a specific good or service is determined by supply and demand. Just as high demand for a consumer product forces its price up, a high demand for money pushes up interest rates. This price of money reflects the limited supply of money, and the demand for it.

Generally, the price of any good or service will *increase* if its supply decreases or if the demand for it increases, or both. Shortages of wheat or corn due to poor weather may cause food prices to rise. In the same way, the price of a good or service will usually *decrease* if its supply increases or if the demand for it decreases, or both. An increase in the number of businesses that provide eyeglasses and contact lenses has lowered the market price of these products.

At times, the price of a certain item may seem to be unaffected by supply and demand, but what is usually happening at such times is that other economic factors are also influencing its price. Although such factors as production costs and competition influence prices, the market forces of supply and demand remain in operation.

Government Actions

The federal government influences the financial planning environment in three main areas. First, tax policies, which provide the federal government with operating funds, have a major impact on the funds available to individuals and on the types of investments that they select.

Second, spending by the federal government influences jobs, prices, and interest rates. Finally, when the federal government spends more than it takes in, as has been the case every year since 1969, its borrowing means that fewer dollars are available for consumers and business. Such borrowing can push interest rates higher.

Financial Institutions

Most people have conducted business with a financial institution. Banks are the most common type of financial institution; other types include savings and loan associations, credit unions, insurance companies, and investment companies. Financial institutions provide services that facilitate financial activities in our economy. They accept savings, handle checking accounts, sell insurance, and make investments on behalf of others.

Many government agencies oversee various financial activities, but the Federal Reserve System (our nation's central bank) has an especially significant responsibility in our economy. *The Fed,* as it is called, is concerned with providing an adequate money supply. It achieves this through borrowing, changing interest rates, and buying or selling government securities. It attempts to make adequate funds available for consumer spending and business expansion while keeping interest rates and consumer prices at an appropriate level.

Foreign Influences

At one point in our history, Brazil's coffee prices were the main foreign influence on our economy. In recent years, the global marketplace has become a daily influence on our financial activities. As Americans buy more foreign goods than they export, more U.S. dollars leave the country. This would reduce the funds available for domestic spending and investment if foreign companies decided not to invest their dollars in the United States. If they decided to spend those dollars elsewhere, the money supply would be reduced and interest rates would rise.

Our economy is affected not only by the financial influence of foreign investors but also by the competition of foreign producers. American companies must compete against foreign companies for the spending dollars of American consumers.

Economic Conditions

Newspapers and business periodicals regularly publish current statistics for a number of economic indicators. Exhibit 1–10 provides an overview of some economic indicators that strongly influence financial decision making. Your personal financial decisions are likely to be influenced most by consumer prices, consumer spending, and interest rates.

Consumer Prices **Inflation** is a rise in the general level of prices. In times of inflation, the buying power of the dollar decreases. If prices increased 5 percent during the last year, items that cost $100 then would cost $105 now. It takes more money to buy the same amount of goods and services.

The main cause of inflation is an increase in demand without a comparable increase in supply. For example, if people have more money to spend because of pay increases or borrowing but the same amounts of goods and services are available, the increased demand will bid up prices for those goods and services.

Inflation is most harmful to people who live on fixed incomes. Due to inflation, retired people whose income does not change are able to afford even smaller amounts of goods and services.

Lenders of money are also adversely affected by inflation. Unless an adequate interest rate is charged, loans repaid by borrowers in times of inflation have less

---

EXHIBIT 1–10   Changing Economic Conditions and Financial Decisions

Economic Factor	What It Measures	How It Influences Financial Planning
Consumer prices	The value of the dollar; changes in inflation	If consumer prices increase faster than your income, you are unable to purchase the same amount of goods and services; higher consumer prices will result in higher interest rates.
Consumer spending	The demand for goods and services by individuals and households	Increased consumer spending is likely to result in increased job opportunities and higher wages; high levels of consumer spending and borrowing can push up consumer prices and interest rates.
Interest rates	The cost of money; the cost of credit when you borrow; the return on your money when you save or invest	Higher interest rates make buying on credit more expensive; higher interest rates make saving and investing more attractive and encourage reducing the amount of debt.
Money supply	The dollars available for spending in our economy	Interest rates tend to be reduced as more people save and invest; but higher saving (and lower spending) may also reduce the number of job opportunities.
Unemployment	The number of individuals without employment who are willing and able to work	Individuals who may become unemployed should reduce their debt level and have an emergency savings fund to take care of their living costs while they are out of work; high unemployment reduces consumer spending and job opportunities.
Housing starts	The number of new homes being built	Increased home building results in more job opportunities, higher wages, more consumer spending, and overall economic expansion.
Trade balance	The difference between a country's exports and its imports	If a country continually exports more than it imports, imported items and foreign travel will cost more.

---

buying power than the money they borrowed. If you pay 10 percent interest on a loan and the inflation rate is 12 percent, the dollars you pay the lender have lost buying power. For this reason, interest rates usually rise in periods of inflation.

The rate of inflation varies. During the late 1950s and the early 1960s, the annual inflation rate was in the 1–3 percent range. During the late 1970s and the early 1980s, the cost of living increased 10–12 percent annually. At a 12 percent annual inflation rate, prices double (and the value of the dollar is cut in half) in about six years. To find out how fast prices (or your savings) will double, use the *rule of 72*—just divide 72 by the annual inflation (or interest) rate. An annual inflation rate of 8 percent, for example, means that prices will double in nine years ($72 \div 8$).

More recently, the annual price increase of most goods and services as measured by the consumer price index has been in the 3–5 percent range. The consumer price index (CPI), published monthly by the Bureau of Labor Statistics, is based on a selected group of goods and services. Although different indexes are computed for various cities, the CPI is probably not a reliable measure of your personal living costs. You do not buy goods and services in the same proportions that are used in calculating the CPI. However, the CPI will give you an indication of changes in prices and in the value of the dollar, and this information can assist you in your financial planning.

Consumer Spending   The total demand for goods and services in the economy influences employment opportunities and the potential for income. As consumer purchasing for an item increases, the financial resources of current and prospective employees are expanded. This situation improves the financial condition of many households.

In contrast, reduced spending causes unemployment. The financial hardships of unemployment are a major concern of business, labor, and government. Retraining programs, income assistance, and job services help individuals adjust to unemployment.

Interest Rates   In the most simple terms, interest rates represent the cost of money. Like everything else, money has a price. The forces of supply and demand influence interest rates. As the amount saved and invested by consumers increases the supply of money, interest rates tend to decrease. But as consumer, business, government, and foreign borrowing increases the demand for money, interest rates also tend to increase.

Interest rates affect financial planning from two perspectives. The earnings you receive as a saver or investor reflect current interest rates as well as a *risk premium* based on such factors as the length of time your funds will be used by others, expected inflation, and the extent of uncertainty about getting your money back. Risk is also a factor in the interest rate you pay as a borrower. Individuals with a poor credit rating pay a higher interest rate than individuals with a good credit rating. Interest rates are central to most financial decisions as they represent the trade-off between the use of funds for future income and its use for future payments.

THE FINANCIAL PLANNING PROCESS

L.O.4
Identify the steps involved in personal financial planning.

Since the United States is one of the richest countries in the world, it is difficult to understand why so many Americans have money problems. The answer seems to be the result of three factors. The first is poor planning. The second is weak habits related to financial activities such as spending and the use of credit. And the third is an extensive number of marketplace influences in the form of advertising, selling efforts, and product availability. Achieving personal financial satisfaction depends on an awareness of your situation, clear goals, and an organized process of financial decision making.

Who Are You?

Your life situation has an important influence on your financial decision making. The factors listed in Exhibit 1–11 are the major influences on the life situation during the various stages of the **adult life cycle**—the stages in the family situation and financial needs of an adult. However, there is no longer what can be called a "typical" American family. During the past few decades, demographic changes in our society have had a significant impact on the traditional nuclear family. Today's society is populated by

- An increased number of single-parent households with children under age 18 (over 7 million as of the early 1990s), 85 percent of which are headed by females.
- Over 27 million two-income couples, two thirds of whom have dependent children.
- Nearly 2 million women who care for both children and parents.

EXHIBIT 1–11   Influences on the Life Situation of Adults

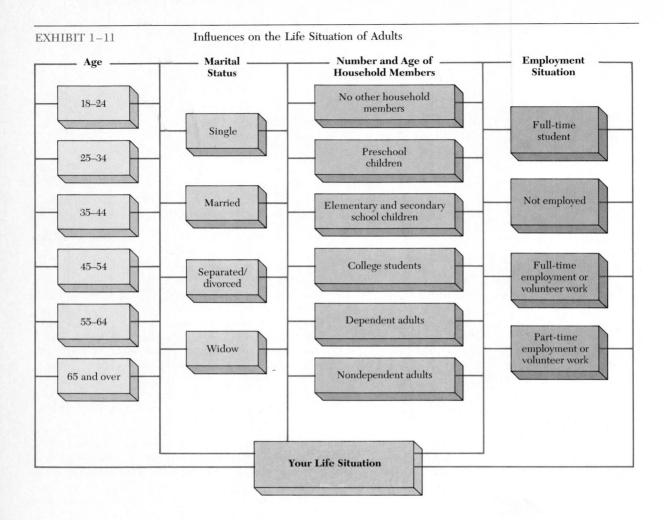

- An increasing number of people (at present, 80 percent of all Americans) who are expected to live past age 65, with close to 50,000 currently more than 100 years old.

In addition to being defined by your family situation, you are defined by your **values**—the ideas and principles that you consider correct, desirable, and important. Values have a direct influence on such decisions as spending now versus saving for the future or continuing school versus getting a job. They also influence the goals of a household, making communication among its members vital. Many money problems result from misunderstandings among family members whose values differ.

What Do You Want?

According to an old saying, "If you don't know where you're going, you might end up somewhere else and not even know it." Goal setting is central to financial decision making. Your financial goals create a basis for planning, implementing, and measuring progress regarding your spending, saving, and investing activities. Exhibit 1–12 offers typical financial activities for various life situations.

EXHIBIT 1–12   Financial Goals and Activities for Various Life Situations

Common Financial Goals and Activities	**Life Situation**	**Specialized Financial Activities**
Obtain appropriate career training.	Young single (18–35)	Establish financial independence. Obtain a disability insurance policy to replace income during prolonged illness. Consider home purchase for tax benefit.
Create an effective financial recordkeeping system.	Young couple with children under 18	Carefully manage the increased need for the use of credit. Obtain an appropriate amount of life insurance for the care of dependents. Use will to name a guardian for children.
Develop a regular savings and investment program.	Single parent with children under 18	Obtain adequate amounts of health, life, and disability insurance. Contribute to a savings and investment fund for college. Name a guardian for children and make other estate plans.
Accumulate an appropriate emergency fund.	Young dual-income couple, no children	Coordinate insurance coverage and other benefits. Develop savings and investment program for changes in life situation (larger house, children). Consider tax-deferred contributions to retirement fund.
Purchase appropriate types and amounts of insurance coverage.	Older couple, no dependent children at home	Consolidate financial assets and review estate plans. Obtain health insurance for postretirement period. Plan retirement housing, living expenses, recreational activities, and part-time work.
Create and implement a flexible budget. Evaluate and select appropriate investments.	Mixed-generation household (elderly individuals and children under 18)	Obtain long-term health care insurance and life/disability income for care of younger dependents. Use dependent care service if needed. Provide arrangements for handling finances of elderly if they become ill. Consider splitting of investment cost, with elderly getting income while alive and principal going to surviving relatives.
Establish and implement a plan for retirement goals. Make will and develop an estate plan.	Older single	Make arrangement for long-term health care coverage. Review will and estate plan. Plan retirement living facilities, living expenses, and activities.

In order to guide your financial decision making, your financial goals should be stated in a manner that takes the following considerations into account.

1. Financial goals should be realistic. Your financial goals should be based on your income and life situation. It is not realistic to plan an annual European vacation on an average income.

2. Financial goals should be stated in specific, measurable terms. Knowing exactly what your goals are will help you create a plan that is designed to achieve them. For example, the goal of "accumulating $5,000 in an investment fund within three years" is a clearer guide to planning than the goal of "putting money into an investment fund."

3. Financial goals should have a time orientation. In the preceding example, the goal was to be achieved in three years. A time frame helps you measure your progress toward your financial goals. Such goals are usually viewed as short-term

objectives (less than two years), intermediate objectives (two to five years), and long-term objectives (more than five years).

4.   Finally, financial goals should imply the type of action to be taken. Your financial goals are the basis for various financial activities.

How Do You Get It?

Successful financial planning is a combination of effective goal setting and good habits related to spending, saving, and investing. The five steps of the financial planning process are shown in Exhibit 1–13. This process for financial planning does not establish a standard. It does not support a particular set of values or prescribe means for attaining particular goals. It applies to persons of any age, any income level, and any life situation.

Analyze Your Current Situation   In this first step of the financial planning process, you must analyze your financial values and goals. This involves identifying how you feel about money and why you feel that way. Is the way you feel about money based on factual knowledge or on the influence of others? Are your financial priorities based on social pressures, household needs, or desires for luxury items? How will economic conditions affect your goals and priorities? The purpose of this analysis is to differentiate your needs from your wants.

In this first step of the financial planning process, you must also determine your current financial situation with regard to income, savings, living expenses, and debts. The personal financial statements discussed in Chapter 3 will provide you

EXHIBIT 1–13
The Financial
Planning Process

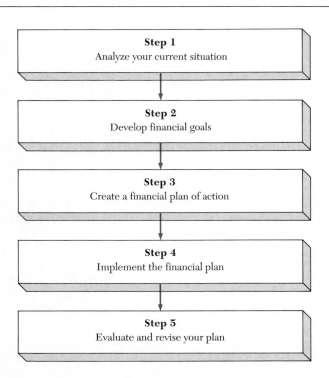

Step 1
Analyze your current situation

Step 2
Develop financial goals

Step 3
Create a financial plan of action

Step 4
Implement the financial plan

Step 5
Evaluate and revise your plan

with the information you need in order to match your goals with your current income and your potential earning power.

Develop Financial Goals　　As previously mentioned, specific financial goals are vital to your financial planning efforts. Others can suggest financial goals, but you must decide which of those goals to pursue. Your financial goals can range from spending all of your current income to developing an extensive savings and investment program for future financial security. The goals you choose will be based on your household situation, your values, and your current financial situation as determined in the first step of this process.

Create a Financial Plan of Action　　The third step of the financial planning process is to develop a plan of action for achieving your financial goals. This requires choosing among the various ways in which those goals can be achieved. For example, you can increase savings by reducing spending or by increasing income through extra time on the job. If you are concerned about year-end tax payments, you can elect to increase the amount withheld for taxes from each paycheck, file quarterly tax payments, or shelter current income in a tax-deferred pension program.

Creating a financial action plan requires the investigation of possible alternatives. To assess how these alternatives will affect your personal and financial situation, you need to obtain information regarding their costs, benefits, and ease of implementation. Although several methods can be used to achieve the same end, because of values, needs, and other factors, these methods may not be equally desirable. For example, you may prefer to increase your savings by participating in a payroll deduction plan instead of taking trips to the bank to make deposits.

Implement the Financial Plan　　This step of the financial planning process may require assistance from others. For example, you may use the services of an insurance agent in purchasing property insurance or the services of an investment broker in purchasing stocks, bonds, or mutual funds. Your own efforts should all be geared toward achieving your financial goals. Specific strategies for the various components of financial planning are the basis of this book; techniques related to saving, spending, borrowing, and investing are presented in the chapters that follow.

Evaluate and Revise Your Plan　　Changes in your income, values, or life situation will require revision of your financial goals and activities. When uncontrollable events affect your financial needs, the financial planning process provides a vehicle for dealing with them by delaying or altering priorities. As you achieve immediate or short-term goals, goals next in priority will come into focus.

Like other kinds of decision making, financial planning is a dynamic process that does not end when you take a particular action. You need to regularly assess your financial decisions. You should make a complete review of your finances at least once a year. Changing personal, social, and economic factors may require more frequent assessments.

• •

FINANCIAL PLANNING CALCULATIONS

Annual Contributions to Meet a Goal

Achieving specific financial goals frequently requires regular additions to a savings or investment account. By using time value of money calculations, you can determine the amount you should save or invest to achieve a specific goal for the future.

Example 1

Jonie Emerson has two children who will start college in 10 years. She plans to set aside $1,500 a year for her children's college education during that period and estimates that she will earn an annual interest rate of 7 percent on her savings. What amount can Jonie expect to have available for her children's college education when they start college?

Calculation:

$1,500 × Future value of a series of deposits,
7%, 10 years
$1,500 × 13.816 (see Exhibit 1–6) = $20,724

Example 2

Don Calder wants to accumulate $50,000 over the next 15 years as a reserve fund for his parents' retirement living expenses and health care. If he earns an average of 8 percent on his investments, what amount must he invest each year to achieve this goal?

Calculation:

$50,000 ÷ Future value of a series of deposits,
8%, 15 years
$50,000 ÷ 27.152 (see Exhibit 1–6) = $1,841.49

Don needs to invest approximately $1,850 a year for 15 years at 8 percent to accumulate the desired financial goal.

• •

FINANCIAL PLANNING IN ACTION: YOUR PERSONAL STRATEGIES

L.O.5
Determine possible strategies for achieving personal financial goals for different life situations.

Throughout life, each individual has needs that the intelligent use of available financial resources can satisfy. Financial planning involves deciding how to obtain, protect, and use those resources.

A comprehensive financial plan can enhance the quality of your life and increase your satisfaction by reducing uncertainty about your future needs and resources. The specific advantages of personal financial planning include

- Increased effectiveness in obtaining, using, and protecting financial resources throughout your life.
- Increased control of financial affairs by preventing excessive debt, bankruptcy, and dependence on others for economic security.
- Improved personal relationships resulting from well-planned and effectively communicated financial decisions.
- A sense of freedom from financial worries that is obtained by looking to the future, anticipating expenses, and achieving personal economic goals.

An organized approach to managing your financial resources will help you avoid the common mistakes listed in Exhibit 1–14. Your personal financial planning comprises eight major components.

Components of Personal Financial Planning

This book is designed to provide you with a framework for the study and planning of personal financial decisions. Exhibit 1–15 presents an overview of the eight major components of personal financial planning along with examples of the

EXHIBIT 1–14

Mistakes That Financial
Planning Can Help You
Avoid

Among the most common financial planning mistakes are the following:

1. Not setting financial goals.
2. Making an unrealistic budget.
3. Maintaining poorly organized financial records.
4. Not establishing a credit history in both spouses' names.
5. Using credit unwisely.
6. Not having enough insurance for your home and valuables.
7. Not having an emergency savings fund.
8. Buying insurance without taking discounts.
9. Failing to shop for the best interest rates.
10. Not insuring lives and earning power.
11. Not putting money to work for you.
12. Paying too much in taxes.
13. Making major financial decisions without professional help.
14. Making spur-of-the-moment investments based on tips.
15. Not having a will.

SOURCE: *15 Money Blunders and How to Avoid Them* (Hartford, Conn.: Aetna Life and Casualty Company).

concerns associated with each of these components. To achieve a successful financial existence, these components must be coordinated through an organized plan and a process of personal choice making.

Obtaining   You will obtain your financial resources (see Exhibit 1–16) from your employment, your investments, or your ownership of a business. Obtaining financial resources is the foundation of financial planning since these resources are the basis of all financial activities.

Planning   Allocating income to cover necessary living expenses through budgeting is a key to achieving goals and planning for future financial security. Efforts to anticipate expenses and financial decisions can also help reduce taxes. The ability to pay your fair share of taxes—no more, no less—is vital to the growth of your financial resources.

Saving   Long-term financial security starts with a regular savings plan for emergencies, unexpected bills, replacement of major items, and the purchase of special goods and services, such as a college education, a boat, or a vacation home. Once a basic savings component has been established, additional money may be used for investments that offer greater financial growth.

A certain amount of savings must be readily available to meet household needs. **Liquidity** refers to financial resources that can be readily converted into usable cash without a loss in value. The need for liquidity will vary based on an individual's age, health, and family situation. Savings plans such as NOW accounts, money market accounts, money market funds, and superNOW accounts earn a good return on your savings while also providing a high degree of liquidity.

EXHIBIT 1–15   Components of Personal Financial Planning

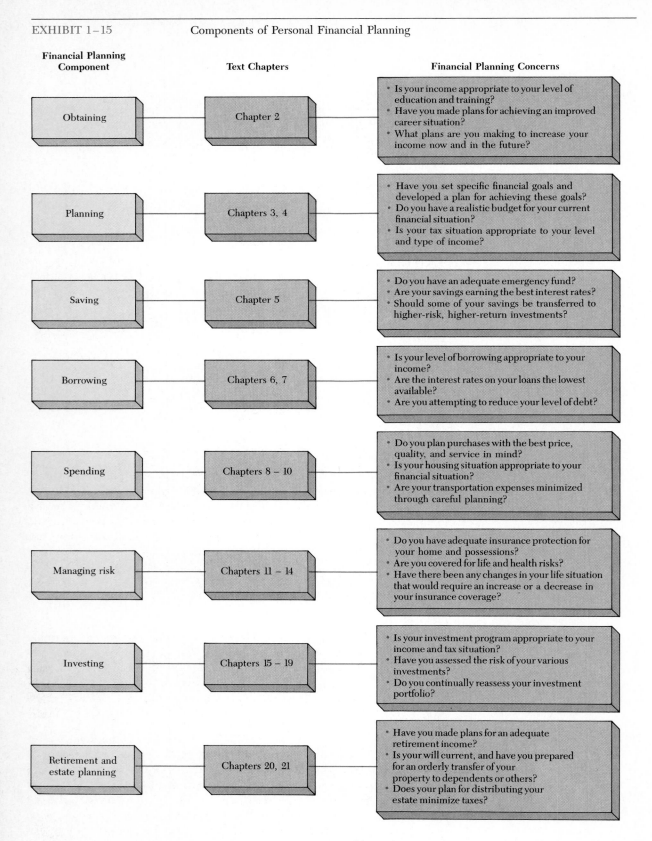

Financial Planning Component

Text Chapters

Financial Planning Concerns

Obtaining — Chapter 2

- Is your income appropriate to your level of education and training?
- Have you made plans for achieving an improved career situation?
- What plans are you making to increase your income now and in the future?

Planning — Chapters 3, 4

- Have you set specific financial goals and developed a plan for achieving these goals?
- Do you have a realistic budget for your current financial situation?
- Is your tax situation appropriate to your level and type of income?

Saving — Chapter 5

- Do you have an adequate emergency fund?
- Are your savings earning the best interest rates?
- Should some of your savings be transferred to higher-risk, higher-return investments?

Borrowing — Chapters 6, 7

- Is your level of borrowing appropriate to your income?
- Are the interest rates on your loans the lowest available?
- Are you attempting to reduce your level of debt?

Spending — Chapters 8 – 10

- Do you plan purchases with the best price, quality, and service in mind?
- Is your housing situation appropriate to your financial situation?
- Are your transportation expenses minimized through careful planning?

Managing risk — Chapters 11 – 14

- Do you have adequate insurance protection for your home and possessions?
- Are you covered for life and health risks?
- Have there been any changes in your life situation that would require an increase or a decrease in your insurance coverage?

Investing — Chapters 15 – 19

- Is your investment program appropriate to your income and tax situation?
- Have you assessed the risk of your various investments?
- Do you continually reassess your investment portfolio?

Retirement and estate planning — Chapters 20, 21

- Have you made plans for an adequate retirement income?
- Is your will current, and have you prepared for an orderly transfer of your property to dependents or others?
- Does your plan for distributing your estate minimize taxes?

EXHIBIT 1–16
Financial Resources
Requiring Management

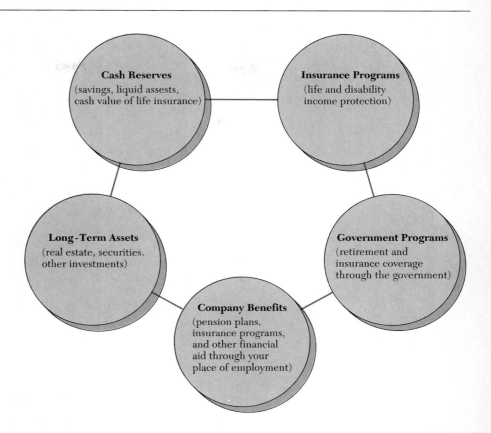

Cash Reserves
(savings, liquid assests,
cash value of life insurance)

Insurance Programs
(life and disability
income protection)

Long-Term Assets
(real estate, securities,
other investments)

Government Programs
(retirement and
insurance coverage
through the government)

Company Benefits
(pension plans,
insurance programs,
and other financial
aid through your
place of employment)

Borrowing   Maintaining control over your credit-buying habits will help you reach your financial goals. Using credit so that you will not have to make excessive credit payments is crucial to successful financial planning. The overuse and misuse of credit is a major cause of personal economic difficulties. **Bankruptcy** is a situation in which a person is not able to pay debts on time. This results in legal proceedings to arrange payments to creditors. Many of the thousands of people who have declared bankruptcy each year could have avoided this trauma through better borrowing and spending decisions.

Spending   Financial planning is not designed to prevent your enjoyment of life but rather to help you obtain the things you want. Too often, however, people buy what they believe they need without considering the financial effect of their purchases. Some individuals shop compulsively and thus are led to financial ruin. You should detail your living expenses and your other financial obligations in a spending plan. Planned spending is necessary to accumulate resources for future financial security.

Managing Risk   Adequate insurance coverage is another consideration in personal financial planning. Certain types of insurance are commonly overlooked in financial plans. The number of people who suffer disabling injuries or diseases at age 50 is greater than the number who die at that age, so individuals may need disability insurance more than they need life insurance. Yet surveys reveal that most people have adequate life insurance, but few have disability insurance. The insurance industry is more aggressive in selling life insurance than in selling disability insurance, thus putting the burden of obtaining adequate disability insurance on the individual.

Many households have excessive or overlapping insurance coverages. Insuring property for more than it is worth may be a waste of money; so may payment by both a husband and a wife for similar health insurance coverage.

Investing   Many types of investment vehicles are available. Those whose principal requirement is long-term safety of their funds should select investment vehicles with minimal risk, such as government securities, corporate bonds, or the stocks of well-established companies.

You can achieve investment diversification by including a variety of assets in your portfolio—for example, stocks, real estate, and collectibles, such as rare coins. Obtaining investment advice is easy; more difficult is obtaining investment advice that is appropriate to your individual needs and goals.

Retirement and Estate Planning   Financial security upon termination of full-time employment is a major goal of most people. But retirement planning also involves thinking about your housing situation, your recreational activities, and possible part-time or volunteer work.

Your transfers of money or property to others should be timed, if possible, to minimize the tax burden of the transfers and to maximize the benefits that those individuals receive. Your knowledge of property transfer methods can help you select the best course of action for funding the current and future living costs, educational expenses, and retirement needs of dependents.

Developing a Flexible Financial Plan

A **financial plan** is a formalized report that summarizes your current financial situation, analyzes your financial needs, and recommends a direction for your financial activities. You can create this document on your own or seek assistance, such as the use of computerized financial plans (see Appendix A). Exhibit 1–17 offers a framework for developing and implementing a financial plan along with examples for several life situations.

As you start to do personal financial planning, assess your current personal and financial situation while also considering social and economic factors. Organize your financial goals so that they can be achieved on the basis of decisions related to spending, saving, investing, and borrowing. Continually communicate with the other members of your household about financial goals and about the financial activities needed to attain them.

Implementing Your Financial Plan

A plan is necessary before you can implement it. But once you have clearly assessed your current situation and identified your financial goals, what do you do next?

EXHIBIT 1–17   Components of a Financial Plan

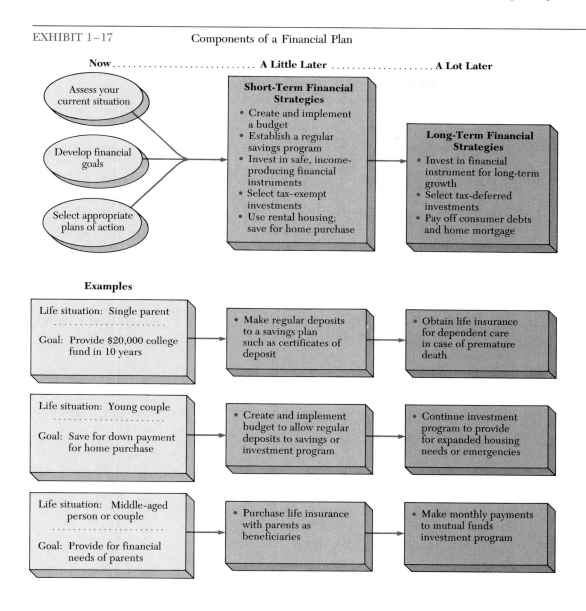

Now . . . . **A Little Later** . . . . **A Lot Later**

Assess your current situation

Develop financial goals

Select appropriate plans of action

Short-Term Financial Strategies
- Create and implement a budget
- Establish a regular savings program
- Invest in safe, income-producing financial instruments
- Select tax-exempt investments
- Use rental housing; save for home purchase

Long-Term Financial Strategies
- Invest in financial instrument for long-term growth
- Select tax-deferred investments
- Pay off consumer debts and home mortgage

Examples

Life situation: Single parent
. . . .
Goal: Provide $20,000 college fund in 10 years

- Make regular deposits to a savings plan such as certificates of deposit

- Obtain life insurance for dependent care in case of premature death

Life situation: Young couple
. . . .
Goal: Save for down payment for home purchase

- Create and implement budget to allow regular deposits to savings or investment program

- Continue investment program to provide for expanded housing needs or emergencies

Life situation: Middle-aged person or couple
. . . .
Goal: Provide for financial needs of parents

- Purchase life insurance with parents as beneficiaries

- Make monthly payments to mutual funds investment program

What you do next is decide how to achieve these goals. The most important strategy for success is the development of financial habits that will contribute to both short-term satisfaction and long-term financial security. Using a set spending plan will help you stay within your income while you save and invest for the future. Having adequate insurance protection will help you prevent financial disasters. Becoming informed on tax and investment alternatives will help you expand your financial resources.

Overall, achieving your financial objectives requires two things: a willingness to learn and appropriate information sources. You must provide the first item; the chapters that follow will provide the second one.

• •

PERSONAL FINANCE JOURNAL
Financial Advice from Experts

Ross Perot, investor and founder of Electronic Data Systems:

- Don't have any credit cards; if you want something, save money until you're able to purchase it.
- Put money into savings, so you have money to invest.
- Don't have making money as the driving force in your life. Money is effective in a very narrow range. It won't buy happiness, and it won't make an unhappy marriage happy.

Lou Dobbs, anchorperson, CNN's *Moneyline:*

- The most boring but the most important: Set a budget and stick to it.
- Whether it's clothing, furniture, or automobiles, buy quality. Quality always pays you back.
- Always read the fine print. It will give you an education. Not reading the fine print will give you *experience.*

Eugene Lang, industrialist and philanthropist:

- Have a long-range objective. Take into account your career ambitions, your present personal circumstances, and your obligations.
- Be willing to take chances, but thoughtfully. Make a rational evaluation of risk. In other words, don't bet the house—unless you're willing to lose it.
- Consult with others who are experienced. But don't let yourself be dominated by them.

William E. Donoghue, financial writer and publisher:

- If you can't afford to live on your full salary, you also can't live on 90 percent of it. So save 10 percent.

SOURCE: *Sylvia Porter's Personal Finance,* July–August 1988, p. 34.

• •

SUMMARY

L.O.1
Analyze the process of making personal financial decisions.

Personal financial planning is the process of managing your money to achieve personal economic satisfaction. The hundreds of decisions we make each day require identification of the basic problem; generation of alternative courses of action; evaluation of these alternatives based on personal, social, and economic factors and selection of the most appropriate alternative; and finally, implementation of the alternative selected.

L.O.2
Determine the personal and financial opportunity costs associated with personal financial decisions.

Every decision involves a trade-off with other things that are given up. Personal opportunity costs include time, effort, and health. Financial opportunity costs are based on the time value of money. Future value and present value calculations enable you to measure the increased value (or lost interest) that results from a saving, investing, borrowing, or purchasing decision.

L.O.3
Assess the personal, social, and economic factors that influence the personal financial planning environment

Financial decisions are affected by personal factors (income, household size, health, values, and goals), social factors (demographic trends and government actions), and economic factors (prices, interest rates, employment opportunities).

L.O.4
Identify the steps involved in personal financial planning.

Personal financial planning involves the following steps: (1) analyze your current needs, wants, values, and financial situation; (2) develop financial goals; (3) create a financial plan of action; (4) implement your plan; and (5) evaluate and revise your plan.

L.O.5
Determine possible strategies
for achieving personal financial
goals for different life
situations.

Successful financial planning requires specific goals combined with spending, saving, investing, and borrowing strategies that are based on your personal situation and that consider various social and economic factors.

GLOSSARY

Adult life cycle   The stages in the family situation and financial needs of an adult.

Bankruptcy   A situation in which a person is not able to pay debts on time.

Economics   The study of how wealth is created and distributed.

Financial plan   A formalized report that summarizes your current financial situation, analyzes your financial needs, and recommends a direction for your financial activities.

Future value   The amount to which current savings will increase based on a certain interest rate and a certain time period; also referred to as compounding.

Inflation   A rise in the general level of prices.

Liquidity   Financial resources that can be readily converted into usable cash without a loss in value.

Opportunity cost   What a person gives up by making a choice.

Personal financial planning   The process of managing your money to achieve personal economic satisfaction.

Present value   The current value for a future sum based on a certain interest rate and a certain time period.

Time value of money   Increases in an amount of money as a result of interest earned.

Values   Ideas and principles that a person considers correct, desirable, and important.

DISCUSSION QUESTIONS

L.O.1   1. What are the main elements of every decision we make?

L.O.1   2. List risks that are associated with financial decisions. How can a person measure the risks of financial decisions?

L.O.1   3. What are common sources of financial planning information? Which of these are likely to be most helpful to you?

L.O.2   4. Explain how an opportunity cost is present in every decision we make.

L.O.3   5. How can future value and present value computations be used to plan and achieve financial goals?

L.O.3   6. What is the relationship between current interest rates and financial opportunity costs?

L.O.3   7. How is financial planning affected by age, marital status, household size, employment situation, and other personal factors?

L.O.3   8. How do supply and demand, government actions, the Federal Reserve System, and foreign companies influence our economy?

L.O.3   9. In what ways does the uncertainty of inflation contribute to the difficulty of personal financial planning?

L.O.4   10. What are the characteristics of useful financial goals?

L.O.4   11. Are the steps of the financial planning process adaptable to all personal situations? Why or why not?

L.O.4   12. Why is it necessary to evaluate the actions you take after making personal financial decisions?

L.O.5   13. What common strategies may be used to achieve personal financial security?

Opening Case Questions

1. What financial planning mistakes did Erika Earnhart make?
2. How did the misuse of credit contribute to Erika's problems?
3. Did Erika's changing household situation affect her financial planning difficulties? Explain.
4. If you were in a situation similar to Erika's, how would your actions differ from her actions?

PROBLEMS AND ACTIVITIES

L.O.1   1. Survey friends, relatives, and other people to determine the process they use when making financial decisions. In what ways do these people consider risk when making financial decisions?

L.O.1   2. Prepare a list of financial planning specialists, library materials, and other resources in your community that can assist people in their personal financial planning. Which of these resources would be most valuable to young persons first starting out on their own? Which would be most valuable to single parents or people getting ready to retire?

L.O.2   3. Create a list of the opportunity costs of going to college for individuals in these life situations—a young single person, a single parent, a married person with no children, and a retired person.

L.O.2   4. Using the time value of money tables in the chapter, calculate the following:
   a. The future value of $450 two years from now at 7 percent.
   b. The future value of $800 saved each year for 10 years at 8 percent.
   c. The amount that a person would have to deposit today (present value) at a 6 percent interest rate in order to have $1,000 three years from now.
   d. The amount that a person would have to deposit today in order to be able to take out $500 a year for 12 years from an account earning 8 percent.

L.O.2   5. Brad Conners plans to buy a town house for $65,000. If the property is expected to increase in value 5 percent each year, what would its approximate value be seven years from now?

L.O.2   6. Eleanore Duncan prepares her own tax return each year. A tax preparer would charge her $60 for this service. Over the course of 20 years, how much does Eleanore gain from preparing her own tax return (assume that she earns 6 percent on a savings account)?

L.O.3   7. Ask people how their spending, saving, and borrowing activities changed when they decided to continue their education, change careers, or have children.

L.O.3   8. Use newspaper or magazine articles to monitor changing economic conditions. Point out how the information you obtain in this way will affect your financial planning decisions.

L.O.3   9. Interview three individuals about the effects of changing consumer prices and interest rates on their financial position and decisions.

L.O.4   10. Use the steps in the financial planning process to develop a plan for a specific area of your personal economic situation. What goals and values do you or members of your household have that will influence this process?

L.O.4   11. Name some financial goals that apply to each of the following life situations:
    a. An unemployed factory worker with two school-age children.
    b. A dual-income couple in their 40s, with no children.
    c. A young couple with a child and another child due in a few months.
    d. A woman who is supporting both her school-age daughter and her retired father.

L.O.5   12. Suggest specific financial activities that would be appropriate to each of the life situations described in the previous item.

L.O.5   13. Obtain advertisements of financial services that could help a person achieve certain financial goals. What questions should a person ask before using these financial services?

LIFE SITUATION   Case 1–1

Emily's Personal Financial Plan

Emily Burton, 23, completed college two years ago with a degree in physical therapy. The major cost of her education was covered by a scholarship. Through wise planning by her parents, Emily has $22,000, which they set aside for her education. This fund consists of savings certificates and stocks that increased in value over the years.

Emily works for a hospital in Lincoln, Nebraska, and earns $26,000 a year. In about three years, she would like to go to graduate school to get a master's degree. Then she would like to buy a house. Emily wants to live on her salary and invest the $22,000 for her education and future needs.

Questions

1. How did Emily benefit from her parents' financial planning?
2. What decisions does Emily need to make regarding her future?
3. How could various personal and economic factors influence Emily's financial planning?
4. What would be the value of Emily's $22,000 in three years if it earned an annual interest rate of 7 percent?

LIFE SITUATION   Case 1–2

The Parkers' Plan for Parenthood

Pam and Brad Parker are in their mid-20s and have no children, but they are considering starting a family in the near future. They both have jobs with very stable companies and good opportunities to advance within their respective organizations. Their combined annual income is $43,000.

Each month, the Parkers spend about $1,800 of their $2,600 after-tax income for rent, utilities, credit payments, and insurance. They owe money on an automobile loan and on a student loan that helped pay Pam's college expenses. The other $800 goes for food, clothing, savings, and miscellaneous expenses. Currently, the Parkers have $2,500 in a savings account.

Questions

1. How could the Parkers benefit from financial planning?
2. Which goals are likely to be priorities in the Parkers' plan?
3. What financial planning resources might be helpful to the Parkers?
4. What financial strategies would you suggest for the Parkers?

SUPPLEMENTARY READINGS

For Additional Information on Financial Planning

Bailard, Thomas E.; David L. Biehl; and Ronald W. Kaiser. *How to Set and Achieve Your Financial Goals.* Homewood, Ill.: Dow Jones-Irwin, 1989.

Consumer Guide to Financial Independence. Foundation for Financial Planning, Two Concourse Parkway, Suite 800, Atlanta, GA 30328.

McWilliams, Bruce G. *Under-33 Financial Plan: Four Painless Steps to Lifelong Prosperity.* Delacorte Press, 1988.

For Additional Information on Personal and Economic Factors That Influence Financial Decisions

Consumer Price Index. Bureau of Labor Statistics. U.S. Department of Labor, 600 E Street, NW, Washington, DC 20212.

The Dow Jones-Irwin Business and Investment Almanac. Homewood, Ill.: Dow Jones-Irwin.

The Wall Street Journal, page A2 for coverage of "The Economy."

For Additional Information on Financial Planning Strategies

Complete Guide to Managing Your Money. Mount Vernon, N.Y.: Consumer Reports Books, 1989.

"1989 Money Guide Special Report: Building Your Fortune." *U.S. News & World Report,* July 17, 1989, pp. 50–66.

Schurenberg, Eric. "The New Gospel of Financial Planning." *Money,* March 1989, pp. 54–77.

2 *Personal Career Strategies*

Managing your financial resources most often starts with obtaining income as a result of employment. A job means that you work regular hours, receive a paycheck, and may experience only limited satisfaction from your employment. In contrast, a career is a commitment to training and growth in a particular field. While both a job and a career contribute to your financial existence, a career usually offers greater opportunities for higher levels of economic and personal fulfillment. Therefore, career selection and development are integral parts of financial planning.

LEARNING OBJECTIVES
After studying this chapter, you will be able to

L.O.1 Recognize the activities associated with career planning and advancement.

L.O.2 Evaluate the factors that influence career choice and employment opportunities.

L.O.3 Implement employment search strategies.

L.O.4 Assess the financial and legal concerns related to obtaining employment.

L.O.5 Analyze the techniques available for career growth and advancement.

OPENING CASE

Getting That First Job

When Kelly Thomas received her B.A. degree from a small college in Maine, she started to look for a job. She sent out many letters and made numerous telephone calls to companies in the towns and cities near her school. Kelly liked that area of the country and wanted to live and work there. Despite her efforts, few businesses were interested in her. After months of disappointment, she expanded her job search to companies in nearby states. Even with this additional effort, Kelly still could not obtain employment.

Steve Bauer has a degree in computer science. While he was in school, his efforts and achievements were outstanding. However, Steve had limited his endeavors to classwork. As he applied for jobs, he discovered that most employers were looking for individuals who had had some practical experience in cocurricular activities. Because of his weakness in this area, Steve had to accept a job with less responsibility than he believed he could handle.

Ellen Mason began her job search by sending hundreds of letters to companies. She sent the same letter to all of these companies despite the fact that they were in different industries. Ellen's letter did not specify what type of employment she was seeking, but since she sent so many letters, she believed that her chances of getting a job were good. Ellen received only a few encouraging responses.

In attempting to obtain employment, these applicants used the approach that they believed was most effective. But limiting the job search to one geographic area, not having appropriate skills and experience, and sending out letters without researching the job situation are common problems of career planning. Also, none of the applicants had formed a clear and carefully planned career search program. Preparing for and obtaining employment is a systematic process. You should begin your career planning activities by deciding how your work will affect your life.

CAREER CHOICE AND YOUR FUTURE

Like any other decision, employment selection involves a trade-off among various factors and requires an ongoing reassessment of the situation. The average person changes jobs about seven times during a lifetime. Most likely, therefore, you will reevaluate your choice of a job on a regular basis.

The lifework you select is a key to your financial existence. You may select a **job,** an employment position that is obtained mainly to earn money. Many people work in one or more jobs during their lives without considering their interests or their opportunities for advancement. Or you may select a **career,** which is a commitment to a profession that requires continued training and offers a clear path for occupational growth. Career decisions are influenced by education, lifestyle, and planning efforts.

Opportunity Costs of Career Decisions

While many factors affect your daily living habits and your financial choices, your employment situation probably affects them most. Your income level, business associates, and available leisure time are a direct result of the work you do. Some people work so that they can pursue their hobbies and recreational activities, while others have a chosen career field that reflects their needs, values, and goals.

Like other decisions, career choice and professional development alternatives have many risks and opportunity costs. In recent years, a large segment of our society has placed family values and personal fulfillment above monetary reward and professional recognition. The many career choices you make will require a continual evaluation of trade-offs related to personal, social, and economic factors. For example:

- Many individuals select employment that is challenging and offers strong personal satisfaction rather than employment in which they can make the most money.
- Individuals may refuse a transfer or promotion that would require moving their families to a new area or reducing their personal time.
- Parents often opt for part-time employment to allow more time for their children.
- Many people have given up secure positions because they preferred the autonomy of operating their own business.

Your ability to assess your personal values, needs, and goals will be an important basis for evaluating the personal and financial opportunity costs of career choice.

The Effect of Education on Income

L.O.1
Recognize the activities associated with career planning and advancement.

Your level of formal training is a determinant of your financial success. Exhibit 2–1 shows the influence of education on annual income. The statistics in this exhibit do not mean that you will automatically earn a certain amount because you have a college degree. The implication of the exhibit is that more education increases your *potential* earning power. However, other factors will also influence your future income. The average monthly earnings of college graduates in the

---

EXHIBIT 2–1
Education and Income

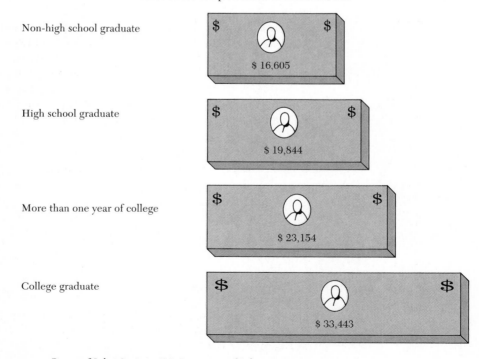

As of the late 1980s, the **average** income for all workers, based on the completed level of education, was:

Non-high school graduate — $ 16,605

High school graduate — $ 19,844

More than one year of college — $ 23,154

College graduate — $ 33,443

SOURCE: Bureau of Labor Statistics, U.S. Department of Labor.

areas of economics, physical/earth sciences, and business/management are higher than those of college graduates in other areas. Although it is true that people with bachelor's degrees earn an average of $1,540 a month and people with associate's degrees earn an average of $1,188 a month, many people with four-year degrees in these fields earn more than people with doctorates.

In addition to formal career training, most successful people, employers, and career counselors stress the importance of certain traits that are adaptable to most work situations. While some of these traits can be acquired in formal school settings, others require experience in other environments. The traits, which successful people usually possess, include

- An ability to work well with others in a variety of settings.
- A desire to do tasks better than they have to be done.
- An interest in reading a wide variety and a large quantity of materials.
- A willingness to cope with conflict and adapt to change.
- An ability to anticipate problems.
- A working knowledge of such computer software as word processing, spreadsheet, and database programs.
- An ability to creatively solve problems.
- A knowledge of research techniques and source materials.
- Well-developed written and oral communication skills.
- An understanding of both their own motivations and the motivations of others.

Career Decision Making

As previously mentioned, your employment choice is not likely to be a one-time decision. Because of changing personal and environmental factors, you will need to continually assess your work situation. Exhibit 2–2 provides a systematic approach to career planning and advancement. As you can see, there are different points of entry, depending on your personal situation.

This process is a suggested framework for planning, changing, or advancing in a career. Your specific strategies will depend on your personal opportunity costs, the alternatives you identify, and your career area. Methods for obtaining employment are quite different for a college professor, an accountant, a computer sales representative, and a government social worker.

FACTORS INFLUENCING CAREER CHOICE

L.O.2
Evaluate the factors that influence career choice and employment opportunities.

Your decision to work in a specific field is influenced by the factors presented in Exhibit 2–3.

Personal Factors

You can identify a satisfying career direction by means of guidance tests that measure your aptitudes, interests, and personal qualities.

What Do You Do Best?   *Aptitudes* are natural abilities that people possess. The ability to work well with numbers, problem-solving skills, and physical dexterity are examples of aptitudes. Certain employment situations require certain competences, and aptitude tests can help identify the tasks at which you will excel.

EXHIBIT 2–2

Stages of Career Planning
and Advancement

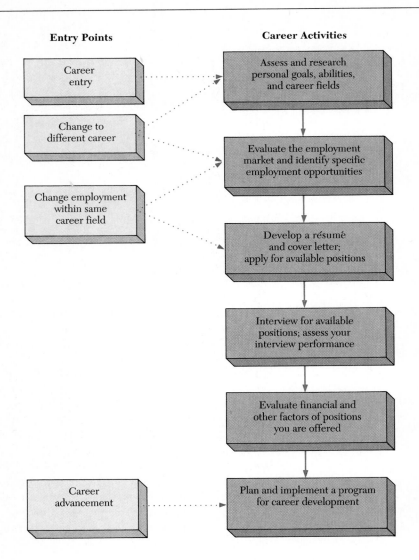

Entry Points

Career entry

Change to different career

Change employment within same career field

Career advancement

Career Activities

Assess and research personal goals, abilities, and career fields

Evaluate the employment market and identify specific employment opportunities

Develop a résumé and cover letter; apply for available positions

Interview for available positions; assess your interview performance

Evaluate financial and other factors of positions you are offered

Plan and implement a program for career development

What Do You Enjoy?   Interest inventories determine the activities that give you the most satisfaction. These instruments measure qualities that are related to various types of work. Individuals with strong social tendencies may be best suited for careers that involve dealing with people, while individuals with investigative interests may be best suited for careers in research areas. Commonly used interest inventories are the *Kuder General Interest Survey* and the *Strong-Campbell Interest Inventory.*

Aptitude tests, interest inventories, and other types of career assessment tests are available at vocational centers and school career counseling offices. You can buy or borrow a book that allows you to take many of these tests at home. For a fee, some testing services will mail you the results of a completed test that you send them.

EXHIBIT 2–3

Factors Influencing Your
Career Selection

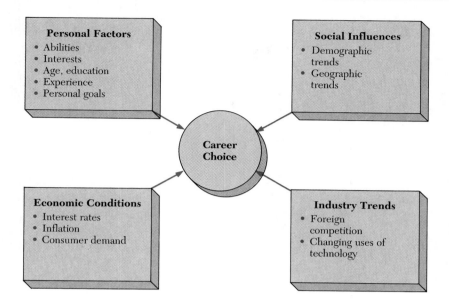

Does a Dream Job Exist?   Test results will not tell you which career to pursue. They will only give you an indication of careers that your aptitudes and interests should lead you to consider. Another important dimension of career selection is your personality. Do you perform best in structured or high-pressure situations, or do you prefer unstructured or creative work environments? The financial aspects of the career are also likely to be a concern.

It has been said that the best job is the one you look forward to on Monday morning. You want a job in which the rewards, location, and work satisfaction are balanced. Some people adapt to any work situation, while others constantly think that the next job will be the best. A vital ingredient in career choice is flexibility, since change will be an integral part of your working life and the job market.

Social Influences

Various demographic and geographic trends are influencing employment opportunities. Demographic trends in our society are affecting the job market in the following ways:

- An increase in the number of working parents is increasing the demand for food service and child care.
- An increase in leisure time among certain segments of the population has resulted in an increased interest in personal health, physical fitness, and recreational products and services.
- An increase in the number of older people has increased the demand for travel services, health care, and retirement facilities.
- An increased demand for additional employment training among some segments of the population has resulted in increased career opportunities for teachers and trainers within business organizations.

With more college-educated people entering the work force, the job market is becoming more competitive. Currently, well over 40 percent of the working people of this country have more than a high school education (about half of them attended college for one to three years); the figure for 1978 was 37 percent.

Changes in the location of jobs continue to influence employment opportunities. At present, the fastest-growing job markets are major cities in California, Florida, and Arizona; Washington, D.C.; Atlanta, Georgia; Norfolk, Virginia; Seattle, Washington; Nassau County, New York; San Antonio, Texas; Boston, Massachusetts; Salt Lake City, Utah; Columbus, Ohio; and Hartford, Connecticut. Geographic location also influences income level. The Bureau of Labor Statistics reports that the mid-Atlantic and north-central areas of the United States have the highest mean earnings.

In considering geographic areas, be sure to assess salary levels. Average incomes are high in such metropolitan areas as Boston, New York, and Chicago, but the prices of food, housing, and other living expenses are also high. What might appear to be a big salary may actually mean a lower standard of living than that of a geographic area with lower salaries and lower living costs.

Economic Conditions

In certain industries, high interest rates, price increases, or reduced demand for goods and services can restrict career opportunities. Unemployment rates are affected by these economic factors. While it is impossible to eliminate the effect of these factors on employment trends, they affect some businesses more than others. For example, high interest rates reduce employment in housing-related industries since people are less likely to buy homes when interest rates are high. Or uncertainty about the stock market results in fewer investment transactions and thus reduces employment opportunities in certain types of financial institutions.

Trends in Industry and Technology

Two factors have reduced manufacturing employment in our economy. First, increased competition from companies in Japan, Germany, and other foreign countries has reduced demand for such American-made products as automobiles and electronic products. Second, automated production methods have reduced the need for manual workers and other entry-level employees in factories.

While career opportunities have dwindled in one sector of our economy, career opportunities in other sectors have grown. Fields that are expected to have the greatest employment potential between now and the year 2000 are

- *Computer technology*—will need systems analysts, computer operators, information systems managers, and repair personnel and technicians for data processing equipment.
- *Health care*—will need medical assistants, physical therapists, physical therapy assistants, home health workers, podiatrists, registered nurses, and health care administrators.
- *Sales and retailing*—will need retail salespeople, marketing representatives, and sales managers with technical knowledge in the areas of electronics, medical products, and financial services.
- *Leisure industry and food services*—will need travel agents, resort and hotel administrators, food preparation workers, and meeting planners.

PERSONAL FINANCE JOURNAL
Self-Employment as a Career Option

More and more individuals are working for themselves rather than for someone else. Each year, more than half a million people start a business. These entrepreneurs are involved in everything from restaurants and gift shops to child care services and computer software.

Would running your own business be an appropriate career for you? That depends on the qualities you possess. Are you a highly motivated, confident individual? Do you have the ability to manage the many different phases of a business? Are you an individual who enjoys challenges and is willing to take risks? Despite the efforts and desires of small-business owners, about 40 percent of the new companies created each year fail within five years.

If you decide that entrepreneurship is for you, there are three main areas of knowledge that can improve your chances for success. First, get to know all aspects of the production, sales, and service of the item you are planning to sell. Second, carefully define your potential customers, select a location, and identify competitors. Finally, consider your financing sources. Most new business owners use a combination of personal funds and loans to get started.

As you start and operate a business, get professional help from experts. A lawyer can assist you in organizing and in obtaining the business permits you need in order to enter certain businesses; and can also assist with the legal matters you encounter during the operation of your company. A local banker can provide financial advice or a loan to expand your business. An accountant can help you handle tax matters and the financial records of the business. Finally, an insurance agent can suggest necessary coverages to protect you from financial disaster.

The career option of small-business management is open to anyone willing to take the risks involved. By the year 2000, women are expected to own half of the small businesses in the United States.

For additional information about starting and operating your own business, contact the Small Business Administration, Attention: Public Information Office, 1441 L Street, NW, Washington, DC 20416.

- *Human resources*—will need recruiters, interviewers, employee benefit administrators, and employment service workers.
- *Financial services*—will need accountants and others with a knowledge of such finance topics as insurance, investments, and taxes.

The demands of industry into the 21st century will include expanded reading and communication skills. More and more employees are being called on to read scientific and technical journals and financial reports, and to write speeches and journal articles. Your career success and potential for advancement are likely to be dependent on these communication skills.

EMPLOYMENT SEARCH STRATEGIES

L.O.3
Implement employment search strategies.

Whether you are looking for your first job or considering a career change, a variety of techniques can assist you in expanding your experience, assessing employment opportunities, and applying for your next position.

Obtaining Employment Experience

A very common concern among people seeking employment is lack of work experience. Part-time or summer employment in your field of interest would be the best situation; if this is not possible, alternatives are available. Most schools offer cooperative education programs and internships. These programs make actual work experience part of your academic studies.

Another source of work-related experience is volunteer work with community organizations. Such work, especially if it is related to your career choice, provides excellent opportunities to acquire skills, establish good work habits, and make contacts. Consider participating in a recycling project, assisting at a senior citizens center, or helping to supervise the park district's youth activities. Any of these efforts will give you valuable experience that is applicable in other work settings.

Class assignments and campus activities are a frequently overlooked source of work-related experience. Too often, students do not see the relationship between school and work. Valuable career skills can be obtained on campus from experience in

- Managing, organizing, and coordinating people and activities as an officer or committee chairperson of a campus organization.
- Public speaking in class, campus, and community presentations.
- Goal setting, planning, supervising, and delegating responsibility in community service and class projects.
- Financial planning and budgeting gained from organizing fund-raising projects, managing personal finances, and handling moneys for campus organizations.
- Conducting research gained from class projects, community involvement, and campus activities.

People who have never been employed or have not been employed recently, such as full-time students or mothers returning to the work force, should view their many experiences at home, in school, at church, and in the community in terms of work skills. The ability to coordinate household resources and activities is comparable to the skills required in a place of business, and sometimes it is more difficult than those skills.

Using Career Information Sources

The career planning and advancement process, like other financial decision making, is enhanced by the use of current and relevant information. Exhibit 2–4 provides an overview of the main sources of career information.

Library Materials   Your school or community library has a wealth of career information ranging from job search guides to in-depth materials on specific careers, employment levels, salaries, and career forecasts. A very comprehensive source of career information is the *Occupational Outlook Handbook,* which is prepared by the Bureau of Labor Statistics, a division of the U.S. Department of Labor. Updated every two years, this extensive volume covers all aspects of career planning and job searching and provides detailed information on jobs in various career clusters. It offers information on approximately 200 occupations. Other helpful government resources related to careers are the *Dictionary of Occupational Titles* and the *Occupational Outlook Quarterly.* These publications supplement the *Occupational Outlook Handbook.*

Mass Media Career Information   Daily news articles and news broadcasts are two more sources of career information. Most newspapers have a column that contains job search tips and career trend data. Newspapers, television, and radio

EXHIBIT 2–4
Career Information Sources

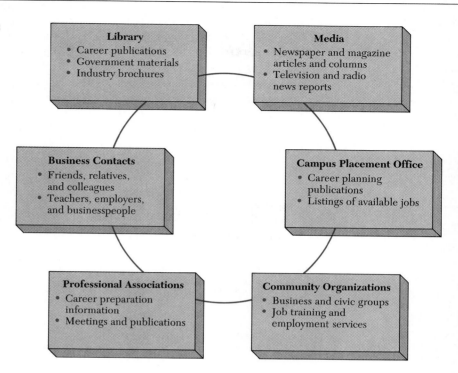

offer helpful information on the economic, social, and business aspects of career planning. Changes in interest rates, consumer preferences, and foreign imports are good indications of the demand for jobs in certain occupational categories.

Magazines are also helpful sources of career information. Timely information is provided by specialized publications such as *National Business Employment Weekly* and by regular features in various periodicals, such as "Job Strategies," which appears each month in *Glamour*.

Campus Placement Office   Your school probably has a career planning and placement service to assist you. This office makes available booklets and other materials on various career planning topics. It will also guide you in creating a résumé and preparing for an interview.

Community Organizations   Every community has a variety of business and civic groups that you can use in your career search. Public meetings featuring industry leaders and business owners provide opportunities to become acquainted with local businesspeople. Members of such organizations as the Chamber of Commerce, Jay-Cees, and Rotary can give you information about current and future jobs in a geographic area.

Professional Associations   Professionals in every career area have organizations that assist them and promote their interests. Organizations of this kind include the American Marketing Association, the Independent Insurance Agents of America, the American Society of Women Accountants, and the National Association of Real Estate Brokers. The *Encyclopedia of Associations* can help you identify organizations in the career areas that interest you. Most of these organizations will provide you with information about career opportunities and about the qualifications you need to enter the professions they represent. Many of them have local chapters and conduct regional meetings.

Business Contacts   Professional contacts can be most helpful in advising you about career preparation and job opportunities. Friends, relatives, the people you meet through community and professional organizations, and the people you have met through school, work, church, or other activities are all potential business contacts. Campus activities such as clubs, sports, and lecture programs will provide you with valuable contacts. You will also meet people who can help you with your career choice if you volunteer for community service activities related to voter registration, recycling centers, or aid to the elderly. Every person you talk to is a potential career contact who may provide information or assistance.

Although the contacts you make may not be able to hire you, if jobs are available, they can refer you to the right person. They can also help you get an **informational interview,** that is, a meeting designed to gather information about a career or an organization. Informational interviews are valuable sources of career planning information because they allow you to interact with people in their actual work setting.

Identifying Job Opportunities

Before you can apply for employment, you need to identify job openings for people with your interests and abilities. Information about career opportunities is available from many of the sources discussed in the previous section. Advertisements in newspapers and professional periodicals are also valuable sources of available positions. Newspapers such as *The Wall Street Journal,* the *New York Times,* the *Chicago Tribune,* and the *Los Angeles Times* have job listings covering a wide geographic area. Local and regional newspapers should also be checked. For opportunities in a specific career field, refer to specialized publications such as *Advertising Age, Marketing News,* the *Journal of Accountancy,* and the *American Banker.*

The various career contacts you develop through community organizations, professional associations, and campus activities will help you identify potential jobs. Your campus placement office probably maintains a list of openings. In addition, many businesses send representatives to campuses to recruit potential employees.

If you want to work in a specific career or for a particular company, conduct research about your interests. Determine what background is needed for your desired occupation, and obtain detailed information about companies for which you would like to work. After learning about your targeted job, present your qualifications to these companies in the form of a letter or a telephone call. Using this method, you can create job opportunities that did not exist previously.

A final source of job leads is an employment agency. This for-profit organization matches job hunters with prospective employers. Often the hiring company pays the fee charged by an employment agency, but be careful of situations where you pay a fee and have no guarantee of getting a job. Government-supported employment services are also available. Contact your state employment service or your state department of labor for further information.

Presenting Yourself to Prospective Employers

Every business must present its product or service to potential customers in an appealing manner. In the same way, you must market yourself to prospective employers by developing a résumé, creating a letter to obtain an interview, and interviewing for available positions.

Résumé Preparation   A **résumé** is a summary of your education, training, experience, and other job qualifications. This personal information sheet is a vital aspect of your employment search. The main components of a résumé are:

1.   *The Personal Data Section.* Here you present your name, address, and telephone number. It may be appropriate to give both a school and home address and telephone number. To avoid discrimination in hiring, you usually do not include your birth date, sex, height, and weight in a résumé unless they are related to specific job qualifications.

2.   *The Career Objective Section.* You may want to omit this section from your résumé because of the problems it might create. A career objective that is too vague will be meaningless to the prospective employer, and a career objective that is too specific might prevent you from being considered for another position within the organization. Many career advisers suggest that your career objective is best communicated in your cover letter.

3.   *The Education Section.* This section should include dates, schools attended, fields of study, and degrees earned. Listing courses directly related to your career field may be appropriate. When your grade point average is exceptionally high, include it to demonstrate your ability to excel.

4.   *The Experience Section.* In this section, you list organizations, dates of involvement, and responsibilities for all previous employment, work-related school activities, and community service. Include significant experiences that demonstrate your ability to perform effectively in a work setting. Maintaining a resource file with information on your work, campus, and community activities will allow you to quickly prepare or update this section.

5.   *The Related Information Section.* Listing honors or awards will communicate your ability to produce quality work. Listing other interests and activities may be appropriate if these relate to your career. However, a long list of this kind might give the impression that work is not your top priority.

6.   *The References Section.* This section lists people who can verify your skills and competences. These individuals may be teachers, previous employers, supervisors, or business colleagues. Be sure to obtain permission from the individuals you plan to use as references. References are usually not included in a résumé, but you will need to have information on references available when a prospective employer requests it.

Three commonly used types of résumés are the chronological résumé, the functional résumé, and the targeted résumé. The first two types are used in a variety of situations while the third type is designed for a specific job. The **chronological résumé** (see Exhibit 2–5) presents your education, work experience, and other information in a reverse time sequence (the most recent item first). This type of résumé is most appropriate for individuals with a continuous school and work record leading to a specific career area. Many people find it to be the best vehicle for presenting their career qualifications.

EXHIBIT 2–5
A Chronological Résumé

CHAD BOSTWICK

SCHOOL ADDRESS	HOME ADDRESS
234B University Drive	765 Cannon Lane
Jasper, MO 54321	Benton, KS 67783
(316) 555-7659	(407) 555-1239

CAREER OBJECTIVE — An entry-level position in medical or health care administration.

EDUCATION — Bachelor of Science in Business Administration and Health Care Marketing, University of South Arkansas, June 1991.

Associate of Arts, Medical Technician Assistant, Arrow Valley Community College, Arlington, Kansas, June 1989

EXPERIENCE — Patient account clerk, University Hospital, Jasper, Missouri, November 1990–present. Researched overdue accounts, created collection method for faster accounts receivable turnover, assisted in training billing clerks.

Sales data clerk, Jones Medical Supply Company, Benton, Kansas, January–August 1989. Maintained inventory records, processed customer records.

CAMPUS ACTIVITIES — Newsletter editor, University of South Arkansas chapter of Financial Management Association, January–June 1991.

Tutor for business statistics and computer lab, 1990–1991.

HONORS — College of Business Community Service Award, University of South Arkansas, June 1991.

Arrow Valley Health Care Society Scholarship, June 1989.

REFERENCES — Furnished upon request.

The **functional résumé** (see Exhibit 2–6) is suggested for individuals with diverse skills and time gaps in their background. This type of résumé emphasizes a person's abilities and skills in such categories as communication, supervision, project planning, human relations, and research. Each section of the résumé provides information on experiences and qualifications rather than dates, places, and job titles. This type of résumé is especially appropriate for individuals who are changing careers or whose most recent experiences are not directly related to the available position.

You may want to develop a résumé for a specific job—that is, a **targeted résumé.** Such a résumé highlights the capabilities and experiences most appropriate to the available position. The format may be similar to that of the chronological or functional résumé, except that it includes a very specific career objective. The targeted résumé takes extra time and research to prepare, but this effort may give you the opportunity to interview for a particularly desirable employment position.

No specific formula exists for the preparation of an effective résumé. However, a résumé must be presented in a professional manner; many candidates are disqualified due to poor ones. Modern word processing equipment and personal computers make the layout process easier. Quick-print businesses will duplicate résumés. Many of these businesses specialize in the preparation and reproduction of personal data sheets.

EXHIBIT 2–6
A Functional Résumé

NANCY FRANK
670 Dove Circle
Reston, ME 01267
(203) 555-6710

CAREER OBJECTIVE
Human resources department position with training responsibilities.

EDUCATION
Master of Arts, Columbia College, Hamilton, New Jersey, 1988
Bachelor of Science, Oral Communications, Martin University, Cooper, New Hampshire, 1983

SUPERVISORY EXPERIENCE
Coordinated conference committees for National Communication Association.
Developed and implemented training program for Ashton Graphics, Harper, Maine.

COMMUNICATION EXPERIENCE
Created training manuals for Benton Printing Company, Reston, Maine.
Wrote press releases for local government agencies, Reston, Maine.

RESEARCH EXPERIENCE
Investigated training problems of large industrial organizations in northeastern United States.

REFERENCES
Furnished upon request.

Limit your résumé to one page if possible. Send a two-page résumé only if you have enough material to fill three pages; then use the most valid information to prepare an impressive two-page data sheet. For best results, seek guidance in preparing and evaluating your résumé. Counselors, the campus placement office, and friends can find errors and suggest improvements.

Thousands of résumés are received by employers each day. As a result of this intense competition, some prospective employees use creative résumés to draw attention to their abilities. Human resource managers have reported receiving résumés in the form of comic strips, wanted posters, advertisements, and menus; résumés attached to balloons, pizzas, and plants; and résumés on videotapes and computer discs. While some of these unusual résumés have been effective, many employers see them as inappropriate gimmicks. The creative approach does work, however, when the job is in a field requiring original thinking, such as advertising, journalism, photography, or public relations.

An Effective Cover Letter   Your résumé presents your qualifications, which must be targeted to a specific organization and job. A **cover letter** is designed to express your interest in a job and obtain an interview. This communication accompanies your résumé and usually consists of an introductory paragraph, one or two development paragraphs, and a concluding paragraph.

The introductory paragraph should get the reader's attention. Indicate your reason for writing by referring to the job or type of employment in which you are interested. Communicate what you have to offer the company based on your experience and qualifications.

The development section should highlight the aspects of your background that specifically qualify you for the job. Refer the employer to your résumé for more details. At this point, you should also elaborate on experiences that will contribute to the organization.

The concluding paragraph should request action from the employer. Ask for the opportunity to discuss your qualifications and potential with the employer in more detail. Include information that will make contacting you convenient, such as telephone numbers and the times when you are available. Close your letter by summarizing how you can benefit the organization.

A separate cover letter should be typed for each of the positions for which you apply. A form cover letter will usually guarantee rejection. Be sure to address your correspondence to the appropriate person in the organization.

A résumé and cover letter are your ticket to the interview. You may possess outstanding qualifications and career potential, but you need an interview to communicate this information. The time, effort, and care you expend in presenting yourself on paper will help you achieve your career goal.

The Job Interview

The interview stage of job hunting is limited to candidates who possess the specific qualifications that the employer wants. Being invited for an interview puts you closer to receiving a job offer.

Preparing for the Interview   Prepare for your interview by obtaining additional information about your prospective employer. The best sources are the company's annual report and other publications that are available to the public. The library has business periodicals and reference volumes with company profiles and current industry news. Attempt to talk with at least one person who is currently employed by the company.

During your research, try to obtain information about the company's past development and current situation. Facts about its operations, competitors, recent successes, planned expansion, and personnel policies will be helpful when you discuss your potential contributions to the company.

Another essential preinterview activity is the development of questions that you would like to ask the interviewer. These questions have two purposes. First, they show that you prepared for the interview. Second, the answers you receive will help you decide whether you would like to work for the company. Some questions to ask in an interview are:

What training opportunities are available to employees who desire to advance?

What do your employees like best about working here?

What plans does the company have for new products or expanded markets?

What actions of competitors are likely to affect the company in the near future?

Also prepare questions on your specific interests and on the particular organization with which you are interviewing. Request information about company policies and employee benefits.

Successful interviewing requires practice. By using a tape recorder or working with friends, you can develop the confidence needed for effective interviewing.

Work to improve your ability to organize ideas, to speak clearly and calmly, and to communicate enthusiasm. Many campus organizations and career placement offices offer opportunities for practice by conducting mock interviews.

As you get ready for the interview, proper dress and grooming will be a consideration. Current employees are the best source of information on how to dress. In general, dress more conservatively than the employees. A business suit is usually appropriate for both men and women. Avoid trendy and casual styles, and don't wear too much jewelry.

The Interview Process   Many companies use a preliminary personal encounter to identify the best candidates. This **screening interview** is an initial meeting, usually brief, with applicants that reduces the pool of job candidates to a workable number. In this situation, interviewees are processed on the basis of overall impression and a few general questions. Screening interviews are frequently conducted on college campuses by corporate recruiters. Success in such an interview qualifies you for closer scrutiny by the employer.

Once you have been judged to be a serious candidate for a job, your next interview can last from one hour to several days. This **in-depth interview,** which is reserved for the finalists in the job search, may involve a series of activities, including responses to questions, meetings with several people on the staff, and a seminar presentation.

When an in-depth interview is conducted, the first few minutes of the interview usually occur in an informal setting. This process is designed to help the interviewee relax and to establish rapport. Next a brief discussion of the available job position may take place. The main part of the interview involves questions to assess your abilities, potential, and personality. Exhibit 2–7 lists some commonly used interview questions. In the last portion of the interview, you are given an opportunity to ask questions.

Most interviewers will conclude the in-depth interview by telling you when you can expect to hear from the company. While waiting, there are two things you should do. First, send a follow-up letter to the company expressing your appreciation for the opportunity to interview. If you don't get the job, this thank-you letter can make a positive impression that improves your chances for future consideration.

Second, do a self-evaluation of your interview performance. Write down the areas that could be improved. Try to remember the questions you were asked that were different from what you expected.

FINANCIAL AND LEGAL ASPECTS OF EMPLOYMENT

When offered an employment position, you should examine a range of factors. Carefully assess the organization, the specific employment position, and the salary and other financial benefits. Also develop an awareness of your legal rights as an employee.

L.O.4
Assess the financial and legal concerns related to obtaining employment

Accepting an Employment Position

Before accepting a position, you may want to do further research about the job and the company. Request information about your specific duties and job

EXHIBIT 2–7

Common Interview
Questions

Education and Training Questions

What experience and training prepare you for this job?
Why are you interested in working for this company?
In addition to going to school, what activities have you engaged in to expand
  your interests and increase your knowledge?
What did you like best about school? What did you like least?

Work and Other Experience Questions

In what types of situations have you done your best work?
Describe the supervisors who motivated you best.
Which of your past accomplishments are you proud of?
Have you ever had to coordinate the activities of several people?
Describe some people whom you have found it difficult to work with.
Describe a situation in which your determination helped you achieve a specific goal.
What situations frustrate you?
Other than past jobs, what experiences have helped prepare you for this job?
What methods do you consider best for motivating employees?

Personal Qualities Questions

What are your major strengths? Your major weaknesses? What have you done to
  overcome your weaknesses?
What do you plan to be doing 5 or 10 years from now?
Which individuals have had the greatest influence on you?
What traits make a person successful?
How well do you communicate your ideas orally and in writing?
How would your teachers and your past employers describe you?
What do you do in your leisure time?
How persuasive are you in presenting ideas to others?

---

expectations. If someone currently has a similar position, ask to talk to that person. If you are replacing a person who is no longer with the company, obtain information about the circumstances of that person's departure.

Another area that you should investigate is the work environment. In the 1980s, the term *corporate culture* emerged. This label refers to such matters as management style, work intensity, dress codes, and social interactions within an organization. For example, some companies have rigid lines of communication, while others have an open-door atmosphere. Are the values, goals, and lifestyles of current employees similar to yours? If not, you may find yourself in an uncomfortable situation that doesn't allow you to perform according to your capabilities.

You should also look into company policies and procedures. For example, how does the company handle salary increases, evaluations of employees, and promotions? Talking with current workers can give you a good indication of the answers to such questions.

Assessing a Compensation Package

Once you have considered your future opportunities and potential satisfaction with a company, you should evaluate the financial benefits of the position. These benefits may be viewed in three time frames:

- Immediate, or short-term, benefits involve current and expected salary, bonuses, and other direct monetary payments.

• •

PERSONAL FINANCE JOURNAL

Careers that Move when You Do

Almost 75 percent of all families are two-income households. If one working spouse relocates for career advancement, the other working spouse may have difficulty in finding employment at the new location. In such situations, flexibility of career direction becomes more important. When her family moved, Joan Senner, an assistant vice president for human resources with a bank, was unable to obtain similar employment. However, her experience in personnel allowed her to get a job with an employment office that eventually led to a better position than the one she had had with the bank.

People in entry-level positions, legal professionals, medical and health care workers, and sales personnel usually have the least trouble in getting a job in a new geographic area. But even individuals with specialized skills can find employment if they are willing to keep an open mind about work opportunities. When his family moved, a former high

school teacher obtained a variety of positions, including insurance agent, park district supervisor, business training specialist, and seminar director for an employment agency.

Flexibility with regard to employment is especially important when a particular geographic area has few jobs available for certain careers. When medical employees are not in demand, but information processing positions offer excellent wages, such flexibility may be crucial to your financial existence. The flexibility may include using your skills and experience to serve a company in an innovative position. Former teachers and counselors, for example, possess an ability to train and guide employees in a way that can improve the overall work environment of an organization. Being willing and able to adapt your talents is vital to continuous employment.

SOURCE: Mary Ellen Schoonmaker, "Careers that Move when You Do," *Working Mother*, December 1985, pp. 28, 30–31.

• •

- Interim benefits include paid holidays and vacation, sick leaves, insurance programs, reimbursement for educational tuition, employee discounts, and recreational facilities. These may be viewed as indirect compensation, whose value may be different for people in different life situations.
- Long-term benefits refer to profit sharing and retirement programs, whose value for employees and their families will be greatest in the future.

Negotiating Salary   Salary is still one of the least discussed topics. Nonetheless, most individuals are concerned about it. Your initial salary will be influenced by your education and training, company size, and salaries for comparable positions. To ensure a fair starting salary, talk to people in similar positions at other companies and check business journals for job ads for information on salary levels for your type of work. In addition, make sure you clearly understand company procedures and policies for granting raises.

Performance quality and work responsibilities are the main influences on salary advances. Meet regularly with your supervisor to obtain performance evaluations and suggestions for professional growth. Communicate your desire for increased work responsibilities and greater financial rewards. Meeting and exceeding organizational expectations should enhance your monetary position. If not, you may wish to consider other employment opportunities.

Comparing Employee Benefits   In recent years, nonsalary employee benefits have been expanded to meet the needs of different life situations. The increasing number of two-income and single-parent households has resulted in a greater need for child care benefits and for leaves of absence to care for newborn children, newly adopted children, and other dependents. The increasing number of older people has increased the need for elder care benefits for employees with dependent parents or grandparents.

Child care benefits are being offered in a variety of forms, ranging from direct payments for child care to facilities on company premises that allow interaction between parent and child during lunch and breaks. Other employee benefits designed to meet the particular needs of employees include flexible work schedules; work-at-home arrangements; legal assistance; counseling for health, emotional, and financial needs; and exercise and fitness programs. Such benefits not only enhance the quality of employees' lives but are also profitable to the organizations that provide them, because happier, healthier employees miss fewer workdays and have a higher level of productivity.

Cafeteria-style employee benefits are programs that allow workers to base their job benefits on a credit system and personal needs. Flexible selection of employee benefits has become quite common. A married employee with children may opt for increased life and health insurance, while a single parent may use benefit credits for child care services. Exhibit 2–8 recommends benefits for certain life situations. Like any other financial decision, the selection of employee benefits involves a trade-off, or opportunity cost, that must be assessed in planning your benefits package.

Two methods that may be used to assess the monetary value of employee benefits are market value calculations and future value calculations.

1.   *Market value* calculations determine the specific monetary value of employee benefits—the cost of the benefits if you had to pay for them. For example, you may view the value of one week's vacation as 1/52 of your annual salary; or you may view the value of a life insurance benefit as what it would cost you to obtain the same coverage. This method can be used to determine the difference between two job offers with different salaries and employee benefits.

2.   *Future value* calculations, as discussed in Chapter 1, can enable you to assess the long-term worth of such employee benefits as pension programs and retirement plans. The future value of payments contributed to a company retirement fund, for example, can be compared to other saving and investment options.

Another factor to consider when determining the value of a pension plan is *vesting*, the point at which retirement payments made by an organization on your behalf belong to you even if you no longer work for the organization. Vesting schedules vary from organization to organization, but all qualified plans (those for which an employer may deduct contributions to the plan for tax purposes) must be fully vested within seven years. Some retirement plans gradually become vested during this period, while others do not have partial vesting but become fully vested at some point within the seven years. Vesting refers only to the employer's contributions to the pension program; employee contributions belong to the employees regardless of the length of their service with the organization.

You should also take tax considerations into account when you assess employment benefits. A *tax-exempt* benefit is one on which you won't have to pay income tax, but a *tax-deferred* benefit will result in the payment of income tax at some future time, such as at retirement. In recent years, the federal government has required that taxes be paid on certain types of nonfinancial benefits. For example, the value of a company car used for personal travel is considered taxable income.

EXHIBIT 2–8

Suggested Employee
Benefits for Different
Life Situations

Life Situation	Recommended Employee Benefits
Single, no children	Disability income insurance to maintain earning power Health insurance Contributions to a retirement program Educational assistance, such as tuition reimbursement
Young family	Comprehensive health insurance Life insurance Child care services
Single parent	Health insurance Life insurance Disability income insurance Dependent care benefits
Married, no children	Health and disability insurance Retirement program contributions Maternity coverage and parental leave (young couple) Long-term health care needs (older couple)
Mixed-generation household	Health and disability insurance Child care services Elder care benefits

NOTE: Although these are the major benefits for the life situations covered, others may also be important. Benefit needs vary by personal situation.

For a benefit plan not to be subject to federal income tax, it must be "nondiscriminatory"—that is, lower-paid workers must be given benefits comparable to those given to highly paid executives. If executives are given life insurance coverage whose premium constitutes a higher proportion of their salaries, the excess value of the insurance premium is taxable. When assessing employment-compensation and benefits, be sure to consider their taxability since an untaxed benefit of lower value may be worth more than a benefit of higher value that is subject to taxation.

Knowing Your Employment Rights

Taxes are only one of the legal aspects of employment. You have various legal rights both during the hiring process and on the job. For example, employers cannot refuse to hire a woman or terminate her employment because of pregnancy, nor can they force her to go on leave at an arbitrary point during her pregnancy. In addition, a woman who stops working because of pregnancy must get full credit for previous service, accrued retirement benefits, and accumulated seniority. Employees should also be aware of these employment rights:

- A person may not be discriminated against in the employment selection process on the basis of age, race, color, religion, sex, or national origin.
- Hiring by federal contractors and subcontractors may not discriminate against individuals with physical or mental handicaps who possess the required competences.
- Minimum wage and overtime pay legislation apply to individuals in certain work settings.
- Workers' compensation (for work-related injury or illness), social security, and unemployment insurance are required benefits.

FINANCIAL PLANNING CALCULATIONS

Tax-Equivalent Employee Benefits

Employee benefits that are nontaxable have a higher financial value than you may realize. A $100 employee benefit on which you are taxed is not worth as much as a nontaxable $100 benefit. This formula is used to calculate the *tax-equivalent value* of a nontaxable benefit:

$$\frac{\text{Value of the benefit}}{(1 - \text{Tax rate})}$$

For example, receiving a life insurance policy with a nontaxable annual premium of $350 is comparable to receiving a taxable employee benefit worth $486 if you are in the 28 percent tax bracket (28 percent is the rate paid on taxable income over $30,000). This tax-equivalent amount is calculated as follows:

$$\frac{\$350}{(1-0.28)} = \frac{\$350}{0.72} = \$486$$

A variation of this formula, which would give the *after-tax* value of an employee benefit, is

Taxable value of the benefit$(1 - \text{Tax rate})$

For the above example, the calculation would be

$$\$486(1 - 0.28) = \$486(0.72) = \$350$$

In other words, a taxable benefit with a value of $486 would have an after-tax value of $350 since you would have to pay $136($486 × 0.28) in tax on the benefit.

These simple calculations can be helpful in assessing and comparing different employee benefits within a company or in considering different jobs. Remember to also consider the value of employee benefits in terms of your personal and family needs and goals.

CAREER DEVELOPMENT TECHNIQUES

L.O.5
Analyze the techniques available for career growth and advancement.

A job is for today, but a career can be for a lifetime. Will you always enjoy the work you do today? Will you be successful in the career you select? These questions cannot be answered right away. But there are a number of skills and attitudes that can lead to a fulfilling work life. Exhibit 2–9 presents some of these ingredients of career success. Other factors can also contribute to job satisfaction. Whether you've just started to work or have been employed many years, a number of activities are available to enhance your career.

Every day of your work life, you can perform duties that will contribute to your career success. Communicating and working well with others will enhance your chances for financial advancement and promotion. Flexibility and an openness to new ideas will help you expand your abilities, knowledge, and career potential.

Develop more efficient work habits. The use of lists, goal setting, note cards, and other time management techniques will help you in this effort. Combine increased productivity with quality. All of your work activities should reflect your best performance. This extra effort will be recognized and rewarded.

Finally, learn to anticipate problems and areas for action. A willingness to assist others and to be creative can help the entire organization and contribute to your work enjoyment and your career growth.

Training Opportunities

Society requires a continual updating of information and skills. Today, there are computerized work situations that did not exist a couple of years ago. Many of the job skills that you will need in the future have yet to be created. Your desire for success is a primary determinant of career and financial advancement, through increased education.

EXHIBIT 2–9   Attitudes for Career Success

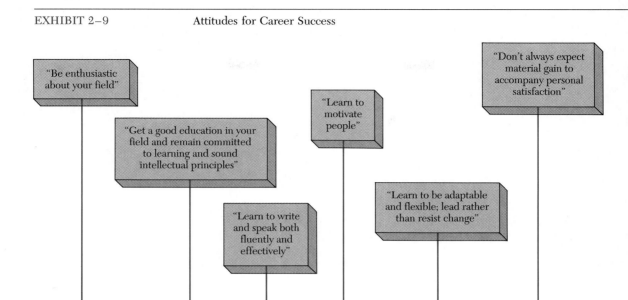

SOURCE: George Gallup, Jr., and Alec M. Gallup, *The Great American Success Story* (Homewood, Ill.: Dow Jones-Irwin, 1986), pp. 167–75.

Various methods for updating and expanding your knowledge are available. Formal methods include company development activities, seminars offered by professional organizations, graduate and advanced college courses. Many companies encourage and pay for such continuing education.

Informal methods for updating and expanding your knowledge include reading and discussion with colleagues. Newspapers, popular magazines, business periodicals, and professional journals offer a wealth of information on business, economic, and social trends. Informal meetings with fellow workers and associates from other companies are also a valuable source of current career information.

Career Paths and Advancement

Throughout your work life, you will need to reassess your employment situation. Like any other financial decisions, previous employment decisions must be reevaluated in light of changing values and goals and of changing economic and social conditions. As shown in Exhibit 2–10, you will evolve through a series of career stages, each with specific tasks and challenges.

A successful technique for coping with the anxieties associated with career development is to gain the support of an established person in your field. A **mentor** is an experienced employee who serves as a teacher and counselor for a less experienced person in a career field. A relationship with a mentor can have such benefits as personalized training, access to influential people, and emotional support during difficult times.

Your efforts to attract a mentor should start with an excellent performance. Show initiative, be creative, and be alert to meeting the needs of others. Maintain visibility and display a desire to learn and grow by asking questions and volunteering for new assignments.

Pepper . . . and Salt

"I'm not sure where my career is going to take me but I'm afraid I might already be there."

From *The Wall Street Journal*, with permission of Cartoon Features Syndicate.

EXHIBIT 2–10   Stages of Career Development: Characteristics and Concerns

Stage	Characteristics	Concerns
Preentry and career exploration stage	• Assess personal interests and set career goals • Obtain necessary training • Gain initial employment	• Matching interests and abilities to employment • Dealing with shock of unfulfilled expectations
Establishment and professional growth stage	• Gain in experience, effectiveness, and respect of colleagues • Concentrate on an area of specialization	• Developing career contacts • Avoiding overinvolvement and career burnout
Advancement and mid-career adjustment stage	• Continue to obtain experience and knowledge to win promotions • Seek new challenges and expanded responsibility	• Finding continued satisfaction • Maintaining sensitivity toward colleagues and subordinates
Late-career and preretirement stage	• Make financial and personal plans for retirement • Assist in training successor	• Determining the extent of professional involvement after retirement • Planning involvement in community activities of personal interest

A prospective mentor should be willing to assist others and to help them grow in both the technical and social areas of a career. Many organizations have implemented formal mentor programs in which an experienced employee is assigned to oversee the career development of a new employee. Many successful mentor relationships involve retired individuals who desire to share their knowledge and experience.

Changing Careers

At some time in their lives, most workers change jobs. This may be done to obtain a better or different position within the same career field or to move into a new career field. Changing jobs may be more difficult than selecting your first job. Unless their present situation is causing mental stress or physical illness, most people are unwilling to exchange the security of an existing position for the uncertainty of an unfamiliar position.

The following situations are frequently indications that it is time to move on:

- Weak motivation toward your current work.
- Physical or emotional distress caused by your job.
- Consistently poor performance evaluations.
- A lack of social interactions with your fellow workers.
- Limited opportunity for salary or position advancement.
- A poor relationship with your superior.

While a decision to change careers may require minor alterations in your life (such as going from retail sales to industrial sales), it might mean extensive retraining and starting at an entry level in a new field. As with every other financial decision, no exact formula exists for deciding whether a career change should be made. However, these guidelines should be followed: First, carefully assess the financial and personal costs and benefits of changing careers in relation to your needs and goals and those of your household. Giving up such benefits as health insurance may be costly to a family, but the expanded career opportunities in a new field may be worth the trade-off. Then determine whether a career change will serve your needs and goals and those of your household while contributing to long-term financial security.

Whether you view a job as a stepping-stone to a higher level or you believe that your present position is also your future, you should continually assess your personal values, your career goals, and the satisfactions that you receive from your work. At the same time, look at your company and its industry to determine whether your personal situation will remain compatible with their situation. These efforts will contribute to a satisfying work life.

SUMMARY

L.O.1
Recognize the activities associated with career planning and advancement.

Career planning and advancement involve the following stages and activities: (1) assess and research personal goals and abilities and career fields; (2) evaluate the employment market and identify specific employment opportunities; (3) develop a résumé and cover letter for use in applying for available positions; (4) interview for available positions; (5) evaluate financial and other factors of the positions you are offered; and (6) plan and implement a program for career development.

L.O.2
Evaluate the factors that influence career choice and employment opportunities.

The selection of a career should be considered in relation to personal abilities, interests, experience, training, and goals; social influences affecting employment such as demographic trends; changing economic conditions; and industrial and technological trends.

L.O.3
Implement employment search strategies.

For successful career planning and development, do the following: Obtain employment or related experiences by working or by participating in campus and community activities. Use career information sources to gain insight into employment fields and to identify job opportunities. Prepare a résumé and cover letter that effectively present your qualifications for a specific employment position. Practice the interview skills that project enthusiasm and competence.

L.O.4
Assess the financial and legal concerns related to obtaining employment.

Evaluate the work environment and compensation package of prospective places of employment. Assess employee benefits on the basis of their market value, future value, and taxability and of your personal needs and goals. Prospective and current employees have legal rights with regard to fair hiring practices and equal opportunity on the job.

L.O.5
Analyze the techniques available for career growth and advancement.

Informal and formal education and training opportunities are available to foster professional development and to facilitate career changes.

GLOSSARY

Cafeteria-style employee benefits   Programs that allow workers to base their job benefits on a credit system and personal needs.

Career   A commitment to a profession that requires continued training and offers a clear path for occupational growth.

Chronological résumé   A data sheet that presents a person's background in a reverse time sequence.

Cover letter   Correspondence that accompanies a person's résumé and expresses interest in a particular job.

Functional résumé   A data sheet that presents a person's background by emphasizing various skills and abilities.

Job   An employment position that a person obtains mainly to earn money, without regard to his or her interests or opportunities for advancement.

In-depth interview   A series of question sessions and other activities that are designed to select one of several candidates for a job.

Informational interview   A visit to a company or with an individual for the purpose of gathering information about a career or an organization.

Mentor   An experienced employee who serves as a teacher and counselor for a less experienced person in a career field.

Résumé   A summary of a person's education, training, experience, and other job qualifications.

Screening interview   An initial meeting with applicants that reduces the pool of job candidates to a workable number.

Targeted résumé   A personal data sheet that is developed for use in applying for a specific job.

DISCUSSION QUESTIONS

L.O.1   1. Based on your work experience and the employment situations of others, how does a *job* differ from a *career*? What factors influence a person to select one or the other?

L.O.1   2. In what ways are career decisions (a first job, a move to another city for a promotion, or a career change) a part of personal financial planning?

L.O.2   3. Give some examples of social, economic, and technological factors that influence career opportunities.

L.O.3   4. How can a person obtain employment-related experiences without working in an employment position?

L.O.3   5. What suggestions would you offer to individuals who want to improve their résumés?

L.O.3   6. How does the information in a cover letter differ from the information in a résumé?

L.O.3   7. How can a person best prepare for an interview?

L.O.4   8. How does a person's life situation influence the importance of certain employee benefits to that person?

L.O.4   9. What types of activities would you recommend to individuals who desire career advancement and professional growth?

L.O.5 10. Should employees be required to take tests every few years to determine the quality of their skills?

Opening Case Questions

1. How could Kelly Thomas improve her chances of finding employment?
2. What practical experience might Steve Bauer have obtained while in college?
3. How might Ellen Mason revise her cover letter?
4. What factors do you consider most important in the career planning and development process?

PROBLEMS AND ACTIVITIES

L.O.1   1. Conduct a survey of currently employed people to determine which school courses contributed most to their career success.

L.O.1   2. Interview an individual who recently made a major career change. Determine what personal and economic factors influenced this decision. What specific career planning activities did he or she use?

L.O.2   3. Prepare a list of work and leisure activities that you enjoy. How could these activities be the basis for selecting a career?

L.O.2   4. Based on a newspaper or magazine article covering current economic news, describe how business conditions will affect demand for certain types of employment.

L.O.3   5. Using the *Occupational Outlook Handbook* and other career information sources, research one or more career areas that interest you. What additional information would you like to have about this career area? How could this information be obtained?

L.O.3   6. Make arrangements for an informational interview at a local company or with someone you know. Prepare a list of questions to ask during the interview.

L.O.4   7. Talk with a human resources manager about the types of employee benefits offered by his or her company.

L.O.4   8. Calculate the future value of a retirement account in which you deposit $2,000 a year for 30 years at an annual interest rate of 8 percent. (Use Tables in Appendix B.)

L.O.4   9. Which types of employee benefits would be most needed by individuals in the following life situations:
   a. A single parent with a preschool child and a child in elementary school.
   b. A two-income couple without children.
   c. A person who has a daughter in college and must also care for an elderly parent.

L.O.4   10. Which of the following employee benefits has the greater value? Use the formula given in the "Financial Planning Calculations" box on page 54 to compare these benefits. (Assume a 28 percent tax rate.)
   a. A nontaxable pension contribution of $4,300 or the use of a company car with a taxable value of $6,325.
   b. A life insurance policy with a taxable value of $450 or a nontaxable increase in health insurance coverage valued at $340.

L.O.5   11. Talk to people employed in various career areas to obtain information about the training and professional development opportunities that they have found most valuable.

LIFE SITUATION   Case 2–1

A Dead-End Career Path

Joanne Nash has tried to get a sales job for three months. She has applied for a position with companies that sell everything from automobiles and electronic products to medical supplies and restaurant equipment. Joanne has always worked in an office. She completed two years of college and took several business courses. She sees sales as a chance to meet interesting people and earn a higher salary.

During interviews, Joanne displays a very pleasant and outgoing personality. The company representatives like talking with her, but they have not offered her a job due to her limited knowledge and her limited sales experience.

Questions

1. As a career counselor, what suggestions would you offer Joanne?
2. What experience might Joanne have that could be adapted to a sales career?
3. How could a specific career objective be valuable to Joanne?
4. What types of career information materials could Joanne use to improve her chances of obtaining a sales job?

LIFE SITUATION   Case 2–2

Where's Bill's Future?

For the past 22 years, Bill O'Connor has been employed by Newton Department Stores. He was promoted from salesclerk to department manager and then to store manager. Currently, as the regional manager for the Mountain Division, Bill is responsible for 14 stores in six states.

Newton was recently sold to BXT Industries, a diversified, multinational company involved in oil exploration, athletic equipment, European resorts, and computer components. Bill is fearful that the takeover will result in a reorganization that would eliminate his job.

Questions

1. What research efforts might Bill take to investigate his future with BXT Industries?
2. What types of career alternatives does Bill have?
3. What should Bill do at this point in his career?

SUPPLEMENTARY READINGS

For Additional Information on Career Planning

Bolles, Richard Nelson. *What Color Is Your Parachute? A Practical Manual for Job-Hunters and Career-Changers.* Berkeley, Calif.: Ten Speed Press, 1990.

"Job Hunting after 50." *Modern Maturity,* June–July 1989, pp. 36–37.

Moskowitz, Milton, and Carol Townsend. "The 60 Best Companies for Working Mothers." *Working Mother,* October 1989, pp. 74–100.

For Additional Information on Employment Opportunities

Moreau, Dan. "Jobs with a Bright Future." *Changing Times,* January 1990, pp. 44–48.

Occupational Outlook Handbook. U.S. Government Printing Office, Washington, DC 20402.

Occupational Outlook Quarterly. U.S. Government Printing Office, Washington, DC 20402.

For Additional Information on Employee Benefits and Career Advancement

Bodnar, Janet. "Make the Most of Your Fringe Benefits." *Changing Times,* September 1989, pp. 93–98.

Managing Your Career. Dow Jones and Co., Educational Service Bureau, Box 300, Princeton, NJ 08543.

Wiatrowski, William J. "Comparing Employee Benefits in the Public and Private Sectors." *Monthly Labor Review,* December 1988, pp. 3–8.

A Working Woman's Guide to Her Job Rights. Consumer Information Center, Pueblo, CO 81009.

3

Money Management Strategy
Financial Statements and Budgeting

Your daily spending and saving decisions are at the center of your financial planning. These decisions must be coordinated with your needs, goals, and personal situation and with financial information. When people watch a baseball or football game, they usually know the score. With financial planning, the score is also important. Various financial records provide information on your wins and losses in the money game. Maintaining financial documents and planning your spending are essential to successful personal financial management. The time and effort you devote to these recordkeeping duties will yield benefits in the form of clear information and informed financial decisions.

LEARNING OBJECTIVES
After studying this chapter, you will be able to:

L.O.1 Recognize the relationships among various money management documents and activities.

L.O.2 Create a system for maintaining personal financial documents.

L.O.3 Develop a personal balance sheet and cash flow statement.

L.O.4 Create and implement a budget.

L.O.5 Calculate needed savings for achieving financial goals.

OPENING CASE

A Money Management Mess

Jeff Conrad completed high school two years ago. Afterward, he continued to live with his parents while attending college across town. He had a part-time job as a sales and inventory clerk at a department store. With his income, he was able to pay his school expenses and save $1,000. Since his parents paid for housing and food, he was able to make car payments, buy clothes, and spend money on entertainment activities.

During the past two years, Jeff never kept track of his spending habits. His financial recordkeeping consisted of depositing half of his income in a checking account and half in a savings account. Whenever he needed to pay a bill or make a purchase, he would write a check. If he didn't have enough money in checking, he would transfer funds from savings to checking. When he decided to get his own apartment, he didn't have a realistic picture of his finances and living expenses.

During the first few months in his apartment, Jeff was able to work full-time and could pay his bills on time. When school started in September, however, his income decreased since he worked fewer hours. Also, he had to use most of his savings to pay for tuition and books. These school costs were higher than those he had paid the previous year.

As time passed, Jeff had other expenses, such as automobile repairs, insurance for his car and other property, and medical bills. The cost of food, electricity, and telephone was higher than he had anticipated. Jeff's financial independence was not as pleasant as he had hoped it would be.

Budgeting and an understanding of living expenses are skills that many people learn only after difficult experiences. An ability to plan and document spending is the starting point of successful money management and effective financial planning.

A PLAN FOR SUCCESSFUL MONEY MANAGEMENT

L.O.1
Recognize the relationships among various money management documents and activities.

Daily financial decisions involve making choices about your use of personal economic resources. Efforts to coordinate daily spending are vital to an overall financial plan. **Money management** refers to the day-to-day financial activities necessary to handle current personal economic resources while working toward long-term financial security.

Opportunity Cost and Money Management

The average consumer can choose from more than 25,000 items in a supermarket, from more than 11,000 periodicals, and from as many as 60 television stations. Daily decision making is a fact of life, and trade-offs are associated with each of the choices made. Selecting an alternative means that you give up something else. In terms of money management decisions, your trade-offs, or *opportunity costs,* can be viewed in these terms:

- Spending money on current living expenses reduces the amount that can be used for saving and investing toward long-term financial security.
- Saving and investing current income reduce the amount that can be spent now.
- Buying on credit results in payments later and a reduction in the amount of future income available for spending.
- Using savings for purchases results in lost interest earnings and in an inability to use them for other purposes.
- Engaging in comparison shopping can save money and improve the quality of purchases but gives up something of value that cannot be replaced—your time.

EXHIBIT 3–1
Major Money Management
Activities

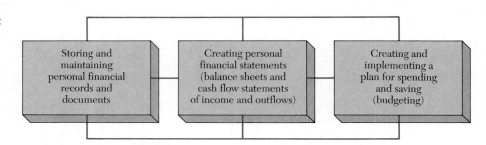

As you develop and implement various money management activities, continually assess the financial and personal costs and benefits associated with money management decisions.

Components of Money Management

As shown in Exhibit 3–1, the three major money management activities are interrelated. Personal financial records and documents are the foundation of systematic resource use. They provide written evidence of business transactions, ownership of property, and legal matters. Personal financial statements enable you to measure and assess your financial position and progress. And your spending plan, or budget, is the driving force of effective money management.

PERSONAL FINANCIAL RECORDS

L.O.2
Create a system for maintaining personal financial documents.

Someone once said that the computer age would result in fewer paper documents. How wrong that person was! Today, computers are generating more paperwork than ever. Much of that paperwork relates to financial matters. Invoices, credit card statements, insurance policies, and tax records are the basis of financial recordkeeping and personal economic choices.

Organized money management requires a system of financial records that provide a basis for

- Handling daily business affairs, including the payment of bills on time.
- Planning and measuring financial progress.
- Completing required tax reports.
- Making effective investment decisions.
- Determining available resources for current and future buying.

As shown in Exhibit 3–2, most financial records are kept in one of two places—a home file or a safe-deposit box. A home file should be used to keep records for current needs and documents with limited value. Your home file may be a series of folders, a cabinet with several drawers, or even a cardboard box. Whatever the method you use, it is most important that your home file be simply organized to allow quick access to required documents and information.

Important financial records and valuable articles should be kept in a location that provides better security than a home file. A **safe-deposit box** is a private storage area at a financial institution that offers maximum security for valuables and difficult-to-replace documents. Access to the contents of a safe-deposit box requires two keys. One key is issued to you; the other is kept by the financial

EXHIBIT 3–2   Where to Keep Your Financial Records

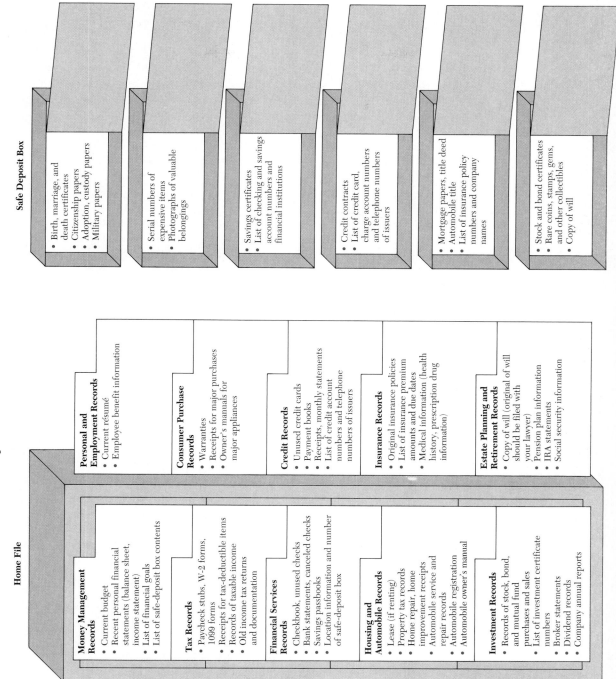

Home File

Money Management Records
- Current budget
- Recent personal financial statements (balance sheet, income statement)
- List of financial goals
- List of safe-deposit box contents

Tax Records
- Paycheck stubs, W-2 forms, 1099 forms
- Receipts for tax-deductible items
- Records of taxable income
- Old income tax returns and documentation

Financial Services Records
- Checkbook, unused checks
- Bank statements, canceled checks
- Savings passbooks
- Location information and number of safe-deposit box

Housing and Automobile Records
- Lease (if renting)
- Property tax records
- Home repair, home improvement receipts
- Automobile service and repair records
- Automobile registration
- Automobile owner's manual

Investment Records
- Records of stock, bond, and mutual fund purchases and sales
- List of investment certificate numbers
- Broker statements
- Dividend records
- Company annual reports

Personal and Employment Records
- Current résumé
- Employee benefit information

Consumer Purchase Records
- Warranties
- Receipts for major purchases
- Owner's manuals for major appliances

Credit Records
- Unused credit cards
- Payment books
- Receipts, monthly statements
- List of credit account numbers and telephone numbers of issuers

Insurance Records
- Original insurance policies
- List of insurance premium amounts and due dates
- Medical information (health history, prescription drug information)

Estate Planning and Retirement Records
- Copy of will (original of will should be filed with your lawyer)
- Pension plan information
- IRA statements
- Social security information

Safe Deposit Box
- Birth, marriage, and death certificates
- Citizenship papers
- Adoption, custody papers
- Military papers

- Serial numbers of expensive items
- Photographs of valuable belongings

- Savings certificates
- List of checking and savings account numbers and financial institutions

- Credit contracts
- List of credit card, charge account numbers and telephone numbers of issuers

- Mortgage papers, title deed
- Automobile title
- List of insurance policy numbers and company names

- Stock and bond certificates
- Rare coins, stamps, gems, and other collectibles
- Copy of will

institution in which the safe-deposit box is located. Items commonly kept in a safe-deposit box include stock certificates, contracts, a list of insurance policies, and valuables such as rare coins and stamps.

The number of financial records and documents may seem overwhelming, but they can easily be organized into 10 basic categories. These categories correspond to the major topics covered in this book. You may not need to use all of the following records and documents at present. However, as your financial situation changes, you will use them.

1. *Money Management Records.* The foundation of your financial records is documents listing your possessions, debts, and spending patterns. A **budget** is a specific plan for spending your income. This device helps an individual or a family control spending while working toward various financial goals.

2. *Personal and Employment Records.* From the day you are born, legal and financial documents are a part of your life. Your birth certificate and later a social security card and, perhaps, a marriage license are among the items that you should keep in your financial records file. Once you are employed, employee benefit information, pension data, and other work records will be added to your recordkeeping system.

3. *Tax Records.* Your annual tax return will be easier to prepare if you keep organized records and documents. Information about income and deductible expenses is necessary. Tax forms, earnings statements, government publications, and articles about changes in tax laws will minimize the burden associated with preparing a tax return.

4. *Financial Services Records.* Most people use one or more services offered by financial institutions. The documents associated with savings and checking accounts are canceled checks, bank statements, savings passbooks, certificates of deposit, and interest earnings reports.

5. *Credit Records.* Buying on credit is a part of most people's lives. The legal agreements between a borrower and a lender, along with payment books, monthly statements, unused credit cards, and other credit-related information, need to be stored carefully.

6. *Consumer Purchase Records.* A receipt provides evidence of payment for a consumer purchase. Some products have a *warranty,* which is a written statement from the manufacturer giving the conditions under which an item can be returned, replaced, or repaired. Expensive items such as appliances and recreational equipment may come with a serial number document and service information booklets.

7. *Housing and Automobile Records.* Housing and transportation are usually the two items on which we incur the largest costs. If you rent, the *lease* is your main document; if you buy a home, you will be concerned with various mortgage papers and real estate documents. Such automobile records as the title, registration report, and service information are also an important part of your financial file.

8. *Insurance Records.* The protection of your belongings and your financial well-being is represented by insurance policies. These are the contractual agreements between you and insurance companies that specify the type, amounts, and costs of coverage for your life, health, home, and automobile.

9. *Investment Records.* Once you have provided for current living expenses and adequate insurance coverage, concentrate on an investment program. The documents for this phase of financial planning include investment research reports, stock and bond certificates, and statements from brokers summarizing transactions.

10. *Estate Planning and Retirement Records.* A fundamental aspect of this area of personal finance is a *will*. This legal document states how a person wants his or her wealth to be distributed after death. Other information related to long-range finances includes social security data, individual retirement account (IRA) statements, and pension plan information.

How long should information be kept? The answer to this question differs for various kinds of items. Such records as birth certificates, wills, and social security data should be kept permanently. Records on property and investments should be kept as long as you own these items. Federal tax laws influence the length of time that tax-related information should be kept. Copies of tax returns and supporting data should be saved for six years. Normally, an audit will go back only three years, but under certain circumstances the Internal Revenue Service may request information six years back. Documents related to the purchase and sale of real estate should probably be kept indefinitely.

PERSONAL FINANCIAL STATEMENTS: MEASURING FINANCIAL PROGRESS

L.O.3
Develop a personal balance sheet and cash flow statement.

Most of the financial documents that we have discussed come from financial institutions, other business organizations, or government. Two documents that you create yourself, the personal balance sheet and the cash flow statement, are called *personal financial statements* or reports. These documents provide information about your current financial position and present a summary of your current income and spending. The main purposes of personal financial statements are to

- Report your current financial position in relation to the value of the items you own and the amounts you owe.
- Measure your progress toward your financial goals.
- Maintain information on your financial activities.
- Provide data that you can use in preparing tax forms or applying for credit.

Your Personal Balance Sheet

The financial position of an individual or a family is a common starting point for financial planning. A **balance sheet,** also known as a net worth statement, specifies what you own and what you owe. A personal balance sheet is prepared to determine your current financial position using the following process:

Items of value	minus	Amounts owed	equals	Net worth

For example, if your possessions are worth $4,500 but you owe $800 to others, your net worth is $3,700.

Listing Items of Value   Available cash and money in bank accounts combined with other items that have a value are the basis of your current financial position. **Assets** are cash and other property that has a monetary value. The balance sheet for Cheryl and Steve Belford (Exhibit 3–3) lists their assets under these three categories:

PERSONAL FINANCE JOURNAL

Welcome to the Real World!

To survive in the real world, remember the following tips:

Insurance premiums are not like stock premiums. You pay them. They don't pay you.

People aren't kidding when they say, "Wash whites separately."

The rate of interest is what kills you, not the down payment.

Cars need not only gasoline but also oil, antifreeze, brake and transmission fluid, and about one fourth of your annual wage for other automobile-related expenses.

Grocery coupons are not socially unacceptable.

Greasy burgers will eventually damage your health; eat good meals.

Buy good stuff. It lasts longer.

Push-ups are just as effective on the living room floor as they are at a $50 a month, $320 a year, Eros Total Body Fitness Center.

If you don't like your job, quit. Otherwise, shut up.

There is no such thing as a self-cleaning oven.

Shower curtains are replaceable.

You are going to need silverware.

No one sells a car because it runs too well.

Never chew red peppers during a job interview.

Get a credit card. Salesclerks are suspicious of cash.

Avoid credit cards. The heck with salesclerks.

Plastic garbage bags are not a luxury item. Look in the bottom of the wastebasket for proof.

Anything-of-the-month clubs are the mail-order equivalent of chronic lower back pain.

You need to hurry up and learn patience.

SOURCE: Wes Smith, "Hey Grads, Your Real Final Exam Awaits," *Chicago Tribune,* June 1, 1986, sec. 3, pp. 1, 4.

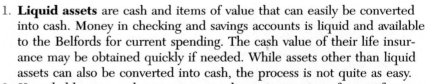

1. **Liquid assets** are cash and items of value that can easily be converted into cash. Money in checking and savings accounts is liquid and available to the Belfords for current spending. The cash value of their life insurance may be obtained quickly if needed. While assets other than liquid assets can also be converted into cash, the process is not quite as easy.

2. *Household assets and possessions* are the major portion of assets for most families. Included in this category are a home, an automobile, and other personal belongings. While these items have value, it is difficult to quickly convert them to cash. You will usually list your possessions on the balance sheet at their original cost. However, these values probably need to be revised over time since a five-year-old television, for example, is worth less now than it was worth when new. Thus, you may wish to list your possessions at their current value (also referred to as *market value*). This method takes into account the fact that such things as a home or jewelry increase in value over time. Estimating current value may be done by looking at ads for the selling price of comparable automobiles, homes, or other possessions.

3. Finally, *investment assets* consist of money set aside for long-term financial needs. The Belfords' investments will be used for such things as financing their children's education, purchasing a vacation home, and plan-

EXHIBIT 3–3   Developing a Personal Balance Sheet

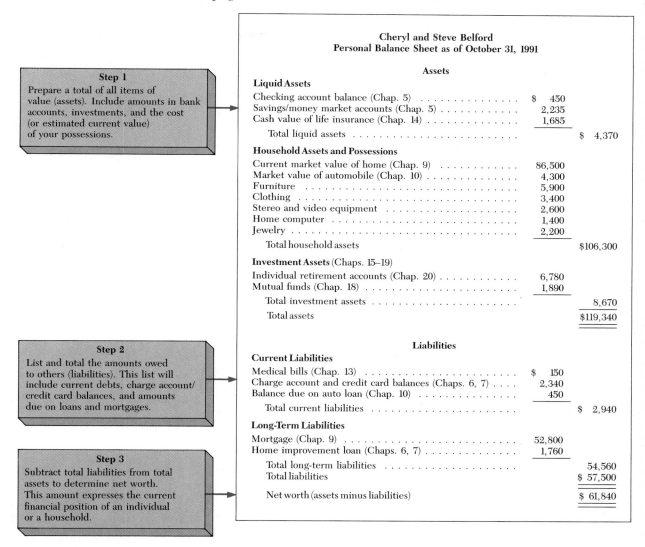

Step 1
Prepare a total of all items of value (assets). Include amounts in bank accounts, investments, and the cost (or estimated current value) of your possessions.

Step 2
List and total the amounts owed to others (liabilities). This list will include current debts, charge account/ credit card balances, and amounts due on loans and mortgages.

Step 3
Subtract total liabilities from total assets to determine net worth. This amount expresses the current financial position of an individual or a household.

Cheryl and Steve Belford
Personal Balance Sheet as of October 31, 1991

Assets

Liquid Assets

Checking account balance (Chap. 5)	$ 450	
Savings/money market accounts (Chap. 5)	2,235	
Cash value of life insurance (Chap. 14)	1,685	
Total liquid assets		$ 4,370

Household Assets and Possessions

Current market value of home (Chap. 9)	86,500	
Market value of automobile (Chap. 10)	4,300	
Furniture	5,900	
Clothing	3,400	
Stereo and video equipment	2,600	
Home computer	1,400	
Jewelry	2,200	
Total household assets		$106,300

Investment Assets (Chaps. 15–19)

Individual retirement accounts (Chap. 20)	6,780	
Mutual funds (Chap. 18)	1,890	
Total investment assets		8,670
Total assets		$119,340

Liabilities

Current Liabilities

Medical bills (Chap. 13)	$ 150	
Charge account and credit card balances (Chaps. 6, 7)	2,340	
Balance due on auto loan (Chap. 10)	450	
Total current liabilities		$ 2,940

Long-Term Liabilities

Mortgage (Chap. 9)	52,800	
Home improvement loan (Chaps. 6, 7)	1,760	
Total long-term liabilities		54,560
Total liabilities		$ 57,500
Net worth (assets minus liabilities)		$ 61,840

NOTE: Various asset and liability items are discussed in the chapters listed next to them.

ning for retirement. Since investment assets fluctuate in value, the amounts listed should reflect their value at the time the balance sheet is prepared.

Determining Amounts Owed   Looking at the Belfords' total assets, you might conclude that they have a strong financial position. But their debts must also be considered. **Liabilities** are amounts owed to others but do not include items not yet due, such as next month's rent. A liability is a debt that you owe now, not something you may owe in the future. Liabilities can be divided into two categories:

1. **Current liabilities** are debts that must be paid within a short time, usually less than a year. These liabilities include such things as medical bills, tax payments, and amounts due for short-term loan and charge accounts.
2. **Long-term liabilities** are debts that are not required to be paid in full until more than a year from now. Common long-term liabilities include auto loans, educational loans, and mortgages. A mortgage is an amount borrowed to buy a house or other real estate that will be repaid over a period of 15 to 30 years. In a similar way, a home improvement loan may be repaid to the lender over the next 5 to 10 years.

The debts listed in the liability section of a balance sheet represent the amount owed at the moment; they do not include future interest payments. However, each debt payment is likely to include a portion of interest. Further discussion of the cost of borrowing is presented in Chapters 6 and 7.

Computing Net Worth   Your **net worth** is the difference between your total assets and your total liabilities. This relationship can be stated as

Assets − Liabilities = Net worth

Net worth is the amount that a person would have if all assets were sold for the listed amounts and all debts were paid in full. Also, total assets equal total liabilities plus net worth. The balance sheet of a business is usually expressed as

Assets = Liabilities + Net worth

As shown in Exhibit 3–3, the Belfords have a net worth of $61,840. Since very few, if any, people liquidate all of their assets, the amount of net worth has a more practical purpose: It is a measurement of your current financial position.

Insolvency is the inability to pay debts when they are due; it occurs when a person's liabilities far exceed his or her available assets. Bankruptcy, a subject discussed in Chapter 7, may be declared by a person in this position.

Net worth can be increased in various ways, including

- Increased earnings from wages, salary, or investments, with higher savings.
- Reduced spending for current living expenses, with higher savings.
- Increased values of investments such as stocks, rare coins, or real estate.
- Reduced amounts owed to others.
- Increased values of personal belongings and other possessions.

Remember, your net worth is *not* money available for use, but an indication of your financial position on a given date.

Evaluating Your Financial Position

Assessing your financial progress with a personal balance sheet can help you achieve your goals. You are experiencing financial improvement if your net worth increases each time you prepare a balance sheet. Your financial status will improve more rapidly if you are able to set aside more money each month for savings and investments.

Like net worth, the relationship between various balance sheet items can give you an indication of your financial position. In general, a lower *debt ratio*— liabilities divided by net worth—indicates a more favorable financial position. For

· ·

PERSONAL FINANCE JOURNAL

What Are Americans Worth?

As of the late 1980s, American households had the following assets and liabilities.

Assets				Liabilities		
Item	**Percentage of Households Possessing This**	**Average Value**		**Item**	**Percentage of Households Possessing This**	**Average Value**
Checking and savings accounts	89.2%	$ 7,445		Home mortgages	38.4%	$34,564
Automobiles	85.9	7,964		Other debt	64.6	3,837
Home	65.7	80,650				
Other real estate	22.4	118,892				
Savings certificates	27.9	31,575				
Retirement accounts	27.3	18,752				
Bonds	20.2	28,116				
Stocks	19.3	81,367				
Pension plans	14.8	26,704				
Business assets	12.4	210,310				

Sources: *American Demographics*, June 1989, p. 20; *Consumer Close-Ups*, Ithaca, N.Y.: 1988–89:4.

· ·

example, if you have $50,000 in debts and a net worth of $25,000, your debt ratio is 2 ($50,000/$25,000); but if you have $25,000 in debts and a net worth of $50,000, your debt ratio is 0.5 ($25,000/$50,000).

Another balance sheet relationship that indicates your financial position is the *current ratio*—liquid assets divided by current liabilities. This relationship indicates how well you will be able to pay your upcoming debts. If you have $4,000 in liquid assets and $2,000 in current liabilities, your current ratio is 2 ($4,000/ $2,000). This means that you have $2 in liquid assets for every dollar in current liabilities.

The debt ratio, the current ratio, and other financial analysis methods, discussed in Chapter 6, can assist you in planning your spending and reaching your financial goals.

Your Cash Flow Statement of Income and Outflows

Each day, financial events can affect your net worth. As you receive a paycheck or pay living expenses, your total assets and liabilities will change. **Cash flow** is the actual inflow and outflow of cash during a given time period. Income from employment will probably represent the most important cash inflow, but other income (such as interest credited to a savings account) should also be considered. In contrast, payments for such things as rent, food, and loans represent cash outflows.

A **cash flow statement** is a summary of cash receipts and payments for a given period, such as a month or a year. This report provides data on your income and spending patterns, information that will be helpful for preparing a budget. A checking account can be used to prepare your cash flow statement. Deposits to the account are your *inflows*; checks written are your *outflows*. In using this system when you do not deposit the entire amounts received, you must, of course, note the undeposited amounts in your cash flow statement.

The process for preparing a cash flow statement is:

| Total cash received during the time period | minus | Cash outflows during the time period | equals | Cash surplus or deficit |

Sources of Income   The preparation of a cash flow statement starts by identifying the cash received during the time period involved. **Income** is the inflows of cash to an individual or a household. For most people, the main source of income is money received from a job. Common income sources include

- Wages, salaries, and commissions.
- Self-employment income.
- Saving and investment income (interest, dividends, rent).
- Gifts, grants, scholarships, and educational loans.
- Payments from government for social security, public assistance, and unemployment benefits.
- Amounts received from pension and retirement programs.
- Alimony and child support payments.

In Exhibit 3–4, notice that Susan Morgan's monthly salary of $2,350 is her main source of income. But she does not have use of the entire amount. **Take-home pay** is a person's earnings after deductions for taxes and other items. Susan's deductions for federal, state, and social security taxes are $470. Her take-home pay is $1,880. This amount plus earnings from savings and investments is the income she has available for use during the current month.

Cash Outflows   Cash payments for living expenses and other items make up the second component of a cash flow statement. Susan Morgan divides her cash outflows into two major categories: fixed expenses and variable expenses. While every individual and household has different cash outflows, these main categories along with the subgroupings used by Susan can be adapted to most situations.

1. *Fixed expenses* are payments that do not vary from month to month. Rent or mortgage payments, installment loan payments, cable television service fees, and a monthly train ticket for commuting to work are examples of constant or fixed cash outflows.

For Susan, another type of fixed expense is the amount she sets aside each month for payments due once or twice a year. For example, Susan pays $240 every March for life insurance. Each month, she records a fixed outflow of $20 for deposit in a special savings account so that the money will be available when her insurance payment is due.

EXHIBIT 3–4   Developing a Cash Flow Statement of Income and Outflows

Step 1

For a set time period, such as a month, record your income from various sources, such as wages, salary, interest or payments from government.

Step 2

Develop categories and record cash payments for the time period covered by the cash flow statement.

Step 3

Subtract the total outflows from the total inflows. A positive number (surplus) represents the amount available for saving and investing. A negative number (deficit) represents the amount that must be taken out of savings or borrowed.

Susan Morgan
Cash Flow Statement for the Month Ended September 30, 1991

Income (cash inflows)

Salary (gross)		$2,350	
Less deductions			
Federal income tax	$235		
State income tax	45		
Social security	190		
Total deductions		$ 470	$1,880
Interest earned on savings			34
Earnings from investments			62
Total income			$1,976

Cash Outflows

Fixed Expenses

Rent	$ 690	
Loan payment	86	
Cable television	43	
Monthly train ticket	147	
Life insurance	20	
Apartment insurance	23	
Total fixed outflows		$1,009

Variable Expenses

Food at home	212	
Food away from home	168	
Clothing	76	
Telephone	52	
Electricity	48	
Personal care (dry cleaning, laundry, cosmetics)	47	
Medical expenses	55	
Recreation/entertainment	78	
Gifts	38	
Donations	45	
Total variable outflows	819	
Total outflows		$1,828
Cash surplus + (or deficit −)		+ $ 148

Allocation of Surplus

Emergency fund savings	30
Savings for short-term/intermediate financial goals	68
Savings/investing for long-term financial security	50
	$148

2. *Variable expenses* are flexible payments that change from month to month. Common examples of variable cash outflows are food, clothing, utilities (such as electricity and telephone), recreation, medical expenses, gifts, and donations. The use of your checkbook or some other recordkeeping system is necessary for an accurate total of cash outflows.

FINANCIAL PLANNING IN ACTION
Measuring Your Financial Progress

A balance sheet is prepared on a periodic basis, such as every three or six months. Between those points in time, your budget and cash flow statement are used to plan and

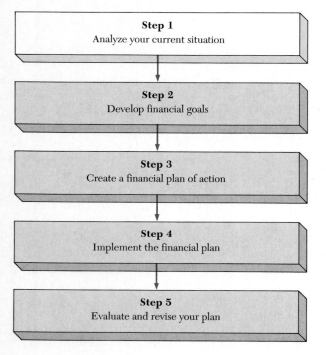

measure your spending and saving activities. For example, during a certain calendar year, you might prepare a balance sheet on January 1, June 30, and December 31. Your budget would serve to plan your spending and saving between these points in time, and your cash flow statement of income and outflows would document your actual spending and saving. This relationship may be illustrated as shown below.

Changes in your net worth are the result of the relationship between cash inflows and outflows. In periods when your outflows exceed your inflows, you must draw upon savings or borrow (buy on credit). When this happens, your lower assets (savings) or higher liabilities (due to the use of credit) result in a lower net worth. When inflows exceed outflows, putting money into savings or paying off debts will result in a higher net worth. In general, the relationship between the cash flow statement and the balance sheet may be expressed as shown below.

Cash Flow Statement	**Balance Sheet**
If cash inflows (income) are greater than cash outflows.......	Net worth increases
If cash outflows (payments) are greater than cash inflows (income)	Net worth decreases

Using a budget, creating a cash flow statement, and developing a balance sheet on a periodic basis will assist you in improving your financial situation.

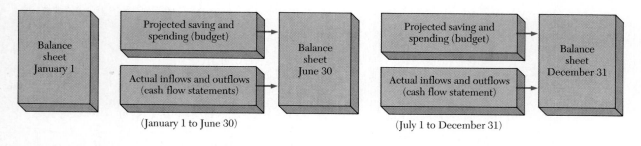

Net Cash Flow   The difference between your income and your outflows can be either a positive (*surplus*) or negative (*deficit*) cash flow. A deficit exists if more cash goes out than comes in during a month. This amount must be made up by withdrawals from savings or by borrowing.

When you have a cash surplus, as Susan did (Exhibit 3–4), this amount is available for saving and investing. Each month, Susan sets aside money for her *emergency fund* in a savings account that she would use to handle unexpected expenses or to pay living costs if she did not receive her salary. She deposits the rest of her cash surplus in savings and investment plans that have two purposes. The first purpose is the achievement of short-term and intermediate financial goals, such as a new car, a vacation, or reenrollment at school; the second purpose is long-term financial security—her retirement.

A cash flow statement provides the foundation for preparing and implementing a spending, saving, and investment plan, discussed in the next section.

THE BUDGETING PROCESS

L.O.4
Create and implement a budget.

Improvements in your financial position are the direct result of an effective budget. Yet a study conducted by *Money* magazine reported that only 23 percent of those surveyed had a planned budget and that another 48 percent only had "somewhat of a budget."[1]

A budget is a fundamental ingredient of successful financial planning. The common financial problems of overusing credit, not having a savings and investment program, and failing to ensure future financial security can all be minimized through budgeting. The main purposes of a budget are to help you

- Live within your income.
- Spend your money wisely.
- Reach your financial goals.
- Prepare for financial emergencies.
- Develop wise financial management habits.

The creation and implementation of a budget may be viewed as a four-phase process (see Exhibit 3–5).

Phase 1: Assessing Your Current Situation

The personal financial statements and documents discussed in the first sections of this chapter provide a starting point for your daily money management activities. In addition, this first phase of the budgeting process involves making some choices based on your personal situation.

Measuring Your Current Financial Position   A personal balance sheet is an effective scorecard for assessing personal economic progress. Increases in net worth as a result of increased assets or decreased debt are tangible evidence of an improved financial position. A regular assessment of your financial standing, as measured with a personal balance sheet, can provide a point of reference for budgeting and money management success.

Determining Your Personal Situation   Each day, you make many decisions that add up to a statement about you. Your *lifestyle* is how you spend your time and money.

The clothes you wear, the food you eat, and your interests contribute to your lifestyle. Some people spend time and money on automobiles or stereo equipment; other people travel, engage in home gardening, or are involved in church

EXHIBIT 3–5
The Budgeting Process

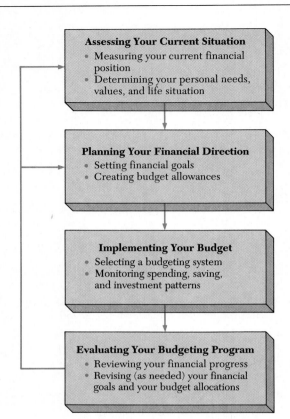

Assessing Your Current Situation
- Measuring your current financial position
- Determining your personal needs, values, and life situation

Planning Your Financial Direction
- Setting financial goals
- Creating budget allowances

Implementing Your Budget
- Selecting a budgeting system
- Monitoring spending, saving, and investment patterns

Evaluating Your Budgeting Program
- Reviewing your financial progress
- Revising (as needed) your financial goals and your budget allocations

or community activities. Each of these actions reflects a lifestyle that is greatly affected by the following factors:

- *Career.* Your job situation will influence the amount of your income, the way you spend your leisure time, and even your choice of the people with whom you wish to associate.
- *Family.* The size of your household and the ages of the people in it will also affect your lifestyle. The spending priorities of a couple without children will be different from those of a couple with several youngsters.
- *Values.* The ideas and beliefs that you regard as important will strongly influence your interests, activities, and purchasing habits.

These factors combine to create planned spending patterns that are reflected in your financial goals.

Phase 2: Planning Your Financial Direction

In this phase of your budgeting activities, you need to be concerned with setting financial goals and deciding budget allocations for various spending and saving categories.

Setting Financial Goals   Future plans are an important dimension of your financial direction. Financial goals are plans for future activities that require you

EXHIBIT 3–6

Common Financial Goals

Personal Situation	Short-Term Goals (less than 2 years)	Intermediate Goals (2–5 years)	Long-Term Goals (over 5 years)
Single person	Complete college Pay off auto loan	Take vacation Pay off education loan Return to school for graduate degree	Buy vacation home Ensure retirement income
Married couple (no children)	Take annual vacation Buy new car	Remodel home Build stock portfolio	Buy retirement home Ensure retirement income
Parent (young children)	Increase life insurance Increase savings	Increase investments Buy new car	Accumulate college fund Move to larger home

to plan your spending, saving, and investing. Exhibit 3–6 gives examples of common financial goals based on life situation and time.

Using your personal financial statements along with a budget can play an important role in achieving financial goals. Your cash flow statement tells you what you have done over a certain time period, such as the past month. Your balance sheet tells you your current financial position—where you are now. And your budget expresses what you would like to do in the future. A budget is a major tool for achieving financial goals by planning spending and saving.

Creating Budget Allowances   The next phase of budgeting is to assign income to spending categories. How much you budget for various items will depend on current needs and on plans for the future. The following sources can assist you in planning your spending:

- Your cash flow statement.
- Sample budgets from government reports.
- Personal financial planning magazines such as *Changing Times* and *Money*.
- Estimates of your future income and expenses and of future cost changes due to inflation.

Exhibit 3–7 provides suggested budget allocations for different life situations. Although this information can be of value when you are creating budget categories, maintaining a detailed record of your spending for several months is a better source for your personal situation. Don't become discouraged about keeping track of your spending. Use a simple system, such as a notebook or your checkbook. Remember, you are developing a budget, which is an *estimate* for spending and saving to help you make better use of your money, not to reduce your enjoyment of life.

A format similar to the one used for the cash flow statement can be the basis for your budget. However, you should regard savings as your first outflow item. A very common budgeting mistake is to save the amount you have left at the end of the month. When that is done, very often *nothing* is left for savings. Since savings

EXHIBIT 3–7		Typical After-Tax Budget, Allocation for Different Life Situations				
	Student	**Young Working Single**	**Couple (children under 18)**	**Single Parent (young children)**	**Parents (children over 18 in school)**	**Couple (over 55; no dependent children)**
Housing (rent or mortgage payment; utilities; furnishings and appliances)	0–25%	30–35%	25–35%	20–30%	25–30%	25–35%
Transportation	5–10	15–20	15–20	10–18	12–18	10–18
Food (at home and away from home)	15–20	15–25	15–25	13–20	15–20	18–25
Clothing	5–12	5–15	5–10	5–10	4–8	4–8
Personal and Health Care (including child care)	3–5	3–5	4–10	8–12	4–6	6–12
Entertainment and Recreation	5–10	5–10	4–8	4–8	6–10	5–8
Reading and Education	10–30	2–4	3–5	3–5	6–12	2–4
Personal Insurance and Pension Payments	0–5	4–8	5–9	5–9	4–7	6–8
Gifts, Donations, and Contributions	4–6	5–8	3–5	3–5	4–8	3–5
Savings	0–10	4–15	5–10	5–8	2–4	3–5

SOURCES: Bureau of Labor Statistics; *American Demographics; Money; The Wall Street Journal.*

are vital to long-term financial security, advisers suggest that they be budgeted as a fixed expense. A suggested budget format is

1. Income   Estimate the amount of available money for a given period of time. A common budgeting period is a month, since many payments, such as rent or mortgage, utilities, and charge accounts, are made during that time frame. In determining available income, only include money that you are sure you'll receive. Bonuses, gifts, or unexpected income should not be considered until the money has actually been received.

If you get paid once a month, planning your budget is easy since you will work with a single amount. But if you get paid weekly or twice a month, you will need to plan how much of each paycheck will go for various expenses. If you get paid every two weeks, plan your spending based on the two paychecks that you will receive each month. Then, during the two months each year that have three paydays, you can put additional amounts in savings, pay off some debts, or make a special purchase.

Budgeting income may be difficult if your earnings vary by season or your income is irregular, as with sales commission. In these situations, attempt to estimate your income based on the past year and on your expectations for the current year. Estimating your income on the low side will help you avoid overspending and financial difficulties.

2. Emergency Fund and Savings   In an attempt to set aside money for unexpected expenses as well as future financial security, the Fraziers (see Exhibit 3–8) have budgeted several amounts for savings and investments. Financial

EXHIBIT 3–8   The Frazier Family Develops and Implements a Monthly Budget

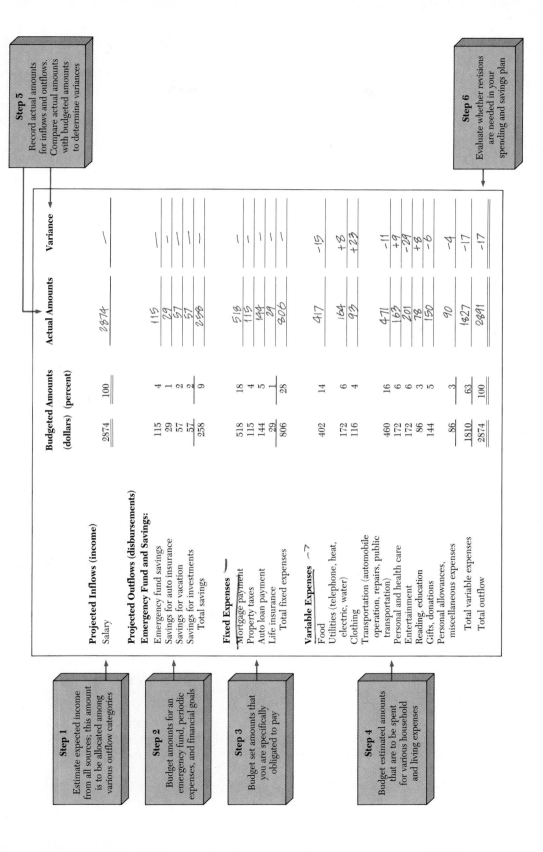

	Budgeted Amounts (dollars)	(percent)	Actual Amounts	Variance
Projected Inflows (income)				
Salary	2874	100	2874	—
Projected Outflows (disbursements)				
Emergency Fund and Savings:				
Emergency fund savings	115	4	115	—
Savings for auto insurance	29	1	29	—
Savings for vacation	57	2	57	—
Savings for investments	57	2	57	—
Total savings	258	9	258	—
Fixed Expenses				
Mortgage payment	518	18	518	—
Property taxes	115	4	115	—
Auto loan payment	144	5	144	—
Life insurance	29	1	29	—
Total fixed expenses	806	28	806	—
Variable Expenses				
Food	402	14	417	−15
Utilities (telephone, heat, electric, water)	172	6	164	+8
Clothing	116	4	93	+23
Transportation (automobile operation, repairs, public transportation)	460	16	471	−11
Personal and health care	172	6	163	+9
Entertainment	172	6	201	−29
Reading, education	86	3	78	+8
Gifts, donations	144	5	150	−6
Personal allowances, miscellaneous expenses	86	3	90	−4
Total variable expenses	1810	63	1827	−17
Total outflow	2874	100	2891	−17

Step 1
Estimate expected income from all sources; this amount is to be allocated among various outflow categories

Step 2
Budget amounts for an emergency fund, periodic expenses, and financial goals

Step 3
Budget set amounts that you are specifically obligated to pay

Step 4
Budget estimated amounts that are to be spent for various household and living expenses

Step 5
Record actual amounts for inflows and outflows. Compare actual amounts with budgeted amounts to determine variances

Step 6
Evaluate whether revisions are needed in your spending and savings plan

advisers suggest that an emergency fund representing three to six months of living expenses be established for use in periods of unexpected financial difficulty. This amount will vary based on a person's life situation and employment stability. A three-month emergency fund is probably adequate for a person with a stable income or secure employment, while a person with erratic or seasonal income may need to set aside an emergency fund sufficient for six months or more of living expenses.

The Fraziers also set aside an amount each month for their automobile insurance payment, which is due every six months. Both this amount and the emergency fund are set aside in a savings or other bank account, and they will grow in value over the months and years. The time value of money, discussed in Chapter 1, refers to increases in an amount of money as a result of interest earned. Savings methods for achieving financial goals are discussed later in this chapter.

3. Fixed Expenses   Definite obligations are the basis for this portion of a budget. As shown in Exhibit 3–8, the Frazier family has fixed expenses for housing, taxes, and credit payments. The family makes a monthly payment of $29 for life insurance. The budgeted total for the Fraziers' fixed expenses is $806, or 28 percent of estimated available income.

4. Variable Expenses   Budgeting variable expenses is not as easy as budgeting savings or fixed expenses. Variable expenses will fluctuate due to household situation, time of year, health, economic conditions, and a wide variety of other factors. A major portion of the Fraziers' planned spending—63 percent of their budgeted income—is for variable living costs.

The Fraziers base their estimates on their needs and desires for the items listed and on changes in the cost of living. The consumer price index is a measure of the general price level of consumer goods and services in the United States. This government statistic indicates changes in the buying power of a dollar. As consumer prices increase due to inflation, people must spend more to buy the same amount.

Changes in the cost of living will vary depending on where you live and what you buy. Between 1980 and 1990, average consumer prices in the United States rose 64.4 percent, but food prices rose 55 percent and the cost of renting a place to live rose 75 percent. In the 1980s, the prices of television sets fell 27 percent and the costs of long-distance phone service fell 15 percent.

As mentioned in Chapter 1, the *rule of 72* can help you budget for price rises. At a 6 percent inflation rate, prices will double in 12 years (72 ÷ 6); at an 8 percent inflation rate, prices will double in only 9 years (72 ÷ 8).

Phase 3: Implementing Your Budget

Selecting a Budgeting System   Although your checkbook will give you a fairly complete record of your expenses, it does not serve the purpose of planning for spending. A budget requires that you outline how you will spend your available income. Various types of budgeting systems exist, from informal procedures to computerized spending plans.

A mental budget is one that exists only in a person's mind. This simple system may be quite appropriate for an individual with limited resources and minimal financial responsibilities. The major drawback of a mental budget is the danger of forgetting what amounts you plan to spend on various items.

A physical budget involves the use of envelopes, folders, or containers to hold the money or slips of paper that represent the amounts allocated for your

. .

FINANCIAL PLANNING CALCULATIONS

Computing Your Own Cost-Of-Living Index

Each month, the Bureau of Labor Statistics (BLS) publishes the consumer price index (CPI). The CPI measures the cost of living based on changes in a selected market basket of goods and services. In addition to the U.S. average CPI, the BLS develops monthly reports for selected large cities.°

While the CPI provides an indication of the cost of living, few people use the exact mix of products and services that is used to compute the monthly index. You can prepare your own consumer price index by monitoring the price of commonly used items over a period of time. For example:

	Base		Time Period 1		Time Period 2	
Item	**Price**	**Index**	**Price**	**Index**	**Price**	**Index**
Gallon of milk	$1.49	100	$1.63	109	$1.78	119
Gallon of gas	$1.09	100	$0.93	85	$1.06	97
Apartment rent	$450	100	$480	107	$510	113

To compute a price index, use the following format:

$1.49   ×   = $1.63   (100)

| | | | |
Base   New   New   Base
price   index   price   index
          number

$$1.49x = 163$$

$$x = \frac{163}{1.49}$$

New index number = 109

This calculation gives you an index number for an individual item. To prepare a personal cost-of-living index, you need to weigh the individual index numbers based on

their proportions of your typical spending patterns—0.2 (20 percent) for food, 0.40 (40 percent) for housing, and so on. A simpler way to estimate your personal cost-of-living index is as follows:

Step 1. List the amounts you spent for various budget categories in the past year.

Step 2. Based on economic prospects and past trends, estimate the price increases for each of these categories in the current year, and add them to 1.0.

Step 3. For each category, multiply these two amounts to get an estimate of your spending in the current year, rounded to the nearest dollar.

Step 4. Total the categories and divide your estimated spending in the current year by your actual spending in the past year.

For example:

	Actual Spending (last year)	**Expected Price Increase + 1.0**	**Estimated Spending (current year)**
Food	$ 3,500	1.06	$ 3,710
Housing (including utilities)	12,180	1.04	12,667
Transportation	3,870	1.07	4,141
Clothing	1,461	1.03	1,505
Personal and medical expenses	2,675	1.09	2,916
	$23,686		$24,939

$$\$24,939 \div \$23,686 = 1.0529$$

The estimated increase in your personal cost of living for the coming year is approximately 5.3 percent.

°For a copy of the latest consumer price index, contact the U.S. Department of Labor, Bureau of Labor Statistics, 441 G Street, NW, Washington, DC 20212.

. .

spending categories. This system allows a person to actually see where the money goes. Envelopes would contain the amount of cash or a note listing the amount to be used for "Food," "Rent," "Clothing," "Auto Payment," "Entertainment," or some other expense.

Financial advisers and experienced money managers recommend the use of a written budget. The exact system and the amount of detail will depend on the time, effort, and information that you put into the budgeting process. A written budget can be kept on notebook paper or in a specialized budgeting book available in office supply stores or bookstores. A common budget format is a spreadsheet that has several sets of monthly columns for comparing budgeted and actual amounts for various expense items.

As the use of personal computers increases, so too does the use of computerized budgeting systems. In addition to creating a spreadsheet budget presentation, a home computer is capable of doing other financial recordkeeping duties such as writing checks and projecting the future value of savings accounts. Software packages ranging in cost from $15 or $25 to several hundred dollars can assist with budgeting and with the preparation of personal financial statements. Information about the use of a personal computer for financial recordkeeping and planning is available through computer stores, books, and articles in such computer magazines as *Personal Computing* (also refer to Appendix C). It takes time and effort to learn the system and enter data, but a computerized budgeting and recordkeeping procedure can yield fast and accurate data for successful financial planning.

Having a budget will not eliminate your financial worries. A budget will work only if you follow it. Changes in income, expenses, and goals will require changes in your budget. Money experts state that a successful budget has the qualities of being

- *Well planned.* A good budget takes time and effort. Planning a budget should involve everyone affected by it. Children can learn important money management lessons by helping develop and use the family budget.
- *Realistic.* If you have a moderate income, don't expect to immediately save enough money for an expensive car or a European vacation. A budget is not designed to prevent you from enjoying life but to help you achieve what you want most.
- *Flexible.* Unexpected expenses and changes in your cost of living will require a budget that can easily be revised. Also, special situations, such as two-income families or the arrival of a baby, may require an increase in certain types of expenses.
- *Clearly communicated.* Unless you and the others affected by a budget are aware of the spending plan, the budget will not be valuable. It should be written and available to all household members. While many variations of written budgets are possible, such budget formats as a notebook or a computerized system are also available.

Monitoring Spending Patterns   After your spending plan has been set, you will need to keep records about your actual income and expenses similar to those you keep in preparing an income statement. In Exhibit 3–8, you will notice that the Fraziers estimated specific amounts for income and expenses. These are presented under "Budgeted Amounts." The family's spending was not always the same as planned. A **budget variance** is the difference between the amount budgeted and the actual amount received or spent. The total variance for the Fraziers was a $17 **deficit** since their actual spending exceeded their planned spending by this amount. The Fraziers would have had a **surplus** if their actual spending had been less than they had planned to spend.

Variances for income should be viewed as the opposite of variances for expenses. Less income than expected would be a deficit, while more income than expected would be a surplus.

Spending more than planned for an item may be justified by reducing spending for another item or by putting less into savings. However, it may be necessary to revise the budget and reevaluate your financial goals and spending patterns.

Phase 4: Evaluating Your Budgeting Program

Like any other decision making, budgeting is a circular, ongoing process. At regular points in your financial existence, you will need to review and perhaps revise your spending plan.

Reviewing Your Financial Progress   The results of your budget may be obvious—having extra cash in checking, falling behind in your bill payments, and so on. But such obvious results may not always be present. Occasionally, you will have to sit down (with other household members, if appropriate) and review areas where spending has been heavier or lighter than expected.

As shown in Exhibit 3–9, you can prepare an annual summary comparing actual spending with budgeted amounts. Such a summary may also be prepared every three or six months. This is easy to do with a spreadsheet computer program. The summary will help you see areas where revisions in your budget may be necessary. This review process is vital to both successful short-term money management and long-term financial security.

Revising Your Goals and Allocations   What should be cut first when there is a budget shortage? This question doesn't have easy answers, and the answers will vary for different household situations. The most common overspending areas are entertainment and food, especially away-from-home meals. Purchasing brand and generic items, buying quality used products, avoiding credit card purchases, and renting rather than buying are common budget adjustment techniques.

At this point of the budgeting process, you should also evaluate, reassess, and revise your financial goals. Are you making progress toward the achievement of your economic objectives? Have changes in personal or economic conditions affected the desirability of certain goals? Have new goals surfaced that should be given a higher priority than those that have been your major concern? Addressing these issues while creating an effective saving method will help assure accomplishment of your financial goals.

EXHIBIT 3–9　　An Annual Budget Summary

Item	Monthly Budget	Jan.	Feb.	Mar.	Apr.	May	June	July	Aug.	Sept.	Oct.	Nov.	Dec.	Annual Totals Actual	Budgeted[*]
						Actual Spending (cash outflows)									
Income	2,730	2,730	2,730	2,730	2,940	2,730	2,730	2,730	2,730	2,850	2,850	2,850	2,850	33,570	32,760
Savings	150	150	150	200	150	90	50	30	100	250	250	150	40	1,610	1,800
Mortgage/rent	826	826	826	826	826	826	826	826	826	826	826	826	826	9,912	9,912
Housing costs (insurance, water, heat, electricity)	190	214	238	187	176	185	188	146	178	198	177	201	195	2,283	2,280
Telephone	50	43	45	67	56	54	52	65	45	43	52	49	47	618	600
Food (at home)	280	287	277	245	234	278	267	298	320	301	298	278	324	3,407	3,360
Food (away from home)	80	67	78	84	87	123	109	89	83	67	76	83	143	1,089	960
Clothing	100	98	78	123	156	86	76	111	124	87	95	123	111	1,268	1,200
Transportation (auto operating costs, auto insurance, auto repairs, public transportation)	340	302	312	333	345	297	287	390	373	299	301	267	301	3,807	4,080
Credit payments	249	249	249	249	249	249	249	249	249	249	249	249	249	2,988	2,988
Insurance (life, health, other)	45	—	—	135	—	—	135	—	—	135	—	—	135	540	540
Personal/health care	140	176	145	187	122	111	156	186	166	134	189	193	147	1,912	1,680
Recreation	80	67	98	123	98	67	45	87	98	65	87	87	111	1,033	960
Reading, education	40	32	54	44	34	39	54	12	38	54	34	76	45	516	480
Gifts, donations	100	102	110	94	87	123	89	95	94	113	87	99	134	1,227	1,200
Personal allowances, miscellaneous expenses	60	89	45	67	54	98	59	54	49	71	65	90	56	797	720
Total	2,730	2,702	2,705	2,964	2,674	2,626	2,642	2,638	2,743	2,892	2,786	2,771	2,864	33,007	32,760

[*]Monthly amount times 12.

SAVING EFFORTS FOR REACHING FINANCIAL GOALS

L.O.5
Calculate needed savings for achieving financial goals.

Saving of current income (as well as investing, which is discussed in Part V) is the basis for an improved financial position and long-term financial security. Common reasons for saving include the following:

- To set aside money for irregular and unexpected expenses.
- To pay for the replacement of expensive items such as appliances or an automobile or to have money for the down payment on a house.
- To buy special items such as home video equipment or recreational equipment or to pay for a vacation.
- To provide for long-term expenses such as the education of children or retirement.
- To earn income from the interest on savings for use in paying living expenses.

Selecting a Savings Technique

In the United States during the late 1980s, personal savings totaled about 4 percent of disposable personal income. For the period from 1950 through 1985, personal savings ranged from 6 to 9 percent of disposable personal income. A low savings rate slows economic growth (because fewer funds are available for borrowing by business), but it also affects the personal financial situation of people who do not have adequate cash for emergencies. In 1989, a *Wall Street Journal*/NBC News poll revealed that only 29 percent of 18–24-year-olds and 49 percent of 35–49-year-olds could raise $3,000 in a few days without borrowing or using a credit card.[2]

Since most people find saving difficult, financial advisers suggest several methods to make it easier. One method is to write a check each payday and deposit it in a special savings account at a distant financial institution. This savings deposit can be a percentage of income, such as 5 or 10 percent, or a specific dollar amount. Always "pay yourself first." To guarantee setting something aside for savings, view savings as a fixed expense in your spending plan.

Another method is payroll deduction, which is available at many places of employment. Under this system, an amount is automatically deducted from your salary and deposited in a savings account or used to purchase U.S. savings bonds.

Finally, saving coins or spending less on certain items can help you save. Each day, put your change in a container. In a short time, you will have enough money to make a substantial deposit in a savings account. You can also increase your savings by taking a sandwich instead of buying your lunch or by not buying snacks or magazines. How you save, however, is less important than saving regularly by making periodic savings deposits that will help you achieve your financial goals.

Calculating Savings Amounts

To achieve your financial objectives, you should convert your savings goals into specific amounts. While certain saving methods mean keeping money at home, that money should be deposited in an interest-earning savings plan on a periodic basis. To earn interest, you must learn to "hide" money, not in your home, but in an account at a financial institution.

Your use of an interest-earning savings plan is vital to the growth of your money and the achievement of your financial goals. Depositing $100 a month in a credit union savings account during the 10-year period ending in mid-1989 would have

EXHIBIT 3–10   Using Savings to Achieve Financial Goals

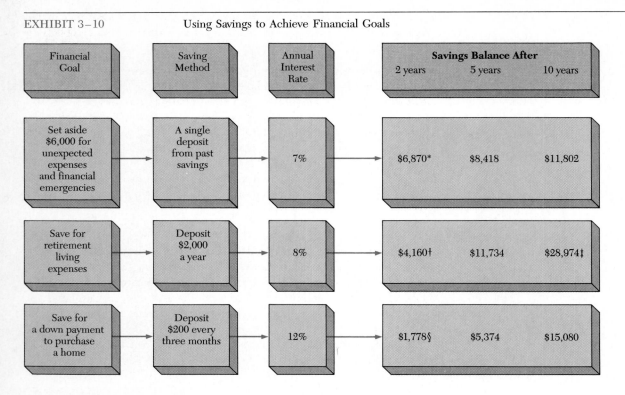

Financial Goal	Saving Method	Annual Interest Rate	Savings Balance After		
			2 years	5 years	10 years
Set aside $6,000 for unexpected expenses and financial emergencies	A single deposit from past savings	7%	$6,870*	$8,418	$11,802
Save for retirement living expenses	Deposit $2,000 a year	8%	$4,160†	$11,734	$28,974‡
Save for a down payment to purchase a home	Deposit $200 every three months	12%	$1,778§	$5,374	$15,080

* Based on the future value of $1 tables in Chapter 1 and Appendix C
† Based on the future value of a series of deposits tables in Chapter 1 and Appendix C
‡ With annual $2,000 deposits, this same retirement account would grow to over $500,000 in 40 years
§ Based on quarterly compounding, which will be explained in Chapter 5

resulted in savings of more than $17,600. Purchasing U.S. savings bonds for an equal amount during the same period would have resulted in savings of more than $19,000. As shown in Exhibit 3–10, such applications of the time value of money, which was introduced in Chapter 1, show how saving efforts achieve financial objectives.

SUMMARY

L.O.1
Recognize the relationships among various money management documents and activities.

L.O.2
Create a system for maintaining personal financial documents.

L.O.3
Develop a personal balance sheet and cash flow statement.

Successful money management requires effective coordination of personal financial records, personal financial statements, and budgeting activities.

An organized system of financial records and documents is the foundation of effective money management. This system should provide ease of access as well as security for financial documents that may be impossible to replace.

A personal balance sheet, also known as a net worth statement, is prepared by listing all items of value (assets) and all amounts owed to others (liabilities). The difference between your total assets and your total liabilities is your net worth. A cash flow statement is a summary of cash receipts and payments for a given period, such as a month or a year. This report provides data on your income and spending patterns.

L.O.4
Create and implement a budget.

The budgeting process involves four phases: (1) assessing your current personal and financial situation; (2) planning your financial direction by setting financial goals and creating budget allowances; (3) implementing your budget; and (4) evaluating your budgeting program.

L.O.5
Calculate needed savings for achieving financial goals.

Future value and present value calculations may be used to compute the increased value of savings for achieving financial goals.

GLOSSARY

Assets   Cash and other property that has a monetary value.

Balance sheet   A financial statement that reports what an individual or a family owns and owes; also called a net worth statement.

Budget   A plan for spending.

Budget variance   The difference between the amount budgeted and the actual amount received or spent.

Cash flow   The actual inflow and outflow of cash for an individual or a household during a given time period, such as a month.

Cash flow statement   A financial statement that summarizes cash receipts and payments for a given period, such as a month or a year.

Current liabilities   Debts that are due within a short time, usually less than a year.

Deficit   The amount by which actual spending exceeds planned spending.

Income   Inflows of cash to an individual or a household.

Insolvency   The inability to pay debts when they are due, because your liabilities far exceed the value of your assets.

Liabilities   Amounts owed to others.

Liquid assets   Cash and items of value that can easily be converted into cash.

Long-term liabilities   Debts that are not required to be paid in full until more than a year from now.

Money management   Day-to-day financial activities necessary to handle current personal economic resources while working toward long-term financial security.

Net worth   The difference between a person's or family's total assets and total liabilities.

Safe-deposit box   A private storage area at a financial institution that offers maximum security for valuables.

Surplus   The amount by which actual spending falls short of planned spending.

Take-home pay   A person's earnings after deductions for taxes and other items.

DISCUSSION QUESTIONS

L.O.1

1. Explain why "successful money management" might mean different things to different people.

L.O.1   2. What are some opportunity costs associated with money management decisions that cannot be measured in monetary terms?

L.O.2   3. What suggestions would you offer to an individual who wants to create a system for organizing and storing financial records and documents?

L.O.2   4. What factors influence the length of time that financial records and documents should be kept?

L.O.3   5. What does a personal balance sheet tell about the financial situation of a person or a household? How can a balance sheet be used for personal financial planning?

L.O.3   6. What information does a cash flow statement offer? How can a cash flow statement assist in the budgeting process?

L.O.4   7. How would such life situations as delayed marriage, deferred parenthood, and divorce influence goal setting and the budgeting process?

L.O.4   8. Why do many people avoid budgeting despite its benefits? How would you persuade a person to practice budgeting?

L.O.4   9. How might the inflation rate as reported in the consumer price index affect budgeting decisions?

L.O.5   10. The amount saved by most people is very low. What efforts to encourage saving could be made by individuals, business organizations, and government? How does increased saving benefit individuals and the economy?

Opening Case Questions

1. What actions could Jeff Conrad have taken to prepare for his financial independence from his parents?

2. What common problems did Jeff encounter because he did not have an organized system of financial records and documents?

3. How effective would Jeff's financial recordkeeping system be for developing personal financial statements and a budget? Explain.

4. What are common savings goals for persons in Jeff's situation? What money management activities would be most effective in achieving these goals?

PROBLEMS AND ACTIVITIES

L.O.1   1. Collect and analyze newspaper and magazine advertisements of services that could make a positive or negative contribution to a person's financial decision-making and money management activities.

L.O.2   2. Contact a local financial institution to obtain information on the cost of a safe-deposit box and the restrictions on its use.

L.O.3   3. Based on the procedures presented in the chapter, prepare your current personal balance sheet and a cash flow statement for the next month. Use this information to assess your financial situation and to plan your financial goals.

L.O.3   4. Based on the following data, compute the total assets, total liabilities, and net worth.

Liquid assets, $3,670   Investment assets, $8,340
Current liabilities, $2,670   Household assets, $89,890
Long-term liabilities, $76,230

L.O.3   5. Talk with several individuals about their cash flow. What are some situations in which they might encounter a cash shortage? How would they cope with a cash shortage?

L.O.3   6. Use the following items to prepare a balance sheet and a cash flow statement. Determine the total assets, total liabilities, net worth, total cash inflows, and total cash outflows.

Rent for the month, $650

Cash in checking account, $450

Spending for food, $345

Current value of automobile, $7,800

Credit card balance, $235

Auto insurance, $230

Stereo equipment, $2,350

Lunches/parking at work, $180

Home computer, $1,500

Clothing purchase, $110

Monthly take-home salary, $1,950

Savings account balance, $1,890

Balance of educational loan, $2,160

Telephone bill paid for month, $65

Loan payment, $80

Household possessions, $3,400

Payment for electricity, $90

Donations to church, $70

Value of stock investment, $860

Restaurant spending, $130

L.O.4   7. Fran Bowen created the following budget:

Food, $350

Transportation, $320

Housing, $950

Clothing, $100

Personal expenses and recreation, $275

She actually spent $298 for food, $337 for transportation, $982 for housing, $134 for clothing, and $231 for personal expenses and recreation. Calculate the variance for each of these categories, and indicate whether it was a *deficit* or *surplus*.

L.O.4   8. Discuss with several individuals how the budget in Exhibit 3–8 (page 81) should be changed. Based on an annual comparison of planned and actual spending, which of the categories in this budget should be revised for the new year?

L.O.4   9. Ask two or three friends or relatives about their budgeting system. Obtain information on how and why they maintain their spending records.

L.O.4   10. Visit a computer store to see a demonstration of money management software for personal financial recordkeeping and budgeting.

L.O.5   11. Conduct a survey of the savings goals and habits of a young single, a young couple, a single parent, and a middle-aged person. Obtain information about their financial security objectives and about the methods they use to save for the future.

L.O.5   12. Use future value and present value calculations (see tables in Appendix B) to determine the following:

a. The future value of a $500 savings deposit after eight years at an annual interest rate of 7 percent.

b. The future value of saving $1,500 a year for five years at an annual interest rate of 8 percent.

c. The present value of a $2,000 savings account that will earn 6 percent interest for four years.

L.O.5   13. Hal Thomas wants to establish a savings fund from which a community organization could draw $800 a year for 20 years. If the account earns 6 percent, what amount would he have to deposit now to achieve this goal?

LIFE SITUATION   Case 3–1

Beth's Unbalanced Books

Beth Lyons is employed as a word processing supervisor for an investment company. She lives in a small house about 20 minutes from work, and she drives a two-year-old car. She is making payments on both the house and the car. Beth has a steady income and can afford to buy many other items. She recently redecorated several rooms in her house, and during each of the past five years she has taken a vacation.

Even though Beth handles business records and documents at work, she is frequently late in making payments to her creditors. Also, the insurance coverage for her home and car is not adequate to cover their value.

Beth has the following assets and liabilities:

Savings/investment account, $800

Market value of automobile, $11,000

Mortgage balance, $66,000

Household possessions, $18,500

Credit card balances, $8,600

Market value of home, $83,000

Checking account balance, $340

Personal loans, $1,700

Questions

1. Which financial documents does Beth need?
2. How could Beth become better organized in handling her personal finances?
3. Compute Beth's net worth based on the data provided.
4. How would a personal balance sheet and a personal cash flow statement assist Beth in her financial planning?

LIFE SITUATION   Case 3–2

Mismanaged Money

Julie and Ralph Palmer have been married six years. They have a combined income of $50,000. With total assets of $110,500, they have only $500 in savings. Their liabilities total $80,600.

Each time the Palmers have a substantial amount of savings, they spend it for such things as vacations, furniture, or home entertainment equipment. Currently, their annual expenses include $11,325 listed as "unaccounted for." This amount is in addition to the amounts they spend for food, housing, utilities, transportation, loan payments, insurance, donations, gifts, and taxes. The Palmers live in a town house, but they would like to buy a detached house.

Questions

1. What is the net worth of the Palmers? What is your opinion of their current financial position?
2. How could the Palmers improve their financial position?
3. What changes would you suggest in the Palmers' budgeting techniques?
4. How could the Palmers be more effective in their financial planning?

SUPPLEMENTARY READINGS

For Additional Information on Money Management and Personal Financial Recordkeeping

Complete Guide to Managing Your Money. Mount Vernon, N.Y.: Consumer Reports Books, 1989.

Managing Your Personal Finances. U.S. Department of Agriculture, Extension Service, Washington, DC 20250.

"Records: Most of Us Squirrel More Paper than Is Necessary." *Money,* September 1988, pp. 157–58.

For Additional Information on Cash Flow Analysis and Budgeting

Consumer Expenditure Survey: Quarterly Data from the Interview Survey. U.S. Department of Labor, Bureau of Labor Statistics, Washington, DC 20212.

"Families of Working Wives Spending More on Services and Nondurables." *Monthly Labor Review,* February 1989, pp. 15–23.

A Guide to Budgeting. National Credit Union Youth Program, Box 391, Madison, WI 53701.

Waldrop, Judith. "A Lesson in Home Economics." *American Demographics,* August 1989, pp. 26–30, 61.

For Additional Information on Savings and Achieving Financial Goals

"How to Set Up a Plan That Takes the Pain out of Saving." *Money,* July 1989, pp. 129–30.

Sebastian, Pamela. "Baby Boomers Find It Hard to Save Money; Will They Do It Later?" *The Wall Street Journal,* February 13, 1989, pp. A1, A4.

"The Secrets of Saving." *Bottom Line/Personal,* June 30, 1989, pp. 7–8.

Williams, Gordon. "Successful Ways to Save." *Reader's Digest,* March 1990, pp. 132–36.

4

Planning Your Tax Strategy

Taxes are a quiet, everyday financial fact of life. You pay certain taxes every time you get a paycheck or make a purchase. But many people concern themselves with taxes only around April of each year. With about one third of each dollar earned going for taxes, an effective tax strategy is a vital component of successful financial planning. If you know and understand the tax rules and regulations, you may be able to reduce your tax liability. Your purchases, investments, and other financial decisions can affect the amount you pay in taxes.

LEARNING OBJECTIVES
After studying this chapter, you will be able to:

L.O.1   Analyze the importance of taxes for personal financial planning.

L.O.2   Calculate taxable income and the amount owed for federal income tax.

L.O.3   Prepare a federal income tax return.

L.O.4   Identify tax assistance sources.

L.O.5   Select appropriate tax strategies for different financial and personal situations.

OPENING CASE

A *Taxing Situation*

Ever since his wife's death, Eric Stanford has faced difficult personal and financial circumstances. His job as a senior sales manager provides him with a substantial income but keeps him away from his daughters, aged 8 and 10, nearly 20 days a month. This requires him to use in-home child care service that takes a large portion of his income. Since the Stanfords' live in a small apartment, this arrangement has been very inconvenient. Moreover, Eric has not taken advantage of the tax benefits of child care expenses.

Due to the costs of caring for his children, Eric has only a minimal amount withheld from his salary for fed-

eral income taxes. This makes more money available during the year, but for the last few years he has had to make large payments in April—another financial difficulty for him.

Although Eric has created an investment fund for his daughters' college education and for his retirement, he has not sought to select investments that offer tax benefits. Overall, he needs to look at several aspects of his tax planning activities in an effort to best serve his current and future financial needs.

TAXES AND FINANCIAL PLANNING

L.O.1
Analyze the importance of taxes for personal financial planning.

Unlike other aspects of financial planning, taxes are affected not only by our personal choices but by a strong external influence—the government. Taxes are vital to society because they provide the funds needed for desired public services. The fairness of taxes is constantly debated. Different types of taxes differ in their effects on an individual's financial situation.

In 1989, the U.S. Census Bureau reported that more than two out of three American households have no money left after paying for taxes and normal living expenses. For most of us, taxes are a significant factor in financial planning. Each year, the Tax Foundation determines how long the average person works to pay taxes. In recent years, "Tax Freedom Day" came about May 4 or 5. This means that in those years a person worked from January 1 until early May to cover his or her tax burden.

In more specific terms, the tax burden for many households is in the 25–30 percent range. This inescapable financial obligation includes the many types of taxes discussed later in this section. To cope with these taxes, common goals related to tax planning include the following:

- Knowing the current tax laws and regulations that affect you.
- Maintaining complete and appropriate tax records.
- Making purchase and investment decisions that can reduce your tax liability.

Your tax planning efforts should be geared toward paying your fair share of taxes while taking advantage of tax benefits appropriate to your personal and financial situation.

Taxes in Our Society

For about two thirds of our nation's history, the federal government did not have the specific constitutional power to directly tax the incomes of individuals. An income tax was imposed briefly during the Civil War. But when the income tax was used again in the 1890s, the U.S. Supreme Court ruled it unconstitutional. In 1913, the states ratified the 16th Amendment to the U.S. Constitution, granting Congress the power to tax personal income.

Taxes have several purposes. Their principal purpose is to finance government activities. As citizens, we expect the government to provide such services as police protection and fire fighting, road maintenance, parks and libraries, and inspection of food, drugs, and other products.

Types of Taxes

Our financial existence is influenced by a variety of taxes. For example, the main sources of federal government revenue are income and social insurance taxes such as social security. Most people pay taxes in four major categories: taxes on purchases, taxes on property, taxes on wealth, and taxes on income.

Taxes on Purchases   You are probably used to paying sales tax on many of your purchases. This state and local tax is added to the purchase price of products. Many states exempt food and drugs from sales tax to reduce the economic burden of this tax on the poor. In recent years, all but five states have had a general sales tax.

An **excise tax** is imposed on specific goods and services, such as gasoline, cigarettes, alcoholic beverages, tires, air travel, and telephone service.

Taxes on Property   The real estate property tax is a major source of revenue for state and local governments. This tax is based on the value of land and buildings. A major concern of homeowners is the increasing amount of real estate property taxes. Retired individuals with a limited pension income may encounter financial difficulties if local property taxes increase at a fast rate.

Personal property taxes are also imposed in some areas. State and local governments may assess taxes on the value of automobiles, boats, furniture, and farm equipment.

Taxes on Wealth   An **estate tax** is imposed on the value of an individual's property at the time of his or her death. This tax is based on the fair market value of the deceased individual's investments, property, and bank accounts less allowable deductions and other taxes.

Money and property passed on to heirs may also be subject to a tax. An **inheritance tax** is levied on the value of property bequeathed by a deceased individual. This tax is paid for the right to acquire the inherited property.

Individuals are allowed to bestow gifts valued at $10,000 or less in a single year without being subject to taxes. Gift amounts greater than $10,000 are subject to federal tax. Amounts given for the payment of tuition or medical expenses are not subject to federal gift taxes. Some states impose a gift tax on amounts that one person, before his or her death, transfers to another person since the action may have been designed to avoid estate and inheritance taxes.

Taxes on Earnings   The two main taxes on your wages and salary are social security and income taxes. Social security taxes are used to finance the retirement, disability, and life insurance benefits of the federal government's social security program. Various features of social security are discussed in Chapters 13 and 20.

Income tax is the major financial planning aspect of taxes for most individuals. Some workers are subject to federal, state, and local income tax. Currently, only seven states do not have a state income tax.

. .

PERSONAL FINANCE JOURNAL

Does a Fair Tax Exist?

Many people believe that the only fair tax is one that someone else pays. However, most people realize that taxes are a financial planning fact and that they must pay their fair share. Three criteria used in assessing the fairness of taxes are the benefits received criterion, the ability to pay criterion, and the payment burden criterion.

Benefits Received   This criterion of tax fairness states that people should pay taxes in proportion to the benefits they receive from the government. An application of this criterion is the use of gasoline taxes and driver's license fees for road construction and repairs.

Equitable as the benefits received criterion may seem, it is very difficult to implement. The value placed on a particular government service is not easily measured. Some individuals may believe that recreational facilities are more important to the community than increased protection of property and citizens' rights; other individuals may hold the opposite view. It is not possible to establish a tax system based entirely on the value of services received.

Ability to Pay   A commonly accepted criterion of tax fairness is that individuals with different amounts of wealth or income should pay different amounts of taxes. Supporters of the ability to pay criterion usually argue that high tax bills hurt the rich less than the poor. This argument is the basis for the *progressive tax,* in which tax rates increase as the level of taxable income increases. Until the 1986 tax reform, the federal income tax was a progressive tax.

Recent tax changes have made the federal income tax more like a *proportional tax,* or a flat tax, with a constant tax rate applied to all levels of the tax base. The new federal tax plan is not completely proportional since it involves two tax brackets for different income levels. Many state and local income taxes are examples of proportional taxes.

Some proportional taxes may seem fair, but they penalize people in low-income groups. For example, when all individuals are charged sales tax on food, low-income people, who use a larger portion of their income for necessities, pay a greater percentage of their total income for sales tax than is paid by people with higher incomes. A *regressive tax* of this kind involves taxes that decrease, as a portion of income, as the tax base increases and tends to place a heavier burden on the poor. For this reason, many states have chosen not to tax the sale of food and medications.

Payment Burden   It has been said that only individuals pay taxes. Although businesses pay property and income taxes, some observers contend that these taxes are passed on to consumers in the form of higher prices. We pay many *indirect* taxes of this kind. In addition to those just mentioned, a portion of building owners' real estate taxes is paid by tenants as part of their rent. Indirect taxes are taxes that can be passed on to someone else, usually in the form of higher prices.

In contrast, *direct* taxes cannot be passed on to someone else. Property taxes paid by homeowners and income taxes paid by individuals are examples of direct taxes. Your awareness of all types of taxes is vital to the success of your personal financial planning and to your long-term economic security.

. .

During the year, your employer will withhold income tax payments from your paycheck or you may be required to make estimated tax payments if you own your own business. Both types of payments are only estimates of your income and social security tax burden. You may need to pay an additional amount, or you may get a tax refund. The next sections will assist you in preparing your federal income tax return and in planning your future tax strategies.

INCOME TAX FUNDAMENTALS

Each year, millions of Americans are required to pay their share of income taxes to the federal government. The process involves computing taxable income, determining the amount of income tax owed, and comparing this amount with the

L.O.2
Calculate taxable income and
the amount owed for federal
income tax.

income tax payments withheld or made during the year. Being aware of the income tax deadlines and of the potential penalties for tax code violations is another basic aspect of the income tax process.

Computing Taxable Income

Taxable income is the net amount of income, after allowable deductions, on which income tax is computed. Exhibit 4–1 presents the components of taxable income and the process used to compute it.

EXHIBIT 4–1
**Computing Taxable Income
and Your Tax Liability**

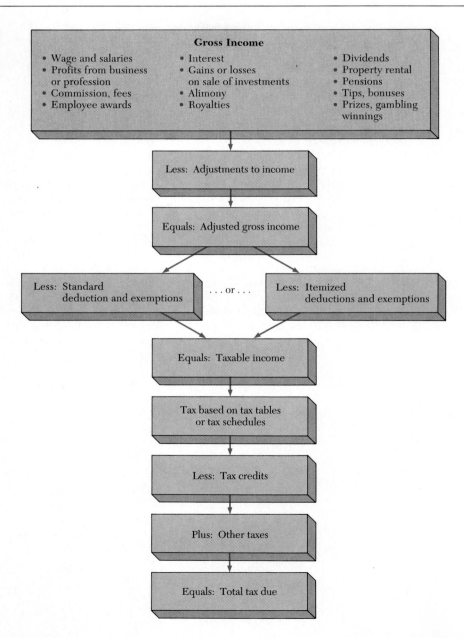

Types of Income   Most, but not all, income is subject to taxation. Your gross, or total, income can consist of several components. **Earned income** is money received by an individual for personal effort. Earned income is usually in the form of wages, salary, commission, fees, tips, or bonuses. **Investment income** (also called portfolio income) is money received in the form of dividends or interest. **Passive income** is the result of business activities in which you do not actively participate, such as a limited partnership.

Other types of income subject to federal income tax include alimony, awards, lottery winnings, and prizes. Cameron Clark, 14, won $30,533 in prizes on the television game show "Wheel of Fortune." In addition to paying California sales tax of $1,154, Cameron had to sell the car stereo, Ping-Pong table, camping gear, water ski equipment, bass guitar, and art drawing table and chair to pay the federal income tax. He did get to keep the Toyota Tercel, Honda Scooter, Gucci watches and Australian vacation.[1]

Total income is also affected by exclusions. An **exclusion** is an amount not included in gross income. For example, the foreign income exclusion allows U.S. citizens working and living in another country to exclude a certain portion ($70,000) of their income from federal income taxes.

Exclusions are also referred to as **tax-exempt income,** that is, income not subject to tax. For example, interest earned on most state and city bonds is exempt from federal income tax. **Tax-deferred income** refers to income that will be taxed at a later date. The earnings on an individual retirement account (IRA) are an example of tax-deferred income. While these earnings are credited to the account now, you do not pay taxes on them until you withdraw them from the account.

Adjustments to Income   **Adjusted gross income (AGI)** is gross income after certain reductions have been made. These reductions, called adjustments to income, include contributions to an individual retirement account (IRA) or a Keogh retirement plan, penalties for early withdrawal of savings, and alimony payments. Adjusted gross income is used as the basis for computing various income tax deductions, such as medical expenses.

Certain adjustments to income, such as tax-deferred retirement plans, are a type of **tax shelter.** Tax shelters are investments that provide immediate tax benefits and a reasonable expectation of a future financial return. In recent years, tax court rulings and changes in the tax code have disallowed various types of tax shelters that were considered abusive.

Deductions   A deduction is an amount subtracted from adjusted gross income to arrive at taxable income. Every taxpayer receives at least the **standard deduction**—a set amount on which no taxes are paid. As of 1989, single people received a standard deduction of $3,100 (married couples, filing jointly, $5,200). Blind and elderly individuals receive higher standard deductions.

Many individuals qualify for more than the standard deduction. **Itemized deductions** are expenses that a taxpayer is allowed to deduct from adjusted gross income.

Common itemized deductions fall into the following categories:

- *Medical and dental expenses,* including doctor's fees, prescription medications, hospital expenses, medical insurance premiums, hearing aids, eyeglasses, and medical travel that has not been reimbursed or paid by others. The amount of this deduction is the medical and dental expenses

Pepper . . . and Salt

"It's still considered income, Mr. Harris, whether you had it spent before you saw it or not."

FROM *The Wall Street Journal,* with permission of Cartoon Features Syndicate.

that exceed 7.5 percent (as of 1989) of adjusted gross income. If your AGI is $20,000, for example, you must have $1,500 in unreimbursed medical and dental expenses before you can claim this deduction. If your medical and dental bills amount to $1,600, you qualify for a $100 deduction.

- *Taxes*—state and local income tax, real estate property tax, and state or local personal property tax.
- *Interest*—mortgage interest, home equity loan interest, and a portion of personal interest (10 percent for 1990). Starting in 1991, no deduction will be allowed for personal interest.
- *Contributions* of cash or property to qualified charitable organizations. Contribution totals greater than 20 percent of adjusted gross income are subject to limitations.
- *Casualty and theft losses*—financial losses resulting from natural disasters, accidents, or unlawful acts. Deductions are for the amount exceeding 10 percent of AGI less $100, for losses *not* reimbursed by an insurance company or other source. In 1989, many residents of the San Francisco area reported casualty losses due to the earthquake damage incurred in October of that year.
- *Moving expenses* when a change in residence is associated with a new job that is at least 35 miles farther from your former home than your old main job location.
- *Job-related and other miscellaneous expenses* such as unreimbursed job travel, union dues, required continuing education, work clothes or uniforms, investment expenses, tax preparation fees, and safe-deposit box rental. The total of these expenses must exceed 2 percent of adjusted gross income to qualify as a deduction. Such miscellaneous expenses as gambling losses to the extent of gambling winnings and physical or mental disability expenses that limit employability are not subject to the 2 percent limit.

The standard deduction *or* total itemized deductions along with the value of your exemptions (see next section) are subtracted from adjusted gross income to obtain your taxable income.

• •

PERSONAL FINANCE JOURNAL

Is It Taxable Income? Is It Deductible?

Certain financial benefits received by individuals are not subject to federal income tax. Indicate whether each of the following items would or would not be included in taxable income when you compute your federal income tax.

	Yes	No
1. Lottery winnings	____	____
2. Child support received	____	____
3. Workers' compensation benefits	____	____
4. Life insurance death benefits	____	____
5. Municipal bond interest earnings	____	____
6. Bartering income	____	____

Indicate whether each of the following items would or would not be deductible when you compute your federal income tax.

	Yes	No
7. Life insurance premiums	____	____
8. The cost of commuting to work	____	____
9. Fees for traffic violations	____	____
10. Mileage for driving to volunteer work	____	____
11. An attorney's fee for preparing a will	____	____
12. Income tax preparation fee	____	____

ANSWERS: 1, 6, 10, 12—yes; 2, 3, 4, 5, 7, 8, 9, 11—no.

NOTE: These taxable income items and deductions are based on the 1989 tax year and may change due to changes in the tax code.

• •

You are required to maintain records to document your tax deductions. Financial advisers recommend that a home filing system (see Exhibit 4–2) be used to store receipts and other forms of expense documentation. Canceled checks will serve as proof of payment for such deductions as charitable contributions, medical expenses, and business-related expenses. Travel expenses must be maintained in a daily log with records of mileage, tolls, parking fees, and away-from-home costs.

Exemptions   An **exemption** is a deduction from adjusted gross income for yourself, your spouse, and qualified dependents. A dependent must not earn more than a set amount unless he or she is under age 19 or is a full-time student under age 23; you must provide more than half of the dependent's support; and the dependent must reside in your home or be a specified relative and must meet certain citizenship requirements.

For 1990, taxable income was reduced by $2,050 for each exemption claimed. This amount is revised annually based on inflation. Increased exemptions and standard deductions eliminate or reduce the taxes paid by many low-income Americans. For 1989, a family of four did not have to pay federal income tax on its first $13,200 of gross income ($5,200 for the standard deduction and $8,000 for four exemptions). After deducting the amounts for exemptions, you obtain your taxable income, which is the amount used to determine taxes owed.

Determining Taxes Owed

Taxable income is the basis for the amount of your income tax. The use of tax rates and the benefits of tax credits are the final phase of the tax computation process.

Tax Rates   Use your taxable income in conjunction with the appropriate tax table or tax schedule. Before 1987, there were 14 tax rates, ranging from 11 to 50 percent. For 1989, the two-rate system for federal income tax was

	Single Taxpayers	**Married Taxpayers**	**Heads of Households**
15 percent on taxable income	Up to $18,550	Up to $30,950	Up to $24,850
28 percent on taxable income	Over $18,550	Over $30,950	Over $24,850

EXHIBIT 4–2

A Tax Recordkeeping System

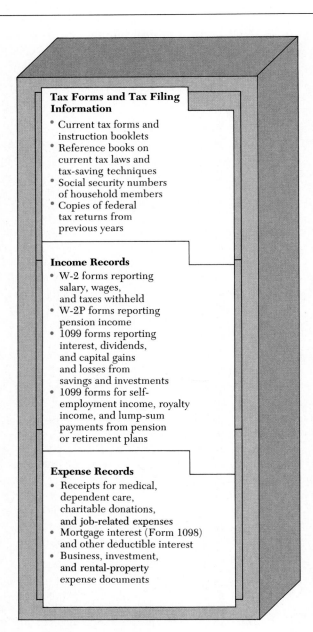

Tax Forms and Tax Filing Information

* Current tax forms and instruction booklets
* Reference books on current tax laws and tax-saving techniques
* Social security numbers of household members
* Copies of federal tax returns from previous years

Income Records

• W-2 forms reporting salary, wages, and taxes withheld
• W-2P forms reporting pension income
• 1099 forms reporting interest, dividends, and capital gains and losses from savings and investments
• 1099 forms for self-employment income, royalty income, and lump-sum payments from pension or retirement plans

Expense Records

• Receipts for medical, dependent care, charitable donations, and job-related expenses
• Mortgage interest (Form 1098) and other deductible interest
• Business, investment, and rental-property expense documents

A separate tax rate schedule exists for married persons who file separate income tax returns. The federal tax code also includes a 5 percent additional tax for persons in higher income categories. This additional tax is designed to eliminate the benefits of the personal exemption and the 15 percent tax bracket for these taxpayers.

The 15 and 28 percent rates are referred to as **marginal tax rates;** these rates are used to calculate tax on your last (and next) dollar of taxable income. After deductions and exemptions, a person in the 28 percent tax bracket pays 28 cents in taxes for every dollar of taxable income in that bracket.

In contrast, your **average tax rate** is based on the total tax due divided by your taxable income. Due to deductions and tax credits, this rate is usually less than a person's marginal tax rate. For example, a person with taxable income of $40,000 and a total tax bill of $4,200 would have an average tax rate of 10.5 percent ($4,200 ÷ $40,000). Self-employed individuals are likely to have a higher average tax rate due to self-employment taxes, which include payments toward future social security benefits.

Taxpayers who benefit from the special treatment given to some kinds of income and receive special deductions may be subject to an additional tax. The *alternative minimum tax (AMT)* is designed to make sure that those who receive tax breaks also pay their fair share of taxes. Further discussion of the AMT is beyond the scope of this book, but additional information may be obtained from the Internal Revenue Service.

Tax Credits   The tax owed may be reduced by a **tax credit,** an amount subtracted directly from the amount of taxes owed. One example of a tax credit is the credit given for child care and dependent care expenses. This amount lowers

FINANCIAL PLANNING CALCULATIONS
Tax Credits versus Tax Deductions

Many individuals confuse tax *credits* with tax *deductions*. Is one better than the other? You might say that the difference is like the difference between *lightning* and the *lightning bug!*

A tax credit, such as eligible child care or dependent care expenses, results in a dollar-for-dollar reduction in the amount of taxes owed. A tax deduction, such as an itemized deduction in the form of medical expenses, mortgage interest, or charitable contributions, reduces the taxable income on which your taxes are based.

Here is how a $100 tax credit compares with a $100 tax deduction:

As you might expect, tax credits are not as readily available as tax deductions. To qualify for a $100 child care tax credit, you may have to spend $500 in child care expenses. In some situations, spending on deductible items may be more beneficial than qualifying for a tax credit. For this reason, a knowledge of tax law and careful financial planning will help you make the best use of both tax credits and tax deductions.

$100 Tax Credit

Reduces your taxes by $100.

$100 Tax Deduction

The amount of your tax reduction depends on your tax bracket. Your taxes will be reduced by $15 if you are in the 15 percent tax bracket, by $28 if you are in the 28 percent tax bracket.

the tax owed by an individual or a couple. A tax credit differs from a deduction in that a tax credit has a full dollar effect in lowering taxes, whereas a deduction reduces the taxable income on which the tax liability is computed.

Payment Methods

Your payment of income taxes to the federal government will be made in one of two ways: through payroll withholding or through estimated tax payments.

Withholding   The pay-as-you-go system, which was started in 1943, requires an employer to deduct an amount for federal income tax from your pay and send it to the government. The withheld amount is based on the number of exemptions and the expected deductions claimed on the W-4 form. For example, a married person with children would have less withheld than a single person with the same salary since the married person will owe less tax at year-end.

After the end of the year, you will receive a W-2 form (Exhibit 4–3), which reports your annual earnings and the amounts that have been deducted for federal income tax, social security, and, if applicable, state income tax. A copy of the W-2 form is filed with your tax return to document your earnings and the amount you have paid in taxes. The difference between the amount withheld and the tax owed is either the additional amount you must pay or the refund you will receive.

Many taxpayers view an annual tax refund as a "windfall," extra money that they can count on each year. But these taxpayers are forgetting the opportunity cost of withholding excessive amounts. In 1988, 75 million American households received an average refund of $875, for a total of $65.625 billion. Invested at 6 percent for a year, these refunds represent over $3.937 billion in lost interest. Some people view their extra tax withholding as "forced savings," but a payroll deduction plan for savings could serve the same purpose and would enable them to earn the interest instead of lending money to the government interest free.

Students and other low-income individuals may file for exemption from withholding if they paid no federal income tax last year and do not expect to pay any in the current year. Dependents may not be exempt from withholding if they have any unearned income and if their total gross income will exceed $500.

EXHIBIT 4–3
W-2 Form

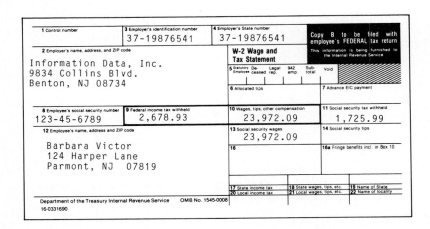

Being exempt from withholding results in not having to file for a refund and allows you to make more use of your money during the year. However, even if federal income tax is not withheld, social security taxes would still be deducted.

Estimated Payments   People with income from savings, investments, independent contracting, royalties, and lump-sum payments from pensions or retirement plans report earnings on Form 1099. People in these situations may be required to make tax payments during the year (April 15, June 15, September 15, and January 15 as the last payment for the previous tax year). These payments are based on the individual's estimate of taxes due at year-end. Underpayment or failure to make these estimated payments can result in penalties and interest charges. These penalties are avoided if withholding and estimated payments total more than your tax liability for the previous year or at least 90 percent of this year's tax.

Deadlines and Penalties

Most people are required to file their federal income tax return each April 15. If you are not able to file on time, Form 4868 can be used to obtain an automatic four-month extension. This extension is for the 1040 form and other documents, but it does not delay your payment liability. You must submit any amount owed with Form 4868 by April 15.

Individuals who make quarterly deposits for estimated taxes must submit their payments by April 15, June 15, and September 15 of the current tax year, with the final payment due by January 15 of the following year.

The Internal Revenue Service (IRS) can impose penalties and interest for violations of the tax code. Failure to file a tax return can result in a 25 percent penalty in addition to the taxes owed.

Underpayment of quarterly estimated taxes requires that you pay interest on the amount that should have been paid. Underpayment due to negligence or fraud can result in penalties of 50 to 75 percent. The good news is that if you claim a refund several months or years late, the IRS will pay you interest. Refunds must be claimed within three years of filing the return or within two years of paying the tax.

FILING YOUR FEDERAL INCOME TAX RETURN

L.O.3
Prepare a federal income tax return.

The annual submission of your federal income tax return requires several decisions and activities. First, you must determine whether you are required to file a return. Next, you must determine which basic form best serves your needs and whether you are required to submit additional schedules or supplementary forms. Finally, you must prepare your return for submission.

Who Must File?

Every citizen or resident of the United States and every U.S. citizen who is a resident of Puerto Rico is required to file a federal income tax return if his or her income is above a certain amount. The amount is based on your *filing status* and other factors such as age. For example, single persons under 65 had to file a return on April 15, 1990 (for tax year 1989), if their gross income exceeded $4,950; single persons over 65 had to file if their gross income exceeded $5,700. The amount required to file will change each year based on changes in the standard deduction and in the allowed personal exemptions. If your gross income is less than this amount but taxes were withheld from your earnings, you will need to file a return to obtain a refund.

Your filing status is affected by such factors as marital status and dependents. The five filing status categories are

- *Single*—never-married, divorced, or legally separated individuals.
- *Married filing joint return*—combines the income of a husband and a wife.
- *Married filing separate return*—each spouse responsible for his or her own tax. Under certain conditions, a married couple can benefit from this filing status.
- *Head of household*—an unmarried individual or a surviving spouse who maintains a household (paying for more than half of the costs) for a child or a dependent relative.
- *Qualifying widow or widower*—an individual whose spouse recently died and who has a dependent.

In some situations, you may have a choice of filing status. In such cases, compute your taxes under the available alternatives to determine which is more advantageous.

Which Tax Form Should You Use?

Although there are nearly 400 federal tax forms and schedules, (see Exhibit 4–4) taxpayers have a choice of three basic forms when filing their income tax. Most recently, 17 percent used Form 1040EZ, 19 percent used Form 1040A, and 64 percent used the regular Form 1040. Your decision on this matter will depend on your type of income, the amount of your income, the number of your deductions, and the complexity of your tax situation.

Form 1040EZ   You may use Form 1040EZ if you are single and claim only your own exemption; if your income consisted only of wages, salaries, and tips and not more than $400 of interest; if your taxable income is less than $50,000; and if you do not itemize deductions or claim any adjustments to income or any tax credits.

Form 1040EZ allows individuals with less complicated situations to file with a minimum of effort. For example, Matthew Collins, a college freshman, had a part-time job at a health center. Since he was single, earned less than the amount needed to file, and had $43 in interest income, Matthew was able to use Form 1040EZ to obtain a refund of income tax withheld during the past year.

Form 1040A   This form would be used by individuals who have less than $50,000 in taxable income from wages, salaries, tips, unemployment compensation, interest, or dividends. With Form 1040A, you can also take deductions for individual retirement account (IRA) contributions and a tax credit for child care and dependent care expenses.

If you qualify for either Form 1040EZ or Form 1040A, you may wish to use one of them to simplify filing your tax return. But you are not required to use either form if the use of the regular Form 1040 lets you pay less tax.

EXHIBIT 4–4   The Most Commonly Used Federal Income Tax Forms

Form	Title	Purpose
1040EZ	Income Tax Return	For single taxpayers with no dependents, taxable income of less than $50,000, no deductions
1040A	Income Tax Return	For taxpayers with taxable income of less than $50,000 and no itemized deductions who may take an IRA deduction and have certain tax credits
1040	Income Tax Return	For taxpayers with more complex tax situations who do not qualify for use of 1040EZ or 1040A
Schedule A	Itemized Deductions	To claim deductions for medical expenses, certain state and local taxes, interest, donations, casualty losses, moving expenses, and other deductible expenses
Schedule B	Interest and Dividend Income	To report interest and/or dividend income of over $400
Schedule C	Profit or Loss from Business or Profession	To report income and expenses from self-employment
Schedule D	Capital Gains and Losses	To report gains and losses on the sale of investments
Schedule E	Supplemental Income Schedule	To report income and expenses from rental property, royalties, partnerships, estates, and trusts
Schedule R	Credit for the Elderly or Disabled	To claim a tax credit for the elderly or disabled in low-income categories
Schedule SE	Social Security Self-Employment Tax	To calculate self-employment social security tax based on profit from a business or profession
2106	Employee Business Expenses	To report employee-related travel expenses and reimbursements for these expenses
2119	Sale of Your Home	To report the sale and/or exchange of your primary place of residence
2441	Credit for Child and Dependent Care Expenses	To calculate the tax credit for child care or dependent care costs for individuals in certain income groups
3903	Moving Expenses	To calculate the deductible expenses related to a change of residence based on job distance restrictions
4562	Depreciation and Amortization	To calculate business depreciation expenses for various types of assets
4684	Casualties and Thefts	To report nonbusiness casualty and theft losses less any reimbursement from insurance or other source
5329	Return for IRA and Qualified Retirement Plans Taxes	To report excess contributions, premature distributions, or excess distributions related to a retirement plan
8283	Noncash Charitable Contributions	To report a charitable deduction of property or services
8606	Nondeductible IRA Contributions	To report contributions to an individual retirement arrangement that are not deductible for tax purposes
8615	Computation of Tax for Children under Age 14 Who Have Investment Income of More than $1,000	To report income and capital gains from investments

Form 1040   Form 1040 is an expanded version of Form 1040A that includes sections for all types of income. You are required to use this form if your income is over $50,000 or if you can be claimed as a dependent on your parents' return *and* you had interest or dividends over a set limit.

Form 1040 makes it possible to itemize your deductions. You can list various allowable expenses (medical costs, home mortgage interest, real estate property taxes) that will reduce your taxable income and the amount you owe the government. You should learn about all the possible adjustments to income, deductions, and tax credits for which you may qualify.

How Is the Federal Income Tax Return Completed?

The major sections of Form 1040 (see Exhibit 4–5) correspond to the components of your income tax discussed in the previous section of this chapter:

1. *Filing Status and Exemptions.* Your tax rate is determined by your filing status and allowances for yourself, your spouse, and each person you claim as a dependent.
2. *Income.* Earnings from your employment (as reported by your W-2 form) and other income, such as savings and investment income, are reported in this section of Form 1040.
3. *Adjustments to Income.* As discussed later in the chapter, if you qualify, you may deduct contributions (up to a certain amount) to an individual retirement account (IRA) or other qualified retirement program.
4. *Tax Computation.* In this section, your adjusted gross income is reduced by your itemized deductions (see Exhibit 4–6) or by the standard

EXHIBIT 4–5   Federal Income Tax Return—Form 1040

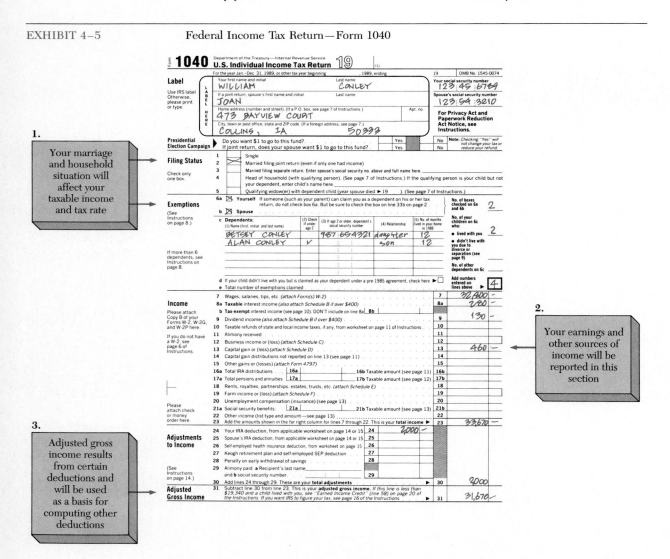

1. Your marriage and household situation will affect your taxable income and tax rate

2. Your earnings and other sources of income will be reported in this section

3. Adjusted gross income results from certain deductions and will be used as a basis for computing other deductions

deduction for your tax situation. In addition, an amount is deducted for each exemption to arrive at your taxable income. That income is the basis for determining the amount of your tax (see Exhibit 4–7).

5. *Tax Credits.* Any tax credits for which you qualify would be subtracted at this point.

6. *Other Taxes.* Any special taxes, such as self-employment tax, would be included at this point.

7. *Payments.* Your total withholding and other payments would be indicated in this section.

8. *Refund or Amount You Owe.* If your payments exceed the amount of income tax you owe, you are entitled to a refund. If the opposite is true, you must make an additional payment.

9. *Your Signature.* Forgetting to sign a tax return is one of the most common filing errors.

EXHIBIT 4–5   *(concluded)*

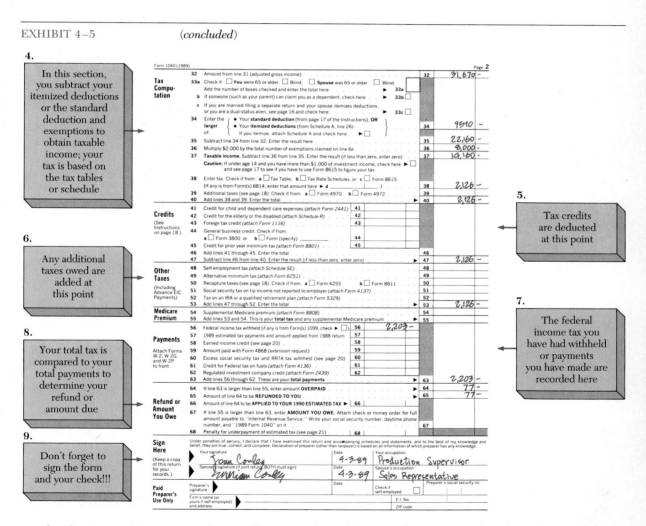

4.
In this section, you subtract your itemized deductions or the standard deduction and exemptions to obtain taxable income; your tax is based on the tax tables or schedule

6.
Any additional taxes owed are added at this point

8.
Your total tax is compared to your total payments to determine your refund or amount due

9.
Don't forget to sign the form and your check!!!

5.
Tax credits are deducted at this point

7.
The federal income tax you have had withheld or payments you have made are recorded here

NOTE: These forms were used in a recent year; the current forms may not be exactly the same. Obtain current income tax forms and current income tax information from your local IRS office, bank, or public library.

EXHIBIT 4–6   Schedule A for Itemized Deductions (Form 1040)

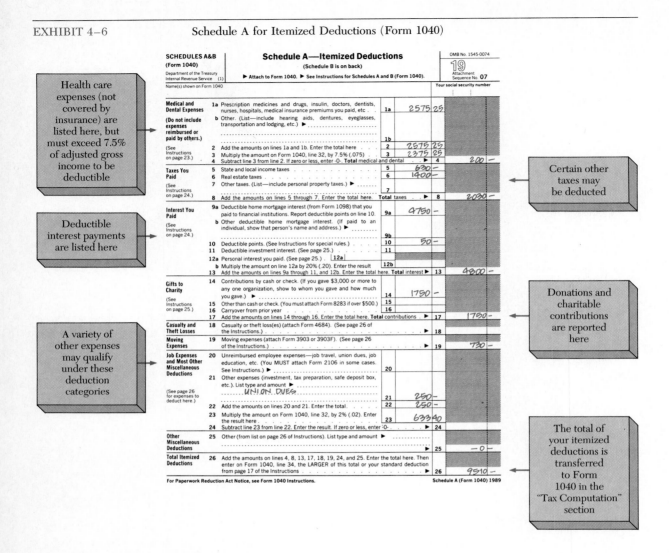

How Are State Income Tax Returns Filed?

All but seven states (Alaska, Florida, Nevada, South Dakota, Texas, Washington, and Wyoming) have a state income tax. In most states, the tax rate ranges from 1 to 10 percent and is based on some aspect of your federal income tax return, such as adjusted gross income or taxable income. For further information on the income tax in your state, contact the state department of revenue.

The states usually require income tax returns to be filed when your federal income tax return is due. To assist in planning your tax activities, see Exhibit 4–8.

TAX ASSISTANCE AND THE AUDIT PROCESS

In the process of completing your federal income tax return, you may seek additional information or assistance. After filing your return, you may be identified for a tax audit; if this happens, several policies and procedures protect your rights.

EXHIBIT 4–7   Tax Tables and Tax Rate Schedules

Tax Table

If line 37 (taxable income) is—		And you are—			
At least	But less than	Single	Married filing jointly *	Married filing sepa- rately	Head of a house- hold
			Your tax is—		
14,000					
14,000	14,050	2,104	2,104	2,104	2,104
14,050	14,100	2,111	2,111	2,111	2,111
14,100	14,150	2,119	2,119	2,119	2,119
14,150	14,200	2,126	2,126	2,126	2,126
14,200	14,250	2,134	2,134	2,134	2,134
14,250	14,300	2,141	2,141	2,141	2,141
14,300	14,350	2,149	2,149	2,149	2,149
14,350	14,400	2,156	2,156	2,156	2,156
14,400	14,450	2,164	2,164	2,164	2,164
14,450	14,500	2,171	2,171	2,171	2,171
14,500	14,550	2,179	2,179	2,179	2,179
14,550	14,600	2,186	2,186	2,186	2,186
14,600	14,650	2,194	2,194	2,194	2,194
14,650	14,700	2,201	2,201	2,201	2,201
14,700	14,750	2,209	2,209	2,209	2,209
14,750	14,800	2,216	2,216	2,216	2,216
14,800	14,850	2,224	2,224	2,224	2,224
14,850	14,900	2,231	2,231	2,231	2,231
14,900	14,950	2,239	2,239	2,239	2,239
14,950	15,000	2,246	2,246	2,246	2,246

Tax Rate Schedules

Schedule X——Use if your filing status is **Single**

If the amount on Form 1040, line 37, is: Over—	But not over—	Enter on Form 1040, line 38	of the amount over—
$0	$18,550	. . . . 15%	$0
18,550	44,900	**$2,782.50 + 28%**	18,550
44,900	93,130	**10,160.50 + 33%**	44,900
93,130	. . . .	Use **Worksheet** below to figure your tax.	

NOTE: These were the federal income tax rates for a recent year. The current rates may vary slightly due to changes in the tax code and adjustments for inflation. Obtain current income tax booklets from your local IRS office, bank, or public library.

L.O.4
Identify tax assistance sources.

Tax Information Sources

As with other aspects of personal financial planning, a variety of materials are available to assist you with your taxes. The Internal Revenue Service offers a wide range of services to taxpayers. Libraries and bookstores offer books and other publications that are updated annually.

IRS Services   If you wish to do your own tax return or just to expand your knowledge of tax regulations, the Internal Revenue Service has four methods of assistance.

1.   *Publications.* The IRS offers hundreds of free booklets and pamphlets. These publications can be obtained at a local IRS office, by mail request, or by a telephone call to the office listed in your tax packet or your local telephone directory. Especially helpful is *Your Federal Income Tax* (IRS Publication 17). Taxpayers may obtain IRS publications and tax forms by calling 1-800-424-FORM.

2.   *Recorded Messages.* The IRS Tele-Tax system allows you access to 150 telephone tax tips covering everything from filing requirements to reporting gambling income. Your push-button phone gives you 24-hour-a-day availability to this recorded information. Again, telephone numbers can be found in your tax packet or your telephone directory.

EXHIBIT 4–8   A Tax Planning Calendar

January	February	March
• Establish a recordkeeping system for your tax information • If you expect a refund, file your tax return for the previous year • Make your final estimated quarterly payment for the previous year for income not covered by withholding	• Check to make sure you received W-2 and 1099 forms from all organizations from which you had income during the previous year; these should have been received by January 31; if not, contact the organization	• Organize your records and tax information in preparation for filing your tax return; if you expect a refund, file as soon as possible

April	May	June
• April 15 is the deadline for filing your federal tax return; if it falls on a weekend, you have until the next business day (usually Monday) • File for an automatic extension for filing your tax forms	• Review your tax return to determine whether any changes in withholding, exemptions, or marital status have not been reported to your employer	• The second installment for estimated tax is due June 15 for income not covered by withholding

July	August	September
• With the year half over, consider or implement plans for a personal retirement program such as an IRA or a Keogh	• Tax returns are due August 15 for those who received the automatic four-month extension	• The third installment for estimated tax is due September 15 for income not covered by withholding

October	November	December
• Determine the tax benefits of selling certain investments by year-end	• Make any last-minute changes in withholding by your employer to avoid penalties for too little withholding • Determine if you qualify for an IRA; if so, consider opening one	• Determine if it would be to your advantage to make any payments for next year before December 31 of the current year • Decide if you can defer income for the current year until the following year

NOTE: Children born before the end of the year give you a full-year exemption, so plan accordingly!

3.   *Toll-Free Hot Line.* You can obtain information on specific problems through an IRS-staffed phone line. The appropriate telephone number can be obtained in the manner described above. You are not asked to give your name when you use this service, so your questions are anonymous.

4.   *Walk-In Service.* You can visit your local or district IRS office to obtain assistance with your taxes. More than 500 of these facilities are available to taxpayers. Be aware, however, that information provided by IRS employees is not always reliable. Various studies in recent years have reported incorrect answers over 30 percent of the time. You can be held liable for taxes owed even though you based your calculations on information provided by IRS employees.

Other Publications   Each year, several tax guides are published and offered for sale. These publications include *J. K. Lasser's Your Income Tax*, the *H&R Block Income Tax Workbook*, and *Consumer Reports Books Guide to Income Tax Preparation*. You can purchase them at bookstores, drugstores, or supermarkets or use them at your library.

Computer Software

More and more taxpayers are making use of personal computers for tax recordkeeping and tax form preparation. A spreadsheet program can be very helpful in maintaining and updating tax data on various income and expense categories. Such software packages as *Tax Preparer, TurboTax,* and *J. K. Lasser's Your Income Tax* allow individuals to complete and print finished versions of needed tax forms and schedules. See Appendix C for additional information.

The IRS has been expanding its acceptance of computer-readable tax forms. Electronic tax filings are expected to increase in number each year and to increase processing efficiency for both the IRS and taxpayers. The IRS is also planning to use computerized *expert systems* to answer tax inquiries. Through a series of on-screen questions, the IRS clerk can first help taxpayers identify their real problem and then provide the real solution. This method is intended to reduce the proportion of incorrectly answered inquiries.

Tax Preparation Services

Over 40 million U.S. taxpayers pay someone to do their income taxes. The fee for this service can range from $40 at a tax preparation service for a simple return, to more than $700 at a certified public accountant for a complicated tax return.

Many people like doing their own taxes. This experience can help you improve your understanding of your actual financial situation. The IRS claims that anyone with an eighth grade education can fill out a 1040 form. The average person takes a little more than two hours to complete Form 1040, compared with 57 minutes for Form 1040A and 22 minutes for the one-page 1040EZ. But doing your own taxes can be complicated, particularly if you have sources of income other than salary. The sources available for professional tax assistance include:

- Tax services ranging from local, one-person operations to national firms such as H&R Block, which has thousands of offices open from January to April each year.

- Enrolled agents—government-approved tax experts who prepare returns and provide tax advice. You may contact the National Association of Enrolled Agents at 1-800-424-4339 for information on enrolled agents in your area.
- The many accountants who offer tax assistance along with their other business services. A certified public account (CPA) with special training in taxes can be valuable in your tax planning and in the preparation of your annual return.
- Attorneys, who usually do not complete tax returns and whose services can be best used when you are involved in a tax-related transaction or when you have a difference of opinion with the IRS.

Even if you hire a professional tax preparer, you are responsible for supplying accurate and complete information. Hiring a tax preparer will not guarantee you're paying the *correct* amount. A *Money* magazine study of 50 tax preparers showed that although they charged fees of from $201 to $2,500, taxes due ranged from $7,202 to $11,881. If your owe more tax because your return contains errors or because you have made entries that are not allowed, it is your responsibility to pay that additional tax plus any interest and penalties.

What if Your Return Is Audited?

The IRS reviews all returns to make sure that they have been properly completed. Computers check all of the arithmetic. If you have made an error, your tax is automatically refigured and you will receive a bill or a refund. If you have made an entry that is not allowed, you will be notified by mail. A **tax audit** is a detailed examination of your tax return by the IRS. In most audits, the IRS requests more information to support the entries on your tax return. You must keep accurate records to support your return. Keep receipts, canceled checks, and other evidence to prove amounts that you claim as valid. Avoiding common filing mistakes (see Exhibit 4–9) helps minimize your chances of an IRS audit.

Who Gets Audited?   In 1988, 1.1 percent of all tax filers—1.1 million people—were audited. While the IRS does not reveal its basis for selecting the returns that it audits, several indicators are evident. Individuals who claim large or unusual deductions increase their chances of an audit. Tax advisers suggest including a brief explanation or a copy of receipts for deductions that may be questioned. Individuals whose incomes are high, who have had large losses due to tax shelters or partnerships, or who have had their income or deductions questioned in the past may also be targeted for an audit.

Types of Audits   The simplest and most common type of audit is the *correspondence audit.* This mail inquiry requires you to clarify or document minor questions about your tax return. You usually have 30 days to provide the requested information, and your response may be by mail.

The *office audit* requires you to visit an IRS office to clarify some aspect of your return. This type of audit usually takes an hour or two. The *field audit* is more complex. It involves having an IRS agent visit you at your home, at your place of business, or at the office of your accountant so that you will have quick access to all pertinent documents and records. A field audit may also be done to verify whether an individual has an office in the home as claimed.

EXHIBIT 4–9

How to Avoid Common Filing Errors

Keep all tax-related information for easy access.

Follow instructions carefully. Many people deduct total medical and dental expenses rather than the amount of these expenses that exceeds 7.5 percent of adjusted gross income.

Use the proper tax rate schedule or tax table column.

Be sure to claim the correct number of exemptions and the correct amount of standard deduction.

Consider the alternative minimum tax that may apply to your situation. Be sure to pay self-employment tax and tax on early IRA withdrawals.

Check your arithmetic several times.

Sign your return (both spouses must sign a joint return), or the IRS won't process it.

Be sure to include the correct social security number(s) and to record amounts on the correct lines.

Attach necessary documentation such as your W-2 forms and required supporting schedules.

Put your social security number, the tax year, and a daytime telephone number on your check—and be sure to sign the check.

Keep a photocopy of your return.

Put the proper postage on your mailing envelope.

Finally, check everything again—and file on time!

Taking care when you file your income tax can result in "many happy returns."

Finally, the *research audit* is a line-by-line investigation of a tax return. Individuals audited in this way are selected at random so that the IRS can obtain information for use in developing future audit procedures. In a research audit, a person is asked to furnish proof for every item on the return, including proof of marriage.

Your Audit Rights   When you are audited, you should be prepared to answer the IRS agent's questions clearly and completely. You may be accompanied by your tax preparer, accountant, or lawyer, who may assist you in answering questions. If you are audited, your attitude can help reduce anxiety and potential hostility. Present substantiating records and receipts in an orderly fashion. Argue in a logical, calm, and confident manner. Keep both the discussion and your answers to the auditor's questions as brief as possible and to the point.

If you disagree with the results of the audit, you may request a conference at the Regional Appeals Office. Although most differences of opinion are settled at this stage, some taxpayers take their cases further. An individual may go to the U.S. tax court, or the U.S. claims court, or the U.S. district court. Some tax disputes have gone as far as the U.S. Supreme Court.

TAX PLANNING STRATEGIES

L.O.5

Select appropriate tax strategies for different financial and personal situations.

Most people want to pay their fair share of taxes—no more, no less. They do this by practicing **tax avoidance,** the use of legitimate methods to reduce one's taxes. This is in contrast to **tax evasion,** which is the use of illegal actions to reduce one's taxes. As shown in Exhibit 4–10, people in different life situations can take advantage of various tax rules. When considering financial decisions in relation to your taxes, you should remember that purchasing, investing, and retirement planning are the areas most affected by tax laws.

EXHIBIT 4–10	Special Tax Situations
Business in your home	You may deduct any ordinary and necessary expenses related to starting and maintaining your business, including a portion of your rent or mortgage if that portion of your home is used exclusively for business. (Individuals who are employed elsewhere but claim an office at home are likely to be challenged by the IRS regarding this deduction.)
Divorced persons	Child support payments have no tax consequences. They are neither deductible by the payer nor included in the income of the recipient. Alimony is tax deductible by the payer and must be included as income by the recipient. Exemptions for children are generally claimed by the parent who has custody for a longer time during the tax year.
Single parents	A single parent may claim "head of household" filing status, which has greater advantages than "single" status. Working parents may qualify for a child care tax credit.
Retired persons	Individuals over age 59 ½ may withdraw tax-deferred funds from a retirement plan without penalty. Of course, these funds must be reported as ordinary income. Social security recipients, as of 1989, may make up to $25,000 if single and up to $32,000 if married without being taxed on their social security benefits. In general, one half of the amount earned above these limits is included in their gross income for computing taxable income. The amount included in gross income cannot exceed one half of their social security benefits.

Consumer Purchasing

The buying decisions most affected by taxes are the purchase of a residence, the use of credit, and job-related expenses.

Place of Residence   Owning a home is one of the best tax shelters available to most individuals. Real estate property taxes and interest on the mortgage are both deductible (as itemized deductions) and thus reduce your taxable income. While renting may seem less expensive than owning, the after-tax cost of owning a home often makes owning financially advantageous. The specific calculations for comparing renting and buying are presented in Chapter 9.

Consumer Debt   Until 1990, some or all of the interest paid on credit cards, charge accounts, and personal loans was deductible for federal income tax purposes; as of 1991, none is deductible. But the current tax laws still leave homeowners plenty of borrowing power for consumer purchases. You can deduct interest on loans (of up to $100,000) secured by your primary or secondary home up to the actual dollar amount you have invested in it—the difference between the market value of the home and the amount you owe on it. These *home equity loans* are discussed in greater detail in Chapters 6 and 9. Current tax laws allow you to use that line of credit to buy a car, to consolidate credit card or other debts, or to finance other personal expenses. Home equity loans, which are in fact second mortgages, are not allowed in a few states.

Job-Related Expenses   As previously mentioned, a variety of work expenses, such as union dues, certain travel and education costs, and business tools, may be included as itemized deductions. Job search expenses are also deductible if you incur them when seeking employment in your current occupational category. Such expenses may include transportation to interviews, résumé preparation and duplication, and employment agency or career counseling fees. Remember that only the portion of these expenses that exceeds 2 percent of adjusted gross income is deductible.

Investment Decisions

A major area of tax planning involves the wide variety of decisions that relate to investing.

Tax-Exempt Investments   Interest income from municipal bonds, which are issued by state and local governments, and other tax-exempt investments is not subject to federal income taxes. While municipal bonds have lower interest rates than other investments, their *after-tax* income may be higher than that of other investments. For example, if you are in the 28 percent tax bracket, earning $100 of tax-exempt income would be worth more to you than earning $125 in taxable investment income. The $125 would have an after-tax value of $90 — $125 less $35 (28 percent of $125) for taxes.

Tax-Deferred Investments   Although, from a tax standpoint, tax-deferred investments, whose income will be taxed at a later date, are less beneficial than tax-exempt investments, they also have financial advantages. As basic opportunity cost tells us, paying a dollar in the future instead of today gives us the opportunity to invest (or spend) it now. Examples of tax-deferred investments include

- Tax-deferred annuities, usually issued by insurance companies. These are discussed in Chapter 20.
- Series EE U.S. Treasury bonds. As of 1990, interest on these bonds is *exempt* from federal income tax if it is used to pay tuition at a college, university, or qualified technical school. Further details are offered in Chapter 5.
- Retirement plans such as IRA, Keogh, or 401(k) plans. The tax implications of these plans are discussed in the next section.

Capital gains, profits from the sale of a capital asset such as stocks, bonds, or real estate, are also tax deferred in that you do not have to pay the tax on these gains until the asset is sold. Capital gains taxation on the sale of your home may be deferred if you buy one of comparable or greater value within 24 months of selling it. Individuals over 55 are allowed a onetime capital gains exclusion of $125,000 when selling a home.

The sale of an investment for less than its purchase price is, of course, a *capital loss*. Capital losses can be used to offset capital gains and up to $3,000 of ordinary income.

Both *short-term* capital gains (on investments held for less than six months) and *long-term* capital gains are taxed as ordinary income. Before 1987, 60 percent of long-term capital gains was excluded from taxable income. This exclusion was intended to encourage investment for economic growth. In recent years, Congress has again considered taxing capital gains at some rate less than the tax on ordinary income.

Self-Employment   Owning your own business has certain tax advantages. Self-employed persons may deduct such expenses as health and life insurance as business costs. However, they may have to pay self-employment tax in addition to the regular tax rate.

Children's Investments   In past years, parents would make investments on their children's behalf and list the children as owners. This process, known as *income shifting*, attempted to reduce the taxable income of parents by shifting the ownership of investments to children in lower tax brackets. Currently, a child under 14 with investment income of more than $1,000 is taxed at the parents' top rate. For investment income under $1,000, the child receives a deduction of $500 and the next $500 is taxed at his or her own rate—which is probably lower than that of the parents. This income-shifting restriction does not apply to children 14 and older, so with such children it is possible to take advantage of the benefits of income shifting.

Retirement Plans

A major tax strategy of working people is the use of tax-deferred retirement plans such as individual retirement accounts (IRAs), Keogh plans, and 401(k) plans. You are allowed to deduct contributions to these plans from current taxable income. These contributions and earnings from the plans are not taxed until they are withdrawn.

When the IRAs were first established, every working person was allowed to deduct up to $2,000 per year for IRA contributions. Today, however, an IRA deduction is available only to individuals who do not participate in employer-sponsored retirement plans or to jointly filing taxpayers whose adjusted gross income is not greater than $40,000 and single taxpayers whose adjusted gross income is not greater than $25,000. IRA contributions are partially deductible for participants in employer-sponsored retirement plans if, when filing jointly, they have an adjusted gross income of between $40,000 and $50,000 or if, when filing individually, they have an adjusted gross income between $25,000 and $35,000. No IRA deduction is allowed for joint and individual filers with adjusted gross incomes of above $50,000 and $35,000, respectively.

Even though an IRA contribution may not be deductible, all working Americans may continue to make annual IRA contributions of up to $2,000. All IRA accounts earn interest on a tax-deferred basis; in other words, you will not have to pay taxes on the earnings of an IRA until you withdraw your money.

A self-employed person or partnership can establish a Keogh plan. You may contribute 20 percent of your annual income, up to a maximum of $30,000, to this tax-deferred retirement plan.

The part of the tax code called 401(k) authorizes a tax-deferred retirement plan sponsored by an employer. This plan allows you to contribute a far greater tax-deferred amount (about $8,000 for 1990) than you can contribute to an IRA. Unlike the IRA, the 401(k) is available to employees at all income levels. These retirement plans are discussed in greater detail in Chapter 20.

Changing Tax Strategies

It has been said that "death and taxes are the only certainties of life." Changing tax laws seem to be another certainty. Each year, the IRS changes the tax form and filing procedures. In addition, Congress frequently passes legislation that changes the tax code. These changes require that you regularly determine how to best take advantage of the tax laws for your personal financial planning. Finally, carefully consider changes in your personal situation and your income level. Your personal tax strategies should be carefully monitored to best serve both your daily living and your long-term financial goals.

SUMMARY

L.O.1
Analyze the importance of taxes for personal financial planning.

Tax planning can influence spending, saving, borrowing, and investing decisions. A knowledge of tax laws and maintenance of accurate tax records are necessary to take advantage of appropriate tax benefits. In addition to an awareness of income taxes, successful financial planning requires an awareness of sales tax, excise tax, property tax, estate tax, inheritance tax, gift tax, and social security.

L.O.2
Calculate taxable income and the amount owed for federal income tax.

Taxable income is determined by subtracting adjustments to income, deductions, and allowances for exemptions from gross income. Your total tax liability is based on the published tax tables or tax schedules less any tax credits.

L.O.3
Prepare a federal income tax return.

The major sections of Form 1040 require the determination or calculation of (1) your filing status, (2) your exemptions, (3) your income from all sources, (4) adjustments to your income, (5) your standard deduction or itemized deductions, (6) tax credits for which you qualify, (7) other taxes you owe, (8) amounts you have withheld or paid in advance, and (9) your refund or the additional amount you owe.

L.O.4
Identify tax assistance sources.

The main sources of tax assistance are IRS services and publications, other publications, computer software, and professional tax preparers such as commercial tax services, enrolled agents, accountants, and attorneys.

L.O.5
Select appropriate tax strategies for different financial and personal situations.

Your tax burden may be reduced through careful planning and financial decisions related to consumer purchasing, the use of debt, investment decisions, and retirement planning.

GLOSSARY

Adjusted gross income (AGI)   Gross income reduced by certain adjustments, such as contributions to an individual retirement account (IRA) and alimony payments.

Average tax rate   Total tax due divided by taxable income.

Capital gain   A profit realized from the sale of a capital asset, such as stocks, bonds, or real estate.

Earned income   Money received by an individual for personal effort, such as wages, salary, commission, fees, tips, or bonuses.

Estate tax   A tax imposed on the value of an individual's property at the time of his or her death.

Excise tax   A tax imposed on specific goods and services, such as gasoline, cigarettes, alcoholic beverages, tires, and air travel.

Exclusion   An amount not included in gross income.

Exemption   A deduction from adjusted gross income for yourself, your spouse, and qualified dependents.

Inheritance tax   A tax levied on the value of property received from a deceased individual.

Investment income   Money received in the form of dividends or interest; also called portfolio income.

Itemized deductions   Expenses that a taxpayer is allowed to deduct from adjusted gross income, such as medical expenses, real estate property taxes, home mortgage interest, charitable contributions, casualty losses, and certain work-related expenses.

Marginal tax rate   The rate used to calculate tax on your last (and next) dollar of taxable income.

Passive income   Money received as a result of business activities in which you do not actively participate.

Standard deduction   A set amount on which no taxes are paid.

Taxable income   The net amount of income, after allowable deductions, on which income tax is computed.

Tax audit   A detailed examination of your tax return by the Internal Revenue Service.

Tax avoidance   The use of legitimate methods to reduce one's taxes.

Tax credit   An amount subtracted directly from the amount of taxes owed.

Tax-deferred income   Income that will be taxed at a later date.

Tax evasion   The use of illegal actions to reduce one's taxes.

Tax-exempt income   Income that is not subject to tax.

Tax shelter   An investment that provides immediate tax benefits and a reasonable expectation of a future financial return.

DISCUSSION QUESTIONS

L.O.1   1. How should a financial plan take account of the effect of taxes?

L.O.1   2. What types of taxes do individuals frequently overlook when making financial decisions?

L.O.2   3. How does tax-exempt income differ from tax-deferred income?

L.O.2   4. What information is needed to compute taxable income?

L.O.2   5. When would a person use the standard deduction instead of itemized deductions?

L.O.2   6. What is the difference between your marginal tax rate and your average tax rate?

L.O.2   7. How does a tax credit affect the amount owed for federal income taxes?

L.O.3   8. In what ways does your filing status affect preparation of your federal income tax return?

L.O.3   9. What factors affect a taxpayer's choice of a 1040 form?

L.O.3   10. In order to get a tax refund, some people make sure that more is withheld from their pay than is necessary. What is your opinion of this action?

L.O.4   11. In what ways could an individual investigate the value of different types of tax assistance sources?

L.O.4   12. What recourse do taxpayers have if they disagree with an audit decision of the Internal Revenue Service?

L.O.5   13. How does tax *avoidance* differ from tax *evasion?*

L.O.5   14. What common tax-saving efforts are available to most individuals and households?

L.O.5   15. What effect can changes in the taxing of capital gains have on economic growth?

Opening Case Questions

1. What are Eric's major financial concerns in his current situation?
2. In what ways might Eric be able to improve his tax planning efforts?
3. Is Eric typical of many people in our society with regard to tax planning? Why?
4. What additional actions might Eric investigate with regard to taxes and personal financial planning?

PROBLEMS AND ACTIVITIES

L.O.1   1. Conduct a survey to determine the extent to which different people consider the tax implications of financial decisions.

L.O.2   2. Research to determine types of income that are exempt from federal income tax. To what extent does a person's life situation (age, marital status, citizenship) influence the taxability of certain income?

L.O.2   3. Thomas Franklin arrived at the following tax information:
Gross salary, $31,780
Interest earnings, $125
Dividend income, $80
One personal exemption, $2,000
Itemized deductions, $3,890
Adjustments to income, $850
What amount would Thomas report as taxable income?

L.O.2   4. If Lola Harper had the following itemized deductions, should she use Schedule A or the standard deduction? The standard deduction for her tax situation is $4,550.
Moving expenses, $1,780
Donations to church and other charities, $930
Medical and dental expenses that exceed 7.5 percent of adjusted gross income, $430
State income tax, $690
Job-related expenses that exceed 2 percent of adjusted gross income, $610

L.O.2   5. What would be the average tax rate for a person who paid taxes of $4,864.14 on a taxable income of $39,870?

L.O.2   6. Based on the following data, would Ann and Carl Wilton receive a refund or owe additional taxes?

Adjusted gross income, $43,190   Itemized deductions, $11,420
Child care tax credit, $80   Federal income tax withheld, $6,784
Amount for personal exemptions,   Average tax rate on taxable income,
  $6,000   25.8%

L.O.3   7. Which 1040 form should each of the following individuals use?
     a. A high school student with an after-school job and interest earnings of
        $480 from savings accounts.
     b. A college student who, due to ownership of property, is able to itemize
        deductions rather than take the standard deduction.
     c. A young entry-level worker with no dependents and income only from
        salary.

L.O.3   8. With the use of the tax table in Exhibit 4–7, determine the amount of
        taxes for the following situations:
     a. A head of household with taxable income of $14,573.
     b. A single person with taxable income of $14,328.
     c. A married person filing a separate return with taxable income of
        $14,632.

L.O.4   9. Use IRS publications and other materials to research a question about
        taxes. Contact an IRS office to obtain an answer to the same question.
        What differences of opinion exist?

L.O.4   10. Contact several tax preparation services to obtain information on their fees
        for preparing a simple federal income tax return. What do you believe ac-
        counts for the difference in these fees?

L.O.5   11. Would you prefer a fully taxable investment earning 10.7 percent or a tax-
        exempt investment earning 8.1 percent?

L.O.5   12. Talk to several friends or relatives about the tax planning actions they have
        taken. How have these actions altered their buying, saving, borrowing, and
        investing decisions?

LIFE SITUATION   Case 4–1

Tax Time for Alicia

Alicia Hamilton needs assistance in preparing her federal income tax return. She
has assembled the following information:

Earnings from wages, $23,340   Interest earned on savings, $125
IRA deduction, $450   Checking account interest, $65
Two exemptions at $2,000 each   Amount withheld for federal income
Current standard deduction for her   tax, $2,349
   filing status, $4,550   Tax credit for child care, $150
Filing status: head of household

Questions

1. What is Alicia's taxable income ? (Refer to Exhibit 4-1, page 98.)
2. What is Alicia's total tax liability? (Use Exhibit 4-7, page 111.) What is her
   average tax rate?
3. Based on her withholding, will Alicia receive a refund or owe additional
   tax? What is the amount?
4. What information sources might Alicia find most helpful in preparing her
   federal income tax return?

LIFE SITUATION   Case 4–2

Taxes and Financial Planning

Bob and Connie Martin have always considered themselves careful in their budgeting and saving activities. They never use credit cards; they pay all bills, including their monthly rent, on time; and they have several thousand dollars in savings certificates. However, tax planning is an area of weakness in what the Martins believe to be good financial planning and money management habits. Each year, they pay much more in taxes than they need to; quite often, they have had to take money out of savings to make their tax payment.

Questions

1. How might the Martins' housing situation be changed for better tax planning?
2. What saving and investment alternatives might reduce the Martins' tax liability?
3. What could the Martins do to prevent having to pay the government tax owed?
4. What additional suggestions with regard to effective tax planning could be offered to the Martins?

SUPPLEMENTARY READINGS

For Additional Information on Filing Your Federal Income Tax Return

Consumer Reports Books Guide to Income Tax Preparation. Mount Vernon, N.Y.: Consumers Union, 1991.

H&R Block Income Tax Guide. New York: Collier Books, 1991.

Holzman, Robert S. *Complete Book of Tax Deductions.* New York: Harper & Row, 1990.

McCormally, Kevin. "Finding Paydirt in the Tax Forms." *Changing Times,* February 1990, pp. 44–52.

U.S. Master Tax Guide. Chicago: Commerce Clearing House, 1991.

Your Federal Income Tax. Publication 17. Washington, D.C.: Internal Revenue Service.

Tax Guide for Small Business. Publication 334. Washington, D.C.: Internal Revenue Service.

For Additional Information on Tax Audits

"How to Survive a Tax Audit." *Consumer Reports,* March 1989, pp. 172–76.

Sydlaske, Janet M., and Richard K. Millcroft. *The Only Tax Audit Guide You'll Ever Need.* New York: John Wiley & Sons, 1990.

For Additional Information on Tax Strategies

Julian Block's Year-Round Tax Strategies for the $40,000-Plus Household. Rocklin, Calif.: Prima Publishing, 1989.

Mendlowitz, Edward. *Aggressive Tax Strategies.* New York: Macmillan, 1989.

Tax Hotline. New York: Boardroom Reports. Monthly Newsletter.

"Tax Report." *The Wall Street Journal,* Wednesdays, p. 1, col. 5.

Tritch, Teresa. "The Taxes You Can No Longer Ignore." *Money,* January 1990, pp. 80–91.

Wool, Robert. "How to Ease Your Total Tax Burden." *Money,* January 1990, pp. 74–77.

COMPREHENSIVE CASE FOR PART I

Sometimes We Fail to Plan

Kendra Winston recently started her first full-time job at Franson and Associates, a real estate development company that builds, rents, and manages shopping centers. While attending college, Kendra held part-time jobs as a receptionist, department store clerk, and assistant manager of a restaurant. She has a degree in business with special interests in finance and marketing.

Franson and Associates offers its employees a very generous package of financial benefits. In addition to paid vacations, holidays, and basic health insurance, Kendra can choose from a variety of supplementary employee benefits. These benefits include company contributions to a pension plan, extra vacation days, additional health insurance, life insurance, and the services of a financial planner.

If Kendra chooses the pension plan as part of her benefits, the company will contribute $750 annually toward her savings for use after retirement. This amount would be in addition to the company's contribution to her regular pension fund.

As an assistant account manager with Franson, Kendra contacts current clients to identify their changing needs. However, the company offers employees a number of opportunities for career advancement and training. These opportunities include employee seminars, management training programs, and tuition reimbursement for college courses. Kendra plans to use one or more of these opportunities to advance her career.

Kendra believes that a single person doesn't need a formal budget. Because of the money she has saved and her current salary, she can now afford many of the things she

dreamed about while growing up. As the second youngest of seven children, she was frequently required to use her older sister's clothing and toys. "But now," as Kendra puts it, "those days are gone; I can afford to enjoy the things I did without when I went to college."

Questions

1. In what ways does Kendra's personal situation influence her financial planning activities and decisions?
2. What are some financial goals that Kendra might want to achieve within the next few years? In the distant future?
3. What factors should Kendra consider in building a savings and investment program? How can a budget contribute to her saving goals?
4. What factors should Kendra consider in determining whether to take advantage of the company's training opportunities?
5. Which of the supplementary employee benefits should Kendra choose? How might these choices change if her life situation changes?
6. If Kendra chooses the pension plan, how much would this portion of her retirement account be worth after 40 years if the contributions to the plan earn 9 percent compounded annually?
7. Based on her life situation, what type of tax planning should Kendra consider?
8. What other financial decisions should Kendra be thinking about at this point in her life?

II

Managing Your
Personal Finances

Part II of *Personal Finance* is concerned with the selection and use of financial services. In Chapter 5, we focus on the changing environment of financial

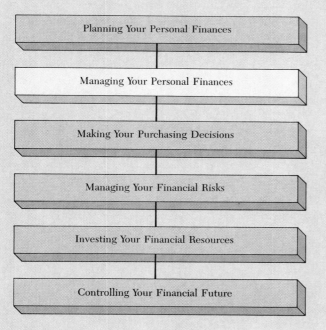

Planning Your Personal Finances

Managing Your Personal Finances

Making Your Purchasing Decisions

Managing Your Financial Risks

Investing Your Financial Resources

Controlling Your Financial Future

institutions and their services. Specifically, we present frameworks for selecting and using savings plans and checking accounts. In Chapters 6 and 7, we offer a comprehensive discussion of consumer credit and its relationship to other financial planning decisions. Chapter 6 provides background information on consumer credit and an overview of the uses and types of credit. It also considers how to establish credit and avoid credit problems. Finally, Chapter 7 analyzes the costs associated with various sources of credit. Part II consists of

5

The Banking Services of Financial Institutions

Many of your financial activities will involve transactions with one or more financial institutions. These organizations provide a variety of services that facilitate your daily payment and savings needs. Someone who says "I'm going to the bank" may be referring to a savings and loan association, a credit union, or even an automatic teller machine in a shopping mall. In recent years, the types and availability of financial services have expanded. A bank is no longer the only source of checking accounts. Mortgages are now available from a wide range of financial institutions. Because many new options have been created for saving, spending, borrowing, and investing your personal economic resources, a basic assessment of the costs and benefits of these services is more necessary than ever.

LEARNING OBJECTIVES
After studying this chapter, you will be able to

L.O.1 Recognize the opportunity costs of selecting and using financial services.

L.O.2 Analyze factors that influence the operating environment of financial institutions.

L.O.3 Evaluate the services offered by different types of financial institutions.

L.O.4 Compare the costs and benefits of different types of savings plans.

L.O.5 Determine the costs and benefits of different types of checking accounts.

OPENING CASE

Checking Out Financial Services

Carla and Ed Johnson have separate checking accounts. They each pay part of the household and living expenses. Carla pays the mortgage and telephone bill, while Ed pays for food and utilities and makes the insurance and car payment. This arrangement allows them the freedom to spend whatever extra money they have each month without needing to explain their actions. Carla and Ed believe that their separate accounts have minimized family disagreements about money. Since they both spend most of their money each month, they have low balances in their checking accounts, resulting in a monthly charge totaling $15.

In the same financial institution where Carla has her checking account, the Johnsons have $600 in a passbook savings account that earns 5.5 percent interest. If the savings account balance exceeded $1,000, they would earn 6 percent. If the balance stayed above $1,000, they would not have to pay the monthly service charge on Carla's checking account. The financial institution has a program that moves money from checking to savings. This program would allow the Johnsons to increase their savings and work toward a secure financial future.

Ed has his checking account at a bank offering an electronic money system that allows a customer to obtain cash at many locations, 24 hours a day. Ed believes that this feature is valuable when cash is needed to cover business expenses and personal spending. For an additional monthly fee, the bank would also provide Ed with a credit card, a safe-deposit box, and a single monthly statement summarizing all transactions.

While most people plan their spending for living expenses, few plan their use of financial services. Therefore, many people are charged high fees for checking accounts and earn low interest on their savings. Despite a wide choice of financial institutions and services, you can learn to compare their costs and benefits. Your awareness of financial services and your ability to evaluate them are vital skills for a healthy personal economic future.

A STRATEGIC PLAN FOR MANAGING CASH

L.O.1
Recognize the opportunity costs of selecting and using financial services.

While many of your financial decisions relate to goals that you hope to achieve in the near or distant future, your daily activities require the use of financial services that facilitate business transactions as well as lead to the achievement of goals. Exhibit 5–1 provides an overview of the use of various financial services in managing cash flows and moving toward financial goals. In simplest terms, the growth of current savings can be achieved only by spending less than is taken in. As discussed in Chapter 3, the savings principle "pay yourself first" is implemented by using various financial services. The use of savings, checking, and other banking accounts provides the foundation for effective financial planning.

Opportunity Costs of Financial Services

When making budget decisions regarding spending and saving, we constantly consider the trade-off between current satisfaction and long-term financial security. In a similar manner, we consider opportunity cost, what is given up when a decision is made, when we evaluate, select, and use financial services. The money you save by shopping around for a low-cost checking account must be balanced against the value of the time you spend in seeking information. Other common trade-offs related to financial services include the following:

- The higher returns of certain long-term savings and investment plans may be achieved at the cost of low liquidity—not being able to obtain your money quickly.

EXHIBIT 5–1   A Plan for Cash Management and the Use of Financial Services

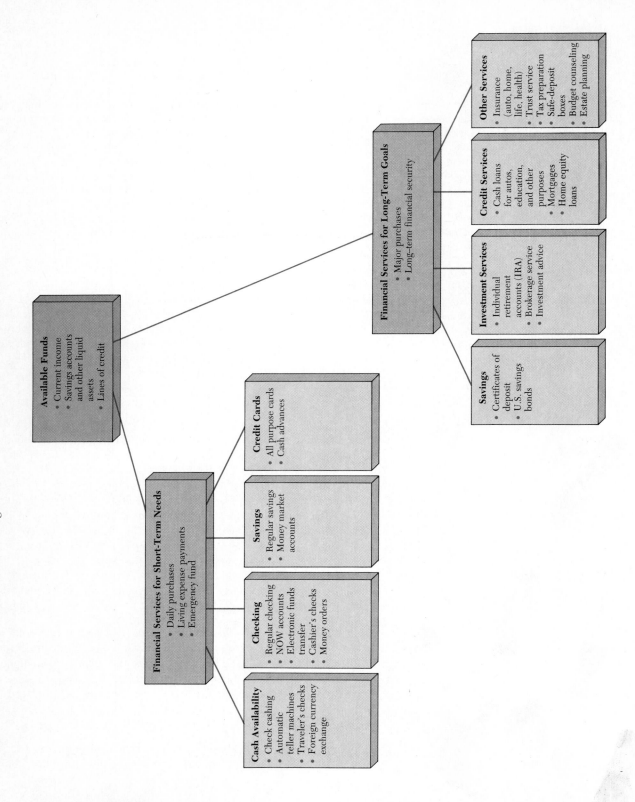

Available Funds
- Current income
- Savings accounts and other liquid assets
- Lines of credit

Financial Services for Short-Term Needs
- Daily purchases
- Living expense payments
- Emergency fund

Cash Availability
- Check cashing
- Automatic teller machines
- Traveler's checks
- Foreign currency exchange

Checking
- Regular checking
- NOW accounts
- Electronic funds transfer
- Cashier's checks
- Money orders

Savings
- Regular savings
- Money market accounts

Credit Cards
- All purpose cards
- Cash advances

Financial Services for Long-Term Goals
- Major purchases
- Long-term financial security

Savings
- Certificates of deposit
- U.S. savings bonds

Investment Services
- Individual retirement accounts (IRA)
- Brokerage service
- Investment advice

Credit Services
- Cash loans for autos, education, and other purposes
- Mortgages
- Home equity loans

Other Services
- Insurance (auto, home, life, health)
- Trust service
- Tax preparation
- Safe-deposit boxes
- Budget counseling
- Estate planning

- The convenience of using a financial institution with 24-hour electronic teller machines or a branch office near your home or place of work must be weighed against potentially higher service costs.
- The "free" checking account that requires you to maintain a $500 minimum balance means lost interest of nearly $400 at 6 percent compounded over 10 years.

Assess potential costs and benefits in both monetary and personal terms so as to choose the financial services that best meet your needs and best help you achieve your economic goals.

An Overview of Financial Services

Banks and other financial institutions offer services that meet a variety of needs. These services fall into four main categories.

Savings   The safe storage of funds for future use is a basic need of every individual. The selection of a savings plan requires consideration of the growth of your money, liquidity, safety, and convenience. These factors are discussed later in this chapter.

Payment Services   The ability to transfer money to others is a necessity for conducting business. Checking accounts and other types of payments will be covered in the final section of this chapter.

Borrowing   Most people use credit sometime during their lives. Credit alternatives range from short-term accounts, such as credit cards and cash loans, to long-term borrowing in the form of a home mortgage. The types and costs of credit are discussed in Chapters 6 and 7.

Other Financial Services   Insurance protection, investment for the future, real estate purchases, tax assistance, and financial planning are additional services that may be needed for a successful economic existence. Many financial plans entail the need to have someone else manage your funds. A **trust** is a legal agreement that provides for the management and control of assets by one party for the benefit of another. This type of arrangement is most commonly created through a commercial bank or a lawyer. A trust may be desirable when parents want to set aside certain funds for their children's education. The investments and money in the trust are managed by a bank, with the necessary amounts going to the children for their educational expenses.

All-Purpose Accounts   To simplify the maze of financial services and to attract customers, many financial institutions offer all-in-one accounts. A **central management account (CMA)**, or central asset account, provides a complete financial services program for a single fee. CMAs were first offered by investment brokers as a method of combining various security investments into a single account. Now banks and other financial institutions offer this service. The all-purpose account will usually include the following:

- A minimum balance of $5,000 or more.
- A checking account.
- One or more all-purpose credit cards.

- A line of credit to obtain quick cash loans.
- Access to various types of investments, such as stocks, bonds, mutual funds, commodities, and government securities.
- Use of an electronic funds transfer system.
- A *sweep* feature in which cash that is not currently invested or needed in the checking account earns a money market interest rate.
- A single monthly statement that summarizes all aspects of the account.

New Services   Interest on checking accounts, variable rate loans, and savings plans with earnings based on market interest rates are the results of the changing financial services environment. The availability of these new banking services has allowed consumers to avoid paying high interest rates on certain types of loans while also receiving competitive returns on their savings. Despite these benefits, many people are paying higher costs for basic banking services. Others can no longer afford to have checking accounts. Since most financial institutions won't cash a check unless you have an account, this creates a dilemma for many low-income consumers. In many ways, a more complex marketplace for financial services is evolving.

THE OPERATING ENVIRONMENT OF FINANCIAL INSTITUTIONS

L.O.2
Analyze factors that influence the operating environment of financial institutions.

In the past, people often had their savings, checking, and loan accounts at the bank closest to their home or their place of work. There was also a limited choice of financial institutions and services. For example, commercial banks were the only organizations that offered checking accounts and most homeowners obtained a mortgage through a savings and loan association. Changing laws, economic conditions, and computer systems have created a very different financial services marketplace.

Legislative Actions

In the early 1980s, two congressional actions significantly changed the role of banks and other financial institutions. The Depository Institutions Deregulation and Monetary Control Act of 1980 made it possible for nonbank financial institutions to offer checking accounts and other services previously limited to banks. It also eliminated restrictions on the amount that a financial institution could pay savers. In 1982, the Garn–St. Germain Depository Institutions Act went further in the deregulation of financial institutions by allowing banks and other organizations to merge. This legislation opened the financial services marketplace to a variety of institutions competing for your banking business.

Increased Competition

Many types of businesses, such as insurance companies, investment brokers, and credit card companies, have become involved in financial services that were previously limited to banks. At the same time, banks have expanded their competitive efforts by opening offices that specialize in such financial services as investments, insurance, or real estate. Increased competition has included the opening of many limited-service offices, sometimes called *nonbank banks*. To avoid certain regulations that still affect full-service banks, these limited-service offices specialize in a particular banking activity, such as savings or personal loans. Nonbank banks have been started by companies involved in types of businesses other than banking, such as Sears, General Motors, and Dreyfus.

Economic Conditions

Changing interest rates, fluctuating consumer prices, and other economic factors also influence financial services. In the late 1970s and early 1980s, high interest rates strongly affected the savings and investment choices of consumers. Savers wanted to earn interest rates that exceeded cost-of-living increases. At the same time, lenders had to charge rates that covered their money costs. This situation resulted in savings plans in which earnings were based on current market interest rates and in loans whose interest rates varied over the borrowing period.

Interest rates and inflation rates are always changing. For successful financial planning, be aware of the current trends and future prospects for interest rates (see Exhibit 5–2). You can learn about these trends and prospects by reading *The Wall Street Journal,* the business section of daily newspapers, and such business periodicals as *Business Week* and *Forbes.*

Technology

In the past, banking transactions had to be conducted during set business hours. Computerized information systems now make 24-hour banking possible. Cash is now available from terminals in food stores, and you can make payments through a home banking system.

Electronic funds transfer (EFT) is a system of making payments and recording receipts through the use of computer data rather than cash and checks. This process involves the use of an **EFT card,** or debit card, which is a plastic access card needed to make computerized banking transactions. The EFT card is called a *debit* card, as opposed to a *credit* card, because when you use it, you are spending existing funds rather than borrowing. Using an EFT card is similar to

EXHIBIT 5–2

Changing Interest Rates and Decisions Related to Financial Services

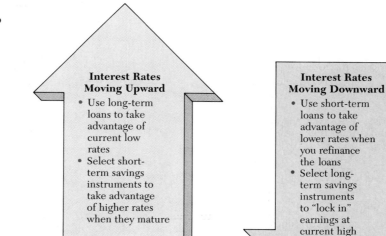

Interest Rates Moving Upward
- Use long-term loans to take advantage of current low rates
- Select short-term savings instruments to take advantage of higher rates when they mature

Interest Rates Moving Downward
- Use short-term loans to take advantage of lower rates when you refinance the loans
- Select long-term savings instruments to "lock in" earnings at current high rates

writing a check, except that the amount of payment is instantly deducted from your account. This instant transfer of funds eliminates the *float*—the time delay between the writing of a check and the deduction from your account.

A lost or stolen EFT card can be expensive. If you notify the financial institution within two days of losing the card, your liability for unauthorized use is $50. If you wait any longer, you can be liable for up to $500 of unauthorized use for up to 60 days. Beyond that time, your liability is unlimited.

The main component of the EFT system is the **automatic teller machine (ATM),** which is a computer terminal at a financial institution or some other location. This terminal allows customers to conduct banking transactions such as transferring amounts among savings, checking, and loan accounts. Some financial institutions have made the terminal very convenient by offering ATMobiles that travel to the customers at their place of employment or some other location. Exhibit 5–3 provides a summary of various EFT transactions.

EXHIBIT 5–3   How Electronic Banking Works

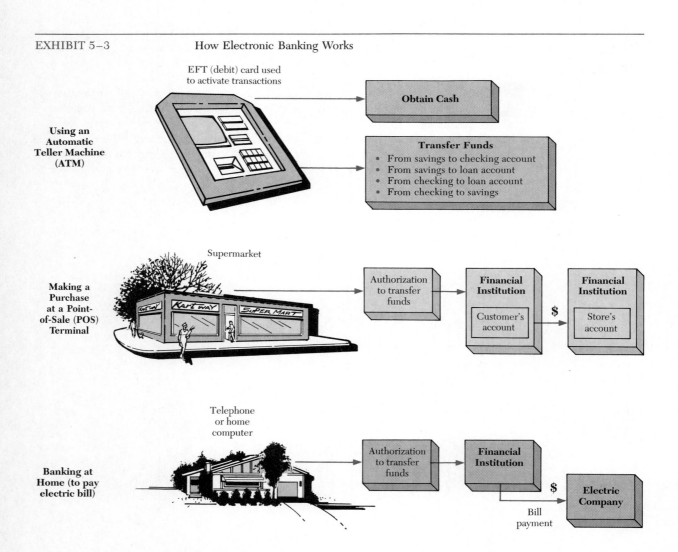

Business Operations of Financial Institutions

Financial institutions accept, store, and use money for the benefit of customers and owners. These main activities of financial institutions may be expressed as follows:

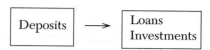

The main sources of funds are deposits made by individuals, businesses, governments, and other financial institutions, including foreign companies and banks. **Demand deposits** are funds held in checking accounts. These funds are very liquid and can quickly flow out of the financial institution. **Time deposits** represent money in savings accounts and certificates. This money will be on deposit longer than the funds in checking accounts.

The money in financial institutions must be put to work so that they can pay interest to savers and earn profit for stockholders. The main interest-earning activities of financial institutions are making loans and investments. Money is lent to businesses and individuals for commercial needs, real estate purchases, consumer buying, and agricultural pursuits. It is also used to purchase investments, mainly government securities. Earnings from loans and investments allow banks and other financial institutions to pay interest on savings, to expand their activities and services, and to grow.

An important business dimension of financial institutions is the role of the Federal Reserve System on our central bank. As shown in Exhibit 5–4, three main actions are taken by the Federal Reserve System to influence the money supply. These actions are designed to make sure that adequate funds are available for economic growth and at the same time to avoid an excessive money supply, which could trigger high inflation. Your awareness of the business and economic operating factors of financial institutions can make for more informed selection and use of their services.

EXHIBIT 5–4   Federal Reserve Actions and the Money Supply

Federal Reserve Action	To Increase Money Supply	To Decrease Money Supply
Changes in *reserve requirements* (the portion of deposits that a bank cannot lend out or invest)	Lower the reserve requirement	Raise the reserve requirement
Changes in the *discount rate* (the interest rate charged by the Federal Reserve System to depository institutions that wish to borrow money)	Lower the discount rate	Raise the discount rate
Open-market operations (the buying and selling of federal government securities by the Federal Reserve System)	Federal Reserve System buys securities so that more money goes into circulation	Federal Reserve System sells securities to reduce the amount of money in circulation

TYPES OF FINANCIAL INSTITUTIONS

L.O.3
Evaluate the services offered by different types of financial institutions.

Despite significant changes in the banking environment, many of the financial institutions with which you are familiar still serve your needs. Most of these institutions have expanded their services to remain competitive. As shown in Exhibit 5–5, financial institutions may be viewed as falling into two major categories.

Deposit-Type Institutions

The financial institutions that most people use on a daily basis serve as intermediaries between suppliers (savers) and users (borrowers) of funds. These deposit-type institutions include commercial banks, savings and loan associations, mutual savings banks, and credit unions.

Commercial Banks   Traditionally, the **commercial bank** has offered the widest range of financial services to individuals, businesses, and government agencies. In addition to checking, savings, and lending services, commercial banks offer many other services. Commercial banks are organized as corporations, with individual investors contributing the capital they need to operate. National banks are chartered by the federal government; state banks, by state governments. State-chartered banks have fewer restrictions placed on them by their regulators.

Savings and Loan Associations   While the commercial bank traditionally served mainly businesses and customers with large amounts of money, the **savings and loan association** traditionally specialized in savings accounts and loans for mortgages. In recent years, savings and loan associations have expanded their offerings to include interest-bearing checking accounts, specialized savings plans, loans to businesses, and other investment and financial planning services. Like banks, savings and loan associations have either federal or state charters.

The high interest rates of the late 1970s and early 1980s resulted in financial difficulties for many savings and loan associations. Many had mortgages locked in at low rates, while savers demanded higher earnings on deposits. In addition, some large savings and loan associations made heavy loans in high-growth and high-cost areas. When an economic downturn occurred in these areas, loans were not paid back, resulting in big losses for the lenders. These difficulties caused failures, mergers, and increased regulation of savings and loan associations.

EXHIBIT 5–5
Types of Financial Institutions

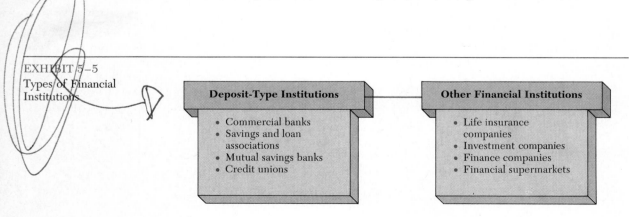

Deposit-Type Institutions	**Other Financial Institutions**
• Commercial banks • Savings and loan associations • Mutual savings banks • Credit unions	• Life insurance companies • Investment companies • Finance companies • Financial supermarkets

Mutual Savings Banks   Another financial institution that concentrates on serving individuals is the **mutual savings bank,** which is owned by depositors and, like the savings and loan association, specializes in savings and mortgage loans. Mutual savings banks are located mainly in the northeastern United States. Unlike the profits of other types of financial institutions, the profits of a mutual savings bank go to the depositors rather than to stockholders.

Credit Unions   Another user-owned financial institution is the **credit union,** a nonprofit, cooperative organization. Traditionally, credit union members had to have a common bond such as work, church, or community affiliation. As the common bond restriction was loosened, the membership of credit unions increased. Today, over 50 million people belong to credit unions.

Credit unions offer low-cost loans and high earnings rates on savings. Many credit unions paid 7 percent on savings accounts when other financial institutions were paying between 5 and 6 percent. Most observers believe that credit unions provide more personal service than other financial institutions. Many credit unions have expanded their services to include checking accounts, credit cards, mortgages, retirement accounts, investment services, and even electronic payment systems. Although credit unions account for only 6 percent of household savings, their growth between 1981 and 1989 was 50 percent.

Other Financial Institutions

Financial services are also available from contractual savings institutions such as life insurance and investment companies, finance companies, and retail organizations.

Life Insurance Companies   While the main purpose of life insurance is to provide financial security for dependents, many life insurance policies contain savings and investment features. Such policies are discussed in Chapter 14. In recent years, life insurance companies have offered a wide variety of financial planning products. "Financial supermarkets" of this kind are discussed later in the section.

Investment Companies   In recent years, various investment companies, also referred to as *mutual funds,* have become involved in banking-type activities. A common service of these organizations is the **money market fund,** a combination savings-investment plan in which the investment company uses your money to purchase a variety of financial instruments. Your earnings are based on the interest received by the investment company. The money market fund usually pays higher interest rates than regular savings accounts, but unlike most banks, savings and loan associations, and credit unions, it is not covered by federal deposit insurance.

Investors in money market funds are usually allowed to write a limited number of checks on their accounts. Each check usually has a minimum limit, such as $250 or $500. The expanded services of investment companies are only one example of the wider range of financial activities now being engaged in by types of businesses other than the traditional financial institutions.

Finance Companies   Making loans to consumers and small businesses is the main function of finance companies. These loans have short and intermediate terms. Finance companies do not accept savings deposits from consumers. As a result of increased competitive pressure from other types of financial institutions, many finance companies have expanded their activities to offer other financial planning services.

Financial Supermarkets   Such financial services as savings, checking, and borrowing have traditionally been offered only by banks and related financial institutions. When you wanted to buy insurance, make a stock investment, or purchase a home, you had to deal with a separate business to meet each of these financial needs. Today, the *financial supermarket*—a large business operation— offers a complete range of financial services. Such organizations allow you to save, make payments, take out loans, apply for a credit card, buy investment securities, insure your property, and purchase real estate through one office. The biggest advantage of financial supermarkets seems to be the convenience of one-stop shopping. You can take care of all your financial needs, and even buy clothes or automotive products, at a single location, such as a Sears outlet. The trade-off for this convenience may be higher costs and less personal service. You must decide what you are willing to give up in order to have convenience. Also, be aware that most of the financial supermarkets do not have federal deposit insurance.

Comparing Financial Institutions

The basic concerns of every financial services customer are simple. Where can I get the best return on my savings? How can I minimize the cost of checking? Will I be able to borrow money when I need it?

As you use financial services, you must decide what you want from the organization that will serve your needs. Because the financial marketplace is constantly changing, you must assess the various services and other factors before selecting the organization that will handle your financial matters (see Exhibit 5–6).

The services offered by the financial institution are likely to be a major factor. Personal service is important to many customers. You may desire a strong working relationship with the institution's staff.

EXHIBIT 5–6

Which Financial Institution Should You Choose to Use?

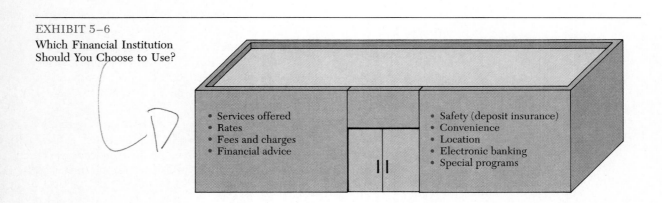

- Services offered
- Rates
- Fees and charges
- Financial advice

- Safety (deposit insurance)
- Convenience
- Location
- Electronic banking
- Special programs

Convenience is another consideration. It may be provided by convenient business hours, conveniently located branch offices and automatic teller machines, and banking by mail service. Convenience and service have a cost; be sure to compare the fees and other charges at several financial institutions.

Finally, safety factors and interest rates should be assessed. Obtain information on the earnings you will receive on your savings and checking accounts and on the amount you will pay for borrowed funds. Most financial institutions have deposit insurance to protect customers against losses, but not all of these institutions are insured by federal government programs. Investigate the type of protection that your money will have.

Your selection of a financial institution should be based on valid information. Never assume that one will provide a better interest rate or service than another. You need to compare banks, savings and loan associations, and credit unions with other providers of financial services.

EVALUATING SAVINGS ALTERNATIVES

As emphasized in Chapter 3, the basis for your attainment of financial goals is the accumulation of funds that results from an effective savings and investment program. This accumulation of funds starts with savings and the evaluation of various savings plans.

L.O.4
Compare the costs and benefits of different types of savings plans.

Types of Savings Plans

Deregulation of savings rates and other changes in financial services have created a wide choice of savings alternatives (Exhibit 5–7). The number of savings plans may seem overwhelming, but they can be grouped into regular savings accounts, club accounts, certificates of deposit, interest-earning checking accounts, money market accounts, and savings bonds. Investment vehicles, such as U.S. Treasury bills, are discussed in later chapters.

Regular Savings Accounts   Traditionally referred to as *passbook accounts*, since savers had a small book showing deposits and withdrawals, regular savings accounts usually involve a low or no minimum balance and allow savers to withdraw money as it is needed. The rate earned on regular savings accounts is usually low. Early in 1986, after interest rates on savings were deregulated, many institutions established an agreement for regular passbook savings in which earnings would vary based on the balance in the account. A typical situation could be as follows:

Balance of . . .	Would Earn . . .
Less than $500	No interest
$500–$9,999	5¾%
$10,000–$24,999	6¼%
$25,000–$49,999	6½%
$50,000 and over	6¾%

Banks, savings and loan associations, and most other financial institutions offer passbook savings plans. A **share account** is a regular savings account at a credit union.

EXHIBIT 5–7   Savings Alternatives

Type of Account	Benefits	Restrictions
Regular savings accounts/passbook accounts/share accounts (credit unions)	Low minimum balance Ease of withdrawal Insured	Low rate of return
Certificates of deposit	Good rate of return Insured	Possible penalty for early withdrawal Minimum deposit
NOW accounts/share drafts (credit unions)	Checking privileges Interest earned Insured	Service charge for going below minimum balance Cost for printing checks; other fees may apply
SuperNOW accounts	Checking privileges Good rate of return Insured	High minimum balance Low return if below a certain balance
Money market accounts	Good rate of return (based on current interest rates) Allows some check writing Insured	High minimum balance No interest or service charge if below a certain balance
Money market funds	Good rate of return (based on current interest rates) Some check writing	Minimum balance Not insured
U.S. savings bonds	Fairly good rate of return (varies with current interest rates) Low minimum deposit Government guaranteed Exempt from state and local income taxes	Long maturity; penalty for withdrawal before five years

Club Accounts   Club accounts are savings plans designed for a certain goal or a certain time of the year. Examples are vacation or Christmas club accounts in which a person makes a weekly deposit and then withdraws a large sum after a set time period, usually a year. Interest on club accounts may be very low; compare them with other savings alternatives.

Certificates of Deposit   Higher earnings result from leaving money on deposit longer. A **certificate of deposit (CD)** is a savings plan that requires you to leave a certain amount on deposit for a set time period (ranging from 30 days to 5, 10, or more years) in order to earn a specified interest rate. These time deposits can be an attractive savings alternative. Although federal law no longer requires a penalty for early withdrawal of CD funds, some financial institutions impose a penalty for cashing in a CD early.

As a result of increased competition among financial service providers, many investment brokers offer a variety of CDs, most at rates higher than those of banks, savings and loan associations, and credit unions. But other factors may offset these higher rates. A brokerage house, unlike other financial institutions, won't give you a free checking account or credit card when you buy a CD. Also, some brokerage houses impose a penalty for cashing it in before the maturity date, making your savings less liquid than they seem to be.

The unique CDs being offered by various financial institutions include

- *Odd-Term CDs.* These CDs have unusual maturities, such as 7, 13, or 15 months, instead of traditional maturities, such as 6 or 12 months. With CDs of this kind, comparing rates may be difficult unless you can find out how much money you will receive at maturity.
- *Bump-Up CDs.* With such CDs, also referred to as rising rate or step-up CDs, the interest rate increases during the term of your deposit. Beware of ads that highlight the last rate, which may be in effect for only the last couple of months of an 18- or 24-month certificate.
- *Promotional CDs.* Some financial institutions have tied the CD rate to such outcomes as the winning of the Super Bowl, the performance of a local sports team, or the success of a presidential candidate. In all cases, the "fun" part may outweigh your economic rewards.
- *Homebuying CDs.* These CDs are used to accumulate funds for a down payment on a house. Financial institutions offer low minimum deposits, no penalties, and high rates to attract customers for this savings plan. The customers are, of course, expected to get their mortgage from the institution at which they obtained the CDs.

When buying and rolling over (buying a new one at maturity) a CD, carefully assess all of its costs and earnings. Do not automatically allow your financial institution to roll over your money into another CD for the same term, since rates may have dropped and you might benefit by using a shorter maturity or by taking your business elsewhere. Also, beware of an investment that looks like a CD but is actually a loan to your bank. Such loans are not federally insured, and the bank can pay you off anytime it likes.[1]

Interest-Earning Checking Accounts A variety of checking accounts can be used as savings vehicles. These interest-earning accounts will be discussed in the next section of this chapter.

Money Market Accounts/Money Market Funds To meet consumer demands for higher savings rates, federal legislation created an account with a floating interest rate. A **money market account** is a savings account that requires a minimum balance and bases earnings on market interest rates. Money market accounts allow savers to write a limited number of checks to make large payments or to transfer money to other accounts. Since money market accounts impose penalties when you go below the required minimum balance, usually $1,000, consider a regular savings account or a payroll deduction savings plan.

Both money market *accounts* and money market *funds* offer earnings based on current interest rates, and both have similar minimum balance restrictions and allow limited check writing. The major difference lies in safety. Since banks and savings and loan associations offer money market accounts, these accounts are covered by federal deposit insurance. This is not true of money market funds, a product of investment and insurance companies. But since money market funds invest mainly in government securities and the securities of creditworthy companies, they are quite safe.

FINANCIAL PLANNING IN ACTION
Understanding Interest Rates

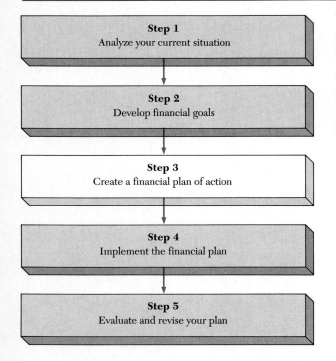

Step 1
Analyze your current situation

Step 2
Develop financial goals

Step 3
Create a financial plan of action

Step 4
Implement the financial plan

Step 5
Evaluate and revise your plan

When people talk about higher or lower interest rates, they could be talking about one of many types of interest rates. Some interest rates refer to the cost of borrowing by business; others refer to the cost of buying a home. Your awareness of various types of interest rates can help you plan your spending, saving, borrowing, and investing. The following information describes the most commonly reported interest rates and gives their *annual average* for selected years.

	1965	1970	1975	1980	1985	1987	1989
Prime rate—an indication of the rate that banks charge large corporations	4.53%	7.91%	7.85%	15.26%	9.93%	8.22%	10.87%
Discount rate—the rate that financial institutions are charged to borrow funds from Federal Reserve banks	4.03	5.95	6.25	11.77	7.69	5.66	6.83
T-bill rate—the yield on short-term (13 weeks) U.S. government debt obligations	3.95	6.39	5.78	11.43	7.48	5.82	8.12
Treasury bond rate—the yield on long-term (30 years) U.S. government debt obligations	4.27	6.86	8.19	11.39	10.97	8.59	8.45
Mortgage rate—the amount being paid by individuals to borrow for the purchase of a new home	5.81	8.45	9.00	12.66	11.55	9.31	10.13
Corporate bond rate—the cost of borrowing for large U.S. corporations	4.49	8.04	8.83	11.94	11.37	9.38	9.26
Certificate of deposit rate—the rate for six-month time deposits at savings institutions	4.43	7.65	6.89	12.99	8.25	7.01	9.09

SOURCES: Board of Governors of the Federal Reserve System and the United States League of Savings Institutions.

U.S. Savings Bonds   In the past, buying savings bonds was a patriotic act rather than a wise savings choice. But as interest rates rose, U.S. savings bonds became less attractive. In order to compete with other savings plans, the Treasury Department now uses a floating interest rate on savings bonds. Their earnings rise and fall based on changes in the level of interest rates. One drawback of U.S. savings bonds is that purchasers earn less if the bonds are redeemed within five years of purchase. U.S. savings bonds have tax advantages: the interest they earn is exempt from state and local taxes, and you do not have to pay the federal income tax on it until the bonds mature or are redeemed.

As of 1990, redeemed Series EE bonds may be exempt from federal income tax if you use the funds to pay tuition and fees at a college, university, or qualified technical school for yourself or a dependent. The bonds must be purchased by an individual who is at least 24 years old, and they must be issued in the names of one or both parents. These provisions have been designed to assist low- and middle-income households, so individuals whose income exceeds a certain amount do not qualify for the exemption.

Over $100 billion in U.S. savings bonds are now being held. Series EE bonds purchased today will continue to earn interest for 30 years, well beyond the maturity date. But holders of U.S. savings bonds should note that those purchased before 1949 are no longer earning interest. For a quick update on U.S. savings bond rates and other information, call 1-800-US BONDS.

Factors Influencing Savings Plan Selection

Your selection of a savings plan will be influenced by the rate of return, tax considerations, liquidity, safety, and restrictions and costs.

Rate of Return   Earnings on savings can be measured by the **rate of return,** or *yield,* which is the percentage of increase in the value of your savings due to earned interest. For example, a $100 savings account that earned $5 after a year would have a rate of return, or yield, of 5 percent. This rate of return was determined by dividing the interest earned ($5) by the amount in the savings account ($100).

Since interest is usually paid more often than once a year, the actual yield on your savings will be greater than the stated interest rate. **Compounding** refers to interest that is earned on previously earned interest. Each time that interest is added to your savings, the next interest is computed on the basis of the new amount in the account. Future value and present value calculations, introduced in Chapter 1, take compounding into account.

The more frequent the compounding, the higher your rate of return, or effective yield, will be. For example, $100 in a savings account that earns 6 percent compounded annually will increase $6 after a year. But the same $100 in a 6 percent account compounded daily will earn $6.19 for the year. Although this difference may seem slight, with large amounts held in savings for long periods of time, far higher differences will result (see Exhibit 5–8).

The rate of return you earn on your savings should be compared with the inflation rate. When the inflation rate was over 10 percent, people whose money

EXHIBIT 5–8

Compounding Frequency
Increases the Savings Yield

It's important to look at the yield on a CD: shorter compounding methods result in higher yields. This chart shows the growth of $10,000 five-year CDs, paying the same rate of 8 percent, but with different compounding methods.

	Compounding Method			
End of Year	**Daily**	**Monthly**	**Quarterly**	**Annually**
1	$10,832.78	$10,830.00	$10,824.32	$10,800.00
2	11,743.91	11,728.88	11,716.59	11,664.00
3	12,712.17	12,702.37	12,682.41	12,597.12
4	13,770.82	13,756.66	13,727.85	13,604.89
5	14,917.62	14,898.46	14,859.46	14,693.28
Effective annual yield	8.33%	8.30%	8.24%	8.00%

SOURCE: United States League of Savings Institutions.

in savings accounts was earning 5 or 6 percent were experiencing a loss in the buying power of that money. In general, as the inflation rate increases, the interest rates offered to savers also increase; this gives you an opportunity to select a savings option that will minimize the erosion of your dollars on deposit.

The balance used for interest computation will also affect the earnings on your savings. Financial institutions use different methods to determine the amount used to compute earnings. These methods include

- *Day of Deposit to Day of Withdrawal (DD/DW)*. Your money earns interest every day that it is on deposit. In general, DD/DW is the most advantageous method for savers.
- *Last In, First Out (LIFO)*. This method assumes that withdrawals are deducted from the most recent deposits. These deposits would not earn interest if withdrawals were made on them.
- *First In, First Out (FIFO)*. This method deducts withdrawals from either the beginning balance of the interest period or the earliest deposit. In either case, an amount on deposit early in the interest period would earn nothing if it were withdrawn before the end of the period.
- *Low Balance*. Interest is based on the lowest balance in the account during the interest period. This method is the least desirable for savers since it results in the fewest dollars earned.

In addition to these interest computation methods, there are combinations of these methods.

Tax Considerations   Like inflation, taxes reduce your earnings on savings. For example, a 10 percent return for a saver in a 28 percent tax bracket means a real return of 7.2 percent (see "Financial Planning Calculations" feature). As discussed in Chapter 4 and as will be discussed further in Part V, several tax-exempt and tax-deferred savings plans and investment programs can increase your real rate of return.

FINANCIAL PLANNING CALCULATIONS

After-Tax Savings Rate of Return

The taxability of the interest on your savings reduces the real rate of return. In other words, you lose some portion of your interest to taxes. This calculation consists of the following steps:

1. Determine your top tax bracket for federal income taxes—15, 28, or 33 percent.
2. Subtract this rate, expressed as a decimal, from 1.0.
3. Multiply the result by the yield on your savings account.
4. The product, expressed as a percentage, is your after-tax rate of return.

For example:

1. You are in the 28 percent tax bracket.
2. $1.0 - 0.28 = 0.72$
3. If the yield on your savings account is 6.25 percent, then $0.0625 \times 0.72 = 0.045$.
4. Your after-tax rate of return is 4.5 percent.

This same procedure may be used to determine the *real rate of return* on savings based on inflation. For example, if you are earning 7 percent on savings and inflation is 10 percent, your real rate of return (after inflation) is 6.3 percent—$.07 \times (1 - 0.10) = 0.063$.

Liquidity   Liquidity allows you to withdraw your money on short notice. Some savings plans have penalties for early withdrawal. With certain types of savings certificates and accounts, early withdrawal may be penalized by a loss of interest or a lower earnings rate.

You should consider the degree of liquidity you desire in relation to your savings goals. To achieve your long-term financial goals, you are likely to trade off liquidity for a higher return on your savings.

Safety   Most savings plans at banks, savings and loan associations, and credit unions are insured by agencies affiliated with the federal government. This protection prevents a loss of money due to the failure of the insured institution.

In recent years, more financial institutions have failed than at any other time since the 1930s. However, savers with deposits covered by federal insurance have not lost any money. Depositors of failed organizations have either been paid the amount in their account or have had the account taken over by a financially stable institution.

In 1989, as a result of financial troubles in the savings and loan industry, the powers of the Federal Deposit Insurance Corporation (FDIC), which provides deposit insurance for banks, were extended to cover savings and loan associations. The FDIC administers separate insurance funds—the Bank Insurance Fund and the Savings Association Insurance Fund. Credit unions may still obtain deposit insurance through the National Credit Union Association (NCUA).

The FDIC insures deposits of up to $100,000 per person per financial institution; a joint account is considered to belong proportionally to each name on the account. If you have a $70,000 account and an $80,000 joint account with a relative in the same financial institution, $10,000 of your savings would not be covered by federal deposit insurance. By using combinations of individual, joint, and trust

Pepper . . . and Salt

ALL DEPOSITS GUARANTEED BY THE FEDERAL GOVERNMENT

SCHWADRON

"Yeah, but who guarantees the federal government?"

From *The Wall Street Journal*, with permission of Cartoon Features Syndicate.

accounts in different financial institutions, it is possible to have federal deposit insurance cover amounts that exceed $100,000. Remember, the maximum coverage of federal deposit insurance is based on each depositor, not on each account.

Since not all financial institutions have federal deposit insurance, investigate this matter when you are selecting a savings plan. Additional information on the regulation and consumer protection aspects of financial institutions is included in Appendix D.

Restrictions and Costs   Other limitations can affect your choice of a savings program. For example, there may be a delay between the time interest is earned and the time it is added to your account. This means that it will not be available for your immediate use. Also, some institutions charge a transaction fee for each deposit or withdrawal. Such fees can become expensive when several transactions are made each month.

Some institutions have promotions offering a *free* gift when a certain savings amount is deposited. For this gift, you will probably have to leave your money on deposit for a certain time period; or you may receive less interest, since some of the institution's earnings may be used to cover the cost of free gifts. Economists tell us that "there is no such thing as a free lunch"; the same holds true for toasters and television sets.

CHOOSING AND USING A CHECKING ACCOUNT

With more than 90 percent of business transactions conducted by check, a checking account is a necessity for most people. Selecting and using a checking account should be based on the types available and consideration of certain factors.

L.O.5
Determine the costs and benefits of different types of checking accounts.

Types of Checking Accounts

As a result of special names and different features, the number of types of checking accounts may seem endless. But such accounts fall into three major categories:

- *Regular checking accounts,* which are likely to have a monthly service charge that, at many financial institutions, can be avoided by maintaining a required minimum balance or by keeping a certain amount in a savings account.
- *Activity accounts,* which charge a fee for each check written, and sometimes for each deposit made, in addition to a monthly service charge but usually do not require a minimum balance. This type of account is most appropriate for individuals who write only a few checks each month and are unable to keep a required amount on deposit.
- *Interest-earning checking accounts,* also referred to as **NOW accounts** at some financial institutions (NOW is an abbreviation for negotiable order of withdrawal), which require a minimum balance. If an account falls below this amount, interest may not be earned and a fee is frequently assessed.

The **share draft account** is an interest-bearing checking account at a credit union. Credit union members write credits, called *share drafts,* against their account balance.

The **superNOW account** benefits customers who keep large amounts in their checking account. This interest-bearing checking account earns a higher rate of interest than that earned by regular savings accounts. But not all of the funds in a superNOW account earn the higher rate. Up to a certain cutoff point, usually $1,000 or $1,500, the rate is similar to that of a NOW account. For amounts above the cutoff point, a higher rate based on current market interest rates is paid. Many people with large amounts in a superNOW account earn a low return compared to other saving and investment alternatives since their balance is not always above the cutoff point.

Beware of checking accounts that offer several services (safe-deposit box, traveler's checks, low-rate loans, and travel insurance) for a single monthly fee. This may sound like a good value, but financial experts observe that such accounts benefit only a small group of individuals who make constant use of the services offered.

Selecting the Best Checking Account

Checking accounts should be evaluated on the basis of restrictions, fees and charges, interest, and special services (see Exhibit 5–9).

Restrictions The most common limitation on checking accounts is the amount that must be kept on deposit to earn interest or avoid a service charge. Until recently, financial institutions also had varying restrictions on the holding period for deposited checks. That is, they require a period of time for checks to clear before you were allowed to use the funds. As of September 1990, the Expedited Funds Availability Act required that funds from local checks be available within two business days and that funds from out-of-town checks be withheld for no more than five business days.

EXHIBIT 5–9

Checking Account Selection Factors

Restrictions
- Minimum balance
- Federal deposit insurance
- Hours and location of branch offices
- Holding period for deposited checks

Fees and Charges
- Monthly fee
- Fees for each check or deposit
- Printing of checks
- Fee to obtain canceled check copy
- Overdraft, stop-payment order, certified check fee
- Fees for preauthorized bill payment, fund transfer, or home banking activity

Special Services
- Direct deposit of payroll and government checks
- 24-hour teller machines
- Overdraft protection
- Banking-at-home
- Discounts or free checking for certain groups (students, senior citizens, employees of certain companies)
- Free or discounted services, such as traveler's checks

Interest
- Interest rate
- Minimum deposit to earn interest
- Method of compounding
- Portion of balance used to compute interest
- Fee charged for falling below necessary balance to earn interest

Fees and Charges   Nearly all financial institutions require a minimum balance or service charges for checking accounts. When using an interest-bearing checking account, you will need to compare your earnings with any service charge or fee. Also consider the cost of lost or reduced interest due to the minimum balance.

Checking account fees have increased in recent years. Such items as check printing, overdraft fees, and stop-payment orders have doubled or tripled in price at some financial institutions. Some institutions will "bait" you with fancy checks at a low price and then charge a much higher price when you reorder.

Interest   As discussed earlier in this chapter, the interest rate, the frequency of compounding, and the interest computation method will affect the earnings on your checking account.

Special Services   Financial institutions may offer checking account customers such extra services as 24-hour teller machines and home banking services. In an effort to attract new accounts, some banks recently offered "buyer protection insurance" to checking account customers. This insurance protects products

FINANCIAL PLANNING CALCULATIONS

Comparing Costs of Checking Accounts

Comparing checking account costs based on interest earned and various service charges and fees can be confusing. To assist with this comparison, the following guideline is offered:

This calculation does not take into account charges and fees for such services as overdrafts, stop payments, ATM use, and check printing. You should also consider these costs when you select a checking account.

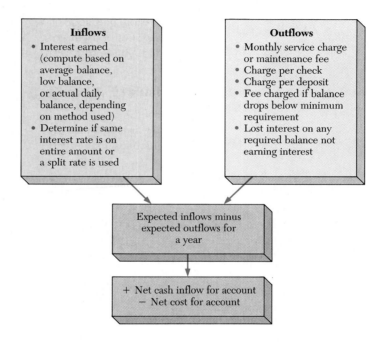

Inflows
- Interest earned (compute based on average balance, low balance, or actual daily balance, depending on method used)
- Determine if same interest rate is on entire amount or a split rate is used

Outflows
- Monthly service charge or maintenance fee
- Charge per check
- Charge per deposit
- Fee charged if balance drops below minimum requirement
- Lost interest on any required balance not earning interest

Expected inflows minus expected outflows for a year

+ Net cash inflow for account
− Net cost for account

---

bought by check against damage or loss and also extends manufacturers' warranties.

Financial institutions are attempting to reduce the paper and postage costs associated with checking accounts. One solution is not to return canceled checks to customers. The financial institution then uses microfilm to store checks and provides customers with statements summarizing the checks written. If a customer requests a copy of a canceled check, the institution reproduces the copy from its microfilm file for a fee.

Overdraft protection is an automatic loan made to checking account customers to cover the amount of checks written in excess of the available balance. This service is convenient but costly. Most overdraft plans make loans based on $50 or $100 increments. An overdraft of just a dollar might trigger a $50 loan and the corresponding finance charges. But overdraft protection can be less costly than the fee charged for a check you write when you do not have enough money on deposit to cover it. That fee is often $10 or $15, or more.

Checking Account Activities

After you select a checking account, several procedures are involved in using the account.

Opening a Checking Account   Deciding on the owner of the account is your starting point for opening a checking account. Only one person is allowed to write checks on an individual account. A joint account has two or more owners, with any authorized person allowed to write checks on the account if it is specified as an "or" account. In contrast, an "and" account with two owners would require the signatures of both owners on checks.

With both an individual account and a joint account, a signature card is required. This document is a record of the official signatures of the persons who are authorized to write checks on an account.

Making Deposits   A deposit ticket is the form used for adding money to your checking account (see Exhibit 5–10). On this document, you list the amounts of the cash and checks you are depositing. Each check you deposit requires an endorsement—your signature on the back of the check—to authorize the transfer of the funds into your account. The following are three common endorsement forms:

- A *blank endorsement* is your signature. This endorsement form should be used only when you are actually depositing or cashing a check, since a check can be cashed by anyone once its back has been signed.
- A *restrictive endorsement* consists of the words *for deposit only* followed by your signature. This endorsement form is especially useful when you are depositing checks by mail.
- A *special endorsement* allows you to transfer a check to an organization or another person. In this endorsement form, the words *pay to the order of* are followed by the name of the organization or person and then by your signature.

An endorsement must be made on the reverse of the left side of the check, using no more than 1½ inches of space from the top. It may be handwritten, typed, rubber-stamped, or printed.

EXHIBIT 5–10

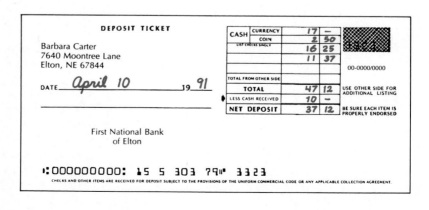

EXHIBIT 5–11

Kenneth Buckley
7828 Carl Drive
Westover, OR 98123

3693

① *February 6,* 19 *91*

PAY TO THE
ORDER OF ② *Midland College* ③ $ *362.75*

④ *Three-hundred sixty-two and 75/100* ————— DOLLARS

Oregon State Employees
Credit Union

MEMO ⑥ *spring tuition*   ⑤ *Kenneth Buckley*

⑈000000000⑈ ⑈505 303079⑈ 3693

Writing a Check   Before writing a check, record the information in your check register and deduct the amount of the check from your balance. Otherwise, you will think that you have more money available than you really do.

The procedure for proper check writing, displayed in Exhibit 5–11, consists of the following steps:

1. Record the current date.
2. Write the name of the person or organization that is receiving the payment.
3. Record the amount of the check in figures.
4. Write the amount of the check in words; checks for less than a dollar should be written as, say, "only 79 cents," with the word *dollars* on the check crossed out.
5. Sign the check in the same way that you signed the signature card when you opened your account.
6. Make a note of the reason for payment, if desired.

Maintaining a Checking Account   Each month, you will receive a *bank statement*, which is a summary of the transactions for a checking account. This document reports deposits made, checks paid, interest earned, and fees for such things as service charges and the printing of checks. The balance reported on the bank statement will probably be different from the balance in your checkbook. The reasons for the difference are checks that you have written but that have not yet cleared, deposits that you have made since the bank statement was prepared, interest added to your account, and deductions for fees and charges.

To determine your true balance, you should prepare a *bank reconciliation*. This report accounts for differences between the bank statement and your checkbook balance. The steps that you take in this process, shown in Exhibit 5–12, are as follows:

1. Compare the checks that you have written over the past month with those reported as paid on your bank statement. Use the canceled checks from the financial institution, or compare your check register with the check numbers reported on the bank statement. *Subtract* from the *bank statement balance* the total of the checks written but not yet cleared.

EXHIBIT 5–12   Reconciling Your Checking Account

The Bank Statement		**Your Checkbook**	
Balance on current bank statement	$ 443.96	Current balance in checkbook	$295.91
Step 1. Subtract outstanding checks (checks that you have written but that have not yet cleared the banking system)	− 311.62	Step 3. Subtract fees or other charges listed on your bank statement	− 15.75
Step 2. Add deposits in transit (deposits that you have made but that have not been reported on this statement)	+ 150.00	Step 4. Add interest earned	+ 2.18
Adjusted cash balance	$ 282.34	Adjusted cash balance	$282.34

2. Determine whether any recent deposits are not on the bank statement. If so, *add* the amount of the deposits to the *bank statement balance.*
3. *Subtract* any fees or charges on the bank statement from your *checkbook balance.*
4. *Add* any interest earned to your *checkbook balance.*

At this point, the revised balances for both your checkbook and the bank statement should be the same. If the two do not balance, attempt to find the error by checking your addition and making sure that every check and deposit was recorded correctly in your checkbook and on the bank statement.

Many people do not take the time to reconcile their accounts, but the failure to do this could cost you money. If the bank subtracts more for a check than the amount for which it was written and you don't complain within a year, the bank may not be liable to correct its error. Regulations for this situation vary from state to state.

Other Payment Methods

While personal checks are the most common payment form, other methods are available. A *certified check* is a personal check with guaranteed payment. The amount of the check is deducted from your balance when the financial institution certifies the check.

A *cashier's check* is the check of a financial institution. A customer may purchase one by paying the amount of the check plus a fee. A *money order* may be purchased in a similar manner from financial institutions, post offices, and stores. Certified checks, cashier's checks, and money orders allow you to make a remittance that the recipient knows is valid.

Finally, *traveler's checks* allow you to make payments when you are away from home. This payment form requires the user to sign each check twice. First, the traveler's checks are signed when they are purchased. Then, to identify the authorized person, they are signed again as they are cashed.

SUMMARY

L.O.1
Recognize the opportunity costs of selecting and using financial services.

A trade-off among such factors as time and effort, convenience, liquidity, safety, and lost earnings must be considered as you evaluate and use various savings and checking services.

L.O.2
Analyze factors that influence the operating environment of financial institutions.

L.O.3
Evaluate the services offered by different types of financial institutions.

L.O.4
Compare the costs and benefits of different types of savings plans.

L.O.5
Determine the costs and benefits of different types of checking accounts.

Legislative actions, increased competition, economic conditions, technology, and the business operations of financial institutions have created a more complex marketplace for users of financial services.

Commercial banks, savings and loan associations, mutual savings banks, credit unions, life insurance companies, investment companies, finance companies, and financial supermarkets should be assessed with regard to product offerings, rates and fees, safety, convenience, and special programs and services available to customers.

Regular savings accounts, certificates of deposit, interest-bearing checking accounts, money market accounts, money market funds, and U.S. savings bonds should be evaluated on the basis of rate of return, tax considerations, liquidity, safety, restrictions, and costs.

Regular checking accounts, activity accounts, and interest-earning checking accounts should be compared with regard to restrictions (such as a minimum balance), fees and charges, interest, and special services.

GLOSSARY

Automatic teller machine (ATM)   A computer terminal that is used to conduct banking transactions.

Central management account (CMA)   An all-in-one bank account that includes savings, checking, borrowing, investing, and other financial services for a single fee; also called a central asset account.

Certificate of deposit   A savings plan requiring that a certain amount be left on deposit for a set time period in order to earn a specified interest rate.

Commercial bank   A financial institution that offers the widest range of financial services to individuals, businesses, and government agencies.

Compounding   Interest that is earned on previously earned interest.

Credit union   A nonprofit, cooperative financial institution that is organized for the benefit of its members.

Demand deposits   Funds in checking accounts.

EFT card   A plastic access card used in computerized banking transactions; also called a debit card.

Electronic funds transfer (EFT)   A system of making payments and recording receipts through the use of computer data rather than cash or checks.

Money market account   A savings account offered by banks, savings and loan associations, and credit unions that requires a minimum balance and bases earnings on market interest rates.

Money market fund   A savings-investment plan offered by investment companies, with earnings based on investments in various financial instruments.

Mutual savings bank   A financial institution that is owned by depositors and specializes in savings and mortgage loans.

NOW account   An interest-bearing checking account; NOW is an abbreviation for negotiable order of withdrawal.

Overdraft protection   An automatic loan made to checking account customers to cover the amount of checks written in excess of the available balance in the checking account.

Rate of return   The percentage of increase in the value of savings as a result of interest earned; also called yield.

Savings and loan association   A financial institution that traditionally specialized in savings and mortgage loans.

Share account   A regular savings account at a credit union.

Share draft account   An interest-bearing checking account at a credit union.

SuperNOW account   An interest-bearing checking account that earns a higher rate of interest than that earned by a regular savings account; requires a high minimum balance.

Time deposits   Money in savings accounts and certificates.

Trust   A legal agreement that provides for the management and control of assets by one party for the benefit of another.

DISCUSSION QUESTIONS

L.O.1   1. Explain why financial services should not be selected only on the basis of monetary factors.

L.O.1   2. What is the relationship between financial services and overall financial planning?

L.O.2   3. Discuss how changing economic conditions will affect your use of financial services.

L.O.2   4. Electronic banking services are being expanded with *smart cards*, which have microcomputer chips for activating and storing data on your financial transactions. What benefits and potential dangers may be associated with this system?

L.O.2   5. How do the actions of the Federal Reserve System affect us on a day-to-day basis?

L.O.3   6. Should retail stores sell insurance and real estate, broker investments, and perform other financial services? What are the major benefits and drawbacks of using a financial supermarket?

L.O.3   7. What factors do consumers usually consider in selecting a financial institution to meet their savings and checking needs?

L.O.4   8. When would a savings plan with high liquidity be preferred over one with a high rate of return?

L.O.4   9. What information should financial institutions be required to disclose to make it easier to compare different types of savings plans?

L.O.4   10. What is the relationship between compounding and calculating the future value of an amount?

L.O.5   11. Are checking accounts that earn interest always better than regular checking accounts? Explain.

L.O.5   12. Is a checking account a necessity in our society? Should the government require financial institutions to provide low-cost checking accounts to people below a certain income level?

Opening Case Questions

1. Which financial services are most important to Carla and Ed Johnson?
2. What efforts are the Johnsons currently making to assess their use of financial services in relation to their other financial activities?

3. How should the Johnsons assess their needs for financial services? On what bases should they compare financial services?

4. What should the Johnsons do to improve their use of financial services?

PROBLEMS AND ACTIVITIES

L.O.1   1. Conduct a survey to determine how the selection and use of financial services have changed in the past few years. Are people making more use of different financial institutions for different financial services than they did in the past?

L.O.2   2. Based on information regarding current economic conditions in *The Wall Street Journal,* the business section of the newspaper, and business magazines, what recommendations for savers and lenders would you make?

L.O.3   3. Collect advertisements offering various financial services. What factors should a person consider before making use of these services and the financial institutions that offer them?

L.O.3   4. Survey a number of individuals to determine their awareness of various types of financial institutions. How knowledgeable are most of them about credit unions, investment companies, and finance companies? Are most of them aware of the expanded services being provided by life insurance companies?

L.O.4   5. Collect advertisements to compare the savings plans of various financial institutions. How easy do the ads make it to evaluate rate of return, frequency of compounding, minimum deposit requirement, safety (federal deposit insurance), and liquidity?

L.O.4   6. What would be common savings goals of a person who buys a five-year CD paying 8.75 percent instead of an 18-month savings certificate paying 7.5 percent?

L.O.4   7. What would be the value of a savings account started with $500 earning 6 percent (compounded annually) after 10 years?

L.O.4   8. Brenda Young desires to have $10,000 eight years from now for her daughter's college fund. If she will earn 7 percent (compounded annually) on her money, what amount should she deposit now? Use the present value of a single amount calculation.

L.O.4   9. What amount would you have if you deposit $1,500 a year for 30 years at 8 percent (compounded annually)? (Use Appendix B.)

L.O.4   10. With a 28 percent marginal tax rate, which would give you a better return on your savings, a tax-free yield of 7 percent or a taxable yield of 9.5 percent? Why?

L.O.5   11. What is the annual opportunity cost of a checking account that requires a $350 minimum balance to avoid service charges? Assume an interest rate of 6.5 percent.

L.O.5   12. What would be the net *annual* cost of the following checking accounts?
   a. Monthly fee, $3.75; processing fee, 25 cents per check; checks written, an average of 22 a month.
   b. Interest earnings of 6 percent with a $500 minimum balance; average monthly balance, $600; monthly service charge of $15 for falling below the minimum balance, which happens three times a year (no interest earned in these months).

L.O.5   13. Based on the following information, determine the true balance of your checking account.

Balance in your checkbook, $356   Balance on bank statement, $472
Service charge and other fees, $15   Interest earned on the account, $4
Total of outstanding checks, $187   Deposits in transit, $60

LIFE SITUATION   Case 5–1

Evaluating Financial Institutions

Barb Kenton is a member of the credit union at her place of work. This financial institution offers regular savings accounts, share draft checking, and a variety of loans. It does not offer electronic banking, mortgages, or investment advice.

Barb's husband, Lance, is a manager at a department store in a local shopping center. Recently, an investment company opened a store in the mall. It offers free checking, low-cost loans, investment assistance, insurance, and real estate service. Lance believes that Barb and he should do business with this nationally known company.

Questions

1. What are the benefits of doing business with the credit union instead of the investment company?
2. What factors should Barb and Lance consider when they compare financial institutions?
3. What recommendations would you make to Barb and Lance about their use of financial services?

LIFE SITUATION   Case 5–2

Comparing Savings Plans

Tom Ward, age 24, has a well-paying job and rents an apartment a few miles from work. Tom keeps his savings in a regular savings account paying 5 percent. His other savings options include the following:

- A money market account paying 6.5 percent with a $1,000 minimum balance.
- A six-month savings certificate paying 6 percent with a $500 minimum balance.
- A two-year savings certificate paying 7 percent with a $1,000 minimum balance.
- A five-year savings certificate paying 8.5 percent with a $1,000 minimum balance.

Tom would like to buy a house in about five years. In about a year or two, he will need to buy a new car. Tom expects a salary increase within the next two months. He plans to use the additional money to buy new furniture for his apartment and to repair the air-conditioning system in his car.

Questions

1. What are Tom's short-term and long-term savings goals? In what ways do these goals conflict?
2. What amount of interest would Tom earn over five years (assume annual compounding) on $1,000 in each of the five savings options? (Some options require the use of Appendix B exhibits.)
3. How does the liquidity of the five savings options compare? How might liquidity affect Tom's selection of a savings plan?
4. What actions do you recommend for Tom?

SUPPLEMENTARY READINGS

For Additional Information on Financial Institutions

Aguilar, Linda. "Still Toe-to-Toe: Banks and Nonbanks at the End of the '80s." *Economic Perspectives,* January–February 1990, pp. 12–23. Federal Reserve Bank of Chicago, Public Information Center, Box 834, Chicago, IL 60690.

Allen, Michael. "Home Banking Gets Another Chance." *The Wall Street Journal,* December 7, 1989, p. B1.

Chambliss, H. Darden, Jr. *Making the Most of Your Money.* Homewood, Ill.: Dow Jones-Irwin, 1990.

Mayer, Martin. "Credit Unions: A Primer." *Modern Maturity,* December 1989– January 1990, pp. 84–90.

Mrkvicka, Edward F., Jr. *The Bank Book: How to Revoke Your Bank's "License to Steal"—and Save up to $100,000.* New York: Harper & Row, 1989.

For Additional Information on Savings Plans

"Banking: The Best Savings Accounts, Certificates of Deposit, and Money-Market Accounts." *Consumer Reports,* August 1988, pp. 495–501.

Jasen, Georgette. "Best Yields May Be Found out of Town." *The Wall Street Journal,* March 2, 1989, p. C1.

The Savings Bonds Question and Answer Book. U.S. Savings Bonds Division, Department of the Treasury, Washington, DC 20226.

Savings Institutions Sourcebook. United States League of Savings Institutions, 1709 New York Avenue, NW, Washington, DC 20006.

Your Insured Deposit. Federal Deposit Insurance Corporation, 550 17th Street, NW, Washington, DC 20429.

For Additional Information on Checking Accounts

"Banking: The Best Deals in Checking Accounts." *Consumer Reports,* July 1988, pp. 455–63.

Check Rights. Federal Reserve Bank of Boston, 600 Atlantic Avenue, Boston, MA 02106.

6

Introduction to Consumer Credit

The use of credit is an important element in personal and family financial planning. When credit is used, needs satisfied in the present are paid for in the future. While the use of credit is often necessary and even advantageous, responsibilities and disadvantages are associated with its use.

LEARNING OBJECTIVES
After studying this chapter, you will be able to

L.O.1 Define consumer credit and analyze its advantages and disadvantages.

L.O.2 Differentiate among various types of credit.

L.O.3 Measure your credit capacity and build your credit rating.

L.O.4 Discover what information creditors look for when you apply for credit.

L.O.5 Choose the steps you can take to avoid and correct credit mistakes.

L.O.6 Evaluate the laws that protect you if you complain about consumer credit.

OPENING CASE

*Pushing Plastic**

For Elmer Hedgpeth, love and credit proved a near-ruinous mix. Caught up in a whirlwind romance with a California woman, the 63-year-old Phoenix resident lived for nearly three years what he wistfully called a "fantasy, the kind you dream about." The once-thrifty former postal worker and his friend frequently embarked on spur-of-the-moment trips to Los Angeles, Las Vegas, or Salt Lake City.

At first, paying the bills with his eight credit cards wasn't a problem because Mr. Hedgpeth regularly drew a cash advance on one card to make payments on another. But then he hit the credit ceilings on all eight cards. With $19,000 in charges, minimum monthly payments of $2,000, and an after-tax monthly income of $1,000, he couldn't meet the payments.

He had to sell his car to help whittle down the debt, and the credit card issuers settled for partial payments. Perhaps worst of all, the romance quickly faded. "About the only way one of these gals will look at a guy is if you've got money," he laments.

But did credit card issuers desert him? Hardly. "I keep getting solicitations in the mail for credit cards," he says incredulously. "I've gotten about three or four. But I just throw them out."

Few products as simple as a credit card carry such a powerful psychological impact. Glorianne Macklin, a 31-year-old Los Angeles restaurant manager, got her first card at age 17. She says, "When I had a credit card, I felt so secure. It was a big ego trip. I was the first in my family to have a credit card. My parents don't believe in them."

Miss Macklin was eventually awash in credit cards. "I had 25 cards—Citibank, First Chicago, Diners Club, American Express, a credit union card. On a vacation to Canada, I got an Eaton's [department store] card. On a trip to San Francisco, I got a Macy's card."

She used her credit cards freely, and periodically she was squeezed financially. On one occasion, her parents bailed her out, and she cut up some cards. But her resolve to trim her spending waned after she moved to Dallas. "It's like an addiction," she says. "I finally maxed out at $16,000."

With creditors chasing after her, she skipped town, leaving no forwarding address, and moved to her parents' home in Los Angeles. "I was getting harassed. It was making me crazy," she says.

The creditors caught up with her. "I knew they'd find me," she says. But living with her parents enabled her to afford a bank loan that paid off her credit card debt. She is determined to live without credit cards despite worries about coping with a financial emergency. "Now," she says, "I carry $200 cash in case my car breaks down, and I pray a lot."

*Adapted from *The Wall Street Journal,* May 22, 1989, p. 1.

WHAT IS CONSUMER CREDIT?

L.O.1
Define consumer credit and analyze its advantages and disadvantages

Credit is an arrangement to receive cash, goods, or services now and pay for them in the future. **Consumer credit** refers to the use of credit for personal needs (except a home mortgage) by individuals and families as contrasted to credit used for business or agricultural purposes.

Although Polonius cautioned, "Neither a borrower nor a lender be," using and providing credit have become a way of life for many individuals in today's economy. In January, you pay a bill for electricity that you used in December. A statement arrives in the mail for medical services that you received last month. You write a check for $40—a minimum payment on a $300 department store bill. With a bank loan, you purchase a new car. These are all examples of using credit, that is, paying later for goods and services obtained now.

For most consumers, there are three alternatives in financing current purchases: they can draw upon their savings, use their present earnings, or borrow against their expected future income. Each of these alternatives has its trade-offs. If savings are repeatedly depleted, there will be little left for emergencies or retirement income. If current income is spent imprudently on luxuries instead of necessities, the family's well-being will eventually suffer. And if future income is pledged to make current credit purchases, there will be little or no spendable income in the future.

Consumer credit is based on trust in the consumer's ability and willingness to pay bills when due. It works because people, by and large, are honest and responsible. But how does consumer credit affect our economy, and how is it affected by our economy?

The Importance of Consumer Credit in Our Economy

Consumer credit dates back to colonial times. While it was originally a privilege of the affluent, it came to be used extensively by farmers. No direct finance charge was imposed; instead, the cost of credit was added to the price of goods. With the advent of the automobile in the early 1900s, installment credit—in which the debt is repaid in equal installments over a specific period of time—exploded on the American scene.

All economists now recognize consumer credit as a major force in the American economy. Any forecast or evaluation of the economy includes consumer spending trends and consumer credit as a sustaining force. To paraphrase an old political expression, as the consumer goes, so goes the U.S. economy.

The movement of the baby boom generation into the age group that tends to use credit most heavily has added to the growth of consumer credit. The 25–44 age group currently represents about 30 percent of the population but holds nearly 60 percent of the debt outstanding. The people in this age group have always been disproportionate users of credit, since consumption is highest as families are formed and homes are purchased and furnished. Thus, while the intensive use of debt by this age group is nothing new, the fact that it has grown rapidly adds to overall debt use.

Uses and Misuses of Credit

Using credit to purchase goods and services may allow consumers to be more efficient or more productive or to lead more satisfying lives. There are many valid reasons for using credit. A medical emergency may cause a person to be strapped for funds. A homemaker returning to the work force may need a car. Or it may be possible to buy an item now for less money than it will cost later. But it is probably not reasonable to finance a Corvette on credit when a Corsica hatchback is all your budget allows.

Using credit increases the amount of money that a consumer can spend to purchase goods and services now. But what is the trade-off? It decreases the amount of money that will be available to spend in the future. However, many people expect their incomes to increase, and they therefore expect to be able to make payments on past credit purchases and still make new purchases.

Here are some trade-offs that you should consider before you decide how and when to buy a car: Do I have the cash I need to make this purchase? Do I want to use my savings for this purchase? Does the purchase fit my budget? Could I use the credit I need for this purchase in some better way? Could I postpone the purchase? What are the opportunity costs of postponing the purchase? (Alternative transportation costs; a possible increase in the price of the car.) What are the dollar costs and the psychological costs of using credit? (Interest; other finance charges; being in debt and responsible for a monthly payment.)

If you decide to use credit, the benefits of making the purchase now (increased efficiency or productivity, a more satisfying life, etc.) should outweigh the costs (financial and psychological) of using credit. Thus, effectively used, credit can help us have more and enjoy more. Misused, credit can result in default, bankruptcy, and loss of reputation.

Advantages of Credit

Consumer credit enables us to have and enjoy goods and services now—a car, a home, education, help in emergencies—and to pay for them through payment plans based on future income.

Charge cards permit the purchase of goods even when funds are low. Customers with previously approved credit may receive other extras, such as advance notice of sales and the right to order by phone or to buy on approval. In addition, many shoppers believe that it is easier to return merchandise that has been purchased on account. Charge cards also provide shopping convenience and the efficiency of paying for several purchases with one monthly payment.

Credit is more than a substitute for cash. Many of the services it provides are taken for granted. Every time you turn on the water tap, flick the light switch, or telephone a friend, you are using credit.

It is also safer to use credit. Charge accounts and credit cards let you shop and travel without carrying a large amount of cash. Credit cards are also used for identification when cashing checks, and the use of credit provides a record of expenses.

Lastly, credit indicates stability. The fact that lenders consider you a good risk usually means that you are a responsible individual. But if you do not pay your debts back on a timely basis, credit has many disadvantages.

Disadvantages of Credit

When considering the use of credit, remember that credit costs money and that it may cause overspending, result in loss of merchandise or income, and tie up your future income.

Perhaps the greatest disadvantage of using credit is the temptation to overspend, especially during periods of inflation. It seems easy to buy today and pay tomorrow using cheaper dollars. But continued overspending leads to serious trouble. Remember the problems faced by Elmer Hedgpeth and Glorianne Macklin, mentioned at the beginning of the chapter? Remember, too, that if payments are not made on time, you may have to give up your home if it has been pledged as collateral for the loan or the merchandise.

Financial and Personal Opportunity Costs

Whether or not credit involves security (something of value to back the loan), failure to pay a loan may result in the loss of income, valuable property, and your good reputation. Further difficulties could be court action and bankruptcy. Misuse of credit can create serious long-term financial problems, damage to family relationships, and a slowing of progress toward goals. Therefore, credit should be approached with caution and must not be used more extensively than your budget permits.

Although credit permits more immediate satisfaction of needs and desires, it does not increase total purchasing power. Credit purchases must be paid for out of future income; therefore, credit ties up the use of future income. Furthermore, if your income does not increase to cover rising costs, your ability to repay credit commitments will be diminished. Before buying goods and services on credit, consider whether they will have lasting value, whether they will increase your personal satisfaction during present and future income periods, and whether your current income will continue or increase.

Finally, credit costs money. It is a service for which you must pay. Paying for purchases over a period of time is more costly than paying cash for them. Making a credit purchase rather than a cash purchase involves one very obvious trade-off: the fact that the purchase will cost more due to monthly finance charges. Depending on the agreement, a direct charge may be applied at the point of purchase as well. In contrast with this explicit example of an opportunity cost involved in making a cash versus credit decision, paying cash involves a less apparent trade-off. By paying cash, you forgo the opportunity to keep the cash in an interest-bearing account. You must decide whether making a credit purchase is worth the extra cost—or whether it is advisable to wait until you can save the necessary money and pay cash. The cost of credit may cancel a bargain.

- -

PERSONAL FINANCE JOURNAL

Helpful Tips about Credit

Always budget your credit spending carefully.

Shop around for the lowest credit rates. The rates sometimes vary tremendously.

Use credit only when doing so is to your advantage.

Buy items on credit that will last at least until the last payment is due. You will receive more satisfaction that way.

Pay your bills on time to ensure that you can continue to use credit.

Understand the credit contract before signing it.

Notify the creditor if, for any reason, you cannot make scheduled payments.

Keep an eye on your credit card when you give it to salespeople. Make certain they use it for your transaction only, and then be sure the card you get back is yours.

Tear up the carbons after you sign credit card receipts. This will make it more difficult for anyone to steal your account number in order to use it for fraudulent purposes.

Do not give your credit card numbers over the phone to anyone unless *you* initiate the call. Ask callers to put their request to you in writing.

Keep your receipts after you make any charges. Compare them with your monthly statement. Carefully read your monthly bill.

If you find any incorrect charges on your monthly credit card statements, notify your credit card issuer in writing.

Keep a list of your credit card numbers and the issuers' phone numbers in a safe place for quick reference in case of loss or theft.

Report your lost or stolen cards at once. Most card issuers have toll-free telephone numbers for this purpose.

Federal law limits your liability for unauthorized charges to $50 per credit card. But you don't have to pay for *any* charges made after you have notified card companies of your loss. After calling, follow up with a telegram or registered letter.

- -

In summary, the use of credit provides immediate access to goods and services, flexibility in money management, safety and convenience, a cushion in emergencies, a means of increasing resources, and a character recommendation if the debt is paid back on a timely basis. But remember, the use of credit is a two-sided coin. An intelligent decision as to its use demands careful evaluation of your current debt, future income, the added cost, and the consequences of overspending.

There are many forms of credit. As a consumer and a borrower, you should select the kind of credit that most appropriately meets your economic and personal needs in given situations. The accompanying box lists a few helpful tips about the use of credit.

TYPES OF CREDIT

L.O.2
Differentiate among various types of credit.

There are two types of consumer credit—closed-end credit and open-end credit. With **closed-end credit,** you pay back onetime loans in a specified period of time and the payments are of equal amounts. With **open-end credit,** loans are made on a continuous basis and you are billed periodically to make at least partial payment. Exhibit 6–1 shows examples of closed-end and open-end credit.

Closed-End Credit
→ like mortage (reehelon)

Closed-end credit is used for a specific purpose and is for a specified amount. Mortgage loans, automobile loans, and installment loans for purchasing furniture or appliances are examples of closed-end credit. An agreement, or contract, lists the repayment terms—the number of payments, the payment amount, and how much the credit will cost. Closed-end payment plans usually involve a written agreement for each credit purchase. A down payment or trade-in may be required, with the balance to be repaid in equal weekly or monthly payments over a period of time. Generally, the seller holds title to the merchandise until the payments have been completed.

The three most common types of closed-end credit are installment sales credit, installment cash credit, and single lump-sum credit. *Installment sales credit* is a loan that allows the consumer to receive merchandise, usually high-priced items

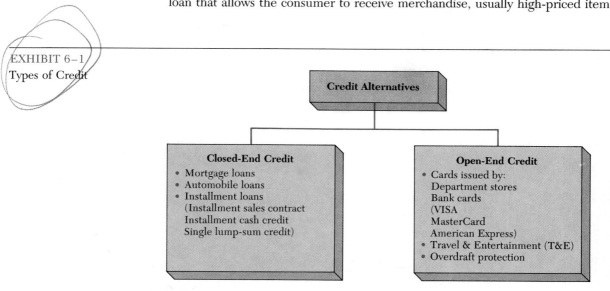

EXHIBIT 6–1
Types of Credit

such as refrigerators or furniture. The consumer makes a down payment and usually signs a contract to repay the balance, plus interest and service charges, in equal installments over a specified period.

Installment cash credit is a direct loan of money for personal purposes, home improvements, or vacation expenses. No down payment is made, and payments are made in specified amounts over a set period.

Single lump-sum credit is a loan that must be repaid in total on a specified day. Lump-sum credit is generally used to purchase a single item.

Open-End Credit

Using a credit card issued by a department store, using a bank credit card (VISA, MasterCard) to make purchases at different stores, charging a meal at a restaurant, and using overdraft protection are examples of open-end credit. As you will see below, you do not apply for open-end credit to make a single purchase, as is done with closed-end credit. Rather, you can use open-end credit to make any purchases you wish if you do not exceed your **line of credit,** the maximum amount of credit you can use. You may have to pay **interest,** a periodic charge for the use of credit, or other finance charges. Some creditors allow you a grace period of 25 to 30 days to pay a bill in full before you incur any interest charges.

All of us have probably had an appointment with a doctor or a dentist that we did not pay for until later. Professionals and small businesses often do not demand immediate payment. *Incidental credit* is a credit arrangement that has no extra costs and no specific repayment plan.

Open-end credit is a form of credit that many retailers use. Customers can purchase goods or services up to a fixed dollar limit at any time. Usually, they have the option of paying the bill in full within 30 days without interest charges or of making stated monthly installments based on the account balance plus interest.

Revolving check credit is a service extended by many banks. It is a prearranged loan for a specified amount that the consumer can use by writing a special check. Repayment is made in installments over a set period. The finance charges are based on the amount of credit used during the month and on the outstanding balance.

Credit Cards   About 25,000 financial institutions participate in the credit card business, and the vast majority of them are affiliated with VISA International or the Interbank Card Association, which issues MasterCard. A bank credit card differs from other credit cards in that it is issued by a bank or other financial institution.

The unique feature of bank credit cards is that they extend a line of credit to the cardholder, much like a bank's consumer loan department. They provide prompt and convenient access to short-term credit for the cardholder, who instructs the bank to pay the merchant immediately and reimburses the bank later. The accompanying box provides a few helpful hints for choosing a credit card.

Don't confuse debit cards with credit cards, although both may look alike. As the name implies, the **debit card** debits your account at the moment you buy goods or services, while the credit card extends credit and delays your payment. Debit cards, unlike credit cards, withdraw money from your account as soon as you make a purchase. Debit cards are used most commonly at automated teller machines, but more and more they are being used to purchase goods at point-of-sale terminals in stores.

FINANCIAL PLANNING IN ACTION

Choosing a Credit Card?

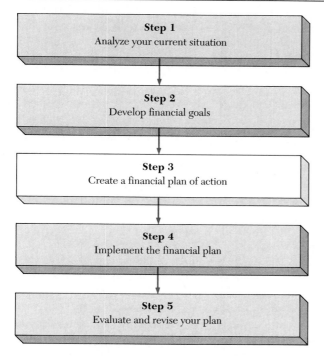

Step 1
Analyze your current situation

Step 2
Develop financial goals

Step 3
Create a financial plan of action

Step 4
Implement the financial plan

Step 5
Evaluate and revise your plan

1. Department stores and gasoline companies are good places to obtain your first credit card. Pay your bills in full and on time, and you will begin to establish a good credit history.

2. Bank cards are offered through banks and savings and loan associations. Fees and finance charges vary considerably (from 12.5 percent to 21.6 percent), so shop around.

3. If you usually pay your bill in full, try to deal with a financial institution with an interest-free grace period, which is the time after a purchase has been made and before a finance charge is imposed, typically 25 to 30 days.

4. If you're used to paying monthly installments, look for a card with a low monthly finance charge. Be sure you understand how that finance charge is calculated. For a list of banks offering low finance charges, send $1, check or money order, to BankCard Holders of America, 560 Hern-

don Parkway, Suite 120, Herndon, VA 22070. Request "Low Interest Rate List." A "No Annual Fee List," a list of banks offering cards with no annual fee, is available for $1.95.

5. Consider the option of obtaining a card from an out-of-state financial institution if it offers better terms than those offered locally.

6. Be aware of some credit cards that offer "no fee" or low interest but start charging interest from the day an item is purchased.

7. Be aware of some credit cards that do not charge annual fees but instead charge a "transaction fee" each time the card is used.

8. If you're only paying the minimum amount on your monthly payments, you need to plan your budget more carefully. The longer it takes for you to pay off a bill, the more interest you pay. The finance charges you pay on an item could end up being more than the item is worth.

9. With a grace period of 25 days, you are actually getting a free loan when you pay bills in full each month.

10. In order to avoid delays that may result in finance charges, follow the card issuer's instructions as to where, how, and when to make bill payments.

11. If you have a bad credit history and problems in getting a credit card, look for a savings institution that will give you a card if you open a savings account with it. Your line of credit will be determined by the amount you have on deposit.

12. Travel and entertainment cards often charge higher annual fees than are charged by most credit cards. Payment usually must be made in full within 30 days of receiving your bill or, typically, no further purchases will be approved on the account.

13. Often, credit cards on your account for a spouse or child (over 18) are available with a minimum additional fee, or no fee at all.

14. Be aware that "debit" cards are not credit cards but simply a substitute for a check or cash. The amount of the sale is immediately subtracted from your checking account.

SOURCES: American Institute of Certified Public Accountants and U.S. Office of Consumer Affairs.

Travel and Entertainment (T & E) Cards   T & E cards are not really credit cards, because the monthly balance is due in full. But most of us think of Diners Club or American Express cards as credit cards because we don't pay the moment we purchase goods or services.

Home Equity Loans   A **home equity loan** is based on the difference between the current market value of your home and the amount you still owe on your mortgage. With such a loan, you can borrow up to $100,000 or more on your home. Depending on the value of the home, you can borrow up to 80 percent of its appraised value, less the amount you still owe on your mortgage.

A home equity loan is usually set up as a revolving line of credit, typically with a variable interest rate. A revolving line of credit is an arrangement whereby borrowings are permitted up to a specified limit and for a specified period. Once the line of credit has been established, you draw from it only the amount you need at any one time.

How much credit do you need? There is no single, universal formula to guide consumers on whether they need credit and on how much credit they can safely handle. People have different wants and needs. In addition, social and economic background and status play a part in what people want and need.

MEASURING YOUR CREDIT CAPACITY

L.O.3
Measure your credit capacity and build your credit rating.

The only way to determine how much credit you can assume is to first learn how to make an accurate and sensible personal or family budget. Budgets, as you learned in Chapter 3, are simple, carefully considered outlines of plans to distribute dollars of earnings. With budgets, you first provide for basic necessities, such as rent, mortgage, food, and clothing. Then you provide for such items as furniture, home furnishings, and other heavy, more durable goods.

Can You Afford a Loan?

Before you take a loan, ask yourself whether you can meet all of your essential expenses and still afford the monthly loan payments. You can make this calculation in two ways. One is to add up all of your basic monthly expenses and then to subtract this total from your take-home pay. If the difference will not cover the monthly payment and still leave funds for other expenses, you cannot afford the loan.

An even more reliable method is to ask yourself what you plan to give up in order to make the monthly loan payment. If you currently save a portion of your income greater than the monthly payment, then you can use these savings to pay off the loan. But if you do not, you will have to forgo spending on entertainment, new appliances, or perhaps even necessities. Are you prepared to make this trade-off? Although it is difficult to precisely measure your credit capacity, there are certain rules of thumb that you can follow.

General Rules of Credit Capacity

Debt Payments-to-Income Ratio   The debt payments-to-income ratio is calculated by dividing your monthly debt payments (not including house payments) by your net monthly income. Experts suggest that you spend no more than 20 percent of your net (after-tax) income on credit payments. Thus, as shown in

Exhibit 6–2, a person making $1,068 per month after taxes should spend no more than $213 on credit payments per month.

The 20 percent estimate is the maximum; however, 15 percent is much better. The 20 percent estimate is based on the average family, with average expenses; it does not take major emergencies into account. If you are just beginning to use credit, you should not consider yourself safe if you are spending 20 percent of your net income on credit payments.

Debt-to-Equity Ratio   The debt-to-equity ratio is calculated by dividing your total liabilities by your net worth. In calculating this ratio, do not include the value of your home and the amount of its mortgage. If your debt-to-equity ratio is about 1, that is, if your consumer installment debt roughly equals your net worth (not including your home or its mortgage), you have probably reached the upper limit of debt obligations.

For example, examine Cheryl and Steve Belford's balance sheet, discussed in Chapter 3. Subtracting the current market value of their home—$86,500—from their total assets of $119,340, the Belfords' remaining assets are worth $32,840. Their total liabilities, $57,500 minus the home mortgage of $52,800, equal $4,700. Therefore, the Belfords' debt-to-equity ratio is $4,700 divided by $32,840, or 0.143 percent. Since this ratio is less than 1, the Belfords are well within their debt limits. In this example, the Belfords should not incur any debts over $32,840.

The debt-to-equity ratio for business firms in general ranges between 0.33 and 0.50. The larger this ratio, the riskier the situation is for lenders and borrowers. Of course, the debt-to-equity ratio can be lowered by paying off debts.

None of the above methods is perfect for everyone; the limits given are only guidelines. Only you, based on the money you earn, your current obligations, and your financial plans for the future, can determine the exact amount of credit you need and can afford. You must be your own credit manager.

Keep in mind that your credit capacity is adversely affected if you cosign a loan for a friend or a relative.

EXHIBIT 6–2
How to Calculate Debt Payments-to-Income Ratio

Monthly gross income	$1,500
Less:	
All taxes	270
Social security	112
Monthly IRA contribution	50
Monthly net income	$1,068
Monthly installment credit payments:	
VISA	25
MasterCard	20
Discover card	15
Education loan	—
Personal bank loan	—
Auto loan	153
Total monthly payments	$ 213
Debt payments-to-income ratio ($213/$1,068)	19.94%

Cosigning a Loan *not good to do*

What would you do if a friend or relative asked you to cosign a loan? Before you give your answer, make sure you understand what cosigning involves. Under a recent Federal Trade Commission rule, creditors are required to give you a notice to help explain your obligations. The cosigner's notice says:

You are being asked to guarantee this debt. Think carefully before you do. If the borrower doesn't pay the debt, you will have to. Be sure you can afford to pay if you have to, and that you want to accept this responsibility.

You may have to pay up to the full amount of the debt if the borrower does not pay. You may also have to pay late fees or collection costs, which increase this amount.

The creditor can collect this debt from you without first trying to collect from the borrower. The creditor can use the same collection methods against you that can be used against the borrower, such as suing you, garnishing your wages, etc. If this debt is ever in default, that fact may become a part of *your* credit record.[1]

Cosigners Often Pay   Some studies of certain types of lenders show that as many as three out of four cosigners are asked to repay the loan. That statistic should not surprise you. When you are asked to cosign, you are being asked to take a risk that a professional lender will not take. The lender would not require a cosigner if the borrower met the lender's criteria for making a loan.

In most states, if you do cosign and your friend or relative misses a payment, the lender can collect from you immediately without pursuing the borrower first. And the amount you owe may be increased—if the lender decides to sue to collect. A lender that wins the case may be able to take your wages and property.

If You Do Cosign   Despite the risks, there may be times when you decide to cosign. Perhaps your son or daughter needs a first loan or a close friend needs help. Here are a few things to consider before you cosign:

1. Be sure you can afford to pay the loan. If you are asked to pay and cannot, you could be sued or your credit rating could be damaged.
2. Before you cosign a loan, consider that even if you are not asked to repay the debt, your liability for this loan may keep you from getting other credit that you may want.
3. Before you pledge property, such as your automobile or furniture, to secure the loan, make sure you understand the consequences. If the borrower defaults, you could lose the property you pledge.
4. Check your state law. Some states have laws giving you additional rights as a cosigner.
5. Request that a copy of overdue payment notices be sent to you, thus allowing you to take action to protect your credit history.

Building and Maintaining Your Credit Rating

If you apply for a charge account, credit card, car loan, personal loan, or mortgage, your credit experience—or lack of it—will be a major factor considered by the creditor. Your credit experience may even affect your ability to get a job or buy life insurance. A good credit rating is a valuable asset that should be nurtured and protected. If you want a good rating, you must use credit with discretion; limit your borrowing to your capacity to repay, and live up to the terms of your contracts. The quality of your credit rating is entirely up to you.

In reviewing your creditworthiness, a creditor seeks information from credit bureaus located in your area.

Credit Bureaus

Across the United States, there are several thousand **credit bureaus** that collect credit information about consumers. Many of these credit bureaus are connected by teletype to centralized computer files that contain data about millions of individuals. From these files, a credit bureau can produce for a subscribing creditor, almost instantaneously, a report about your past and present credit activity.

Who Provides Data to Credit Bureaus?

Credit bureaus obtain their data from banks, finance companies, merchants, credit card companies, and other creditors. These sources regularly send reports to credit bureaus containing information about the kinds of credit they extend to customers, the amount and terms of that credit, and customers' paying habits. Credit bureaus also collect some information from other sources, such as court records.

What's in Your Credit Files?

As shown in a sample credit report (Exhibit 6–3), the credit bureau file contains your name, your address, your social security number, and your birth date. It may also include the following information:

Your employer, position, and income.
Your former address.
Your former employer.
Your spouse's name, social security number, employer, and income.
Whether you own your home, rent, or board.
Checks returned for insufficient balance.

Your credit file may also contain detailed credit information. Each time you buy from a reporting store on credit or take out a loan at a bank, a finance company, or some other reporting creditor, a credit bureau is informed of your account number and of the date, amount, terms, and type of credit. As you make payments, your file is updated to show the outstanding balance, the number and the amounts of payments past due, and the frequency of 30-, 60-, or 90-day latenesses. Your record may indicate the largest amount of credit you have had and the maximum limit permitted by the creditor. Each inquiry about you may be recorded. If you have been refused credit, that may also be entered into your file. If this has happened frequently, a creditor may be wary; he will at least want to consider the reasons for the refusals. Any suits, judgments, or tax liens against you may appear as well. However, a federal law protects your rights if the information in your credit file is erroneous.

Fair Credit Reporting

You can see that fair and accurate credit reporting is vital to both creditors and consumers. Therefore, Congress enacted the **Fair Credit Reporting Act** of 1971, which regulates the use of credit reports, requires the deletion of obsolete information, and gives the consumer access to his or her file and the right to have

EXHIBIT 6–3   Sample Credit Report

CONFIDENTIAL

EQUIFAX SERVICES/RETAILERS COMMERCIAL AGENCY CREDIT REPORT (INDIVIDUAL)

Report Made By Equifax Services ☒ Retailers ☐

Acct. No. 00000	File No. & Requestor's Name 1821 Faye	Macon, GA **OFFICE**

Date 7/15/90

NAME (& Spouse) BRYAN, JOHN A. (MARY)

Address Macon, GA, 248 Poplar St., N.E.

Emp-Occ. Johnson Realty Co., Salesman

Bus. Add. Macon, GA, 301 Main St., S.W.

REPORT FROM (If not city in heading) (State whether former addr., etc.)

Transaction: Books
Amount $ 200
Mo. Notes $ 10

1. Time known by each source? — 1. 3, 3, 1, 2yrs
2. Are name and address correct as given above? — 2. yes
3. About what is age? (If around 21 verify if possible.) — 3. 33
4. Is applicant married, single, divorced or widowed? No. dependents? — 4. married   No. dependents 2
5. Name of employer? (Give name of firm.) — 5. Johnson Realty Co.
6. What is nature of business? (State the kind of trade or industry.) — 6. Real Estate
7. Position held—how long with present employer? (If less than 1 year, explain.) — 7. Salesman   How long? 1½ yrs
8. Work full time steadily? (If not, how many days per week?) — 8. yes
9. Are prospects for continued employment regarded as good? — 9. yes
10. What would you estimate NET WORTH? — 10. $ 8,500
11. List principal assets (Real estate, cash, stocks, bonds, etc.). — 11. Car, equity in home, personals
12. Does applicant own home, rent or board? — 12. buying
13. What is ANNUAL EARNED INCOME from work or business? — 13. $ 18,000   Exact ☐   Estimated ☒
14. ADDED ANNUAL income from investments, rentals, pensions, disability, etc. — 14. $ none   Source:
15. If spouse employed, give name of employer. — 15. A&B Insurance Co.
  a. Position held—approximate ANNUAL INCOME. — a. Clerk (part- Income $ 5,000
  b. Approximate number of years employed. — b. 2   time)
16. Any foreclosures, garnishments, suits, judgments or bankruptcies known to sources? (If yes, explain below.) — 16. no
17. Any factors that may affect doing business with applicant on a credit basis? — 17. no
18. CREDIT RECORD: Set out CREDIT RECORD in tabular form below.
19. BUSINESS-FINANCES: Comment on present and any past business connections developed, irregular employment or lack of stability. Cover subject's financial position, giving breakdown on worth.
20. RESIDENCE: Show how long subject has lived at this address and former addresses, if developed.

Comment when information developed on credit responsibility or financial difficulties may affect earnings or paying ability.

Trade Line	How Long Selling	Date Last Sale	Highest Credit	Terms of Sale	Amount Owing	Amount Past Due	Paying Record
Sundial Finance Company	2 yrs	10/89	1200	24 x $35	885	–	prompt
Al's Dept. Store	9/79	10/86	100	30 days	–	–	30 days
GA State Bank		7/84	3850	48x $80.20	962.40	–	as agreed
FROM FILE DATED 8/14/88							
Al's Dept. Store	9/86	–	264	10 mos.	none	none	as agreed
GA State Bank	11/83	–	1321	24 x $65	none	none	as agreed

BUSINESS FINANCES: John A. Bryan is employed as shown. He sells on a commission basis and has been successful in this work. His employer expects his earnings to increase. Prior to this employment, he was an insurance salesman for A&B Insurance Co. for two years, where he was well regarded. His wife is employed by this company. Their worth is composed of equity in home, auto (83 Chev.), household goods, personal effects and cash.

RESIDENCE: Prior to buying their present home 6 months ago, they rented an apartment at 29 Maple Lane, N.W., Macon for 1 year. They have one child age 2.

Equifax Services Inc.
Equifax Services Ltd.
Form 62LE.—2-78 U.S.A.

SOURCE: Courtesy of Equifax Services, Inc.

erroneous data corrected. Furthermore, the act allows only authorized persons to obtain your credit report.

Who May Obtain a Credit Report?

Your credit report may be issued only to properly identified persons for approved purposes. It may be furnished in response to a court order or in accordance with your own written request. It may also be provided to someone who will use it in connection with a credit transaction, an employment application, the underwriting of insurance, or some other legitimate business need or in the determination of eligibility for a license or other benefit granted by a governmental agency. Your friends and neighbors may not obtain credit information about you. If they request such information, they may be subject to fine and imprisonment.

Time Limits on Adverse Data

Most of the information in your credit file may be reported for only seven years. If you have declared personal bankruptcy, however, that fact may be reported for 10 years. After 7 years or 10 years, the information in your credit file can't be disclosed by a credit reporting agency unless you are being investigated for a credit application of $50,000 or more, for an application to purchase life insurance of $50,000 or more, or for employment at an annual salary of $20,000 or more.

Incorrect Information in Your Credit File

Credit bureaus are required to follow reasonable procedures to ensure that subscribing creditors report information accurately. However, mistakes may occur. Your file may contain erroneous data or records of someone with a similar name. When you notify the credit bureau that you dispute the accuracy of information, it must reinvestigate and modify or remove inaccurate data. You should give the credit bureau any pertinent data you have concerning an error. If reinvestigation does not resolve the dispute to your satisfaction, you may place a statement of 100 words or less in your file, explaining why you think the record is inaccurate. You may also want to place a statement in your file to explain a period of delinquency caused by some unexpected hardship, such as serious illness, a catastrophe, or unemployment, that cut off or drastically reduced your income. The credit bureau must include your statement about disputed data—or a coded version of that statement—with any report it issues about you. At your request, the credit bureau must also send a correction to any recipient of a report in the preceding six months if the report was for a credit check or in the preceding two years if the report was for employment purposes.

What Are the Legal Remedies?

Any consumer reporting agency or user of reported information that willfully or through negligence fails to comply with the provisions of the Fair Credit Reporting Act may be sued by the consumer. If the agency or the user is found guilty, the consumer may be awarded actual damages, court costs, and attorney's fees, and in the case of willful noncompliance, punitive damages as allowed by the court. The action must be brought within two years of the occurrence or within two years after the discovery of material and willful misrepresentation of information. An unauthorized person who obtains a credit report under false pretenses may be fined up to $5,000 or imprisoned for one year, or both. The same penalties apply to anyone who willfully provides credit information to someone not authorized to receive it.

Exhibit 6–4 outlines the steps you can take if you are denied credit.

EXHIBIT 6–4   What if You're Denied Credit?

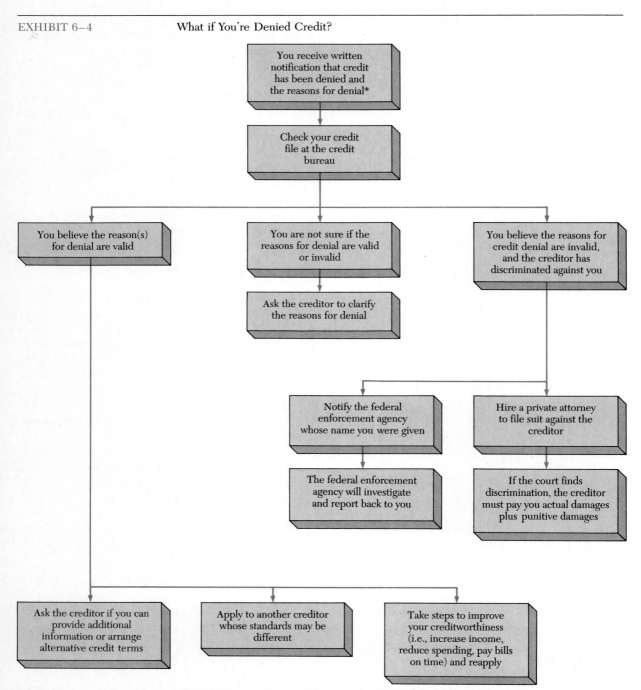

*If a creditor receives no more than 150 applications during a calendar year, the disclosures may be oral.
SOURCE: Reprinted, courtesy of Office of Public Information, Federal Reserve Bank of Minneapolis, Minneapolis, MN 55480.

APPLYING FOR CREDIT

A Scenario from the Past

Mary and John Jones, whose joint income is more than enough for payments on their dream house, are turned down for a mortgage loan. The lender says that Mary might become pregnant and leave her job.

It is illegal for creditors to ask or assume anything about a woman's childbearing plans. It is even illegal to discourage the Joneses from applying for a loan because Mary is of childbearing age. And Mary's income must be acknowledged fully by a lender.

L.O.4
Discover what information creditors look for when you apply for credit.

When you are ready to apply for credit, you should know what creditors think is important in deciding whether you are creditworthy. You should also know what they cannot legally consider in their decisions.

The **Equal Credit Opportunity Act (ECOA)** starts all credit applicants off on the same footing. It states that race, color, age, sex, marital status, and certain other factors may not be used to discriminate against you in any part of a credit dealing. Credit rights of women are protected under the ECOA. Women should build and protect their own credit history, using the checklist shown in Exhibit 6–5.

EXHIBIT 6–5

Women's Checklist to Build and Protect Their Own Credit History

It is simple and sensible to build and protect your own credit history. Here are some steps to get you started:

If You Are Single

Open a checking or savings account, or both.
Apply for a local department store card.
Take out a small loan from your bank.
Make timely payments.

If You Are Already Married

Establish credit in your maiden name or your first name.
Open your own accounts.
Try to have separate credit card accounts in your own name.
Review your joint accounts. Make sure that creditors report your credit history to credit bureaus in both names.

If You Are Getting Married

Write to your creditors and ask them to continue maintaining your credit file separately. You can choose to use your first name and your maiden name (Sue Smith), your first name and your husband's last name (Sue Jones), or your first name and a combined last name (Sue Smith-Jones).
Once you have picked a name, use it consistently.

If You Have Recently Been Separated or Divorced·

Close all of your joint accounts. Your credit record could suffer if your ex-partner is delinquent.
Meet your creditors and clear your credit record if your ex-partner has hurt your credit rating.

If You Are Widowed

Notify all creditors and tell them whether you or the executor of the estate will handle payment.
Transfer all existing joint loans to your name alone. You may also want to renegotiate repayment terms.
Transfer joint credit card accounts to your name alone, or reapply for new accounts.
Seek professional advice, if needed.

EXHIBIT 6–5
(*concluded*)

And Remember That

A creditor *cannot*

1. Refuse you individual credit in your own name.
2. Require a spouse to cosign a loan. Any creditworthy person can be your cosigner if one is required.
3. Ask about your birth control practices or family plans or assume that your income will be interrupted to have children.
4. Consider whether you have a telephone listing in your own name.

A creditor *must*

5. Evaluate you on the same basis as applicants who are male or who have a different marital status.
6. Consider income from part-time employment.
7. Consider reliable alimony, child support, or separate maintenance payments.
8. Consider the payment history of all joint accounts that accurately reflects your credit history.
9. Report the payment history on an account if you use the account jointly with your spouse.
10. Disregard information on accounts if you can prove that it does not reflect your ability or willingness to repay.

SOURCE: Reprinted, courtesy of Office of Public Information, Federal Reserve Bank of Minneapolis, Minneapolis, MN 55480.

What Creditors Look For

When a lender extends credit to its customers, it recognizes that some customers will be unable or unwilling to pay for their purchases. Therefore, lenders must establish policies for determining who will receive credit. Most lenders build their credit policies around the five Cs of credit: **character, capacity, capital, collateral,** and **conditions** (see accompanying feature).

Creditors use different combinations of the above facts to reach their decisions. Some creditors set unusually high standards, and others simply do not make certain kinds of loans. Creditors also use different kinds of rating systems. Some rely strictly on their own instinct and experience. Others use a credit-scoring or statistical system to predict whether you are a good credit risk. They assign a certain number of points to each characteristic that has proven to be a reliable sign that a borrower will repay. Then they rate you on this scale.

Typical questions in a credit application are shown in Exhibit 6–6, and Exhibit 6–7 shows how your credit application might be scored. In addition, during the loan application process, lenders may evaluate many of the following criteria to determine whether you are a good credit risk.

Age   Many older persons have complained about being denied credit because they were over a certain age. Or when older persons retired, their credit may have been suddenly cut off or reduced.

The ECOA is very specific about how a person's age may be used in credit decisions. A creditor may ask your age, but if you're old enough to sign a binding contract (usually 18 or 21 years old, depending on state law), a creditor may not turn you down or decrease your credit because of your age, may not ignore your retirement income in rating your application, may not close your credit account or require you to reapply for it because you reach a certain age or retire, and may not

..

PERSONAL FINANCE JOURNAL

The Five Cs of Credit

Here is what lenders look for in determining your creditworthiness:

Credit History

1. **Character:** Will You Repay the Loan?
   What is your attitude toward credit obligations?
   Have you used credit before?
   Do you pay your bills on time?
   Have you ever filed for bankruptcy?
   Do you live within your means?

Stability

How long have you lived at your present address?
Do you own your home?
How long have you been employed by your present employer?

Income

2. **Capacity:** Can You Repay the Loan?
   Your salary and occupation?
   Place of occupation?
   How reliable is your income?
   Any other sources of income?

Expenses

Number of dependents?
Do you pay any alimony or child support?
Current Debts?

Net Worth

3. **Capital:** What Are Your Assets or Net Worth?
   What are your assets?
   What are your liabilities?
   What is your net worth?

Loan Security

4. **Collateral:** What if You Don't Repay the Loan?
   What assets do you have to secure the loan?
   (Car, home, furniture?)
   What sources do you have besides income?
   (Savings, stocks, bonds, insurance?)

Job Security

5. **Conditions:** What General Economic Conditions Can Affect Your Repayment of the Loan?
   How secure is your job?
   How secure is the firm you work for?

SOURCE: Adapted from William M. Pride, Robert J. Hughes, and Jack R. Kapoor, *Business,* 2nd ed. (Boston: Houghton Mifflin, 1988), pp. 464–66. Copyright 1988, Houghton Mifflin Company.

..

EXHIBIT 6–6

Sample Credit Application Questions

Amount of loan requested
Proposed use of the loan
Your name and birth date
Social security and driver's license numbers
Present and previous street address
Present and previous employers and their addresses
Present salary
Number of ages of dependents

Other income and sources of other income
Have you ever received credit from us?

If so, when and at which office?
Checking account number, institution, and branch
Savings account number, institution, and branch
Name of nearest relative not living with you
Relative's address and telephone number

Information regarding joint applicant
The same questions as above

Marital status of the applicant
Marital status of the joint applicant

EXHIBIT 6–7   How Is a Consumer's Application Scored?

To illustrate how credit scoring works, consider the following example which uses only five factors to determine whether someone is creditworthy. (Most systems use 6 to 15 factors.)

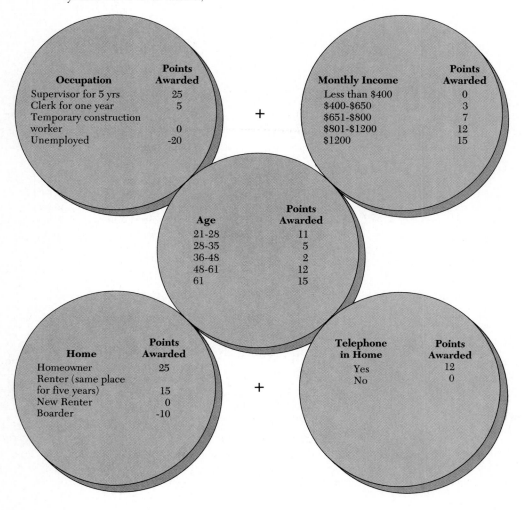

Occupation	Points Awarded
Supervisor for 5 yrs	25
Clerk for one year	5
Temporary construction worker	0
Unemployed	-20

Monthly Income	Points Awarded
Less than $400	0
$400-$650	3
$651-$800	7
$801-$1200	12
$1200	15

Age	Points Awarded
21-28	11
28-35	5
36-48	2
48-61	12
61	15

Home	Points Awarded
Homeowner	25
Renter (same place for five years)	15
New Renter	0
Boarder	-10

Telephone in Home	Points Awarded
Yes	12
No	0

deny you credit or close your account because credit life insurance or other credit-related insurance is not available to persons of your age.

Remember that while declining income may be a handicap if you are older, you can usually offer a solid credit history. The creditor has to look at all the facts of your particular situation and to apply the usual standards of creditworthiness to it.

Public Assistance   You may not be denied credit because you receive social security or public assistance. But, as is the case with age, certain information related to this source of income could have a bearing on your creditworthiness.

Housing Loans   The ECOA covers your application for a mortgage or a home improvement loan. It bans discrimination because of such characteristics as your race, color, or sex or because of the race or national origin of the people in the neighborhood where you live or want to buy your home. Creditors may not use any appraisal of the value of your property that considers the race of the people in your neighborhood.

What if Your Application Is Denied?

Ask Questions if Your Application Is Denied   The ECOA gives you the right to know the specific reasons for denial if you receive a notice that your application was denied. If the denial was based on a credit report, you are entitled to know the specific information in the credit report that led to the denial. After you receive this information from the creditor, you should visit or telephone the local credit bureau to find out what information it reported. The bureau cannot charge for disclosure if you ask to see your file within 30 days of being notified of a denial based on a credit report. You may ask the bureau to investigate any inaccurate or incomplete information and correct its records.

AVOIDING AND CORRECTING CREDIT MISTAKES

L.O.5
Choose the steps you can take to avoid and correct credit mistakes.

Has the department store's computer ever billed you for merchandise that you returned to the store or never received? Or has a credit company every charged you for the same item twice or failed to properly credit a payment on your account?

The best way to maintain your credit standing is to repay your debts on time. But there may still be complications. To protect your credit and to save your time, your money, and your future credit rating, you should learn how to correct the mistakes and misunderstandings that may tangle your credit accounts. If there is a snag, first try to deal directly with the creditor. The credit laws can help you settle your complaints.

The Fair Credit Billing Act (FCBA), passed in 1975, sets procedures for promptly correcting billing mistakes, for refusing to make credit card or revolving credit payments on defective goods, and for promptly crediting your payments.

The act defines a billing error as any charge for something you did not buy or for something bought by a person not authorized to use your account. Also included among billing errors is any charge that is not properly identified on your bill, that is for an amount different from the actual purchase price, or that was entered on a date different from the purchase date. A billing error may also be a charge for something that you did not accept on delivery or that was not delivered according to agreement.

Finally, billing errors include errors in arithmetic; failure to reflect a payment or other credit to your account; failure to mail the statement to your current address, provided you notified the creditor of an address change at least 20 days before the end of the billing period; and questionable items or items on which you need additional information.

In Case of Error

If you think your bill is wrong or you want more information about it, follow these steps. First, notify the creditor *in writing* within 60 days after the bill was mailed. Be sure to write to the address that the creditor lists for billing inquiries, to give the creditor your name and account number, and to say that you believe the bill contains an error and what you believe the error to be. State the suspected amount of the error or the item you want explained. Then pay all the parts of the bill that are not in dispute.

While waiting for an answer, you do not have to pay the disputed amount or any minimum payments or finance charges that apply to it.

The creditor must acknowledge your letter within 30 days, unless your bill can be corrected sooner. Within two billing periods, but in no case longer than 90 days, either your account must be corrected or you must be told why the creditor believes the bill is correct. If the creditor made a mistake, you do not pay any finance charges on the disputed amount. Your account must be corrected, and you must be sent an explanation of any amount you still owe.

If no error is found, the creditor must promptly send you an explanation of the reasons for that determination and a statement of what you owe, which may include any finance charges that have accumulated and any minimum payments that you missed while you were questioning the bill. You then have the time usually given on your type of account to pay any balance. If you are still not satisfied, you should notify the creditor within the time allowed to pay your bill.

Maintaining Your Credit Rating

A creditor may not threaten your credit rating while you are resolving a billing dispute. Once you have written about a possible error, a creditor is prohibited from giving out information that would damage your credit reputation to other creditors or credit bureaus. And until your complaint has been answered, the creditor may not take any action to collect the disputed amount.

After the creditor has explained the bill, you may be reported as delinquent on the amount in dispute and the creditor may take action to collect if you do not pay in the time allowed. Even so, you can still disagree in writing. Then the creditor must report that you have challenged your bill and give you the name and address of each recipient of information about your account. When the matter has been settled, the creditor must report the outcome to each recipient

Pepper . . . and Salt

"We're sorry about the mistake, sir—our administrative computer is chewing out our billing computer right now."

From *The Wall Street Journal,* with permission of Cartoon Features Syndicate.

of information. Remember that you may also place your version of the story in your credit record.

Defective Goods or Services

Your new sofa arrives with only three legs. You try to return it; no luck. You ask the merchant to repair or replace it; still no luck. The Fair Credit Billing Act provides that you may withhold payment on any damaged or shoddy goods or poor services that you have purchased with a credit card, as long as you have made a real attempt to solve the problem with the merchant. This right may be limited if the card was a bank credit card or a travel and entertainment credit card or any other credit card not issued by the store where you made your purchase. In such cases, the sale must have been for more than $50 and it must have taken place in your home state or within 100 miles of your home address.

COMPLAINING ABOUT CONSUMER CREDIT

L.O.6
Evaluate the laws that protect you if you complain about consumer credit.

First try to solve your problem directly with the creditor. Only if that fails should you bring more formal complaint procedures. Here's the way to file a complaint with the federal agencies responsible for administering consumer credit protection laws.

Complaints about Banks

If you have a complaint about a bank in connection with any of the federal credit laws or if you think that any part of your business with a bank has been handled in an unfair or deceptive way, you may get advice and help from the Federal Reserve System. You don't need to have an account at the bank to file a complaint. (see Exhibit 6–8 for the complaint form.)

Protection under Consumer Credit Laws

You may also take legal action against a creditor. If you decide to file a lawsuit, here are important consumer credit laws you should know.

Truth in Lending and Consumer Leasing Acts   If any creditor fails to disclose information required under the Truth in Lending Act or the Consumer Leasing Act, or gives inaccurate information, or does not comply with the rules about credit cards or the right to cancel them, you may sue for actual damages, that is, any money loss you suffer.

Class action suits are also permitted. A class action suit is one filed on behalf of a group of people with similar claims.

Equal Credit Opportunity Act   If you think you can prove that a creditor has discriminated against you for any reason prohibited by the ECOA, you may sue for actual damages plus punitive damages (that is, damages for the fact that the law has been violated) of up to $10,000.

Fair Credit Billing Act   A creditor who fails to comply with rules applying to the correction of billing errors automatically forfeits the amount owed on the item in question and any finance charges on it, up to a combined total of $50, even if the bill was correct. You may also sue for actual damages plus twice the amount of any finance charges.

EXHIBIT 6–8   Complaint Form to Report Violations of Federal Credit Laws

COMPLAINT FORM   **Federal Reserve System**

Name _____   Name of Bank _____

Address _____   Address _____
                 Street   City   State   Zip
_____
  City   State   Zip

Daytime telephone _____   Account number (if applicable) _____
            (include area code)

The complaint involves the following service: Checking Account ☐   Savings Account ☐   Loan ☐

   Other: Please specify _____

I have attempted to resolve this complaint directly with the bank: No ☐   Yes ☐

   If "No", an attempt should be made to contact the bank and resolve the complaint.

   If "Yes", name of person or department contacted is _____
                                                                        Date

MY COMPLAINT IS AS FOLLOWS (Briefly describe the events in the order in which they happened, including specific
dates and the bank's actions to which you object. Enclose copies of any pertinent information or correspondence that
may be helpful. Do not send us your only copy of any document):

_____
_____
_____
_____
_____
_____
_____
_____
_____
_____
_____

This information is solicited under the Federal Trade Commission Improvement Act. Providing the information is voluntary; complete information is necessary to expedite investigation of your complaint. Routine use of the information may include disclosing it to bank(s) or others involved or to other governmental agencies as deemed appropriate.

Date _____   Signatures _____

                                                        _____

SOURCE: Board of Governors of the Federal Reserve System.

Fair Credit Reporting Act   You may sue any credit reporting agency or creditor for violating the rules about access to your credit records and the correction of errors in your credit file. Again, you are entitled to actual damages plus such punitive damages as the court may allow if the violation is proven to have been intentional.

Exhibit 6–9 summarizes the major federal consumer credit laws. The Federal Reserve System has set up a separate office in Washington—the Division of Consumer and Community Affairs—to handle consumer complaints. This division also writes regulations to carry out the consumer credit laws, enforces these laws for state-chartered banks that are members of the Federal Reserve System, and helps banks comply with these laws.

The Federal Reserve System is advised by the Consumer Advisory Council, a panel of experts in consumer credit, representing both business and consumer interests across the country. The council meets four times a year, and its meetings are open to the public.

EXHIBIT 6–9   Summary of Federal Consumer Credit Laws

Act (date effective)	Major Provisions
Truth in Lending (July 1, 1969)	Provides specific cost disclosure requirements for the annual percentage rate and the finance charges as a dollar amount.
	Requires disclosure of other loan terms and conditions.
	Regulates the advertising of credit terms.
	Provides the right to cancel a contract when certain real estate is used as security.
(January 25, 1971)	Prohibits credit card issuers from sending unrequested cards. Limits a cardholder's liability for unauthorized use of a card to $50.
(October 1, 1982)	Requires that disclosures for closed-end credit (installment credit) be written in plain English and appear apart from all other information.
	Allows credit customer to request an itemization of the amount financed, if the creditor does not automatically provide it.
Fair Credit Reporting Act (April 24, 1971)	Requires disclosure to consumers of the name and address of any consumer reporting agency that supplied reports used to deny credit, insurance, or employment.
	Gives a consumer the right to know what is in his file, to have incorrect information reinvestigated and removed, and to include his version of a disputed item in the file.
	Requires credit reporting agencies to send the consumer's version of a disputed item to certain businesses or creditors.
	Sets forth identification requirements for consumers wishing to inspect their files.
	Requires that consumers be notified when an investigative report is being made.
	Limits the time that certain information can be kept in a credit file.
Fair Credit Billing Act (October 28, 1975)	Establishes procedures for consumers and creditors to follow when billing errors occur on periodic statements for revolving credit accounts.
	Requires creditors to send a statement setting forth these procedures to consumers periodically.
	Allows consumers to withhold payment for faulty or defective goods or services (within certain limitations) when purchased with a credit card.
	Requires creditor to promptly credit customers' accounts and to return overpayments if requested.
Equal Credit Opportunity Act (October 28, 1975)	Prohibits credit discrimination based on sex and marital status.
	Prohibits creditors from requiring women to reapply for credit upon a change in marital status.
	Requires creditors to inform applicants of acceptance or rejection of their credit application within 30 days of receiving a completed application.
	Requires creditors to provide a written statement of the reasons for adverse action.
(March 23, 1977)	Prohibits credit discrimination based on race, national origin, religion, age, or the receipt of public assistance.
(June 1, 1977)	Requires creditors to report information on an account to credit bureaus in the names of both husband and wife if both use the account and both are liable for it.
Fair Debt Collection Practices Act (March 20, 1978)	Prohibits abusive, deceptive, and unfair practices by debt collectors.
	Establishes procedures for debt collectors contacting a credit user.
	Restricts debt collector contacts with a third party.
	Specifies that payment for several debts be applied as the consumer wishes and that no money be applied to a debt in dispute.

SOURCE: *Managing Your Credit*, rev. ed. (Prospect Heights, Ill.: Money Management Institute, Household Financial Services, 1988), p. 36. © Household Financial Services, Prospect Heights, Illinois.

SUMMARY

Consumer credit is the use of credit by individuals and families for personal needs. Among the advantages of using credit are purchasing goods when they are needed and paying for them gradually, meeting financial emergencies, achieving convenience in shopping, and establishing a credit rating. But credit costs money, encourages overspending, and ties up future income.

Closed-end and open-end credit are two types of consumer credit. With closed-end credit, the borrower pays back a onetime loan in a specified period of time and with a specified number of payments. With open-end credit, the borrower is permitted to take loans on a continuous basis and is billed for partial payments periodically.

Two general rules of thumb for measuring credit capacity are the debt payments–to–income ratio and the debt-to-equity ratio. In reviewing your creditworthiness, a creditor seeks information from credit bureaus in your area.

Creditors determine creditworthiness on the basis of the five Cs: character, capacity, capital, collateral, and conditions.

You are responsible for building and maintaining your credit rating. Credit bureaus collect credit information and reveal it to creditors. In the event of a billing error, notify the creditor in writing within 60 days.

The Fair Credit Reporting Act gives you the right to know what your credit file contains. Erroneous information must be corrected to your satisfaction; if not, you may enter your version.

GLOSSARY

Capacity   The borrower's financial ability to meet credit obligations.

Capital   The borrower's assets or net worth.

Character   The borrower's attitude toward his or her credit obligations.

Closed-end credit   Onetime loans that the borrower pays back in a specified period of time and in payments of equal amounts; also called installment credit if paid in more than one payment.

Collateral   A valuable asset that is pledged to assure loan payments.

Conditions   The general economic conditions that can affect a borrower's ability to repay a loan.

Consumer credit   The use of credit for personal needs (except a home mortgage).

Credit   An arrangement to receive cash, goods, or services now and pay for them later.

Credit bureau   A reporting agency that assembles credit and other information on consumers.

Debit card   Subtracts the amount of a purchase from the buyer's account at the moment the purchase is made.

Equal Credit Opportunity Act (ECOA)   Bans discrimination in the extension of credit on the basis of race, color, age, sex, or marital status.

Fair Credit Billing Act (FCBA)   Sets procedures for promptly correcting billing mistakes, for refusing to make credit card payments on defective goods, and for promptly crediting payments.

Fair Credit Reporting Act   Regulates the use of credit reports, requires the deletion of obsolete information, and gives the consumer access to his or her file and the right to have erroneous data corrected.

Home equity loan   A loan based on the market value of a home less the mortgage on it.

Interest   The dollar cost of borrowing money.

Line of credit   The dollar amount, which may or may not be borrowed, that a lender is making available to a borrower.

Open-end credit   A line of credit, extended by many retailers, in which loans are made on a continuous basis and the borrower is billed periodically to make at least partial payment.

Revolving check credit   A prearranged loan from a bank for a specified amount; also called a bank line of credit.

DISCUSSION QUESTIONS

L.O.1   1.   Why does consumer credit play an important role in our economy?

L.O.1   2.   Evaluate uses and misuses of credit.

L.O.2   3.   Distinguish between open-end and closed-end credit. Explain when one type is better than the other.

L.O.3   4.   What steps will you take to measure your credit capacity? Which method will you use to determine your credit limit, and why?

L.O.3   5.   Will you cosign a loan for a friend or a relative? Why or why not?

L.O.3   6.   How would you go about building and maintaining your credit rating?

L.O.4   7.   What are the five Cs of credit? How do creditors evaluate the five Cs in granting or denying credit?

L.O.5   8.   Why is it important to maintain your credit rating?

L.O.6   9.   Evaluate the laws that protect you if you must complain about consumer credit.

Opening Case Questions

1.   How did Elmer Hedgpeth misuse credit, and why?
2.   Did credit card issuers desert Elmer Hedgpeth? If not, why?
3.   How did Glorianne Macklin misuse her credit cards? What would you have done if you were in a similar situation?

PROBLEMS AND ACTIVITIES

L.O.1   1.   Survey friends and relatives to determine the process they used in deciding whether or not to use credit to purchase an automobile or a major appliance. What risks and opportunity costs did they consider?

L.O.1   2. Think about the last three major purchases you have made.
    a. Did you pay cash? Why?
    b. If you paid cash, what opportunity costs were associated with the purchase?
    c. Did you use credit? If so, why?
    d. What were the financial and psychological opportunity costs of using credit?

L.O.2   3. Prepare a list of similarities and differences in the reasons that the following individuals might have for using credit:
    a. A teenager.
    b. A young adult.
    c. A growing family of four.
    d. A retired couple.

L.O.2   4. A few years ago, Michael Tucker purchased a home for $100,000. Today, the home is worth $150,000. His remaining mortgage balance is $50,000. Assuming that Michael can borrow up to 80 percent of the market value, what is the maximum amount he can borrow?

L.O.3   5. Louise McIntyre's monthly gross income is $2,000. Her employer withholds $400 in federal, state, and local income taxes and $160 in social security taxes per month. Louise contributes $80 per month for her IRA. Her monthly credit payments for VISA, MasterCard, and Discover card are $35, $30, and $20, respectively. Her monthly payment on an automobile loan is $285. What is Louise's debt payments–to–income ratio? Is Louise living within her means?

L.O.3   6. Calculate your net worth based on your present assets and liabilities.

L.O.3   7. Referring to your net worth statement, determine your safe credit limit. Use debt payments–to–income and debt-to-equity formulas.

L.O.4   8. What changes might take place in your personal net worth during different stages of your life? How might these changes affect your credit limits?

L.O.4   9. Survey credit representatives such as bankers, managers of credit departments in retail stores, managers of finance companies, credit union officers, managers of credit bureaus, and savings and loan officers. Ask what procedures they follow in granting or refusing a loan.

L.O.5   10. Bring to class examples of credit-related problems of individuals or families. Suggest ways in which these problems might be solved.

L.O.6   11. Compile a list of places that can be called to report dishonest credit practices, to get advice and help with credit problems, and to check out a creditor's reputation before signing a contract.

LIFE SITUATION   Case 6–1

Applying for Credit and Getting It

Betty Carson applied for credit at Friendly Finance Company. She was denied credit and received a form letter stating that information had been obtained from a consumer reporting agency. The letter included the name, address, and phone number of Anytown Credit Bureau.

Betty called Anytown Credit Bureau to find out what information it had given the finance company. She was told that it generally did not give out such information on the phone but that she could come to the office to learn the contents of her credit file. Betty said that she would be able to come at 1 P.M. on Monday.

When Betty arrived at the credit bureau, she was asked to show her driver's license and one other piece of identification. A trained interviewer talked with her and revealed that the inquiry from Friendly Finance Company was the only inquiry about her that the credit bureau had received during the past six months. The only other information in her file was that an account held five years earlier with AAA Department Store had been paid. Betty was surprised at the lack of credit information in her file, but she explained that until recently she had lived in a different state. The interviewer asked whether she could provide the names of her creditors there. The credit bureau would then check with those firms and add any new credit information. Betty did so and then applied for credit again at Friendly Finance Company. This time, she was granted credit.

Questions

1. Why do you think Ms. Carson was denied credit?
2. Was it legal for the Friendly Finance Company to deny her credit request?
3. How could Ms. Carson have avoided being denied credit the first time?

SOURCE: *Your Credit Rights,* rev. ed. (Minneapolis: Federal Reserve Bank of Minneapolis, 1988), p. 65. © 1988 by Federal Reserve Bank of Minneapolis. Reprinted, courtesy of Office of Public Information, Federal Reserve Bank of Minneapolis, Minneapolis, MN 55480.

LIFE SITUATION Case 6–2

Measuring Hank's Credit Capacity

Hank Hansen is 24 years old, single, and employed as a computer operator at a local manufacturing company. He recently purchased a two-bedroom condominium, and he plans to marry his high school sweetheart when she graduates from college in two years.

Hank's net monthly income is $2,000. He spends the following amounts each month for essential items:

Mortgage loan	$ 600
Utilities	130
Food	260
Transportation	130
Clothing	40
Medical expenses	40
Total	$1,200

Hank wants to buy a $10,000 car, and he has a down payment of $2,000. He figures that automobile insurance will be about $900 a year but that if he buys this new, fuel-efficient car, he will save about $30 a month on transportation.

Questions

1. How much can Hank spend on credit payments each month?
2. What percentage of his net monthly income can Hank spend safely on credit (not including housing) payments?
3. Will Hank get a loan from a bank if he applies for it?

SUPPLEMENTARY READINGS

For Additional Information on Credit Management

Bailard, Thomas E.; David L. Biehl; and Ronald W. Kaiser. *How to Set and Achieve Your Financial Goals.* Homewood, Ill.: Dow Jones-Irwin, 1989.

Complete Guide to Managing Your Money. New York: Consumer Reports Books, 1989.

Consumer Guide to Financial Independence. Foundation for Financial Planning, Two Concourse Parkway, Suite 800, Atlanta, GA 30328.

Managing Your Credit. Prospects Heights, Ill.: Money Management Institute, Household Financial Services, 1988.

For Additional Information on Home Equity Loans

Home Equity Lending: Boon or Bane? FRBSF Weekly Letter. San Francisco: Federal Reserve Bank of San Francisco, June 2, 1989.

Home Equity Lines of Credit. Federal Reserve Bulletin. Washington, D.C.: Board of Governors of Federal Reserve System, June 1988.

For Additional Information on Credit Cards

Bank Credit Card Boom: Some Explanations and Consequences. Cleveland: Federal Reserve Bank of Cleveland, March 1, 1988.

Choosing and Using Credit Cards: Facts for Consumers. Washington, D.C.: Federal Trade Commission, December 1988.

"Pushing Plastic." *The Wall Street Journal,* May 22, 1989, p. 1.

Using Plastic: A Young Adult's Guide to Credit Cards. Washington, D.C.: Federal Trade Commission, January 1989.

For Additional Information on Credit Card Problems

Building a Better Credit Record. Washington, D.C.: Federal Trade Commission, n.d.

Consumer Handbook to Consumer Protection Laws. Washington, D.C.: Board of Governors of Federal Reserve System, December 1987.

Your Guide to Consumer Credit. Chicago: American Bar Association, Public Education Division, 1988.

NOTE: All Federal Reserve bank publications can be ordered by writing to Publications Services, MS 138, Board of Governors, Federal Reserve System, Washington, DC 20551. All Federal Trade Commission publications referred to here can be obtained free by writing to Federal Trade Commission, 6th & Pennsylvania Avenues, NW, Washington, DC 20580.

7

Choosing a Source of Credit
The Costs of Credit Alternatives

All of us can get into credit difficulties if we do not understand how and when to use credit. Credit problems are rarely identical. Consumers are motivated by the desire for a higher standard of living, persuasive advertising, ignorance of the real cost of credit, lack of realistic planning, impatience, and a desire to live beyond their means. When, as a result, credit problems begin to arise, they lack the skills to deal with those problems and to find alternative solutions.

LEARNING OBJECTIVES
After studying this chapter, you will be able to

L.O.1 Analyze the major sources of consumer credit.

L.O.2 Determine the cost of credit by calculating interest with various interest formulas.

L.O.3 Develop a plan to manage your debts.

L.O.4 Evaluate various private and governmental sources that assist consumers with debt problems.

L.O.5 Assess the choices in declaring personal bankruptcy.

OPENING CASE

Financing Sue's Omni America

After shopping around, Sue Wallace decided on the car of her choice, an Omni America. The dealer quoted her a total price of $8,000. Sue decided to use $2,000 of her savings as a down payment and borrow $6,000. The salesperson wrote this information on a sales contract that Sue took with her when she set out to find financing.

When Sue applied for a loan, she discussed loan terms with the bank lending officer. The officer told her that the bank's policy was to lend only 80 percent of the total price of a new car. Sue showed the officer her copy of the sales contract, indicating that she had agreed to make a $2,000, or 25 percent, down payment on the $8,000 car, so this requirement caused her no problem. Although the bank was willing to make 48-month loans at an annual percentage rate of 15 percent on new cars, Sue chose a 36-month repayment schedule. She felt that she could afford the higher payments, and she knew that she would not have to pay as much interest if she paid off the loan at a faster rate. The bank lending officer provided Sue with a copy of the Truth-in-Lending Disclosure Statement shown here.

Truth-in-Lending Disclosure Statement (Loans)

ANNUAL PERCENTAGE RATE	FINANCE CHARGE	Amount Financed	Total of Payments 36
The cost of your credit as a yearly rate.	The dollar amount the credit will cost you.	The amount of credit provided to you or on your behalf.	The amount you will have paid after you have made all payments as scheduled.
15 %	$ 1,487.64	$ 6,000.00	$ 7,487.64

You have the right to receive at this time an itemization of the Amount Financed.

☒ I want an itemization.   ☐   I do not want an itemization.

Your payment schedule will be:

Number of Payments	Amount of Payments	When Payments Are Due
36	$ 207.99	1st of each month

The disclosure statement gathers all of the most important information about the loan. For example, the "Finance Charge" is the sum of all the costs of the credit, including all of the charges that Sue must pay before and during the term of the loan. Although interest is commonly the largest part of the finance charge, other charges may be included. For example, Sue might be required to pay a credit report fee. The amount that Sue will receive from the bank is the "Amount Financed."

The "Total of Payments" is the sum of the amount financed and the finance charge. If Sue makes her monthly payments on time, this is the entire amount that she will pay the bank.

The "Annual Percentage Rate" (APR) is perhaps the most important item shown on the disclosure statement. By relating the finance charge to the amount financed, it provides a percentage figure that Sue may use to compare the costs of obtaining a loan from various lenders.

Sue decided to compare the APR that she had been offered with the APR offered by another bank, but the 20 percent APR of the second bank (Bank B) was more expensive than the 15 percent APR of the first bank (Bank A). Here is her comparison of the two loans:

	Bank A 15 Percent APR	Bank B 20 Percent APR
Amount financed	$6,000.00	$6,000.00
Finance charge	1,487.64	2,027.28
Total of payments	7,487.64	8,027.28
Monthly payments (36)	207.99	222.98

The 5 percent difference in the APRs of the two banks meant that Sue would have to pay $15 extra every month if she got her loan from the second bank. Of course, she got the loan from the first bank.

SOURCES OF CONSUMER CREDIT

L.O.1
Analyze the major sources of consumer credit.

We all have short- or long-term needs for money or credit. Whether your furnace quit in the middle of January or short-term disability has limited your monthly income, unexpected incidents can create a need for several hundred or several thousand dollars.

Financial institutions, the sources of credit, come in all shapes and sizes. They play an important role in our economy, and they offer a broad range of financial services.

Nearly two thirds of all families owe nonmortgage consumer debt averaging more than $6,000. This level of debt usually costs between $600 and $1,200 in finance charges annually. By evaluating your credit options, you can reduce your finance charges. You can reconsider your decision to borrow money; you can discover a less expensive type of loan; or you can find a lender that charges a lower interest rate.

Before deciding whether to borrow money, ask yourself these three questions: Do I need a loan? Can I afford a loan? Can I qualify for a loan? The affordability of loans and the qualifications required to obtain loans were discussed in the last chapter. Here we wrestle with the first question.

In two situations in which many borrow, credit should be avoided. The first situation is one in which you do not need or really want a product that will require financing. Easy access to installment loans or possession of credit cards sometimes encourages consumers to make expensive purchases that they later regret. The solution to this problem is simple: After you have selected a product, resist any sales pressure to buy immediately and take a day to think it over.

The second situation is one in which you can afford to pay cash. Consider the trade-offs and opportunity costs involved. For example, paying cash is almost always cheaper than using credit. A $4,000 used car financed over a four-year period at 15 percent will cost approximately $1,200 in finance charges. On the other hand, if you paid for the car with $4,000 withdrawn from a passbook savings account or a money market account paying 7 percent and then deposited the equivalent of the monthly car payments into that account for four years, you would lose only $500 in interest. Thus, paying cash would cost you about $700 less than borrowing. Of course, this difference in cost will vary depending on such factors as the loan rate, the savings yield, and the willingness to replenish savings after having withdrawn them to make a purchase.

What Kind of Loan Should You Seek?

As discussed in the last chapter, there are two types of credit—closed-end and open-end credit. Because installment loans carry a lower interest rate, they are the less expensive credit option for loans that are repaid over a period of many months or years. However, because credit cards usually provide a float period—days when no interest is charged—they represent the cheaper way to make credit purchases that are paid off in a month or two. Also, once you have a credit card, using it is always easier than taking out an installment loan. An alternative to a credit card is a T & E card, such as an American Express or Diners Club card, which requires full payment of the balance due each month but does not impose a finance charge.

In seeking an installment loan, think first of borrowing from a bank or a credit union. There are, however, other credit sources, some of which are less expensive.

Inexpensive Loans   Parents or family members are often the source of the least expensive loans. They may charge you only the interest they would have earned if they had not made the loan—as little as the 5 percent they would have earned on a passbook account. Such loans, however, can complicate family relationships.

Also relatively inexpensive is money borrowed on financial assets held by a lending institution—for example, a bank certificate of deposit or the cash value of a whole life insurance policy. The interest rate on such loans typically ranges from 8 to 12 percent. But the trade-off is that your assets are tied up until the loan has been repaid.

Medium-Priced Loans   You can often obtain medium-priced loans from commercial banks and credit unions. New car loans, for example, may cost 11 to 16 percent; used car loans and home improvement loans may cost slightly more.

Borrowing from credit unions has several advantages. These institutions provide free credit life insurance, they are generally sympathetic to borrowers with legitimate payment problems, and they provide personal service. Nearly 55 million Americans belong to the nation's 16,700 credit unions, and the number of credit union members has been growing steadily.

Of course, you must join a credit union and pay membership fees to use its services. Some credit unions require members to be enrolled three to six months before they are allowed to take out loans, but others allow borrowing on the first day of membership.

In the past, the nonprofit status and lower costs of credit unions usually enabled them to provide better terms on loans and savings than those offered by commercial institutions. However, National Credit Unions Association data indicate that for comparable loans the average loan rate of credit unions has been higher than that of banks since 1985.

Expensive Loans   The most expensive loans are available from finance companies, retailers, and banks through credit cards. Finance companies often lend to those who cannot obtain credit from banks or credit unions. Typically, the interest ranges from 15 percent to 30 percent. If you are denied credit by a bank or a credit union, you should question your ability to afford the higher rate of a loan company.

EXHIBIT 7–1   Summary of Sources of Consumer Credit and Comparisons of Major Features

The following table outlines the major sources of consumer loans. It attempts to generalize the information and to give an average picture of each source in regard to the type of credit available, lending policies, and customer services. Due to the

Credit Source	Commercial Banks	Consumer Finance Companies
Type of loan	Single-payment loans Personal installment loans Passbook loans Check-credit plans Credit card loans Second mortgages	Personal installment loans Second mortgages
Lending policies	Seek customers with established credit history Often require collateral or security Prefer to deal in large loans, such as auto, home improvement, and home modernization, with the exception of credit card and check-credit plans Determine repayment schedules according to the purpose of the loan Vary credit rates according to the type of credit, time period, customer's credit history, and the security offered May require several days to process a new credit application	Often lend to consumers without established credit history Often make unsecured loans Often vary rates according to the size of the loan balance Offer a variety of repayment schedules Make a higher percentage of small loans than other lenders Maximum loan size limited by law Process applications quickly, frequently on the same day as the application is made

Cost	Lower than some lenders because they
	   Take fewer credit risks
	   Lend depositors' money, which is a relatively inexpensive source of funds
	   Deal primarily in large loans, which yield a larger dollar income without an increase in administrative costs
		Higher than some lenders because they
		   Take greater risks
		   Must borrow and pay interest on money to lend
		   Deal frequently in small loans, which are costly to make and yield a small amount of income

Services	Offer several types of consumer credit plans May offer financial counseling Handle credit transactions confidentially	Provide credit promptly Make loans to pay off accumulated debts willingly Design repayment schedules to fit the borrower's income Usually offer financial counseling Handle credit transactions confidentially

dramatic fluctuations in interest rates during the 80s, it is no longer possible to provide a common range of annual percentage rates for each source of credit. Check with your local lender for current interest rates.

Study and compare the differences to determine which source can best meet your needs and requirements.

Credit Unions	Life Insurance Companies	Savings and Loan Associations
Personal installment loans Share draft–credit plans Credit card loans Second mortgages	Single-payment or partial payment loans	Personal installment loans (generally permitted by state-chartered savings associations) Home improvement loans Education loans Savings account loans Second mortgages
Lend to members only Make unsecured loans May require collateral or cosigner for loans over a specified amount May require payroll deductions to pay off loan May submit large loan applications to a committee of members for approval Offer a variety of repayment schedules	Lend on cash value of life insurance policy No date or penalty on repayment Deduct amount owed from the value of policy benefit if death or other maturity occurs before repayment	Will lend to all creditworthy individuals Often require collateral Loan rates vary, depending on size of loan, length of payment, and security involved

Lower than some lenders because they
  Take fewer credit risks
  Lend money deposited by members, which is less expensive than borrowed money
  Often receive free office space and supplies from the sponsoring organization
  Are managed by members whose services, in most cases, are donated
  Enjoy federal income tax exemptions
	Lower than some lenders because they
	  Take no risk
	  Pay no collection costs
	  Secure loans by cash value of policy
		Lower than some lenders because they
		  Lend depositors' money, which is a relatively inexpensive source of funds
		  Secure most loans by savings accounts or real estate

Design repayment schedules to fit the borrower's income Generally provide credit life insurance without extra charge May offer financial counseling Handle credit transactions confidentially	Permit repayment at any time Handle credit transactions confidentially	Often offer financial counseling Specialize in mortgages and other housing-related loans Handle credit transactions confidentially

SOURCE: *Managing Your Credit* (Prospect Heights, Ill.: Money Management Institute, Household Financial Services, 1988), pp. 18–19. © Household Financial Services, Prospect Heights, Illinois.

Borrowing from car dealers, appliance stores, department stores, and other retailers is also relatively expensive. The interest rates charged by retailers are usually similar to those charged by finance companies, frequently 20 percent or more.

Banks lend funds not only through installment loans but also through cash advances on MasterCard or VISA cards. More than 107 million Americans carry bank credit cards. In 1989, the average interest rate on bank credit cards was 18.28 percent and the average annual fee was $16.97.

There is, however, one type of loan from finance companies that is currently less expensive than most other credit. Loans of this kind, which can often be obtained at a rate under 10 percent, are available from the finance companies of major automakers—General Motors Acceptance Corporation, Ford Motor Credit Corporation, and others. But a car dealer that offers you such a rate may be less willing to discount the price of the car or to throw in free options.

Exhibit 7–1 summarizes the major sources of consumer credit—commercial banks, consumer finance companies, credit unions, life insurance companies, and savings and loan associations.

Today, borrowing and credit are more complex than ever. As more and more types of financial institutions offer financial services, your choices of what and where to borrow grow wider. Shopping for credit is just as important as shopping for an automobile, furniture, or major appliances.

COST OF CREDIT

L.O.2
Determine the cost of credit by calculating interest with various interest formulas.

Which is the less expensive choice—a three-year, $6,000 loan at 14 percent APR with a monthly payment of $205.07 or a four-year, $6,000 loan at 14 percent APR with a monthly payment of $163.96?

The **Truth in Lending law** of 1969 was a landmark piece of legislation. For the first time, creditors were required to state the cost of borrowing as a dollar amount so that you, and Sue Wallace in the opening case, would know exactly what the credit charges were and thus could compare credit costs and shop for credit.

If you are thinking of borrowing money or opening a credit account, your first step should be to figure out how much it will cost you and whether you can afford it. Then you should shop for the best terms. As you learned in the opening case, two key concepts that you should keep in mind are the finance charge and the annual percentage rate.

The Finance Charge and the Annual Percentage Rate (APR)

Credit costs vary. By remembering the finance charge and the APR, you can compare credit prices from different sources. Under the Truth in Lending law, the creditor must inform you, in writing and before you sign any agreement, of the finance charge and the APR.

The **finance charge** is the total dollar amount you pay to use credit. It includes interest costs and sometimes other costs, such as service charges, credit-related insurance premiums, or appraisal fees.

For example, borrowing $100 for a year might cost you $10 in interest. If there were also a service charge of $1, the finance charge would be $11. The **annual percentage rate (APR)** is the percentage cost (or relative cost) of credit on a yearly basis. The APR is your key to comparing costs, regardless of the amount of credit or how much time you have to repay it.

Suppose you borrow $100 for one year and pay a finance charge of $10. If you can keep the entire $100 for the whole year and then pay it all back at once, you are paying an APR of 10 percent:

Amount Borrowed	Month Number	Payment Made	Loan Balance
$100	1	0	$100
	2	0	100
	3	0	100
	.	.	.
	.	.	.
	.	.	.
	.	.	.
	12	100	0
		(plus $10 interest)	

On the average, you had a full use of $100 throughout the year. To calculate the average use, add the loan balance during the first and last month, then divide by 2.

$$\text{Average balance} = \frac{\$100 + \$100}{2} = \$100$$

But if you repay the $100 and the finance charge (a total of $110) in 12 equal monthly payments, you don't get the use of the $100 for the whole year. In fact, as shown below, you get the use of less and less of that $100 each month. In this case, the $10 charge for credit amounts to an APR of 18.5 percent.

Amount Borrowed	Month Number	Payment Made	Loan Balance
$100	1	0	$100.00
	2	8.33	91.67
	3	8.33	83.34
	4	8.33	75.01
	5	8.33	66.68
	6	8.33	58.35
	7	8.33	50.02
	8	8.33	41.69
	9	8.33	33.36
	10	8.33	25.03
	11	8.33	16.70
	12	8.33	8.37

Note that you are paying 10 percent interest even though you had the use of only $91.67 during the second month, not $100. During the last month, you owed only $8.37 (and had the use of $8.37), but the $10 interest is for the entire $100. As calculated in the previous example, the average use of the money during the year is $100 + $8.37 divided by 2, or $54.18.

The accompanying "Financial Planning Calculations" feature shows how the APR can be calculated.

FINANCIAL PLANNING CALCULATIONS

The Arithmetic of the Annual Percentage Rate (APR)

There are two ways to calculate the APR—an APR formula and the APR tables. The APR tables are more precise than the formula. The formula, given below, only approximates the APR:

$$r = \frac{2 \times n \times I}{P(N + 1)}$$

where

- r = Approximate APR
- n = Number of payment periods in one year (12, if payments are monthly; 52, if weekly)
- I = Total dollar cost of credit
- P = Principal, or net amount of loan
- N = Total number of payments scheduled to pay off the loan

Let us compare the APR when the $100 loan is paid off in one lump sum at the end of the year and when the same loan is paid off in 12 equal monthly payments. The stated annual interest rate is 10 percent for both loans.

Using the formula, the APR for the lump sum loan is

$$r = \frac{2 \times 1 \times \$10}{\$100(1 + 1)} = \frac{\$20}{\$100(2)} = \frac{\$20}{\$200} = 0.10, \text{ or 10 percent}$$

Using the formula, the APR for the monthly payment loan is

$$r = \frac{2 \times 12 \times \$10}{\$100(12 + 1)} = \frac{\$240}{\$100(13)} = \frac{\$240}{\$1,300}$$
$$= 0.1846, \text{ or 18.46 percent (rounded to 18.5 percent)}$$

Pepper . . . and Salt

"May I have $125,000 Dad?—I have a chance to buy into a clinic.

From *The Wall Street Journal*, with permission of Cartoon Features Syndicate.

All creditors—banks, stores, car dealers, credit card companies, finance companies—must state the cost of their credit in terms of the finance charge and the APR. The law says that you must be shown these two pieces of information before you sign a credit contract. The law does not set interest rates or other credit charges, but it does require their disclosure so that you can compare credit costs and tackle the trade-offs.

Tackling the Trade-Offs[1]

When you choose your financing, there are trade-offs between the features you prefer (term, size of payments, fixed or variable interest, or payment plan) and the cost of your loan. Here are some of the major trade-offs you should consider.

Term versus Interest Costs   Many people choose longer-term financing because they want smaller monthly payments. But, as Sue Wallace in the opening case learned, the longer the term for a loan at a given interest rate, the greater the amount that must be paid in interest charges. Consider the following analysis of the relationship between the term and interest costs.

A Comparison   Even when you understand the terms a creditor is offering, it's easy to underestimate the difference in dollars that different terms can make. Suppose you're buying a $7,500 car. You put $2,500 down, and you need to borrow $6,000. Compare the three credit arrangements below.

	APR	Length of Loan	Monthly Payment	Total Finance Charge	Total Cost
Creditor A	14%	3 years	$ 205.07	$1,382.52	**$7,382.52**
Creditor B	14	4 years	**163.96**	1,870.08	7,870.08
Creditor C	**15**	4 years	166.98	2,015.04	8,015.04

How do these choices compare? The answer depends partly on what you need. The lowest-cost loan is available from Creditor A. If you are looking for lower monthly payments, you could repay the loan over a longer period of time. However, you would have to pay more in total costs. A loan from Creditor B—also at a 14 percent APR, but for four years—will add about $488 to your finance charge.

If that four-year loan were available only from Creditor C, the APR of 15 percent would add another $145 to your finance charges. Other terms—such as the size of the down payment—will also make a difference. Be sure to look at all the terms before you make your choice.

Lender Risk versus Interest Rate   You may prefer financing that requires fixed payments or only a minimum of up-front cash. But both of these requirements can increase your cost of borrowing because they create more risk for your lender.

If you want to minimize your borrowing costs, you may need to accept conditions that reduce your lender's risk. Here are a few possibilities:

Variable Interest Rate. With this type of loan, you share the interest rate risks with the lender. Therefore, the lender may offer you a lower initial interest rate than it would offer with a fixed rate loan.

A Secured Loan. If you pledge property or other assets as collateral, you'll probably receive a lower interest rate on your loan.

Up-Front Cash. Many lenders feel that you have a higher stake in repaying a loan if you pay cash for a large portion of what you are financing. Doing so may give you a better chance of getting the other terms you want. Of course, by making a large down payment, you forgo interest that you might have earned in a savings account.

A Shorter Term. As you have learned, the shorter the period of time for which you borrow, the less the chance that something will prevent you from repaying and the less the risk to the lender. Therefore, you may be able to borrow at a lower interest rate if you accept a shorter-term loan.

In the next section, you will see how the above-mentioned trade-offs can affect the cost of closed-end and open-end credit.

Calculating the Cost of Credit

The two most common methods of calculating interest are compound and simple interest formulas; perhaps the most basic method is the simple interest calculation. Simple interest on the declining balance, add-on interest, bank discount, and compound interest are variations of simple interest.

Simple Interest   **Simple interest** is the interest computed on principal only and without compounding; it is the dollar cost of borrowing money. This cost is based on three elements: the amount borrowed, which is called the principal; the rate of interest; and the amount of time for which the principal is borrowed.

The following formula may be used to find simple interest:

Interest = Principal × Rate of interest × Time
  or I = P × r × T

Example 1   Suppose you have persuaded your relative to lend you $1,000 to purchase a lap-top computer. Your relative agreed to charge only 5 percent interest, and you agreed to repay the loan at the end of one year. Using the simple interest formula, the interest will be 5 percent of $1,000 for one year, or $50, since you have the use of $1,000 for the entire year.

I = $1,000 × 0.05 × 1
  = $50

Using the APR formula discussed earlier,

$$\text{APR} = \frac{2 \times n \times I}{P(N + 1)} = \frac{2 \times 1 \times \$50}{\$1,000(1 + 1)} = \frac{\$100}{\$2,000} = 0.05, \text{ or 5 percent}$$

Note that the stated rate, 5 percent, is also the annual percentage rate.

Simple Interest on the Declining Balance   When more than one payment is made on a simple interest loan, the method of computing interest is known as the **declining balance method.** Since you pay interest only on the amount of the original principal that has not yet been repaid, the more frequent the payments, the smaller the interest paid will be. Of course, the amount of credit you have at your disposal is also smaller.

Example 2   Using simple interest on the declining balance to compute interest charges, the interest on a 5 percent, $1,000 loan repaid in two payments—one at the end of the first half year and another at the end of the second half year—would be $37.50, as follows.

First payment:

$$I = P \times r \times T$$

$$= \$1,000 \times 0.05 \times \frac{1}{2}$$

$$= \$25 \text{ interest plus } \$500, \text{ or } \$525$$

Second payment:

$$I = P \times r \times T$$

$$= \$500 \times 0.05 \times \frac{1}{2}$$

$$= \$12.50 \text{ interest plus the remaining balance of } \$500, \text{ or } \$512.50$$

Total payment on the loan:

$$\$525 + \$512.50 = \$1,037.50$$

Using the APR formula,

$$APR = \frac{2 \times n \times I}{P(N + 1)} = \frac{2 \times 2 \times \$37.50}{\$1,000(2 + 1)} = \frac{\$150}{\$3,000} = 0.05, \text{ or 5 percent}$$

Note that under simple interest on the declining balance method, the stated rate, 5 percent, is also the annual percentage rate. The add-on interest, bank discount, and compound interest calculation methods differ from the simple interest method as to when, how, and on what balance interest is paid. For these methods, the real annual rate, or the annual percentage rate, differs from the stated rate.

Add-On Interest   When the **add-on interest method** is used, interest is calculated on the full amount of the original principal. The interest amount is immediately added to the original principal, and payments are determined by dividing principal plus interest by the number of payments to be made. When only one payment is required, this method produces the same APR as the simple interest method. However, when two or more payments are to be made, use of the add-on method results in an effective rate of interest that is greater than the stated rate.

Example 3   Consider, again, the two-payment loan in Example 2. Using the add-on method, interest of $50 (5 percent of $1,000 for one year) is added to the $1,000 borrowed, giving $1,050 to be repaid—half (or $525) at the end of the first half year and the other half at the end of the second half year.

Even though your relative's stated interest rate is 5 percent, the real interest rate is

$$APR = \frac{2 \times n \times I}{P(N + 1)} = \frac{2 \times 2 \times \$50}{\$1,000(2 + 1)} = \frac{\$200}{\$3,000} = 0.066, \text{ or 6.6 percent}$$

Note that using the add-on interest method means that no matter how many payments are to be made, the interest will always be $50. As the number of payments increases, you have use of less and less credit over the year. For example, if four quarterly payments of $262.50 are made, you have use of $1,000 during the first quarter, around $750 during the second quarter, around $500 during the third quarter, and around $250 during the fourth and final quarter. Therefore, as the number of payments increases, the true interest rate, or APR, also increases.

Various other methods of determining the cost of credit, such as the bank discount method, the compound interest formula, amortization, and the use of tables, are presented in the end-of-chapter appendix.

Cost of Open-End Credit   As discussed earlier, open-end credit includes credit cards, department store charge plates, and check overdraft accounts that allow you to write checks for more than your actual balance. Open-end credit can be used again and again, until you reach a prearranged borrowing limit. The Truth in Lending law requires that open-end creditors let you know how the finance charge and the APR will affect your costs.

First, they must tell you how they calculate the finance charge. Creditors use various systems to calculate the balance on which they assess finance charges. Some creditors add finance charges after subtracting payments made during the billing period; this is called the **adjusted balance method.** Other creditors give you no credit for payments made during the billing period; this is called the **previous balance method.** Under the third method, the **average daily balance method,** creditors add your balances for each day in the billing period and then divide by the number of days in the period.

Here is a sample of the three billing methods:

	Adjusted Balance	Previous Balance	Average Daily Balance
Monthly interest rate	1½%	1½%	1½%
Previous balance	$400	$400	$400
Payments	$300	$300	$300 (payment on 15th day)
Interest charge	**$1.50** ($100 × 1.5%)	**$6.00** ($400 × 1.5%)	**$3.75** (average balance of $250 × 1.5%)

As the example shows, the finance charge varies for the same pattern of purchases and payments.

Second, creditors must tell you when finance charges on your credit account begin, so that you know how much time you have to pay your bills before a finance charge is added. Some creditors, for example, give you 30 days to pay your balance in full before imposing a finance charge.

The Truth in Lending law does not set the rates or tell the creditor how to make interest calculations. It only requires that the creditor tell you the method that will be used. You should ask for an explanation of any terms you don't understand.

Cost of Credit and Expected Inflation   As you have seen, interest rates specify when you must pay future dollars to receive current dollars. Borrowers and lenders, however, are less concerned about dollars, present or future, than about the goods and services those dollars can buy—their purchasing power.

Inflation erodes the purchasing power of money. Each percentage point increase in inflation means a decrease of approximately 1 percent in the quantity of goods and services that can be purchased with a given quantity of dollars. As a result, lenders, seeking to protect their purchasing power, add the expected rate of inflation to the interest rate they charge. You are willing to pay this higher rate because you expect inflation to enable you to repay the loan with cheaper dollars.

If a lender expects, for example, a 4 percent inflation rate for the coming year and desires an 8 percent return on its loan, it would probably charge you a 12 percent nominal or stated rate (a 4 percent inflation premium plus an 8 percent "real" rate).

Return to Example 1, in which you borrowed $1,000 from your relative at the bargain rate of 5 percent for one year. If, during that year, the inflation rate was 4 percent, your relative's real rate of return was only 1 percent (5 percent stated interest minus 4 percent inflation rate) and your "real" cost was not $50 but only $10 ($50 minus $40 inflation premium).

Cost of Credit and Tax Considerations   Before the Tax Reform Act of 1986, all of the interest you paid on consumer credit reduced your taxable income. The new law did not affect the deductibility of home mortgage interest, but beginning in 1991 you can no longer deduct interest paid on consumer loans.

When you borrow from a bank or another lender, you usually arrange to repay the loan with interest by a specific date in a number of installments. But after several payments, you may decide to repay the entire loan at an earlier date than the one originally scheduled. How is interest calculated if you repay the loan early?

When the Repayment Is Early: The Rule of 78's

Creditors use tables based on a mathematical formula called the **rule of 78's,** or sometimes "the sum of the digits," to determine how much interest you have paid at any point in a loan. This formula dictates that you pay more interest at the beginning of a loan, when you have the use of more of the money, and that you pay less and less interest as the debt is reduced. Because all of the payments are the same in size, the part going to pay back the amount borrowed increases as the part representing interest decreases.

The laws of several states authorize the use of the rule of 78's as a means of calculating finance charge rebates when you pay off a loan early. The Truth in Lending law requires that your creditor disclose whether or not you are entitled to a rebate of the finance charge if the loan is paid off early.

Read the accompanying feature to learn how to use the rule of 78's.

Credit Insurance

Credit insurance ensures the repayment of your loan in the event of death, disability, or loss of property. The lender is named the beneficiary and directly receives any payments made on submitted claims.

There are three types of credit insurance: credit life, credit accident and health, and credit property. The most commonly purchased type of credit insurance is credit life insurance, which provides for the repayment of the loan if the borrower dies.

Credit accident and health insurance, also called credit disability insurance, repays your loan in the event of a loss of income due to illness or injury. Credit property insurance provides coverage for personal property purchased with a loan. It may also insure collateral property, such as a car or furniture.

FINANCIAL PLANNING CALCULATIONS
The Rule of 78's

How to Use the Rule of 78's

The first step is to add up all the digits for the number of payments scheduled. For a 12-installment loan, add the numbers 1 through 12:

$1 + 2 + 3 + 4 + 5 + 6 + 7 + 8 + 9 + 10 + 11 + 12 = 78$

The answer—"the sum of the digits"—explains how the rule was named. One might say that the total interest is divided into 78 parts for payment over the term of the loan.

In the first month, before making any payments, the borrower has the use of the whole amount borrowed and therefore pays 12/78 of the total interest in the first payment; in the second month, he still has the use of 11 parts of the loan and pays 11/78 of the interest; in the third, 10/78; and so on down to the final installment, 1/78.

Adding all the numbers in a series of payments is rather tedious. One can arrive at the answer quickly by using this formula:

$$\frac{N}{2} \times (N + 1)$$

is the number of payments. In a 12-month loan, it looks like this:

$$\frac{12}{2} \times (12 + 1) = 6 \times 13 = 78$$

A Loan for Ann and Dan

Let us suppose that Ann and Dan Adams borrow $3,000 from the Second Street National Bank to redecorate their home. Interest comes to $225, and the total of $3,225 is to be paid in 15 equal installments of $215.

Using the rule of 78's, we can determine how much of each installment represents interest. We add all the numbers from 1 through 15:

$$\frac{15}{2} \times (15 + 1) = 7.5 \times 16 = 120$$

The first payment will include 15 parts of the total interest, or 15/120; the second, 14/120; and so on.

Notice in the following table that the interest decreases with each payment and that the repayment of the amount borrowed increases with each payment.

Payment No.	Interest	Reduction of Debt	Total Payment
1	$ 28.13	$ 186.87	$ 215.00
2	26.25	188.75	215.00
3	24.37	190.63	215.00
4	22.50	192.50	215.00
5	20.63	194.37	215.00
6	18.75	196.25	215.00
7	16.87	198.13	215.00
8	15.00	200.00	215.00
9	13.13	201.87	215.00
10	11.25	203.75	215.00
11	9.37	205.63	215.00
12	7.50	207.50	215.00
13	5.63	209.37	215.00
14	3.75	211.25	215.00
15	1.87	213.13	215.00
	$225.00	$3,000.00	$3,225.00

How Much Is the Rebate?

Now let's assume that Ann and Dan want to pay off the loan with the fifth payment. We know that the total interest is divided into 120 parts. To find out how many parts will be rebated, we add up the numbers for the remaining 10 installments, which will be prepaid:

$$\frac{10}{2} \times (10 + 1) = 5 \times 11 = 55$$

Now we know that 55/120 of the interest will be deducted as a rebate; it amounts to $103.12.

$$\frac{55}{120} \times \$225 = \frac{\$12,375}{120}$$
$$= \$103.12$$

We see that Ann and Dan do not save two thirds of the interest (which would be $150) by paying off the loan in one third of the scheduled time. But the earlier they repay the loan, the higher the portion of interest they do save. The rule of 78's favors lenders.

SOURCE: *The Rule of 78's* (Philadelphia: Federal Reserve Bank of Philadelphia, May 1989).

MANAGING YOUR DEBTS

L.O.3
Develop a plan to manage your debts.

A sudden illness or the loss of your job may make it impossible for you to pay your bills on time. If you find that you cannot make your payments, contact your creditors at once and try to work out a modified payment plan with them. If you have paid your bills promptly in the past, they may be willing to work with you. Do not wait until your account is turned over to a debt collector. At that point, the creditor has given up on you.

Automobile loans present special problems. Most automobile financing agreements permit your creditor to repossess your car anytime you are in default on your payments. No advance notice is required. If your car is repossessed, you may have to pay the full balance due on the loan, as well as towing and storage costs, to get it back. If you cannot do this, the creditor may sell the car. Try to solve the problem with your creditor when you realize that you will not be able to meet your payments. It may be better to sell the car yourself and pay off your debt than to incur the added costs of repossession.

If you are having trouble paying your bills, you may be tempted to turn to a company that claims to offer assistance in solving debt problems. Such companies may offer debt consolidation loans, debt counseling, or debt reorganization plans that are guaranteed to stop creditors' collection efforts. Before signing with such a company, investigate it. Be sure you understand what services the company provides and what they will cost you. Do not rely on oral promises that do not appear in your contract. Also, check with the Better Business Bureau and your state or local consumer protection office. They may be able to tell you whether other consumers have registered complaints about the company.

A constant worry for a debtor who is behind in payments is the fear of debt collection agencies. However, as you will see in the next section, a federal agency protects certain legal rights that you possess in your dealings with such agencies.

Debt Collection Practices

The Federal Trade Commission enforces the **Fair Debt Collection Practices Act (FDCPA),** which prohibits certain practices by agencies that collect debts for creditors. The act does not apply to creditors that collect debts themselves. While the act does not erase the legitimate debts that consumers owe, it does regulate the ways in which debt collection agencies do business.

Exhibit 7–2 summarizes the steps you may take if a debt collector calls.

Consumer Credit Counseling

Bill Kenney is a vigorous, healthy man in his early 30s. He has a steady job with an annual income of $30,000 a year. Bill, his wife, and their two children enjoy a comfortable life; a new car is parked in the driveway of their home, a home furnished with such modern conveniences as a new microwave oven, a new freezer, an electric washer and dryer, a videocassette recorder, and a large-screen color television set.

However, Bill Kenney is in debt. He is drowning in a sea of bills; most of his income is tied up in repaying debts. Foreclosure proceedings on his home have been instituted, while several stores have court orders to repossess practically every major appliance in it. His current car payment is overdue, and three charge accounts at local stores are several months delinquent.

This case is neither exaggerated nor isolated. Unfortunately, a large number of people are in the same floundering state. The problem of these people is immaturity. Mature consumers have certain information; they demonstrate

EXHIBIT 7–2   What if a Debt Collector Calls?

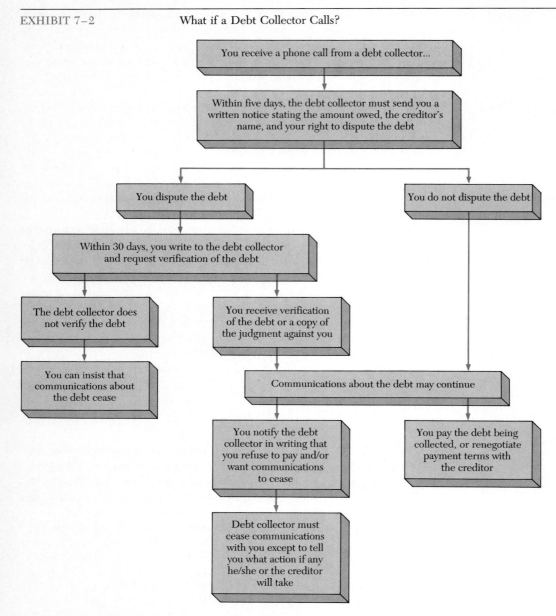

SOURCE: Reprinted, courtesy of Office of Public Information, Federal Reserve Bank of Minneapolis, Minneapolis, MN 55480.

self-discipline, control of impulses, and sound judgment; they accept responsibility for money management; and they are able to postpone and govern expenditures when overextension of credit appears likely. As shown in Exhibit 7–3, overextension of credit is the second most common reason why consumers are unable to pay their bills on time.

Referring to overindebtedness as the nation's number one family financial problem, a nationally noted columnist on consumer affairs lists the following as frequent reasons for indebtedness:[2]

EXHIBIT 7–3
Why Consumers Don't Pay

Reason for Default	Primary or Contributing Cause of Default (percent of cases)	
Loss of income		48
Unemployment	24	
Illness	16	
Other	8	
Overextension		25
Defective goods or services or other perceived consumer fraud		20
Fraudulent use of credit		4
Other		3

SOURCE: Reprinted, courtesy of Office of Public Information, Federal Reserve Bank of Minneapolis, Minneapolis, MN 55480.

1. *Emotional problems,* such as the need for instant gratification, as in the case of a man who can't resist buying some costly sports equipment, or of a woman who lets herself be talked into an expensive purchase by a door-to-door salesperson.
2. *The use of money to punish,* as in the case of a husband who buys a new car without consulting his wife, who in turn makes an expensive purchase to get even.
3. *The expectation of instant comfort* among young couples who assume that they can have immediately, by use of the installment plan, the possessions that their parents acquired after years of work.
4. *Keeping up with the Joneses,* which is more apparent than ever, not only among families with more money but among limited-income families too.
5. *Expensive indulgence of children,* often because of both parents' emotional needs, but also sometimes because the two parents are in competition with each other or lack adequate communication with each other (they buy independently).
6. *Misunderstanding or lack of communication among family members.* For example, a salesperson selling an expensive freezer visited a Memphis family. Although the freezer was beyond the means of this already over-indebted family, and too large for its needs anyway, the husband thought that his wife wanted it. Not until later, in an interview with a counselor, did the wife relate her concern when she signed the contract; she had wanted her husband to say no.
7. *The amount of the finance charges,* which can push a family over the edge of ability to pay, especially when it borrows from one company to pay another and these charges pyramid.

Exhibit 7–4 lists the 10 danger signals of potential debt problems.

The Serious Effects of Debt

If the causes of indebtedness vary, so too do a mixture of other personal and family problems that frequently occur with the overextension of credit.

EXHIBIT 7–4

The 10 Danger Signals of
Potential Debt Problems

1.   Paying only the minimum balance each month on credit card bills
2.   Increasing the total balance due each month on credit accounts
3.   Missing payments, paying late, or paying some bills this month and others next month
4.   Intentionally using the overdraft or automatic loan features on checking accounts or taking frequent cash advances on credit cards
5.   Using savings to pay normal bills such as groceries or utilities
6.   Receiving second or third notices from creditors
7.   Not talking to your spouse about money, or . . . talking only about money
8.   Depending on overtime, moonlighting, or bonuses to meet normal expenses
9.   Using up your savings
10. Borrowing money to pay old debts

If your household is experiencing more than three of these warning signals, it's time to examine your budget for ways to reduce expenses.

SOURCE: *Advice for Consumers Who Use Credit* (Silver Springs, MD.: Consumer Credit Counseling Service of Maryland, Inc., n.p., n.d.).

Loss of a job because of garnishment proceedings may occur in a family that has a disproportionate amount of its income tied up in debts. Another possibility is that such a family may be forced to neglect vital areas. In the frantic effort to rob Peter to pay Paul, family skimping may seriously affect diet, the educational needs of children, and the protection of the family's health. Excessive indebtedness may also result in heavy drinking, a neglect of children, marital difficulties, and drug abuse. But help is available to those debtors who seek it.

CONSUMER CREDIT COUNSELING SERVICES

L.O.4
Evaluate various private and governmental sources that assist consumers with debt problems.

A **Consumer Credit Counseling Service (CCCS)** is a local, nonprofit organization affiliated with the National Foundation for Consumer Credit. It provides debt counseling services for families and individuals with serious financial problems. It is not a charity, a lending institution, or a governmental or legal institution. It is supported by contributions from banks, consumer finance companies, credit unions, merchants, and other community-minded firms and individuals.

What a CCCS Does

Credit counselors are aware that most people who are in debt over their heads are basically honest people who want to clear up their indebtedness. Too often, the problems of such people arise from a lack of planning or a miscalculation of what they earn. Therefore, the CCCS is just as concerned with preventing the problems as with solving them. As a result, its activities are divided into two parts:

1.   Aiding families with serious debt problems by helping such families manage their money better and by setting up a realistic budget and plan for expenditures.
2.   Helping prevent debt problems by teaching the necessity of family budget planning, providing education to people of all ages regarding the pitfalls of unwise credit buying, suggesting techniques for family budgeting, and encouraging credit institutions to provide full information about the

costs and terms of credit and to withhold credit from those who cannot afford to repay it.

How a CCCS Works

Anyone overburdened by credit obligations can phone, write, or visit a CCCS office. There are over 200 CCCS offices all over the nation. The CCCS requires that an application for credit counseling be completed, and then an appointment is arranged for a personal interview with the applicant.

CCCS counseling is usually free. However, when the CCCS administers a debt repayment plan, it sometimes charges a nominal fee to help defray administrative costs.

In addition to the counseling services of the CCCS, nonprofit counseling services are sometimes provided by universities, military bases, credit unions, and state and federal housing authorities. These organizations are likely to charge little or nothing for such assistance. You can also check with your local bank or consumer protection office to see whether it has a listing of reputable, low-cost financial counseling services.

But what if the debtor is suffering from an extreme case of financial woes? Is there any relief? The answer is yes—bankruptcy proceedings.

DECLARING PERSONAL BANKRUPTCY

L.O.5
Assess the choices in declaring personal bankruptcy.

Unfortunately for some, bankruptcy has become an acceptable tool of credit management. During the last five years, the personal bankruptcy rate has increased 16 percent annually. Recently, roughly half a million people declared bankruptcy.[3]

Executives at VISA USA cite one big spender who took $350,000 in cash from 30 credit cards to the gaming tables of Las Vegas. A few throws of the dice later, he became another personal bankruptcy statistic. Another former VISA customer bought a Jaguar and then declared bankruptcy as a way to "stretch out the car payments," said Kenneth Crone, director of the bankruptcy recovery program at VISA.[4]

Debt burden, unemployment, divorce rates, and household net worth are all indicators of personal bankruptcies. However, the Bankruptcy Recovery Act of 1978, which made personal bankruptcy easier, is also considered an important cause of the increase in personal bankruptcies (see Exhibit 7–5).

The U.S. Bankruptcy Act of 1978: The Last Resort

If your situation is hopeless, you have two choices in declaring personal bankruptcy: Chapter 7 and Chapter 13 bankruptcy.

Chapter 7 Bankruptcy   In **Chapter 7 bankruptcy,** a debtor is required to draw up a petition listing his or her assets and liabilities. The debtor submits the petition to a U.S. district court and pays a filing fee. A person filing for relief under the bankruptcy code is called a debtor; the term *bankrupt* is not used.

"The purpose of bankruptcy under Chapter 7 is to grant to the honest debtor who is overwhelmed by his debts a chance to make a fresh start in life and remain a useful member of society by relieving him of the oppressive burden of his debts."[5]

The discharge of debts in Chapter 7 does not affect alimony, child support, certain taxes, fines, certain debts arising from educational loans, or debts that you fail to disclose properly to the bankruptcy court. At the request of a creditor, the bankruptcy judge may also exclude from the discharge debts resulting from loans

EXHIBIT 7–5

Increase in Personal
Bankruptcies (per 1,000
Persons) since Enactment
of U.S.Bankruptcy Act
of 1978.

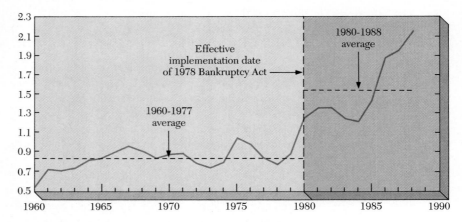

SOURCE: Division of Bankruptcy, Administrative Office of the U.S. Courts, Washington, D.C.

you received by giving the lender a false financial statement. Furthermore, debts arising from fraud, embezzlement, drunken driving, larceny, or certain other willful or malicious acts may also be excluded.

Chapter 13 Bankruptcy   In a **Chapter 13 bankruptcy,** a debtor with a regular income proposes to a bankruptcy court a plan for extinguishing his or her debts from future earnings or other property over a period of time. In such a bankruptcy, you normally, keep all or most of your property.

During the period that the plan is in effect, which can be as long as five years, you make regular payments to a Chapter 13 trustee. The trustee, in turn, distributes the money to your creditors. Under certain circumstances, the bankruptcy court may approve a plan permitting you to keep all of your property even though you repay less than the full amount of your debts. Certain debts not dischargeable in Chapter 7, such as those based on fraud, may be discharged in Chapter 13 if you successfully complete your plan. To file a Chapter 13 bankruptcy, you must have regular income and not more than $100,000 in unsecured debts or $350,000 in secured debts.

Effect of Bankruptcy on Your Job and Your Future Credit

Different people have different experiences in obtaining credit after they file a bankruptcy case. Some find obtaining credit more difficult. Others find obtaining credit easier because they have relieved themselves of their prior debts or because creditors know that they cannot file another bankruptcy case for a period of time. Obtaining credit may be easier for people who file a Chapter 13 bankruptcy and repay some of their debts than for people who file a Chapter 7 bankruptcy and make no effort to repay their debts. The bankruptcy law prohibits your employer from discharging you simply because you have filed a bankruptcy case.

Should a Lawyer Represent You in a Bankruptcy Case?

You have the right to file your own bankruptcy case and to represent yourself at all court hearings. In any bankruptcy case, however, you must complete and file with a bankruptcy court several detailed forms concerning your property, debts, and financial condition. Many people find it easier to complete these forms with the assistance of experienced bankruptcy counsel. In addition, you may discover, especially if you own a substantial amount of property or if your creditors object to the discharge of your debts, that your case will develop complications. Then you will require the advice and assistance of a lawyer.

What Are the Costs?   The monetary costs to the debtor under Chapter 13 include the following:

1.   *Court Costs.* A $60 filing fee must be paid to the clerk of the court at the time the debtor's petition is filed. The filing fee may be paid in up to four installments if authorization is granted by the court.
2.   *Attorney's Fees.* These fees are usually the largest single item of cost. Often the attorney does not require them to be paid in advance at the time of filing but agrees to be paid in installments after receipt of a down payment.
3.   *Trustee's Fees and Costs.* The trustee's fees are established by the bankruptcy judge in most districts and by a U.S. trustee in certain other districts.

Although it is possible to reduce these costs by purchasing the legal forms in a local stationery store and completing them yourself, an attorney is strongly recommended.

There are also psychological costs. For example, obtaining credit in the future may be difficult since bankruptcy reports are retained in credit bureaus for 10 years. Therefore, the extreme step of declaring personal bankruptcy should be taken only when no other options for solving financial problems exist.

SUMMARY

L.O.1
Analyze the major sources of consumer credit.

The major sources of consumer credit are commercial banks, savings and loan associations, credit unions, finance companies, life insurance companies, and family and friends. Each of these sources has unique advantages and disadvantages.

L.O.2
Determine the cost of credit by calculating interest with various interest formulas.

L.O.3
Develop a plan to manage your debt.

Compare the finance charge and the annual percentage rate as you shop for credit. Under the Truth in Lending law, creditors are required to state the cost of borrowing so that you can compare credit costs and shop for credit.

The Fair Debt Collection Practices Act prohibits certain practices by debt collection agencies. Debt has serious effects if a proper plan for managing it is not implemented.

L.O.4
Evaluate various private and governmental sources that assist consumers with debt problems.

If you cannot meet your obligations, contact your creditors immediately. Before signing up with a debt consolidation company, investigate it thoroughly. Better yet, contact your local Consumer Credit Counseling Service.

L.O.5
Assess the choices in declaring personal bankruptcy.

A debtor's last resort is to declare bankruptcy, permitted by the U.S. Bankruptcy Act of 1978. Consider the financial and psychological costs of bankruptcy before taking this extreme step.

KEY FORMULAS

A Reference Guide

Page	Topic	Formula
196	Calculating annual percentage rate (APR)	$\text{APR} = \dfrac{2 \times \text{Number of payment periods in one year} \times \text{Dollar cost of credit}}{\text{Loan amount (Total number of payments to pay off the loan} + 1)}$ $= \dfrac{2 \times n \times I}{P(N + 1)}$
198	Calculating simple interest	$\text{Interest (in dollars)} = \text{Principal borrowed} \times \text{Interest rate} \times \text{Length of loan in years}$ $I = P \times r \times T$
215	Calculating compound interest	$\text{Total future value of a loan} = \text{Principal} (1 + \text{Rate of interest})^{\text{Time in years}}$ $F = P(1 + r)^T$
217	Calculating total monthly payment (principal + interest) on a conventional loan	$\text{Monthly payment} = \dfrac{\text{Loan} \times \text{Monthly interest rate} \times (1 + \text{Monthly interest rate})^{\text{Time in months}}}{(1 + \text{Monthly interest rate})^{\text{Time in months}} - 1}$ $MP = P \times \dfrac{i \times (1 + i)^T}{(1 + i)^T - 1}$
202	Rule of 78's	$\dfrac{\text{Number of Payments}}{2} \times (\text{Number of payments} + 1)$ $\dfrac{N}{2} \times (N + 1)$ Example: In a 12-month loan, $\dfrac{12}{2} \times (12 + 1) = 6(13) = 78$

GLOSSARY

Add-on interest method   A method of computing interest in which interest is calculated on the full amount of the original principal.

Adjusted balance method   The assessment of finance charges after payments made during the billing period have been subtracted.

Annual percentage rate (APR)   The percentage cost (or relative cost) of credit on a yearly basis. The APR yields a true rate of interest for comparisons with other sources of credit.

Average daily balance method   A method of computing finance charges that uses a weighted average of the account balance throughout the current billing period.

Chapter 7 bankruptcy   Grants the honest debtor a chance to make a fresh start in life by relieving him or her of the oppressive burden of debts.

Chapter 13 bankruptcy   A voluntary plan that a debtor with regular income develops and proposes to a bankruptcy court.

Consumer Credit Counseling Service (CCCS)   A local, nonprofit organization that provides debt counseling services for families and individuals with serious financial problems.

Credit insurance   Any type of insurance that ensures repayment of a loan in the event that the borrower is unable to repay it.

Declining balance method   A method of computing interest when more than one payment is made on a simple interest loan.

Fair Debt Collection Practices Act (FDCPA)   A federal law, enacted in 1978, that regulates debt collection activities.

Finance charge   The total dollar amount paid to use credit.

Previous balance method   A method of computing finance charges that gives no credit for payments made during the billing period.

Rule of 78's   A mathematical formula to determine how much interest has been paid at any point in a loan.

Simple interest   Interest computed on the principal only and without compounding.

Truth in Lending law   A federal law that requires that the annual percentage rate (APR) and the finance charge be disclosed as a dollar amount.

DISCUSSION QUESTIONS

L.O.1   1. What questions should you ask yourself before deciding whether to borrow money?

L.O.1   2. What are your trade-offs and opportunity costs if you pay cash or use credit for a purchase?

L.O.2   3. How does the Truth in Lending law help you when you shop for credit?

L.O.2   4. When you choose financing, what are the trade-offs between the features you prefer (term, size of payments, fixed or variable interest, or payment plan) and the cost of your loan?

L.O.2   5. How are the simple interest, simple interest on the declining balance, and add-on interest formulas used in determining the cost of credit?

L.O.3   6. How would you handle your debts if a sudden illness or the loss of your job makes it impossible for you to pay your bills on time?

L.O.3   7. What is the Fair Debt Collection Practices Act, and how does it help you if a debt collector is after you?

L.O.4   8. What is a Consumer Credit Counseling Service (CCCS)? How does a CCCS help consumers who are in debt?

L.O.5   9. What factors would you consider in assessing the choices in declaring personal bankruptcy?

L.O.5   10. Why should personal bankruptcy be the choice of last resort?

Opening Case Questions

1. Estimate Sue Wallace's opportunity cost of paying $2,000 from her savings to finance her car.

2. Do you agree with Sue's decision to pay $2,000 cash and borrow $6,000? Explain.
3. What other options were available to Sue in financing her car?
4. If you had been in Sue's situation, what actions different from hers would you have taken?

PROBLEMS AND ACTIVITIES

L.O.1   1. Survey friends and relatives to find out how they determine the need for credit.

L.O.1   2. Prepare a list of sources of inexpensive loans, medium-priced loans, and expensive loans in your area. What are the trade-offs in obtaining a loan from an "easy" lender?

L.O.2   3. Dorothy Zwayer lacks cash to pay for a $600 dishwasher. She could buy it from the store on credit by making 12 monthly payments of $52.74 each. The total cost would then be $632.88. Instead, Dorothy decides to deposit $50 a month in the bank until she has saved enough money to pay cash for the dishwasher. One year later, she has saved $642 — $600 in deposits plus interest. When she goes back to the store, she finds that the dishwasher now costs $660. Its price has gone up 10 percent—the current rate of inflation. Was postponing her purchase a good trade-off for Dorothy?

L.O.2   4. You have been pricing a compact disc player in several stores. Three stores have the exact same price of $300. Each of these stores charges 18 percent APR, has a 30-day free ride, and sends out bills on the first of the month. On further investigation, you find that Store A calculates the finance charge by using the average daily balance method, that Store B uses the adjusted balance method, and that Store C uses the previous balance method. Assume that you purchased the disc player on May 5 and that you made a $100 payment on June 15. What will the finance charge be if you made your purchase from Store A? from Store B? from Store C?

L.O.2   5. What is the interest cost and the total amount due on a six-month loan of $1,500 at 13.2 percent simple annual interest?

L.O.2   6. Return to the example of Ann and Dan discussed in "Financial Planning Calculations: The Rule of 78's." Assume that Ann and Dan pay off their loan with the 11th payment. How much interest will they save? Remember that the interest over 15 months is divided into 120 parts and that you need to know how many payments will be prepaid. Fill in the blanks:

$$\frac{N}{2} \times (N + 1) = \frac{}{2} \times (\underline{\quad} + 1) = \underline{\quad} \times \underline{\quad} = \underline{\quad}.$$

Now multiply the rebate fraction by the total amount of interest on the loan: $\underline{\quad} \times \underline{\quad} = \$\underline{\quad}$ rebate.

L.O.3   7. Your friend is drowning in a sea of overdue bills and is being harassed by a debt collection agency. Prepare a list of the steps that he or she should take if the harassment continues.

L.O.4   8. Visit a local office of the Consumer Credit Counseling Service. What assistance can debtors obtain from this office? What is the cost of this assistance, if any?

L.O.4   9. Prepare a list of counseling organizations other than the Consumer Credit Counseling Service that assist debtors in distress.

L.O.5   10. Create a list of reasons why people declare personal bankruptcy. What are the financial and psychological opportunity costs of choosing a bankruptcy option?

LIFE SITUATION   Case 7–1

Richard's Automobile Loan

After visiting several automobile dealerships, Richard Welch selects the car he wants. He likes its $10,000 price, but financing through the dealer is no bargain. He has $2,000 cash for a down payment, so he needs an $8,000 loan. In shopping at several banks for an installment loan, he learns that interest on most automobile loans is quoted at add-on rates. That is, during the life of the loan, interest is paid on the full amount borrowed even though a portion of the principal has been paid back. Richard borrows $8,000 for a period of four years at an add-on interest rate of 11 percent.

Questions

1. What is the total interest on Richard's loan?
2. What is the total cost of the car?
3. What is the monthly payment?
4. What is the annual percentage rate (APR)?

LIFE SITUATION   Case 7–2

Shirley's Predicament

Shirley Watson wishes to buy a freezer that now costs $600. Since the current inflation rate is 5 percent, she expects the freezer to cost $630 if she postpones the purchase for a year. If she buys it now, she estimates that it would save her $150 in food costs during the next year. It would enable her to purchase food at special sales and in larger quantities and to preserve vegetables from her garden. However, operating the freezer would increase her electricity bill. Shirley can use one of the following options in purchasing the freezer:

Option 1   Buy the freezer now, using $600 she has in a savings account that earns interest at an annual rate of 6 percent.

Option 2   Buy the freezer now, using credit at an annual rate of 10 percent. She would make 12 monthly payments of $52.50 each.

Option 3   Postpone the purchase until she saves an additional $600. Her savings earn interest at an annual rate of 6 percent.

Questions

1. What trade-offs should Shirley consider in deciding whether to buy the freezer now or later?
2. If Shirley wants to buy the freezer now, what trade-offs should she consider in deciding whether to use credit or pay cash from her savings?

SUPPLEMENTARY READINGS

For Additional Information on Sources of Consumer Credit

Choosing and Using Credit Cards. Washington, D.C.: Federal Trade Commission, December 1988.

Managing Your Credit. Prospects Heights, Ill.: Money Management Institute, Household Financial Services, 1988.

Understanding Credit. Rockville, Md.: National Education Association Special Services, September 1988.

Using Plastic: A Young Adult's Guide to Credit Cards. Washington, D.C.: Federal Trade Commission, 1989.

For Additional Information on Calculating Interest on Loans

ABCs of Figuring Interest. Chicago: Federal Reserve Bank of Chicago, December 1986.

Ledesma, Rodolfo G. *How to Use Credit Wisely.* Great Barrington, Mass.: American Institute for Economic Research, April 1989.

Paying a Loan Off Early. Philadelphia: Federal Reserve Bank of Philadelphia, May 1989.

For Additional Information on Consumer Credit Protection

Some General Information Concerning Chapter 7 of the Bankruptcy Code. Washington, D.C.: Division of Bankruptcy, Administrative Office of the U.S. Courts, n.d.

Truth in Lending: What It Means for Consumer Credit. Philadelphia: Federal Reserve Bank of Philadelphia, n.d.

Your Credit Rating. Philadelphia: Federal Reserve Bank of Philadelphia, July 1989.

APPENDIX   Other Methods of Determining the Cost of Credit

Bank Discount Method   When the *bank discount rate* method is used, interest is calculated on the amount to be paid back and you receive the difference between the amount to be paid back and the interest amount. That is, your relative lends you $1,000 less $50 (interest at 5 percent), or $950.

Example 1   Using the APR formula, you find that the true interest rate, or the annual percentage rate, is 5.263 percent, not the stated 5 percent.

$$APR = \frac{2 \times n \times I}{P(N + 1)} = \frac{2 \times 1 \times \$50}{\$950(1 + 1)} = \frac{\$100}{\$1,900} = 0.05263, \text{ or } 5.263 \text{ percent.}$$

Compound Interest   Unlike simple interest, *compound interest* is the interest paid on the original principal *plus* the accumulated interest. With interest compounding, the greater the number of periods for which interest is calculated, the more rapidly the amount of interest on interest and interest on principal builds.

Annually compounding means that there is only *one* period annually for the calculation of interest. With such compounding, interest charges on a *one-year* loan are identical whether they are figured on a simple interest basis or on an annual compound basis. However, a new interest formula, based on the simple interest formula, must be used if there is annual compounding for two or more years or if there is compounding with more than one compound period per year.

Compound Formula   A compact formula that describes compound interest calculations is

$$F = P(1 + r)^T$$

where

F = Total future repayment value of a loan (principal *plus* total accumulated or compound interest)
P = Principal
r = Rate of interest per year, or annual interest rate
T = Time in years

Before the compound interest formula can be used for *multiple*-period compounding, two important adjustments must be made.

First, adjust the *annual* interest rate (r) to reflect the number of compound periods per year. For example, a 5 percent annual rate of interest, compounded half-yearly, works out to 2.5 percent (5 percent divided by 2) per half year.

Second, adjust the time factor (T), which is measured in years, to reflect the *total* number of compound periods. For example, your loan for one year compounded half-yearly works out to two compound periods (1 year multiplied by 2 compound periods per year) over the length of the loan.

Example 2   Suppose that your relative compounds interest semiannually and that you make two payments, six months apart. Using the compound interest formula, here is the annual percentage rate:

$$
\begin{aligned}
F &= P(1 + r)^T \\
&= \$1,000(1 + 0.05)^{1 \times 2} \\
&= \$1,000(1 + 0.025)^2 \\
&= \$1,000(1.050625) \\
&= \$1,050.625
\end{aligned}
$$

That is, you are paying $50.63 in interest for a one-year $1,000 loan. Now, using the APR formula, you find that the APR is 6.75 percent.

$$\begin{aligned}
\text{APR} &= \frac{2 \times n \times I}{P(N + 1)} \\
&= \frac{2 \times 2 \times \$50.63}{\$1,000(2 + 1)} \\
&= \frac{\$202.52}{\$3,000} \\
&= 0.0675, \text{ or } 6.75 \text{ percent}
\end{aligned}$$

If your relative chose to compound interest daily (365 compound periods per year), the solution to this problem would be quite complicated. A calculator or a compound interest table can help make interest calculations more manageable. See Appendix B for compound interest tables.

The following table summarizes the effects on the APR when the interest on a one-year, $1,000 loan is calculated using the simple interest, declining balance, add-on interest, bank discount, and compound interest methods.

Method	Amount Borrowed	Stated Interest	Total Interest	Number of Payments	APR
°Simple interest	$1,000	5%	$50	1	5 %
°Declining balance	1,000	5	37.50	2	5
°Add-on	1,000	5	50	2	6.6
Bank discount	1,000(−50)	5	50	1	5.26
Compound interest	1,000	5	50.63	2	6.75

°Discussed in the chapter.

The methods of calculating interest described here are just some of the more common methods in use. As you have seen, the method of interest calculation can substantially affect the amount of interest paid, and you should be aware not only of the stated or nominal interest rates but also of how the stated rates are used in calculating total interest charges. Furthermore, the simple interest and bank discount methods assume that you have the full use of the principal over the length of the loan. Rather than making periodic payments, you are obligated to repay the loan in one or two lump sums. Most borrowers, however, are unable to repay loans, especially home loans (mortgages) and auto loans, in one or two lump-sum payments. They must make equal periodic payments to pay off a loan and interest over the length of the loan. This concept is known as amortization.

Amortization   *Amortization* is the process of gradually reducing a debt through scheduled periodic payments. For example, if a five-year auto loan is repaid in 60 equal monthly payments, each of these payments is applied to reduce the principal and pay interest on the total amount borrowed. Over the initial years of the loan, most of the monthly payment is used to pay interest; the rest reduces the principal. As the loan approaches maturity, more of the monthly payment is used to pay off the principal than to pay interest.

The following formula can be used to calculate the monthly payment (principal and interest) on an installment loan or a conventional mortgage loan:

$$\frac{\text{Monthly}}{\text{payment}} = \frac{\text{Loan} = \text{Monthly interest rate} \times (1 + \text{Monthly interest rate})^{T \times 12}}{(1 + \text{Monthly interest rate})^{T \times 12} - 1}$$

Because a monthly mortgage payment is required, both the annual interest rate and the total length of the loan must be adjusted by 12 (months).

Example 3   On a 30-year mortgage loan for $60,000 at a 12 percent annual interest rate, what is the monthly payment (MP)? Substitute the numbers into the formula:

$$MP = \$60,000 \times \frac{\dfrac{0.12}{12} \times 1 + \dfrac{0.12^{30 \times 12}}{12}}{1 + \dfrac{0.12^{30 \times 12}}{12} - 1}$$

$$= \$60,000 \times \frac{(0.01) \times (1 + 0.01)^{360}}{(1 + 0.01)^{360} - 1}$$

$$= \$60,000 \times \frac{(0.01) \times (35.9496)}{(35.9496) - 1}$$

$$= \$60,000 \times \frac{0.359496}{34.9496}$$

$$= \$60,000 \times 0.010286$$

$$= \$617.17$$

Use of Tables   Finding the monthly payment on a mortgage or consumer installment loan may become rather complicated when the problem must be solved manually. Fortunately, the use of tables can ease the task. Notice how easily the problem in Example 3 is solved by using the table on the following page.

Just find the P&I constant for 12 percent and a 30-year term, which is 10.29 for a $1,000 loan. Since the loan in Example 3 is for $60,000, multiply 10.29 by 60. The result, $617.40, is fairly close to the $617.17 found by using the formula.

Example 4   What is the total finance charge on a 30-year, $60,000 loan at a 10.5 percent annual interest rate?

Using the table, you find that the constant for a 10.5 percent, $1,000 loan with a 30-year term is 9.15. Since the loan is for $60,000, multiply the constant by 60 ($1,000 × 60). The result is a $549 monthly payment, which includes principal and interest.

For a 30-year loan, you must make 360 monthly payments of $549, totaling $197,640. Since you borrowed $60,000 but repaid $197,640, the difference must be the finance charge, which amounts to $137,640! Surprised?

You will come to a similar conclusion if you use the monthly payment formula presented in Example 3.

P & I Constants per $1,000 of Loan Amount

Interest Rate	15 Years	20 Years	25 Years	30 Years	Interest Rate	15 Years	20 Years	25 Years	30 Years
6.00%	8.44	7.16	6.44	6.00	10.62%	11.13	10.07	9.53	9.24
6.12	8.51	7.24	6.52	6.08	10.75	11.21	10.15	9.62	9.33
6.25	8.57	7.31	6.60	6.16	10.87	11.29	10.24	9.71	9.43
6.37	8.64	7.38	6.67	6.24	11.00	11.37	10.32	9.80	9.52
6.50	8.71	7.46	6.75	6.32	11.12	11.44	10.41	9.89	9.62
6.62	8.78	7.53	6.83	6.40	11.25	11.52	10.49	9.98	9.71
6.75	8.85	7.60	6.91	6.49	11.37	11.60	10.58	10.07	9.81
6.87	8.92	7.68	6.99	6.57	11.50	11.68	10.66	10.16	9.90
7.00	8.99	7.75	7.07	6.65	11.62	11.76	10.75	10.26	10.00
7.12	9.06	7.83	7.15	6.74	11.75	11.84	10.84	10.35	10.09
7.25	9.13	7.90	7.23	6.82	11.87	11.92	10.92	10.44	10.19
7.37	9.20	7.98	7.31	6.91	**12.00**	12.00	11.01	10.53	**10.29**
7.50	9.27	8.06	7.39	6.99	12.12	12.08	11.10	10.62	10.38
7.62	9.34	8.13	7.47	7.08	12.25	12.16	11.19	10.72	10.48
7.75	9.41	8.21	7.55	7.16	12.37	12.24	11.27	10.81	10.58
7.87	9.48	8.29	7.64	7.25	12.50	12.33	11.36	10.90	10.67
8.00	9.56	8.36	7.72	7.34	12.62	12.41	11.45	11.00	10.77
8.12	9.63	8.44	7.80	7.42	12.75	12.49	11.54	11.09	10.87
8.25	9.70	8.52	7.88	7.51	12.87	12.57	11.63	11.18	10.96
8.37	9.77	8.60	7.97	7.60	13.00	12.65	11.72	11.28	11.06
8.50	9.85	8.68	8.05	7.69	13.12	12.73	11.80	11.37	11.16
8.62	9.92	8.76	8.14	7.78	13.25	12.82	11.89	11.47	11.26
8.75	9.99	8.84	8.22	7.87	13.37	12.90	11.98	11.56	11.36
8.87	10.07	8.92	8.31	7.96	13.50	12.98	12.07	11.66	11.45
9.00	10.14	9.00	8.39	8.05	13.62	13.07	12.16	11.75	11.55
9.12	10.22	9.08	8.48	8.14	13.75	13.15	12.25	11.85	11.65
9.25	10.29	9.16	8.56	8.23	13.87	13.23	12.34	11.94	11.75
9.37	10.37	9.24	8.65	8.32	14.00	13.32	12.44	12.04	11.85
9.50	10.44	9.32	8.74	8.41	14.12	13.40	12.53	12.13	11.95
9.62	10.52	9.40	8.82	8.50	14.25	13.49	12.62	12.23	12.05
9.75	10.59	9.49	8.91	8.59	14.37	13.57	12.71	12.33	12.15
9.87	10.67	9.57	9.00	8.68	14.50	13.66	12.80	12.42	12.25
10.00	10.75	9.65	9.09	8.78	14.62	13.74	12.89	12.52	12.35
10.12	10.82	9.73	9.18	8.87	14.75	13.83	12.98	12.61	12.44
10.25	10.90	9.82	9.26	8.96	14.87	13.91	13.08	12.71	12.54
10.37	10.98	9.90	9.35	9.05	15.00	14.00	13.17	12.81	12.64
10.50	11.05	9.98	9.44	9.15					

COMPREHENSIVE CASE FOR PART II

Confusion in the Financial Services Marketplace

Chuck Ellis recently spent a lot of time reading advertisements for financial services in the business section of the newspaper. Among them were the following:

"Reduce Your Taxes with a Tax-Deferred Savings Account"

"Our Electronic Banking System Gives You a Personal Banker 24 Hours a Day"

"Auto Loans at 6.9% (some restrictions apply)"

"Fast, Easy Loans for Any Purpose (amount based on the value of your home)"

"Free Checking Account and No Charge for a Safe-Deposit Box with Convenience Savings ($5,000 minimum balance required)"

After seeing these and many other ads, Chuck complained to his friend Beverly, "I thought gathering information was supposed to make financial planning easier, but I'm just more confused!"

"What's the big deal?" asked Beverly, "Just put some money in a savings account each month, and get a checking account at the bank near work." This was how Beverly handled her financial activities.

"But it seems that some savings accounts pay more interest than others and that not all checking accounts charge the same fees," said Chuck. "In fact, some checking accounts can earn you money instead of costing you money."

"The fees and extra interest are really not worth the time and effort you're giving to them," said Beverly. "Besides, my bank has several 24-hour electronic teller machines that make the fees worth it."

"Well, you obviously have your ideas on this matter and I have mine," said Chuck. "Personally, I think a little bit of effort can result in some wise financial choices."

"Come on, let's get something to eat," suggested Beverly. "And I'll buy," she added.

"Now that's the best financial deal of the day," said Chuck.

When Beverly paid for the meal with a bank credit card, Chuck commented, "I thought you said you could get cash at any time from your bank's electronic teller machines?"

"Well," sighed Beverly, "you have to have money in the account to withdraw cash."

"Maybe a person's money management habits and financial planning are affected by the way he or she chooses financial services," said Chuck as he picked up a newspaper to look at the ads placed by various financial institutions.

"OK," said Beverly, "maybe I could make better choices of financial services."

Questions

1. How do Chuck's and Beverly's viewpoints with regard to selecting and using financial services reflect the importance of various opportunity costs? Is one viewpoint necessarily better than the other? Explain your answer.

2. How can a person's use of financial services influence his or her success in financial planning?

3. How helpful were the financial services ads that Chuck read? What additional information would he need to effectively evaluate these services?

4. How important should the amount of interest be as a consideration in selecting a savings plan or a financial institution?

5. What considerations should influence a person's selection of the place and type of his or her checking account?

6. Using one institution for all of your financial services can be convenient. Describe a situation in which it would be better to use more than one financial institution.

III

Making Your Purchasing Decisions

Part III of *Personal Finance* considers the spending phase of financial planning. First, in Chapter 8, we discuss the costs and benefits associated with daily buying decisions. The process used in making such decisions suggests a research procedure that can be adapted to any purchasing situation. In Chapter 8, we also describe effective buying strategies and actions that can be used to resolve consumer complaints. In Chapter 9, we offer a comprehensive presentation of housing alternatives and costs. The selection of a place to live is examined from the perspective of your needs, financial resources, and life situation. The renting, buying, and building options are carefully analyzed. Affordability and housing costs are emphasized in an effort to take both short-term personal satisfaction and long-term financial security into account. Finally, in Chapter 10, we provide a framework for assessing transportation needs and costs. In addition, we present practical suggestions for buying a used car, selecting and financing a new car, and maintaining your car. Part III consists of

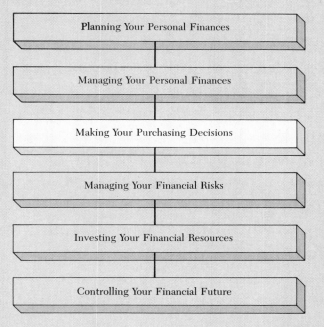

8

Consumer Purchasing Strategies and Legal Protection

Every person involved with personal financial planning is also a consumer. Regardless of our age, income, or household situation, each day we all use a variety of goods and services. Our daily buying decisions require a trade-off between current spending and saving for the future. Various purchasing techniques can assist us in getting the most for our money. Wise buying decisions can contribute to both our current personal satisfaction and our long-term financial security.

LEARNING OBJECTIVES

After studying this chapter, you will be able to

L.O.1   Analyze the financial implications of consumer purchasing decisions.

L.O.2   Evaluate the alternatives in consumer purchasing decisions.

L.O.3   Implement strategies for effective purchasing.

L.O.4   Identify areas of potential consumer dissatisfaction.

L.O.5   Evaluate the legal alternatives available to consumers.

. .

OPENING CASE

Buyer Beware

Each month, John and Tina Harper had difficulty in making ends meet. They had three children, and their housing, food, and other living expenses were constantly increasing. One day at work, a friend told John about a food-buying plan that would help the Harpers save money. For a monthly payment of $165, all the food they needed would be delivered and they would also qualify for a new refrigerator. Since the Harpers viewed this plan as a way to save money and since they also needed a new refrigerator, they signed up for the plan.

After making two payments, the Harpers were notified by the company with which they had signed up that delivery of their refrigerator had been delayed due to production problems. Meanwhile, they had received less food than they needed, so they still had to spend money for groceries.

Two months later, the refrigerator still hadn't arrived and the Harpers were paying more for food than they had

paid before they joined the plan. Two weeks later, the Harpers stopped receiving food from the company. "Well, I guess we won't have to make any more payments," commented John, "since we aren't receiving any of the services we were paying for." He attempted to notify the company of his intention to stop making payments, but its phone had been disconnected and its office was empty. He sighed, saying, "Now our food expenses can return to the amount they were before we got involved in this deal."

But the Harpers' problems weren't over. A few months later, a collection agency notified them that they still owed $495 for several months of service. The contract they had signed obligated them to pay for a minimum of eight months.

Such consumer problems occur frequently. People get involved in expensive situations that they could have avoided if they had known all the facts when they were making their purchasing choices.

. .

FINANCIAL IMPLICATIONS OF CONSUMER DECISIONS

L.O.1
Analyze the financial implications of consumer purchasing decisions.

Your daily buying habits are affected by a wide variety of factors that can be grouped into three major categories: economic, social, and personal (see top section of Exhibit 8–1). These factors are the basis for the spending, saving, and investing that lead to the achievement of personal financial goals. In very simple terms, the only way you can have long-term financial security is by not spending all of your current income. In addition, as shown in Exhibit 8–1 (bottom section), overspending leads to misuse of credit and financial difficulties.

Overspending patterns may arise from various personal and social factors. Overspenders include the following character types:

- *Depression spenders*—shop as a method of obtaining an emotional boost.
- *Me-too buyers*—use credit cards to purchase items that they cannot afford, because friends have these items.
- *"I gotta have it" buyers*—purchase every new item on the market, and are heavy users of home shopping television networks.
- *Cashless buyers*—use credit cards for *every* purchase.
- *Credit card collectors*—try to impress others by having every credit card on the market.[1]

Overspending patterns frequently result from the absence of a systematic decision process for making purchases.

Throughout your life, you have made buying decisions that reflect a wide range of factors. As discussed throughout this book, the opportunity costs of such decisions should be considered in order to maximize the satisfaction obtained from available financial resources. Commonly overlooked trade-offs of buying decisions include:

EXHIBIT 8–1   Consumer Buying Influences and Their Financial Implications

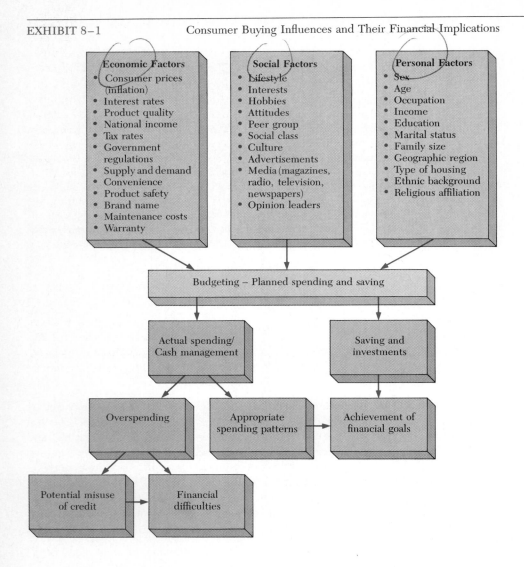

- Paying a higher price over time when purchasing items on credit that may be required now.
- Buying less expensive unknown brands that may be of poor quality.
- Selecting less expensive brands that may present difficulties when trying to obtain service or repairs.
- Ordering by mail that saves time and money but may make it harder to return, replace, or repair purchases.
- Taking time and effort to comparison-shop so as to save money and obtain better after-sale service, if that's what you want.

Your buying decisions reflect many aspects of your personality, life situation, values, and goals. Combine this with the complexity of the marketplace, and you have a situation that requires some analysis when you make purchases.

CONSUMER PURCHASING: A RESEARCH-BASED APPROACH

L.O.2
Evaluate the alternatives in consumer purchasing decisions.

While many factors affect your purchasing habits, your actual shopping decisions are based on a specific decision-making process. Exhibit 8–2 presents an overview of the steps that could be taken to ensure effective purchasing. This consumer buying process will be most valuable with large purchases, such as appliances, sports equipment, home improvements, or vacations. When you buy such items, you should take the time and effort needed to get the most for your money. However, you probably make many routine purchases of low-cost items—food, clothing, and the like—without thinking about them, and often this may be exactly what you should do. Following all of the steps in the consumer buying process for such items may not be the best use of your time. But taking time to evaluate all of your purchases can improve the satisfaction you receive from each dollar you spend.

Preshopping Activities

In the first phase of the research-based consumer purchasing approach, you define your needs while obtaining relevant information. These activities are the foundation for buying decisions that help achieve your personal goals.

Problem Identification   Objective decision making with regard to purchases must start without a planned course of action. Some people always buy the same brand when another brand at a lower price may serve their needs as well or when another brand at the same price may provide better quality. A narrow view of the problem is a weakness in problem identification. You may think that the problem is the need to get a car when the real problem is the need for transportation.

EXHIBIT 8–2
A Research-Based Approach to Consumer Purchases

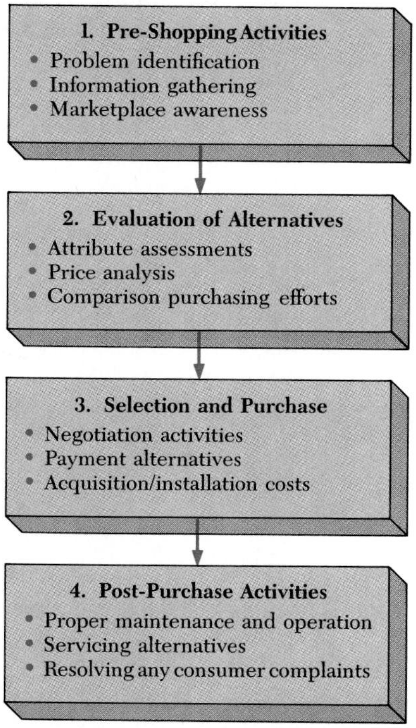

1. Pre-Shopping Activities
- Problem identification
- Information gathering
- Marketplace awareness

2. Evaluation of Alternatives
- Attribute assessments
- Price analysis
- Comparison purchasing efforts

3. Selection and Purchase
- Negotiation activities
- Payment alternatives
- Acquisition/installation costs

4. Post-Purchase Activities
- Proper maintenance and operation
- Servicing alternatives
- Resolving any consumer complaints

Information Gathering   Information is power. The better informed you are, the more likely you are to make the purchasing choice that best serves your interest. Knowing the least expensive place to buy an item or being aware of the ingredients of a food product can enhance your financial and physical well-being.

Some people spend very little, if any, time on gathering and evaluating information relevant to their purchases. At the other extreme are people who spend more time and effort than necessary on obtaining consumer information. While information is necessary for wise purchasing, too much information can create confusion and frustration.

The best course of action lies somewhere between these two extremes. Many of your simple, routine purchases may not require any information other than experience, but your large, expensive buying should involve some information gathering.

The main sources of information available to consumers are personal contacts, business organizations, media stories and reports, independent testing organizations, and government agencies. The information received from each of these sources should be evaluated for reliability, completeness, relevance, and objectivity.

1. Personal Contacts   Besides gaining knowledge from every purchase you make, you can learn from the buying experiences of the people with whom you associate. The information that they can give you on product performance, brand quality, and prices provides a valuable foundation for the information gathering phase of the buying process.

2. Business Organizations   Advertising is the most common type of consumer information. Each day, you are exposed to several hundred ads that appear along the road, in publications, at stores, and on television and radio. Exhibit 8–3 lists common techniques used in advertising to influence consumers. Advertising that

EXHIBIT 8–3	Common Advertising Techniques
Product quality ads	Demonstrate a product Present scientific evidence Emphasize quality, brand, price, or other characteristic
Comparative ads	Direct presentation of competitive brands
Endorsement ads (or testimonials)	May involve one of the following: (a) Plain folks, average consumers expressing their support of the product or service (b) Corporate representative or character—a company executive or an animated person or animal (c) Famous person or company spokesperson—someone with high visibility, usually an entertainment or sports personality
Humorous ads	Use comedy to draw attention to a product or to stimulate sales
Lifestyle ads	Present the product or service in a common situation to which potential customers can relate—people at work, at home, or in recreational settings
Emotional ads	Obtain the attention and response of consumers by appealing to their feelings and desires—fear, guilt, sex, love, pleasure, convenience, safety, economy, beauty, popularity, power, security, and status

provides information about product price, quality, and availability can be helpful. But many ads appeal to emotions and provide little assistance when purchases are made.

Other information sources provided by business organizations are the product label and the package. Like advertising, a product label can contain helpful information, such as information on content, weight, and price, as well as features that are designed only to stimulate sales.

3. Media Information　　Among the most valuable, easily available, and least expensive consumer information sources are data from television, radio, newspapers, and magazines. Besides offering advertisements, these communication systems provide purchasing advice and general consumer information. Many magazines and newspapers present regular columns and special articles on such topics as wise spending, budgeting, and insurance. Special topic magazines can also be helpful when you are buying such products as automobiles, boats, cameras, stereos, video recorders, or sports equipment.

4. Independent Testing Organizations　　For over 50 years, Consumers Union has been providing information about the quality of products and services. Each month, *Consumer Reports* magazine presents test results on items ranging from automobiles, vacuum cleaners, and personal computers to hand soap, orange juice, and hot dogs. As our economy has become more service oriented, Consumers Union has increased its coverage of such subjects as apartment renting, health care, insurance, investments, legal services, tax preparers, and banking.

Underwriters Laboratories (UL) is a business-sponsored organization that tests products for electrical and fire safety. Items that pass its tests can display the UL symbol. This emblem provides consumers with an assurance that the product has met rigorous safety standards.

5. Government Agencies　　Local, state, and federal government funds are used to provide publications and other information services for consumers. Beyond providing printed information, government agencies work to inform consumers through toll-free telephone numbers and displays at shopping centers, county fairs, and libraries. Appendix D details government sources on various consumer purchasing topics.

Marketplace Awareness　　Expanded awareness of the buying environment results from your preshopping research efforts. This includes an awareness of

- Store and mail-order sources of the item you desire.
- Available brands and features.
- Pricing techniques for the item.
- The most reliable sources of information.

Based on these marketplace factors, you can create and evaluate a list of product attributes in the second phase of the research-based consumer purchasing approach.

Evaluation of Alternatives

Every purchasing situation is likely to have several acceptable alternatives. These alternatives are based on various questions that you might ask yourself. Is it possible to delay the purchase or to do without the item? Will you pay for the item with cash, or will you buy it on credit? Which brands should you consider? How do the price, quality, and service compare at different stores? Is it possible to rent the item instead of buying it? Considering such alternatives will result in more effective purchasing decisions.

Attribute Assessments   Each alternative needs to be evaluated on the basis of such factors as personal values and goals, available time and money, the costs of each alternative, the benefits of each alternative, and your specific needs with regard to product size, quality, quantity, and features. Exhibit 8–4 is an example of a consumer buying matrix that may be used to evaluate alternatives. In this exhibit, a person is considering the purchase of one of three brands of personal computers based on features, performance, style, and warranty. Each computer is rated for each attribute, and the rating number is multiplied by the weight

---

EXHIBIT 8–4   Consumer Buying Matrix

Item __PERSONAL COMPUTER__

Information Sources/Comments __Consumer Magazine/ Brand C slow compared to others tested__
__Friend / Brand B performs well__

Attribute	Weight	Brand A Price $1,150 Rating (1-10)	Weighted Score	Brand B $1,029 Rating (1-10)	Weighted Score	Brand C $899 Rating (1-10)	Weighted Score
Features	.3	6	1.8	8	2.4	10	3
Performance	.4	9	3.6	7	2.8	5	2
Style	.1	8	.8	8	.8	7	.7
Warranty	.2	9	1.8	6	1.2	4	.8
■ Totals	1.0		8.0		7.2		6.5

assigned to that attribute. This process results in an objective assessment of several purchase alternatives.

This type of buying matrix can be used for different products or services at different stores. You should consider various attributes, such as location, price, and services provided. The result obtained with the buying matrix may not be the computer you select. Factors related to the place of purchase and shopping procedures should also be considered.

As you research various consumer purchases, you will need to identify the attributes important to you. Helpful sources for this task are friends who own the product, salespeople, and periodicals such as *Consumer Reports* or specialized magazines covering computers, photography equipment, stereo systems, and so on. The specific attributes will vary depending on the product or service. When buying a cordless telephone, you might consider sound quality, ring loudness, number memory, and the range of use; you might assess a microwave oven on the basis of size, ease of operation, power settings, and exterior finish; and you are likely to select a provider of services on the basis of training, qualifications, experience, and reputation. As previously mentioned, independent testing organizations can assist you in evaluating the desirable attributes.

Price Analysis   Research studies have shown that price variations can occur for all types of products. For a single-lens reflex camera, prices may range from under $200 to well over $500. The price of aspirin may range from less than 50 cents to over $3 for 100 five-grain tablets. While there may be differences in the cameras,

---

PERSONAL FINANCE JOURNAL
Buying Services Is Different

You can actually see a microwave oven in action, and you can view recordings made by a camcorder. But how do you go about comparing and evaluating education, child care, home improvements, automobile repairs, or other services? With increasing incomes and expanded leisure time, our society is increasing the amount it spends on services. Many have estimated that in the future over 80 percent of our purchases will be for services. Renting furniture, leasing a car, traveling to a vacation resort, and buying computer time are becoming more common.

Buying services presents special problems. First, services are intangible, so it is difficult to assess their quality. Second, services must be performed before their actual quality can be judged. This limits comparison shopping. Finally, variations among sources of services can be great. For example, two home improvement firms charging the same price may provide very different end results.

Your primary decision in selecting a service concerns the type of business you choose. National firms usually provide fast service at a low cost. In contrast, local businesses may be more concerned with quality and customer satisfaction. Certain types of services, such as automobile repair shops and beauty parlors, require certification in some states. Investigate this aspect of the companies you plan to patronize.

When obtaining price information for expensive services, get written estimates of the costs, the work to be performed, the time it will take, and the terms of payment. Such estimates will help assure that you get what you are paying for. Also get information about the guarantee the company offers for customer satisfaction.

For services, the main indicator is the reputation of the business. The experiences of previous customers can help you in choosing service organizations.

the aspirin are the same in quantity and quality. Differences in quality (based on information from others and on your personal evaluation of product attributes) need to be assessed in relation to prices. When the quality and quantity are the same (as with the aspirin), the lowest price is likely to be the most valid choice except, perhaps, if the place of purchase is not convenient.

When the prices and quality are different (as in the buying matrix example), you have two alternatives. If all of the choices are within your available resources, you may purchase the item with the highest number of weighted "quality points." Or you may divide the price of each item by its quality points to determine which item gives you the best value per dollar spent.

Always be cautious of the common belief that "you get what you pay for." Many studies have revealed low relationships between price and quality, especially for expensive, highly technical products. To obtain the best value for your dollar, other comparison shopping activities are suggested.

Comparison Purchasing Efforts   Many people view comparison shopping as a large waste of time to save a few cents. While this may be true in certain situations, you can benefit from comparison shopping when

- Buying expensive or complex items.
- Buying items that you purchase often.
- Comparison shopping can be done easily (as with advertisements or several mail-order catalogs).
- Different sellers offer different prices and services, creating a competitive environment.
- Product quality or prices vary greatly.[2]

The next major section of this chapter provides additional details on comparison shopping techniques.

Selection and Purchase

If you've done your research and evaluations, the next phase should be easy. You are ready to make your purchase after a few last-minute activities and decisions.

When certain types of products are purchased, such as real estate or automobiles, negotiation of price is usually involved. Negotiation may also be used in other buying situations in an effort to obtain a lower price or additional features. Two vital factors in negotiation are (1) having all the necessary information about the product and buying situation and (2) dealing with a person who has the authority to give you a lower price or additional features, such as the owner or store manager.

The payment process should be considered in terms of the costs and benefits of using cash or credit. Paying cash gives you the benefit of not paying finance charges, but remember that you also have the opportunity costs of not earning interest on the amount paid and of not having the amount in savings for potential financial emergencies. Before using credit, also evaluate the various financial and opportunity costs based on

- Different places to borrow.
- Different types of credit accounts.

- Different down payment amounts.
- Different lengths of time to complete payments.

Decisions about using credit can be made in a more intelligent manner by reviewing the material in Chapters 6 and 7.

The final aspect of the purchase phase is getting all acquisition and installation costs in writing. Many bargains have disappeared due to the "add-on" costs of hookup charges, delivery fees, and the like. Know exactly what you are getting for the agreed purchase price.

Postpurchase Activities

Several postpurchase tasks are involved in most buying situations. Maintenance and ownership costs may be associated with the purchased item. Correct use can result in improved performance and fewer long-term repairs. When repairs not covered by a warranty are necessary, obtaining the repair service should follow a pattern similar to that followed in making the original purchase. Investigate, evaluate, and negotiate a variety of servicing options.

In some situations, you may not be satisfied with a purchase. A wide variety of grounds for complaint can occur. It is vital that you know these grounds and be able to cope with situations in which they exist. The final two sections of this chapter discuss the handling of consumer complaints and the legal alternatives available to consumers.

One final point about the purchasing process. Remember that it is an ongoing activity that continually requires reevaluation. You have to consider not only what you have learned from gathering information on products and services and from buying experiences but also changes in your values, goals, personal resources, and life situation. These changes will make every purchasing decision a new experience with different alternatives and different opportunity costs.

PRACTICAL PURCHASING STRATEGIES

L.O.3
Implement strategies for effective purchasing.

In using the purchasing approach discussed in the preceding section, six shopping techniques should be considered (see Exhibit 8–5).

Timing Your Purchases

Have you ever noticed that certain items are offered at lower than usual prices at the same time each year? Or that certain types of news can influence the prices of various goods and services? Bargains can be obtained by buying winter clothing in midwinter or late winter or by buying summer clothing in midsummer or late summer. Many people save by buying holiday items and other products at reduced prices in late December and early January, when retail sales are slow. These are just a few examples of the ways in which savings can be achieved by buying certain items at times of the year when retailers offer special promotions and reduced prices.

Weather reports and other news can also help you plan your purchasing strategies. Crop failure can quickly result in higher prices for certain food products. Changing economic conditions and political difficulties in foreign countries can result in higher prices and reduced supplies of products desired by American consumers. An awareness of such situations can help you buy while prices are relatively low.

EXHIBIT 8–5

A Framework for Practical
Purchasing Strategies

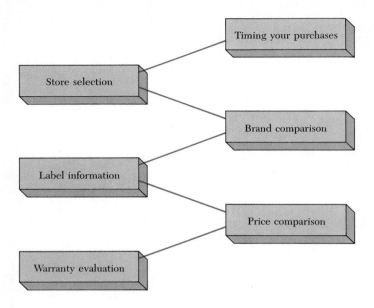

Store Selection

Your decision to shop at a particular store is probably influenced by the variety of its merchandise and the quality of its brands. Also important are the store's policies with regard to such matters as check cashing, exchanges, and frequency of sales. Most stores offer customers various services, including free parking and delivery, telephone and mail orders, and product advice. Finally, your selection of a store is affected by store hours, location, reputation, and the accessibility of shopping alternatives. Exhibit 8–6 provides an overview of the major types of retailers based on a breakdown into three groups: traditional stores, contemporary retailers, and nonstore shopping.

Because of social, economic, and technological influences, a variety of alternatives to store shopping have evolved. One alternative is the **cooperative,** a nonprofit organization created so that its member-owners can save money on certain products or services. As discussed in Chapter 5, a credit union is an example of a financial services cooperative. Food cooperatives, usually based in a community group or church, buy grocery items in large quantities. The money saved by these bulk purchases is passed on to the co-op's members in the form of lower food prices than they would pay at a supermarket. Although most food co-ops have a limited scope, some have thousands of members and have expanded their service to provide low-cost groceries to nonmembers. Cooperatives have also been organized to provide less expensive child care, recreational equipment, health care, cable television, and burial services.

Another nonstore shopping option is *buying clubs,* organizations that allow members to purchase brand name products at prices lower than those charged by retail stores. Since most buying clubs charge expensive initiation fees, you usually have to buy hundreds of dollars of merchandise to break even. For example, if you paid $500 to join a buying club and saved 25 percent on the items you purchased, you would have to spend $2,000 to cover the cost of membership.

EXHIBIT 8–6   Types of Retailers

	Benefits	**Limitations**
Traditional Stores		
Department stores	Wide variety of products grouped by department	Possible inexperience or limited knowledge of sales staff
Specialty stores	Wide selection of a specific product line; knowledgeable sales staff	Prices generally higher; location and shopping hours may not be convenient
Discount stores	Convenience of parking; low prices	Self-service format; minimum assistance from sales staff
Contemporary Retailers		
Convenience stores	Convenience of location; long hours; fast service	Prices generally higher than those of other types
Catalog showroom	Brand name items; discount prices	Limited services from sales staff; no delivery or installation
Factory outlet	Brand name items; low prices	May offer only "seconds" or "irregulars"; few services; returns may not be allowed
Hypermarket	Full supermarket combined with general merchandise discount store	Clerks not likely to offer specialized service or product information
Nonstore Shopping		
Cooperative	Nonprofit, member owned and operated, resulting in lower prices	Limited product line; few customer services; may sell only to members
Buying club	Brand name items available at low prices	Expensive membership fees; showroom locations may not be convenient
Direct selling (mail order, telephone sales, home demonstrations, cable television home shopping)	Convenience; saves time and, perhaps, money	Delays in delivery; companies may not give what they promise; difficult to return purchases and get refunds

Brand Comparison

Comparison shopping is the process of considering alternative stores, brands, and prices. In contrast, **impulse buying** is unplanned purchasing. While some impulse buying may be acceptable, too much can cause financial problems.

Since food and other products come in different brands, customers have a choice. Brand name products are highly advertised items that are available in many stores. You are probably familiar with such brands as Green Giant, Nabisco, Del Monte, Kellogg's, Kraft, Levi's, Sony, Kodak, and Tylenol. Brand name products are usually more expensive than nonbrand products but offer a consistency of quality for which many people are willing to pay.

Store brand products, sold by one chain of stores, are low-cost alternatives to famous name products. These products have labels that identify them with a specific chain, such as Safeway, Kroger, A&P, Osco, Walgreen's, and K mart. Since store brand products may be manufactured by the same companies that produce their brand name counterparts, they give consumers an opportunity to save money.

For many products, a third brand alternative is the plain package, nonbrand **generic item.** Introduced in the late 1970s, the generic alternatives for certain products provide customers with a low-cost choice. While, for some items, the generic equivalent may be lower in quality than the national and store brands, other items, such as plain aspirin, bleach, granulated sugar, and salt, are equal in quality to the national and store brands.

Label Information

Certain types of label information can be helpful for buying decisions, but other package data are nothing more than advertising. Federal law requires that a label on all food products contain information on the common name of the product, the name and address of the manufacturer or distributor, the net weight of the product, and a list of the ingredients in decreasing order of weight. Product labeling for appliances includes information on operating costs that can assist you in selecting the most energy-efficient models of refrigerators, washing machines, and air conditioners.

Open dating—information that tells consumers about the freshness or shelf life of a perishable product—is also found on labels. Open dating was originally used for bakery and dairy products, but it is now also used for many other kinds of foods. Such phrases as "Use before May 1992" or "Not to be sold after October 8" are found on most grocery items.

Price Comparison

Unit pricing uses a standard unit of measurement to compare the prices of packages of different sizes. An 8-ounce package of breakfast cereal selling for $1.52 would have a unit price of 19 cents per ounce, while an 11-ounce package selling for $1.98 would have a unit price of 18 cents per ounce. The package that has the lowest unit price may not be the best buy for you since it may contain more food than you will use before the food spoils. Some stores are using computerized visual displays that inform customers of current selling prices and unit costs.

Two common techniques that offer customers reduced prices are coupons and rebates. Each year, billions of coupons are distributed on packages and through newspapers, magazines, and the mail. These coupons are especially valuable if you already intend to buy the product. A **rebate** is a partial refund of the price of a product. This technique was originally used to promote sales of automobiles, but it is now used in selling clothing, home appliances, food products, and alcoholic beverages.

The following guidelines are helpful in comparing prices:

- The more convenience a store offers (location, hours, sales staff), the more likely it is that the store will charge higher prices.
- The more ready-to-use a product is (convenience foods, preassembled toys, furniture), the higher its price is likely to be.
- The largest package is usually the best buy. Be sure to use unit pricing to compare packages of different sizes, different brands, and different stores.
- A "sale" may not always mean saving money. The sale price of one store may be higher than the regular price of another store.[3]

Warranty Evaluation

Most products come with some guarantee of quality. A **warranty** is a written guarantee from the manufacturer or distributor of a product that specifies the

• •

FINANCIAL PLANNING CALCULATIONS
The Net Present Value of a Consumer Purchase

The time value of money (see Chapter 1 and Appendix B) may be used to evaluate the financial benefits of buying home appliances. For example, when a washing machine and a clothes dryer are purchased, the money saved by not having to drive to and use a Laundromat could be considered a cash *inflow* (since money not going out is like money coming in). The cost of the appliances would be the current cash *outflow*. If the appliances have an expected life of 10 years, the *net present value* calculations might be as shown in the table below.

This calculation format can be used to assess the financial benefits of a consumer purchase by comparing the cost savings achieved by the purchase over time with the current price of the item purchased.

Step 1.	Estimated amount saved on weekly washing and drying at Laundromat: $4.75 times 52 weeks	$ 247.00
	Savings from not driving to Laundromat: six miles a week at 15 cents a mile times 52 weeks	46.80
	Total annual savings	$ 293.80
Step 2.	Multiply annual savings by the present value of a series (Exhibit 1–7 in Chapter 1 or Exhibit B–4 in Appendix B) for 6 percent of 10 years (6 percent is the average expected return from a savings account).	× 7.360 $ 2,162.37
Step 3.	Subtract the cost of the washing machine and the clothes dryer.	− 875.00
	The result is the net present value of the savings obtained by buying the appliances.°	$ 1,287.37

°A negative net present value would indicate that the financial aspects of the purchase are not desirable.

• •

conditions under which the product can be returned, replaced, or repaired. Retailers of a product that costs more than $15 and has a warranty are required by federal law to make this document available to customers before they buy the product. Frequently, this disclosure is printed in a catalog or on the product carton.

An *express warranty,* usually in written form, is created by the seller or manufacturer and has two forms—the full warranty and the limited warranty. Full warranties state that a defective product can be fixed or replaced in a reasonable amount of time. Limited warranties cover only certain aspects of a product, such as parts, or require the buyer to incur part of the costs for shipping or repairs.

An *implied warranty* is the result of a product's intended use or of other suggested understandings that are not in writing. For example, the implied warranty of title indicates that the seller has the right to sell the product. The implied warranty of merchantability guarantees that the product is fit for the ordinary uses for which it is intended: a toaster must toast bread, and a stereo must play records or tapes. Since implied warranties vary from state to state, contact your state consumer protection office for additional information on them.

A **service contract** is an agreement between a business and a consumer to cover the repair costs of a product. Even though service contracts are frequently called extended warranties, they are not warranties. For a fee, they insure the

---

EXHIBIT 8–7
Wise Buying Techniques:
A Summary

Compare brands of similar products to determine which is best for your intended use.

Compare stores and other sources of buying with regard to prices, services offered, product quality, and return privileges.

Read and evaluate label information.

Use coupons for products that you buy regularly or are trying out.

Use unit pricing to compare packages of different sizes.

Use open dating to determine the freshness and shelf life of perishable products.

Use various consumer information sources to assist you with your buying decisions.

Consider the nutritional value and the health aspects of the foods you buy.

Evaluate and compare the warranties of different brands.

Read product testing reports to determine which items are the safest and have the highest quality.

Plan your purchases to take advantage of sales and special offers.

Consider the time and effort it takes to evaluate alternatives and go to different stores.

---

buyer of a product against losses due to the cost of certain repairs. Owners of automobiles, home appliances, and other equipment buy these contracts to protect themselves against large repair expenses. In general, service contracts are very profitable for businesses since many more people buy them than need repair service. So buying a service contract may not be the best use of your money.

Exhibit 8–7 provides a summary of techniques that can assist you in your buying decisions.

COPING WITH CONTINUING CONSUMER CONCERNS

L.O.4
Identify areas of potential consumer dissatisfaction.

Every business transaction is a potential problem. Consumer protection experts suggest that to prevent being taken by deceptive business practices, such as those listed in Exhibit 8–8, you should

1. Do business with reputable companies that have a proven record of satisfying customers.
2. Avoid signing contracts and other documents that you do not understand.
3. Be cautious about offerings that seem too good to be true—they probably are!
4. Compare the cost of buying on credit with the cost of paying cash; also compare the interest rates offered by the seller with those offered by a bank or a credit union.
5. Not be in a hurry to get a good deal; successful con artists depend on your impulse buying.

Most customer difficulties are the result of defective products, low quality, short product lives, unexpected costs, and poor repairs. These problems are most commonly associated with the products and services listed in Exhibit 8–9. A variety of protections have been created to assist consumers in avoiding deceptive advertising, unclear contracts, and other fraudulent business practices.

EXHIBIT 8–8   Common Consumer Frauds Related to Financial Planning

Area of Personal Finance	Examples of Deceptive or Illegal Business Practices
Career planning	Employment agencies or vocational schools that *guarantee* you a job; work-at-home opportunities that offer you the chance to "earn easy money"
Tax planning	Tax preparers who *guarantee* you a refund
Consumer credit	Companies that offer credit with little or no down payment; credit counselors who offer easy solutions to your credit problems
Financial services	Someone posing as a bank examiner or other "official" who asks you to withdraw a large sum of money from a bank account
Consumer purchases	Advertised specials that are good for a "limited time only" or seem "too good to be true"
	"Rent-to-own" agreements that can result in paying 200 to 500 percent more than the retail price for home appliances, furniture, and electronic equipment
Housing	Home repair companies that offer the "free" inspections and then have "special offers" on needed repairs; mortgage brokers who offer to help pay off your mortgage faster but make use of your money for their own purposes
Insurance	Insurance coverage on fairly rare events such as air travel and cancer; mail-order health or life insurance that offers low coverage for high rates
Investments	Offerings of special investments, such as "penny stocks" (those selling for less than $5 a share), that promise quick profits, claim "inside information," deny broker commissions, or pressure you to invest quickly without written information
Retirement	Financial planners who offer to manage your retirement funds at a low fee or no fee or who offer you complete retirement living at one low price

EXHIBIT 8–9

Areas of Common
Consumer Complaints

Motor vehicle repairs	Home remodeling, home improvement companies
Mail-order purchases	Credit card companies
Magazine subscriptions	Banks and savings and loan associations
Used and new motor vehicle dealers	Department stores
Landlord-tenant relations	Insurance companies
Investment brokers	Contests and sweepstakes
Direct selling companies	Dry cleaning, laundry companies
Computers	

SOURCES: Wisconsin Department of Justice, Arkansas Attorney General, Council of Better Business Bureaus.

Consumer Protection Efforts

Every generation has unique consumer problems. At one time in our history, people were endangered by contaminated meat, poorly labeled foods, and adulterated drugs. More recently, food additives, radiation from color televisions, and automobile safety have been of concern.

In the 1960s, Congress enacted a broad range of consumer protection laws to supplement some of the earlier consumer protection legislation. Most of the states also passed laws and created various consumer protection offices within their governmental structures. In general, a vast mechanism was formed to help consumers cope with potential marketplace difficulties. An attitude of consumerism has become embedded among individuals, businesses, and public officials. The consumer movement resulted in

- Increased awareness among consumers regarding sources of product information and actions that they could take when dissatisfied.
- Acceptance by business that the health, safety, and well-being of individuals are vital to consumer satisfaction and company profits.
- Laws and government offices to assist consumers.
- Initiatives by community organizations to inform consumers, protest marketplace injustices, and lobby legislative regulatory bodies.
- A recognition of basic consumer rights and responsibilities.

In March 1962, President Kennedy delivered his Consumer Bill of Rights address to Congress. At that time, he identified four fundamental consumer rights: the right to be informed, the right to choose, the right to safety, and the right to be heard.

As with any right, each of these rights is accompanied by certain responsibilities. For example, the right to be informed requires that you seek out, evaluate, and use available resources about products and services. And the right to safety demands that you read warning labels and use products properly. The consumer rights identified by President Kennedy are the foundation for various channels that have been established to resolve marketplace dilemmas.

Resolving Consumer Complaints

You will probably never be completely satisfied with every purchase you make. Most consumers have problems related to poor quality, inadequate service, defective products, or incorrect pricing. The process for resolving differences between buyers and sellers includes the steps presented in Exhibit 8–10. To help ensure success when you make a complaint, keep a file of receipts, names of people you have talked to, dates of attempted repairs, copies of letters you have written, and costs you have incurred. This information can document your arguments.

EXHIBIT 8–10

Suggested Steps for Resolving Consumer Complaints

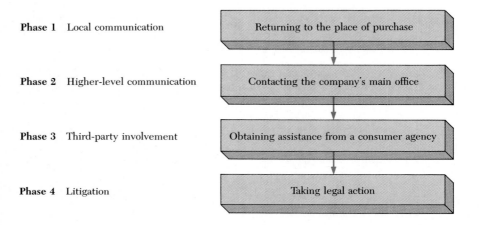

Phase 1   Local communication — Returning to the place of purchase

Phase 2   Higher-level communication — Contacting the company's main office

Phase 3   Third-party involvement — Obtaining assistance from a consumer agency

Phase 4   Litigation — Taking legal action

Returning to the Place of Purchase   Most consumer complaints are resolved at the original sales location. Since most business firms are concerned with their reputation for honesty and fairness, retailers will usually honor legitimate complaints. As you talk with the salesperson, customer service person, or store manager, you should avoid yelling, threatening a lawsuit, or asking for unreasonable action. In general, a calm, rational, but persistent approach is recommended.

Contacting the Company's Main Office   Most consumer advisers suggest that you express your dissatisfaction at the corporate level if your problem is not resolved at the local store. A letter like the one shown in Exhibit 8–11 provides the communication necessary. Addresses of companies that you may wish to contact can be obtained from the *Consumer's Resource Handbook,* published by

EXHIBIT 8–11   Sample Complaint Letter

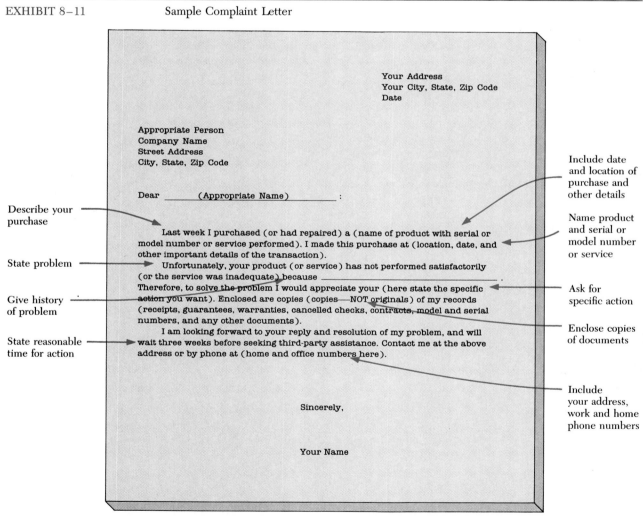

Keep copies of your letter and all related documents and information

SOURCE: *Consumer's Resource Handbook* (Washington, D.C.: U.S. Office of Consumer Affairs, 1990).

the U.S. Office of Consumer Affairs; Standard & Poor's *Register of Corporations, Directors, and Executives;* and Dun & Bradstreet's *Million Dollar Directory.* You can obtain a company's hot line number by using a directory of toll-free numbers in the library or by calling 1-800-555-1212, which is the toll-free information number. Some companies print the toll-free hot line number on product packages.

Obtaining Assistance from a Consumer Agency   If you do not receive satisfaction from the company, several consumer, business, and government organizations are ready to serve you. These include national organizations specializing in such issues as automobile safety, nuclear energy, and nutrition and local organizations that handle complaints, conduct surveys, and provide legal assistance.

The Better Business Bureaus are a network of offices throughout the country that resolve complaints against local merchants. Since Better Business Bureaus are sponsored by local business organizations, companies are not obligated to respond to the complaints they handle. The Better Business Bureau in your area can be of most value to you before your make a purchase. Its files will tell you about the experiences of others who dealt with a firm with which you are planning to do business.

The Better Business Bureau and other organizations provide third-party assistance, or **mediation,** for settling grievances. In mediation, an impartial person tries to resolve a difference between a customer and a business through discussion and negotiation.

Arbitration is the settlement of a difference by a third party—the arbitrator— whose decision is legally binding. After both sides agree to abide by the arbitrator's decision, each side presents its case to the arbitrator. Arbitrators are selected from a pool of volunteers. The major automobile manufacturers and many industry organizations have arbitration programs.

A vast network of government agencies is also available to consumers. Problems with local restaurants or food stores may be handled by a city or county health department. Every state has a variety of agencies to handle problems involving deceptive advertising, fraudulent business practices, banking, insurance companies, and utility rates.

Federal agencies that are available to help resolve consumer difficulties and provide information are listed in Appendix D. When you are uncertain about which agency to use, contact the U.S. Office of Consumer Affairs in Washington. This office can help channel your concern to the most appropriate consumer protection agency.

LEGAL OPTIONS FOR CONSUMERS

L.O.5
Evaluate the legal alternatives available to consumers.

If all of the previously mentioned avenues of action fail to bring about resolution of a consumer complaint, legal action might be appropriate. Several legal alternatives are available.

Small Claims Court

Every state has a system of courts to settle minor legal differences. In a **small claims court,** a person may file a claim for legal matters involving amounts under a set limit. The maximum amount varies from state to state; most states have a limit of $750 to $5,000.

Before resorting to the small claims court, you should become familiar with its location, procedures, and fees. During the court hearing, you are allowed to present your case. Your evidence should include contracts, receipts, photographs, and other items that prove your position. You may also use witnesses to testify on your behalf.

Although obtaining a favorable judgment in a small claims court may be easy, the collection process is frequently difficult. Since the defendant may not appear, you may have to pay a sheriff to serve a court order or you may have to use a collection agency to get your money.

Class Action Suits

Occasionally, a number of people have the same problem—for example, people who claim to have been injured by a defective product, customers who believe that a utility company has overcharged them, or travelers who believe that they have been cheated by a charter tour business. Such people may qualify for a **class action suit.** A class action suit is a legal action taken by a few individuals on behalf of all the people who have suffered the same alleged injustice. These people, called a *class,* are represented by one lawyer or by a group of lawyers working together.

Once a situation qualifies as a class action suit, all of the affected persons must be notified of the suit. At this point, an individual may decide not to participate in the class action suit or may decide to file an individual lawsuit. If the court ruling is favorable to the class, the funds awarded may be divided among all of the persons involved, used to reduce rates in the future, or assigned to public funds for government use.

Using a Lawyer

When small claims court or a class action suit is not appropriate, you may seek the services of an attorney. The most common sources of available lawyers are referrals from people you know, the local branch of the American Bar Association, and telephone directory listings. Lawyers advertise in newspapers, on television, and in other media. However, you must be aware that impressive advertising does not mean competent legal counsel.

Deciding when to use a lawyer is difficult. In general, straightforward legal situations, such as appearing in small claims court, renting an apartment, or defending yourself on a minor traffic violation, usually do not require legal counsel. But for more complicated matters, such as writing a will, settling a real estate purchase, or suing for injury damages caused by a product, it is probably wise to obtain legal assistance.

When selecting a lawyer, you should consider several questions. Is the lawyer experienced in your type of case? How will you be charged—on a flat fee basis, at an hourly rate, or on a contingency basis? Is there a fee for the initial consultation? How and when will you be required to make payment for services?

Other Legal Alternatives

The cost of legal services is frequently a problem, especially for low-income consumers. A **legal aid society** is one of a network of publicly supported community law offices that provide legal assistance to consumers who cannot afford their own attorney. These community agencies provide legal assistance at a minimal cost or without charge.

Because of increased competition among lawyers, other ways to cut the cost of legal assistance are available. Prepaid legal services are programs that provide unlimited or reduced-fee legal assistance for a set fee. Some of these programs provide certain basic services, such as telephone consultation and preparation of a simple will, for an annual fee ranging from $50 to $150 or more. More complicated legal assistance would require an additional fee, usually at a reduced rate. Other programs do not charge an advance fee but allow members to obtain legal services at discount rates. There are also comprehensive plans in which a high prepaid fee covers the legal needs of most families. In general, prepaid legal programs are designed to prevent minor troubles from becoming complicated legal problems.

• •

PERSONAL FINANCE JOURNAL:

Is It Legal?

The following situations are common problems for consumers. How would you respond to the question at the end of each situation?

	Yes	No
1. A store advertised a bottle of shampoo as "the $1.79 size, on sale for 99¢." If the store never sold the item for $1.79 but the manufacturer's recommended price was $1.79, was this a legitimate price comparison?	_____	_____
2. You purchase a stereo system for $650. Two days later, the same store offers the same item for $425. Is this legal?	_____	_____
3. You receive a sample of flower seeds in the mail. You decide to plant them to see how well they will grow in your yard. A couple of days later, you receive a bill for the seeds. Do you have to pay for the seeds?	_____	_____
4. A store has a "going out of business sale—everything must go" sign in its window. After six months, the sign is still there. Is this a deceptive business practice?	_____	_____
5. A 16-year-old, injured while playing ball at a local park, is taken to a hospital for medical care. The parents refuse to pay the hospital since they didn't request the service. Can the parents be held legally responsible for the charges?	_____	_____
6. You purchase a shirt for a friend. The gift doesn't fit, but when you return to the store, you are offered an exchange, since the store policy is not to give cash refunds. Is this legal?	_____	_____
7. A manufacturer refuses to repair a motorcycle that is still under warranty. The manufacturer can prove that the motorcycle was used improperly. If this is true, must the manufacturer honor the warranty?	_____	_____
8. If an employee of a store incorrectly marks the price of an item, is the store obligated to sell the item at the incorrect price?	_____	_____

Circumstances, interpretations of the law, and store policies, as well as state and local laws, can affect the above situations. The generally accepted answers would be: 1, 3, 7, and 8 —no; 2, 4, 5, and 6 —yes.

• •

Personal Consumer Protection

While a vast array of laws, agencies, and legal tools is available to protect your rights, none of these will be valuable to you unless you use them. To achieve a successful financial existence, you must be aware of and use the various information sources available to consumers and you must make effective purchasing decisions.

SUMMARY

L.O.1
Analyze the financial implications of consumer purchasing decisions.

Daily buying decisions are influenced by a variety of economic, social, and personal factors. Overspending and poor money management are frequent causes of the overuse of credit and other financial difficulties.

L.O.2
Evaluate the alternatives in consumer purchasing decisions.

A research-based approach to consumer buying starts with problem identification, information gathering, and increased marketplace awareness. In this approach, purchase alternatives are assessed on the basis of quality, price, performance, style, company reputation, and service.

L.O.3
Implement strategies for effective purchasing.

Timing purchases, comparing stores and brands, using label information, computing unit prices, and evaluating warranties are common strategies for effective purchasing.

L.O.4
Identify areas of potential consumer dissatisfaction.

Defective products, low quality, short product lives, unexpected costs, poor repair service, deceptive advertising, unclear contracts, and fraudulent business practices are the most common causes of customer difficulties.

L.O.5
Evaluate the legal alternatives available to consumers.

Small claims court, class action suits, and the services of a lawyer are legal means for handling consumer problems that cannot be resolved through communication with the business involved or through the help of a consumer protection agency.

GLOSSARY

Arbitration   The settlement of a difference by a third party whose decision is legally binding.

Class action suit   A legal action taken by a few individuals on behalf of all the people who have suffered the same alleged injustice.

Cooperative   A nonprofit organization created so that member-owners can save money on certain products or services.

Generic item   A plain package, nonbrand version of a product, offered at a lower price than that of the brand version or versions.

Impulse buying   Unplanned purchasing.

Legal aid society   One of a network of publicly supported community law offices that provide legal assistance to consumers who cannot afford their own attorney.

Mediation   The attempt by a third party to resolve a difference between two parties through discussion and negotiation.

Open dating   Information on freshness or shelf life found on the package of a perishable product.

Rebate   A partial refund of the price of a product.

Service contract   An agreement between a business and a consumer to cover the repair costs of a product.

Small claims court   A court that settles legal differences involving amounts under a set limit and employs a process in which the litigants do not use a lawyer.

Unit pricing   The use of a standard unit of measurement to compare the prices of packages of different sizes.

Warranty   A written guarantee from the manufacturer or distributor of a product that specifies the conditions under which the product can be returned, replaced, or repaired.

DISCUSSION QUESTIONS

L.O.1   1. What factors commonly influence the daily buying decisions of individuals and households? Which of these factors seem to be overlooked by most people?

L.O.1   2. What is the relationship between daily buying decisions and overall financial planning?

L.O.2   3. What are the benefits and drawbacks of using advertising to gather information about a consumer purchase?

L.O.2   4. What relationship exists between the life situation of an individual and the attributes that the individual desires in a consumer purchase?

L.O.2   5. Why is buying services more difficult than buying products?

L.O.3   6. Is the benefit from always shopping at the same store greater than the benefit from expending time and effort to take advantage of lower prices and special sales at various stores?

L.O.3   7. In what ways can the labeling on food and other products be deceptive?

L.O.3   8. How does a service contract differ from a warranty? What rights do purchasers of products have even if there is no written warranty?

L.O.4   9. The frequent avoidance of certain behaviors results in consumer problems and complaints. What are those behaviors?

L.O.4   10. How does arbitration differ from mediation?

L.O.5   11. Describe some situations in which the use of a lawyer would probably be desirable.

Opening Case Questions

1. What actions should the Harpers have taken before joining the food-buying plan?
2. How can the Harpers avoid paying the additional $495?
3. In what ways could effective financial planning help the Harpers cope with their situation?

PROBLEMS AND ACTIVITIES

L.O.1   1. Use advertisements, recent news articles, and personal observations to point out the economic, social, and personal factors that influence the purchases of the people in the following life situations:

         a. A retired person.

         b. A single parent with children aged five and nine.

         c. A dual-income couple with no children.

         d. A person with a dependent child and a dependent parent.

L.O.2   2. Use a recent issue of *Consumer Reports* to evaluate different brands of a product. Talk to several people about their experience with the product.

L.O.2   3. Develop a framework for evaluating different types of consumer information. Consider the objectivity, accuracy, clarity, and usefulness of advertisements, articles in consumer magazines, recommendations from friends, comments from sales personnel, the findings of consumer testing organizations, and information in government publications.

L.O.3   4. Survey consumers regarding their brand loyalty. For which types of products do individuals always buy a certain brand? What factors influence the selection of a certain brand?

L.O.3   5. Calculate the unit price of each of the following items:

Item	Price	Size	Unit Price
Motor oil	$1.95	2.5 gal.	____ cents/gal.
Cereal	2.17	15 oz.	____ cents/oz.
Canned fruit	0.89	13 oz.	____ cents/oz.
Facial tissue	2.25	300 tissues	____ cents/100 tissues
Shampoo	3.96	17 oz.	____ cents/oz.

L.O.3   6. What would be the net present value of a microwave oven that costs $159 and will save you $68 a year in time and food away from home? Assume an average return on your savings of 7 percent.

L.O.4   7. Conduct a survey of individuals who had a complaint about a product or a company. What difficulties did they encounter? What action did they take? Was the complaint resolved in a satisfactory manner?

L.O.4   8. Collect examples of magazine and newspaper advertisements that seem "too good to be true." Why are these ads deceptive? Should government agencies take action with regard to any of the ads?

L.O.4   9. Obtain information from various companies that offer "rent-to-buy" agreements. Compare the regular purchase price of an appliance with the cost of the appliance under a rent-to-buy agreement.

L.O.5   10. Prepare a survey of the legal services available to students and others in your community. Compare the fees charged and the services provided by individual lawyers and other sources of legal assistance.

LIFE SITUATION   Case 8–1

Comparing Computers

Jeanne Wilson is planning to purchase a home computer. Friends have suggested a variety of brands and models. Also, Jeanne has heard about certain features that she would like to have on her computer. She plans to use it to prepare school reports, to assist her in home money management, and to practice playing chess.

Jeanne likes the personal computer she uses at her part-time job, but the cost of that computer is more than she can afford. A friend has an inexpensive model that can handle most of the information processing that Jeanne wants to do now. But this model may not be able to handle the information processing that she hopes to do in the future.

Questions

1. How should Jeanne define the problem with regard to her planned purchase of a home computer?
2. What information sources are available to Jeanne?
3. What factors should Jeanne consider in evaluating her alternatives in buying a home computer?

LIFE SITUATION   Case 8–2

A Cool Consumer Problem

Al Emory bought a new window air conditioner three weeks ago. A few days ago, the unit overheated and started a small fire in his apartment. Al's rug and drapes were damaged, and Al suffered some minor burns that required medical treatment.

The day after the fire, Al returned to the store where he bought the air conditioner. He asked that the purchase price of the air conditioner be refunded, and he wanted the store to pay for his property damage and medical costs. The store's customer service manager was willing to give Al the refund for the air conditioner but said that he was not authorized to make any additional payments.

Questions

1. What actions might Al have taken to avoid buying a potentially defective air conditioner?
2. What additional courses of action can Al take to resolve his complaint?
3. What types of legal action may be appropriate in this situation?

SUPPLEMENTARY READINGS

For Additional Information on Consumer Purchasing

Buying Guide Issue, Consumer Reports. Consumers Union, 256 Washington Street, Mount Vernon, NY 10553.

Cude, Brenda J. *Shop Smart to Buy More for Less.* Urbana, Ill.: Cooperative Extension Service, University of Illinois, April 1989.

Home Furnishings and Equipment. Money Management Institute, Household Financial Services, 2700 Sanders Road, Prospect Heights, IL 60070.

Moreau, Dan. "Appliance Service Contracts: Why the Dealer Wins." *Changing Times,* January 1989, pp. 83–84, 86.

For Additional Information on Consumer Problems

Blumberg, Paul. *The Predatory Society: Deception in the American Marketplace.* New York: Oxford University Press, 1989.

Consumer's Resource Handbook. U.S. Office of Consumer Affairs, Washington, DC 20201.

Greer, Rebecca E. "Be Safer in the 90's: New Warnings from Ralph Nader." *Woman's Day,* October 24, 1989, pp. 32, 36, 38–39.

Harris, Marlys. "You May Already Be a Victim of Fraud." *Money,* August 1989, pp. 75–80, 85–89, 91.

Paulson, Morton C. "You Have Definitely Won a Fabulous Prize." *Changing Times,* August 1989, pp. 34–36, 38, 40.

For Additional Information on Legal Alternatives

The American Lawyer: When and How to Use One. American Bar Association, Public Education Division, 750 North Lake Shore Drive, Chicago, IL 60611.

Nasar, Sylvia. "Best Ways to Get Your Money Back." *Money,* April 1989, pp. 149–53, 156–58.

Warner, Ralph. *Everybody's Guide to Small Claims Court.* National Edition, 1990. Nolo Press, 950 Parker Street, Berkeley, CA 94710.

9

The Finances of Housing

Whether you rent an apartment, own a house, or live in a mobile home, the cost of your place of residence is a major budget item. Due to the economic significance of a housing decision, careful consideration of housing alternatives is vital. The type and location of the residence, renting versus buying, and financing are only a few of the factors that you should consider before you make this decision. The choice of housing is a major aspect of your personal finances.

LEARNING OBJECTIVES
After studying this chapter, you will be able to

L.O.1 Evaluate available housing alternatives.

L.O.2 Analyze the costs and benefits associated with renting.

L.O.3 Implement the home buying process.

L.O.4 Calculate the costs associated with purchasing a home.

L.O.5 Develop a strategy for selling a home.

OPENING CASE

Housing Decisions

When Mark and Valerie Bowman first saw the house, they didn't like it. This could have been because it was a dark, rainy day. They viewed the house more favorably on their second visit, which they had expected to be a waste of time. Despite cracked ceilings, the need for a paint job, and a kitchen built in the 1950s, the Bowmans saw a potential for creating a place that they could call their own.

Beth Franklin purchased her condominium four years ago. She got a mortgage rate of 12.5 percent, which was very good then. Recently, when interest rates had dropped, Beth was considering refinancing her mortgage at a lower rate.

Matt and Peggy Zoran had been married for five years and were still living in an apartment. Several of Zorans'

friends had purchased homes recently, but Matt and Peggy were not sure that they wanted to follow this example. Although they liked their friends' homes and had viewed photographs of homes currently on the market, they also liked the freedom from responsibility that they had as renters.

Buying a home that needs improvement, refinancing a mortgage when interest rates decline, and deciding to rent instead of buying a home are just a few of the housing strategies used by individuals and families. The logical investigation of housing options and costs is an integral part of your overall financial decision making.

EVALUATING HOUSING ALTERNATIVES

L.O.1
Evaluate available housing alternatives.

If you walk down any residential street, you are likely to see a variety of housing types. What makes people select a certain type of housing? As you assess various housing choices, you will identify the factors that will influence your choice. Your needs, lifestyle, and financial resources will determine whether you decide to rent, buy, or have a home built. In assessing these alternatives, you must make use of reliable housing information.

Your Lifestyle and Your Choice of Housing

While the concept of lifestyle—how a person spends his or her time and money—may seem intangible, it materializes in your consumer purchases. Every buying decision is a statement about your lifestyle. Thus, your lifestyle, as well as your values, needs, desires, and attitudes, is reflected in your choice of a place to live. For example, some people may want a kitchen that is large enough for family-oriented, home-cooked meals. In contrast, a career-oriented person may want a lavish bathroom or a home spa in which he or she can escape from the pressures of work. Among the lifestyle factors that influence housing choices are status, fashion, individualism, and ecological concerns. As you select housing, you will probably consider the alternatives in Exhibit 9–1 as ways of meeting your needs and expressing your lifestyle.

While personal preferences and tastes are the foundation of your housing decision, financial factors may modify your final choice. Traditional financial guidelines suggest that "you should spend no more than 25 or 30 percent of your take-home pay on housing" or that "your home should cost about 2½ times your annual income." Because of changes in our economy and society, these guidelines are no longer completely valid. Some sort of financial guideline is necessary to determine the amount you should spend on housing. A budget and the other financial records discussed in Chapter 3 can assist you in evaluating your income, living costs, and other financial obligations to determine an appropriate amount for your housing payment.

EXHIBIT 9–1   Different Housing for Different Life Situations

Life Situation	Possible Housing Types
Young single	Due to possible job transfer, rental housing because it requires limited maintenance activities and offers mobility
	Purchase home or condominium for financial and tax benefits
Single parent	Rental housing that provides an environment for children and appropriate home security
	Purchase low-maintenance housing that meets the financial and social needs of family members
Young couple, no children	Rental housing that offers convenience and flexibility of lifestyle
	Purchase housing for financial benefits and the building of long-term financial security
Couple, young children	Rental housing that provides appropriate facilities for children and is situated in a family-oriented area
	Home that meets the financial and other needs of the family
Couple, children no longer at home	Rental housing that offers convenience and flexibility for changing needs and financial situations
	Purchase housing that requires minimum maintenance and meets lifestyle needs
Retired person	Rental housing that meets financial, social, and physical needs
	Purchase housing that requires minimum maintenance, offers convenience, and provides needed services

Opportunity Costs of Housing Choices

While the selection of housing is usually based on life situation and financial factors, also consider what you are giving up when you live in a certain area or in a certain type of residence. The opportunity costs of your housing decision will vary, but some common trade-offs include

- The savings and investment interest lost on the money you use for a down payment when you buy a home.
- The interest lost on your security deposit when you rent an apartment.
- The time and cost of commuting to work when you live in an area that offers less expensive housing or more living space.
- The loss of tax advantages and equity growth when you rent a city apartment in order to be close to your place of work.
- The time and money you spend when you repair and improve a lower-priced home.
- The time and effort needed when you have a home built to your personal specifications.

A housing decision, like every other financial choice, requires consideration of what you give up in time, effort, and money as well as consideration of the obvious costs, such as monthly rental or mortgage payments.

Renting versus Buying Your Housing

Choosing between renting and buying your place of residence is an essential decision in the selection of housing. You will probably be able to resolve this dilemma by evaluating various lifestyle and financial factors. Exhibit 9–2 can help you assess the renting and buying alternatives. Mobility is a primary motivator of renters, while buyers usually want permanence.

EXHIBIT 9–2 Housing Alternatives

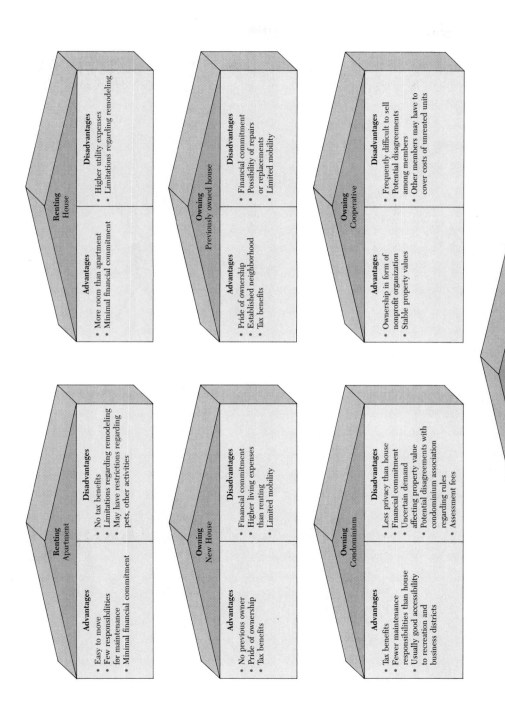

Renting
Apartment

Advantages
- Easy to move
- Few responsibilities for maintenance
- Minimal financial commitment

Disadvantages
- No tax benefits
- Limitations regarding remodeling
- May have restrictions regarding pets, other activities

Renting
House

Advantages
- More room than apartment
- Minimal financial commitment

Disadvantages
- Higher utility expenses
- Limitations regarding remodeling

Owning
New House

Advantages
- No previous owner
- Pride of ownership
- Tax benefits

Disadvantages
- Financial commitment
- Higher living expenses than renting
- Limited mobility

Owning
Previously owned house

Advantages
- Pride of ownership
- Established neighborhood
- Tax benefits

Disadvantages
- Financial commitment
- Possibility of repairs or replacements
- Limited mobility

Owning
Condominium

Advantages
- Tax benefits
- Fewer maintenance responsibilities than house
- Usually good accessibility to recreation and business districts

Disadvantages
- Less privacy than house
- Financial commitment
- Uncertain demand affecting property value
- Potential disagreements with condominium association regarding rules
- Assessment fees

Owning
Cooperative

Advantages
- Ownership in form of nonprofit organization
- Stable property values

Disadvantages
- Frequently difficult to sell
- Potential disagreements among members
- Other members may have to cover costs of unrented units

Owning
Manufactured home (mobile home)

Advantages
- Less expensive than other ownership options
- Flexibility in selection of home features and appliances

Disadvantages
- May be difficult to sell in future
- Financing may be difficult to obtain
- Construction quality may be poor

Economic conditions can also influence your choice between renting and buying. Between 1973 and 1982, when housing prices increased by nearly 150 percent, buying a house made sound financial sense. In just a few years, a person was able to make a large profit from the sale of a home. Since then, lower inflation rates have had a stabilizing effect on housing prices.

As you can see in the "Financial Planning Calculations" feature, the choice between renting and buying is usually not clear. In general, renting is less costly in the short run, but home ownership also has certain financial advantages.

• •

FINANCIAL PLANNING CALCULATIONS

Renting versus Buying Your Place of Residence

Comparing the costs of renting and buying involves consideration of a variety of factors. The following framework and example provide a basis for assessing these two housing alternatives. The apartment in the example has a monthly rent of $700, and the home costs $85,000. Although the numbers in this example favor buying, remember that in any financial decision, calculations provide only part of the answer. You must also consider your personal needs and values and assess the opportunity costs associated with renting and buying.

	Example
Rental Costs	
Annual rent payments	$ 8,400
Renter's insurance	170
Interest lost on security (amount of security deposit times after-tax savings account interest rate)	80
Total annual cost of renting	$8,650
Buying Costs	
Annual mortgage payments	$ 10,500
Property taxes (annual costs)	2,000
Homeowners insurance (annual premium)	400
Estimated maintenance and repairs (1%)	850
After-tax interest lost on down payment and closing costs	1,030
Less (financial benefits of home ownership): Growth in equity	− 264
Tax savings for mortgage interest (annual mortgage interest times tax rate)	− 2,866
Tax savings for property taxes (annual property taxes times tax rate)	− 560
Estimated annual appreciation (3%)°	− 2,550
Total annual cost of buying	$8,540

°This is a nationwide average; actual appreciation of property will vary by geographic area and economic conditions.

• •

Housing Information Sources

As with other consumer purchases, much information is available on housing. Start your data search with basic resources such as this book and books available in libraries. Consult the weekly real estate section in your newspaper. That section carries useful articles about renting, buying, financing, remodeling, and other housing topics. Other helpful information sources are friends, local real estate agents, and government agencies (see Appendix D). Your current and future housing decisions should be based on sound, up-to-date information.

RENTING YOUR RESIDENCE

L.O.2
Analyze the costs and benefits associated with renting.

At some point in your life, you are likely to rent your place of residence. You may rent when you are first on your own and cannot afford to buy a home or later in life when you want to avoid the activities required to maintain your own home. In 1989, over 36 percent of U.S. households lived in rental units.

As a tenant, you pay for the right to live in a residence owned by someone else. When choosing a rental unit, you should consider the available types of rented housing and the advantages, disadvantages, and costs of renting. Exhibit 9–3 presents the activities involved in finding and living in a rental unit.

Selecting a Rental Unit

An apartment is the most common type of rented housing. Apartments range from modern high rises and luxury suburban complexes with extensive recreational facilities to simple one- and two-bedroom units in quiet, family-oriented neighborhoods.

EXHIBIT 9–3    Housing Rental Activities

The Search

> Select a geographic area and rental cost appropriate to your life situation and needs
> Compare costs and facilities between comparable rental units
> Talk to current and past residents of the rental unit and geographic area

Before Signing a Lease

> Make sure all agreements regarding the starting date of the lease, costs, and facilities are clearly presented in writing
> Talk to a lawyer about any aspects of the lease on which you are not clear
> Note in writing, signed by the owner, the condition of the rental unit
> If you'll have a roommate, make sure you are compatible and, remember, even if both names are on the lease, one person can be held responsible for the full rent

Living in Rental Property

> Keep all facilities and appliances in good operating condition
> Contact the owners regarding repairs for which they are responsible
> Respect the rights of others when playing the stereo and having parties
> Obtain renter's insurance to cover your personal belongings and potential liability situations (see Chapter 12)

At the End of the Lease

> Clean the apartment and prepare for your departure; leave it in the same condition as when you moved in
> Provide the landlord with information where your security deposit is to be sent
> Require that any deductions from your security deposit be documented

People who need more room should consider renting a house. The increased space will cost you more money, and you will probably have more responsibility for maintaining the property. People who need less space may rent a room in a house, over a garage, or in a basement.

The main sources of information on available rental units are newspaper ads, real estate and rental offices, and people you know. When comparing rental units, consider the factors presented in Exhibit 9–4.

Advantages of Renting

The advantages of renting include mobility, fewer responsibilities, and lower initial costs.

Mobility   Renting gives you mobility when a change of location becomes necessary or desirable. A new job, a rent increase, the need for a larger apartment, or the desire to live in a different community can make relocation necessary. It is easier to move when you are renting than when you own a home. After you have completed school and started your career, renting will make it easier for you to move in response to job demands.

Fewer Responsibilities   Renters have fewer responsibilities than homeowners because they usually do not have to be concerned with maintenance and repairs. However, they are expected to do regular household cleaning. Renters also have fewer financial concerns. Their main housing costs are rent and utilities, while homeowners incur expenses related to property taxes and upkeep.

EXHIBIT 9–4   Selecting an Apartment

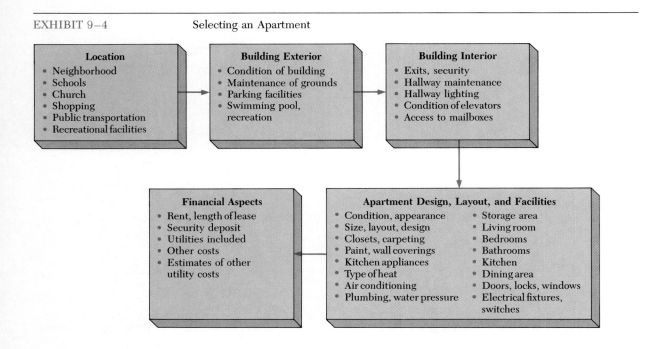

Lower Initial Costs   It is less expensive to take possession of a rental unit than to buy a home. While new tenants may have to pay a security deposit, a new homebuyer usually has to make a high down payment—several thousand dollars at the least.

Disadvantages of Renting

Renting offers few financial benefits, imposes a restricted lifestyle, and entails legal concerns.

Few Financial Benefits   Renters do not have the financial advantages that homeowners have. They get no tax deductions for mortgage interest and property taxes. They do not benefit from the increased value of real estate. They are subject to rent increases over which they have little control.

Restricted Lifestyle   When you rent, the types of activities that you can pursue in your place of residence are generally limited. Noise from a stereo system or parties is usually monitored closely. Restrictions regarding pets and decoration are often imposed.

Legal Concerns   Most tenants sign a **lease,** the legal document that defines the conditions of a rental agreement. This document provides the following information:

- A description of the property, including the address.
- The name and address of the owner/landlord (the *lessor*).
- The name of the tenant (the *lessee*).
- The effective date of the lease.
- The length of the lease.
- The amount of the security deposit.
- The amount and due date of the monthly rent.
- The location at which the rent must be paid.
- The date and amount due of charges for late rent payments.
- A list of the utilities, appliances, furniture, or other facilities that are included in the rental amount.
- The restrictions regarding certain activities (pets, remodeling).
- The tenant's right to sublet the rental unit.
- The charges for damages or for moving out of the rental unit later than the lease expiration date.
- The conditions under which the landlord may enter the apartment.

Standard lease forms include many terms and conditions that you may not want to accept. The fact that a lease is printed does not mean that you must accept it as is. Negotiate with the landlord about lease terms and conditions that you consider unacceptable.

Some leases give you the right to *sublet* the rental unit. Subletting may be necessary if you must vacate the premises before the lease expires. The privilege of subletting allows you to have another person take over rent payments and live in the rental unit.

Most leases are in writing, but oral leases are also valid. With such a lease, one party to the lease must give a 30-day notice to the other party before terminating the lease or imposing a rent increase.

A lease provides protection to both the landlord and the tenant. The tenant is protected from rent increases during the term of the lease unless the lease has a provision allowing a rent increase. In most states, too, the tenant of a leased dwelling unit cannot be locked out or evicted without a court hearing. The lease gives the landlord the right to take legal action against a tenant for nonpayment of rent or destruction of property.

Costs of Renting

A security deposit is usually required when you sign a lease. This is an amount of money held by the landlord to cover the cost of any damages that may be done to the rental unit during the lease period. The security deposit is usually one month's rent.

Several state and local governments require that the landlord pay you interest on your security deposit. After you vacate a rental unit, your security deposit should be refunded within a reasonable time. Many states require that it be returned within 30 days of the end of the lease. If money is deducted from your security deposit, you have the right to an itemized list of the costs of any repairs or maintenance.

As a renter, besides paying the monthly rent, you will incur other living expenses. For many apartments, water is covered by the rent, but other utilities are not. If you rent a house, you will probably pay for heat, electricity, water, and telephone. When you rent, you should obtain insurance coverage for your personal property. Renter's insurance is discussed in Chapter 12.

THE HOME BUYING PROCESS

L.O.3
Implement the home buying process.

Owning a home is a financial goal of many people. This goal is achieved through the activities shown in Exhibit 9–5. Each phase of the home buying process involves decisions that require an assessment of your current and future financial situation. You must determine what you can afford to spend when you buy a home, and you must consider the trade-offs associated with home ownership. In addition, you must evaluate the various types of home ownership.

What Are the Benefits of Home Ownership?

Whether you purchase a house, a condominium, or a manufactured home, you can enjoy the pride of ownership, financial benefits, and lifestyle flexibility.

Pride of Ownership   Having a place to call their own is a primary motive of many homebuyers. Stability of residence and a personalized living location can be important. Pride of ownership may be reflected in involvement in civic and community activities.

Financial Benefits   Home ownership has financial benefits. One benefit is the deductibility of mortgage interest and real estate tax payments for federal income tax purposes. A potential benefit is increases in the value of the property. Finally, homeowners in most states may be able to borrow against their equity in their homes. *Equity* is the value of the home less the amount still owed on the mortgage.

EXHIBIT 9–5

The Home Buying Process

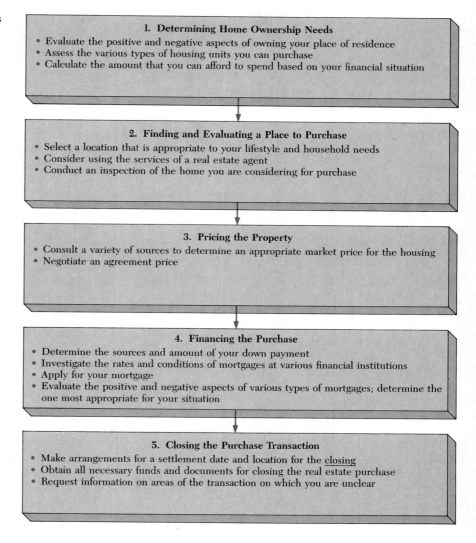

1. Determining Home Ownership Needs
- Evaluate the positive and negative aspects of owning your place of residence
- Assess the various types of housing units you can purchase
- Calculate the amount that you can afford to spend based on your financial situation

2. Finding and Evaluating a Place to Purchase
- Select a location that is appropriate to your lifestyle and household needs
- Consider using the services of a real estate agent
- Conduct an inspection of the home you are considering for purchase

3. Pricing the Property
- Consult a variety of sources to determine an appropriate market price for the housing
- Negotiate an agreement price

4. Financing the Purchase
- Determine the sources and amount of your down payment
- Investigate the rates and conditions of mortgages at various financial institutions
- Apply for your mortgage
- Evaluate the positive and negative aspects of various types of mortgages; determine the one most appropriate for your situation

5. Closing the Purchase Transaction
- Make arrangements for a settlement date and location for the closing
- Obtain all necessary funds and documents for closing the real estate purchase
- Request information on areas of the transaction on which you are unclear

Lifestyle Flexibility   While renting gives you greater mobility, home ownership gives you more opportunity to express your individuality. Homeowners have greater freedom than renters in decorating and redesigning their dwelling units and in entertaining friends.

What Are the Drawbacks of Home Ownership?

The American Dream of buying your own home does not guarantee a glamorous existence. This investment has financial risks, limited mobility, and higher living costs.

Financial Risks   Among the financial risks associated with buying a home are difficulty in obtaining the money needed for a down payment. Obtaining mortgage financing may also be a problem, due to your personal situation or current economic conditions. Finally, changing property values in an area can affect your financial investment.

Limited Mobility   Home ownership does not provide the ease in changing living location that renters have. If changes in your situation make it necessary for you to sell your home, doing so may be difficult. High interest rates can result in a weak demand for housing.

Higher Living Costs   As most homeowners will verify, owning your place of residence can be expensive. The homeowner is financially responsible for maintenance and must bear the costs of repainting and repairs for plumbing, roofing, and appliances. The homeowner must also fund home improvements.

Real estate taxes are a major expense of homeowners. In the 1980s, when the federal government cut various services in an attempt to reduce its budget, state and local governments accepted the responsibility for many of these services. This resulted in higher property taxes. Even for homeowners who no longer have mortgage payments, higher property values and higher tax rates mean higher real estate taxes. These higher taxes affect the homeowner more directly than they affect the renter, who pays for them in the form of higher rent, and it is harder for the homeowner to counter their effects by moving to less expensive housing.

What Types of Housing Can Be Purchased?

Several options are available to the person who wants to buy a home. Single-family dwellings are the most popular type of housing. These residences include previously owned houses, new houses, and custom-built houses. Older houses are preferred by people who want a certain style and quality of housing.

Multiunit dwellings—dwellings that comprise more than one living unit—include duplexes and town houses. A duplex is a building that contains two separate homes. A town house is a building that contains two, four, or six single-family living units. While multifamily housing appeals to some people, others want more privacy than it affords.

A **condominium** is an individually owned housing unit in a building with a number of such units. Individual ownership does not include the common areas, such as hallways, outside grounds, and recreational facilities. These areas are owned by the condominium association, which consists of the people who own the housing units. The condominium association oversees the management and operation of the housing complex. The condominium owners are charged a monthly fee to cover the maintenance, repairs, improvements and insurance for the building and the common areas. A condominium is not a type of building structure; it is a legal form of home ownership. Many housing units previously rented as apartments have been converted to condominiums, with individuals purchasing their living units. These conversions created difficulties for people who could not or did not want to buy the units they rented but were profitable to the owners of those units.

Cooperative housing is a form of housing in which a building containing a number of units is owned by a nonprofit organization whose members have the right to live in the units by paying rent. The living units of a co-op, unlike condominiums, are not owned by the residents but by the co-op. Rents in a co-op can increase quickly if living units become vacant, since the maintenance costs of the building must be covered by the remaining residents.

Finally, a **manufactured home** is a housing unit that is fully or partially assembled in a factory before being moved to the living site. There are two basic types of manufactured homes. One type is the prefabricated home, whose components are built in the factory and then assembled at the housing site. This type of housing has become more popular since mass production helps keep its costs lower, allowing more people to buy a home.

The second type of manufactured home, generally purchased by middle- and low-income families, was previously called a *mobile home.* However, since very few mobile homes are moved from their original site, the term is no longer accurate. These housing units are usually less than 1,000 square feet in size, but they usually offer the same features as a conventional house—for example, fully equipped kitchens, fireplaces, cathedral ceilings, and whirlpool baths. The site for a mobile home may be either purchased or leased in a development specifically designed for such housing units.

The safety of mobile homes is continually debated. Fires do not occur any more frequently in these housing units than in other types of homes. But due to the size and construction of mobile homes, a fire spreads faster in them than in conventional houses. Manufacturers' standards for the fire safety of mobile homes are higher now than they were in the past. Still, when a fire occurs in a mobile home, the unit is usually completely destroyed.

Another common concern about mobile homes is that they frequently depreciate in value. When this occurs, an important benefit of home ownership is eliminated. The possibility of depreciation may also make it difficult to obtain financing for the purchase of a mobile home.

Building Your Own Home

Some people want a home built according to their specifications. Before you begin such a project, be sure you possess the knowledge, the money, and the perseverance that are needed to complete it.

When choosing a contractor to coordinate the project, be sure to consider the following:

Does the contractor have the experience needed to handle the type of building project you require?

Does the contractor have a good working relationship with the architect, materials suppliers, electricians, plumbers, carpenters, and other personnel needed to complete the project?

What assurance do you have about the quality of the materials used and of the finished home?

What arrangements have to be made for payments during the construction process?

What delays in the construction process will be considered legitimate?

Your written contract should include a time schedule, cost estimates, a description of the work, and a payment schedule.

As much as 25 percent of the cost of a new house can be saved by supervising its construction. Home building suppliers and owners of homes under construction can suggest quality tradespeople. Inexpensive blueprints are available from the U.S. Department of Housing and Urban Development; these building plans can save you thousands of dollars in architect's fees.

How Much Can I Afford to Spend?

As you determine how much of your budget will be spent on your purchased home, consider the price of the house as well as its size and quality.

Price   The amount you can afford to spend for a house will be affected by the cash you have available for a down payment, by your regular income, and by your current living expenses and financial obligations. Other factors that you should consider are the current mortgage rates, the potential future value of the property you want to buy, and your ability to make monthly mortgage payments and to cover other living costs, maintenance, repairs, and home improvements. To determine how much you can afford to spend on a home, you can have a loan officer at a mortgage company or other financial institution *prequalify* you. This service is usually provided without charge.

Size and Quality   You may not get all the features you want in your first home, but financial advisers suggest that you should get into the housing market by purchasing what you can afford. Studies show that the most desired features in a home are a basement, a large garage, abundant closet and storage space, and a large, modern kitchen. As you move up in the housing market, your second or third home can include more of the features you want.

Ideally, the home you buy will be in good condition. In certain circumstances, however, you may be willing to buy a *handyman's special*—a home that needs work but that you are able to get at a lower price because of its poor condition. Then you will need to put more money into the house for repairs and improvements or to invest *sweat equity* by doing some of the work yourself. Home improvement information and assistance are available from hardware stores and other home product retailers.

Finding and Evaluating a Home

Next, you should select a location, consider using the services of a real estate agent, and conduct a home inspection.

Selecting a Location   An old adage of real estate people is that "the three most important factors to consider when buying a home are location, location, and location!" Perhaps you prefer an urban, a suburban, or a rural setting. Or perhaps you want to live in a small town or in a resort area near a lake or skiing facilities. In selecting a neighborhood, consider the character of the community. Is there a strong community spirit and high neighbor involvement? Compare your values and lifestyle with those of current residents.

Be aware of **zoning laws**—restrictions on how the property in an area can be used. The location of businesses and the anticipated construction of industrial buildings may influence your decision to settle in a particular area.

If you have or plan to have a family, you should assess the school system. Educators recommend that schools be evaluated on the basis of variety of programs, the achievement level of students, the percentage of students who go on to college, the dedication of faculty members, the available facilities, and the involvement of parents. Homeowners without children also benefit from strong schools since the educational advantages of a community affect property values.

Utilizing the Services of Real Estate Agents   A real estate agent can help you assess your housing needs and determine the amount you can afford to spend on a home. Real estate agents will have information on the communities in which you are interested. The Multiple Listing Service used by real estate agents is a directory of the homes that are available for purchase in a geographic area. This system provides a fast method of searching the market for homes that meet your personal and financial needs.

Finally, a real estate agent can be helpful in presenting your offer to the seller, negotiating a settlement price, assisting you in obtaining financing, and representing you at the closing. Your real estate agent can recommend lawyers, insurance agents, inspectors, and mortgage companies that will serve your needs.

Since the real estate agent's commission is paid by the seller in a housing sale, the services of the real estate agent are provided without cost to the buyer. However, most states allow homebuyers to hire a real esate agent who, for a fee, works on their behalf.

Conducting a Home Inspection   Before reaching your decision about a specific home, conduct a complete evaluation of the property. This evaluation can help minimize future problems. Do not assume that because someone now lives there, everything is in proper working condition. Being cautious and aggressive will save you headaches and unplanned expenses. The mortgage company will usually conduct an *appraisal* to determine the fair market value of the property; although the appraisal is not a detailed inspection, it nonetheless assesses the condition of the home. Exhibit 9–6 presents a more detailed format for inspecting a home. A home purchase agreement may include the right to have a contractor or several professionals (roofer, plumber, electrician) inspect the property.

Pricing the Property

After you select a home you desire, your efforts must turn to determining an initial offer price and negotiating a final buying price.

Determining the Home Price   What price should you offer for the home? The main factors you should consider are recent sales prices in the area, the current demand for housing, the length of time the home has been on the market, the owner's need to sell, the financing options, and the features and condition of the home. Each of these items can affect your offer price. For example, you will have to offer a higher price in times of low interest rates and high demand for homes. On the other hand, a home that has been on the market for over a year could mean an opportunity to offer a lower price. The services of an appraiser can assist you in assessing the current value of the home you wish to buy.

Your offer will be in the form of a purchase agreement, or contract (see Exhibit 9–7). This document constitutes your legal offer to purchase the home. Usually, your first offer price will not be accepted.

Negotiating the Purchase Price   If your initial offer is accepted, you have a valid contract to buy the home. But if your offer is rejected, you have several options, depending on the actions of the seller. A counteroffer from the owner indicates a willingness to negotiate a price settlement. If the counteroffer is only slightly lower than the asking price, you are probably expected to move closer to

EXHIBIT 9–6

Conducting a Home
Inspection

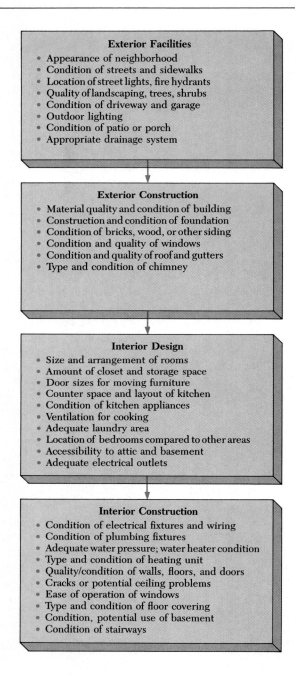

Exterior Facilities
- Appearance of neighborhood
- Condition of streets and sidewalks
- Location of street lights, fire hydrants
- Quality of landscaping, trees, shrubs
- Condition of driveway and garage
- Outdoor lighting
- Condition of patio or porch
- Appropriate drainage system

Exterior Construction
- Material quality and condition of building
- Construction and condition of foundation
- Condition of bricks, wood, or other siding
- Condition and quality of windows
- Condition and quality of roof and gutters
- Type and condition of chimney

Interior Design
- Size and arrangement of rooms
- Amount of closet and storage space
- Door sizes for moving furniture
- Counter space and layout of kitchen
- Condition of kitchen appliances
- Ventilation for cooking
- Adequate laundry area
- Location of bedrooms compared to other areas
- Accessibility to attic and basement
- Adequate electrical outlets

Interior Construction
- Condition of electrical fixtures and wiring
- Condition of plumbing fixtures
- Adequate water pressure; water heater condition
- Type and condition of heating unit
- Quality/condition of walls, floors, and doors
- Cracks or potential ceiling problems
- Ease of operation of windows
- Type and condition of floor covering
- Condition, potential use of basement
- Condition of stairways

that price with your next offer. If the counteroffer is quite a bit off the asking price, you are closer to the point where you can split the difference with the seller to arrive at the purchase price. If no counteroffer is forthcoming, you may wish to make another offer to see whether the seller is willing to do any negotiating on the price. In times of high demand for housing, negotiating is minimized; this is referred to as a *seller's market* since the current homeowner is likely to have several offers for the property. In contrast, when home sales are slow, a *buyer's*

EXHIBIT 9–7
The Components of a
Home Purchase Agreement

In a real estate transaction, the contract between a buyer and a seller contains the following information:

1. The names and addresses of the buyer and seller.
2. A description of the property.
3. The price of the property.
4. The amount of the mortgage that will be needed.
5. The amount of the earnest money deposit.
6. The date and time of the closing.
7. Where the closing will take place.
8. Provision for extension of the closing date.
9. Provision for disposition of the deposit money if something goes wrong.
10. Adjustments to be made at the closing.
11. Details of what is included in the sale—home appliances, drapes, carpeting, and other items.
12. Special conditions of the sale.
13. Inspections that the buyer can make before the closing.
14. Property easements, such as the use of an area of the property for utility lines or poles.

SOURCE: *Homeownership: Guidelines for Buying and Owning a Home* (Richmond: Federal Reserve Bank of Richmond).

market exists and a homebuyer is likely to be able to purchase the property at a lower price.

When you buy a previously owned home, your negotiating power is based on current market demand and the current owner's need to sell. When you buy a new home, a slow market may mean lower prices or an opportunity to obtain various amenities (fireplace, higher-quality carpeting) from the builder at little or no cost.

Once a price has been agreed upon, the purchase contract becomes the basis for the transaction. At this time, the buyer must deposit **earnest money**—a portion of the purchase price that the buyer deposits as evidence of good faith to show that the purchase offer is serious. At the closing of the home purchase, the earnest money is applied toward the down payment.

Home purchase agreements often contain a *contingency clause.* This contract condition states that the agreement is binding only if a certain event occurs. For example, a real estate contract may stipulate that the contract will be invalid if the buyer does not obtain financing for the purchase within a certain time or it may make the purchase of a home contingent on the sale of the buyer's currently owned home.

FINANCING THE HOME PURCHASE

L.O.4
Calculate the costs associated with purchasing a home.

After you have decided to purchase a specific home and have agreed upon a price, you will probably borrow to buy the home. Financing a home purchase requires obtaining a mortgage, being aware of the types of mortgages, and settling the real estate transaction.

Obtaining a Mortgage

To finance your home purchase, you will need to obtain funds for a down payment, meet certain requirements of your lending institution, and assess different types of mortgages.

Down Payment Sources   How much cash you have available for a down payment will affect the size of the mortgage loan you require. A large down payment, such as 20 percent or more, will make it easier for you to obtain a mortgage.

Personal savings, pension plan funds, sales of investments or other assets, and assistance from relatives are the most common sources of down payment money. Parents can help their children in the purchase of a home by giving them a cash gift or a loan, depositing money with the lender to reduce the interest rate of the loan, cosigning the loan, or acting as comortgagors.

Private mortgage insurance (PMI) is usually required if the down payment is less than 20 percent. This coverage protects the lender from financial loss due to default. PMI charges, which are paid by the borrower, vary depending on the amount of the down payment. They may be paid in full at closing, but they are usually financed over the life of the mortgage.

Qualifying for a Mortgage   Do you have the funds you need for a down payment? Do you earn enough to make mortgage payments while also covering other living expenses? Do you have a favorable credit rating? Unless you pay cash for a home, you will be required to respond affirmatively to these questions in order to obtain financing. A **mortgage** is a long-term loan on a specific piece of property, such as a home or other real estate. Payments on a mortgage are made over an extended period, for example, 15 or 30 years. Financial institutions such as banks, savings and loan associations, credit unions, mortgage companies, and insurance companies are the most common home financing sources.

To qualify for a mortgage, you must meet criteria similar to those that must be met for other loans. The home you buy will serve as the security, or collateral, for the mortgage loan. The current level of interest rates will affect the amount and cost of your mortgage.

The major factors that affect the affordability of your mortgage are your income, other debts, the amount available for a down payment, the length of the loan, and current mortgage rates. The results calculated in Exhibit 9–8 are

1. The monthly mortgage payment you can afford.
2. The mortgage amount you can afford.
3. The home purchase price you can afford.

These sample calculations are typical of the calculations made by most financial institutions, but the actual qualifications for a mortgage will vary by lender and by the type of mortgage you apply for. In addition, current mortgage interest rates will affect the amount of the mortgage loan for which you qualify.

The mortgage loan for which a person can qualify is larger when interest rates are low than when they are high. For example, a person who can afford a monthly mortgage payment of $700 will qualify for a 30-year loan of

$86,995 at 9 percent
$79,765 at 10 percent
$73,503 at 11 percent
$68,052 at 12 percent
$63,279 at 13 percent
$59,078 at 14 percent
$55,360 at 15 percent

EXHIBIT 9–8   Housing Affordability and Mortgage Qualification Amounts

	Example A	Example B
Step 1. Determine your monthly gross income (annual income divided by 12).	$36,000 ÷ 12	
Step 2. With a down payment of at least 10 percent, lenders use 28 percent of monthly gross income as a guideline for TIPI (taxes, insurance, principal, and interest), 36 percent of monthly gross income as a guideline for TIPI plus other debt payments.	$ 3,000 × .36 ───── $ 1,080	3,000 × .28 ───── $ 840
Step 3. Subtract other debt payments (such as payments on an auto loan) and an estimate of the monthly costs of property taxes and homeowners insurance	− 180 − 200	— − 200
Affordable monthly mortgage payment	$ 700	640
Step 4. Divide this amount by the monthly mortgage payment per $1,000 based on current mortgage rates—a 10 percent, 30-year loan, for example (see Exhibit 9–9)—and multiply by $1,000	÷ $ 8.78 × $ 1,000	÷ $ 8.78 × $ 1,000
Affordable mortgage amount	$79,727	$72,893
Step 5. Divide your affordable mortgage amount by 1 minus the fractional portion of your down payment (1 − .1, for example, with a 10 percent down payment).	÷ .9	÷ .9
Affordable home purchase price	$88,585	$80,992

NOTE: The two ratios used by lending institutions (Step 2) and other loan requirements are likely to vary based on a variety of factors, including the type of mortgage, the amount of the down payment, your income level, and current interest rates. If you have other debts, lenders will calculate both ratios and then use the one that allows you greater flexibility in borrowing.

EXHIBIT 9–9

Mortgage Payment Factors *(Principal and Interest Factors per $1,000 of Loan Amount)*

Term Rate	30 Yrs.	25 Yrs.	20 Yrs.	15 Yrs.
7.5%	$ 6.99	$ 7.39	$ 8.06	$ 9.27
8.0	7.34	7.72	8.36	9.56
8.5	7.69	8.05	8.68	9.85
9.0	8.05	8.39	9.00	10.14
9.5	8.41	8.74	9.32	10.44
10.0	8.78	9.09	9.65	10.75
10.5	9.15	9.44	9.98	11.05
11.0	9.52	9.80	10.32	11.37
11.5	9.90	10.16	10.66	11.68
12.0	10.29	10.53	11.01	12.00
12.5	10.67	10.90	11.36	12.33
13.0	11.06	11.28	11.72	12.65
13.5	11.45	11.66	12.07	12.98
14.0	11.85	12.04	12.44	13.32
14.5	12.25	12.42	12.80	13.66
15.0	12.64	12.81	13.17	14.00

As interest rates rise, fewer people are able to afford the cost of an average-priced home.

When you compare costs at several mortgage companies, the interest rate you are quoted is not the only factor you should consider. The required down payment and the points charged will affect the interest rate. **Points** are prepaid interest charged by the lender. Each *discount point* is equal to 1 percent of the loan amount and should be viewed as a premium being paid for obtaining a lower mortgage rate. In deciding whether to take a lower rate with more points or a higher rate with fewer points, do the following:

Step 1.   Determine the difference between the monthly payments that must be made to the two lenders.

Step 2.   Determine the difference between the points charged by the two lenders.

Step 3.   Divide the result in Step 2 by the result in Step 1. This will tell you how many months it will take for the lower monthly payment to offset the higher cost of the points.

If you plan to live in your home longer than the time calculated in Step 3, it is better to pay the points and take the lower mortgage rate. This decision will, of course, be affected by the amount of funds available to pay the points at the time of closing. If you will probably sell your home sooner than the time calculated in Step 3, take the higher mortgage rate with fewer discount points.

Obtaining a mortgage requires the potential borrower to submit an application form containing personal and financial data. Most lenders charge a loan application fee of between $100 and $300.

Once the loan application has been reviewed, an interview is usually scheduled. At this meeting, the lender requests additional information and gives the potential borrower an opportunity to prove employment, level of income, ownership of assets, and amounts owed.

Other common charges associated with the mortgage application process are loan origination fees, property appraisal fees, and a credit report charge. The final decision to grant the loan is based on the creditworthiness of the potential borrower and an evaluation of the home, including its location, condition, and value.

The loan commitment is the financial institution's decision to provide the funds needed to purchase a specific property. At this point, the purchase contract for the home becomes legally binding. The approved mortgage application usually locks in an interest rate for 45 to 60 days.

Types of Mortgages

The major categories of mortgages are fixed rate, fixed payment mortgages and adjustable rate, variable payment mortgages (see Exhibit 9–10). In addition, creative financing offers other types of mortgages that include the buydown and the shared appreciation mortgage. You should also be familiar with second mortgages (home equity loans) and refinancing.

Fixed Rate, Fixed Payment Mortgages   The main types of home loans in this category include the conventional mortgage, government-guaranteed financing programs, and the balloon mortgage.

1.   The **conventional mortgage** has equal payments over 15 or 30 years based on a fixed interest rate. This mortgage offers homebuyers certainty about future loan payments. The mortgage payments are set at a level that allows **amortization** of the loan. That is, the balance owed is reduced with each payment. Since the amount borrowed is large, the payments made during the early years of the mortgage are applied mainly to interest, with only small reductions in the principal of the loan. As the amount owed declines, the monthly payments have

EXHIBIT 9–10   Types of Mortgage Loans

Loan Type	Benefits	Drawbacks
1. Fixed rate, fixed payment		
a. Conventional 30-year mortgage	Fixed monthly payments for 30 years provide certainty of principal and interest payments.	Higher initial rates than adjustables.
b. Conventional 15-year mortgage	Lower rate than 30-year fixed; faster equity buildup and quicker payoff of loan.	Higher monthly payments.
c. FHA/VA fixed rate mortgages (30-year and 15-year)	Low down payment requirements and fully assumable with no prepayment penalties.	May require substantial points; may have application red tape and delays.
d. "Balloon" loans (3–10-year terms)	May carry discount rates and other favorable terms, particularly when the loan is provided by the homeseller.	At the end of the 3–10-year term, the entire remaining balance is due in a lump-sum or "balloon" payment, forcing the borrower to find new financing.
2. Adjustable rate, variable payment		
a. Adjustable rate mortgage (ARM)—payment changes on one-year, three-year, and five-year schedules	Lower initial rates than fixed rate loans, particularly on the one-year adjustable. Generally assumable by new buyers. Offers possibility of future rate and payment decreases. Loans with rate "caps" may protect borrowers against increases in rates. In some cases, may be convertible to fixed rate plans after three years.	Shifts far greater interest rate risk onto borrowers than fixed rate loans. Without "caps," may also sharply push up monthly payments in future years.
b. Graduated payment mortgage (GPM)—payment increases by prearranged increments during first five–seven years, then levels off	Allows buyers with marginal incomes to qualify. Higher incomes over next five–seven years expected to cover gradual payment increases. May be combined with adjustable rate mortgage to further lower initial rate and payment.	May have higher annual percentage rate (APR) than standard fixed rate or adjustable rate loans. May involve negative amortization— increasing debt owed by lender.
c. Growing equity mortgage (GEM)—contributes rising portions of monthly payments to payoff of principal debt. Typically pays off in 15–18 years rather than 30.	Lower up-front payments, quicker loan payoff than conventional fixed rate or adjustable.	May have higher effective rates and higher down payments than other loans in the marketplace. Tax deductions for interest payments decrease over time.

SOURCE: *Real Estate Today*, National Association of Realtors.®

an ever greater impact on the loan balance. Near the end of the mortgage term, nearly all of each payment is applied to the balance.

For example, a $75,000, 30-year, 10 percent mortgage would have monthly payments of $658.18. The payments would be divided as follows:

	Interest		Principal	Remaining Balance
For the first month	$625.00	($75,000 × .10 × 1/12)	$ 33.18	$74,966.82 ($75,000 − $33.18)
For the second month	624.72	($74,966.82 × .10 × 1/12)	33.46	74,933.36 ($74,966.82 − $33.46)
For the 360th month	5.41		649.54	— 0 —

In the past, many conventional mortgages were *assumable*. This feature allowed the homebuyer to continue with the seller's original agreement. Assumable mortgages were especially attractive if the mortgage rate was lower than market interest rates at the time of the sale. Due to volatile interest rates, very few assumable mortgages are currently offered by lending institutions.

2.   Government-guaranteed financing programs include insured loans by the Federal Housing Authority (FHA) and loans guaranteed by the Veterans Administration (VA). These government agencies do not provide the mortgage money, but they do help homebuyers obtain low-interest, low–down payment loans.

To qualify for an FHA-insured loan, an individual must meet a few conditions related to the down payment and fees. Most low- and middle-income people in our society can qualify for the FHA loan program. The minimum down payment ranges from 3 to 5 percent, depending on the amount of the loan. This lower down payment makes it easier for a person to purchase a home. FHA-insured loans have interest rates lower than market interest rates since the FHA's involvement reduces the risk for the lending institution. The borrower is required to pay a fee for insurance that protects the lender against financial loss due to default. Despite the protection given the lender, the lower-than-market interest rate can result in extra prepaid interest, *points,* as a condition of the loan.

The VA-guaranteed loan program assists eligible veterans of the armed services in purchasing a home. As with the FHA program, the funds from VA loans come from a financial institution or a mortgage company and the risk is reduced by government participation. A VA loan can be obtained without a down payment. The points charged by the lending institution must be paid by the homeseller, but the veteran is usually responsible for other charges, such as origination and funding fees.

Both FHA-insured loans and VA-guaranteed loans can be attractive financing alternatives and are assumable by future owners when the house is sold to qualifying individuals. Both impose limits on the amount that can be borrowed, however, and a backlog of processing applications and approving loans can occur during periods of high demand for housing.

3.   The historically high mortgage rates of the early 1980s (Exhibit 9–11) helped stimulate various innovative lending plans for homebuyers. One such plan is the **balloon mortgage,** which has fixed monthly payments and a very large final payment, usually after three, five, or seven years. This financing plan is designed for individuals who wish to buy a home during periods of high interest rates but expect to be able to refinance the loan before or when the balloon payment is due. Many financial counselors advise against the use of a balloon mortgage since you

---

EXHIBIT 9–11

Mortgage Rates through the Years

The national average of interest rates paid for new home loans in the years listed was as follows:

1965	5.81%	1984	12.38%
1970	8.45	1985	11.58
1975	9.00	1986	9.82
1978	9.56	1987	9.31
1980	12.66	1988	9.19
1982	15.14	1989	10.13

SOURCE: *Savings Institution Sourcebook* (Chicago: United States League of Savings Institutions, 1989).

have to pay mortgage processing and closing costs when you refinance. Moreover, not being able to refinance in time could result in a major financial loss.

Adjustable Rate, Variable Payment Mortgages   This category includes adjustable rate mortgages, graduated payment mortgages, and growing equity mortgages.

4.   Adjustable rate and flexible payment mortgages give individuals a better opportunity to buy homes in times of high interest rates. The **adjustable rate mortgage (ARM),** also referred to as a flexible rate mortgage or a variable rate mortgage, has an interest rate that increases or decreases during the life of the loan based on changes in market interest rates. When mortgage rates were at record highs, many people took out variable rate home loans based on the expectation that interest rates would eventually go down. ARMs usually have a lower initial interest rate than fixed rate mortgages, but the risk of future interest rate increases resides with the borrower, not the lender.

A **rate cap** restricts the amount that the interest rate can increase during the loan term. This limit prevents the borrower from paying an interest rate significantly higher than the one in the original agreement. Most rate caps limit increases (or decreases) in your mortgage rate to two percentage points in a year and to no more than six points over the life of the loan.

A **payment cap** keeps the payments on an adjustable rate mortgage at a given level or limits the amount to which those payments can rise. When mortgage payments do not rise but interest rates do, the amount owed can increase in months in which the mortgage payment does not cover the interest owed. This increased loan balance, called *negative amortization,* means that the amount of your home equity is decreasing instead of increasing. As a result of such increases in the amount owed, the borrower usually has to make payments for a period longer than the one originally planned.

Consider several factors when you evaluate adjustable rate mortgages. First, consider the frequency of and the restrictions on allowed changes in interest rates. Second, consider the frequency of and the restrictions on changes in the monthly payment. Third, investigate the possibility that the loan will be extended due to negative amortization and find out whether the mortgage agreement limits the amount of negative amortization. Finally, find out what index the lending institution will use to set the mortgage interest rate over the term of the loan. A lending institution will revise the rate for an adjustable rate mortgage based on changes in the rates on U.S. Treasury securities, the Federal Home Loan Bank Board's mortgage rate index, or its own cost-of-funds index.

Convertible ARMs allow the homebuyer to change an adjustable rate mortgage to a fixed rate mortgage during a certain period, such as the time between the second year and the fifth year of the loan. A conversion fee, typically between $250 and $500, must be paid to obtain the fixed rate, which is usually 0.25 to 0.50 percent higher than the current rates for conventional 30-year mortgages.

5.   A **graduated payment mortgage** is a financing agreement in which payments rise to different levels every 5 or 10 years during the term of the loan. During the early years, the payments are relatively low. This mortgage is especially beneficial to individuals who anticipate increases in income in future years.

6.   A **growing equity mortgage** provides for increases in payments that allow the amount owed to be paid off more quickly. With such a mortgage, a person would be able to pay off a 30-year home loan in 15 to 18 years. A growing equity

mortgage may be desired by high-income individuals who want to quickly build equity in their homes.

Creative Financing   In an effort to assist first-time buyers and others, home builders and financial institutions have created mortgages that make it easier to purchase a home and pay off the loan.

7.   A **buy down** is an interest rate subsidy from a home builder or a real estate developer that reduces the mortgage payments during the first few years of the loan. This assistance is intended to stimulate sales among homebuyers who cannot afford conventional financing. After the buy-down period, the mortgage payments increase to the level that would have existed without the financial assistance.

8.   The **shared appreciation mortgage (SAM)** is an arrangement in which the borrower agrees to share the increased value of the home with the lender when the home is sold. This agreement provides the homebuyer with a below-market interest rate and with lower payments than those of a conventional loan. To obtain these conditions, the borrower typically has to agree to give the lending institution 30–50 percent of the home's appreciation when the home is sold. Shared appreciation agreements are also common when parents provide financial assistance for the purchase of a home.

Additional Home Financing   After your primary mortgage has been established, you may consider making use of your equity or seeking a lower interest rate.

9.   A **second mortgage,** more commonly called a *home equity loan,* allows a homeowner to borrow on the paid-up value of the property. Traditional second mortgages allow a homeowner to borrow a lump sum against the equity and to repay it in monthly installments. More recently, lending institutions have offered a variety of home equity loans, including a line-of-credit program that allows the borrower to obtain loan funds by writing a check. A home equity loan makes it possible to deduct the interest on consumer purchases in income tax returns, but it entails the risk of losing the home if required payments on both the first and second mortgages are not made. To help prevent this financial disaster, some states restrict the use of home equity loans. In Texas, for example, a second mortgage may be used only for home improvement expenses.

10. Plans are being offered to assist individuals with low incomes who have a high equity in their home. **Reverse mortgages** provide the elderly homeowner with tax-free income in the form of a loan that is paid back (with interest) when the home is sold or the homeowner dies. These financing plans have two main formats. A *reverse mortgage annuity* guarantees the homeowner a monthly income for life. In contrast, a reverse mortgage may have a set term at the end of which the loan would be due. This format is likely to offer a higher monthly income, but it confronts the elderly person with the prospect of selling the home before he or she desires to do so. Reverse mortgages are expected to be increasingly available through both government agencies and private lending institutions.

11. During the term of your mortgage, you may want to **refinance** your home—that is, to obtain a new mortgage on your current home at a lower interest rate. Before taking this action, be sure that the costs of refinancing do not offset the savings of a lower interest rate. Refinancing is most advantageous when you can get a mortgage rate 2 or 3 percent lower than your current rate and when you plan to own your present home for at least two more years. Also be sure to consider the tax deductibility of refinancing costs.

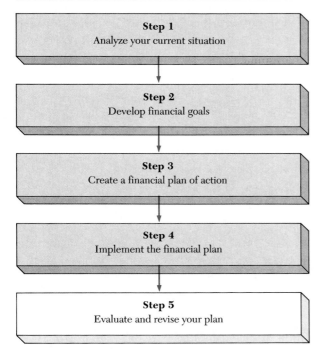
Closing the Transaction

The *closing* involves a meeting of the buyer, seller, and lender of funds, or representatives of each party, to complete the transaction. Documents are signed, last-minute details are settled, and appropriate amounts are paid. A number of expenses are incurred at the closing. The **closing costs,** also referred to as settlement costs, are the fees and charges paid when a real estate transaction is completed (see Exhibit 9–12).

Title insurance is a closing cost. This coverage has two phases. First, the title company defines the boundaries of the property being purchased and conducts a search to determine whether the property is free of claims, such as unpaid real estate taxes. Second, during the mortgage term the title company protects the owner and the lender against financial loss resulting from future defects in the title and from other unforeseen property claims not excluded by the policy.

Also due at closing time is the fee for recording the deed. The **deed** is the document that transfers ownership of property from one party to another. Mortgage insurance is another possible closing cost. If required, mortgage insurance protects the lender from loss as a result of a mortgage default.

EXHIBIT 9–12

Components of a Closing
Statement

At the transaction settlement of a real estate purchase and sale, the buyer and seller will encounter a variety of expenses that are commonly referred to as closing costs.

	Cost Range Encountered	
	By the Buyer	**By the Seller**
Title search fee	$50–$150	—
Title insurance	$100–$600	$100–$600
Attorney's fee	$50–$700	$50–$700
Property survey	—	$100–$400
Appraisal fee	$100–$300	—
Recording fees; transfer taxes	$15–$30	$15–$30
Credit report	$25–$75	—
Termite inspection	$50–$150	—
Lender's origination fee	1–3% of loan amount	—
Reserves for home insurance and property taxes	Varies	—
Interest paid in advance (from the closing date to the end of the month)	Varies	—
Real estate broker's commission	—	5–7% of purchase price

NOTE: These amounts—paid, of course, by the buyer—are in addition to the down payment.

The Real Estate Settlement Procedures Act of 1974 was enacted to assist homebuyers in understanding the closing process and closing costs. This legislation requires that loan applicants be given certain information, including an estimate of the closing costs, before the actual closing. Obtaining this information as early as possible will allow you to plan for the closing costs.

At the time of closing and when you make your monthly payments, you will probably have to deposit money that will be used to pay home-related expenses. For example, the lender will require that you have property insurance on the home. An **escrow account** is money, usually deposited with a financial institution, for the payment of property taxes and homeowners insurance. This account protects the lender from financial loss due to unpaid real estate taxes or damage from fire or other hazards. Some states require that interest be paid on the amount in an escrow account.

As a new homebuyer, you might also consider purchasing an agreement that affords you protection against the cost of defects in the home. Implied warranties created by state laws may cover some problem areas, but other repair costs can also occur. Home builders and real estate sales companies offer warranties to buyers. Coverage purchased from the Home Owners Warranty Corporation includes protection against structural, wiring, and plumbing defects and defects in the heating system and other mechanical systems. About one fourth of the nation's home builders participate in this program, which offers a 10-year warranty on new homes. Or a new homeowner may wish to purchase from a real estate company such as Electronic Realty Associates (ERA) or Century 21, a service contract that warrants appliances, plumbing, air-conditioning systems, the heating unit, and other items for one year. As with any service contract, you must decide whether the coverage provided and the chances of repair expenses justify the cost.

SELLING YOUR
PLACE OF
RESIDENCE

L.O.5
Develop a strategy for selling
a home.

Most of the people who buy a home will eventually be on the other side of the transaction. Selling your home requires preparing it for selling, setting a price, and deciding whether to sell it yourself or to sell it through a real estate agent.

Preparing Your Home for Selling

The effective presentation of your home can result in a fast, financially favorable sale. Real estate salespeople recommend that you make needed home repairs and paint the exterior and interior areas. Clear the garage and exterior areas of toys, debris, and old vehicles, and keep the lawn cut and the leaves raked. Keep the kitchen and bathroom clean. Avoid offensive odors by removing garbage and keeping pets and their areas clean. Remove excess furniture and dispose of unneeded items to make the house and its closets and storage areas look larger. When showing your home, open drapes and turn on lights to give it a pleasant atmosphere. This effort will give your property an improved image and enable you to sell it sooner.

Determining the Selling Price

Putting a price on your home can be a difficult decision. You face the risk of not selling it immediately if the price is too high, and you may not get a fair settlement if the price is too low. An **appraisal,** which is an estimate of the current value of the property, can provide a good indication of the price you should set for it. Your asking price will be influenced by the recent selling price of comparable homes in your area, demand in the housing market, and the availability of financing based on current mortgage rates.

The home improvements you have made may or may not increase the selling price. A hot tub or an exercise room may have no value for potential buyers of your home. Among the most desired improvements are energy-efficient features, a remodeled kitchen, an additional or remodeled bathroom, added rooms and storage space, a converted basement, a fireplace, and an outdoor deck or patio.

The time to think about selling your home is when you buy it and every day you live in it. Daily maintenance, timely repairs, and home improvements will increase the future sales price.

Sale by Owner

Each year, about 10 percent of home sales are made by the owner. If you decide to sell your home without the use of a real estate professional, price the home and then advertise it through local newspapers and through a flier describing it in detail. Obtain a listing sheet from a real estate office as an example of the information to include on your flier. Distribute the flier through stores and other public areas.

When selling your own home, obtain information on the availability of financing and on the qualifications required for financing. This information will help you and potential buyers to determine whether a sale is possible. Use the services of a lawyer or title company to assist you with the contract, the closing, and other legal matters.

Require potential buyers to provide their names, addresses, telephone numbers, and background information, and show your home by appointment only. As a security measure, show it only when two or more adults are at home. Selling

Pepper . . . and Salt

GREENHILLS REALTY

"Your ad made my house sound so great I've decided not to sell it."

From *The Wall Street Journal,* with permission of Cartoon Features Syndicate.

your own home can save you several thousand dollars in commission, but it requires an investment in time and effort.

let take about 6%

Listing with a Real Estate Agent

If you decide to sell your home with the assistance of a real estate agent, you can probably choose among many real estate businesses in your area. These businesses range from firms owned by one person to nationally advertised companies. Primary selection factors should be the real estate agent's knowledge of all aspects of your community and the willingness of the real estate agent to actively market your home.

Your real estate agent will provide you with various services. These services include suggesting a selling price, making potential buyers and other agents aware of your home, providing advice on features to highlight, conducting showings of your home, and handling the financial aspects of the sale. The real estate agent can be especially helpful in screening potential buyers to determine whether they will be able to qualify for a mortgage.

SUMMARY

L.O.1
Evaluate available housing alternatives.

Your needs, life situation, and financial resources are the major factors that will influence your selection of housing. You should assess renting and buying alternatives in terms of their financial and opportunity costs.

L.O.2
Analyze the costs and benefits associated with renting.

The main advantages of renting are that it offers mobility, imposes fewer responsibilities, and requires lower initial costs. The main disadvantages of renting are that it offers few financial benefits, imposes a restricted lifestyle, and entails legal concerns.

Home buying involves five major stages: (1) determining home ownership needs, (2) finding and evaluating a property to purchase, (3) pricing the property, (4) financing the purchase, and (5) closing the purchase transaction.

The costs associated with purchasing a home include the down payment, mortgage origination costs, and closing costs such as a deed fee, prepaid interest, attorney's fees, payment for title insurance and a property survey, and an escrow account for homeowners insurance and property taxes.

When selling a home, you must decide whether to make certain repairs and improvements, determine a selling price, and choose between selling it yourself and using the services of a real estate agent.

GLOSSARY

Adjustable rate mortgage (ARM)   A home loan with an interest rate that can change during the mortgage term due to changes in market interest rates; also called a flexible rate mortgage or a variable rate mortgage.

Amortization   The reduction of a loan balance through payments made over a period of time.

Appraisal   An estimate of the current value of a property.

Balloon mortgage   A home loan with fixed monthly payments and a large final payment, usually after three, five, or seven years.

Buy down   An interest rate subsidy from a home builder or a real estate developer that reduces a homebuyer's mortgage payments during the first few years of the loan.

Closing costs   Fees and charges paid when a real estate transaction is completed; also called settlement costs.

Condominium   An individually owned housing unit in a building with a number of such units.

Conventional mortgage   A fixed rate, fixed payment home loan.

Cooperative housing   A form of housing in which a building containing a number of housing units is owned by a nonprofit organization whose members rent the units.

Deed   The document that transfers ownership of property from one party to another.

Earnest money   A portion of the price of a home that the buyer deposits as evidence of good faith to indicate a serious purchase offer.

Escrow account   Money, usually deposited with a financial institution, for the payment of property taxes and homeowners insurance.

Graduated payment mortgage   A home financing agreement in which payments rise to different levels during the loan term.

Growing equity mortgage   A home loan agreement in which payment increases allow the amount owed to be paid off more quickly.

Lease   A legal document that defines the conditions of a rental agreement.

Manufactured home   A housing unit that is fully or partially assembled in a factory before being moved to the living site.

Mortgage   A long-term loan on a specific piece of property, such as a home or other real estate.

Payment cap   A limit on the payment increases for an adjustable rate mortgage.

Points   Prepaid interest charged by a lending institution for a mortgage; each discount point is equal to 1 percent of the loan amount.

Rate cap   A limit on the increases in the interest rate charged on an adjustable rate mortgage.

Refinance   The process of obtaining a new mortgage on a home in order to get a lower interest rate or a more favorable loan agreement.

Reverse mortgage   A loan, based on the equity in a home, that provides the elderly homeowner with tax-free income and is paid back with interest when the home is sold or the homeowner dies.

Second mortgage   A cash advance based on the paid-up value of a home; also called a home equity loan.

Shared appreciation mortgage (SAM)   A home loan agreement in which the borrower agrees to share the increased value of the home with the lender when the home is sold.

Title insurance   Insurance that during the mortgage term protects the owner or the lender against financial loss resulting from future defects in the title and from other unforeseen property claims not excluded by the policy.

Zoning laws   Restrictions on how the property in an area can be used.

DISCUSSION QUESTIONS

L.O.1   1. Give examples that show how a person's employment and household situation could influence his or her selection of housing.

L.O.1   2. What are some commonly overlooked opportunity costs associated with a housing decision?

L.O.2   3. How can the experiences of others be helpful in finding and renting an apartment or a house?

L.O.2   4. Which components of a lease are likely to be most negotiable?

L.O.3   5. What specific financial, personal, and economic factors could indicate that a situation is right for the purchase of housing?

L.O.3   6. What guidelines would you suggest regarding the amount that individuals should spend on the purchase of a house?

L.O.3   7. How can the quality of the local school system benefit even the homeowners who do not have school-age children?

L.O.4   8. What factors affect a person's ability to qualify for a mortgage?

L.O.4   9. Under what conditions would you recommend the use of an adjustable rate mortgage?

L.O.4   10. How do closing costs affect your ability to afford a home purchase?

L.O.5   11. What factors should you consider when you are deciding whether to sell your home yourself or to use the services of a real estate agent?

Opening Case Questions

1. How could the Bowmans have benefited from buying a home that needed improvements?

2. How might Beth Franklin have found out when mortgage rates were at a level that would make refinancing her condominium more affordable?

3. Although the Zorans had good reasons for continuing to rent, what factors might make it desirable for an individual or a family to buy a home?

PROBLEMS AND ACTIVITIES

L.O.1   1. What type of housing would you suggest for people in the following life situations?
   a. A single parent with two school-age children.
   b. A two-income couple without children.
   c. A person with both dependent children and a dependent parent.
   d. A couple near retirement with grown children.

L.O.1,2   2. Based on the following data, would you recommend buying or renting?

Rental Costs	**Buying Costs**
Annual rent, $7,380	Annual mortgage payments, $9,800
Insurance, $145	($9,575 is interest)
Security deposit, $650	Property taxes, $1,780
	Insurance/maintenance, $1,050
	Down payment/closing costs, $4,500
	Growth in equity, $225
	Estimated annual appreciation, $1,700

Assume an after-tax savings interest rate of 6 percent and a tax rate of 28 percent.

L.O.2   3. Using newspaper advertisements and information from rental offices, prepare an oral or written presentation comparing the costs, facilities, and features of available apartments in your area.

L.O.2   4. Interview a lawyer and a landlord to obtain their views on common problems associated with renting. How do their views on tenant-landlord relations differ?

L.O.3   5. Visit the sales offices of condominiums, new housing developments, and mobile home companies. Based on the information you obtain, what are the benefits and the potential problems of these types of housing?

L.O.3   6. Interview a real estate agent about the process involved in selecting and buying a home. Ask about housing prices in your area and about the services that the agent offers. What does the agent think will happen to housing prices and interest rates over the next six months?

L.O.4   7. Estimate the affordable monthly mortgage payment, the affordable mortgage amount, and the affordable home purchase price for the following situation (see Exhibit 9–8):
   Monthly gross income, $2,950
   Down payment to be made— 15 percent of purchase price
   Other debt (monthly payment), $160
   Monthly estimate for property taxes and insurance, $210
   30-year loan at 10.5 percent.

L.O.4   8. Talk with people who have different types of mortgages. What suggestions can they offer about obtaining and selecting a home financing plan?

L.O.4   9. How can a person determine whether to pay more discount points or make a higher monthly payment when obtaining a mortgage?

L.O.4   10. Based on Exhibit 9–9, what would be the monthly mortgage payments for each of the following situations?

   a. A $40,000, 15-year loan at 11.5 percent.

   b. A $76,000, 30-year loan at 9 percent.

   c. A $65,000, 20-year loan at 10 percent.

   What relationship exists between the length of the loan and the monthly payment? How does the mortgage rate affect the monthly payment?

L.O.5   11. Visit a couple of open houses for homes on sale. What features seemed to appeal most to potential buyers? What efforts were made to attract potential buyers to the open houses?

LIFE SITUATION   Case 9–1

Hunting for a Home

Dan and Lia Schultz were recently married and are looking for a permanent residence. Dan, a computer operator, is learning programming as a part-time student. Lia works part-time as a receptionist and is taking courses toward a degree in health care administration. They have $2,000 in a savings account.

Dan and Lia are considering renting an apartment that has a monthly rent of $575 and requires a $600 security deposit. They are also looking into a condominium that they can buy with a $2,300 down payment and monthly mortgage payments of $730.

Questions

1. What personal and household factors should Dan and Lia consider before choosing their housing?
2. What positive and negative aspects of the two housing alternatives mentioned above should Dan and Lia consider?
3. Besides the two housing alternatives mentioned above, what other alternatives might be available to Dan and Lia?
4. What future events might affect the current choice made by Dan and Lia?
5. What should Dan and Lia do?

LIFE SITUATION   Case 9–2

Selecting a Mortgage

Michelle Dean is planning to buy a small house instead of continuing to rent. This house will cost $82,000, and she will be able to make a down payment of $22,000. While applying for a mortgage, Michelle was given the choice between a fixed rate mortgage and a variable rate mortgage. The payments on the fixed rate mortgage will be $80 more a month than those on the variable rate mortgage. If interest rates rise, however, the payments on the variable rate mortgage may increase.

Questions

1. What financial factors should Michelle consider before buying a home?
2. Under what circumstances should Michelle take the variable rate mortgage?
3. What factors could cause interest rates to rise and Michelle's monthly payment to increase?
4. What action should Michelle take?

SUPPLEMENTARY READINGS

For Additional Information on Renting

Donnelly, Barbara. "Formula May Determine if Buying a Home or Renting Is Way to Go." *The Wall Street Journal,* January 23, 1990, pp. C1, C19.

Landlords and Tenants. American Bar Association, Public Education Division, 750 North Lake Shore Drive, Chicago, IL 60611.

Moskovitz, Myron, and Ralph Warner. *Tenants' Rights.* Nolo Press, 950 Park Street, Berkeley, CA 94710.

Saltzman, Amy. "To Buy or Rent Is a Question for the '90s." *U.S. News & World Report,* April 17, 1989, pp. 68–70.

For Additional Information on Home Buying

Affordable Housing: Manufactured Homes. Circular 1299. Cooperative Extension Service, University of Illinois, Urbana, IL 61801.

Bob Vila's Guide to Buying Your Dream House. Boston: Little, Brown, 1990.

Irwin, Robert. *Tips and Traps When Buying a Home.* New York: McGraw-Hill, 1990.

Kiernan, Michael. "Deciding whether to Move or Improve." *U.S. News & World Report,* April 17, 1989, pp. 71, 73.

Reilly, John W. *The Language of Real Estate.* 3rd ed. Chicago: Longman Financial Services, 1989.

Updegrave, Walter L. "It's Time to Rethink Your Biggest Investment." *Money,* June 1989, pp. 69–74, 76.

For Additional Information on Financing and Selling a Home

"Do You Know Where Your Mortgage Is?" *Consumer Reports,* July 1989, p. 441.

Eisenson, Marc. *A Banker's Secret: Your Mortgage Is a Great Investment.* Good Advice Press, Box 78, Elizaville, NY 12523.

Irwin, Robert. *Tips and Traps When Selling a Home.* New York: McGraw-Hill, 1990.

Thompson, Terri. "Finding the Way to Pay for Your Dream." *U.S. News & World Report,* April 17, 1989, pp. 74–75.

Thomsett, Michael C. *How to Sell Your Home for Top Dollar.* Homewood, Ill.: Dow Jones-Irwin, 1989.

10 *Transportation Options and Costs*

Few of us live, work, and shop within a small geographic area. Most of us need transportation in order to go to work or school or for other reasons. Transportation, and more specifically the automobile, has become a necessity for most of the people in our society. For over 75 years, the automobile has affected the way we live and the way we do business. The financial demands of transportation make it necessary to carefully plan this expenditure. Your selection and use of transportation alternatives are a fundamental component of your personal financial plan.

LEARNING OBJECTIVES
After studying this chapter, you will be able to

L.O.1 Analyze the factors that influence transportation decisions.

L.O.2 Investigate the process of buying a used car.

L.O.3 Develop a strategy for purchasing a new car.

L.O.4 Determine the costs associated with owning and operating an automobile.

L.O.5 Recognize the legal and social concerns associated with automobile ownership.

OPENING CASE

On the Road Again!

Andrew and Jill Nagel have never owned a car during their 17 years of marriage. Work is a short commute by train or bus; taxi service takes care of their need to get to shopping, the theater, or friends in town. Several times a year, the Nagels rent a car for use on a weekend trip or on an extended visit with friends. Owning a car is not a necessity for everyone in our society. Andrew has said a number of times, "Living in the city is expensive enough. If we had to have a car, it would be impossible to control our finances in a sane manner."

Mike and Patty Owen both work, so they both need cars. Both of their teenage sons also have cars, with which they get to school and their part-time jobs. But wait—the Owens are still one car short. Their daughter goes to the college across town, so she needs a car or a ride. Coordinating work, school, and other schedules so as to satisfy the transportation needs of all the Owens can be a major task. And the Owens also have to satisfy the financial demands of being a four-car family.

In transportation decisions, needs, lifestyles, and financial resources are intertwined. Most individuals and families are required to make important value judgments and economic choices regarding the transportation component of their financial planning efforts.

THE BASICS OF SELECTING TRANSPORTATION

L.O.1
Analyze the factors that influence transportation decisions.

Like housing and food, transportation is usually a major consumer expense. Daily needs and desires require financial allocations for travel to work, school, and other activities. While transportation is clearly a basic need for most individuals, that need can be met in many ways. As shown in Exhibit 10–1, a variety of personal, social, and economic factors determine the ways in which you will meet it.

Your Lifestyle and Transportation

Many aspects of your life are affected by the relationship between needs and desires and your ability to pay for the transportation required to satisfy them. Your financial situation impels you to make a rational transportation decision. However, emotional factors are also involved. A desire for convenience may be a primary motivator of the travel modes you choose. Such factors as luxury, style, and appearance can also affect your choices, especially if you need to project a certain business or professional image.

If simplicity characterizes your lifestyle, this may be reflected in your use of a bicycle as your primary vehicle. The bicycle is a transportation alternative that provides convenience and low-cost operation and has health and fitness benefits as well.

Transportation Opportunity Costs

Like every other financial decision, the transportation decision should consider the monetary and personal opportunity costs of the alternative chosen. The wisest choice for your personal and financial situation will be achieved when your transportation decision is made in light of

- The possible inconvenience of depending on public transportation.
- The money saved by using public transportation instead of owning your own vehicle.

- The savings and investment income lost on the down payment used to finance a vehicle.
- The differences in the operating costs (gas mileage, insurance, depreciation) of vehicles of different models and sizes.
- The trade-off between the higher insurance and depreciation costs of a new car and the higher repair costs of a used car.

You need to consider these factors as you narrow down your selection among public transportation and various purchase alternatives.

The Public Transportation Option

Some people do not want the problems associated with owning and operating an automobile. Other people cannot afford an automobile. **Mass transit** refers to systems of public transportation, such as bus or train lines, that allow the fast, efficient movement of many people. Many people select mass transit to fill their transportation needs. As the demand for public transportation has increased, government has made efforts to upgrade and expand it. Modern buses and additional intracity train routes, supported by public funds, have made this travel alternative more attractive.

A person's lifestyle will affect the use of public transportation. Some of the people whose primary work and other activities take place within areas served by mass transit systems enjoy the convenience and the avoidance of traffic and parking difficulties that these systems offer. Others use public transportation to

---

EXHIBIT 10–1

A Decision-Making Model for Purchasing Transportation

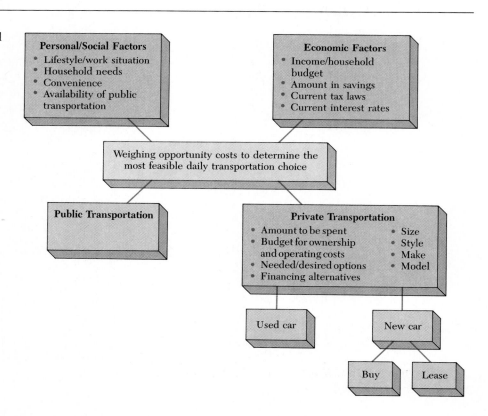

save time and money. Still others use it to reduce the pollution caused by automobile emissions.

Some Fundamental Purchasing Decisions

Buying an automobile involves a number of choices and alternatives. The process should begin with some basic decisions related to finances and to vehicle size, style, and model.

Budget Your financial situation will be a major influence on your decisions. If housing, food, clothing, and other living expenses account for most of your income, your spending on transportation will require tight control. But if money is available, you may elect to use a large portion of your available resources to buy and operate an automobile.

Size Consumers can choose from over 200 different types of automobiles. This maze of choices can be reduced by first deciding what car size you want (see Exhibit 10–2).

EXHIBIT 10–2

Lifestyle and Other Influences on the Selection of a Vehicle Size

Minicompact   Subcompact
Compact

- Less expensive to buy and operate
- Appropriate for individuals and small households
- Limited passenger and cargo space

Midsize (intermediate)

- Provides adequate passenger and cargo space for most households
- Appropriate for older drivers, more comfortable than small cars, easier to handle than larger cars

Full-Size

- Appropriate for use by households with more than four passengers or for use with business customers
- Higher purchase price and operating costs

Minivan
Full-Size Van

- Offers extra passenger and cargo space at a reasonable purchase price and reasonable operating costs
- Appropriate for households and businesses that need to transport groups of people or additional cargo

Pickup Truck

- Useful for travel in areas with a rough terrain
- Practical for use in certain types of business activities

Style   Body style is most influenced by the number of doors you prefer. Do you want a two- or four-door vehicle? Will your needs be better served by a hatchback or a station wagon? Or does your lifestyle call for a convertible, a minivan, or a pickup truck?

Make and Model   The specific model is your final consideration. Most manufacturers offer twin models with different names. For example, certain Mercury models are also available as Fords. General Motors has similar models of Buicks, Chevrolets, Oldsmobiles, and Pontiacs. For many years, the Chevrolet Camaro and the Pontiac Firebird have had twin bodies. The Dodge Caravan and Plymouth Voyager are twin minivans. Foreign competitors also have duplications among their models. The Dodge Colt, for example, is a twin of the Mitsubishi Mirage.

New or Used: Which Is for You?

Since most people buy an automobile, a primary decision is whether to buy a new automobile or a used one. This decision is based primarily on financial factors. Can you afford the costs associated with buying a new automobile? A used car is less expensive to buy than a new car.

Your decision to buy a new automobile will be influenced by your financial resources and by economic conditions. Your income and your financial situation may allow you to buy a new car regularly. Or increased prices and high interest rates may impair your ability to buy a new car. Such economic factors will frequently modify your decision on whether to buy a new or used car.

Automobile Information Sources

Readily available data sources related to automobiles include industry information, media sources, financial institutions, product testing organizations, and government agencies.

Industry Information   Automobile manufacturers are a primary source of information. Promotional brochures provide data about models, styles, and options on currently available vehicles. Automobile dealers can provide price information.

Media Sources   Many newspapers have special sections on automobile purchasing and maintenance. Specialized periodicals such as *Motor Trend* and *Car and Driver* provide in-depth data about automobile specifications and maintenance procedures.

Financial Institutions   Banks, savings and loan associations, finance companies, and other organizations that finance automobile purchases also provide information. *Car Facts,* an educational program of the Credit Union National Association, helps credit union members make sound auto-buying and -financing decisions. This program makes available a trained auto adviser and a library of printed resources to help credit union members select, shop for, and finance an automobile.

Testing and Rating Organizations   Each April, *Consumer Reports* gives the results of the automobile testing efforts of Consumers Union. This annual sum-

PERSONAL FINANCE JOURNAL

Automobile Testing at Consumers Union

How would you like to buy 35 new cars a year? That's exactly what Consumers Union, publisher of *Consumer Reports,* does. To provide readers with accurate test results, it inspects, drives, and crashes today's most popular models. It buys these vehicles in the same manner as you would buy a car. That is, Consumers Union has shoppers bargain with dealers for the best price.

The testing process for a car starts with a 50-item inspection of the car's features. The car's cargo space and seating comfort and the location and convenience of its gauges, switches, and pedals are evaluated. To determine the ease of starting in cold weather, the car is not kept in a garage. The climate control features of the car are tested under different conditions.

During road testing, engineers take turns driving each car over a 195-mile course and record their comments and impressions on tape and in writing. This test drive examines the car's noise level and its ability to maintain a steady course, the ease of steering and control, fuel economy, and the comfort of the ride with various passenger loads.

The sports car track phase of the investigation includes acceleration timing measurements, measurements of the braking distance at different speeds, tests of the control of the car during quick stops, and avoidance maneuver tests that use swerves similar to those that may be needed to avoid a collision. Finally, low-speed bumper crashes are conducted to determine the extent of vehicle damage. After two impacts at five miles per hour and one corner impact at three miles per hour, a professional estimates the cost of repairs.

The data from this extensive research are used to develop an overall rating for each vehicle. Ratings are combined with information from readers of *Consumer Reports* on their experiences with various models. The resulting frequency-of-repair charts and tables can provide a valuable indication of your potential satisfaction with a particular automobile.

SOURCE: "How CU Tests and Rates Cars," *Consumer Reports,* April 1989, pp. 218–19. Copyright 1989 by Consumers Union of United States, Inc., Mount Vernon, NY 10553. Excerpted by permission from *Consumer Reports,* April 1989.

---

mary provides extensive data about quality, price, safety, and performance. Other automobile ratings are published by *Changing Times* and *Consumers Digest.*

Government Agencies   The Federal Highway Administration monitors automobile operating costs and the safety features of highways. The National Highway Traffic Safety Administration provides test results to inform consumers about the safety and performance features of motor vehicles. The Federal Trade Commission regulates automobile sales practices and provides information about used car purchase disclosures, deceptive advertising, and financing. See Appendix D for additional information sources.

THE USED CAR OPTION

L.O.2
Investigate the process of buying a used car.

The average cost of a used car is about $8,000 less than the average cost of a new car, which was close to $16,000 in early 1990. New cars cost an average of 37.7 cents a mile to own and operate; used cars cost an average of 25.8 cents a mile. While many people prefer a previously owned vehicle, higher new car prices have created increased demand for used cars, resulting in higher costs for such cars. The process of buying a used car starts with an assessment of the places that sell previously owned vehicles and with an awareness of the consumer protection available to used car buyers. Next, a complete inspection is appropriate to ensure the quality of the used car you are getting. Finally, price negotiation is likely to be involved.

Used Car Sources

Americans spend over $100 billion a year to purchase more than 18 million used cars. New car dealers usually have a good supply of used vehicles. These automobiles are late-model vehicles that have been received as trade-ins for new car purchases. New car dealers generally give you a better warranty on a used car than do other sellers, and have a service department that reconditions the cars they sell. These services mean higher used car prices at new car dealers.

Used car dealers specialize in the sale of previously owned vehicles. They usually offer vehicles that are older than those offered by new car dealers. They are unlikely to have a service department, and if they give you a warranty, its coverage is very limited. In exchange for these shortcomings, however, you will probably be able to obtain a lower price from a used car dealer than from a new car dealer.

Individuals selling their own cars are another very common source of used cars. A private party sale can be a good bargain if the vehicle was well maintained; it can also be a nightmare. Since few consumer protection regulations cover private party sales, additional caution is suggested if you are considering the purchase of a used car from a private party.

Other used car sources include auctions and dealers that sell automobiles previously owned by businesses, auto rental companies, and government agencies. Each year, the General Services Administration of the federal government sells over 40,000 used vehicles. Some are luxury cars seized by federal drug law enforcement agents, but most are three-year-old sedans and station wagons. For further information, contact the General Services Administration, Washington, DC 20405. Beware of advertisements offering this information for a fee.

Government automobiles and the automobiles of auto rental companies are usually serviced regularly, but most of them have many different drivers or, as with police vehicles, undergo extreme use. Care must be taken to avoid an automobile of this kind that seems to be in good shape but has undergone extreme use.

Consumer Protection for Used Car Buyers

The Federal Trade Commission requires businesses that sell used cars to place a buyers guide sticker in the window of a car that is available for sale. This disclosure must state whether the car comes with a warranty and, if so, what specific warranty protection the dealer will provide. If no warranty is offered, the car is sold "as is" and the dealer assumes no responsibility for any repairs, regardless of any oral claims. About one half of all the used cars sold by dealers come without a warranty, and if you buy such a car, you must pay for any repairs that are needed to correct problems.

While a used car may not have an express warranty, most states have implied warranties that protect basic rights of the used car buyer. An implied warranty of merchantability means that the product is guaranteed to do what it is supposed to do. Thus, the used car is guaranteed to run—at least for a while!

The buyers guide required by the FTC encourages you to have the used car inspected by a mechanic and to get all promises in writing. You are also provided with a list of the 14 major systems of an automobile and some of the major problems that may occur in these systems. This list can be helpful in comparing the vehicles and warranties offered by different dealers. FTC used car regulations do not apply to vehicles purchased from private owners. Limited information may be available, but ask the seller whether you can see the receipts for maintenance and repairs.

You should follow two general rules when you buy a used car. First, buy your car from a source that gives some assurance of the car's reliability. Second, make a detailed investigation of the car's condition and performance potential.

The Inspection Process

The appearance of a used car can be deceptive. A well-maintained engine may be found inside a body with unsightly rust; a clean, shiny exterior may conceal major operational problems. A used car inspection as outlined in Exhibit 10–3 should be conducted.

Have a trained and trusted mechanic of *your* choice check the car to estimate the costs of current or potential repairs. This service will help avoid surprises when the vehicle becomes yours.

Although federal law makes odometer tampering illegal, the problem still exists. Mileage may be turned back to give a vehicle a newer appearance. Signs of possible odometer fraud are the failure of digits to line up straight and the presence of broken plastic in the speedometer case. If the brake pedal, tires, or upholstery look very old or very new for the number of miles shown on the odometer, there may have been odometer tampering.

Before making your final decision, find out whether there have been any safety recalls on the car. If so, have the necessary adjustments been made? Information about recalls may be obtained from the National Highway Traffic Safety Administration, a division of the U.S. Department of Transportation. This agency has an auto safety hot line for consumers (1-800-424-9393).

Used Car Price Negotiation

The final phase in buying a used car is agreeing on a price. You can begin to determine a fair price by checking newspaper ads for the prices of comparable vehicles. Other sources of current used car prices are *Edmund's Used Car Prices* and the National Automobile Dealers Association's *Official Used Car Guide,* commonly called the *blue book.* These publications are available at banks, credit unions, libraries, and bookstores. Since the blue book is updated monthly, some automobile sellers and buyers use the *black book,* a weekly report of automobile auction sales published by National Auto Research of Gainesville, Georgia.

The basic price of a used car is also influenced by a number of other factors. The number of miles that the car has been driven and the car's special features and options will directly affect its price. A low-mileage car will have a higher price than a comparable car with high mileage. The overall physical condition of the car and the demand for the given model also influence price.

Used car prices follow the trend of new car sales. If more people buy new cars and trade in or sell their present cars, the increased supply of used cars keeps their prices down. But when the demand for new cars is low and people keep their present cars longer, the prices of used cars increase.

EXHIBIT 10–3
Checking Out a Used Car

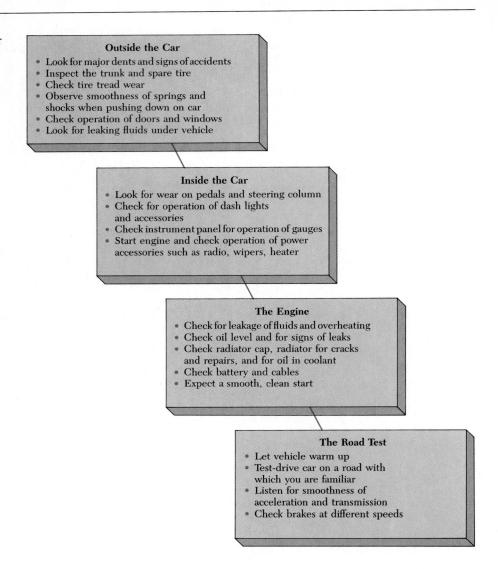

Outside the Car
- Look for major dents and signs of accidents
- Inspect the trunk and spare tire
- Check tire tread wear
- Observe smoothness of springs and shocks when pushing down on car
- Check operation of doors and windows
- Look for leaking fluids under vehicle

Inside the Car
- Look for wear on pedals and steering column
- Check for operation of dash lights and accessories
- Check instrument panel for operation of gauges
- Start engine and check operation of power accessories such as radio, wipers, heater

The Engine
- Check for leakage of fluids and overheating
- Check oil level and for signs of leaks
- Check radiator cap, radiator for cracks and repairs, and for oil in coolant
- Check battery and cables
- Expect a smooth, clean start

The Road Test
- Let vehicle warm up
- Test-drive car on a road with which you are familiar
- Listen for smoothness of acceleration and transmission
- Check brakes at different speeds

PURCHASING A NEW CAR

L.O.3
Develop a strategy for purchasing a new car.

Gathering information, selecting options for your new car, and bargaining for price are the primary phases of buying a new car.

Gathering Information

An important source of price information is on every new car. The **sticker price,** displayed in printed form on the vehicle, is the suggested retail price of a new car and its optional equipment. This information label presents the base price of the car as well as details about the costs of accessories and other items. The dealer's cost, or *invoice price,* is an amount less than the sticker price. The difference between the sticker price and the dealer's cost is the range available for negotiation. This range is larger for full-size, luxury cars; subcompacts usually do not have a wide negotiation range (see Exhibit 10–4).

EXHIBIT 10–4

Estimated Dealer Cost Factors as a Percentage of List Price

The following cost factors are an indication of the dealer's cost (in relation to the list price) for vehicles of various sizes. This information can help you in negotiating the sales price for a car or other vehicle. The cost factors shown exclude shipping charges and sales tax.

Mini- and subcompacts	.94 to .90
Compacts	.90 to .87
Intermediate size	.86 to .82
Full-size	.85 to .80
Small vans	.89 to .86
Full-size vans, pickup trucks	.84 to .80

NOTE: If consumer demand for certain types of vehicles is strong, you are more likely to pay close to the list price for them.

SOURCES: *Sylvia Porter's Personal Finance,* November 1988, p. 33; *Consumer Reports,* April 1990, pp. 235–57.

Information about the dealer's cost may be obtained from several sources. *Edmund's New Car Prices,* available in libraries and bookstores, is quite helpful. More sophisticated car cost data can be obtained from computerized services. Such data are also available from Consumers Union, publisher of *Consumer Reports.* For a minimal fee, a prospective buyer can obtain information about standard features, options, and costs. The Consumer Reports Auto Price Service is a worksheet that allows you to select the options you desire and to compute two totals, one for the suggested list price and the other for the dealer's cost. This information is used to bargain for the best deal.

Also helpful in planning your purchase of a new car is a knowledge of economic conditions in the automobile industry. A monthly report of car sales is published in *The Wall Street Journal* and the business section of newspapers. When automobile sales are lower than they were in previous months and years, your chances of getting a better price are improved.

Your prospects for obtaining a favorable deal may also be influenced by the time of day, the month, and the year. You will usually get the best attention during the morning or early afternoon. Salespeople may give you a better price near the end of the month in order to make a quota. Finally, some experts recommend that you buy your new car at the end of the model year (in late summer), winter, or early spring, when sales are very slow.

Selecting Options

Optional equipment can be grouped into three categories. The first category comprises mechanical devices that improve performance and ease of operation, such as larger engines, special transmissions, power steering, power brakes, and cruise control. The second category, comfort and convenience options, includes reclining seats, air-conditioning, stereo systems, power locks, rear window defoggers, and tinted glass. The third category consists of aesthetic features that add to the vehicle's visual appeal, such as metallic paint, special trim, and plush upholstery.

Color is an option that may make your car safer. Tests that involved viewing vehicles on backgrounds of concrete, meadows, and snow determined that the most visible colors were luminous orange, white (although white was difficult to see in snow and bright sunshine), light shades of orange, gray, and blue and that the colors most difficult to see were browns, greens, dark gray, dark blue, and black. Cars whose colors are the same as the colors of cars in company ads will probably have the best resale value since these ads probably use the colors that research has shown to be most appealing.

Several options may be available for a single price. For example, a convenience package may include power door locks, power windows, power mirror adjustment, and a push-button trunk opener. The package price may save you money, but do you want all of these items? Remember, too, that these power items will increase the operating cost of the vehicle by reducing fuel efficiency.

You may save money on optional equipment by selecting the deluxe edition of a model. Items that cost extra with the basic, low-price edition may be included as standard equipment with the higher-priced limited edition. Again, be sure that you want all of the options and compare the prices of the two editions to make sure that the cost difference is justified by the additional accessories (see Exhibit 10–5). Your willingness to accept different editions or comparable models of a different make will improve your negotiating position.

An option that you may want to do without is a *service contract*. This agreement can cover the cost of repairs not included in the warranty provided by the manufacturer. Service contracts range in price from $200 to over $1,000, but they do not always include everything you might expect. Most of these contracts contain a listing of parts that are not covered as well as other provisions. Failure of the engine cooling system is covered by all service contracts, but some service contracts exclude coverage of such failures if they are caused by over-heating.

Because of costs and exclusions, service contracts may not be a wise financial decision. You can minimize your concern about expensive repairs by setting aside a fund of money to pay for them. Then, if repairs are needed, the money to pay for them will be available. If the automobile performs as expected, you will be able to use the money in other ways. Most people spend less on repair costs than they would be charged for a service contract.

Price Bargaining

You should start your price bargaining by comparing the prices of similar automobiles at several dealers. This information will provide you with background on selling prices in relation to the sticker price. Be prepared to be flexible about the kind of car you choose. Your determination to buy a certain make, model, and style will weaken your negotiating position.

EXHIBIT 10–5
Dealer Costs for Popular Options

Item/Make, Model	Dealer Cost	List Price
Automatic four-speed transmission/Ford Mustang LX Sport	$437	$515
Cruise control/Buick LeSabre	149	175
Air-conditioning/Chevrolet Celebrity	659	775
AM–FM stereo cassette/Mazda 626 DX	342	450
Power windows/Pontiac Grand Am	242	285
Power steering/Toyota Tercel	214	250

SOURCE: *The Complete Car Cost Guide, 1989* (San Jose, Calif.: IntelliChoice).

Use dealer's cost information in your effort to get a vehicle price that is only a couple of hundred dollars over the dealer's cost. The closer your price is to the dealer's cost, the better the deal you are getting. Don't be fooled by an offer of a price far below the sticker price; the dealer's cost is the number that should concern you.

Will you receive a better deal by purchasing a car off the lot or by ordering one from the factory? The answer is not clear. Selling a car in stock helps a dealer clear inventory, but you may not get a good price deal on the car if it is in high demand among potential buyers. Moreover, the car on the lot may have options you don't want. Ordering a car means waiting several weeks or months, but it eliminates the dealer's inventory carrying cost.

When dealing with a car salesperson, be cautious of two deceptive techniques. **Lowballing** occurs when a new car buyer is quoted a very low price that add-on costs increase before the deal is concluded. **Highballing** occurs when a new car buyer is offered a very high price for a trade-in vehicle, with the extra amount made up by increasing the price of the new car. To prevent confusion in determining the true price of the new car, do not mention a trade-in vehicle until the cost of the new car has been settled. Then ask how much the dealer is willing to pay for your old car. If the offer price is not acceptable, sell the old car on your own.

To avoid the time and effort involved in price bargaining, you may wish to use a **car buying service,** a business that helps a person obtain a specific new car at a reasonable price with little effort. Also referred to as auto brokers, such businesses offer desired models with options for a price ranging between $50 and a couple of hundred dollars over the dealer's cost. First, the auto broker charges the customer a small fee for price information on desired models. Then, if you decide to buy a car, the auto broker arranges the purchase with a dealer near your home. Car buying services are frequently available through credit unions, churches, community organizations, and motor clubs.

Manufacturers and dealers may offer financing to assist you in your automobile purchase. Until the new car price has been set, however, you should not indicate that you intend to use the dealer's credit plan. Studies have revealed that low-cost loans are frequently offset by increased vehicle prices.

Before the sale is complete, you must sign a **sales agreement,** the legal document that contains the specific details of an automobile purchase. As with any contract, make sure that you understand the sales agreement before signing it. Also, be sure that everything you expect from the deal is presented in the sales agreement. If an item isn't in writing, you have no assurance that it will be included.

The sales agreement or another receipt will serve as proof of any deposit you pay. Obtain in writing the conditions that would allow you to get back your deposit. Make your deposit as small as possible to cut your losses in case you cancel the deal and are unable to get a refund.

Financing an Automobile Purchase

You may pay cash for your car, but since automobiles are very expensive, many people buy them on credit.

Financing Sources   As discussed in Chapter 7, car loans are available from banks, credit unions, consumer finance companies, and other financial institutions. Many lenders will preapprove you for a certain loan amount. This lets you know how much you can afford to spend on your car. It also separates financing from the process of negotiating the price of the car.

Dealer financing is another option. In an effort to make automobile buying more attractive, General Motors Acceptance Corporation, Ford Motor Credit Company, and Chrysler Financial Corporation have created new types of credit plans, such as balloon payment loans, variable rate loans, and special loans to meet the needs of recent college graduates. With a balloon payment loan, which is illegal in some states, for 48 months you make payments that are smaller than the payments on a regular loan. After 48 months, you have the options of continuing to make payments until the balance has been paid; returning the car to the dealer for a fee; or selling the car, paying off the loan, and keeping any leftover funds.

Obtaining the Best Financing   The lowest interest rate or the lowest payment does not necessarily mean the best credit plan.

You must select the length of your auto loan carefully. Otherwise, after two or three years the value of your car may be less than the amount you still owe on it; this is sometimes referred to as upside-down or *negative equity*. If you default on your loan or sell the car at this time, you would have to pay the difference—a very unpleasant financial situation!

The annual percentage rate (APR) is the best indicator of the true cost of credit. The federal Truth in Lending law requires that the APR be clearly stated in advertising and other communications. Low payments may seem to be a good deal, but they mean that you will be paying longer and that your total finance

"Just take a look at this onboard computer. It can figure square roots, percentages and the interest rate of your monthly installment."

From *The Wall Street Journal,* with permission of Cartoon Features Syndicate.

charges will be higher. Consider both the APR and the finance charge when you compare the credit terms of different lenders.

Automobile manufacturers frequently offer opportunities for low-interest financing. They may offer rebates at the same time, giving buyers a choice between a rebate and a low-interest loan. Although most people take the low-interest financing, the rebate is more advantageous under certain conditions (see Exhibit 10–6).

The Leasing Alternative

When federal tax laws eliminated deductions for consumer loan interest and sales tax, buying an automobile had fewer financial benefits and leasing became a more attractive alternative. **Leasing** is a contractual agreement under which monthly payments are made for the use of an automobile over a set time period—usually three, four, or five years. At the end of the lease term, the vehicle is returned to the leasing company.

The advantages of leasing an automobile include the following:

- Leasing requires only a small cash outflow for the security deposit, which usually amounts to two monthly payments, whereas buying requires a large cash outflow for the purchase price or a down payment.
- The monthly lease payments are likely to be lower than the monthly financing payments on a purchased automobile.
- Individuals can afford to lease a more expensive automobile than they would be able to buy on credit.
- The lease agreement provides detailed records for individuals who use their automobiles for business purposes.

Common drawbacks of automobile leasing include the following:

- You have no ownership interest in the vehicle.
- You must be able to meet requirements similar to those that must be met in qualifying for credit.
- You may be subject to additional costs for such things as extra mileage, certain needed repairs, or even a move to another state.

EXHIBIT 10–6

Comparing Rebates and Special Financing: An Example

	Auto Manufacturer Financing	Financial Institution Financing (Bank, Credit Union)
Annual percentage rate	6.9%	11.5%
Vehicle price	$12,500	$12,500
Down payment	$ 2,500	$ 2,500
Manufacturer's rebate	—	$ 1,500
Loan amount	$10,000	$ 8,500
Term of loan	48 months	48 months
Monthly payment	$ 239.00	$ 221.75
Total payment (not including down payment)	$11,472	$10,644

Total savings using financial institution, $828

. .

FINANCIAL PLANNING CALCULATIONS
Buying versus Leasing an Automobile

To compare the costs of purchasing and leasing a vehicle, the following framework can be used:

Purchase Costs

Total vehicle cost, including sales tax ($15,000)

Down payment (or full amount if paying cash)	$ 2,000
Monthly loan payment: $336 × 48-month length of financing (This item is zero if vehicle is not financed.)	16,128
Opportunity cost of down payment (or total cost of the vehicle if it is bought for cash): $2,000 × 4 years of financing/ownership × 6 percent	480
Less: Estimated value of vehicle at end of loan term/ownership period	−3,000
Total cost to buy	$15,608

Leasing Costs

Security deposit ($300)

Monthly lease payments: $300 × 48-month length of lease	$14,400
Opportunity cost of security deposit: $300 security deposit × 4 years × 6 percent	72
End-of-lease charges (if applicable)°	1,500
Total cost to lease	$15,972

°With a closed-end lease, charges for extra mileage or excessive wear and tear; with an open-end lease, end-of-lease payment if appraised value is less than estimated ending value.

. .

EXHIBIT 10–7

Terms and Conditions of an Automobile Lease

Initial Costs	**Continuing and End-of-Lease Costs**
Security deposit	Monthly payment
Advance payments	Length of agreement (number of payments)
Insurance requirements	Mileage charges (for exceeding the mileage specified in the lease agreement)
Sales tax and license fees	Charges for excessive wear and tear
"Capitalized cost reduction" (really a down payment) to reduce amount of monthly payments	End-of-lease and disposition charges

Individuals who lease automobiles are protected by the Consumer Leasing Act, administered by the Federal Trade Commission, which requires disclosure of various terms and conditions of the leasing agreement (see Exhibit 10–7).

Automobiles and other vehicles are commonly leased through a car dealer or an auto leasing company. Your lease payments are based on the length of the agreement (shorter leases have higher monthly payments) and the expected value of the vehicle at the completion of the lease, referred to as the *residual value*.

With a *closed-end,* or "walk-away," lease, which is the more common type, you return the vehicle at the end of the lease after paying any additional costs for damage or extra mileage. With such a lease, you are committed for the full term; getting out early will probably require a large fee. Since you have no risk with regard to the residual value of the car, your payments are higher with a closed-end lease than with an open-end lease.

An *open-end,* or "finance," lease, which is easier to terminate than a closed-end lease, may require you to pay the difference between the expected value of the leased automobile specified in the lease and the amount for which the leasing company sells it. The current market value will probably be determined by an independent appraiser. If the appraised value is equal to (or greater than) the estimated ending value specified in the lease, you will not owe another amount. But if the appraised value is less than that value, you will be required to make an *end-of-lease* payment.

Before entering into a leasing agreement, thoroughly investigate its costs and benefits in relation to your driving and financial situation.

FINANCIAL ASPECTS OF AUTOMOBILE OWNERSHIP

L.O.4
Determine the costs associated with owning and operating an automobile.

Most people spend more of their income on an automobile and related expenses than on any other item except housing and food. For many households, when insurance, license plates, and road taxes are included, the amount spent on an automobile exceeds the amount spent on food. Over a period of 50 years, you can expect to spend over $200,000 on automobile costs; this is seven times as much as the average person spends on education.

Automobile Operating Costs

Your driving costs will vary based on two main factors—the size of your automobile and the number of miles you drive. The American Automobile Association recently estimated that, given an annual mileage of 10,000, a subcompact would cost 30.6 cents a mile; a midsize car, 38.2 cents; and a full-size car, 42 cents.[1] These cost estimates are reached by considering two categories of expenses:

Fixed Ownership Costs	Variable Operating Costs
Depreciation	Gasoline and oil
Interest on auto loan	Tires
Insurance	Maintenance and repairs
License, registration, taxes, and fees	Parking and tolls

Fixed Ownership Costs   The largest fixed expense associated with a new automobile is **depreciation,** the loss in the vehicle's value due to time and use. Since money is not paid out for depreciation, many people do not consider it an actual expense. But this decreased value of an automobile is a cost that owners incur as they use the automobile and time goes by. Not all automobiles depreciate. Very old vehicles in excellent condition may *appreciate,* or increase in value.

While depreciation is considered a fixed cost of automobile ownership, the actual amount of the decreased value depends on two factors—the amount that the automobile is used and the care that is taken to maintain it. Low-mileage, well-maintained automobiles retain a larger portion of their original value than do other automobiles. Also, certain high-quality, expensive models, such as BMWs or Cadillacs, depreciate at a slower rate than other models.

Another fixed ownership cost is the interest charge for financing your automobile purchase. This charge is based on the loan amount, the interest rate, and the length of time it will take you to pay off the loan.

Other fixed costs associated with automobile ownership are insurance, license and registration fees, and taxes. Since fixed costs are fairly constant, they are easier to anticipate than variable costs.

Variable Operating Costs   Some automobile expenses are directly related to operation and vary in relation to the amount of use. The costs of such items as gasoline, oil, and tires increase with the number of miles that an automobile has been driven. Planning for expenses of this kind is made easier if the number of miles you drive during a given period of time is more or less uniform. Unexpected trips will increase such costs.

As your car gets older, maintenance and repair costs usually increase. You should expect to replace such relatively low-priced components as fan belts, hoses, the battery, or the muffler. Budgeting a certain amount of savings for more costly repairs, such as the repair of brakes, can help minimize their financial burden.

Automobile Expense Records   An awareness of the total cost of owning and operating an automobile can be valuable in your overall financial planning. Exhibit 10–8 presents a summary of the major expenses for three sizes of automobiles.

An automobile expense record should include the dates of odometer readings. Recording your mileage each time you buy gas will allow you to compute the fuel efficiency of your car. For tax-deductible travel, the Internal Revenue Service requires specific information on the mileage, location, date, and purpose of trips. You can use a notebook to keep records of your regular operating expenses, such as gas, oil, parking, and tolls. You should also keep files on your maintenance, repair, and replacement part costs. Finally, you should record such infrequent expenditures as insurance payments and license and registration fees (see Exhibit 10–9).

Proper Maintenance

People who sell, repair, or drive automobiles for a living state that regular vehicle care is one of your best investments. While owner's manuals and articles suggest mileage or time intervals for certain servicing, more frequent oil changes or tune-ups can minimize major repair expenses and maximize the life of your car.

The systems of your car that should be monitored and maintained on a regular basis are the engine, cooling system, transmission, brakes, steering mechanism, exhaust components, and suspension. Exhibit 10–10 presents additional details on automobile maintenance. It is not intended to be a complete guide, but it should serve as a reminder of areas that could result in expensive problems.

Automobile Servicing Sources

Automobile maintenance and repair service is offered by a variety of businesses.

Car Dealers   The service department of a car dealer offers a wide range of car care activities. Since car dealers are required to perform routine maintenance, major repairs, and body work, they have a complete inventory of parts for most vehicles. The service charges of car dealers are generally higher than those of other types of servicing facilities.

EXHIBIT 10–8   Annual Costs for New Automobiles (Based on 15,000 Miles a Year, Ownership for Four Years)

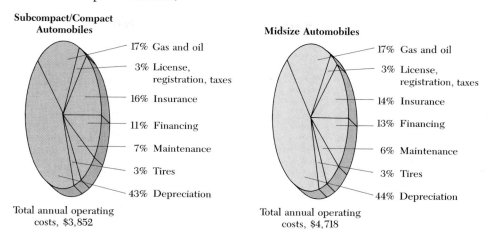

Subcompact/Compact Automobiles

- 17% Gas and oil
- 3% License, registration, taxes
- 16% Insurance
- 11% Financing
- 7% Maintenance
- 3% Tires
- 43% Depreciation

Total annual operating costs, $3,852

Midsize Automobiles

- 17% Gas and oil
- 3% License, registration, taxes
- 14% Insurance
- 13% Financing
- 6% Maintenance
- 3% Tires
- 44% Depreciation

Total annual operating costs, $4,718

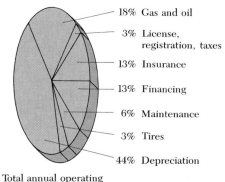

Full-Size Automobiles

- 18% Gas and oil
- 3% License, registration, taxes
- 13% Insurance
- 13% Financing
- 6% Maintenance
- 3% Tires
- 44% Depreciation

Total annual operating costs, $5,232

SOURCES: *Your Driving Costs* (Falls Church, Va.: American Automobile Association, 1989); and U.S. Department of Transportation data.

Service Stations   Local gas stations often provide convenience and reasonable prices for routine maintenance and most repair needs. The number of full-service gas stations has declined in recent years due to lower profits and competition from other types of automobile servicing businesses. Today, most people buy gas at a combination gas station and convenience food store. For automobile servicing, drivers must consider other alternatives.

Automobile Repair Shops   Independent repair shops serve a wide variety of automobile servicing needs at fairly competitive prices. As with any service, the quality of these repair shops varies. Research the satisfaction of previous customers before doing business with an automobile repair shop.

Department and Discount Stores   Mass merchandise retailers such as Sears and K mart offer convenient, low-cost automobile service. These retailers usually emphasize the sale of tires, batteries, mufflers, and other replacement parts. As required, they will also replace brakes and do oil changes or tune-ups at moderate prices.

EXHIBIT 10–9   Estimating Annual Automotive Ownership and Operating Costs

Model Year _1991_ — Make, Size, Model _Dodge Caravan LE_

Fixed Ownership Costs

1. Depreciation
$ _18,000_ purchase price
divided by _6_ years
estimated life of
vehicle* $ _3,000_

2. Interest on Auto Loan
Cost of financing
the vehicle if buying
on credit $ _700_

3. Insurance
Cost of liability
and property insurance
on the vehicle
for the year $ _600_

4. License, Registration Fee, and Taxes
Cost of registering
vehicle for state and
city license fees $ _50_

Variable Operating Costs

5. Gasoline
_12,000_ estimated miles per
year divided by _20_ miles
per gallon times the
$ _1.20_ average price of gasoline
per gallon $ _720_

6. Oil Changes
Cost of regular
oil changes
during the year $ _54_

7. Tires
Cost of tires purchased
during the year $ _110_

8. Maintenance/Repairs
Cost of planned
or other
expected maintenance $ _156_

9. Parking and Tolls
Regular fees for
parking and highway
toll charges $ _310_

Total Fixed Costs $ _4,350_
Divided by miles driven
equals fixed cost
per mile   _36.25_ ¢

Total Variable Costs $ _1,350_
Divided by
miles driven
equals variable cost
per mile   _11.25_ ¢

Total Costs $ _5,700_
Divided by
miles driven
equals total cost
per mile   _47.5_ ¢

*This estimate of vehicle depreciation is based on a *straight-line* approach—equal depreciation each year. A more realistic approach would be larger amounts in the early years of ownership, such as 25–30 percent the first year and 30–35 percent the second year. Most cars lose 90 percent of their value by the time they are seven years old.

Specialty Shops   These limited-service businesses offer a single product or maintenance effort at a reasonable price with fast, quality results. Mufflers, tires, automatic transmissions, and oil changes are among the replacement parts or services that automobile specialty businesses provide.

Since automobile maintenance and repairs can be expensive, be sure to seek out competent service for your money. To avoid unnecessary expense, be aware of the common repair frauds presented in Exhibit 10–11. Remember to deal with

EXHIBIT 10–10   Extended Vehicle Life through Proper Maintenance

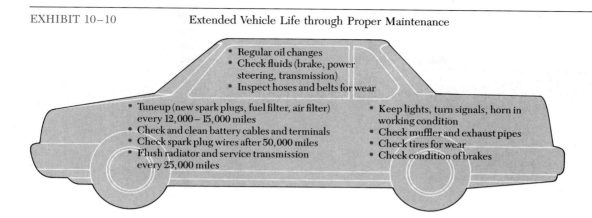

- Regular oil changes
- Check fluids (brake, power steering, transmission)
- Inspect hoses and belts for wear

- Tuneup (new spark plugs, fuel filter, air filter) every 12,000 – 15,000 miles
- Check and clean battery cables and terminals
- Check spark plug wires after 50,000 miles
- Flush radiator and service transmission every 25,000 miles

- Keep lights, turn signals, horn in working condition
- Check muffler and exhaust pipes
- Check tires for wear
- Check condition of brakes

EXHIBIT 10–11

Common Automobile
Repair Frauds

The vast majority of automobile servicing sources are fair and honest. But sometimes dollars are wasted when consumers fall prey to the following tricks:

When checking the oil, the attendant may put the dipstick only partway down and then use it to show that you need oil.

An attendant can cut a fan belt or puncture a hose. Carefully watch when someone checks under your hood.

A garage employee may put some liquid on your battery and then try to convince you that it is leaking and you need a new battery.

Removing air from a tire instead of adding air to it can make an unwary driver open to buying a new tire or to paying for a patch on a tire that is in perfect condition.

The attendant may put grease by a shock absorber or on the ground and then tell you that your present shocks are dangerous and you need new ones.

You may be charged for two gallons of antifreeze with a radiator flush, when only one gallon is put in.

Dealing with reputable businesses and having a basic knowledge of your automobile are the best methods of preventing deceptive repair practices.

---

enterprises with whose reputation you are familiar. Be sure to get a written, detailed estimate in advance as well as a detailed, paid receipt for the service that was done.

Many individuals avoid problems and minimize costs by working on their own vehicles. This can be especially worthwhile for routine maintenance and minor repairs, such as oil changes, tune-ups, and replacement of belts, hoses, and batteries. Many books on automobile servicing are available at libraries and bookstores. Also, local high schools and colleges frequently offer courses on the basics of automobile maintenance.

Selling Your Automobile

At some time, you may be on the selling side of an automobile transaction. The decision to sell a car on your own may result from a low trade-in offer from a dealer. This process starts with an awareness of the documents that must be filed with your state department vehicle registration agency. Contact this agency to obtain the necessary forms as well as information on the regulations that affect the sale of an automobile.

Use current advertisements in local newspapers along with the used car pricing guides discussed earlier to assist you in setting a sales price. Maintenance and minor repairs will help improve your car's appearance and increase its price and customer appeal.

Next, make others aware of the car. Put a "For Sale" sign with a telephone number on it. Place it in a location that will allow many people to see it. Information about the car can be distributed through stores, church, or community bulletin boards. Advertisements in local newspapers will increase the number of people who are aware that the car is for sale.

Require people who are interested in buying your car to provide you with their addresses and telephone numbers, and have them make appointments to see and test-drive the car. As a precaution, be sure to accompany prospective buyers on the road test. If you have kept a file of maintenance and repair receipts, use this information to document the condition of the car. In negotiating price, consider the condition, mileage, and potential demand.

When completing the transaction, be sure to meet the associated legal requirements, such as the payment of title, vehicle registration, and other fees. To avoid getting a bad check or handling large amounts of cash, insist that the car be paid for with a cashier's check or a money order. Provide the buyer with a receipt stating the details of the transaction.

LEGAL AND SOCIAL CONCERNS OF AUTOMOBILE OWNERS

L.O.5
Recognize the legal and social concerns associated with automobile ownership.

Each day, our transportation habits affect many aspects of our lives. The legal, energy, environmental, and safety concerns associated with owning and operating an automobile can influence our financial decisions related to transportation.

Consumer Protection for New Car Buyers

New car warranties provide buyers with some assurance of quality. These warranties vary in the time and mileage of the protection they offer and in the parts they cover. The main conditions of a warranty are the coverage of basic parts against manufacturer's defects; the power train coverage for the engine, transmission, and drivetrain; and the corrosion warranty, which usually applies only to holes due to rust, not to surface rust. Other important conditions of a warranty are a statement regarding whether the warranty is transferable to other owners of the car and details on the charges, if any, that will be made for major repairs in the form of a *deductible*.

Some automobile manufacturers make free repairs or adjustments on certain parts even after the warranty period. This free service, sometimes called a *secret warranty,* is usually the result of the manufacturer's decision to correct design faults that owner complaints have brought to its attention. Information on secret warranties may be obtained from dealers and the National Highway Traffic Safety Administration.

In the past, when major functional problems occurred with a new car and warranty service didn't solve the difficulty, many consumers lacked a course of action. As a result, 45 states and the District of Columbia enacted *lemon laws* that required a refund for the vehicle after the purchaser had made repeated attempts to obtain servicing. In general, these laws apply to situations in which a person has attempted four times to get the same problem corrected and to situations in which the vehicle has been out of service for more than 30 days within 12 months of purchase or the first 12,000 miles. The terms of the state laws vary; contact your state consumer protection office for details.

The lemon laws triggered the various arbitration programs of automobile manufacturers. These programs were discussed in Chapter 8. Although the manufacturers' intention was to resolve the complaints of auto buyers by means of arbitration, some critics say that these arbitration programs have not been effective since the automobile manufacturers fund and control them.

Energy Conservation

Before the mid-1970s, when a gas tank could be filled for a couple of dollars, **fuel efficiency,** the number of miles per gallon, was not a major consumer concern. But as gas prices rose, demand increased for automobiles that provided more miles per gallon. Each year, the Environmental Protection Agency (EPA) conducts tests to determine the fuel efficiency of automobiles sold in the United States. EPA mileage information can guide you in selecting an automobile that will give you the fuel efficiency you desire. Since the EPA tests are conducted under laboratory conditions, the mileage you get from your car will probably differ from the EPA figure.

Environmental Concerns

An **emission control device** is a mechanism in a vehicle that reduces air pollution from the vehicle's exhaust system. When such devices were originally mandated, they were criticized as costly and as reducing fuel efficiency. Today, there is general acceptance of emission control devices since technology has helped reduce their cost and minimize their effect on fuel efficiency. The environmental efforts of the federal government have been supplemented by the efforts of heavily populated areas such as Chicago and its suburbs, which conduct emission control tests to assure that vehicles meet required pollution control standards. The elimination of leaded gasoline is another environmental action that has been taken as a result of automotive pollution.

Despite these environmental efforts, auto emissions are considered a possible cause of atmospheric warming. In addition, the American Lung Association estimates that motor vehicle pollution is responsible for $40 billion to $50 billion in health care costs each year and as many as 120,000 deaths.

Automobile Safety

With the publication of *Unsafe at Any Speed* in the mid-1960s, Ralph Nader ushered in a new era of automobile safety. Since then, a number of efforts made by government, industry, and individual consumers have resulted in safer vehicles and fewer highway deaths and injuries. Among these efforts were required seat belts, windshields that safely shatter into small pieces upon impact, crash-resistant fuel tanks, and warning signals to encourage seat belt use. Another safety effort was the passage of child seat belt laws by all 50 states. Although these laws vary by state, in general young children are required to ride in a safety seat specifically designed for transporting them in automobiles. Older children (usually over three or five years old, depending on the state) may use regular seat belts.

As of 1990, all motor vehicles sold in the United States are required to have "passive restraints"—either air bags or automatic seat belts. Concerns that have been expressed about air bags are unfounded: they will not inflate when a bump is hit or a low-speed collision occurs. But even if an air bag inflates while a car is being driven, this would not cause problems. Since the air bag inflates and starts to deflate in about 1/25 of a second, the test drivers who participated in research on this question were all able to maintain control of their vehicles when the air bag inflated. Air bags provide protection that is not possible with other safety devices. An air bag, for example, saved the life of an 81-year-old woman whose car smashed into a tank truck when the combined speed of the two vehicles was 95 miles per hour.

SUMMARY

L.O.1
Analyze the factors that influence transportation decisions.

Lifestyle, household needs, and financial situation are the main influences on transportation decisions.

L.O.2
Investigate the process of buying a used car.

The purchase of a used car requires assessment of the sources of used cars, awareness of consumer protection for used car buyers, inspection of the vehicle, and negotiation of a price.

L.O.3
Develop a strategy for purchasing a new car.

When buying a new car, obtain vehicle and dealer cost information, select desired options, compare the price and service offered by different dealers, and negotiate the price. As needed, investigate and compare financing and leasing alternatives.

L.O.4
Determine the costs associated with owning and operating an automobile.

The fixed ownership costs of an automobile are depreciation, interest on financing, insurance, license and registration fees, and taxes. The variable operating costs of an automobile are the costs of gasoline, oil, tires, maintenance, repairs, parking, and tolls.

L.O.5
Recognize the legal and social concerns associated with automobile ownership.

Warranty conditions, the arbitration process, fuel efficiency, emission control devices, and automobile safety are among the legal and social concerns that affect the owners of automobiles.

GLOSSARY

Car buying service   A business that helps a person obtain a specific new car at a reasonable price with minimal effort; also called an auto broker.

Depreciation   The loss in value of an automobile—or other asset—due to time and use.

Emission control device   A mechanism in a vehicle that reduces air pollution from the vehicle's exhaust system.

Fuel efficiency   The number of miles per gallon obtained by an automobile.

Highballing   A sales technique in which a very high price is offered for a trade-in vehicle, with the extra amount made up by increasing the price of the new car.

Leasing   A contractual agreement under which a person makes monthly payments for the use of an automobile over a set period of time.

Lowballing   A sales technique in which a new car buyer is quoted a very low price that add-on costs increase before the deal is concluded.

Mass transit   Systems of public transportation, such as bus or train lines, that allow the fast, efficient movement of many people.

Sales agreement   The legal document that contains the specific details of an automobile purchase.

Sticker price   The suggested retail price, displayed in printed form on the vehicle, of a new automobile and its optional equipment.

DISCUSSION QUESTIONS

L.O.1   1. Why do many people base the purchase of an automobile on emotion rather than good financial planning?

L.O.1   2. How could public transportation be made more appealing? What benefits would individuals and society derive from the increased use of public transportation?

L.O.2   3. How could a person assess the available sources on the purchase of a used car?

L.O.2   4. What aspects of a used car's condition should be inspected most carefully?

L.O.3   5. What information could be most helpful in negotiating the price of a new car?

L.O.3   6. In what situations might it be more beneficial to lease a car rather than buy one?

L.O.4   7. Why should depreciation, for which no money is paid, be considered an operating expense of a vehicle?

L.O.4   8. What types of preventive maintenance are likely to extend the life of an automobile?

L.O.5   9. Is the buyer of a new car adequately protected from financial difficulties and personal inconvenience when major defects occur in the car? Provide evidence for your position.

L.O.5 10. Should federal or local governments limit the use of automobiles in highly populated areas? Explain your answer.

Opening Case Questions

1. What personal or financial changes in their lives might impel Andrew and Jill Nagel to purchase an automobile?

2. Do the Owens have four cars because of their needs, their lifestyle, or their financial situation? Do you see any alternatives for this family?

PROBLEMS AND ACTIVITIES

L.O.1   1. Talk to people who make regular use of public transportation. Why do they use it? How does their transportation budget compare with that of people whose primary means of transportation is an automobile?

L.O.2   2. Compare the prices that several businesses charge for comparable used cars. What factors account for the differences in the prices charged by these businesses?

L.O.2   3. Conduct a survey of friends and relatives who have purchased a used car? What did they do to get the best deal? Based on their experiences, what would they do differently now?

L.O.3   4. Observe the behaviors and conversation patterns of new car shoppers and auto salespeople. Based on your observations, what suggestions would you offer new car buyers?

L.O.3   5. In the following situation, which would be more beneficial—purchasing the vehicle or leasing it? Justify your answer.

Vehicle cost, $18,000	Security deposit, $300
Down payment, $3,000	Monthly lease payment, $315
Monthly loan payment, $330	Loan/lease length, 60 months
Estimated value at end of loan term, $4,500	End-of-lease charges, $1,100
Opportunity cost interest rate, 6 percent	

L.O.3   6. Analyze advertisements that offer rebates or low-cost financing to car buyers. What factors should a consumer consider in choosing among the discount or low-cost credit terms offered in these advertisements?

L.O.4   7. Compare the prices that different types of automotive service businesses charge for the purchase and installation of a new battery, a muffler, shock absorbers, or tires.

L.O.4   8. Calculate the approximate operating cost of the following vehicle:

Annual depreciation, $2,500	Annual mileage, 13,200
Current year's loan interest, $650	Miles per gallon, 24
Insurance, $680	Average gasoline price, $1.18 per gallon
License and registration fees, $65	Oil changes/repairs, $370
	Parking/tolls, $420

L.O.4   9. Create a framework for evaluating places to which you could take your vehicle for servicing.

L.O.5   10. Survey auto owners on the safety features that they believe should be standard equipment on vehicles.

LIFE SITUATION   Case 10–1

Drive or Ride?

Carissa Meyer uses a two-year-old car to travel to her office management job, a trip of about four miles each day. About twice a month, Carissa drives to another city for regional staff meetings. In addition to gas and other operating costs,

Carissa pays a daily parking fee of $4.50. In contrast, monthly public transportation tickets are $42 and allow unlimited travel for 30 days on the city transit system. Even though public transportation offers Carissa obvious cost savings, she prefers to drive to work.

Questions

1. What factors may have influenced Carissa's decision to drive to work?
2. How much could Carissa save each month if she used public transportation?
3. If Carissa decided to sell her car, how would her living expenses change? How could not having a car affect her job situation?

LIFE SITUATION　Case 10–2

Vehicle Shopping

Jessica and David Gill needed a new car. Their current automobile was seven years old, had been driven 93,000 miles, and needed major repairs. They had $2,700 for a down payment. After talking with several friends and visiting three new car dealers, the Gills couldn't decide what type of car to buy or how much to spend. A few days later, however, Jessica and David bought a full-size car that cost $15,000.

Questions

1. What additional actions could the Gills have taken before buying a new car?
2. What car buying alternatives were not considered by Jessica and David?
3. What financial factors did the Gills forget to consider?
4. For future car buying, what suggestions would you make to the Gills?

SUPPLEMENTARY READINGS

For Additional Information on Purchasing Used Cars

Gillis, Jack. *The Used Car Book*. New York: Harper & Row, 1990.

"How to Find a Good Used Car." *Consumer Reports,* April 1990, pp. 273–76.

For Additional Information on Purchasing New Cars

The Complete Car Cost Guide, 1990. IntelliChoice, Inc., 1135 South Saratoga-Sunnyvale Road, San Jose, CA 95129.

The Complete Small Truck Cost Guide, 1990. IntelliChoice, Inc., 1135 South Saratoga-Sunnyvale Road, San Jose, CA 95129.

Gillis, Jack. *The Car Book*. New York: Harper & Row, 1990.

"Good Reasons to Lease Your Next Car." *Changing Times,* September 1989, pp. 77–82.

Guiles, Melinda Grenier. "The Pitches and Pitfalls of Auto Leasing." *The Wall Street Journal,* July 19, 1990, p. B1.

"How to Shop Smart for a New Car." *Consumer Reports,* April 1990, pp. 203–7.

For Additional Information on Automobile Operating Costs

Henry, Ed. "Sorry, That's Out of Warranty." *Changing Times,* March 1990, pp. 53–54, 56–57.

Silver, Marc. "The Out-of-Warranty Blues." *U.S. News & World Report,* October 30, 1990, pp. 73–75.

What Your Car Really Costs. Great Barrington, Mass.: American Institute for Economic Research, 1990.

Your Automobile Dollar. Money Management Institute, Household Financial Services, 2700 Sanders Road, Prospect Heights, IL 60070.

Your Driving Costs. American Automobile Association, 8111 Gatehouse Road, Falls Church, VA 22047.

COMPREHENSIVE CASE FOR PART III

The Cost of Financial Independence

After 16 years of school, during which he depended on his parents, Jason Matthews was starting his own household. He rented a one-bedroom apartment that was 8 miles away from the company he worked for as an assistant product manager. Some furniture, dishes, towels, and linens that he was able to obtain from his parents and friends helped reduce his move-in costs. He planned to use some of the $1,100 he had in savings to buy additional furniture, decorations for his apartment, and new speakers for his stereo.

Jason realized that before making these planned household purchases, he had to budget for transportation costs. Currently, he was driving a seven-year-old car that needed major repairs. He was thinking about using his savings for a down payment on a car that was in better condition. In the process of examining purchasing alternatives, he found the following ads for cars that seemed to meet his needs:

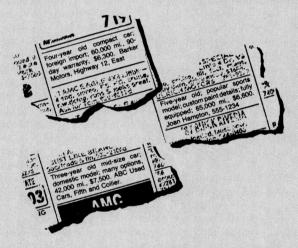

If he selected the vehicle in the first ad, the financing could be handled through the dealer's financing plan. Otherwise, he would use a bank or a credit union to finance the automobile purchase.

Besides budgeting transportation costs, Jason had to budget money for food and to take the time and effort needed to go grocery shopping. While eating at various types of restaurants was convenient, even the fast-food restaurants were more costly than eating at home. Jason usually went to the grocery store whenever he needed something. He didn't shop consistently at any one store, but would shop at the store nearest to the location of the activity in which he happened to be engaged. When selecting brands, he chose the items with which he was most familiar.

Besides budgeting various household, automobile, and food costs, Jason had to budget other expenses, such as electricity and telephone bills. He also had to buy clothing appropriate for his job.

Financial independence can be very pleasant and enjoyable, but it is expensive. Just when you think you've got all of your expenses covered, it's time to make your automobile payment, to pay your apartment insurance premium, or to buy your mother a birthday gift.

Questions

1. What major influences are affecting Jason's spending habits?
2. Other than relying on personal experience, how can a person anticipate the types and amounts of the expenses for housing, transportation, food, clothing, and other necessities that he or she will encounter?
3. Prepare a list of the items and costs that are necessary to start living on your own.
4. What actions should Jason take before deciding which car to buy? Should he keep the car he now has, or should he buy another car? What opportunity costs must he consider in this decision?
5. What food-buying habits should Jason develop? What are some wise buying techniques that he might consider?
6. How will Jason's spending affect his overall financial existence and his future financial security?

IV

Insuring Your Resources

Part IV of *Personal Finance* offers material designed to help you protect your financial resources. In Chapter 11, we present an overview of insurance and of its importance in your financial plan. We suggest

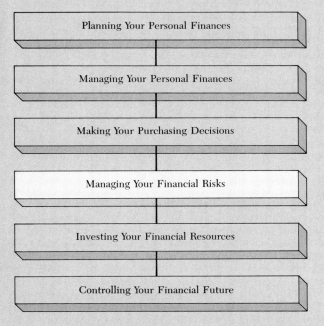

Planning Your Personal Finances

Managing Your Personal Finances

Making Your Purchasing Decisions

Managing Your Financial Risks

Investing Your Financial Resources

Controlling Your Financial Future

how you can plan your personal insurance program and what steps you should take in purchasing insurance. Next, in Chapter 12, we discuss the risks and coverages associated with your home and automobile. In Chapter 13, we examine health care and medical insurance, analyzing the benefits and limitations of various health coverages. Finally, in Chapter 14, we consider the importance of life insurance for your personal financial plan. This chapter discusses types of life insurance, the features of different types of life insurance policies, and the activities involved in buying life insurance. Part IV consists of

11

Personal Risks and Insurance

Insurance deals with property and people. The beneficial impact of insurance on people and businesses in America is so great that we can hardly imagine how our society would function without it. By providing protection against the many risks of financial uncertainty and unexpected losses, insurance makes it possible for people to plan confidently for the future.

LEARNING OBJECTIVES
After studying this chapter, you will be able to

L.O.1 Explain the meaning of insurance and outline its early development.

L.O.2 Interpret the nature of insurance.

L.O.3 Define risk management and evaluate the methods of managing risk.

L.O.4 Assess the bases of insurance.

L.O.5 Plan and purchase your personal insurance coverage intelligently.

OPENING CASE

*Insurance Ads Starring Celebrities**

When Art Linkletter appeared on television in Washington State to plug a seemingly low-cost life insurance plan for the elderly, state regulators panned his act. They called the ads, promoting National Home Life Assurance Company, false and misleading and ordered the ads off the air.

Insurance regulators in California proposed giving the hook to comedian Dick Van Dyke's television ads for National Benefit Insurance Company, a unit of Primerica Company. A California insurance commissioner said that the ads are deceptive and that they will be banned unless the company shows why they shouldn't be.

Driven by consumer complaints, regulators in a growing number of states clamped down on television insurance ads featuring celebrities. The targets were commercials for "guaranteed acceptance" life insurance for the elderly and medigap policies, health insurance promoted as a supplement to Medicare.

Consumer groups and regulators said that these celebrity ads often wildly exaggerated benefits, understated or omitted policy exclusions and exceptions, and sold policies of questionable value by mixing fear with the trust engendered by celebrities.

"When the stars come out, it's a good idea to stay wide awake and hang on to your wallet," said Dick Marquardt, Washington's insurance commissioner, who is perhaps the most vocal critic of celebrity insurance advertising. Besides Mr. Linkletter's ads, Washington in the past year banned ads featuring Tennessee Ernie Ford and the late Lorne Greene and has gotten companies to withdraw others by Ed McMahon and Dick Van Dyke.

Florida regulators have proposed rules that would bar celebrities from discussing insurance premiums or benefits in ads unless they pass insurance licensing exams. At least 15 other states have shown interest in toughening regulations to curb alleged abusive practices.

The insurance industry defends the use of celebrities. According to the American Council of Life Insurance, a 645-member trade group in Washington, D.C., the problem is confined to a relatively small number of ads that may require adjustment but shouldn't be banned. The council also says that when asked to do so by regulators, most insurers and their spokesmen will voluntarily change commercials to lessen perceived misunderstanding of consumers.

In this chapter, you will learn, among other things, what insurance is and how to choose an insurance agent and an insurance company.

*Adapted from Ken Wells, "Insurance Ads Starring Celebrities Are Target of Crackdown by States," *The Wall Street Journal*, May 5, 1988, p. 27.

INSURANCE: AN INTRODUCTION

L.O.1
Explain the meaning of insurance and outline its early development.

Your decisions about insurance will be easier if you keep a few fundamentals in mind. First, you should know what insurance is supposed to do. Basically, its purpose is to help protect you and your family against financial hardship due to hazard, accident, death, and the like. Rebuilding your home after a fire, paying a large court judgment, or providing for your family in the event of your early death may require more money than you have. Dealing with damage to your car or theft of your property, however, may be within your means.

To select the right insurance, then, you must know your risks. Start by looking at your property and your family responsibilities. Think about the chances of mishaps or events that could cause major trouble or expense. It is wise to insure against them. Do not insure against little losses that will not hurt. Unless yours is one of the few families that can afford all the protection they need, you should insure the greater risks first.

A little study before you see an insurance agent will help you make your money go as far as it can in fitting you with proper insurance. An agent will answer questions and advise you on details, but the final decision is yours. You can choose from many kinds of insurance. Figuring out how much insurance you need and how much you can spend for it will help you decide which kind to buy.

How much insurance you buy depends largely on what you can afford. Young families can seldom buy all the insurance they need. However, you should aim at an amount that will give you the money you need to live on and pay sickness, funeral, or other expenses—keeping in mind other sources of income that you will be able to fall back on, such as savings and social security benefits. Then you should buy what you can.

Choosing the amounts and kinds of insurance that fit your needs will take continued study. Insurance problems will always be with you as your situation and responsibilities change. That usually makes it desirable to choose an agent in whom you have full confidence and with whom you can work out a sensible insurance program. The agents recommended by your parents, friends, relatives, neighbors, or bankers are likely to be the best for you.

What Insurance Is

Insurance is protection. Although there are many types of insurance, they all have on thing in common—they give you the peace of mind that comes from knowing that money will be available to meet the needs of your survivors, to pay medical expenses, to protect your home and belongings, and to cover personal or property damage caused by your car. Thus, the principle of all insurance is the same: it protects people against possible financial loss.

Life insurance replaces income that would be lost if the policyholder should die. Health insurance helps meet medical expenses when the policyholder gets sick or helps replace income lost when illness makes it impossible for the policyholder to work. Automobile insurance helps cover property and personal damage caused by the policyholder's car.

What an Insurance Company Is

An **insurance company,** or **insurer,** is a risk-sharing firm that agrees to assume financial responsibility for losses that may result from an insured risk. A person joins the risk-sharing group (the insurance company) by purchasing a contract (a **policy**). Under the policy, the insurance company agrees to assume the risk for a fee (the **premium**) paid periodically by the person (the **insured** or the **policyholder**).

Tackling the Trade-Offs

Insurance provides protection against many risks of financial uncertainty and unexpected losses. The financial trade-offs of not obtaining the right amount and type of insurance can be disastrous. Consider the following trade-offs of being without insurance:

1. What will happen to your family if you die prematurely without an adequate amount of life insurance? Weigh the yearly cost of insurance premiums against the benefits that your family will receive if your financial support stops with your death.
2. What if you become permanently disabled and unable to support your family? Again, consider the psychological and financial costs versus the benefits of disability income.
3. What if you have unexpected medical or automobile accident expenses and you have no major medical or automobile insurance? Most people will agree that

the cost of such insurance protection is a better trade-off than not having the insurance coverage.

4.   What might happen if your property is stolen, destroyed, or damaged and you are not insured against such losses?

5.   What if a repairperson sues you for an injury suffered from falling down the stairs of your house and you don't carry liability insurance?

Since these trade-offs are not acceptable alternatives, most Americans are covered by some type of insurance for most of their lives.

Early Insurance Developments

The insurance policy is a relatively recent development. The concept of insurance, however, is not new. The idea of transferring the risk of loss from the individual to a group originated thousands of years ago. When a family's hut burned down, for instance, the entire tribe would rebuild it. Traces of rudimentary insurance practices may be seen among the few primitive tribes that still exist.

The first American insurance company, the Friendly Society for the Mutual Insuring of Houses against Fire, was formed in 1735. A fire put it out of business in 1740.

In 1752, Benjamin Franklin was instrumental in founding a fire insurance company, the Philadelphia Contributorship for the Insurance of Houses from Loss by Fire. Also known as Hand in Hand, it is America's oldest continuously operated fire insurance company. The Insurance Company of North America, founded in 1792, was the first U.S. insurance company to underwrite large risks. By the close of the 18th century, 14 insurance companies had been formed in the United States.

NATURE OF INSURANCE.

L.O.2
Interpret the nature of insurance.

You face risks every day. You can't cross the street without some danger that you'll be hit by a car. You can't own property without taking the chance that it may be lost, stolen, damaged, or destroyed. Insurance companies offer financial protection against such dangers and losses by promising to compensate the insured for a relatively large loss in return for the payment of a much smaller, but certain, expense, called the premium.

Risk, peril, and hazard are important terms in insurance. While in popular use these terms tend to be interchangeable, each of them has a distinct, technical meaning in insurance.

Risk refers to the uncertainty as to loss that faces a person or property covered by insurance. Uncertainty of loss exists for the insured. Insurance companies frequently refer to the person or property insured as the risk.

Peril is the cause of a possible loss. It is the contingency that causes someone to take out insurance. People buy policies for financial protection against such perils as fire, windstorm, explosion, robbery, and accident.

Hazard increases the likelihood of loss through some peril. For example, defective house wiring is a hazard that increases the likelihood of the peril of fire.

Types of Risk

The most common risks are classified as personal risk, property risks, and liability risks.

Personal risks are the uncertainties surrounding loss of income or life due to premature death, illness, disability, old age, and unemployment.

EXHIBIT 11–1   Types of Insurance Available for Certain Risks

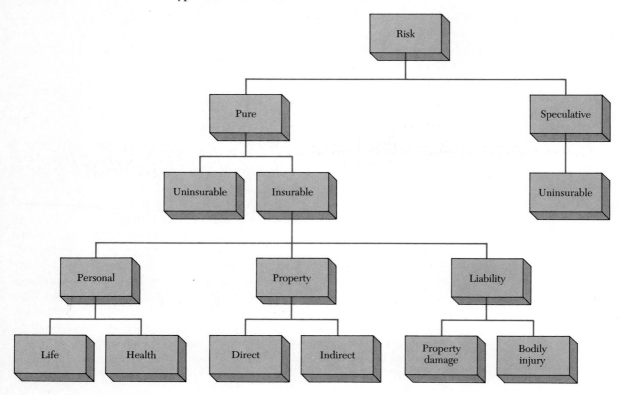

SOURCE: David L. Bickelhaupt, *General Insurance,* 11th ed. (Homewood, Ill.: Richard D. Irwin, 1979), p. 11. Copyright 1983, Richard D. Irwin, Inc.

Property risks are the uncertainties of direct or indirect losses to personal or real property due to fire, wind, accident, theft, and other hazards.

Liability risks are possible losses due to negligence resulting in bodily harm or property damage to others. Such harm or damage could be caused by an automobile, professional misconduct, injury on one's property, and so on.

Personal risks, property risks, and liability risks are types of **pure risk** (see Exhibit 11–1), or insurable risk, since there would always be a chance of loss if the specified events occurred. Pure risks are accidental and unintentional risks for which the nature and financial cost of the loss can be predicted. Such risks are insurable.

A **speculative risk** is one in which there is a chance of either loss or gain. Starting a small business that may or may not succeed is an example of speculative risk. So is gambling. Speculative risks are legally defined as uninsurable.

RISK MANAGEMENT

Risk management is an organized strategy for protecting and conserving assets and people. It helps reduce financial losses caused by destructive or damaging events. Risk management is a long-range planning process. The risk management needs of people change at various points in the life cycle. If you understand risks and how to manage them, you can provide better protection for yourself and your family against the effects of personal risks, property risks, and liability risks. In this

L.O.3
Define risk management and evaluate methods of managing risk.

way, you can reduce your financial losses and thereby improve your chances for economic, social, physical, and emotional well-being throughout life. Since most families cannot afford to cover all risks, they need to understand how to obtain the best protection that they can afford. A combination of strategic alternatives to cover major risks is usually advisable. Exhibit 11–1 shows what types of insurance are available to cover certain risks.

Methods of Managing Risk[1]

Most people think of risk management as buying insurance. But insurance is not the only method of dealing with risk, and in certain situations other methods may be less costly. In this section, we will discuss the five general risk management techniques.

Risk Avoidance   You can avoid the risk of an automobile accident by not riding in a car. General Motors can avoid the risk of product failure by not introducing new models. Risk avoidance would be practiced in both instances, but at a very high cost. You might have to give up your job, and General Motors might lose out to competitors that introduce new models.

There are, however, situations in which risk avoidance is a practical technique. At the personal level, individuals avoid risks by not smoking or by not walking through high-crime neighborhoods. At the business level, jewelry stores avoid losses through robbery by locking their merchandise in vaults before closing. Obviously, no person or business can avoid all risks. By the same token, however, no one should assume that all risks are unavoidable.

Risk Reduction   It may be possible to reduce risks that cannot be avoided. You can reduce the risk of injury in an auto accident by wearing a seat belt. You can install smoke alarms and fire extinguishers to protect life and reduce potential damage in case of fire.

Risk Assumption   Risk assumption is the act of taking on responsibility for the loss or injury that may result from a risk. Generally, it makes sense to assume a risk when the potential loss is too small to worry about, when effective risk management has reduced the risk, when insurance coverage is too expensive, and when there is no other way of obtaining protection against a loss. For instance, you might decide not to purchase collision insurance on an older car. Then, if an accident occurs, you would bear the costs of fixing the car.

Self-insurance is the process of establishing a monetary fund that can be used to cover the cost of a loss. Self-insurance does not eliminate risks; it only provides means for covering losses. Many people self-insure by default, not by choice.

Risk Pooling   Pooling is cooperative participation to spread expenses from losses among a group of people (the pool). This reduces the cost of risk coverage to individuals. Group life insurance and health insurance plans are examples of pooling.

Risk Shifting   The most common method of dealing with risk is to shift, or transfer, it to an insurance company or some other organization.

Exhibit 11–2 summarizes various risks and appropriate strategies for managing them.

EXHIBIT 11–2   Examples of Risks and Risk Management Strategies

| Risks | | Strategies for Reducing Financial Impact | | |
Personal Events	**Financial Impact**	**Personal Resources**	**Private Sector**	**Public Sector**
Disability	Loss of one income Loss of services Increased expenses Other losses	Savings, investments Family observing safety precautions Other resources	Disability insurance Other strategies	Disability insurance

Illness	Loss of one income
	Catastrophic hospital
	  expenses
	Other losses
		Health-enhancing
		  behavior
			Health insurance
			Health maintenance
			  organizations
			Other strategies
				Military health
				Medicare, Medicaid

Death	Loss of one income
	Loss of services
	Final expenses
	Other expenses
		Estate planning
		Risk reduction
		Other resources
			Life insurance
			Other strategies
				Veteran's life
				  insurance
				Social security
				  survivor's benefit

Retirement	Decreased income
	Other expenses
		Savings
		Investments
		Hobbies, skills
		Other resources
			Retirement and/or
			  pensions
			Other strategies
				Social security
				Pension plan for
				  government
				  employees

Property loss	Catastrophic storm
	  damage to property
	Repair or
	  replacement cost of
	  theft
		Property repair and
		  upkeep
		Security plans
		Other resources
			Automobile insurance
			Homeowners
			  insurance
			Flood insurance
			  (joint program with
			  government)
				Flood insurance
				  (joint program with
				  business)

Liability	Claims and
	  settlement costs
	Lawsuits and legal
	  expenses
	Loss of personal
	  assets and income
	Other expenses
		Observing safety
		  precautions
		Maintaining property
		Other resources
			Homeowners
			  insurance
			Automobile insurance
			Malpractice insurance
			Other strategies	

INSURANCE IN OPERATION

L.O.4
Assess the bases of insurance.

Insurance is not a gamble. It provides protection because it is based on proven principles—on truths or rules of science that explain how things act. These principles are supported by extensive records that insurance companies have kept for many decades. The principles, or laws, include human mortality, probability, and the law of large numbers.

Human Mortality

As you will see in Chapter 14, life insurance companies compile their own mortality tables, based on their own experiences with their policyholders, and these tables are revised regularly. It is from these tables that such companies secure the basic data they need in order to establish the cost of life insurance.

Probability and the Law of Large Numbers

At first glance, it may seem strange that a combination of individual risks would result in the reduction of total risk. The principle that explains this phenomenon is called the **law of large numbers,** sometimes loosely termed the law of averages or the law of probability. However, the law of large numbers is only a part of the subject of probability, which is not a law but a field of mathematics.

Probability is the mathematics of chance. The word *chance* is one we use very frequently. Like many words, it is used in a variety of ways. We may say that we took a chance crossing the street or that we took a chance on a raffle. We discuss the chances that a football team will win its next game or that our next missile will reach the moon. We may say "I haven't a chance of getting an A" or "I'm sure the professor wouldn't give us a test today." However, the notion of chance is given a definite mathematical meaning when we define probability.

In order to set premiums, an insurance company must know how to measure the risks against which people are buying insurance. A fire insurance company must have some way of knowing how many fires will occur. An automobile insurance company must be able to predict the number of accidents involving injury, loss of life, and property damage. A life insurance company must know what the expected number of deaths will be in a given group of policyholders.

How will these companies make their estimates? How will they estimate the probability that (1) an 18-year-old male driver will be involved in an automobile accident this year? (2) a new all-brick house in your community will burn? (3) a 70-year-old man will be hospitalized this year? (4) a 16-year-old person will die before reaching age 17?

In order to arrive at such estimates, data must be collected. The automobile insurance company has to gather data on 18-year-old male drivers in order to find out how many accidents this group of drivers has. The fire insurance company must compile statistics on fires among all-brick houses in communities with good fire departments. The life insurance company must have statistics that show how many 16-year-olds die.

Data for the above probabilities must be based on large numbers of events. The law of large numbers assumes that seemingly chance incidents actually have a predictable pattern if enough such incidents are observed. This means that the longer the number insured for a particular risk are observed, the more accurately the expected losses can be predicted.

The **actuary** makes all of the probability calculations used by insurance companies. Actuaries are highly specialized insurance company mathematicians who have been professionally trained in the risk aspects of insurance. Their functions include determining proper insurance rates and conducting various aspects of insurance research. Interested in being an actuary? Read the accompanying feature.

Principle of Indemnity

Indemnity is a legal doctrine that limits recovery under an insurance policy to the lesser of the actual cash value of a loss or the amount that will restore the insured to his or her financial position prior to the loss. To indemnify is to restore lost value or to compensate for damage or loss sustained. Property and liability insurance contracts, for example, are contracts of indemnity; they provide for the compensation of the amount of loss or damage. Thus, if you have insured your house with a replacement value of $90,000 for $120,000 and the house burns down, the most that an insurance company will reimburse you is $90,000, not $120,000. Consequently, there is no point in insuring any item for more than its value.

• •

PERSONAL FINANCE JOURNAL
The Actuarial Profession

To choose a career intelligently, you must know and understand yourself and your interests, abilities, and ambitions. And then you must select a type of work that will provide a satisfying outlet for your talents and energy. If you are skilled in math and are looking for a career in which you can make a worthwhile contribution to society, consider becoming an actuary. Actuaries work with facts, figures, and people, and they must possess the curiosity and drive needed to find answers to complex questions.

An actuary is a business professional who uses mathematical skills to define, analyze, and solve business and social problems. Actuaries are disciplined problem solvers who create and manage insurance and pension programs to reduce the financial impact of the expected and unexpected things that happen to people, such as illnesses, accidents, unemployment, and premature death. That's why people buy insurance and participate in pension plans—to protect themselves financially.

College training is not specifically required to become an actuary, but such training is almost essential to pass the actuarial examinations you'll have to take for professional qualification. Good all-around preparation for an actuarial career is a mathematics or statistics major, a business administration major with a math or statistics minor, or an economics major with a math or statistics minor. Your math courses should include calculus, probability, and statistics. Some colleges and universities have specific undergraduate or graduate programs in actuarial science.

Actuarial salaries compare favorably with salaries in other professions that require similar skills and training. In the actuarial profession, as in any profession, certain factors will help determine your salary. These are

- Your ability, imagination, creativity, and integrity.
- Your education and experience, and how well you apply them.
- Your employer—whether you work in private industry, government, consulting, education, or for yourself.
- The law of supply and demand.

Actuarial salaries vary geographically, but broadly estimated salary ranges in 1989 indicated the following earning potential at various experience levels:

No exams	$22,000–$26,000
One exam	$24,000–$28,000
Two exams	$26,000–$30,000
SOA new associates (five exams)	$35,000–$48,000
CAS and SOA new fellows (10 exams)	$47,000–$57,000
Fellows (several years' experience)	$55,000–$100,000 and up

SOURCE: *The Actuarial Profession* (Schaumburg, Ill.: Casualty Actuarial Society and Society of Actuaries, 1989), pp. 4–18.

• •

An important principle stems from the doctrine of indemnity; this principle is known as insurable interest.

Insurable Interest

The principle of *insurable interest* is basic to the structure of insurance. In property insurance, an exposure to a financial loss must exist to create an insurable interest. The law requires an insurable interest so that insurance policies are neither gambling devices nor tools for those who would profit deliberately from destroying the property of others. In life insurance, an insurable interest is any reasonable expectation of financial loss caused by the death of the person whose life is insured. Thus, husband and wife, partners in a hardware store, the lender of a home mortgage, and parents and their children have an insurable interest in a life insurance policy. But college roommates and an employer and most employees do not have an insurable interest in a life insurance policy because the death of a roommate or an employee does not cause a financial loss to the other roommate or the employer. Related to the principle of insurable interest is the concept of insurable risk.

Insurable Risk

As discussed earlier, only pure risks (not speculative risks) are insurable. Insurable risks have the following characteristics: they are common, definite, accidental, not excessively catastrophic, not trivial, calculable, and economically affordable.

Insurable Risks Are Common to a Large Number of People   For example, a fire insurance company cannot write insurance covering only 100 or 150 homeowners for loss of their homes. Remember, the law of large numbers plays a vital role in insurance. In life insurance, many persons are needed in each age, health, and occupational classification.

Insurable Risks Are Definite   The loss should be difficult to counterfeit. Death comes closest to perfection in meeting this criterion. An insured can collect disability insurance more easily from an automobile accident than from illness because auto accident disability is more definite.

Insurable Risks Are Accidental or Fortuitous   The loss should be beyond the control of the insured. An insured will not collect insurance by deliberately setting his or her house on fire.

Insurable Risks Frequently Are Not Excessively Catastrophic   Losses must be individually random; that is, no loss can be connected with any other loss. No insurer can afford to write insurance for a type of loss that is likely to happen to a very large percentage of insureds. A life insurer would go bankrupt if all of its policyholders died prematurely, as would a fire insurer whose policyholders all lost their homes by fire. That's why catastrophic losses, such as mass destruction of property and life in a war, are not insurable. Life insurers insert war clauses in new policies when war seems imminent.

Insurable Risks Are Not Trivial   The peril covered by insurance should be capable of producing a loss so large that the insured could not bear it without financial hardship. For example, you would not buy a life insurance policy on your pet parakeet or insurance against breakage of a shoestring. The loss involved is too small to warrant the time, effort, and expense necessary to insure against the occurrence.

Insurable Risks Are Calculable   Some probabilities can be determined by logic alone—for example, the probabilities in the flip of a coin. Others must be determined by tabulating experience and projecting that experience into the future. Mortality tables, for example, are tabulations of past experiences that are used to calculate the number of deaths for a group of people of the same age, sex, and so forth.

Some chances of loss, however, are incalculable—that is, they cannot be determined either by logic or from experience. Unemployment is an example of an incalculable cost because it occurs with such irregularity that no one has yet succeeded in determining its future incidence. In such cases, insurers rely heavily on subjective rather than objective probabilities in estimating the chance of loss.

Insurable Risks Are Economically Affordable   Theoretically, an insurance company could issue a life insurance policy to a 99-year-old male. But the premium (the cost) would be so prohibitive that the policy would be neither feasible for the insured nor practical for the insurer—because the law of large numbers is inoperative at that age level.

PLANNING A PERSONAL INSURANCE PROGRAM

L.O.5
Plan and purchase your personal insurance coverage intelligently.

Because each individual and each family has its own needs and goals—many of which change over the years—a financial security insurance program should be tailored to those needs and goals and to the changes they undergo.

If you buy a pair of shoes, for example, you know it will fit because the size is right. But the feet of people who wear the same size of shoes differ somewhat. So if your shoes were custom made, you would give more attention to making sure that each part of the shoes fitted you exactly. The same is true of a well-planned insurance program.

In the early years of marriage, when the children are young and the family is growing, most families need certain kinds of insurance protection. This protection may include fire insurance on an apartment or a house, life and disability insurance for the breadwinner, and adequate health insurance (with maternity benefits for the wife) for the whole family.

Later, when the family has a higher income and different financial requirements, its protection needs will change. There will be long-range provision for the children's education, more life insurance to match higher income and living standards, and revised health insurance protection. Still later, when the children have grown and are on their own, there will be consideration of retirement benefits, further changing the family's personal insurance program.

In the accompanying feature, we suggest several guidelines to follow in planning your insurance program.

Set Your Goals[2]

In managing risks, your goals are to minimize personal, property, and liability risks. Your insurance goals should define what you expect to do about covering the basic risks present in your life situation. Covering the basic risks means providing a financial resource to cover costs resulting from a loss.

Suppose your goal is to buy a new car. You must plan to make the purchase and to protect yourself. Auto insurance on the car lets you enjoy the car without worrying that an auto accident might leave you worse off, financially and physically, than before.

Each individual has unique goals. Social attitudes, income, age, family size, experience, and responsibilities enter into the goals you set—and the insurance you buy must reflect those goals. In general, financial advisers say that a basic risk management plan must set goals to reduce

1. Potential loss of income due to the premature death, illness, accident, or unemployment of a wage earner.
2. Potential loss of income and extra expense resulting from the illness, disability, or death of a spouse.
3. Additional expenses due to the injury, illness, or death of other family members.
4. Potential loss of real or personal property due to fire, theft, or other hazards.
5. Potential loss of income, savings, and property due to personal liability.

FINANCIAL PLANNING IN ACTION

How Can You Plan an Insurance Program?

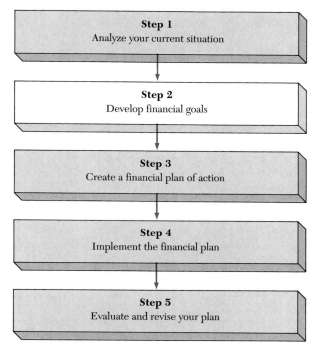

Step 1
Analyze your current situation

Step 2
Develop financial goals

Step 3
Create a financial plan of action

Step 4
Implement the financial plan

Step 5
Evaluate and revise your plan

Seek advice from a competent and reliable insurance adviser.

Determine what insurance is required to provide the family with sufficient protection if the breadwinner dies.

Consider what portion of the needed family protection is met by social security and by group insurance, if any.

Decide what other needs must be met by insurance (funeral expenses, savings, retirement annuities, etc.).

Decide what types of insurance best meet your needs.

Plan on an insurance program and stick to it except for periodic reviews of changing needs and changing conditions.

Don't buy more insurance than you need or can afford.

Don't drop one policy for another—unless the new policy provides the same coverage for less money.

Plan to Reach Your Goals

Planning is a sign of maturity, a way of taking control of life instead of letting life happen to you. What risks do you face? Which of them can you afford to take without having to back away from your goals? What resources—public programs, personal strengths, or private risk-sharing plans—are available to you?

To understand and use the resources at your command, you need good information. In insurance, this means a clear picture of the available insurance, the strength and reliability of different insurers, and the comparative costs of the coverage you need.

Put Your Plan into Action

As you carry out your plan, you obtain financial and personal resources, budget them, and use them to reach your risk management goals. If, for example, you find that the insurance protection you have is not enough to cover your basic risks, you may act to purchase additional coverage, to change the kind of insurance coverage you have, to restructure your personal or family budget to cover additional insurance costs, and to strengthen your savings or investment programs to reduce the long-term risk of economic hardship.

The best risk management plans have an element of flexibility. Savings accounts, for example, are available as emergency funds for any number of sudden financial problems. The best insurance plan is also flexible enough to respond to changing life situations. Your goal should be an insurance program that expands (or contracts) with the changing size of your protection needs.

Check Your Results

Evaluate your insurance plan periodically. Among the questions you should ask yourself are: Does it work? Does it adequately protect my plans and goals? An effective risk manager consistently checks the outcomes of decisions and is alert to changes that may reduce the effectiveness of the current risk management plan.

A young working couple may be entirely happy with their life and health insurance coverage. But when they add an infant to the family, it's time to review the protection plans. Suddenly, the risk of financial catastrophe to the family (should one or both parents die or be disabled) is much greater. Yesterday's decisions about insurance coverage are in need of revision.

The needs of a single person differ from those of a family, a single parent, a couple, or a group of unrelated adults living in the same household. All of these people face similar risks, but their financial responsibility to others differs greatly. In each case, the vital question is: Have I provided the financial resources and risk management strategy needed to take care of my basic responsibilities for my own well-being and the well-being of others?

To put your risk management plan to work, you must answer four basic questions: What should be insured, and for how much? What kind of insurance should be bought, and from whom?

What Should Be Insured?

As stated earlier, insurance decisions should be planned to cover clearly defined risks. The questions center on goals again. What do you want your insurance protection to do? Protect a big-ticket purchase (car, home)? Provide income for your family if you should die or become totally disabled? Cover the risk of theft or fire at your home? Before purchasing insurance, you should work to develop a clear sense of the purposes you want insurance to serve.

How Much Insurance?

A proper insurance plan covers all unaffordable losses. Properly used, insurance pays for major losses that would cause real economic hardship if left uncovered. A rule of thumb is that you absorb minor loss and insure major loss. No sensible person will pay the cost of buying an insurance policy against the loss of trivial possessions: pens, hats, costume jewelry, and so forth. Such losses can be absorbed into the personal budget without creating financial problems. But what if the economic loss were $50,000 — the fee for a surgical technique required by a member of the family? Such a loss could not be absorbed by most people; therefore, it should be insured against.

Answering the question how much requires a hard analysis of what you need to protect your economic well-being and what you can afford to pay for protection.

Need Analysis   Taking an inventory of your personal finances is a good way to start thinking about the protection you need. The inventory should list your assets, such as real estate, savings and investments, and personal property; your liabilities, such as outstanding loans, charge accounts, and mortgages; and your estimated income and expenses. If you are dealing with life and health insurance, estimate what your income and expenses would be if the wage earner died or were disabled; in other insurance situations, an estimate will indicate how much leeway your income and expenses give you in meeting smaller losses. In short, the expected loss minus the assets available to cover it roughly equals the amount of insurance needed.

Affordability   When major economic losses are possible, few of us can afford to be without adequate protection. A sudden illness in the family, for instance, could cause a six-figure medical bill. The question, then, isn't just "What can I afford?" but "How can I afford to buy the insurance I need?"

Affording protection may require a shift in the way you manage resources: extending a saving program or cutting down on nonessential spending. Above all, look for ways to get the best protection for the least money.

What Kind of Insurance?

Consumers should be aware of the variety of available insurance products. In the next three chapters, we will discuss the range of life, health, and property insurance products that are available to consumers. Variety makes it possible for you to find flexible insurance plans tailored to your special needs. Young families, for instance, can protect their income with low-cost term life insurance that fits their budgets. Before making a commitment to one insurance plan, look over the variety of available products. If the first policy you review isn't a good fit, you can assume that there is another plan better suited to your insurance needs.

From Whom to Buy?

Look for insurance coverage from financially strong companies with professionally qualified representatives. It is not unusual for a relationship with an insurance company to extend over a period of 20, 30, even 50 years. For that reason alone, consumers should choose carefully when they decide on an insurance company or an insurance agent. Fortunately, you do have a choice of sources.

Sources   Protection is available from a wide range of private and public sources, among which are insurance companies and their representatives; private groups, such as employers, labor unions, and professional or fraternal organizations; government programs, such as Medicare and social security; and other sources, such as financial institutions and manufacturers offering credit insurance.

Rating Insurance Companies   Some of the strongest, most reputable insurance companies in the nation provide excellent insurance coverage at reasonable costs. In fact, the financial strength of an insurance company may be a major factor in holding down premium costs for consumers.

Locate an insurance company by checking the reputations of local agencies. Ask members of your family, friends, or colleagues about the insurers they prefer.

PERSONAL FINANCE JOURNAL
Guidelines for Choosing an Insurance Agent

1. The agent is available when he or she is needed. Clients sometimes have problems that need immediate answers. These problems can occur on weekends and evenings.
2. The agent wants the client to have a balanced financial plan. Each part of the plan should be necessary to the client's overall financial protection.
3. The agent does not pressure the client. The client should be free to make a rational decision about insurance coverage.

4. The agent keeps up with changes in his or her field through education. Agents often attend special classes or study on their own so that they can serve their clients better.
5. As a professional, the agent is happy to answer questions. He or she wants the client to know exactly what is being paid for in an insurance policy.

SOURCE: American Council of Life Insurance.

For a more official review, look for a copy of *Best's Agents Guide* or *Best's Insurance Reports* in the public library. The Best's ratings are an authoritative guide to the financial stability of the nation's insurers. Best's has five rating classifications: A+ or A (excellent), B+ (very good), B (good), C+ (fairly good), and C (fair). In addition, *Consumer Reports, Changing Times,* and *Money* periodically provide consumer satisfaction ratings on various types of insurance and insurance companies.

Choosing Your Insurance Agent   An insurance agent handles the technical side of insurance. But that's only the beginning. The really important part of the agent's job is to apply his or her knowledge of insurance to help you select the proper kind of protection within your financial boundaries.

Choosing a good agent is among the most important steps in the process of building your insurance program. How do you find an agent? One of the best ways to begin is by asking your parents, friends, neighbors, and others for their recommendations. You may also want to know something about an agent's membership in professional groups. Agents who belong to a local Life Underwriters Association are often among the more experienced agents in their communities. A **Chartered Life Underwriter (CLU)** is a life insurance agent who has passed a series of college-level examinations on insurance and related subjects. Such agents are entitled to use the designation CLU after their names.

Once you have learned of an agent who sounds promising, you must decide which policy is right for you. The best way to do this is to talk to your agent. Remember, this does not obligate you to buy insurance.

You can size up an agent by asking yourself a few questions about the advice he or she offers. How does the agent explain that a particular type of policy is right for you? Does the agent describe in detail the benefits that you can receive? Does the policy fit in with the rest of your financial picture—social security, company pension, group life insurance, health insurance, and your savings plan?

Understanding Your Insurance Policy

According to the Insurance Information Institute, a common consumer complaint is that people do not know enough about the insurance they are paying for and do not know whether or not they are paying too much for it. The informed consumer questions the agent or company representative and reads insurance contracts for complete understanding of their terms and clauses. In the past, people felt intimidated by the legal terminology of most insurance policies. The simplified writing of contracts for auto and homeowners insurance has eased the burden of reading and understanding these documents.

Understanding the various parts of an insurance policy is vital to knowing whether the proper coverage has been purchased. A general policy has the following components.

The Declaration   The declaration is a separate sheet that is fastened to the policy. It is a statement about the property to be insured, and it takes up such matters as deductibles and the amount of coverage.

The Insuring Agreement   This section explains who and what various coverages of the policy protect.

The Conditions   This section explains the duties and obligations of both the insurer and the policyholder.

The Exclusions   This section describes the properties, losses, and perils that are not covered.

Endorsements   An **endorsement** is a written document that modifies the policy in some way, perhaps adding or deleting coverage.

To be properly informed about buying insurance, there is no substitute for sitting down and talking with an agent or a company representative. Communication is the key to better learning.

How to File an Insurance Claim

Sustaining a loss is frustrating, but the problem can be compounded if care is not taken to secure proper information about the loss prior to filing a claim.

The Insurance Information Institute advises all policyholders to review their policies (both auto and homeowners) *before* a loss to ensure proper coverage and clarify any uncertainties.

The institute offers the following general tips:

1.   Maintain receipts on all purchases. Providing receipts will help the insurance company reimburse the policyholder fairly for a loss. Receipts leave no doubts as to the value of a piece of property.
2.   Contact the police after a loss, and obtain a written police report, if possible.
3.   Take notes about what happened, and include the names of the persons to contact.
4.   In the case of an auto accident, get the names of all the parties involved, including witnesses, along with addresses, telephone numbers, driver's license numbers, and license plate numbers.
5.   In the case of a homeowners claim, list all damaged or stolen property. Locate original receipts whenever possible, including repair receipts. Gather repair estimates or estimates of the value of property.
6.   Contact the insurance company or the agent as soon as possible.

..

Insurance premiums can account for a substantial portion of the household budget. You can reduce the amount you spend on insurance in these ways.

Comparison Shopping   Insurance premiums for similar coverage vary widely from one company to the next. Check the rates of several companies before making a decision.

Deductibles   A deductible is the money you must pay toward a loss before the insurance will pay—the larger the deductible, the lower the premium. A large deductible can result in large savings on the premium.

Group Insuring   Group plans usually result in a substantial premium savings over individual plans—especially with health insurance. Consider joining a group insurance plan at the place you work, through your credit union, or through a social organization.

Self-Insuring   You can sometimes insure yourself against a loss. For example, if your car has a low value, say about $1,000, you can save on your automobile insurance

premium by dropping the collision insurance and putting $1,000 in a savings account, where it can earn interest. Later, if you damage the car, money for repairs would come from this savings account.

Fewer Payments   You can usually save a few dollars by paying your insurance premiums once or twice a year instead of breaking them down into monthly payments.

Preventive Measures   Being a good insurance risk can also result in lower premiums. For example, nonsmokers often qualify for lower life or health insurance premiums. Alarms in a house or an apartment may qualify you for a reduction in homeowners insurance rates, and safe driver rates are available from most auto insurers.

When cutting premium costs, beware of underinsuring. Find out whether your insurance will rebuild your house and replace your belongings at current prices. Underinsuring could cause considerable financial stress if your insurance does not restore you to your prior financial position after a loss.

..

SUMMARY

L.O.1
Explain the meaning of insurance and outline its early development.

L.O.2
Interpret the nature of insurance.

L.O.3
Define risk management and evaluate the methods of managing risk.

L.O.4
Assess the bases of insurance.

L.O.5
Plan and purchase your personal insurance coverage intelligently.

Insurance is protection. The principle of all insurance is the same: People buy insurance policies to protect themselves against possible financial loss. Although the insurance policy is a recent development, the concept of insurance is quite old.

Risk, peril, and hazard are important terms in insurance. Risk refers to a chance of loss with respect to the person, liability, or property of the insured. Peril is the cause of a possible loss, such as fire, windstorm, explosion, theft, or riot. Hazard is the presence of a condition that increases the likelihood of loss through some peril. Risks can be personal, property, or liability risks.

Risk management, a long-range planning process, is an organized strategy for protecting and conserving assets and persons. The five general risk management techniques are risk avoidance, risk reduction, risk assumption, risk pooling, and risk shifting.

All insurance is based on the principles of human mortality, probability, and the law of large numbers. The three most basic principles in insurance are indemnity, insurable interest, and insurable risk. Insurable risks are common to a large number of people. These risks are common, definite, accidental, not excessively catastrophic, not trivial, calculable, and economically affordable.

In planning a personal insurance program, you set your goals, make a plan to reach your goals, put your plan into action, and check your results. In purchasing your insurance coverage, you should ask these basic questions: What should be insured? How much insurance is needed and affordable? What kind of insurance should be bought? From whom should it be bought? Once you have purchased an insurance policy, you should understand its various parts and learn how to file an insurance claim.

GLOSSARY

Actuary   A highly specialized insurance company mathematician who has been professionally trained in the risk aspects of insurance.

Chartered Life Underwriter (CLU)   A life insurance agent who has passed a series a college-level examinations on insurance and related subjects.

Endorsement   A written document that modifies an insurance policy.

Hazard   Increases the likelihood of loss through some peril.

Indemnity   A legal doctrine that limits recovery under an insurance policy.

Insurance   Protection against possible financial loss.

Insurance company   A risk-sharing firm that assumes financial responsibility for losses that may result from an insured risk.

Insured   A person who is covered by an insurance policy.

Insurer   An insurance company.

Law of large numbers   The longer the number insured for a particular risk are observed, the more accurately the expected losses can be predicted; also called the law of averages or the law of probability.

Peril   The cause of a possible loss.

Policy   A written contract of insurance.

Policyholder   A person who owns an insurance policy.

Premium   The amount of money that a policyholder is charged for an insurance policy.

Probability   The mathematics of chance.

Pure risk   A risk in which there is only a chance of loss; only pure risks are insurable; also called insurable risk.

Risk   Chance or uncertainty of loss; also used to mean "the insured."

Self-insurance   The process of establishing a monetary fund that can be used to cover the cost of a loss.

Speculative risk   A risk in which there is a chance of either loss or gain.

DISCUSSION QUESTIONS

L.O.1   1. Discuss this statement: "How much insurance you buy depends largely on what you can afford."

L.O.1   2. What are the financial and psychological trade-offs for not obtaining the right amount and type of insurance?

L.O.2   3. Why are personal risks, property risks, and liability risks called pure risks?

L.O.2   4. Distinguish between pure and speculative risks.

L.O.3   5. Evaluate various methods of managing risks.

L.O.4 6. How do insurance companies secure the basic data that they use to establish the cost of life insurance?

L.O.4 7. What is an assumption in the law of large numbers?

L.O.4 8. Why is the principle of insurable interest basic to the structure of insurance?

L.O.5 9. What should be your goals in managing risks?

L.O.5 10. What steps must you take in planning your personal insurance program?

L.O.5 11. Who rates insurance companies?

Opening Case Questions

1. Should state insurance regulators be authorized to pull false and misleading life insurance commercials off the air? Why or why not?

2. Are insurance advertisements more credible when celebrities appear on radio or television commercials? Why or why not?

3. In your opinion, should insurance advertisements by celebrities be banned?

PROBLEMS AND ACTIVITIES

L.O.1 1. Think about the last three times you bought automobile, home, life, or health insurance. List reasons why you purchased these insurance coverages.

L.O.1 2. Survey friends and relatives to determine their reasons for purchasing various kinds of insurance coverages.

L.O.2 3. Prepare a list of the risks you face every day. Classify these risks as personal, property, and liability risks.

L.O.3 4. Write down the provisions that you will make to cover personal, property, and liability risks.

L.O.4 5. Flip a coin 100 times and observe the outcome. How many heads and tails did you observe? What is the principle that explains these results? How do insurance companies apply this principle to determine insurance premiums?

L.O.4 6. Lee and Kim Nguyen paid $120,000 for their home two years ago. Today, its market value is $150,000. The Nguyens have a $180,000 homeowners insurance policy. If their home is completely destroyed by fire, what is the maximum reimbursement that they can expect from the insurance company (not including reimbursement for personal property)?

L.O.5 7. Plan your personal insurance program by listing your short- and long-term financial goals. What steps must you take to reach these goals?

L.O.5 8. Compile a list of the various insurance sources used by your family and neighbors. Evaluate these sources, and classify them as private or public sources.

L.O.5 9. Ask a qualified insurance agent what a competent insurance agent can and will do to help you purchase various types of protection.

L.O.5 10. List the risks that you or your family will probably face over the next four years. Then list the personal, private, and public resources that you will use to reduce the financial impact of each of these risks.

L.O.5 11. Examine your or your parents' life insurance and automobile insurance policies. What are the major components of each of these policies?

L.O.5 12. Obtain sample insurance policies from an insurance agent or broker, and analyze the similarities and differences among their definitions, coverages, exclusions, limitations on coverage, and amounts of coverage.

L.O.5 13. Contact your state legislative representatives for copies of state bills and laws that are intended to regulate insurance. Analyze the bills and laws to learn their basic provisions, the ease and cost of enforcing them, and their consequences for consumers.

LIFE SITUATION   Case 11–1

Buying Adequate Insurance Coverage

Kathy Jones was a junior at Glenbard High School. She had two younger sisters. Her father, the manager of a local supermarket, had take-home pay of $2,000 a month. He had a small group health insurance policy and a $20,000 life insurance policy. He said that he could not afford to buy additional insurance. All of his monthly salary was used to meet current expenses, including car and house payments, food, clothing, transportation, children's allowances, recreation and entertainment, and vacation trips.

One evening, Kathy was talking with her father about insurance, which she was studying in an economics course. She asked what kind of insurance program her father had for their family. This question started Mr. Jones thinking about how well he was planning for his wife and children. Since the family had always been in good health, Mr. Jones felt that additional health and life insurance was not essential. Maybe after he received a raise in his salary and after his daughter was out of high school, he could afford to buy more insurance.

Questions

1. Do you think Kathy's father was planning wisely for the welfare of his family? Can you suggest ways in which this family could have cut monthly expenses and thus set aside some money for more insurance?

2. Although Mr. Jones's salary was not big enough to buy insurance for all possible risks, what protection do you think he should have had at this time?

3. Suppose Mr. Jones had been seriously injured and unable to work for at least a year. What would his family have done? How might this situation have affected his children?

LIFE SITUATION   Case 11–2

The Importance of Planning Ahead

Michael Beale worked in a gift shop in the city. His take-home pay was about $1,600 a month. He had a four-year-old son, and he and his wife were expecting another child. Last year, he told his insurance agent that he felt his family was sufficiently protected with a $40,000 life insurance policy and a hospital expense health insurance policy.

His shop was successful, and he felt that additional protection was not necessary. Besides, he felt that he would have plenty of time to save for his children's education. Then, several months ago, he was injured when he fell from a ladder. The accident left him disabled and unable to work.

Questions

1. Did Mr. Beale have the right kind of insurance protection for his family? How will his disability affect the welfare of his growing children?
2. If Mr. Beale didn't think he had any financial worries, why should he have considered loss of income insurance?
3. What are some ways in which Mr. Beale's insurance program could have been improved?

SUPPLEMENTARY READINGS

For Additional Information on General Insurance Topics

Bailard, Thomas E.; David L. Biehl; and Ronald W. Kaiser. *How to Buy the Right Insurance at the Right Price.* Homewood, Ill.: Dow Jones-Irwin, 1989.

Mehr, Robert I. *Fundamentals of Insurance.* 2nd ed. Homewood, Ill., Richard D. Irwin, 1986.

Pride, William M.; Robert J. Hughes; and Jack R. Kapoor. *Business.* 2nd ed. chap. 18. Boston: Houghton Mifflin, 1988.

Your Insurance Dollar. Prospect Heights, Ill.: Money Management Institute, Household Financial Services, 1988.

12 | *Home and Automobile Insurance*

Since most people invest a large amount of money in a home and a vehicle for transportation, protecting these assets from loss must be a concern. Each year, homeowners and renters lose billions of dollars from more than 3 million burglaries, 500,000 fires, and 200,000 instances of damage from other hazards. The cost of injuries and property damage caused by automobiles is also very great. Most people use insurance to reduce their chances of economic loss from these risks. Becoming familiar with the types and costs of property and liability coverages available to individuals is a vital component of personal financial planning.

LEARNING OBJECTIVES
After studying this chapter, you will be able to

L.O.1   Discuss the importance of property and liability insurance.

L.O.2   Explain the insurance coverages and policy types available to homeowners and renters.

L.O.3   Analyze the factors that influence the coverage amount and cost of home insurance.

L.O.4   Identify the important types of automobile insurance coverages.

L.O.5   Evaluate the factors that affect the cost of automobile insurance.

· ·

OPENING CASE

Household Insurance Decisions

Doug and Brenda Patterson have two children, Heidi, 22, and Chuck, 17. They have fire insurance on their home, and they are considering the purchase of a burglary policy since they collect antiques and have four rare items as well as a number of other pieces.

The Patterson's dog, Ruffy, is one of the most popular pets in the neighborhood. Ruffy can be seen playing with children almost every day.

Heidi shares an apartment with a friend, Ruth Bowman. Since Heidi and Ruth don't have much furniture or other belongings, they have decided not to get insurance. Although they are assuming some risks, they are also saving the cost of insurance.

Chuck Patterson drives to school each morning, then to his part-time job. He also uses his car for social trips on evenings and weekends. He has the minimum amount of automobile liability insurance required by the state.

As you can see, the Pattersons have some financial risks that they could reduce with insurance. Damage to their home and property, harm done by their pet, injuries to people in their dwelling, and automobile accidents causing property damage and injuries are a few of the areas in which the Pattersons might consider purchasing additional insurance. Striking the proper balance between too much insurance and not enough insurance is a difficult financial decision. Knowing the risks and the available coverages related to your home and your automobile can help you make your property and liability insurance choices.

· ·

THE ROLE OF PROPERTY AND LIABILITY INSURANCE IN YOUR FINANCIAL PLAN

L.O.1
Discuss the importance of property and liability insurance.

Every aspect of personal financial decision making involves a trade-off among alternatives. Many events that might effect your home or your automobile—for example, having your home robbed or being involved in an automobile accident—can result in great financial losses. The price you pay for home and automobile insurance may be viewed as an investment in financial protection against such losses. Although the costs of home and automobile insurance may seem high, the financial losses from which that insurance protects you is much higher. Property and liability insurance offer protection from financial losses that may arise from a wide variety of situations.

An automobile insurance company once paid $3,600 for damages to a car in an accident caused by a mouse. The critter apparently got into the car while it was parked and then crawled up the driver's pants leg when the car was on an interstate highway. The driver lost control of the vehicle and crashed into a roadside barrier.

Another claim resulted when a barbecued steak fell off a 17th-floor balcony and dented a car.

A weather report recommended that homeowners "crack" their windows to minimize damage from an approaching hurricane. Instead of opening the windows slightly, one individual used a hammer to crack them. The damage was covered by a home insurance policy.[1]

While these incidents have a humorous side, most accidents—and the property losses and legal actions connected with them—do not. The main types of risks related to a home and an automobile are property damage or loss and your responsibility for injuries to others or damage to the property of others.

Potential Property Losses

Houses, automobiles, furniture, clothing, and other personal belongings represent a substantial financial commitment. Property owners face two basic types of risks. The first type is physical damage that may be caused by such hazards as fire, wind, water, and smoke. These hazards can cause destruction of your property or temporary loss of its use. For example, if a windstorm causes a large tree branch to break your automobile windshield, you lose the use of the vehicle while it is being repaired. The second type of risk faced by property owners is the threat of robbery, burglary, vandalism, or arson.

Liability Protection

In a wide variety of circumstances, a person can be judged legally responsible for injuries or damages to others. For example, if a child walks across your property, falls, and sustains severe injuries, the child's family can sue you. Or if you accidentally damage a rare painting while assisting a friend with home repairs, the friend can take legal action against you to recover the cost of the painting.

Liability is legal responsibility for the financial cost of another person's losses or injuries. In many situations, your legal responsibility can be caused by **negligence**—failure to take ordinary or reasonable care. Doing something in a careless manner, such as improperly supervising children at a swimming pool or not removing items from a frequently used staircase, may be ruled as negligence in a liability lawsuit.

Another type of legal responsibility is **vicarious liability,** a situation in which a person is held responsible for the actions of another person. If financial or physical harm to others is caused by the behavior of a child, the parent may be held responsible; if it is caused by the activities of an employee, the employer may be held responsible.

Liability lawsuits can affect society as well as individuals. The settlements for such cases result in higher insurance premiums and higher prices for goods and services. In an effort to keep liability insurance costs down, most states have taken action to limit damage awards. The purpose of these legislative measures is to keep insurance premiums reasonable for businesses and consumers. Florida's liability award limit, for example, was imposed on the condition that premiums be reduced for insurance customers.

PRINCIPLES OF HOME AND PROPERTY INSURANCE

L.O.2
Explain the insurance coverages and policy types available to homeowners and renters.

Your home and your personal belongings are a major portion of your assets. Loss of some or all of these possessions could cause financial disaster. Whether you rent your dwelling or own a house, condominium, or manufactured home, property insurance is vital to you. **Homeowners insurance** is coverage for your place of residence and its associated financial risks, such as damage to personal property and injuries to others (see Exhibit 12–1).

Homeowners Insurance Coverages

A homeowners policy provides coverages for the building and other structures, additional living expenses, personal property, personal liability and related coverages, and specialized coverages.

EXHIBIT 12–1
Home Insurance Coverages

Building and other
structures

Loss of use/necessary
living expenses while
home is unhabitable

Personal property

Personal liability
and related coverages

Building and Other Structures   The main component of homeowners insurance is protection against financial loss due to damage or destruction to a house or other structures. Your dwelling and attached structures are covered for fire and other damages. Detached structures on the property, such as a garage, toolshed, or bathhouse, are also protected. Finally, trees, shrubs, and plants are included in the coverage.

Additional Living Expenses   If a fire or other damage prevents the use of your home, additional living expense coverage pays for the cost of living elsewhere. While your home is being repaired, this coverage reimburses you for the cost of living in a temporary location. Some policies limit additional living expense coverage to 10–20 percent of the home's coverage and limit payments to a maximum of 6–9 months; other policies pay the full cost incurred for up to a year.

Personal Property   Your household belongings, such as furniture, appliances, and clothing, are covered for damage or loss up to a portion of the insured value of the home, usually 55, 70, or 75 percent. For example, a home insured for $80,000 might have $56,000 of coverage for household belongings.

Personal property coverage may have limits for the theft of certain items, such as $1,000 for jewelry, $2,000 for firearms, and $2,500 for silverware. Items whose value exceeds these limits can be protected with a **personal property floater,** which covers the damage or loss of a specific item of high value. A floater requires a detailed description of the item and periodic appraisals to verify its current value. This coverage protects the item regardless of its location, which insures the item while you are traveling with it or transporting it.

Floaters to protect home computers and related equipment are recommended. This additional coverage can prevent financial loss due to damage or loss of your computer. Contact your insurance agent to determine whether the equipment is covered against damage from spilled drinks, mischievous pets, dropping, or power surges.

Personal property coverage usually provides protection against the loss or damage of an article that you take with you when you leave home. For example, possessions that you take with you when you go on vacation or use while you are living at school are usually covered up to a limit stated in the policy. Property that you rent, such as a video recorder or a rug shampoo machine, is insured while it is in your possession.

In case of damage or loss of property, you must be able to prove both ownership and value. A **household inventory** is a list or other documentation of personal belongings, with purchase dates and cost information. You can get a form for such an inventory from an insurance agent. Exhibit 12–2 provides a reminder of the items that should be included in the inventory. For items of special value, you should have receipts, serial numbers, brand names, model names, and written appraisals of value.

Your household inventory can include photographs or a video recording of your home and its contents. Make sure that the closet and storage area doors are open. On the back of the photographs indicate the date and the value of the object. Regularly update your inventory, photos, and appraisal documents; also keep a copy of each document in a secure location such as a safe-deposit box.

Personal Liability and Related Coverages   Each day, we face the risk of financial loss due to injuries to others or damage to property for which we are responsible. The following are examples of this risk:

- A neighbor or guest falls on your property, resulting in permanent disability.
- A spark from burning leaves on your property starts a fire that damages a neighbor's roof.
- A member of your family accidentally breaks an expensive glass statue while at another person's house.

In each of these situations, you could be held responsible for the costs incurred. The personal liability component of a homeowners policy protects you from financial losses resulting from legal action or claims against you or family members due to damages to the property of others. This coverage includes the cost of your legal defense.

Not all of the individuals who come to your property are covered by your liability insurance. While a baby-sitter and others who assist you occasionally are probably covered, regular employees, such as a housekeeper or a gardener, may

EXHIBIT 12–2   Household Inventory Contents

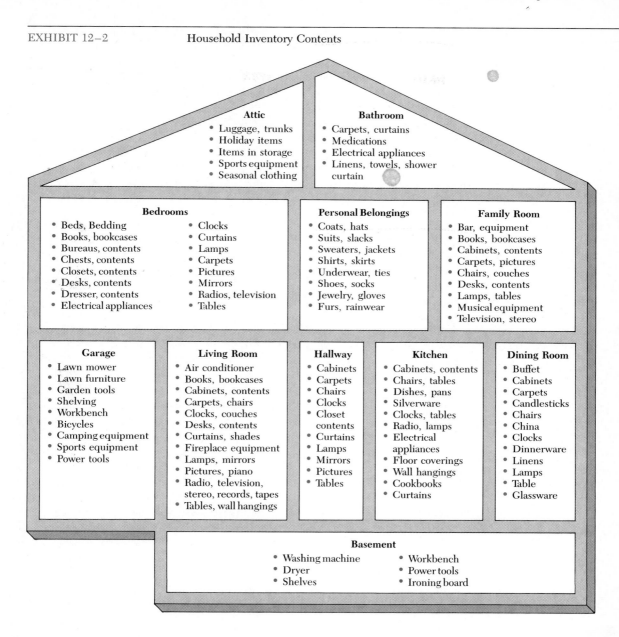

Attic
- Luggage, trunks
- Holiday items
- Items in storage
- Sports equipment
- Seasonal clothing

Bathroom
- Carpets, curtains
- Medications
- Electrical appliances
- Linens, towels, shower curtain

Bedrooms
- Beds, Bedding
- Books, bookcases
- Bureaus, contents
- Chests, contents
- Closets, contents
- Desks, contents
- Dresser, contents
- Electrical appliances
- Clocks
- Curtains
- Lamps
- Carpets
- Pictures
- Mirrors
- Radios, television
- Tables

Personal Belongings
- Coats, hats
- Suits, slacks
- Sweaters, jackets
- Shirts, skirts
- Underwear, ties
- Shoes, socks
- Jewelry, gloves
- Furs, rainwear

Family Room
- Bar, equipment
- Books, bookcases
- Cabinets, contents
- Carpets, pictures
- Chairs, couches
- Desks, contents
- Lamps, tables
- Musical equipment
- Television, stereo

Garage
- Lawn mower
- Lawn furniture
- Garden tools
- Shelving
- Workbench
- Bicycles
- Camping equipment
- Sports equipment
- Power tools

Living Room
- Air conditioner
- Books, bookcases
- Cabinets, contents
- Carpets, chairs
- Clocks, couches
- Desks, contents
- Curtains, shades
- Fireplace equipment
- Lamps, mirrors
- Pictures, piano
- Radio, television, stereo, records, tapes
- Tables, wall hangings

Hallway
- Cabinets
- Carpets
- Chairs
- Clocks
- Closet contents
- Curtains
- Lamps
- Mirrors
- Pictures
- Tables

Kitchen
- Cabinets, contents
- Chairs, tables
- Dishes, pans
- Silverware
- Clocks, tables
- Radio, lamps
- Electrical appliances
- Floor coverings
- Wall hangings
- Cookbooks
- Curtains

Dining Room
- Buffet
- Cabinets
- Carpets
- Candlesticks
- Chairs
- China
- Clocks
- Dinnerware
- Linens
- Lamps
- Table
- Glassware

Basement
- Washing machine
- Dryer
- Shelves
- Workbench
- Power tools
- Ironing board

require worker's compensation coverage. Most homeowners policies provide a basic personal liability coverage of $100,000, but additional amounts are frequently recommended. An **umbrella policy**, also called a personal catastrophe policy, supplements your basic personal liability coverage. This added protection covers you for such personal injury claims as libel, slander, defamation of character, and invasion of property. Extended liability policies are sold in amounts of $1 million or more and are especially useful to individuals with substantial net worth. If you are a business owner, you may also need other types of liability coverages.

Medical payments coverage pays the cost of minor accidental injuries on your property and minor injuries caused by you, family members, or pets away from home. Settlements under medical payments coverage are made without determining fault. This protection allows fast processing of small claims, generally up to $5,000. Suits for more severe personal injuries are covered by the personal liability portion of the homeowners policy.

Should you or a family member accidentally damage the property of others, the *supplementary coverage* of homeowners insurance is designed to pay for these minor mishaps. This protection is usually limited to $500 or $1,000. Again, payments are made regardless of fault. Any property damage claims for greater amounts would require action under the personal liability coverage.

Specialized Coverages   Homeowners insurance does not cover losses from floods and earthquakes. Therefore, people living in areas with these two risks need to obtain special coverage. In various communities, the National Flood Insurance Program makes flood insurance available. This protection is a coverage separate from your homeowners policy. An insurance agent or the Federal Emergency Management Agency of the Federal Insurance Administration can give you additional information about this coverage.

Earthquake insurance can be obtained as an **endorsement,** or addition of coverage, to your homeowners policy. Since the most severe earthquakes occur in the Pacific Coast region, most of the insurance against this risk is bought by people in that region. You should remember, however, that every state is vulnerable to earthquakes and that this insurance coverage is available in all areas for an additional charge. Insurance against both floods and earthquakes is frequently required by lenders for a mortgage to buy a home in an area that faces these risks.

Renters Insurance

For people who rent, home insurance coverages include personal property protection, additional living expenses, and personal liability and related coverages. Protection against financial loss due to damage or loss of personal property is the main component of renters insurance. While 9 out of 10 homeowners have insurance, only 3 out of 10 renters are covered. Quite often, renters believe that they are covered under the insurance policy of the building owner. In fact, the building owner's property insurance does not cover the personal property of tenants unless the building owner can be proven negligent. If needed repairs for wiring caused a fire and damaged a tenant's furniture, the renter may be able to collect for damages from the building owner. Renters insurance is relatively inexpensive and provides protection from financial loss due to many of the same risks covered in homeowners policies.

Home Insurance Policy Forms

Until the mid-1950s, a person had to buy separate insurance coverage for fire, theft, and other risks. Since then, the insurance industry has created a series of homeowners and renters policies that provide package protection. The primary types of home insurance policies are the basic, broad, special, tenants, condominium owners, and modified coverage forms.

EXHIBIT 12–3   Types of Home Insurance Policies

Basic Form (HO-1)	Broad Form (HO-2)	Special Form (HO-3)	Tenants Form (HO-4)
• Fire, lightning • Windstorm, hail • Explosion • Riot or civil commotion • Aircraft • Vehicles • Smoke • Vandalism or malicious mischief • Theft • Glass breakage • Volcanic eruption	Covers all basic form risks plus • Falling objects • Weight of ice, snow, or sleet • Discharge of water or steam • Tearing apart of heating system or appliance • Freezing • Accidental damage from electric current	Covers all basic and broad forms risks plus any other risks except those specifically excluded from the policy such as • Flood • Earthquake • War • Nuclear accidents	Covers personal belongings against the risks covered by the basic and broad forms of the homeowners policies **Condominium Form (HO-6)** Covers personal belongings and additions to the living unit

The other major coverages of each policy are
• Personal liability
• Medical payments
• Additional living expenses

Basic Form   As presented in Exhibit 12–3, the *basic form* (HO–1) of homeowners insurance, also referred to as fire and extended coverage, protects your home and property against 11 risks. Although this policy is adequate for many situations, such as a summer home, it does not cover damage from falling objects, the weight of ice, or freezing. Insurance companies are phasing out use of the basic form in most states.

Broad Form   The *broad form* (HO–2) expands the basic coverage by including protection against several additional risks (see Exhibit 12–3). It also increases the coverage for such risks as theft and vehicle damage.

Special Form   The *special form* (HO–3) of homeowners policy covers the building for all causes of loss or damage except those specifically excluded by the policy. Common exclusions are flood, earthquake, war, and nuclear accidents (also see Exhibit 12–4). Personal property is covered for the risks listed in the policy.

Tenants Form   The *tenants form* (HO–4) protects the personal property of renters against the specific risks listed in the policy. As mentioned, renters insurance does not include coverage on the building or other structures.

Other Policy Forms   *Condominium owners insurance* (HO–6) protects your personal property and any additions or improvements you make to the living unit, such as bookshelves, electrical fixtures, and wall or floor coverings. Insurance on the building and other structures is purchased by the condominium association.

Finally, the *modified coverage form* (HO–8), or older home policy, covers residences with a high replacement cost compared to their current market value. For example, decorative woodwork in a Victorian home would be very costly to duplicate. HO–8 coverage pays for the restoration of property, but not necessarily

EXHIBIT 12–4

Not Everything's Covered

Certain personal property is specifically excluded from the coverage provided by home-owners insurance:

Articles separately described and specifically insured, such as jewelry, furs, boats, or expensive electronic equipment.

Animals, birds, or fishes.

Motorized land vehicles, except those used to service an insured's residence that are not licensed for road use.

Any device or instrument for the transmission and recording of sound, including any accessories or antennas, while in or upon motor vehicles. This includes stereotape players, stereotapes, and citizens band radios.

Aircraft and parts.

Property of roomers, boarders, and other tenants who are not related to any insured.

Property contained in an apartment regularly rented or held for rental to others by any insured.

Property rented or held for rental to others away from the residence premises.

Business property in storage, or held as a sample, or for sale, or for delivery after sale.

Business property pertaining to business actually conducted on the residence premises.

Business property away from the residence premises.

SOURCE: George E. Rejda, *Principles of Insurance* (Glenview, Ill.: Scott, Foresman, 1982). Copyright 1982 by Scott, Foresman and Company. Reprinted by permission.

with the same materials as those used in the original. This homeowners policy provides the same coverages as the basic form at a more reasonable cost because the homes are older and more difficult to replace.

Manufactured housing units and mobile homes usually qualify for insurance coverage with conventional policies. But certain mobile homes may require a special arrangement and higher rates since their construction makes them more prone to fire and wind damage. The cost of mobile home insurance coverage is most affected by location and by the method used to attach the housing unit to the ground. This type of property insurance is quite expensive; a $20,000 mobile home costs about as much to insure as a $60,000 house.

In addition to the property and liability risks previously discussed, home insurance policies include coverage for

- Credit card fraud, check forgery, and counterfeit money.
- The cost of removing damaged property.
- Emergency removal of property to protect it from damage.
- Temporary repairs after a loss to prevent further damage.
- Fire department charges in areas with such fees.

HOME INSURANCE COST FACTORS

Financial losses caused by fire, theft, wind, and other risks amount to billions of dollars each year. Since most homeowners have a mortgage on their property, the lending institution will require that you have insurance. When purchasing

EXHIBIT 12–5   Determining the Amount of Home Insurance You Need

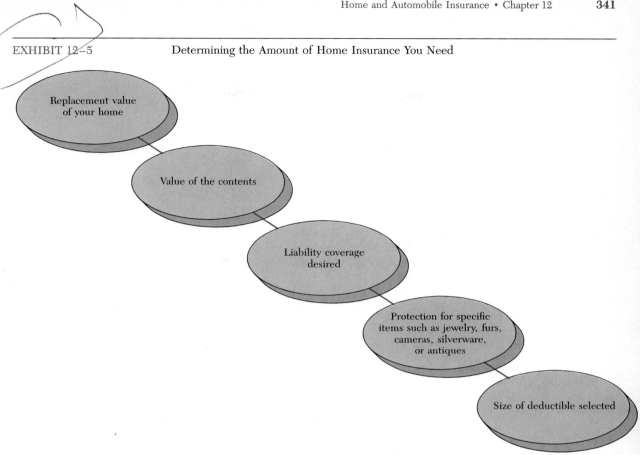

Replacement value
of your home

Value of the contents

Liability coverage
desired

Protection for specific
items such as jewelry, furs,
cameras, silverware,
or antiques

Size of deductible selected

L.O.3
Analyze the factors that influence the coverage amount and cost of home insurance.

insurance, you can get the best value for each premium dollar by selecting the appropriate amount of coverage and by being aware of the factors that affect insurance costs.

How Much Coverage Do You Need?

Several factors determine how much insurance coverage you need for your home and property (see Exhibit 12–5). Your insurance protection should be based on the amount of money you need to rebuild or repair your house, not on the amount you paid for it. As construction costs increase, you should increase the amount of coverage. In recent years, most insurance policies have had a built-in inflation clause that increases the coverage as property values increase. This increased coverage is based on an index of property values and on the cost of living in your area.

Most homeowners insurance policies contain a provision requiring that the building be insured for at least 80 percent of the replacement value. Under this **coinsurance clause,** the homeowner must pay for part of the losses if the property is not insured for the specified percentage of the replacement value. Only 80 percent is required because even if your property is completely destroyed, the land and the building foundation will probably still be usable.

When you insure for less than the 80 percent minimum, the insurance company will base its payment of claims on the portion of coverage carried (see "Personal Financial Calculations" feature). Any coverage over the amount needed to meet the 80 percent coinsurance clause is wasted spending since it would not increase the maximum amount that the insurance company would pay you for your loss. The coinsurance requirement is an important reason to monitor the value of your home and adjust the policy amount accordingly.

If you are financing a home, the lending institution will require you to have property insurance in an amount that covers its financial investment. Remember, too, that the amount of insurance on your home will determine the coverage on the contents. Personal belongings are generally covered up to an amount equal to 50 percent of the insurance on the dwelling.

Insurance companies base claim settlements on one of two methods. Under the **actual cash value (ACV)** method, the payment you receive is based on the current replacement cost of a damaged or lost item less depreciation. This means that you would get $180 for a five-year-old television set that cost you $400 and had an estimated life of eight years if the same set now costs $480. Your settlement amount is determined by taking the current cost of $480 and subtracting five years of depreciation from it—$300 for five years at $60 a year.

Under the **replacement value** method for settling claims, you receive the full cost of repairing or replacing a damaged or lost item; depreciation is not considered. However, many companies limit the replacement cost to 400 percent of the item's actual cash value. Replacement value coverage is about 10 to 20 percent more expensive than ACV coverage.

[handwritten margin notes: like if bought roverhings yrs. ago, at 10 bucks, still get 10 bucks even though it's worth more now (ACV)]

[handwritten margin note: cost more but will totally replace]

What Factors Affect Home Insurance Costs?

The main influences on the premium paid for home and property insurance are the location of the home, the coverage amount and policy type, discounts, and company differences.

FINANCIAL PLANNING CALCULATIONS
Coinsurance Claim Settlements

Property insurance companies require that your home be insured for at least 80 percent of its replacement value. The amount that such a company will pay for damage is based on the following formula:

$$\frac{\text{Amount of insurance coverage}}{0.80 \times \text{Replacement cost of building}} \times \frac{\text{Amount of property}}{\text{damage or loss}} = \frac{\text{Insurance}}{\text{company}}_{\text{payment}}$$

For example, a $100,000 home with $60,000 of insurance would be below the 80 percent limit. Wind damage of $8,000 to the roof of the house in this situation would mean a settlement of $6,000 ($60,000/$80,000 × $8,000 = $6,000).

Location of Home   The location of the residence affects insurance rates. So, too, do the efficiency of the fire department and the frequency of the thefts in an area. If more claims have been filed in an area, the rates for those living there will be higher.

The type of home and the construction materials also influence the costs of insurance coverage. A brick house, for example, would cost less to insure than a similar house made of wood. Also, the age and style of the house can cause more potential risks and thus increase insurance costs.

Coverage Amount and Policy Type   The policy you select and the financial limits of coverage are other factors that affect the premium you pay. It costs more to insure a $90,000 home than a $70,000 home. The special form of homeowners policy costs more than either the basic form policy or the broad form policy.

The cost of your insurance is also affected by the amount of the deductible in your policy. If you increase the amount of your deductible, your premium will be lower since the company will pay out less in claims. The most common deductible amount is $250. Increasing the deductible from $250 to $500 or $1,000 can reduce the premium 15 percent or more.

Home Insurance Discounts   Most companies offer incentives that reduce home insurance costs. Your premium may be lower if you have smoke detectors or a fire extinguisher. Deterrents to burglars, such as dead bolt locks or an alarm system, can save you money. Some companies even offer home insurance discounts to policyholders who are nonsmokers.

Company Differences   Studies have shown that you can save up to 25 percent on homeowners insurance by comparing companies. Contact both insurance agents who work for one company and independent agents who represent several. The information you obtain in this way will enable you to compare rates.

Don't select a company on the basis of price alone. Also consider service and coverage. Not all companies settle claims in the same way. For example, a number of homeowners had two sides of their houses dented by hail. Since the type of siding used in these houses was no longer available, all of the siding had to be replaced. Some insurance companies paid for the complete replacement of the siding, while others only paid for the replacement of the damaged areas.[2] State insurance commissions, other government agencies, and consumer organizations can provide information about the reputation of insurance companies. *Consumer Reports* regularly publishes a satisfaction index of property insurance companies based on speed of settling claims, claim settlement amounts, and ease of reaching a claim representative.

AUTOMOBILE INSURANCE COVERAGES

L.O.4
Identify the important types of automobile insurance coverages.

The National Traffic Safety Administration estimates that alcohol use is a factor in 65 percent of automobile accidents. Each year, such accidents result in thousands of highway deaths and injuries and over $30 billion in costs. Together with other kinds of automobile accidents, they create a risk associated with the major type of transportation in our society that affects a great number of people financially and emotionally. Automobile insurance cannot eliminate the financial costs of automobile accidents, but it does reduce their impact.

A **financial responsibility law** is state legislation that requires drivers to prove their ability to cover the cost of damage or injury caused by an automobile accident. All states have such laws to protect the public from physical harm and property damage losses caused by drivers. When there are injuries or significant property damage in an accident, the drivers involved are required to file a report with the state and to show financial responsibility. As of 1990 over 40 states had compulsory automobile insurance laws. In other states, most people meet the financial responsibility requirement by buying insurance, since very few people have the financial resources needed to meet this legal requirement on their own. Exhibit 12–6 presents each state's minimum limits for financial responsibility. These amounts represent the minimum state requirement; higher coverage is frequently recommended to protect the financial assets of individuals.

The main coverages of automobile insurance can be grouped into two categories—bodily injury coverages and property damage coverages (see Exhibit 12–7). Other coverages include wage loss insurance and towing service.

EXHIBIT 12–6
Automobile Financial Responsibility/Compulsory Insurance Minimum Limits (As of January 1990)

State	Liability Limits	State	Liability Limits
Alabama	20/40/10	Montana°	25/50/5
Alaska°	50/100/25	Nebraska°	25/50/25
Arizona°	15/30/10	Nevada°	15/30/10
Arkansas°	25/50/15	New Hampshire	25/50/25
California°	15/30/5	New Jersey°	15/30/5
Colorado°	25/50/15	New Mexico°	25/50/10
Connecticut°	20/40/10	New York°	10/20/5†
Delaware°	15/30/10	North Carolina°	25/50/10
District of Columbia°	10/20/5	North Dakota°	25/50/25
Florida°	10/20/5	Ohio°	12.5/25/7.5
Georgia°	15/30/10	Oklahoma°	10/20/10
Hawaii°	35/unlimited/10	Oregon°	25/50/10
Idaho°	25/50/15	Pennsylvania°	15/30/5
Illinois°	20/40/15	Rhode Island	25/50/25
Indiana°	25/50/10	South Carolina°	15/30/5
Iowa°	20/40/15	South Dakota°	25/50/25
Kansas°	25/50/10	Tennessee	25/50/10
Kentucky°	25/50/10	Texas°	20/40/15
Louisiana°	10/20/10	Utah°	20/40/10
Maine°	20/40/10	Vermont°	20/40/10
Maryland°	20/40/10	Virginia	25/50/10
Massachusetts°	10/20/5	Washington°	25/50/10
Michigan°	20/40/10	West Virginia°	20/40/10
Minnesota°	30/60/10	Wisconsin	25/50/10
Mississippi	10/20/5	Wyoming°	25/50/10
Missouri°	25/50/10		

°State with compulsory automobile liability insurance.
†50/100 in cases where injury results in death.
SOURCES: Insurance Information Institute and American Insurance Association.

Bodily Injury Coverages

Most of the money that automobile insurance companies pay in claims is for the legal expenses of injury lawsuits, medical expenses, and related expenses. The main bodily injury coverages are bodily injury liability, medical payments, and uninsured motorists protection. The development of no-fault systems in a number of states has influenced the process of settling bodily injury claims.

Bodily Injury Liability   The coverage provided by **bodily injury liability** is for the risk of financial loss due to legal expenses, medical expenses, lost wages, and other expenses associated with injuries caused by an automobile accident for which you were responsible. This insurance protects you from extensive financial losses.

Bodily injury liability is usually expressed as a split limit, such as 10/20 or 100/300. These amounts represent thousands of dollars of coverage. The first number (see Exhibit 12–8) is the limit for claims that can be paid to one person; the second number is the limit for each accident; the third number is discussed below in the "Property Damage Coverages" section.

Medical Payments   While bodily injury liability pays for the costs of injuries to persons who were not in your automobile, **medical payments** covers the costs of health care for people who were injured in your automobile, including yourself. This protection covers friends, car pool members, and others who ride in your vehicle. Medical payments insurance also provides medical benefits if you or a member of your family is struck by an automobile or injured while riding in another person's automobile.

Uninsured Motorists Protection   If you are in an accident caused by a person without insurance, **uninsured motorists protection** covers the cost of injuries to

EXHIBIT 12–7
Automobile Insurance
Coverage

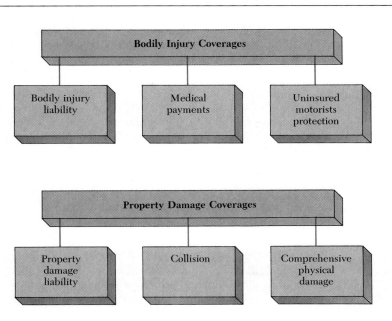

EXHIBIT 12–8
Automobile Liability
Insurance Coverage

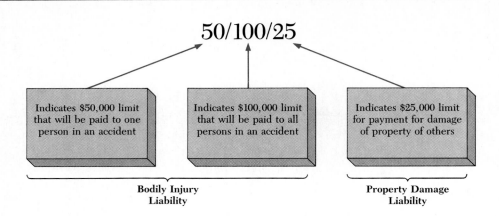

you and your family, but, in most states, not property damage. This insurance also provides protection against financial losses due to injuries caused by a hit-and-run driver or by a driver who has less coverage than the cost of your injuries.

No-Fault Insurance Difficulties in settling claims for medical expenses and personal injuries resulted in the creation of the **no-fault system,** under which drivers involved in an accident collect medical expenses, lost wages, and related injury costs from their own insurance company. The system is intended to provide fast and smooth methods of paying for damages without taking the legal action frequently necessary to determine fault.

In 1971, Massachusetts was the first state to implement no-fault insurance. As of 1990, 28 states had some variation of the system. While no-fault automobile insurance was intended to reduce the time and cost associated with the settlement of automobile injury cases, it has not always achieved these results. One reason for continued difficulties is that no-fault systems vary from state to state. Some no-fault states set limits on medical expenses, lost wages, and other claim settlements, whereas other states allow lawsuits under certain conditions, such as permanent paralysis or death. And some states include property damage in no-fault insurance. Michigan's system, in which policies provide unlimited compensation for medical and rehabilitation costs and up to $114,384 for lost income, is considered by many to be the ideal no-fault system. Drivers should investigate the coverages and implications of no-fault insurance in their state.

Property Damage Coverages

The three coverages that protect you from financial loss due to the damage of the property of others and damage to your vehicle are property damage liability, collision, and comprehensive physical damage.

Property Damage Liability When you damage the property of others, **property damage liability** protects you against financial loss. This coverage applies mainly to other vehicles, but it also includes damage to street signs, lampposts, buildings, and other property. Property damage liability protects you and others covered by your policy when you are driving another person's automobile with his or her permission. The policy limit for property damage liability is frequently given with your bodily injury coverages. The last number in the groups 50/100/25 and 100/300/50 is for property damage liability ($25,000 and $50,000, respectively).

Collision   When your automobile is involved in an accident, **collision** insurance pays for the damage to the automobile regardless of who is at fault. But if another driver caused the accident, your insurance company would try to recover the repair costs for your vehicle from the other driver's property damage liability coverage. The insurance company's right to recover the amount it pays for the loss from the person responsible for the loss is called *subrogation*.

The amount you can collect with collision insurance is limited to the retail value of the automobile at the time of the accident. This amount is usually based on the figures provided by some appraisal service, such as the *Official Used Car Guide* of the National Association of Automobile Dealers. If you have an automobile with many add-on features or one that is several years old and has been restored, you should obtain a documented statement of its condition and value before an accident occurs.

Comprehensive Physical Damage   Another protection for your automobile involves financial losses from damage to it caused by a risk other than a collision. **Comprehensive physical damage** covers you for such risks as fire, theft, glass breakage, falling objects, vandalism, wind, or hail, or damage caused by hitting an animal. Certain articles in your vehicle, such as some types of radios and stereo equipment, may be excluded from this insurance. These articles may be protected by the personal property coverage of your home insurance. As with collision, comprehensive coverage applies only to your car and claims are paid without considering fault.

Both collision and comprehensive coverage are commonly sold with a *deductible* to help reduce insurance costs. If a broken windshield costs $250 to replace and you have a $100 deductible on your comprehensive coverage, the insurance company would pay $150 of the damage. Deductibles keep insurance premiums lower by reducing the number of small claims that the company pays.

Other Automobile Coverages

In addition to the basic bodily injury and property damage coverages of automobile insurance, other protection is available. Wage loss insurance will reimburse you for any salary or income lost due to injury in an automobile accident. Wage loss insurance is required in states with a no-fault insurance system; in other states, it is available on an optional basis.

Towing and emergency road service pays for the cost of breakdowns and mechanical assistance. This coverage can be especially beneficial on long trips or during inclement weather. Towing and road service pays for the cost of getting the vehicle to a service station or starting it when it breaks down on the highway, but not for the cost of repairs. If you belong to an automobile club, towing coverage may be included in your membership. Purchasing duplicate coverage as part of your automobile insurance could waste money.

PERSONAL FINANCE JOURNAL

Are You Covered?

Quite often, we believe that our insurance will cover various financial losses. For each of the following situations, name the type of home or automobile insurance that would protect you.

1. While you are on vacation, clothing and other personal belongings are stolen. _____

2. Your home is damaged by fire, and you have to live in a hotel for several weeks. _____

3. You and members of your family suffer injuries in an automobile accident caused by a hit-and-run driver. _____

4. A delivery person is injured on your property and takes legal action against you. _____

5. Your automobile is accidentally damaged by some people who are playing baseball. _____

6. A person takes legal action against you for injuries you caused in an automobile accident. _____

7. Water from a local lake rises and damages your furniture and carpeting. _____

8. Your automobile needs repairs because you hit a tree. _____

9. You damaged a valuable tree when your automobile hit it, and you want to pay for the damage. _____

10. While riding with you, in your automobile, your nephew is injured in an accident. He incurs various medical expenses. _____

ANSWERS: (1) Personal property coverage of home insurance; (2) additional living expenses of home insurance; (3) uninsured motorists protection; (4) personal liability coverage of home insurance; (5) comprehensive physical damage; (6) bodily injury liability; (7) flood insurance—requires coverage separate from home insurance; (8) collision; (9) property damage liability of automobile insurance; (10) medical payments.

AUTOMOBILE INSURANCE COSTS

L.O.5
Evaluate the factors that affect the cost of automobile insurance.

Automobile insurance premiums reflect the amounts an insurance company pays for injury and property damage claims. Your automobile insurance is directly related to coverage amounts and such factors as the vehicle, your place of residence, and your driving record.

The Amount of Coverage

"How much coverage do I need?" This question affects the amount you pay for insurance. Our legal environment and constantly increasing property values influence coverage amounts.

Legal Concerns   As discussed, every state has laws that require or encourage automobile liability insurance coverage. Since very few people can afford to pay an expensive court settlement with their personal assets, most drivers buy automobile liability insurance.

Until the mid-1970s bodily injury liability coverage of 10/20 was considered adequate. In fact, some states still have these amounts as their minimum limits for financial responsibility. But in recent injury cases some people have been awarded millions of dollars, so legal and insurance advisers now recommend 100/300. An umbrella policy can provide additional liability coverage of up to $1 million, as discussed earlier in this chapter.

Property Values Just as medical expenses and legal settlements have increased, so too has the cost of automobiles. Therefore, a policy limit of more than $5,000 or $10,000 for property damage liability is appropriate; $50,000 or $100,000 is suggested.

The higher cost of automobile replacement parts also contributes to the need for increased property damage coverage. The list price for a 1989 Nissan Maxima was $17,499. The Alliance of American Insurers determined that purchasing its parts individually would cost $60,755, not including labor!

Automobile Insurance Premium Factors

The premium you pay for automobile insurance is influenced by several factors. The main factors are automobile type, rating territory, and driver classification.

Automobile Type The year, make, and model of your automobile have a strong impact on your automobile insurance costs. Expensive replacement parts and complicated repairs due to body style cause higher rates. Also, certain makes and models are stolen more often than others. According to the Highway Loss Data Institute, the Plymouth Colt, Ford Escort, and Plymouth Reliant have low theft records, whereas the Chevrolet Camaro, Pontiac Sunbird, Corvette, and Mercedes have high theft records. Occupant injury data for various types of vehicles also affect the rates paid.

Rating Territory In most states, your rating territory is the place of residence that is used to determine your automobile insurance premium. Different geographic locations have different costs due to differences in the number of claims made. For example, fewer accidents and less vandalism occur in rural areas than in large cities. In 1988, 119,940 vehicles were stolen in New York City, 57,331 in Los Angeles, and 45,012 in Chicago. These cities had the highest incidence of automobile theft.

Driver Classification You are compared with other drivers to set your automobile insurance premium. **Driver classification** is a category based on the driver's age, sex, marital status, driving record, and driving habits; the driver's category is used to determine his or her automobile insurance rates. In general, young, unmarried male drivers have more accidents and can expect to pay higher premiums (see Exhibit 12–9). In recent years, some states have barred the use of sex as a factor in setting insurance premiums. As a result, young female drivers have had premium increases of from $200 to over $1,000. Insurance companies argue that young male drivers should pay more than young female drivers since they have more moving violations, license suspensions, and revocations.

Your driver classification is also influenced by accidents and traffic violations. A poor driving record will increase your insurance costs. Finally, you will pay less for insurance if you do not drive to work than if you use your automobile for business purposes. Belonging to a car pool instead of driving to work alone can reduce your insurance costs.

The number of claims you have filed with your insurance company also affects your insurance premiums. Expensive liability settlements or extensive property damage will increase your rates. If you have many expensive claims or a poor

EXHIBIT 12–9
Fatal Motor Vehicle
Accidents by Age of Driver

(Numbers represent drivers in fatal accidents per 100,000 drivers in each age group.)

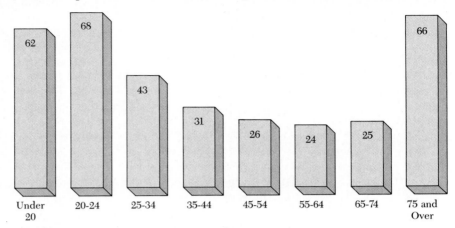

| Under 20 | 20-24 | 25-34 | 35-44 | 45-54 | 55-64 | 65-74 | 75 and Over |
| 62 | 68 | 43 | 31 | 26 | 24 | 25 | 66 |

SOURCE: *Accident Facts* (Chicago: National Safety Council, 1988), p. 54.

driving record, your company may cancel your policy, and it is then usually difficult to obtain coverage from another company. To deal with this problem, every state has an **assigned risk pool** consisting of people who are unable to obtain automobile insurance. Some of these people are assigned to each of the insurance companies operating in the state. They pay several times the normal rates, but they do get coverage. Once they establish a good driving record, they can reapply for insurance at the regular rates. Critics of the assigned risk system contend that under this system good drivers help cover the costs of poor drivers. However, if assigned risk drivers were in accidents without insurance, the potential financial burden on society might be even greater.

Reducing Automobile Insurance Premiums

Methods to help lower your automobile insurance costs include comparing companies and taking advantage of discounts.

Comparing Companies Rates and service vary among automobile insurance companies. Among companies in the same area, premiums can vary as much as 100 percent. If you relocate, don't assume that the company offering the best rates in your former area also offers the best rates in your present area.

Also consider the service provided by the local insurance agent. Will this company representative be available to answer questions, change coverages, and handle claims as needed? A company's reputation for handling automobile insurance claims and other matters can be checked with such sources as *Consumer Reports* magazine or your state insurance department.

Premium Discounts The best way to keep your rates down is to establish and maintain a safe driving record. Avoiding accidents and traffic violations will mean lower automobile insurance premiums. In addition, most insurance companies offer premium discounts for various reasons. Drivers under 25 can qualify for

PERSONAL FINANCE JOURNAL

What to Do If You Have an Auto Accident

No one plans to have an auto accident, but each year more than 18 million auto accidents occur. If you are involved in such an accident, you should take the following actions:

- Stop your vehicle, turn off your ignition, and remain at the scene of the accident.
- Obtain the names and addresses of other drivers, passengers, and witnesses; make notes regarding the circumstances of the accident.
- Obtain a copy of any police accident report; file the necessary accident documents with your insurance company and state or local government agencies.

- Provide assistance to anyone who is injured; seek medical assistance if needed; DO NOT MOVE the injured person – that should be done by medical personnel.
- Assist in the preparation of a police report, if required, by providing your name, address, license number, and vehicle and insurance information.

reduced rates by completing a driver training program and maintaining good grades in school. If a young driver is away at school without a car, the family is likely to get a reduction in its automobile premium since he or she will not be using the vehicle on a regular basis.

Installing security devices such as a fuel shutoff switch, a second ignition switch, or an alarm system will decrease your chances of theft and thus lower your comprehensive insurance costs. Equipping your automobile with air bags may qualify you for a discount. Being a nonsmoker can qualify you for lower automobile insurance premiums. Discounts are also offered for participating in a car pool and insuring two or more vehicles with the same company. Ask your insurance agent about other methods for lowering your automobile insurance rates.

Increasing the amount of deductibles will result in a lower premium. Also, some people believe that an old car is not worth the amount paid for the collision and comprehensive coverages and therefore dispense with them. But before doing this, be sure to compare the value of your car for getting you to school or work with the cost of these coverages.

If you change your driving habits, get married, or alter your driving status in other ways, be sure to notify the insurance company. Premium savings can result. Also, some employers make group automobile insurance available to workers. As with other types of group insurance plans, the cost of such insurance is usually less than the cost of an individual policy.

Before you buy a car, find out which makes and models have the lowest insurance costs. This information can result in a purchasing decision that is beneficial to your overall financial existence.

SUMMARY

L.O.1
Discuss the importance of property and liability insurance.

Owners of homes and automobiles face the risks of property damage or loss and the risks of legal actions by others for the costs of injuries or property damage. Property and liability insurance offer protection from financial losses that may arise from a wide variety of situations faced by owners of homes and users of automobiles.

L.O.2
Explain the insurance coverages and policy types available to homeowners and renters.

Homeowners insurance includes protection for the building and other structures, additional living expenses, personal property, and personal liability. Renters insurance includes the same coverages except protection for the building and other structures, which is the concern of the building owner, not the tenant. The main types of home insurance policies are the basic, broad, special, tenants, and condominium forms. These policies differ in the risks and property they cover.

L.O.3
Analyze the factors that influence the coverage amount and cost of home insurance.

The amount of home insurance coverage is determined by the replacement cost of your dwelling and your personal belongings. The cost of home insurance is influenced by the location of the home, the coverage amount, the policy type, discounts, and company differences.

L.O.4
Identify the important types of automobile insurance coverages.

Automobile insurance is used to meet the financial responsibility laws of the state and to protect drivers against financial losses associated with bodily injury and property damage. The major types of automobile insurance coverages are bodily injury liability, medical payments, uninsured motorists, property damage liability, collision, and comprehensive physical damage.

L.O.5
Evaluate the factors that affect the cost of automobile insurance.

The cost of automobile insurance is affected by the amount of coverage, the automobile type, the rating territory, the driver classification, company differences, and premium discounts.

GLOSSARY

Actual cash value (ACV)   A claim settlement method in which the insured receives payment based on the current replacement cost of a damaged or lost item, less depreciation.

Assigned risk pool   Consists of people unable to obtain automobile insurance due to poor driving or accident records who obtain coverage at high rates through a state program that requires insurance companies to accept some of them.

Bodily injury liability   Coverage for the risk of financial loss due to legal expenses, medical costs, lost wages, and other expenses associated with injuries caused by an automobile accident for which you were responsible.

Coinsurance clause   A policy provision that requires a homeowner to pay for part of the losses if the property is not insured for the specified percentage of the replacement value.

Collision   Automobile insurance that pays for damage to the insured's car when it is involved in an accident.

Comprehensive physical damage   Automobile insurance that covers financial loss from damage to your vehicle caused by a risk other than a collision, such as fire, theft, glass breakage, hail, or vandalism.

Driver classification   A category based on the driver's age, sex, marital status, driving record, and driving habits; used to determine automobile insurance rates.

Endorsement   An addition of coverage to a standard insurance policy.

Financial responsibility law   State legislation that requires drivers to prove their ability to cover the cost of damage or injury caused by an automobile accident.

Homeowners insurance   Coverage for your place of residence and its associated financial risks.

Household inventory   A list or other documentation of personal belongings, with purchase dates and cost information.

Liability   Legal responsibility for the financial cost of another person's losses or injuries.

Medical payments   Home insurance that pays the cost of minor accidental injuries on your property; also automobile insurance that covers the costs of health care for people injured in your car.

Negligence   Failure to take ordinary or reasonable care in a situation.

No-fault system   An automobile insurance program in which drivers involved in an accident collect medical expenses, lost wages, and related injury costs from their own insurance company.

Personal property floater   Additional property insurance to cover the damage or loss of a specific item of high value.

Property damage liability   Automobile insurance coverage that protects you against financial loss when you damage the property of others.

Rating territory   The place of residence that is used to determine your automobile insurance premium.

Replacement value   A claim settlement method in which the insured receives the full cost of repairing or replacing a damaged or lost item.

Umbrella policy   Supplementary personal liability coverage; also called a personal catastrophe policy.

Uninsured motorists protection   Automobile insurance coverage for the cost of injuries to you and members of your family caused by a driver with inadequate insurance or by a hit-and-run driver.

Vicarious liability   A situation in which a person is held legally responsible for the actions of another person.

DISCUSSION QUESTIONS

L.O.1   1. What property and liability risks do many people overlook?

L.O.1   2. How could a person's life situation influence the need for various types of property and liability insurance?

L.O.2   3. What is covered under the personal property portion of home insurance?

L.O.2   4. How do renters insurance policies differ from other home insurance policies?

L.O.2   5. What reasons would explain the fact that most renters do not have property and liability insurance?

L.O.3   6. What are the major factors that influence the cost of home insurance?

L.O.3   7. What actions can a person take to reduce the cost of home insurance?

L.O.4   8. Should all of the states require automobile liability insurance? Give reasons for your answer.

L.O.4   9. Which automobile insurance coverages do you consider the most important for good personal financial planning?

L.O.4   10. How does collision coverage differ from comprehensive physical damage coverage?

L.O.5   11. What factors influence how much a person pays for automobile insurance?

L.O.5   12. Should female drivers be charged less than male drivers for comparable automobile insurance coverage? Should unmarried drivers be charged more than married drivers? Give reasons for your answers.

L.O.5   13. What actions can a person take to reduce the cost of automobile insurance?

L.O.5   14. What actions should government agencies take to reduce automobile accidents and highway injuries?

Opening Case Questions

1. What additional insurance coverages might the Pattersons consider obtaining?

2. What factors should the Pattersons consider in deciding whether they require additional coverages?

3. How could the Pattersons' home and auto insurance coverages affect other aspects of their financial planning?

4. What efforts can the Pattersons make to reduce the amount they pay for property and liability insurance?

PROBLEMS AND ACTIVITIES

L.O.1   1. Contact financial planners and insurance agents to obtain examples of financial difficulties encountered by individuals who lacked adequate home or automobile insurance.

L.O.2   2. Talk to several friends and relatives about their household inventory records. In case of damage or loss, would they be able to prove the value of their personal belongings?

L.O.2   3. Interview an insurance agent about the cost differences among various forms of home insurance policies. Which form is most commonly used? What type of coverage does the agent recommend for most homeowners?

L.O.2　4.　Examine a homeowners or renters insurance policy. What coverages does the policy include? Does the policy contain any unclear features or wording?

L.O.3　5.　If a $130,000 home was insured for $100,000, based on the 80 percent coinsurance provision, how much would the insurance company pay on a $5,000 claim?

L.O.3　6.　For each of the following situations, what amount would the insurance company pay?

　　a.　Wind damage of $785; the insured has a $500 deductible.

　　b.　Theft of a stereo system worth $1,300; the insured has a $250 deductible.

　　c.　Vandalism that does $375 of damage to a home; the insured has a $500 deductible.

L.O.4　7.　The insured has 25/50/10 automobile insurance coverage. If two other people are awarded $35,000 each for injuries in an auto accident in which the insured was judged at fault, how much of this judgment would insurance cover?

L.O.5　8.　Obtain automobile insurance rates from agents representing three companies. What might be reasons for the differences in these rates?

L.O.5　9.　Conduct an informal survey of consumer attitudes toward regulation of drunk drivers. Are current penalties appropriate for the driving violations of such drivers?

LIFE SITUATION　Case 12–1

Selecting Home Insurance

Kyle Gelwicks recently bought a home for $83,000 in an area with many older homes that are being remodeled and improved with new roofs and room additions. The home has a current replacement value of $90,000. Kyle has about $6,000 worth of personal belongings other than his automobile. He has a busy work schedule, and he travels to other cities several times each month. He is not sure what type or amount of home insurance he should have.

Questions

1.　As a homeowner, what financial risks does Kyle face?
2.　How should Kyle determine the amount of insurance he needs on his home?
3.　What types of home insurance are available to Kyle?
4.　What type of policy and amount of coverage would you recommend?

LIFE SITUATION　Case 12–2

Reducing Auto Insurance Costs

Melissa Sutherland owns a four-year-old automobile that she drives to work each day. She also uses it for visits to friends and for vacations. She drives about 14,000 miles a year. Currently, Melissa has full insurance coverage for all types of bodily injury and property damage. The amount she pays each year for this coverage increases as the value of her car decreases. She would like to reduce her living expenses for automobile insurance while assuming some of the risk of financial loss associated with driving her car.

Questions

1. What automobile insurance coverage could Melissa eliminate?
2. What other actions could Melissa take to reduce the cost of her automobile insurance?
3. How would changes in Melissa automobile insurance coverages affect her financial risks?
4. What actions should Melissa take?

SUPPLEMENTARY READINGS

For Additional Information on Property and Liability Insurance

Plawin, Paul. "Insurance Myths You Probably Believe." *Changing Times,* August 1989, pp. 31–33.

Your Insurance Dollar. Money Management Institute, Household Financial Services, 2700 Sanders Road, Prospect Heights, IL 60070.

For Additional Information on Home Insurance

"Before Disaster Strikes: How to Protect Everything You Own." *Money,* February 1990, pp. 54–63, 66.

"Homeowner's Insurance." *Complete Guide to Managing Your Money,* pp. 256–75. Mount Vernon, N.Y.: Consumer Reports Books, 1989.

How to File an Insurance Claim. Insurance Information Institute, 110 William Street, New York, NY 10038.

"How to Make Your Home Secure." *Consumer Reports,* February 1990, pp. 96–109.

"Insuring Your Home." *Consumer Reports,* September 1989, pp. 572–78.

For Additional Information on Automobile Insurance

"Auto Insurance." *Consumer Reports,* October 1988, pp. 622–36.

Auto Insurance: Critical Choices for the 1900s. Insurance Information Institute, 110 William Street, New York, NY 10038.

Henry, Ed. "Car Insurance: Dial Up a Better Deal." *Changing Times,* April 1990, pp. 43–48.

"How Efficient Is Your Auto Insurer?" *Journal of American Insurance,* Third Quarter 1989, pp. 6–9. Alliance of American Insurers, 1501 Woodfield Road, Schaumburg, IL 60173.

Paulson, Morton C. "The Compelling Case for No-Fault Insurance." *Changing Times,* July 1989, pp. 49–52.

"10 Ways to Cut the Cost of Car Insurance." *Changing Times,* July 1988, pp. 47, 50–54.

"Will Your Car Coverage Vanish?" *U.S. News & World Report,* January 9, 1989, p. 62.

13

Health Care and Disability Insurance

Health insurance is one way in which people protect themselves against economic losses due to illness, accident, or disability. The coverage is available through private insurance companies, service plans, health maintenance organizations, and government programs. Employers often offer health insurance as part of an employee benefit package, called group health insurance, and health care providers sell it to individuals.

LEARNING OBJECTIVES

After studying this chapter, you will be able to

L.O.1 Explain why the costs of health insurance and health care have been increasing.

L.O.2 Define health insurance and disability income insurance and explain their importance in financial planning.

L.O.3 Recognize the need for disability income insurance.

L.O.4 Analyze the benefits and limitations of the various types of health care coverages.

L.O.5 Evaluate private sources of health insurance and health care.

L.O.6 Appraise the sources of government health programs.

· ·

OPENING CASE°

The Demise of Cost Watchdogs?

For the past 20 years, Alvin Saidiner had been a tireless crusader against rising medical costs. "Nobody had ever heard of cost containment when I got into it in 1967," he boasted. But the 55-year-old pharmacist from Burbank, California, was himself paying a high price.

His company, PCC/Drug Data Systems, Inc., was despised by hospitals and health care trade groups—and no wonder. Mr. Saidiner reviewed the cost of drugs on hospital bills and recommended on average that his clients—mostly insurance firms—refuse payment on about 40 percent of the tab.

For three years, Mr. Saidiner had been embroiled in a lawsuit filed by the California Association of Hospitals and Health Systems and 123 of its member hospitals, which claimed that they had unfairly been denied payments. Because Mr. Saidiner's firm is known as one of the most aggressive in the field, other auditors of medical costs are closely following the case. A win by the hospitals could lead these auditors to tone down their own cost containment efforts.

Even if Mr. Saidiner wins the suit, the litigation has raised questions about his methods and frightened off clients. While employers and insurers are looking for ways to cut medical costs, few want to go to court.

The suit, filed in federal court in Los Angeles, accused PCC and the other defendants of conspiring "to fix and pay arbitrarily established and unreasonably low prices." The plaintiffs contended that in the past six years PCC had cost California hospitals more than $58 million in denied charges.

In a countersuit, Mr. Saidiner claimed that the hospitals' real purpose was simply to drive him out of business. "It's

sham litigation," he charged. PCC was seeking treble damages totaling $42 million, three times the $14 million that Mr. Saidiner estimated to be the value of his business before it was ruined by the suit.

Three years ago, PCC had 1,400 clients nationwide and close to $5 million in annual revenues. This year, PCC will be lucky to pull in $300,000. PCC has laid off 25 people since the lawsuit was filed in March 1986, and its staff has shrunk to 9, including Saidiner's wife and the Saidiners' 28-year-old daughter. "Our phones don't ring any more," Mrs. Saidiner says.

Other cost containment firms typically audit entire hospital bills, but PCC audits only the charges for drugs and supplies. This approach is irksome to hospitals, whose markups on these products are "often in the realm of 800 percent to 1,000 percent," say Gregory Johnson, an associate in the San Francisco office of a major benefits consulting firm.

Take, for example, a bill that PCC reviewed for Chevron Corporation. Presbyterian Intercommunity Hospital in Whittier, California, charged a patient $270.50 for intravenous solutions. PCC calculated the hospital's actual cost at just $9 and recommended payment of $69.50. The hospital also charged $23.50 for eight iron capsules that PCC said cost $1.04; PCC recommended payment of $4.80. The hospital is disputing the recommendations.

°Adapted from Rhonda L. Rundle, "Hospital Groups Try to Pull Off Cost Watchdogs," *The Wall Street Journal*, August 16, 1989, p. B1.

· ·

HEALTH CARE COSTS

L.O.1
Explain why the costs of health insurance and health care have been increasing.

The soaring costs of medical care have forced employers such as Chevron Corporation to retain the services of cost containment or utilization review firms.

In a survey of 1,600 employers conducted in 1988, A. Foster Higgins, Inc., a benefits research firm based in New York, found that 75 percent of them had adopted cost controls.[1] Employer medical costs were up 20.5 percent in 1989, and they are still climbing.[2] Moreover, as the following cases illustrate, skyrocketing medical costs have affected everyone—not just employers.

> Greg Greene of Vacaville, California, was a data circuits installer at Pacific Telesis whose daughter, Katherine, had surgery to patch a hole in her heart in May 1989, when she was five months old. Katherine's hospital bill totaled almost $100,000. "Even if you're asked to pay just 10 percent of the bill from your own pocket, it is a huge amount," he said. Worse, an infection picked up in the hospital led to the removal of her sternum, and she may require costly reconstructive surgery as she grows.[3]

Linda Kasinowski designs circuits at AT&T's Oakton, Virginia, regional headquarters. In 1986, the younger of her two daughters, Katrina, then two years old, was diagnosed as leukemic. The family spends "thousands of dollars" on related health costs. Ms. Kasinowski's husband, able to work only from time to time as a carpenter, has his own medical expenses that often outstrip his income. "I've often felt like I'm working to pay doctors," Ms. Kasinowski says.[4]

How much do the doctors charge? Exhibit 13–1 shows typical physician charges in 1988 for selected services and procedures and the approximate times spent on each of these tasks.

Remember the Opening Case—$270.50 for intravenous solutions, and $23.50 for eight iron capsules? And, as Exhibit 13–2 shows, the cost of one day's care in a hospital can be as much as $1,500.[5]

Since 1988, the premiums for many health care plans have increased between 10 percent and 30 percent. In 1989, HMOs increased their premiums by an average of 17 percent, according to a survey conducted by the Group Health Association of America, Inc., an HMO trade organization. Almost half of the HMOs surveyed also said that they were forcing patients to pay slightly more out

---

EXHIBIT 13–1   How Much Doctors Charge—and Who Pays

Procedure	Approximate Time	Typical Charge
Reading a chest X ray	One minute	$10–$15
Office visit with family practitioner	15 minutes	$25
Office visit with internist	15 minutes	$30
Office visit with psychiatrist	50 minutes	$100–$150
Removing a lipoma*	20 minutes	$300
Administering anesthesia during surgery	One hour	$400–$500
Hernia repair	30 minutes– one hour	$750
Cesarean section	30 minutes– one hour	$1,500
Hip replacement	Three hours	$3,000

Where the money for the U.S. health dollar comes from and where it goes (in cents).

Who Pays

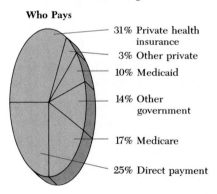

- 31% Private health insurance
- 3% Other private
- 10% Medicaid
- 14% Other government
- 17% Medicare
- 25% Direct payment

Where It Goes

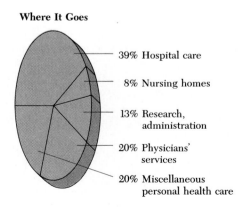

- 39% Hospital care
- 8% Nursing homes
- 13% Research, administration
- 20% Physicians' services
- 20% Miscellaneous personal health care

*A benign tumor, made of fat tissue, under the skin.

SOURCE: *The Wall Street Journal,* September 9, 1988, p. 19; based on data from Prudential Insurance Company of America and the Health Care Financing Administration.

of pocket.[6] Many employers concluded that HMOs weren't delivering promised savings over conventional insurance plans, whose rates rose 20.4 percent in 1989.[7]

Why Does Health Care Cost So Much?

The high and rising costs of health care are attributable to many factors, including

- The use of sophisticated and high-priced equipment.
- More and better-trained medical personnel who command high earnings.
- Increases in the variety and frequency of treatments.
- Innovative but costly treatment of some illnesses, such as heart ailments, end-stage renal disease, AIDS, and cancer.
- The increased longevity of the population.
- The increased ability of people to pay for health care because they have private health insurance or are eligible for Medicare or Medicaid.
- Too many hospital beds and too much duplication of highly expensive services, equipment, and facilities.

Because third parties—private health insurers and government—pay so much of the nation's health care bill, hospitals, doctors, and patients too often lack the incentive to make the most economical use of health care services.

What Is Being Done about the High Costs of Health Care?

In the private sector, concerned groups such as employers, labor unions, health insurers, health care professionals, and consumers have undertaken a wide range of innovative activities to contain the costs of health care. These activities include the following:

EXHIBIT 13–2

Cost of Care
(*Average Charge per Day*)

It costs less to be sick in a Danville, Virginia, hospital than in a San Jose, California, hospital.

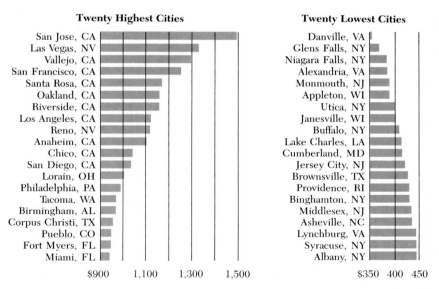

SOURCE: *The Wall Street Journal*, January 6, 1988, p. 19; based on data from Equicor Equitable HCA Corporation.

- Programs to carefully review health care fees and charges and the use of health care services.
- Establishment of incentives to encourage preventive care and to provide more services out of the hospital where this is medically acceptable.
- Involvement in community health planning to help achieve a better balance between health needs and health care resources.
- Encouragement of prepaid group practice and other alternatives to fee-for-service arrangements.
- Community health education programs that motivate people to take better care of themselves.

What Can You Do to Reduce Health Care Costs?

The best way to avoid the high cost of sickness is to stay well. The prescription is the same as it has always been:

1. Eat a balanced diet, and keep your weight under control.
2. Avoid smoking, and don't drink to excess.
3. Get sufficient rest and relaxation.
4. Drive carefully, and watch out for accident and fire hazards in the home.

Learn to minimize, through intelligent self-care, the need for medical attention.

It is also essential, however, to find a personal physician and to follow his or her orders. Have a periodic physical checkup, especially for blood pressure, signs of diabetes, and symptoms of cancer.

Finally, take part in community health activities and support programs to clean up the environment or to further medical research.

HEALTH CARE INSURANCE AND FINANCIAL PLANNING

L.O.2
Define health insurance and disability income insurance, and explain their importance in financial planning.

Although this country spent $618.4 billion on health care in 1989, the number of Americans without basic health insurance has been growing. Statistics provided by the Blue Cross and Blue Shield Association in December 1989 illustrate the depth of the problem:

- Approximately 37 million people in the United States, or 15.5 percent of the population, were without health insurance.
- Of those people, 32 percent, or 12 million, were children.
- Of the uninsured under 65 years of age, more than 78 percent were employed or the dependents of employed persons.
- Approximately 53 million people may have been underinsured.[8]

A growing number of students have been uninsured because of the growth of an older student population not covered by family policies. Today, 40 percent of college students are older than 25.

What Is Health Insurance?

Health insurance is a form of protection whose primary purpose is to alleviate the financial burdens suffered by individuals because of illness or injury. Health insurance includes both medical expense insurance and disability income insurance.[9]

Health insurance, like other forms of insurance, reduces the financial burden of risk by dividing losses among many individuals. It works in the same ways as life insurance, homeowners insurance, or automobile insurance. You pay the insurance company a specified premium, and the company guarantees you some degree of protection. As with the premiums and benefits of other types of insurance, the premiums and benefits of health insurance are figured on the basis of average experience. To establish rates and benefits, insurance company actuaries rely on general statistics that tell them how many people in a certain population group will become ill and how much their illnesses will cost.

Because you feel young and healthy, you may overlook the very real need for disability income insurance. Disability income insurance protects your most valuable asset—your ability to earn income. Most people are more likely to lose their income due to disability than due to death. The fact is that for all age groups disability is more likely than death. At age 62, disability is twice as likely as death. At age 42, it is more than four times as likely as death. And at age 22, it is 7½ times as likely as death.[10] If you have no disability income protection, you are betting that you will not be disabled, and that could be a very costly bet.

Medical expense insurance and disability income insurance are an important part of your financial planning. To safeguard your family's economic security, both protections should be a part of your overall insurance program.

There are many ways in which individuals, or groups of individuals, can obtain health insurance protection. Planning a health insurance program takes careful study because the protection should be shaped to the needs of the individual or family. For many families, however, the task is simplified because the group health insurance they obtain at work already provides a foundation for their coverage.

Group Health Insurance

Group plans comprise more than 85 percent of all the health insurance issued by life insurance companies. Most of these plans are employer sponsored, and the employer often pays part or all of their cost. Group insurance will cover you and your immediate family.

The protection provided by group insurance varies from plan to plan. The plan may not cover all of your health insurance needs, or benefits may be lost if you lose your job. In such cases, you will have to start thinking about replacing your insurance or supplementing it with individual health insurance.

Individual Health Insurance

Individual health insurance covers either one person or a family. If the kind of health insurance you need is not available through a group or if you need coverage in addition to the coverage that a group provides, then you should obtain an individual policy—a policy tailored to your particular needs—from the company of your choice. This requires careful shopping because coverage and cost vary from company to company.

So find out what your group insurance will pay for and what it won't. Make sure you have enough insurance, but don't try to overinsure, because that costs money.

Supplementing Your Group Insurance

A sign that your group coverage needs supplementing would be its failure to provide benefits for the major portion of your medical care bills, mainly hospital, doctor, and surgical charges.

If, for example, your group policy will pay only $150 per day toward a hospital room and the cost in your area is $300, you should look for an individual policy that covers most of the other amount. Similarly, if your group policy will pay for only about half of the going rate for surgical procedures in your area, you need individual coverage for the other half.

In supplementing your group health insurance, consider the health insurance benefits that your employer-sponsored plan provides to your spouse. Most group policy contracts have a **coordination of benefits (COB)** provision. The COB is a method of integrating the benefits payable under more than one health insurance plan so that the benefits received from all sources are limited to 100 percent of allowable medical expenses.

If you have any questions about your group plan, you should be able to get answers from your employer, your union, or your association. But if you have questions about an individual policy, talk with your insurance company representative.

You should understand the various types of coverages that are available to you or your family.

DISABILITY INCOME INSURANCE

L.O.3
Recognize the need for disability income insurance.

Disability income insurance benefits provide regular cash income lost by employees as the result of an accident, illness, or pregnancy. Disability income insurance is probably the most neglected form of available insurance protection. Many people who insure their houses, cars, and other property fail to insure their most valuable resource—their earning power. Disability can cause even greater financial problems than death. In fact, disability is often called the living death. Disabled persons lose their earning power while continuing to incur normal family expenses. In addition, they often face huge expenses for the medical treatment and special care required by their disability.

Generally, disability income policies are divided into two types: (1) those that provide benefits for up to two years (short-term policies) and (2) those that provide benefits for a longer period, usually for at least five years but often to age 65 or for life (long-term policies).

Definition of Disability

There are different definitions of disability. Some policies define it as simply being unable to do your regular work, while others are stricter. In a stricter policy, a dentist who is unable to do his or her regular work because of a hand injury, but can earn income through related duties, such as teaching dentistry, would not be considered permanently disabled.

Good disability plans pay when you are unable to work at your regular job; poor disability plans pay only when you are unable to work at any job. A good disability plan will also make partial disability payments when you return to work on a part-time basis.

Tackling the Trade-Offs

Here are some important trade-offs that you should consider in purchasing disability income insurance. Weigh the costs and benefits in making your decision.

Waiting or Elimination Period   Benefits don't begin on the first day you are disabled. There is a waiting or elimination period that usually lasts between 30 and 90 days. Some waiting periods may be as long as 180 days. Generally, disability income policies with longer waiting periods have lower premiums. If you have substantial savings, the reduced premiums of a policy with a long waiting period may be attractive. But if you need every paycheck to cover your bills, you are probably better off paying the increased premium for a short waiting period.

Duration of Benefits   The maximum time that a disability income policy will pay benefits may be a few years, to age 65, or for life. You should seek a policy that pays benefits for life. If you become permanently disabled, it would be financially disastrous for your benefits to end at age 55, or age 65.

Amount of Benefits   You should aim for a benefit amount that when added to your other income will equal 60–70 percent of your gross pay. Of course, the greater the benefits, the greater the cost.

Accident and Sickness Coverage   Consider both accident and sickness coverage. Some disability income policies will pay only for accidents, but you want to be insured for illness too.

Guaranteed Renewability   Ask for noncancelable and guaranteed renewable coverages. Either coverage will protect you against having your insurance company drop you if your health turns bad. The premium for these coverages is higher, but the coverages are well worth the extra cost. Furthermore, look for a disability income policy that waives premium payments while you are disabled.

See whether you qualify for a lower premium if you agree to forgo part of your monthly benefit when social security or workers' compensation benefits begin. Most disability income policies coordinate their benefits with these benefits.

Sources of Disability Income

Before you buy disability income insurance, remember that you may already have some form of such insurance. This coverage may come to you through your employer, social security, or workers' compensation.

Employer   Many, but not all, employers provide disability income protection for their employees through group insurance plans. Your employer may have some form of wage continuation policy that lasts a few months or an employee group disability plan that provides long-term protection. In most cases, your employer pays part or all of the cost of this plan.

Social Security   Most of the salaried workers in the United States participate in the social security program. In this program, your benefits are determined by your salary and by the number of years you have been covered under social security. Your dependents also qualify for certain benefits, as shown in Exhibit 13–3.

Workers' Compensation   If your accident or illness occurred at your place of work or resulted from your type of employment, you could be entitled to workers' compensation benefits in your state. Like social security benefits, these benefits are determined by your earnings and your work history.

Other possible sources of disability income include Veterans Administration pension disability benefits, civil service disability benefits for government workers, state vocational rehabilitation benefits, state welfare benefits for low-income people, Aid to Families with Dependent Children, group union disability benefits, automobile insurance that provides benefits for disability from an auto accident, and private insurance programs, such as credit disability insurance that covers loan payments when you are disabled.

The availability and extent of these and other disability income sources vary widely in different parts of the country. Be sure to look into such sources carefully before calculating your need for additional disability income insurance.

EXHIBIT 13–3

Approximate Monthly Disability Benefits if the Worker Became Disabled in 1989 and Had Steady Earnings

To use the table, find the age and earnings closest to your age and earnings in 1988.

		Disabled Worker's Earnings in 1988							
Worker's Age	Worker's Family	$10,000	$15,000	$20,000	$25,000	$30,000	$35,000	$40,000	$45,000 or More*
25	Disabled worker only	$455	$585	$ 715	$ 845	$ 908	$ 969	$1,030	$1,100
	Disabled worker, spouse, and child†	683	878	1,072	1,267	1,363	1,454	1,545	1,650
35	Disabled worker only	453	581	710	838	905	962	1,015	1,055
	Disabled worker, spouse, and child†	679	872	1,065	1,257	1,357	1,443	1,522	1,583
45	Disabled worker only	452	580	709	837	895	933	963	986
	Disabled worker, spouse, and child†	679	871	1,063	1,256	1,343	1,399	1,445	1,480
55	Disabled worker only	452	580	708	823	872	898	918	934
	Disabled worker, spouse, and child†	678	871	1,063	1,235	1,308	1,347	1,377	1,401
64	Disabled worker only	450	577	705	818	862	885	904	919
	Disabled worker, spouse, and child†	675	866	1,057	1,227	1,293	1,328	1,356	1,378

*Earnings equal the social security wage base from age 22 through 1988.
†Equals the maximum family benefit.
NOTE: The accuracy of these estimates depends on the pattern of the worker's earnings in prior years.
SOURCE: Social Security Administration, 1989.

Calculating Your Disability Income Insurance Requirement

Once you have found out what your benefits from the numerous public and private disability income sources would be, you should determine whether those benefits are sufficient to meet your disability income needs. If the sum of your disability benefits approaches your after-tax income, you can safely assume that should disability strike, you'll be in good shape to pay your day-to-day bills while recuperating.

You should know how long you would have to wait before the benefits begin (the waiting or elimination period) and how long they would be paid (the benefit period).

But what if—as is often the case—social security and other disability benefits are not sufficient to support your family? In that case, you may want to consider buying disability income insurance to make up the difference. Exhibit 13–4 can help you determine whether you have enough income protection for you and your family. You should list your monthly expenses and compare them with the income you can expect to receive from the total disability benefits you now have.

EXHIBIT 13–4   Determining Your Disability Income Insurance Needs

Your Monthly Expenses	Today	When Disabled	**Substitute Income to Pay Expenses When Disabled**	Monthly Benefit	Waiting Period	Benefit Period
Mortgage or rent (include property taxes)	$_____	$_____	Group disability insurance (from your employer or union)	$_____	_____	_____
Utilities (oil, gas, electric, water, phone)	$_____	$_____	Social Security	$_____	_____	_____
Home maintenance and repairs	$_____	$_____	State plans	$_____	_____	_____
Food	$_____	$_____	Workers' compensation	$_____	_____	_____
Clothing	$_____	$_____	Credit disability (in some auto loans or home mortgages)	$_____	_____	_____
Insurance			Other income sources (stocks, bonds, spouse's income)	$_____	_____	_____
Auto $____						
Home $____						
Life $____						
Health $____						
Total	$_____	$_____	Total income when disabled (B)		_____	
Installment payments (including auto)	$_____	$_____				
Transportation (gas, oil, maintenance, parking, etc.)	$_____	$_____				
Medical and dental care	$_____	$_____				
Education	$_____	$_____				
Family spending money	$_____	$_____				
Recreation, entertainment, hobbies, vacation, dues	$_____	$_____				
Total monthly expenses when disabled (A)		$_____				

If B is equal to or greater than A, you do not need to purchase disability income insurance. However, if B is less than A, you need to purchase disability income insurance to make up the difference.

SOURCE: Health Insurance Association of America.

This calculation will keep you from buying more insurance than you need. What's wrong with overinsuring? First, it is almost always unwise to buy more of anything than you really need. Second, many overinsured people take far more time than they need to return to work.

Don't expect to insure yourself for your full salary. Most insurers limit benefits from all sources to no more than 70–80 percent of your take-home pay. For example, if you are earning $400 a week, you could be eligible for disability insurance of about $280–$320 a week. You will not need $400 because while you are disabled, your work-related expenses will be eliminated and your taxes will be far lower.

TYPES OF HEALTH INSURANCE COVERAGES

L.O.4
Analyze the benefits and limitations of the various types of health care coverages.

With today's high cost of health care, it makes sense to be as well insured as you can afford to be. Combining the group plan that is available where you work with the individual policies offered by insurance companies will enable you to put together enough coverage to give you peace of mind. A good health insurance plan should

- Offer basic coverage for hospital and doctor bills.
- Provide at least 120 days' hospital room and board in full.
- Provide at least a $250,000 lifetime maximum for each family member.
- Pay at least 80 percent for out-of-hospital expenses after a yearly deductible of $250 per person or $500 per family.
- Impose no unreasonable exclusions.
- Limit your out-of-pocket expenses to no more than $3,000–$5,000 a year, excluding dental, optical, and prescription costs.

Several types of health insurance coverage are available under group and individual policies.

Hospital Expense Insurance

Hospital expense insurance pays part or all of hospital bills for room, board, and other charges. Frequently, a maximum amount is allowed for each day in the hospital, up to a maximum number of days. More people have hospital insurance than any other kind of health insurance.

Surgical Expense Insurance

Surgical expense insurance pays part or all of the surgeon's fees for an operation. A policy of this kind usually lists a number of specific operations and the maximum fee allowed for each. The higher the maximum fee allowed in the policy, the higher the premium charged. Surgical expense insurance is often bought in combination with hospital expense insurance.

Physician's Expense Insurance

Physician expense insurance helps pay for physician's care that does not involve surgery. Like surgical expense insurance, it lists maximum benefits for specific services. Its coverage may include visits to the doctor's office, X rays, and lab tests. This type of insurance is usually bought in combination with hospital and surgical insurance. The three types of insurance are called **basic health insurance coverage.**

Major Medical Expense Insurance

Major medical expense insurance protects against the large expenses of a serious injury or a long illness. It adds to the protection offered by basic health insurance coverage. The costs of a serious illness can easily exceed the benefits under hospital, surgical, and physician's expense policies. Major medical pays the bulk of the additional costs. The maximum benefits payable under major medical insurance are high—$50,000, $100,000, or even more.

Because major medical insurance offers such a wide range of benefits and provides high maximums, it contains two features to help keep the premium within the policyholder's means.

One of these features is a **deductible** provision that requires the policyholder to pay a basic amount before the policy benefits begin—for example, the first $500 per year under an individual plan and a lesser amount under a group plan. (Sometimes part or all of the deductible amount is covered by the benefits of a basic hospital and surgical plan.)

The other feature is a **coinsurance** provision that requires the policyholder to share the expenses beyond the deductible amount. Many policies pay 75 or 80 percent of expenses above the deductible amount. The policyholder pays the rest.

Some major medical policies contain a **stop-loss** provision. This requires the policyholder to pay up to a certain amount, after which the insurance company pays 100 percent of all remaining covered expenses. Typically, the out-of-pocket payment is between $3,000 and $5,000.

Comprehensive Major Medical Insurance

Comprehensive major medical insurance is a type of major medical insurance that has a very low deductible amount, often $200 or $300, and is offered without any separate basic plan. This all-inclusive health insurance helps pay hospital, surgical, medical, and other bills.

Many major medical policies have specific maximum benefits for certain expenses, such as hospital room and board and the cost of surgery.

Hospital Indemnity Policies

A **hospital indemnity policy** pays benefits only when you are hospitalized, but these benefits, stipulated in the policy, are paid to you in cash and you can use the money for medical, nonmedical, or supplementary expenses. While such policies have limited coverage, their benefits can have wide use. The hospital indemnity policy is not a substitute for basic or major medical protection but a supplement to it. Many people buy hospital indemnity policies in the hope that they will make money if they get sick, but the average benefit return does not justify the premium cost.

Dental Expense Insurance

Dental expense insurance provides reimbursement for the expenses of dental services and supplies and encourages preventive dental care. The coverage normally provides for oral examinations (including X rays and cleanings), fillings, extractions, inlays, bridgework, and dentures as well as oral surgery, root canal therapy, and orthodontics.

Dental coverage is generally available through insurance company group plans, prepayment plans, and dental service corporations.

Vision Care Insurance

A recent interesting development in health insurance coverage has been vision care insurance, which has been offered, usually to groups, by an increasing number of insurance companies and prepayment plans.

Dread Disease and Cancer Insurance Policies

Dread disease and cancer policies, which are usually solicited through the mail, in newspapers and magazines, or by door-to-door salespeople working on commission, are notoriously poor values. Their appeal is based on unrealistic fears, and a number of states have prohibited their sale. Such policies provide coverage only for very specific conditions and are no substitute for comprehensive insurance.

National Insurance Consumer Organization (NICO), based in Alexandria, Virginia, advises that cancer or dread disease insurance is simply a bad buy, citing its narrow coverage. "If you have a heart attack, cancer insurance doesn't do any good," says Robert Hunter, president of NICO.

Long-Term Care Insurance

Long-term care insurance (LTC), virtually unknown a decade ago, is growing faster than any other form of insurance in the country. More than 1 million policies are in force, and half have been sold in just the past three years.[11]

Long-term care is day-in, day-out help that you could need if you ever have an illness or a disability that lasts a long time and leaves you unable to care for yourself. You may or may not need lengthy care in a nursing home, but you might need help at home with daily activities such as dressing, bathing, or doing household chores.

The annual premium of LTC policies can range from under $300 up to $15,000, depending on your age and the choices you make. The older you are when you enroll, the higher your annual premium. Typically, individual insurance plans are sold to the 50–80 age group, pay benefits for a maximum of 2–6 years, and carry a dollar limit on the total benefits that will be paid.[12]

An insurance company usually allows you a minimum of 10 days to review your health insurance policy, so be sure to check the major provisions that affect your coverage. Deductible, coinsurance, and stop-loss provisions were discussed under major medical expense insurance. Here are other major provisions.

Major Provisions in a Health Insurance Policy

All health insurance policies have certain provisions in common. It is important for you to understand what your policy covers because the most comprehensive policy may be of little value if a provision in small print limits or denies benefits.

Eligibility   The eligibility provision defines who is entitled to benefits under the policy. Age, marital status, and dependency requirements are usually specified in this provision. For example, foster children are usually not automatically covered under the family contract, but stepchildren may be. Check with your insurance company to be sure.

Assigned Benefits   When you assign benefits, you sign a paper allowing your insurance company to make payments to your hospital or doctor. Otherwise, the payments will be made to you when you turn in your bills and claim forms to the company.

Inside Limits   A policy with inside limits will pay only a fixed amount for your hospital room, no matter what the actual rate is, or it will cover your surgical expenses only to a fixed limit, no matter what the actual charges are. For example, if your policy has an inside limit of $200 per hospital day and you are in a $300-a-day hospital room, you will have to pay the difference.

Service Benefits   In a service benefits provision, insurance benefits are expressed in terms of entitlement to receive specified hospital or medical care rather than entitlement to receive a fixed dollar amount for each procedure. Service benefits are always preferable to a coverage stated in dollar amounts.

Benefit Limits   The benefit limits provision defines the maximum benefits possible, in terms of either a dollar amount or a number of days in the hospital. Many policies today have benefit limits ranging from $250,000 to unlimited payments.

Exclusions and Limitations   The exclusions and limitations provision specifies the conditions or circumstances for which the policy does not provide benefits. For example, the policy may exclude coverage for preexisting conditions, cosmetic surgery, or routine checkups.

Coordination of Benefits   As discussed earlier, the coordination of benefits provision prevents you from collecting benefits from two or more group policies that would in total exceed the actual charges. Under this provision, the benefits from your and your spouse's policies are coordinated to allow you up to 100 percent payment of your covered charges.

Cancellation and Termination   This provision explains the circumstances under which an insurance company can terminate your health insurance policy. It also explains your right to convert a group contract into an individual contract.

In this section, we have discussed ten types of health insurance coverages and eight of their major provisions. A natural question is: How should you choose among these many types of coverages?

Which Coverage Should You Choose?

Now that you are familiar with the available types of health insurance and some of their major provisions, how do you choose one? The most important thing to understand is that the more money you are ready to pay for health insurance, the more coverage you can get.

When it comes to medical insurance, you have three choices. You can buy (1) basic, (2) major medical, or (3) both basic and major medical.

If your pocketbook is very limited, then it is a toss-up between choosing a basic plan and choosing a major medical plan. In many cases, either plan will handle the lion's share of your hospital and doctor bills. In the event of an illness involving catastrophic costs, however, you will need the protection given by a major medical policy. Ideally, you should get a basic plan and a major medical supplementary plan. Or you should get a comprehensive major medical policy that combines the values of both these plans in a single policy.

A Comparison   Let's look at the hypothetical cases of the Jones family, which has basic and major medical coverage, and the Brown family, which has only the basic coverage.

Let's suppose that the breadwinner in each of these families requires a coronary bypass operation. Both breadwinners recover—after heart surgery and a hospital stay lasting eight days.

The Jones family has a major medical policy that pays 80 percent of the total bills up to a maximum of $250,000 after the family pays a $5,000 deductible. To offset this deductible, the family also has a basic hospital-surgical expense policy paying $150 a day toward hospital room and board for 180 days ($300 a day for time in an intensive care unit), with an additional in-hospital allowance of $1,000 and a $1,500 maximum benefit for surgery.

On the other hand, the Browns have an identical basic policy but no major medical policy.

Exhibit 13–5 shows about what the bills would amount to for the two families. It illustrates the importance of major medical coverage in handling catastrophic bills—bills that are not likely to hit the average family but that most definitely can.

In choosing your coverage, be sure to analyze the costs and benefits of your health insurance policy.

Tackling the Trade-Offs

The benefits of health insurance policies differ, and the differences in benefits can have a significant impact on your premiums. Consider the following trade-offs.

EXHIBIT 13–5
Hospital Cost for Two
Families

Services	Charges
Hospital daily room and board, 5 days at $400 a day (intensive care) plus 10 days at $200 a day, semiprivate accommodation	$ 4,000
Additional in-hospital services such as operating room, operation of heart-lung machine, and X-ray laboratory tests	1,400
Private duty nursing (2 days)	400
Surgeon's fee, including in-hospital postoperative consultation and care	3,300
Cardiologist's fee	1,300
Out-of-hospital physician services only	700
Total expenses	$11,100
Paid by basic insurance	$ 5,500
Paid by major medical	4,880
Total paid by Jones's insurance	10,380
Total paid by Brown's insurance	5,500
Total paid by Jones°	720
Total paid by Brown	5,600

°Deductible, coinsurance, and certain miscellaneous expenses.

SOURCE: *What You Should Know about Health Insurance,* Consumer Series (Washington, D.C.: Health Insurance Association of America, n.d.), p. 11.

Reimbursement versus Indemnity   A reimbursement policy provides benefits that depend on the actual expenses you incur. But an indemnity policy provides specified benefits, regardless of whether the actual expenses are greater or less than the benefits.

Inside Limits versus Aggregate Limits   A policy with inside limits stipulates maximum benefits for specific expenses, such as the maximum reimbursement for daily hospital room and board. Other policies may place a limit only on the total amount of coverage, such as $1 million major expense benefits, or may have no limits.

Deductibles and Coinsurance   The cost of a health insurance policy can be greatly affected by the size of the deductible (the amount that you must pay toward medical expenses before the insurance company pays), the degree of coinsurance, and the share of medical expenses that you must pay (for example, 20 percent).

Out-of-Pocket Limit   A policy that limits the total of the coinsurance and deductibles that you must pay (for example, $2,000) will limit your financial risk, but it will also increase the premium.

Benefits Based on Reasonable and Customary Charges   A policy that covers "reasonable and customary" medical expenses limits reimbursement to the usual charges of medical providers in an area and helps avoid overcharging.

Before you look into private sources of health insurance and health care, make sure that you have considered the trade-offs.

PRIVATE SOURCES OF HEALTH INSURANCE AND HEALTH CARE

L.O.5
Evaluate private sources of health insurance and health care.

Health insurance is available from more than 800 private insurance companies, from service plans such as Blue Cross/Blue Shield, from health maintenance organizations, from preferred provider organizations, from governmental programs such as Medicare, and from fraternal organizations and trade unions.

Private Insurance Companies

Insurance companies sell health insurance through either group or individual policies. Of these two types, group health insurance represents about 90 percent of the medical expense insurance and 80 percent of the disability income insurance.

The policies issued by insurance companies provide for payment either directly to the insured for reimbursement of expenses incurred or, if assigned by the insured, to the provider of services.

Most private insurance companies sell health insurance policies to employers, which in turn offer the benefits to employees and their dependents, as fringe benefits. The premiums may be wholly or partially paid by employers.

Hospital and Medical Service Plans

Blue Cross and Blue Shield are statewide organizations similar to commercial health insurance companies. Each state has its own Blue Cross and Blue Shield.

Blue Cross plans provide *hospital care benefits* on essentially a "service type" basis. Through a separate contract with each member hospital, Blue Cross reimburses the hospital for covered services provided to the insured.

Blue Shield plans provide benefits for *surgical and medical services* performed by physicians. The typical Blue Shield plan provides benefits similar to those provided under the benefit provisions of hospital-surgical policies issued by insurance companies.

The rates and coverages of Blue Cross and Blue Shield are administered locally. Both organizations have contracts with participating hospitals and doctors that set the amounts they will pay for the covered services. These amounts are often less than the amounts charged to cash patients and insurance companies. The "Blues" always pay the hospital or doctor directly.

During the 1970s and 1980s, increasing health care costs spurred the growth of managed care. **Managed care** refers to prepaid health plans that provide comprehensive health care to members. Managed care is offered by health maintenance organizations, preferred provider organizations, and traditional indemnity insurance companies.[13]

Health Maintenance Organizations (HMOs)

Prepaid managed care is designed to make the provision of health care services cost effective by controlling their use. Health maintenance organizations are an alternative to basic and major medical insurance plans. A **health maintenance organization** is a health insurance plan that directly employs or contracts with selected physicians, surgeons, dentists, and optometrists to provide you with health care services in exchange for a fixed, prepaid monthly premium. HMOs operate on the premise that maintaining your health through preventive care will minimize future medical problems.

The preventive care provided by HMOs includes periodic checkups, screening programs, diagnostic testing, and immunizations. HMOs also provide a comprehensive range of other health care services. These services are divided into two categories—basic and supplemental. *Basic health services* include inpatient, outpatient, maternity, mental health, substance abuse, and emergency care. *Supplemental services* include vision, hearing, and pharmaceutical care, which are usually available for an additional fee.

Your membership in a typical HMO should cover office visits, routine checkups, hospital and surgical care, eye exams, laboratory and X-ray services, hemodialysis for kidney failure, and mental health services. See the accompanying feature for tips on how to use and choose an HMO.

In 1989, HMOs were increasing their premiums an average of 16.5 percent according to a survey conducted by Group Health Association of America.[14] Almost half of the HMOs surveyed also said that they were requiring patients to pay slightly more out of pocket. Recent studies indicate that patients generally experience greater satisfaction with traditional fee-for-service medicine than with HMOs because with the former specialists and hospitals are more readily available, waits are shorter, and relationships between patient and doctor are better.[15] Some HMOs have abandoned the principles that the HMOs pioneered, including comprehensive coverage for all members at a flat, prepaid rate. They have been charging fees for doctor's visits and prescriptions or adjusting their rates to reflect the health prospects of different employee groups, a change that will increase costs for older workers.[16]

How to Use an HMO

When you first enroll in an HMO, you must choose a plan physician (family practitioner, internist, pediatrician, or obstetrician-gynecologist) who provides or arranges for all of your health care services. It is extremely important that you receive your care through the plan physician. If you don't, you are responsible for the cost of the service rendered.

The only exceptions to the requirement that care be received through the plan physician are medical emergencies. A medical emergency is a sudden onset of illness or a sudden injury that would jeopardize your life or health if it were not treated immediately. In such instances, you may use the facilities of the nearest hospital emergency room. All other care must be provided by hospitals and doctors under contract with the HMO.

How to Choose an HMO

If you decide to enroll in an HMO, you should consider these additional factors:

1. *Accessibility.* Since you must use plan providers, it is extremely important that they be easily accessible from your home or office.

2. *Convenient Office Hours.* Your plan physician should have convenient office hours.

3. *Alternative Physicians.* Should you become dissatisfied with your first choice of a physician, the HMO should allow you the option of changing physicians.

4. *Second Opinions.* You should be able to obtain second opinions.

5. *Type of Coverage.* You should compare the health care services offered by various HMOs, paying particular attention to whether you will incur out-of-pocket expenses or copayments.

6. *Appeal Procedures.* The HMO should have a convenient and prompt method of resolving problems and disputes.

7. *Price.* You should compare the prices charged by various HMOs to see that you are getting the most services for your health care dollar.

Preferred Provider Organizations

Preferred provider organizations (PPOs) combine the best elements of the fee-for-service and HMO systems. PPOs offer the services of doctors and hospitals at discount rates or give breaks in copayments and deductibles. An insurance company or your employer contracts with a PPO to provide specified services at predetermined fees to PPO members.

PPOs provide their members with essentially the same benefits that HMOs offer. However, unlike HMOs, which require you to seek care from HMO providers only (except for emergency treatment), PPOs allow members to use a preferred provider—or someone else—each time a medical need arises. What makes PPOs popular is that they combine free choice of physicians with low-cost care. In 1989, HMOs and PPOs were servicing more than 23 percent of the U.S. population, up from 3 percent in the 1970s.[17]

Health Associations

Health associations (not to be confused with HMOs) are usually local organizations designed to provide routine and emergency health care more conveniently in relatively isolated areas. These organizations usually operate one or more clinics and employ a small number of physicians, dentists, and supporting staff.

For a nominal fee of $15 to $30 per year, anyone can join a health association. Membership entitles you to participate in the association's programs and allows you to make appointments with doctors and dentists at the association's clinics.

Health associations provide no health insurance, however. You are responsible for any charges. You must have your own insurance. Aside from the convenience offered by health association membership, there is another advantage. Health associations participating in Medicare must agree to accept Medicare payment as payment in full. Thus, if you have a Medicare supplemental policy that does not cover the difference between Medicare's reasonable fee and the actual cost, membership in a health association may be wise.

Home Health Agencies

Home health care providers furnish and are responsible for the supervision and management of preventive medical care in a home setting in accordance with a medical order. Rising hospital care costs, new medical technology, and the increasing number of the elderly and infirm have helped make home care one of the fastest-growing areas of the health care industry. Other factors that have contributed to the growth of home health care are government support through Medicare and Medicaid program payments, the inclusion of home health care in an increasing number of health insurance policies, and the tendency of hospitals to discharge patients before they have fully recovered. As shown in Exhibit 13–6, providing health care in the home is less expensive than providing it in hospitals.

Spending on home health care has been growing at an annual rate of about 20 percent for the past few years. This rapid growth reflects (1) the increasing proportion of older people in the U.S. population, (2) the lower costs of home health care compared to the costs of institutional health care, (3) insurers' active support of home health care, and (4) Medicare's promotion of home health care as an alternative to institutionalization.[18]

Employer Self-Funded Health Plans

Certain types of health insurance coverage are made available by plans that employers, labor unions, fraternal societies, or communities administer. Usually, these groups provide the amount of protection that a specific group of people desires and can afford.

EXHIBIT 13–6

Average Costs of Home Care and Hospital Care in 1987

Type of Care	At Home	In Hospital
Intensive course of treatment, per day	$25–$200	$300–$500
Care for a ventilator-dependent person, per year	21,192	270,830
Care for an AIDS patient, per day	94	773
Care for quadriplegic patient with spinal cord injury, per month	13,931	23,862
Care for patient with neurological disorder and respiratory problems (excluding cost of equipment), per month	196	17,783
Care for infant care with breathing and feeding problems, per month	20,209	60,970
Routine skilled nursing care, per month	750	2,000

SOURCE: National Association for Home Care.

It is important to note that self-funded groups must assume the financial burden if the medical bills are greater than the amount covered by premium income. While private insurance companies have the assets needed in such situations, self-funded plans often do not. The results can be disastrous.

In addition to the private sources of health insurance and health care discussed in this section, there are government health care programs covering over 32 million people.

GOVERNMENT HEALTH CARE PROGRAMS

L.O.6
Appraise the sources of government health programs.

Public opinion polls consistently show that Americans are unhappy, if not disgusted, with the nation's health care system. Increasingly, businesses and citizens have been calling for some kind of national health program.[19]

Federal and state governments offer health coverage in accordance with laws that define the premiums and benefits they can offer. Specific requirements as to age, occupation, length of service, and family income may be used to determine eligibility for coverage. Two sources of government health insurance are Medicare and Medicaid.

Medicare

Medicare is a federal health insurance program for people 65 or older, people of any age with permanent kidney failure, and certain disabled people. The program is administered by the Health Care Financing Administration. Local Social Security Administration offices take applications for Medicare, assist beneficiaries in filing claims, and provide information about the program.

Medicare has two parts—hospital insurance (Part A) and medical insurance (Part B). *Hospital insurance* helps pay for inpatient hospital care and certain follow-up care. *Medical insurance* helps pay for your doctor's services and many other medical services and items.

Hospital insurance is financed from part of the social security tax. Voluntary medical insurance is financed from the monthly premiums paid by people who have enrolled for it and from general federal revenues.

Hospital Insurance Benefits Medicare hospital insurance helps pay for inpatient hospital care, inpatient care in a skilled nursing facility, home health care, and hospice care.

Part A pays for all covered services for inpatient hospital care after you pay a single annual deductible ($560 in 1989). Once you meet this deductible, Medicare pays for all medically necessary inpatient hospital care for the remainder of the calendar year, regardless of the costs, the length of your stay, or the number of times you are hospitalized during the year.

Medical Insurance Benefits Medicare medical insurance helps pay for your doctor's services and for a variety of other medical services and supplies that are not covered by hospital insurance. Each year, as soon as you meet the annual medical insurance deductible, medical insurance will pay 80 percent of the approved charges for the covered services that you receive during the rest of the year. In 1989, the annual deductible was $75.

Exhibit 13–7 presents a summary of the benefits that were available through Part A and Part B of Medicare in 1989. Note that Medicare does not pay the

EXHIBIT 13–7

Medicare (Part A): Hospital Insurance—Covered Services per Calendar Year

Service	Benefit	Medicare Pays°	You Pay°
Hospitalization Semiprivate room and board, general nursing, and miscellaneous hospital services and supplies.	Unlimited days of reasonable and necessary care	All but $560 of first hospital stay	$560 of first stay each calendar year†
Skilled Nursing Facility Care . . . In a facility approved by Medicare.‡	First eight days Additional 142 days	All but $25.50 a day All	$25.50 a day for the first eight days
Home Health Care	Visits limited to medically necessary skilled care	Full cost of services 80% of approved amount for durable medical equipment	Nothing for services 20% of approved amount for durable medical equipment
Hospice Care Available to terminally ill	As long as doctor certifies need	All but limited costs for outpatient drugs and inpatient respite care	Limited cost sharing for outpatient drugs and inpatient respite care
Blood	Blood	All but first 3 pints	For first 3 pints

°These figures are for 1989 and are subject to change each year.

†If you pay the deductible during December, you do not have to pay it again if you remain a patient in or are readmitted to the hospital in January of the following year.

‡Medicare and private insurance will not pay for most nursing home care. You pay for custodial care and most care in a nursing home.

Medicare (Part B): Medical Insurance—Covered Services per Calendar Year

Service	Benefit	Medicare Pays	You Pay
Medical Expense Physician's services, inpatient and outpatient medical services and supplies, physical and speech therapy, ambulance, etc.	Medicare pays for medical services in or out of the hospital.	80% of approved amount (after $75 deductible)	$75 deductible° plus 20% of balance of approved amount (plus any charge above approved amount)†
Home Health Care	Visits limited to medically necessary skilled care	Full cost of services 80% of approved amount for durable medical equipment (after $75 deductible)	Nothing for services 20% of approved amount for durable medical equipment (after $75 deductible)
Outpatient Hospital Treatment	Unlimited if medically necessary	80% of approved amount (after $75 deductible)	Subject to deductible plus 20% of balance of approved amount
Blood	Blood	80% of approved amount (after $75 deductible and starting with 4th pint)	First 3 pints plus 20% of approved amount (after $75 deductible)

°Once you have had $75 of expense for covered services in 1989, the Part B deductible does not apply to any further covered services you receive for the rest of the year.

†You pay for charges higher than the amount approved by Medicare unless the doctor or supplier agrees to accept Medicare's approved amount as the total charge for services rendered.

SOURCE: U.S. Department of Health and Human Services, 1989.

entire cost of all the services that it covers. You or your insurance company must pay certain deductibles and make copayments. A deductible is an initial dollar amount that Medicare does not pay, and a copayment is your share of the expenses for covered services above the deductible.

Medigap

Medicare was never intended to pay all medical costs. To fill the gap between Medicare payments and medical costs not covered by Medicare, many companies sell medigap insurance policies. **Medigap insurance,** intended to supplement Medicare, is not sold or serviced by the federal government or state governments. Do not believe the claims of advertising or agents that Medicare supplement insurance is a government-sponsored program.

Do You Need Medigap Insurance?   If you are a Medicare beneficiary enrolled in a prepayment plan, such as an HMO, you may not need a Medicare supplement policy. Low-income people who are eligible for Medicaid (discussed next) generally do not need medigap insurance.

Whether you need health insurance in addition to Medicare is a matter that you should discuss with someone who understands insurance and your financial situation. The best time to do this is before you reach age 65.

In considering the purchase of a medigap policy, make sure that you

- Shop carefully and compare the medigap policies.
- Don't buy more medigap policies than you need. Duplicate coverage is costly and unnecessary. One comprehensive policy is better than several policies with overlapping or duplicate coverage.
- Examine the alternatives. Consider continuing the group coverage you have at work, joining an HMO, buying a long-term care insurance policy, or buying a Medicare supplement policy.
- Check for preexisting condition exclusions that reduce or eliminate coverage of your existing health problems.
- Check your right to renew the policy.
- Don't buy from a person who cannot prove that he or she is licensed.
- Take your time. Don't be pressured by the claim that an offer is limited to a short enrollment period. Professional salespeople will not rush you.

Medicaid

Title XIX of the Social Security Act provides for a program of medical assistance to certain low-income individuals and families. In 1965, the program, known as Medicaid, became federal law.

Medicaid is administered by each state within certain broad federal requirements and guidelines. Financed by both state and federal funds, it is designed to provide medical assistance to groups or categories of persons who are eligible to receive payments under one of the cash assistance programs, such as Aid to Families with Dependent Children and Supplemental Security Income. The states may also provide Medicaid to the medically needy, that is, to persons who fit into one of the categories eligible for public assistance.

Many members of the Medicaid population are also covered by Medicare. Where such dual coverage exists, most state Medicaid programs pay for the Medicare premiums, deductibles, and copayments and for services not covered by Medicare.

To qualify for federal matching funds, state programs must include inpatient hospital services; outpatient hospital services; laboratory and X-ray services; skilled nursing and home health services for individuals aged 21 and older; family planning services; early and periodic screening, diagnosis, and treatment for individuals under 21; and physicians' services in the home, office, hospital, or nursing home or elsewhere.

The accompanying "Financial Planning in Action" feature provides some consumer tips on health and disability insurance.

FINANCIAL PLANNING IN ACTION

Final Consumer Tips on Health and Disability Insurance

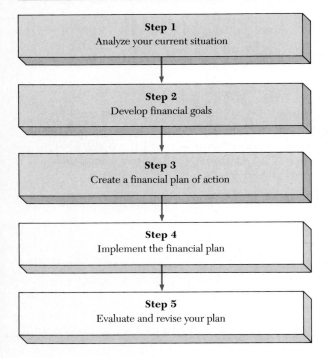

Step 1
Analyze your current situation

Step 2
Develop financial goals

Step 3
Create a financial plan of action

Step 4
Implement the financial plan

Step 5
Evaluate and revise your plan

1. If you pay your own premiums directly, try to arrange for paying them on an annual or quarterly basis rather than a monthly basis. It is cheaper.

2. Policies should be delivered to you within 30 days. If not, contact your insurer and find out, in writing, why. If a policy is not delivered in 60 days, contact the state department of insurance.

3. When you receive a policy, take advantage of the free look provision. You have 10 days to look it over and to obtain a refund if you decided that it is not for you.

4. Unless you have a policy with no inside limits, read your contract over every year to see whether its benefits are still in line with medical costs.

5. Don't replace a policy because you think it is out-of-date. Switching may subject you to new waiting periods and new exclusions. Rather, add to what you have if necessary. But . . .

6. Don't keep a policy because you've had it a long time. You don't get any special credit from the company for being an old customer.

7. Don't try to make a profit on your insurance by carrying overlapping coverages. Duplicate coverage is expensive. Besides, most group policies now contain a coordination of benefits clause limiting benefits to 100 percent.

8. Use your health emergency fund to cover small expenses.

9. If you're considering the purchase of a dread disease policy such as cancer insurance, understand that it is supplementary and that it will pay for only one disease. You should have full coverage before you consider it. Otherwise, it's a gamble.

10. Don't lie on your insurance application. If you fail to mention a preexisting condition, you may not get paid. You can usually get paid, even for that condition, after one or two years have elapsed if during that period you have had no treatment for the condition.

11. Keep your insurance up-to-date. Some policies adjust to inflation better than others. Some make sure that their benefits have not been outdistanced by inflation. Review your policies annually.

12. Never sign a health insurance application—such applications are lengthy and detailed for individually written policies—until you have recorded full and complete answers to every question.

SOURCE: Health Insurance Association of America.

SUMMARY

Health care costs have gone up faster than the rate of inflation. Among the reasons for high and rising health care costs are the use of high-priced equipment and personnel, increases in the variety and frequency of treatments, innovative but costly treatment of some illnesses, third-party payments, too many hospital beds and too much duplication of facilities, and the lack of incentive to make the most economical use of health care services.

Health insurance is protection that provides payment of benefits for covered sickness or injury. Disability income insurance protects your most valuable asset—your ability to earn income.

Health insurance and disability income insurance are two protections against economic losses due to illness, accident, or disability. Both protections should be a part of your overall insurance program to safeguard your family's economic security.

Disability income insurance benefits provide regular cash income lost by employees as the result of an accident, illness, or pregnancy.

Sources of disability income insurance include your employer, social security, workers' compensation, the Veterans Administration, the federal government and state governments, unions, and private insurance.

Five basic types of health insurance are available under group and individual policies: hospital expense insurance, surgical expense insurance, physician's expense insurance, major medical expense insurance, and comprehensive major medical insurance. The benefits and limitations of each policy differ. Ideally, you should get a basic plan and a major medical supplementary plan. Or, you should get a comprehensive major medical policy that combines the values of both of these plans in a single policy.

Health insurance and health care are available from private insurance companies, hospital and medical service plans such as Blue Cross/Blue Shield, health maintenance organizations (HMOs), preferred provider organizations (PPOs), health associations, home health agencies, and employer self-funded health plans.

The federal government and state governments offer health coverage in accordance with laws that define the premiums and benefits. Two well-known government health programs are Medicare and Medicaid.

GLOSSARY

Basic health insurance coverage   Hospital expense insurance, surgical expense insurance, and physician's expense insurance.

Blue Cross   An independent, nonprofit membership corporation that provides protection against the cost of hospital care.

Blue Shield   An independent, nonprofit membership corporation that provides protection against the cost of surgical and medical care.

Coinsurance   A provision under which both the insured and the insurer share the covered losses.

Comprehensive major medical insurance   A type of major medical insurance that has a very low deductible.

Coordination of benefits (COB)   A method of integrating the benefits payable under more than one health insurance plan.

Deductible   An amount that the insured must pay before benefits by the insurance company become payable.

Disability income insurance   Provides payments to replace income when an insured is unable to work.

Health maintenance organization (HMO)   A health insurance plan that provides a wide range of health care services for a fixed, prepaid monthly premium.

Hospital expense insurance   Pays part or all of hospital bills for room, board, and other charges.

Hospital indemnity policy   Pays stipulated daily, weekly, or monthly cash benefits during hospital confinement.

Long-term care insurance (LTC)   Provides day-in, day-out care for long-term illness or disability.

Major medical expense insurance   Pays most of the costs exceeding those covered by the hospital, surgical, and physician's expense policies.

Managed care   Prepaid health plans that provide comprehensive health care to members.

Medigap insurance   Supplements Medicare by filling the gap between Medicare payments and medical costs not covered by Medicare.

Physician's expense insurance   Provides benefits for doctor's fees for nonsurgical care, X rays, and lab tests.

Preferred provider organization (PPO)   Provides services of doctors and hospitals at discount rates.

Stop-loss   A provision under which an insured pays a certain amount, after which the insurance company pays 100 percent of the remaining covered expenses.

Surgical expense insurance   Pays part or all of the surgeon's fees for an operation.

DISCUSSION QUESTIONS

L.O.1   1.   Why does health care cost so much? What is being done about the high costs of health care? What can you do about them?

L.O.2   2.   Why are health insurance and disability income insurance of vital importance in personal financial planning?

L.O.2   3.   What factors should you consider in supplementing your group health insurance?

L.O.3   4.   What are important trade-offs in the purchase of disability income insurance?

L.O.4   5.   What are major benefits and limitations of various types of health care coverages?

L.O.4   6.   Which health insurance coverages would you choose, and why?
L.O.5   7.   Why has the growth of HMOs slowed?
L.O.6   8.   What benefits do Medicare and Medicaid provide?

Opening Case Questions

1.   Why do California hospitals and health care trade groups despise PCC/ Drug Data Systems, Inc.?
2.   Do you think that the California hospitals have been unfairly denied payments? Why?
3.   Do you believe that the lawsuit filed against PCC by the California Association of Hospitals and Health Systems is "sham litigation"? Why?

PROBLEMS AND ACTIVITIES

L.O.1   1.   List health services that you and other members of your family have used during the past year. Assign an approximate dollar cost to each of these services, and identify the financial resources (savings, health insurance, government sources, etc.) that were used to pay for the services.
L.O.1   2.   Make a list of things that you can do to reduce your and your family's health care costs.
L.O.2   3.   Develop a list of hazardous occupations and a list of hazardous hobbies or recreational activities. How do these occupations, hobbies, and activities affect your health and disability insurance?
L.O.2   4.   Make a list of the benefits included in your employee benefit package, such as health insurance, disability insurance, and life insurance. Discuss the importance of such a benefit package to the consumer.
L.O.3   5.   Review several disability income insurance plans. Look for the following terms, and develop a definition for each: maximum benefit, benefit period, waiting period, and cancellation clause.
L.O.4   6.   Contact health insurance companies in your area, and collect information on the coverages that these companies provide (group, individual, disability, supplemental, etc.). Also collect information on the services provided by the HMOs in your area. Compare the provisions and benefits of the various plans. List advantages and disadvantages of each plan.
L.O.5   7.   Obtain sample health insurance policies from insurance agents or brokers, and analyze the policies for definitions, coverages, exclusions, limitations on coverage, and amounts of coverage. In what ways are the policies similar? In what ways are they different?
L.O.6   8.   Write to the U.S. Department of Health and Human Services, Health Care Financing Administration, Baltimore, MD 21207, and ask for the latest edition of *Guide to Health Insurance for People with Medicare*. On the basis of the information contained in this source, describe the changes that have been made in the hospital insurance and medical insurance provided by Medicare.

LIFE SITUATION   Case 13–1

Premium Refunds Are a Healthy Incentive

An Ohio company is holding down medical costs with "wellness dividends." Famous Supply Company, a building products distributor in Akron, decided in 1984 to make its 500 employees shoulder more of the cost of their health benefits. The insurance deductible was increased to $150 from $100, and employees, for the first time, were required to pay a monthly premium for medical coverage: $25 for individuals and $50 for families.

The problem, says Craig Raub, the company's controller, was that employees who rarely submitted claims felt that they were being penalized. The company, therefore, began offering refunds to employees who stay healthy.

Any employee who hasn't submitted a claim for a year gets back two thirds of his or her premium as a dividend. A family, for instance, would get a check for $400, two thirds of its $600 annual payment. People who submit a small number of claims can still be eligible for a dividend. Total dividends paid last year: $58,000.

Mr. Raub acknowledges that the program can be viewed as discouraging people to visit a doctor when they need care. But he says that the system has made employees more conscious about their medical bills and their health. That, in turn, has enabled Famous Supply to keep increases in health care costs below the national average of 12 to 15 percent.

"When there's a little bit of incentive to control costs," he says, "people get smarter about how they use" health benefits.

Questions

1. Do you think that the use of "wellness dividends" will spread from Famous Supply to other U.S. companies? What are the pros and cons of such dividends for the employees? For the employer?
2. Do you agree that "when there's a little bit of incentive to control costs, people get smarter about how they use" health benefits? Explain your answer.

SOURCE: Glenn Ruffenach, "Premium Refunds Are a Healthy Incentive," *The Wall Street Journal*, August 22, 1989, p. B1.

LIFE SITUATION   Case 13–2

Health Care Benefits for Live-In Mates

Employers are starting to consider providing benefits to unmarried mates of employees, but the practice still faces financial, tax, and insurance problems. Moreover, the employers face political opposition from conservative groups that see homosexuals as the main beneficiaries.

Still in an embryonic state, partner benefits and policies have been adopted in recent years by almost a dozen employers. Such cities as Madison, Wisconsin, and Berkeley, California, have led the way in awarding sick and bereavement leave to workers with unmarried mates.

The impetus behind the drive is simple. Of an average worker's total annual compensation, 40 percent will be paid out in benefits next year, up from 35.4 percent in 1975, according to Hewitt Associates, a benefits consulting firm. And with health care costs surging, health coverage is an especially coveted benefit for unmarried partners who don't already have it.

The lack of health care benefits is nettlesome to Alix Olson and Martha Popp. Ms. Olson, a city police detective, can't get health coverage for Ms. Popp, her companion of 13 years, or Ms. Popp's two children. "We take our kids to school, we pay our taxes," says Ms. Popp, a substitute teacher without health coverage. "Then to turn around and not be allowed to have benefits—it wears away on you."

Questions

1. Do you think employers should provide health care benefits to live-in mates? Why or why not?
2. Why are health care benefits especially coveted by employees?
3. Why is the lack of health care benefits nettlesome to Alix Olson and Martha Popp?

SOURCE: William Celis III, "Benefits for Live-In Mates of Workers Face Obstacles," *The Wall Street Journal,* July 25, 1989, p. B1.

SUPPLEMENTARY READINGS

For Additional Information on Health Insurance Topics

Choice Time: Thinking Ahead of Long-Term Care. Hartford, Conn.: Aetna Life Insurance and Annuity Company, May 1989.

Health Insurance. Rockville, Md.: National Education Association, December 1988.

For Additional Information on Medicare Coverage

"Beyond Medicare." *Consumer Reports,* June 1989, pp. 375–86.

Capitani, Joseph and Richard A. Kuenster. "The Retiree's Quest for Health Coverage." *Best's Review,* July 1989, p. 38.

Guide to Health Insurance for People with Medicare. Washington, D.C.: U.S. Department of Health and Human Services, 1989.

For Additional Information on Disability Income Insurance

Disability. Washington, D.C.: U.S. Department of Health and Human Services, 1989.

Disability Income Insurance. Rockville, Md.: National Education Association Special Services, December 1988.

14

Life Insurance

You probably own some life insurance—through a group plan where you work, as a veteran, or through a policy you bought yourself. Perhaps you are considering the purchase of additional life insurance to keep pace with inflation or to cover your growing family. If so, you should prepare for that purchase by learning as much as possible about life insurance and how it can apply to your needs.

This chapter will help you make decisions about life insurance. It describes what life insurance is and how it works, the major types of life insurance coverages, and how you can use life insurance to protect your family.

LEARNING OBJECTIVES

After studying this chapter, you will be able to

L.O.1 Define life insurance and describe its purpose and principle.

L.O.2 Determine your life insurance needs.

L.O.3 Distinguish between the two types of life insurance companies and analyze various types of life insurance policies issued by them.

L.O.4 Select important provisions in life insurance contracts.

L.O.5 Create a plan to buy your life insurance.

L.O.6 Recognize how annuities provide security.

• •

OPENING CASE*

Whole Life Bounces Back as Insurers Sweeten Returns

Ten years after the Federal Trade Commission rocked insurers by denouncing their bread-and-butter product as a bad investment, the much-maligned whole life policy is selling like hotcakes again.

Whole life is a type of insurance that combines death benefits with a savings account in which investment earnings build up tax free. Its comeback was sparked when insurers raised the interest rates paid on the policy's savings to make it more competitive with other investments. Equally important, a much-ballyhooed rival product—universal life—left some buyers and sellers disappointed.

Buyers of savings-oriented insurance "are clearly getting a higher percentage of the available interest rates" than they got a decade ago, says William T. Potvin, a Touche Ross & Co. insurance consultant. And companies are footing the bill through narrower profit margins.

But new pitfalls have emerged for consumers. It's hard to compare whole life policies because their features vary so much. In addition, critics say, some sellers of whole life policies are creating unreasonably high expectations about investment returns as they scramble to outdo competitors.

"There are more misleading sales presentations going on—and more misunderstanding from the prospective customers—than there were 10 years ago," says Charles E. Rohm, a senior vice president of Principal Financial Group, an insurer based in Des Moines, Iowa. A key selling point for whole life and other savings-oriented policies is that the competing term life coverage—which doesn't have a savings component and is cheaper initially—becomes extremely expensive as a person gets older. On a traditional whole life policy, the annual premium is fixed and part of the money goes into the savings side in early years to cover higher death benefits payments later.

The high initial rates on universal life led some sellers to proclaim the new product a major improvement. "It's clear that universal life is not better than whole life today [as an investment]. They are about the same thing," says James H. Hunt, an actuary and a director of the National Insurance Consumer Organization in Alexandria, Virginia.

*Condensed from Karen Slater, "Whole Life Bounces Back as Insurers Sweeten Returns," *The Wall Street Journal,* June 22, 1989, p. C1.

• •

LIFE INSURANCE: AN INTRODUCTION

L.O.1
Define life insurance and describe its purpose and principle.

Consumer awareness of life insurance has changed very little over the years. Life insurance is still more often sold than bought. In other words, while most people actively seek to buy insurance for their property and health, most people avoid a life insurance purchase until they are approached by an agent. Let us see what life insurance is.

The Meaning of Life Insurance

Life insurance is neither mysterious nor difficult to understand. It works in the following manner. A person joins a risk-sharing group (an insurance company) by purchasing a contract (a policy). Under the policy, the insurance company promises to pay a sum of money at the time of the policyholder's death to the person or persons selected by him or her (the beneficiaries). In the case of an endowment policy, the money is paid to the policyholder (the insured) if he or she is alive on the future date (the maturity date) named in the policy. The insurance company makes this promise in return for the insured's agreement to pay it a sum of money (the premium) periodically.

The Purpose of Life Insurance

Life insurance is purchased primarily to provide an immediate estate that did not previously exist. Most people buy life insurance to protect someone who depends on them from financial losses caused by their death. That "someone" could be the nonworking spouse and children of a single-income family. It could be the wife or husband of a two-income family. It could be an aging parent. It could be a business partner or a corporation.

Here are typical examples of uses that are made of life insurance proceeds:

Paying off a home mortgage or other debts at the time of death by way of a decreasing term policy.

Providing lump-sum payments through an endowment to children when they reach a specified age.

Providing an education or income for children.

Making charitable bequests after death.

Providing a retirement income.

Accumulating savings.

Establishing a regular income for survivors.

Setting up an estate plan.

Making estate and death tax payments.

Life insurance is one of the few ways to provide liquidity at the time of death.

The Principle of Life Insurance

The principle of home insurance discussed in Chapter 12 can be applied to the lives of persons. From records covering many years and including millions of lives, mortality tables have been prepared that show the number of deaths for various age groups during any year. In the 1950s, the life insurance industry developed and the National Association of Insurance Commissioners (NAIC) approved a mortality table known as the Commissioners 1958 Standard Ordinary (CSO) Mortality Table. In 1980, the NAIC approved a new Standard Ordinary Mortality Table based on experience during 1970–75 (Exhibit 14–1). Unlike the 1958 CSO Table, which combined the mortality experience of males and females, the 1980 CSO Table separates the experience by sex.

An Example   The data in the 1980 CSO Table can be used to illustrate the insurance principle for lives of human beings. Let us assume that a group of 100,000 males, aged 29, wish to contribute a sufficient amount to a common fund each year so that $1,000 can be paid to the dependents of each group member who dies during the year. A glance at Exhibit 14–1 shows that the death rate for males at age 29 is 1.71 per thousand; therefore, 171 members of the group can be expected to die during the year.

Thus, each of the 100,000 members must contribute $1.71 at the beginning of the year in order to provide $1,000 for the dependents of each of the 171 who will die before the end of the year. If the survivors desire to continue the arrangements the following year, each of the remaining 99,829 members alive at the beginning of the next year, when they will be 30 years old, must contribute $1.73

Life insurance is *sold,* not bought.

"You are now insured against fire, flood, theft, liability, sickness, accident, death and any attempts on my part to sell you more insurance."

From *The Wall Street Journal*, with permission of Cartoon Features Syndicate.

in order to protect the dependents of the 173 individuals in the group who will die during that year.

If the group of 100,000 were females, aged 29, the per member cost for providing $1,000 of benefits to those who died during the year would be $1.30 since the female mortality rate per 1,000 is 1.30 at 29 years of age. This example may make it easier for you to see why life insurance premiums are usually less for females than for males.

How Long Will You Live?

Life expectancy, shown in Exhibit 14–1, does not indicate the age at which a person has the highest probability of dying. For example, the exhibit shows that the life expectancy of a male at the age of 30 is 43.24 years. This does not mean that males 30 years old will probably die at the age of 73.24 years. It means that 43.24 is the average number of years that all males alive at 30 years of age will still live.

But all of them will die sometime, and all could die soon. Covering the financial need arising from the risk of untimely death is the function of life insurance. Modern life insurance policies are designed to meet almost every circumstance in which there is loss of earning power.

EXHIBIT 14–1   1980 Commissioners Standard Ordinary Mortality Table

Age	Male Mortality Rate per 1,000	Male Expectancy, Years	Female Mortality Rate per 1,000	Female Expectancy, Years	Age	Male Mortality Rate per 1,000	Male Expectancy, Years	Female Mortality Rate per 1,000	Female Expectancy, Years
0	4.18	70.83	2.89	75.83	50	6.71	25.36	4.96	29.53
1	1.07	70.13	0.87	75.04	51	7.30	24.52	5.31	28.67
2	0.99	69.20	0.81	74.11	52	7.96	23.70	5.70	27.82
3	0.98	68.27	0.79	73.17	53	8.71	22.89	6.15	26.98
4	0.95	67.34	0.77	72.23	54	9.56	22.08	6.61	26.14
5	0.90	66.40	0.76	71.28	55	10.47	21.29	7.09	25.31
6	0.85	65.46	0.73	70.34	56	11.46	20.51	7.57	24.49
7	0.80	64.52	0.72	69.39	57	12.49	19.74	8.03	23.67
8	0.76	63.57	0.70	68.44	58	13.59	18.99	8.47	22.86
9	0.74	62.62	0.69	67.48	59	14.77	18.24	8.94	22.05
10	0.73	61.66	0.68	66.53	60	16.08	17.51	9.47	21.25
11	0.77	60.71	0.69	65.58	61	17.54	16.79	10.13	20.44
12	0.85	59.75	0.72	64.62	62	19.19	16.08	10.96	19.65
13	0.99	58.80	0.75	63.67	63	21.06	15.38	12.02	18.86
14	1.15	57.86	0.80	62.71	64	23.14	14.70	13.25	18.08
15	1.33	56.93	0.85	61.76	65	25.42	14.04	14.59	17.32
16	1.51	56.00	0.90	60.82	66	27.85	13.39	16.00	16.57
17	1.67	55.09	0.95	59.87	67	30.44	12.76	17.43	15.83
18	1.78	54.18	0.98	58.93	68	33.19	12.14	18.84	15.10
19	1.86	53.27	1.02	57.98	69	36.17	11.54	20.36	14.38
20	1.90	52.37	1.05	57.04	70	39.51	10.96	22.11	13.67
21	1.91	51.47	1.07	56.10	71	43.30	10.39	24.23	12.97
22	1.89	50.57	1.09	55.16	72	47.65	9.84	26.87	12.28
23	1.86	49.66	1.11	54.22	73	52.64	9.30	30.11	11.60
24	1.82	48.75	1.14	53.28	74	58.19	8.79	33.93	10.95
25	1.77	47.84	1.16	52.34	75	64.19	8.31	38.24	10.32
26	1.73	46.93	1.19	51.40	76	70.53	7.84	42.96	9.71
27	1.71	46.01	1.22	50.46	77	77.12	7.40	48.04	9.12
28	1.70	45.09	1.26	49.52	78	83.90	6.97	53.45	8.55
29	1.71	44.16	1.30	48.59	79	91.05	6.57	59.35	8.01
30	1.73	43.24	1.35	47.65	80	98.84	6.18	65.99	7.48
31	1.78	42.31	1.40	46.71	81	107.48	5.80	73.60	6.98
32	1.83	41.38	1.45	45.78	82	117.25	5.44	82.40	6.49
33	1.91	40.46	1.50	44.84	83	128.26	5.09	92.53	6.03
34	2.00	39.54	1.58	43.91	84	140.25	4.77	103.81	5.59
35	2.11	38.61	1.65	42.98	85	152.95	4.46	116.10	5.18
36	2.24	37.69	1.76	42.05	86	166.09	4.18	129.29	4.80
37	2.40	36.78	1.89	41.12	87	179.55	3.91	143.32	4.43
38	2.58	35.87	2.04	40.20	88	193.27	3.66	158.18	4.09
39	2.79	34.96	2.22	39.28	89	207.29	3.41	173.94	3.77
40	3.02	34.05	2.42	38.36	90	221.77	3.18	190.75	3.45
41	3.29	33.16	2.64	37.46	91	236.98	2.94	208.87	3.15
42	3.56	32.26	2.87	36.55	92	253.45	2.70	228.81	2.85
43	3.87	31.38	3.09	35.66	93	272.11	2.44	251.51	2.55
44	4.19	30.50	3.32	34.77	94	295.90	2.17	279.31	2.24
45	4.55	29.62	3.56	33.88	95	329.96	1.87	317.32	1.91
46	4.92	28.76	3.80	33.00	96	384.55	1.54	375.74	1.56
47	5.32	27.90	4.05	32.12	97	480.20	1.20	474.97	1.21
48	5.74	27.04	4.33	31.25	98	657.98	0.84	655.85	0.84
49	6.21	26.20	4.63	30.39	99	1,000.00	0.50	1,000.00	0.50

SOURCE: American Council of Life Insurance.

DETERMINING YOUR LIFE INSURANCE NEEDS

L.O.2
Determine your life insurance needs.

You should consider a number of factors before you buy insurance. These factors include your present and future sources of income, other savings and income protection, group life insurance, group annuities (or other pension benefits), and social security. But first you should determine whether you need life insurance.

Do You Need Life Insurance?

If your death would cause financial stress for your spouse, children, parents, or anyone you want to protect, then you should consider purchasing life insurance. Your stage in the life cycle and the type of household you live in will influence this decision. Single persons living alone or with their parents usually have little or no need for life insurance. A two-earner couple may have a moderate need for life insurance, especially if they have a mortgage or other large debts. Households with small children most often have the greatest need for life insurance. Families may also want small amounts of insurance to cover burial expenses for children and other household members or may decide to self-insure for this purpose.

Determining Your Life Insurance Objectives

Before you consider types of life insurance policies, you must decide what you want your life insurance to do for you and your dependents.

First, how much money do you want to leave to your dependents if you should die today? Will you require more or less insurance protection to meet their needs as time goes on?

Second, when would you like to be able to retire? What amount of income do you feel you and your spouse would need then?

Third, how much will you be able to pay for your insurance program? When you are older, are you most likely to earn more than, the same as, or less than you do now? Are the demands on your family budget for other expenses of living likely to be greater or less as time goes on?

When you have considered these questions and developed some approximate answers, you are ready to select the types and amounts of life insurance policies that will help you accomplish your objectives.

Once you have decided on what you want your life insurance to accomplish, the next difficult question is to decide how much to buy.

Estimating Your Life Insurance Requirements

How much life insurance should you carry? This question is important for every person who owns or intends to buy life insurance. Because of the various factors involved, the question cannot be answered by mathematics alone. Nevertheless, an insurance policy does put a price on the life of the person insured and methods are therefore needed to estimate what that price should be.

There are four general methods for determining the amount of insurance you might need: the easy method, the Dink method, the "nonworking" spouse method, and the thorough method.[1]

The Easy Method   Simple as this method is, it is remarkably useful. It is based on the insurance agent's rule of thumb that a "typical family" will need approximately 70 percent of your salary for seven years before it adjusts to the financial consequences of your death.

In other words, for a simple estimate of your life insurance needs, just multiply your current gross income by 5.

Example:

$24,000 current income × 5 = $120,000

Your figures:

$_____ current income × 5 = $_____

This method assumes that your family is "typical." You may need more insurance if you have four or more children, if you have above-average family debt, if any member of your family suffers poor health, or if your spouse has poor employment potential.

The Dink (Dual Income, No Kids) Method   If you have no dependents and your spouse earns as much as or more than you do, you have very simple insurance needs. Basically, all you need to do is ensure that your spouse will not be unduly burdened by debts should you die. Here is an example of the Dink method:

	Example	Your Figures
Funeral expenses	$ 5,000	$
One half of mortgage	60,000	
One half of auto loan	7,000	
One half of credit card balance	1,500	
One half of personal debt	1,500	
Other debts	1,000	_____
Total insurance needs	$76,000	$

This method assumes that your spouse will continue to work after your death. If your spouse suffers poor health or is employed in an occupation with an uncertain future, you should consider adding an insurance cushion to see him or her through hard times.

The "Nonworking" Spouse Method   Insurance experts have estimated that extra costs of up to $9,000 a year may be required to replace the services of a homemaker in a family with small children. These extra costs may include the cost of a housekeeper, baby-sitting, more meals out, additional carfare, laundry services, and so on. They do not include the lost potential earnings of the surviving spouse, who must often take time away from the job to care for the family.

To estimate how much life insurance a homemaker should carry, multiply the number of years before the youngest child reaches age 18 by $9,000.

Example:

10 years × $9,000 = $90,000

Your figures:

_____ years × $9,000 = $_____

If the wage-earning spouse's job is not demanding or if there are teenage children, the $9,000 figure can be reduced. If the wage earner's job is especially demanding, if there are more than two children under the age of 13, or if anyone in the family suffers poor health or has special needs, the $9,000 figure should be adjusted upward.

The Thorough Method   The first three methods assume that you and your family are "typical" and ignore such important factors as social security and the rate of return that your survivors can earn if they invest the life insurance benefits they receive. Exhibit 14–2 provides a detailed worksheet for a thorough estimation of your life insurance needs.

The first four items on the worksheet are self-explanatory, but when you get to the section on expected living expenses, you'll need to subtract income expenses to see how much the insurance benefit should provide your spouse each year (Item 5D). Then you must assume an investment strategy that is either "conservative" or "aggressive." Use the table of investment rate factors to find the factor that corresponds to your chosen strategy and the number of years until your spouse reaches 90. Multiply this factor by the net annual living expenses (Item 5D) to get the amount needed to give your spouse enough income to meet expected living expenses.

Add the fund for total living expenses (Item 5G) to the sum of the first four items, and then subtract any assets you have at the moment. The result is your life insurance needs.

Although this method is quite thorough, you may feel that it does not address all of your special needs. If so, you should obtain further advice from an insurance expert or a financial planner.

EXHIBIT 14–2
Worksheet to Calculate
Your Life Insurance Needs

Expenses You'll Need to Cover	Example	Your Family
1. Funeral, estate taxes, etc.	$ 5,000	
2. Settling of nonmortgage debt	2,500	
3. Emergency fund	5,000	
4. College fund	76,800	
5. Expected living expenses:		
A. Expected average living expenses	29,000	
B. Expected spouse's average annual income after taxes	− 22,500	
C. Annual social security benefits	− 5,000	
D. Net annual living expenses (A − B − C)	1,500	
E. Years until spouse is 90	55	
F. Investment rate factor°	× 22	
G. Total living expenses (D × F)	$ 33,000	
6. Total monetary needs (1 + 2 + 3 + 4 + 5G)	$ 122,300	
7. Total investment assets in hand	− 10,000	
8. Life insurance needs (6 − 7)	$ 112,300	

°Table of Investment Rate Factors:

Years until spouse is 90	25	30	35	40	45	50	55	60
Conservative investment	20	22	25	27	30	31	33	35
Aggressive investment	16	17	19	20	21	21	22	23

SOURCE: Adapted from a chart developed by financial advisers Bailard, Biehl & Kaiser, Inc., of San Mateo, California. Originally printed in the April 2, 1984, edition of *The Wall Street Journal.*

As you determine your life insurance needs, don't forget to consider the life insurance you may already have. You may already have ample coverage through your employer and through mortgage and credit life insurance that you have purchased.

You can purchase the new or extra life insurance you need from two types of life insurance companies. Mutual life insurance companies sell participating policies, while stock life insurance companies generally sell nonparticipating policies.

TYPES OF LIFE INSURANCE COMPANIES AND LIFE INSURANCE POLICIES

L.O.3
Distinguish between the two types of life insurance companies and analyze various types of life insurance policies issued by them.

Types of Life Insurance Companies

There are two types of life insurance companies: stock life insurance companies, owned by shareholders, and mutual life insurance companies, owned by their policyholders. About 94 percent of U.S. life insurance companies are stock companies, and about 6 percent are mutuals.

Stock companies generally sell nonparticipating (or nonpar) policies, while mutual companies specialize in the sale of participating (or par) policies. A **participating policy** has a somewhat higher premium than a **nonparticipating policy,** but annually a part of the premium is refunded to the policyholder. This refund is called the *policy dividend.*

Which Type Should You Buy?

There has been long and inconclusive debate on whether stock companies or mutual companies offer the least expensive life insurance. You should check with both stock and mutual companies to determine which type of company offers the best policy for your particular needs at the lowest price.

If you wish to pay exactly the same premium each year, you should choose a nonparticipating policy, with its guaranteed premiums. However, you may prefer life insurance whose annual price reflects the company's experience with its investments, the health of its policyholders, and its general operating costs—that is, a participating policy.

Both mutual insurance companies and stock insurance companies sell three basic types of life insurance—term, whole life, and endowment insurance. In the next section, you will learn about the various types of insurance coverages.

Types of Life Insurance Policies

Exhibit 14–3 shows the common types of policies issued by life insurance companies. We will discuss not only these common types but also more fashionable new types, and we will examine the purposes for which each type is best suited.

Term Life Insurance

Term insurance is protection for a specified period of time, usually 1, 5, 10, or 20 years or up to age 65. A term insurance policy pays a benefit only if you die during the period that it covers. If you stop paying the premiums, the

EXHIBIT 14–3   Major Types and Subtypes of Life Insurance

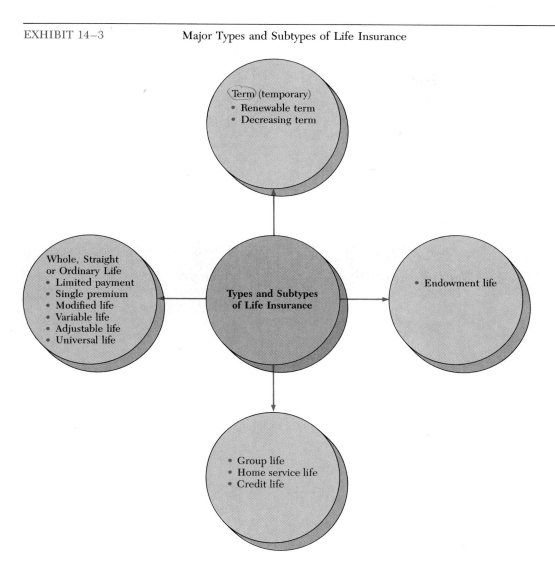

insurance stops. Term insurance is therefore sometimes called temporary life insurance.

Many insurance agents will dissuade you from buying low-cost term insurance, and for an unsurprising reason—their commissions. "Given the same face amount, the agents will make 5 to 10 times as much selling whole life or universal as opposed to term," notes James Hunt, a director of the National Insurance Consumer Organization. An agent or a financial planner may tell you, "Term premiums are wasted because you have nothing left after paying premiums for many years." However, in buying term insurance, as in buying automobile insurance, you purchase pure insurance protection. And the money you save by buying term insurance instead of whole life insurance is hardly wasted if you invest it or use it to meet other needs.

Renewability Option   The coverage of term insurance ends at the end of the term, but it can be continued for another term if you have a renewable option. For example, the term insurance of Teachers Insurance and Annuity Association is renewable at your option for successive five-year periods to age 70 without medical reexamination. Level premiums are paid during each five-year period. The premiums increase every five years.

Conversion Option   If you have convertible term insurance, you can exchange it for a whole life policy without a medical examination and at a higher premium. The premium for the whole life policy stays the same for the rest of your life.

Decreasing Term Insurance   Term insurance is also available in a form that pays less to the beneficiary as time passes. The insurance period you select might depend on your age or on how long you decide the coverage will be needed. For example, a decreasing term contract for 25 years might be appropriate as coverage of a mortgage loan balance on a house because the coverage would decrease as the balance on the mortgage decreases. You could get the same result by purchasing annual renewable term policies of diminishing amounts during the period of the mortgage loan. An annual renewable policy would offer more flexibility to change coverage if you were to sell the house or remortgage it. Mortgage insurance, therefore, is a form of decreasing term insurance, decreasing to keep pace with the principal balance on your mortgage loan.

There are sound reasons for using term policies for both permanent and temporary life insurance requirements. *Consumer Reports* and many financial advisers recommend term insurance for both purposes because it provides maximum protection for each premium dollar. Since term life provides protection only, however, it has no cash value. Whole life insurance, on the other hand, does have cash value.

Whole Life Insurance

The most common type of permanent life insurance is the **whole life policy** (also called a straight life policy or an ordinary life policy), in which you pay a specified premium each year for as long as you live. In return, the insurance company pays a stipulated sum to the beneficiary when you die. The amount of your premium depends primarily on the age at which you purchase the insurance.

One important feature of the whole life policy is its cash value. Cash value is an amount that increases over the years and that you receive if you give up the insurance. A table in the whole life policy enables you to tell exactly how much cash value it has (see Exhibit 14–4).

Cash value policies may make sense for those who can afford them or for those who must be forced to save. But you should not have too low a death benefit because you'd like the savings component of a cash life policy. James Hunt of National Insurance Consumer Organization suggests that you explore other savings and investment strategies before investing your money in such a policy. Read the accompanying "Financial Planning in Action" feature to find out how haggling with your insurance agent can boost your insurance returns.

EXHIBIT 14–4

An Example of Guaranteed
Cash Values

Plan and Additional Benefits	Amount	Premium	Years Payable
Whole life (premiums payable to age 90)	$10,000	$229.50	55
Waiver of premium (to age 65)		4.30	30
Accidental death (to age 70)	10,000	7.80	35

A premium is payable on the policy date and every 12 policy months thereafter. The first premium is $241.60.

Table of Guaranteed Values

End of Policy Year	Cash or Loan Value	Paid-up Insurance	Extended Term Insurance	
			Years	Days
1	$ 14	$ 30	0	152
2	174	450	4	182
3	338	860	8	65
4	506	1,250	10	344
5	676	1,640	12	360
6	879	2,070	14	335
7	1,084	2,500	16	147
8	1,293	2,910	17	207
9	1,504	3,300	18	177
10	1,719	3,690	19	78
11	1,908	4,000	19	209
12	2,099	4,300	19	306
13	2,294	4,590	20	8
14	2,490	4,870	20	47
15	2,690	5,140	20	65
16	2,891	5,410	20	66
17	3,095	5,660	20	52
18	3,301	5,910	20	27
19	3,508	6,150	19	358
20	3,718	6,390	19	317
Age 60	4,620	7,200	18	111
Age 65	5,504	7,860	16	147

Paid-up additions and dividend accumulations increase the cash values; indebtedness decreases them.

Direct Beneficiary	Helen M. Benson, wife of the insured		
Owner	Thomas A. Benson, the insured		
Insured	Thomas A. Benson	**Age and Sex**	37 Male
Policy Date	November 1, 1990	**Policy Number**	000/00
Date of Issue	November 1, 1990		

SOURCE: *Sample Life Insurance Policy* (Washington, D.C.: American Council of Life Insurance, n.d.) p. 2.

FINANCIAL PLANNING IN ACTION

Haggling Can Boost Insurance Returns

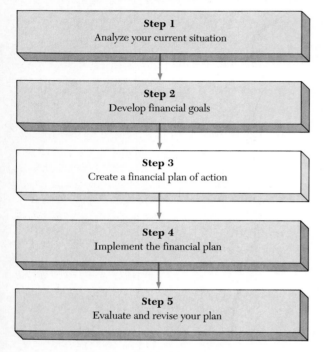

Step 1
Analyze your current situation

Step 2
Develop financial goals

Step 3
Create a financial plan of action

Step 4
Implement the financial plan

Step 5
Evaluate and revise your plan

Psst. Here's a little secret for people planning to invest in an insurance product: Haggling with your agent can often mean higher investment returns.

Unknown to most investors, some insurers offer two or more products that are essentially the same, except for the size of the commissions paid to agents and others who sell them. The product that pays the most to the agent is typically the one that's least generous to the investor.

The differences can be significant. Consider two annuity contracts offered by United Services General Life Company, a unit of Equitable of Iowa Companies.

With one of these annuities, the commission to the person selling the contract is 4.25 percent of the money that the investor pays in; with the other, the commission is 8.5 percent. The lower-commission annuity offers 8.62 percent interest for the first year, while the higher-commission annuity offers 8 percent. The lower-commission annuity also has a lower surrender charge, or penalty for pulling out of the contract in the first several years.

The Trade-Off

The trade-off between commissions and policy benefits is simply a matter of mathematics. While commissions on insurance products are paid by the companies, the policy buyers ultimately bear this cost. Because the policy buyers don't pay the commission directly, most of them probably have no idea how much it is. And insurance agents have no incentive to tell clients about a low-commission, high-benefit product when they would prefer to sell a high-commission version.

"The choice would be obvious. It's like saying 'Do you want this for $125, $110, or $100?'" says John Branton, whose Philadelphia marketing firm helps Equitable of Iowa sell a range of annuities. "It puts the agent in the moral dilemma" of benefiting either himself or his client, says Jack E. Bobo, executive vice president of the National Association of Life Underwriters, a Washington-based trade group of life insurance agents.

SOURCE: Condensed from Karen Slater, "Haggling Can Boost Insurance Returns," *The Wall Street Journal*, August 3, 1989, p. C1.

Nonforfeiture Clause   Another important feature of the whole life policy is the **nonforfeiture clause.** This provision allows you not to forfeit all accrued benefits. For example, if you decide not to continue paying premiums, you can exercise certain options with your cash value.

To see the workings of the whole life policy and its cash value, let us suppose that a 30-year-old woman wants to buy $30,000 worth of coverage. She might pay an annual premium of $435 for a whole life policy with no policy dividends. Here's how the cash would grow:

Age 35 $1,830
Age 40   4,260
Age 45   6,990
Age 50   9,960

A substantial reserve is accumulated by the insurance company during the early years of the whole life policy in order to pay the benefits in the later years when your chances of dying are greater. At first, the basic premium for whole life insurance is higher than that for term insurance; however, the premium for a whole life policy remains constant throughout your lifetime, whereas the premium for a term policy increases with each renewal.

Several types of whole life insurance have been developed to meet different objectives. A few of the popular types are discussed next.

Limited Payment Policy   One type of whole life policy is called the limited payment policy. Under the limited payment plan of insurance, you pay premiums for a stipulated period, usually 20 or 30 years, or until you reach a specified age, such as 60 or 65 (unless your death occurs earlier). However, you remain insured for life and the company will pay the face amount of the policy at your death. Because the premium payment period for a limited payment policy is shorter than that for a whole life policy, the annual premium is larger.

A special form of the limited payment plan is the single-premium policy. In this type of contract, you make only one premium payment.

Under the Tax Reform Act of 1986, annuities (to be discussed later in this chapter) and single-premium whole life insurance have retained their tax-deferred benefits. You pay no federal, state, or local income tax on the interest, dividends, or capital gains that your money earns while the policy remains in force. Increases in cash value are taxed only if and when they are distributed to you. Furthermore, beneficiaries pay no income tax on the policy proceeds.

Variable Life Insurance Policy   The cash values of a variable life insurance policy fluctuate according to the yields earned by a separate fund, which can be a stock fund, a money market fund, or a long-term bond fund. A minimum death benefit is guaranteed, but the death benefit can rise above that minimum, to a level that depends on the earnings of the dollars invested in the separate fund. The premium payments for a variable life policy are fixed.

Adjustable Life Insurance Policy   The adjustable life insurance policy is another relatively new type of whole life insurance. You can change such a policy as your needs change. For example, if you want to increase or decrease your coverage, you can change either the premium payments or the period of coverage.

Universal Life   Subject to certain minimums, **universal life** insurance is designed to let you pay premiums at any time in virtually any amount. The amount of insurance can be changed more easily in a universal life policy than in a traditional policy. The increase in the cash value of a universal life policy reflects the interest earned on short-term investments. Thus, the universal life policy clearly combines term insurance and investment elements.

EXHIBIT 14–5   How Life Insurance Market Breaks Down

Share of New-Policy Premiums

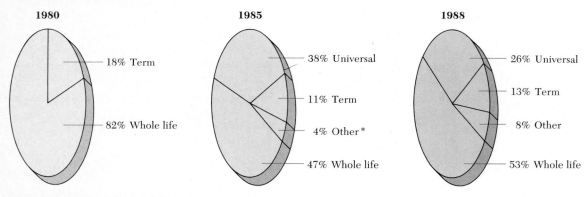

1980

18% Term

82% Whole life

1985

38% Universal

11% Term

4% Other*

47% Whole life

1988

26% Universal

13% Term

8% Other

53% Whole life

*"Variable" policies with mutual-fund investment options
SOURCE: *The Wall Street Journal,* June 22, 1989, p. C1; based on data from Life Insurance Marketing and Research Association, Hartford, Connecticut.

Universal life is actually a more flexible version of whole life insurance. As you learned in the Opening Case, when universal policies were first offered, in 1979, they paid much higher interest rates than whole life, and sales of universal life skyrocketed. In 1985, six years after being introduced, universal accounted for a strong 38 percent of new insurance sales and whole life accounted for only 47 percent, down sharply from its 82 percent share in 1980 (see Exhibit 14–5). Then, just as suddenly, sales of universal slowed. In 1988, universal was down to 26 percent of new policy premiums and whole life, at 53 percent, had a 2-to-1 lead.[2]

Like the details of other types of policies, the details of universal life policies vary from company to company. The key distinguishing features of universal life policies are explicit, separate accounting to the policyholders of (1) the charges for the insurance element, (2) the charges for company expenses (commissions, policy fees, etc.), and (3) the rate of return on the investment (cash value) of the policy. The rate of return is flexible; it is guaranteed to be not less than a certain amount (usually 4 percent), but it may be more, depending on the insurance company's decision.

Since your primary reason for buying a life insurance policy is the insurance component, the cost of that component should be your primary consideration. Thus, universal life policies, which offer a high rate of return on the cash value but charge a high price for the insurance element, should generally be avoided.

Endowment Life Insurance

Endowment life insurance pays your beneficiary a tax-free death benefit after a specified number of years if you die within that period. However, if you don't die, it pays you the same amount. Endowment life is expensive, and recent tax law changes have made it less attractive than it was.

Exhibit 14–6 compares some important features of term, whole life, universal life, and endowment policies.

EXHIBIT 14–6 Comparison of Term, Whole Life, Universal Life, and Endowment Insurance

Type of Policy	Period Covered	Cash Value	Insurance Protection	Premium	Coverage	Comments
Term						
Level	For a stated number of years, such as 1, 5, 20	None	High	Stays the same until renewal	Stays the same	Pure insurance coverage
Decreasing	For a stated number of years, such as 1, 5, 20	None	High	Stays the same	Decreases	Least expensive type of insurance
Whole Life						
Straight	Whole life	Low	Moderate	Stays the same	Stays the same	Part insurance, part savings
Limited payment	Whole life	Low	Moderate	Stays the same	Stays the same	Paid up after a certain number of years
Universal Life	Varies	Low to high	Low to high	Varies	Varies	Combines renewable term insurance with a savings account paying market interest rates
Endowment	For a stated period of time	High	Low	Stays the same	Stays the same until paid up	Savings accumulation No insurance protection after policy has been paid up

Over the years, variations on term, whole life, and endowment insurance have been developed. The details of these policies may differ among companies. So check with individual companies to determine the best policy for your needs.

Other Types of Life Insurance Policies

Group Life Insurance Policy   During recent decades, group life insurance has become widely popular. A group insurance plan insures a large number of persons under the terms of a single policy without medical examination. In general, the principles that apply to other forms of insurance also apply to group insurance.

Fundamentally, group insurance is term insurance, which was described earlier. Usually, the cost of group insurance is split between an employer and the employees in such a way that the cost of insurance per $1,000 is the same for each employee, regardless of age. The employer pays a larger portion of the costs of the group policy for older employees. Group insurance is therefore a rare bargain for older employees, but even younger employees usually find it inexpensive.

In 1988, group life coverage totaled $3 trillion, or almost 41 percent of all life coverage. Group life insurance has grown significantly during the past decade, with increases in the coverage of group members' dependents as well as that of the members themselves.[3]

Credit Life Insurance   Credit life insurance is used to repay a personal debt should the borrower die before doing so. It is based on the belief that "no person's debts should live after him or her." It was introduced in the United States in 1917, when installment financing and purchasing became popular.

Credit life insurance policies for auto loans and home mortgages are not the best buy for the protection that these policies offer. Instead, buy the decreasing term insurance discussed earlier; it's cheaper.

Modern life insurance policies contain numerous provisions whose terminology can be confusing. However, an understanding of these provisions is very important for the insurance buyer.

In our dynamic economy, inflation and interest rates change often. Therefore, experts recommend that you reevaluate your insurance coverage every two years. Be sure, of course, to update your insurance whenever your situation changes dramatically. For example, the birth of another child or an increase in your home mortgage can boost your insurance needs greatly.

IMPORTANT PROVISIONS IN A LIFE INSURANCE CONTRACT

L.O.4
Select important provisions in life insurance contracts.

Your life insurance policy is valuable only if it meets your objectives. When your objectives change, however, it may not be necessary to give up the policy. Instead, study the policy carefully and discuss its provisions with your agent. Here are some of the most common provisions.

Naming Your Beneficiary

An important provision in every life insurance policy is the right to name your beneficiary. A **beneficiary** is a person who is designated to receive something, such as life insurance proceeds, from someone.

Under group insurance, you can name one or more persons as contingent beneficiaries who will receive your policy proceeds if the primary beneficiary dies before you do.

The Grace Period

When you buy a life insurance policy, the insurance company agrees to pay a certain sum of money under specified circumstances and you agree to pay a certain premium regularly. The grace period allows 28 to 31 days to elapse, during which time the premium may be paid without penalty. After that time, the policy lapses if the premium has not been paid.

Policy Reinstatement

A lapsed policy can be put back in force—reinstated—if it has not been turned in for cash. To reinstate the policy, you must again qualify as an acceptable risk and you must pay overdue premiums with interest. There is a time limit on reinstatement.

Incontestability Clause

The **incontestability clause** stipulates that after the policy has been in force for a specified period (usually two years), the insurance company cannot dispute its validity during the lifetime of the insured for any reason, including fraud. One reason for this provision is that the beneficiaries should not be forced to suffer because of acts of the insured.

Suicide Clause

The **suicide clause** provides that if the insured dies by suicide during the first two years that the policy is in force, the death benefit will equal the amount of the premium paid. After two years, the suicide becomes a risk covered by the policy and the beneficiaries of a suicide receive the same benefit that is payable for death from any other cause. In the early 20th century, policies were issued in which no benefit was ever payable in the event of suicide.

Automatic Premium Loans

Under this option, which the insured may elect, if the insured does not pay the premium within the grace period, the insurance company automatically pays it out of the policy's cash value if that cash value is sufficient. This prevents the insured from inadvertently allowing the policy to lapse.

Misstatement of Age Provision

This provision says that if the company finds out that the insured's age was incorrectly stated, it will pay the benefits that the insured's premiums would have bought if his or her age had been correctly stated. The provision sets forth a simple procedure to resolve what could otherwise be a complicated legal matter.

Policy Loan Provision

A loan from the insurance company is available on a whole life or endowment policy after the policy has been in force for one, two, or three years, as stated in the policy. This feature, known as the policy loan provision, permits the owner of the policy to borrow any amount up to the cash value of the policy.

Riders to Life Insurance Policies

An insurance company can change the provisions of a policy by attaching a rider to the policy. A **rider** is any document attached to the policy that modifies its coverage by adding or excluding specified conditions or altering its benefits. A whole life insurance policy may include a waiver of premium disability benefit or an accidental death benefit, or both.

Waiver of Premium Disability Benefit Under this provision, the company waives any premiums that are due after the beginning of total and permanent disability. In effect, the company pays them. The disability must occur before you reach a certain age, usually 60, and before the policy matures if it is an endowment.

The waiver of premium rider may sometimes be desirable, but don't buy it if the added cost prevents you from carrying needed basic life insurance.

Accidental Death Benefit Under this provision, the insurance company pays twice the face amount of the policy if the insured's death results from an accident. The accidental death benefit is often called **double indemnity.** Accidental death must occur within a certain time after the injury, usually 90 days, and before the insured reaches a certain age, usually 60 or 65.

The accidental death benefit, however, is expensive. Moreover, your chances of dying in the exact manner stated in the policy are very small, and so are the chances that your beneficiary will collect the double payment.

Guaranteed Insurability Option This option allows you to buy specified additional amounts of life insurance at stated intervals without proof of insurability. Thus, even if you do not remain in good health, you can increase the amount of your insurance as your income rises. This option is desirable if you anticipate the need for additional life insurance in the future.

Now that you know the various types of life insurance policies and the major provisions of and riders to such policies, you are ready to make your buying decisions.

BUYING YOUR LIFE INSURANCE

L.O.5
Create a plan to buy your life insurance.

You should consider a number of factors before buying life insurance. As discussed earlier in this chapter, these factors include your present and future sources of income, other savings and income protection, group life insurance, group annuities (or other pension benefits), and social security.

In this section, you will learn how life insurance companies price their products.

Comparing Policy Costs

Each life insurance company designs the policies it sells to make them attractive and useful to many policyholders. One policy may have features that another policy doesn't have; one company may be more selective than another company; one company may get a better return on its investments than another company. These and other factors affect the price of life insurance policies.

In brief, the price that a company charges for a life insurance policy is affected by five factors: the company's cost of doing business, the return on its investments, the mortality rate that it expects among its policyholders, the features contained in its policy, and competition among companies with comparable policies.

FINANCIAL PLANNING CALCULATIONS	
Determining the Cost of Insurance	

In determining the cost of insurance, don't overlook the time value of money. You must include as part of that cost the interest (opportunity cost) you would earn on money if you did not use it to pay insurance premiums. For many years, insurers did not assign a time value to money in making their sales presentations. Only recently has the insurance industry widely adopted interest-adjusted cost estimates.

If you fail to consider the time value of money, you may get the false impression that the insurance company is giving you something for nothing. Here is an example. Suppose that you are 35 and that you have a $10,000 face amount, 20-year limited-payment, participating policy. Your annual premium is $210, or $4,200 over the 20-year period. Your dividends over the 20-year payment period total $1,700, so that your total net premium is $2,500 ($4,200 − $1,700). Yet the cash value of your policy at the end of 20 years is $4,600. If you disregard the interest that your premiums could otherwise have earned, you might get the impression that the insurance company is giving you $2,100 more than you paid ($4,600 − $2,500). But if you consider the time value of money (or its opportunity cost), the insurance company is not giving you $2,100. What if

you had deposited the annual premiums in a savings account? At 8 percent interest (plus a $25 policy fee), your account would have accumulated to $6,180 in 20 years. Therefore, instead of having been given $2,100 by the insurance company, you have paid the company $1,580 for 20 years of insurance protection:

Premiums you paid over 20 years	$4,200
Time value of money	1,980 ($6,180 − $4,200)
Total cost	6,180
Cash value	4,600
Net cost of insurance	1,580 ($6,180 − $4,600)

Be sure to request interest-adjusted indexes from your agent; if he or she doesn't give them to you, look for another agent. As you have seen in the example, the costs of insurance companies can be compared by combining premium payments, dividends, cash value buildup, and present value analysis into an index number. But as you learned in the Opening Case, policy features vary so much that it's hard to compare them. Hard, yes; impossible, no.

The price of life insurance policies varies therefore considerably among life insurance companies. Moreover, a particular company will not be equally competitive for all policies. Thus, one company might have a competitively priced policy for 24-year-olds but not for 35-year-olds.

Ask your agent to give you interest-adjusted indexes. An **interest-adjusted index** is a method of evaluating the cost of life insurance by taking into account the time value of money. Combining premium payments, dividends, cash value buildup, and present value analysis into an index number makes possible a fairly accurate cost comparison among insurance companies. The lower the index number, the lower is the cost of the policy.

The accompanying "Financial Planning Calculations" feature shows how to use an interest-adjusted index to compare the costs of insurance.

Obtaining a Policy

A life insurance policy is issued after you submit an application for insurance and the insurance company accepts the application. The application usually has two parts. In the first part, you state your name, age, sex, what type of policy you desire, how much insurance you want, your occupation, and so forth. In the second part, you give your medical history. While a medical examination is frequently required for ordinary policies, usually no examination is required for group insurance.

The company determines your insurability by means of the information in your application, the medical examination, and the inspection report. Ninety-eight percent of all applicants are found to be insurable.

Examining a Policy: Before the Purchase

When you buy a life insurance policy, read every word of the contract and, if necessary, ask your agent for a point-by-point explanation of the language. Many insurance companies have rewritten their contracts to make them more understandable. Remember that these are legal documents and that you should be familiar with what they promise, even though technical terms are used.

Examining a Policy: After the Purchase

After you buy new life insurance, you have a 10-day "free look" period, during which you can change your mind. If you do so, the company will return your premium without penalty.

It's a good idea to give your beneficiaries and your lawyer a photocopy of your policy. Your beneficiaries should know where the policy is kept, because in order to obtain the insurance proceeds, they will have to send it to the company upon your death, along with a copy of the death certificate.

Choosing Settlement Options

A well-planned life insurance program should cover the immediate expenses resulting from the death of the insured, but that is only one of its purposes. In most instances, the primary purpose of life insurance is to protect dependents against a loss of income resulting from the premature death of the primary breadwinner. Thus, selecting the appropriate settlement option is an important part of designing a life insurance program. Perhaps the most common settlement options are lump-sum payment, limited installment payment, life income option, and proceeds left with the company.

Lump-Sum Payment   In the lump-sum payment option, the company pays the face amount of the policy in one installment to the beneficiary or to the estate of the insured. This form of settlement is the most widely used option.

Limited Installment Payment   This option provides for payment of the life insurance proceeds in equal periodic installments for a specified number of years after your death.

Life Income Option   Under the life income option, payments are made to the beneficiary for as long as the beneficiary may live. The amount of each payment is based primarily on the sex and attained age of the beneficiary at the time of the insured's death.

Proceeds Left with the Company   Under this option, the life insurance proceeds are left with the insurance company at a specified rate of interest. The company acts as trustee and pays the interest to the beneficiary. The guaranteed minimum interest rate paid on the proceeds varies among companies.

Read your policy diligently, and know its benefits and limitations. The accompanying feature provides a comprehensive insurance policy checklist.

Switching Policies

Think twice if someone suggests that you replace the whole life insurance you already own. Before you give up this protection, make sure you are still insurable (check medical and any other qualification requirements). Also remember that you are now older than you were when you purchased your policy and that a new policy will cost more because of your age. Moreover, the older policy may have provisions that are not duplicated in some of the new policies. We are not saying that you should reject the idea of replacing your present policy, but rather that you should proceed with caution. We recommend that you ask your agent or company for an opinion about the new proposal, so as to get both sides of the argument.

As you have seen so far, life insurance provides a set sum at your death. But if you want to enjoy benefits while you are still alive, you might consider annuities. An annuity protects you against the risk of outliving your assets.

PERSONAL FINANCE JOURNAL

Do You Know What Is in Your Life Insurance Policy?

Read your life insurance policy, and know its benefits and restrictions. The following questions will help you know what is in your present policy and in those policies that you may buy in the future.

1. Which insurance company issued the policy?
2. What type of policy is it?
3. What is the face value of the policy?
4. What is the *annual* premium if paid annually? What is the *annual* premium if paid quarterly? What is the *annual* premium if paid semiannually? What is the *annual* premium if paid monthly?
5. Who is the beneficiary? Who is the contingent beneficiary (the person who receives the policy proceeds at the death of the insured if the first beneficiary is deceased)?
6. How long is the grace period?
7. If the premium is unpaid at the end of the grace period, does this policy automatically lapse?
8. May the insured reinstate the policy if it has lapsed?
9. When does the policy become incontestable (during the time the policy is contestable, the company can seek release from the policy if it is discovered that false statements of a material nature were made in the application for insurance)?
10. Is there an annual dividend on the policy? If so, what will be the anticipated annual dividend this year? At the end of the 10th policy year? At the end of the 20th policy year?
11. If the policy pays dividends, what choices do you have as to how they will be used?
12. How soon after issue may a policy loan be made?
13. What rate of interest is charged on money borrowed from the policy?
14. What is the cash value or loan value of this policy in its 5th year? In its 10th year? In its 15th year? In its 20th year?
15. What nonforfeiture provisions are available if the policy is allowed to lapse?
16. May this policy be converted to any other type of policy?
17. What settlement options does this policy have?
18. Does this policy include a provision for waiver of premium in event of disability? If so, what is the additional premium charge for this provision?
19. If this is a term policy, is it guaranteed renewable?
20. What other pertinent information about the policy do you want to note?

SOURCE: *Life Insurance Teacher's Guide* (Washington, D.C.: American Council of Life Insurance, 1982), p. 32.

FINANCIAL PLANNING WITH ANNUITIES

L.O.6
Recognize how annuities provide security.

An **annuity** is a financial contract written by an insurance company to provide you with a regular income. Generally, you receive the income monthly, with payments often arranged to continue as long as you live. The payments may begin at once or at some future date. The annuity is often described as being the opposite of life insurance. It pays while you live; life insurance pays when you die.

However, fundamental to the annuity principle, as to the life insurance principle discussed earlier, is the predictable mortality experience of a large group of individuals. By determining the average number of years that a large number of persons of a given age group will live, the insurance company can calculate the annual amount that can be paid to each person in the group for his or her entire life.

For example, for annuity purposes, the life expectancy of males aged 76 is about 10 years (see Exhibit 14–7). Thus, if 1,000 males aged 76 each pay a $10,000 premium (a total of $10 million), each can be guaranteed a payment of $1,000 per year for life. Those who live beyond the 10-year average have their "excess" payments funded by those who die before 10 years have elapsed.

Because the annual payouts per premium amount are determined by average mortality experience, annuity contracts are more attractive for persons whose present health, living habits, and family mortality experience suggest that their

EXHIBIT 14–7
1971 Individual Annuity Mortality Table°

Age of Male	Deaths per 1,000	Life Expectancy (Years)	Age of Male	Deaths per 1,000	Life Expectancy (Years)
51	5.86	27.99	71	28.34	13.11
52	6.46	27.15	72	30.93	12.48
53	7.09	26.33	73	33.80	11.86
54	7.74	25.51	74	36.97	11.26
55	8.42	24.71	75	40.49	10.67
56	9.12	23.91	76	44.39	10.10
57	9.85	23.13	77	48.72	9.55
58	10.61	22.35	78	53.50	9.01
59	11.41	21.59	79	58.79	8.50
60	12.25	20.83	80	64.60	7.99
61	13.13	20.08	81	70.90	7.51
62	14.07	19.34	82	77.67	7.05
63	15.08	18.61	83	84.94	6.60
64	16.19	17.89	84	92.87	6.16
65	17.41	17.17	85	101.69	5.74
66	18.77	16.47	86	111.65	5.34
67	20.29	15.77	87	123.05	4.95
68	21.99	15.09	88	136.12	4.57
69	23.89	14.42	89	151.07	4.21
70	26.00	13.76	90	168.04	3.87

°In order to build in a safety factor, the number of deaths per thousand for annuity purposes is somewhat lower than actual experience. This results in the assumption of a higher than actual life expectancy.

SOURCE: *Annuities from the Buyer's Point of View,* Economic Education Bulletin (Great Barrington, Mass.: American Institute for Economic Research, July 1988), p. 122.

lives are likely to be longer than average. As a general rule, annuities are not advisable for persons in poor health, though this rule has its exceptions.

Why Buy Annuities?

A prime reason for buying an annuity is to give you retirement income for the rest of your life. We will discuss retirement income in Chapter 20, "Retirement Planning."

Although people have been buying annuities for many years, the appeal of fixed annuities has increased recently because of rising interest rates and the relative safety of annuities as compared to securities. A *fixed annuity* is a contract stating that the annuitant (the person who is to receive the annuity) will receive a fixed amount of income over a certain period or for life. A *variable annuity*, on the other hand, is a plan under which the monthly payments will vary because they are based on the income received from stocks or other investments.

Some of the recent growth in the use of annuities can be attributed to the passage of the Employee Retirement Income Security Act (ERISA) of 1974. Annuities are often purchased for individual retirement accounts (IRAs), which were made possible by the act. They may also be used in Keogh-type plans for the self-employed. As you will see in Chapter 20, contributions to both IRA and Keogh plans are tax deductible up to specified limits.

What about Taxes?

When you buy an annuity, the interest on the principal, as well as the interest compounded on that interest, builds up free of current income tax. The Tax Reform Act of 1986 preserves the tax advantages of annuities (and insurance) but curtails deductions for IRAs. With an annuity, there is no maximum annual contribution. And if you die during the accumulation period, your beneficiary is guaranteed no less than the amount invested.

Exhibit 14–8 shows the difference between an investment in an annuity and an investment in a certificate of deposit. Remember, federal income tax on an annuity is deferred, whereas the tax on interest earned on a certificate of deposit must be paid currently.

As with any other hot product, however, the advantages of annuities are tempered by drawbacks. In the case of variable annuities, these drawbacks include reduced flexibility and fees that lower investment return.

EXHIBIT 14–8
Tax-Deferred Annuities versus Taxable CDs°

End of Year	8.5 Percent Tax-Deferred Annuity	8.5 Percent Taxable CD	Difference
5	$ 15,037	$13,191	$ 1,846
10	22,610	17,400	5,210
20	51,120	30,275	20,845
30	115,583	52,678	62,905

°This illustration assumes a $10,000 investment and a 33 percent federal income tax rate.
SOURCE: Miller & Schroeder Financial, Inc., *Newsletter/Inventory,* July 1989, p. 3.

SUMMARY

Life insurance is a contract between an insurance company and a policyholder
under which the company agrees to pay a specified sum to a beneficiary upon the
death of the insured.

Most people buy life insurance to protect someone who depends on them from
financial losses caused by their death.

Fundamental to the life insurance principle is the predictable mortality experience of a large group of individuals.

In determining your life insurance needs, you must first determine your insurance
objectives and then use the easy method, the Dink method, the "nonworking"
spouse method, or the thorough method. The thorough method is recommended.

The two types of life insurance companies are stock companies, owned by
stockholders, and mutual companies, owned by policyholders. In general, stock
companies sell nonparticipating policies and mutual companies sell participating
policies.

The three basic types of life insurance are term, whole life, and endowment
policies. There are many variations and combinations of these types.

The naming of the beneficiary, the grace period, policy reinstatement, the
incontestability and suicide clauses, automatic premium loans, the misstatement
of age provision, and the policy loan provision are important provisions in most life
insurance policies. Common riders in life insurance policies are the waiver of
premium disability benefit, the accidental death benefit, and the guaranteed
insurability option.

Before buying life insurance, consider your present and future sources of income,
group life insurance, group annuities (or other pension benefits), and social
security. Then compare the costs of life insurance policies. Examine your policy
before and after the purchase, and choose appropriate settlement options.

An annuity is the opposite of life insurance. It pays while you live; life insurance
pays when you die. An annuity provides you with a regular income during your
retirement years. Annuities are given favorable income tax treatment under the
Tax Reform Act of 1986.

GLOSSARY

Annuity   A contract that provides an income for a specified period of time.

Beneficiary   A person who is designated to receive something, such as life
insurance proceeds, from someone.

Cash value   The cash surrender value of a life insurance policy.

Double indemnity   A benefit under which the company pays twice the face
value of the policy if the insured's death results from an accident.

Endowment life insurance   Provides payment after a specified number of
years to the insured (if living) or the beneficiary.

Incontestability clause   A provision stating that the insurer cannot dispute the validity of a policy after a specified period.

Interest-adjusted index   A method of evaluating the cost of life insurance by taking into account the time value of money.

Nonforfeiture clause   A provision that allows the insured not to forfeit all accrued benefits.

Nonparticipating policy   Life insurance that does not provide policy dividends; also called a nonpar policy.

Participating policy   Life insurance that provides policy dividends; also called a par policy.

Rider   A document attached to a policy that modifies its coverage.

Suicide clause   A provision stating that if the insured dies by suicide, the death benefit will equal the amount of the premium paid.

Term insurance   Protection for a stated period.

Universal life   A policy that combines term insurance and investment elements.

Whole life policy   A plan of insurance for the whole of life, with a specified premium payable for life; also called a straight life policy or an ordinary life policy.

DISCUSSION QUESTIONS

L.O.1   1. How can the principle of home insurance be applied to the lives of persons?

L.O.1   2. What does a life insurance mortality table indicate?

L.O.2   3. Analyze the four methods of determining life insurance requirements. Which method is best, and why?

L.O.3   4. Assess the following types of life insurance policies, and discuss their advantages and disadvantages:
    a. Term life insurance.
    b. Whole life insurance.
    c. Limited payment policy and single-premium policy.
    d. Endowment policy.
    e. Universal life insurance policy.
    f. Variable life insurance policy.
    g. Flexible premium variable life insurance policy.
    h. Group life insurance policy.

L.O.4   5. Which of the provisions in a life insurance contract are important to you? Why?

L.O.5   6. How do you compare the costs of life insurance policies? What are the five factors that affect the cost of a life insurance policy?

L.O.6   7. Why do people buy annuities? Which type of annuity might you purchase? Why?

Opening Case Questions

1. Why has the much-ballyhooed universal life insurance left some buyers and sellers disappointed?

2. Why would the sales presentations for life insurance be more misleading in 1989 than they were a decade ago?

3. Why have new pitfalls for consumers emerged in life insurance sales presentations?

PROBLEMS AND ACTIVITIES

L.O.1 1. Ask an insurance company to send you its annual report. State how that report can assist you in planning to buy your life insurance.

L.O.1 2. Assume that a group consists of 100,000 male members, aged 35, who wish to contribute each year an amount to a common fund sufficient to pay $1,000 to the dependents of each group member who dies during the year. Use the mortality table in Exhibit 14–1 to determine
   a. How many members of the group can be expected to die during the year.
   b. What amount each of the 100,000 members must contribute at the beginning of the year to provide $1,000 for the dependents of those who die before the end of the year.

L.O.2 3. You are the wage earner of a "typical family" with $30,000 gross annual income. Use the easy method to determine how much life insurance you should carry.

L.O.2 4. You and your spouse are in good health and have reasonably secure careers. You each make about $28,000 annually. You own a home with an $80,000 mortgage, and you owe $10,000 on car loans, $5,000 in personal debts, and $3,000 on credit card loans. You have no other debts. You don't have any plans to increase the size of your family in the near future. Estimate your total insurance needs using the Dink method.

L.O.2 5. Tim and Allison are married and have two children, aged 4 and 7. Allison is a "nonworking" spouse who devotes all of her time to household activities. Estimate how much life insurance Tim and Allison should carry.

L.O.2 6. Use Exhibit 14–2 as a worksheet to calculate your own life insurance needs.

L.O.3 7. Obtain premium rates for $25,000 whole life, universal life, and term life policies from local insurance agents. Compare the costs and provisions of these policies.

L.O.4 8. Examine your life insurance policies and the life insurance policies of other members of your family. Note the contractual provisions of each policy. What does the company promise to do in return for premiums?

L.O.5 9. Review the settlement options on your family's life insurance policies, and discuss with your family which option would be the best choice for them at this time.

L.O.5 10. Contact your state insurance department to get information about whether your state requires interest-adjusted cost disclosure.

L.O.6 11. Assume that you have $10,000 to invest for 10 years. You can invest in a certificate of deposit at 8.5 percent or a 10-year tax-deferred annuity at 8.5 percent. Assume a 33 percent federal tax bracket. Use Exhibit 14–8 to find your accumulated account values. Which investment is better, and by how much?

LIFE SITUATION Case 14–1

Identifying the Need for and Amount of Life Insurance

Joanne Kitsos was a 27-year-old single parent. She and her four-year-old son, Brad, lived in a small two-bedroom apartment. Since graduating from high school, Joanne had been employed as a secretary for an insurance company. Brad stayed at a day-care center while Joanne worked.

Joanne found it very difficult to maintain a home for herself and her son on her $13,000 salary. She was often forced to borrow money from her parents. She had a small Christmas savings account in her company's credit union, a $5,000 term life insurance policy, and a $2,000 debt with a local furniture store.

Joanne's two major goals were (1) to increase her income and (2) to protect her income should she become unable to work. She approached her employer to find out how she could progress in her company. She learned that the company had an upward mobility program for employees who had been with it at least five years. Interested employees were given company-paid on-the-job training and college courses to learn one of several jobs. Joanne quickly applied for admission to the program. Within several months, she was able to secure an entry-level position as a computer operator and an accompanying raise in salary.

Joanne then turned her attention toward protecting her income and providing for Brad's future education. She bought a $25,000 term life insurance policy on herself; the policy had a disability rider under which she would be paid if she became disabled and could not work. Joanne had always been unable to stick to a savings plan—withdrawing money as quickly as she deposited it. So she took out a $5,000 endowment policy on Brad that would come due when he was 18 and contribute to his college education. The policy also gave him life insurance protection as long as the premiums were paid.

Questions

1. Was purchasing term insurance and an endowment policy the right decision for Joanne? Why?
2. Did Joanne need additional life insurance? Why?

LIFE SITUATION Case 14–2

Pam's Stage One

Pam is single, aged 21, and a college senior in excellent health. She has no dependents and no plans for marriage. She wants to get established in her career before settling down. She is working part-time to supplement her college grant and meet school and living expenses. She does not receive any support from her widowed mother, who works and just meets her own living expenses.

Pam plans to go to graduate school for her Master of Business Administration degree before looking for a full-time job.

Questions

1. Analyze Pam's need for life insurance. How much life insurance, if any, does she need at this time?
2. What kind of insurance should Pam choose? What options should she select?

SUPPLEMENTARY READINGS

For Additional Information on Life Insurance

Bailard, Thomas E.; David L. Biehl; and Ronald W. Kaiser. *How to Buy the Right Insurance at the Right Price.* Homewood, Ill.: Dow Jones-Irwin, 1989.

Brownlie, William D. *The Life Insurance Buyer's Guide.* New York: McGraw-Hill, 1989.

Life Insurance. Rockville, Md.: National Education Association Special Services, September 1988.

Life Insurance and Annuities: From the Buyer's Point of View. Economic Education Bulletin. Great Barrington, Mass.: American Institute for Economic Research, March 1988.

Lynch, Kerry Anne. *How to Plan for the Harvest Years.* Economic Education Bulletin. Great Barrington, Mass.: American Institute for Economic Research, July 1988.

COMPREHENSIVE CASE FOR PART IV

An Insurance Plan for Fran

Changes in a person's life situation frequently seem to occur in clusters. Fran Voss recently had some major ups and downs in her life situation. She was promoted to district manager of a software development company; her divorce settlement, in which she received custody of her six-year-old son, was finalized; and she learned that her mother could no longer live alone.

Fran's two-income household with one dependent has become a one-income household with two dependents. This change has had a major impact on her insurance needs. Fran's current life insurance coverage is equal to twice her annual salary before her promotion. Fran can purchase a whole life insurance policy from a local agent, or she can obtain additional term insurance through her company. Fran's son is still a beneficiary on one of his father's life insurance policies.

When Fran and her husband were together, both of their jobs provided health insurance, so the family's health insurance was adequate. Fran's son is still covered by his father's policy, and her mother is covered by Medicare. But Fran needs to reevaluate her health and disability coverage and to consider coverage for her mother for expenses not paid by Medicare. Fran can obtain expanded health insurance coverage through her employer, but this would mean paying a portion of the premium or giving up other employee benefits.

To assist her mother with errands and local travel, Fran must purchase a larger car. This purchase is likely to increase the cost of her automobile insurance.

Questions

1. What should be Fran's major objectives in planning her new life insurance program? What factors should she consider in determining how much life insurance coverage she needs? What choice of additional life insurance would you recommend to her? Why?

2. As a result of Fran's changed household situation, what new types of health insurance risks does she face? What are the main health insurance coverages that she should select?

3. What trade-offs exist for Fran in the choice between paying for additional health insurance coverage and reducing other employee benefits.

4. Before purchasing a new car, what actions can Fran take that might minimize her automobile insurance costs? How can Fran reduce her automobile insurance costs once she has purchased a new car?

5. What other areas of personal and financial risk should Fran consider if she wants to develop a complete risk management program? What actions would you recommend to her for dealing with these risk areas?

V

Investing Your Financial Resources

In Part V of *Personal Finance,* we consider how you can increase your financial resources and achieve your economic goals by putting your dollars to work. In Chapter 15, we take up the fundamentals of a

| Planning Your Personal Finances |
| Managing Your Personal Finances |
| Making Your Purchasing Decisions |
| Managing Your Financial Risks |
| Investing Your Financial Resources |
| Controlling Your Financial Future |

personal investment program. In Chapter 16, we examine the details associated with stock investments. In Chapter 17, we present material on investment in various types of bonds. In Chapter 18, we discuss mutual funds, vehicles that enable investors to diversify. Finally, in Chapter 19, we look at real estate and at more speculative investments such as commodities and collectibles. Part V consists of

15

Fundamentals of Investing

There are people who get rich quick by buying and selling an investment at just the right time. These people often seem to hit it lucky without formulating a plan, using investment information, or examining investment alternatives. Sooner or later, however, their luck plays out and they lose money. Over a long period of time, there is no substitute for systematically evaluating potential investments. If you expect your investment program to earn money for you, you must be willing to expend some time and effort in gathering and analyzing the information you need to make quality decisions. In developing your personal investment plan, you can choose from many different types of investment opportunities. One very safe method of accumulating money is the traditional savings account. You can also purchase common stock, preferred stock, bonds, mutual funds, commodities, or collectibles. Each of these investment alternatives has advantages and disadvantages, which we will examine in detail. We will also look at financial information and investment services that help you evaluate your possible choices.

LEARNING OBJECTIVES
After studying this chapter, you will be able to

L.O.1 Explain why it is to your advantage to prepare for and establish an investment program.

L.O.2 Describe how the factors of safety, risk, income, growth, and liquidity affect your investment options.

L.O.3 Identify the major types of investment alternatives available to investors.

L.O.4 Recognize the role of the professional financial planner in your investment program and the sources of financial information that can reduce investment risks.

418

• •

OPENING CASE

Basic Rules for Investing

Bob Martin, 48 and single, had never thought much about saving money or establishing an investment program. He had always enjoyed life and spent everything he could lay his hands on. He always had a new car, bought designer clothes, enjoyed dating, and went on nice vacations. He had almost $3,000 in a savings account, which he thought should be enough to get him through any emergency. In his own words, he was looking forward to the future because he seemed to be on the right track.

But something happened last week that made Bob sit back and take a long, hard look at the track he was really on. Alex Newton, one of his best friends had decided to take their firm's early retirement option. The fact that Alex was going to retire was upsetting, but even more upsetting was the fact that Alex was only two years older than Bob. How could he afford to retire at 50?

Alex had started saving money when he graduated from college. Later, he began investing in what he referred to as quality, long-term stocks and bonds. Early retirement had been one of his long-term goals. He wanted to travel now and eventually to open a small ski-repair business in the Colorado Rockies.

Alex's retirement made Bob sit back and examine his own financial condition. He knew he would never be able to retire unless he changed his lifestyle. That's why he made an appointment with a financial planner who worked for Barns and Barnett Investment Consultants. After a two-hour exploratory meeting, he left the consultant's office with some basic ideas on how to get started. According to the consultant, Bob had to take some logical steps if he was going to change his current financial picture. The consultant made the following suggestions:

1. *Plan Your Financial Future.* Determine short-term and long-term financial objectives that are important to you.

2. *Learn to Budget.* Most people spend money without thinking. A better approach is to determine which expenditures are important and which are unnecessary.

3. *Keep Accurate Records.* A good recordkeeping system lets you see where your money is going. Most experts believe that establishing such a system is one of the most important steps in financial planning.

4 *Take Advantage of Windfalls.* You should use unexpected inheritances, tax refunds, bonuses, and other windfalls to achieve the long-term investment goals of your financial plan.

5. *Reevaluate Your Investment Plan.* Your financial goals and objectives may change over time. You should be able to change your investment plan to meet revised goals and objectives.

Although Bob realized that his financial planning was long overdue, he felt encouraged after his conversation with the consultant. He was excited by the prospect of achieving added security through an increase in his savings and of fulfilling some of his long-term financial objectives through the purchase of quality investments.

For more information, see Wilbur Cross, *Investor Alert:* (New York: Andrews & McMeel, 1988); *Fortune/1989 Investor's Guide* (*Fortune* magazine publishes an updated edition of its investor's guide in the fall of each year); "Where Does All the Money Go?" *Consumer Reports,* September 1986, p. 581; and "Taking Charge of Your Finances," *Parade Magazine,* February 1, 1987, p. 12b.

• •

PREPARING FOR AN INVESTMENT PROGRAM

L.O.1
Explain why it is to your advantage to prepare for and establish an investment program.

Bob Martin, the man in the Opening Case, spent money on new cars, designer clothes, dating, and vacations and yet never got around to starting an investment program. He had never planned for retirement or even thought of starting an investment program until one of his best friends opted for early retirement. Only then did he realize that it was time to consider his financial future.

Simply put, Bob's lifestyle illustrates the problem of making some wrong decisions. His decision to spend *all* of his money on cars, clothes, dating, and vacations was one option. Establishing an investment program was an option that he could have chosen. Like other decisions, the decision to start an investment program is one that you must make for yourself. In fact, that decision may be the most important element in the whole investment process. No one is going to make you establish a financial plan. No one is going to make you save the money necessary to fund an investment program. These things won't be done unless you want to do them.

Personal investment is the use of one's personal funds to earn a financial return. The overall objective of investing is to earn money with money. But that objective is completely useless for the individual investor because it is so vague. The *specific* goals that you want to accomplish must be the driving force behind your investment program.

Establishing Investment Goals

To be useful, investment goals must be specific and measurable. They must be tailored to the particular financial needs of the individual. Some financial planners suggest that investment goals be stated in terms of money: By December 31, 1999, I will have total assets of $120,000. Other financial planners believe that investors are more motivated to work toward goals that are stated in terms of the particular things they desire: By January 1, 1998, I will have accumulated enough money to purchase a second home in the mountains. How the goals are stated depends on the individual to whom they apply. The following questions may help you establish valid investment goals:

1. What will I use the money for, and what will the consequences be if I do not obtain it?
2. How much money do I need to satisfy my investment goals?
3. How will I obtain the money?
4. How much risk am I willing to assume in my investment program?
5. How long will it take me to obtain the money?
6. What possible economic or personal conditions could alter my investment goals?
7. Considering my economic circumstances, are the above goals reasonable?
8. Am I willing to make the sacrifices necessary to ensure that my investment goals are met?

Investment objectives must always be oriented toward the future. In Chapter 3, objectives were classified as short term, intermediate, or long term. These classifications are also useful in planning an investment program. For example, an investor may establish a short-term objective of accumulating $3,000 in a savings account over the next 18 months. The $3,000 may then be used to finance intermediate or long-term investment objectives.

Performing a Financial Checkup

Before beginning an investment program, you must make sure your personal financial affairs are in order. In this section, we will examine different factors that you must consider before making your first investment.

Learn to Live within Your Means   Many potential investors must learn to live within their means before an investment program can become a reality. Many individuals regularly spend more than they make. They purchase items on credit and then must make monthly installment payments and pay finance charges that range between 14 and 24 percent. To remedy this situation, credit purchases should be limited to only the necessities or to purchases required to meet

FINANCIAL PLANNING IN ACTION

An Obvious Need for Financial Planning

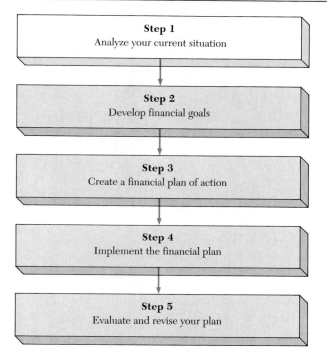

Step 1
Analyze your current situation

Step 2
Develop financial goals

Step 3
Create a financial plan of action

Step 4
Implement the financial plan

Step 5
Evaluate and revise your plan

Mike Denton, 36, was a chemical engineer employed by Exxon Corporation. During 1989, he earned $62,000. Julie, his wife, earned $32,000 a year as a medical technician for a local hospital. Since their marriage, three years ago, they had purchased two new BMWs and a new home in an exclusive Houston suburb. They each had American Express and VISA credit cards, which they used to purchase

almost anything they wanted. According to Mike, everything seemed to be right on track.

One year later, everything was off track. It all started when Mike lost his job—he simply got the boot. Since he had always taken his well-paying job for granted, he and Julie had never thought much about money. Now that he was unemployed, they were suffering because they had not done any financial planning. He was trying not only to find another job but also to pay the monthly bills on a lot less money.

When Mike lost his job, the Dentons had $2,800 in the bank and their monthly expenses totaled more than $4,500. Until Mike found a new job, they had to find a way to live on Julie's $32,000 salary. First, they sold one of the BMWs. Next, they took out a bank loan to pay off their credit card debts. Finally, they put their home up for sale, but they were unable to sell it because of the depressed Houston economy. Eventually, they lost their home when the mortgage company foreclosed on it. They then moved to a one-bedroom apartment.

Fifteen months after losing his job at Exxon, Mike Denton got another engineering job and he and Julie began to rebuild their lives. They both vowed to develop a financial plan. They had learned their lesson well, and they didn't want to make the same mistakes again.

For more information on financial planning, see "Where Does All the Money Go?" *Consumer Reports,* September 1986, p. 581; Don Hayner, "Four Steps to Building A Financial Base," *Chicago Sun-Times,* Sunday, January 8, 1989, p. 57; William Gese, "7 Deadly Investment Sins," *Changing Times,* July 1989, p. 54+; and Walter Updegrave, "Where to Invest Your Money Now," *Money,* July 1989, p. 60+;

emergency situations. A good rule of thumb is to limit installment payments to 10 to 20 percent of your net monthly pay after taxes. Eventually, the amount of cash remaining after the bills are paid will increase and can be used to start a savings program or finance other investment projects. A word of caution: corrective measures take time, and it is impossible to improve a bad situation overnight.

Provide Adequate Insurance Protection   The topic of insurance was discussed in detail in Part IV, and it is not our intention to cover that topic again. However, it is essential for individuals to consider their insurance needs before beginning an investment program. The types of insurance and the amount of coverage will vary from one person to the next. Before you start investing, you should examine the amount of your insurance coverage for life insurance, hospitalization, the family home and other real estate holdings, automobiles, and any other assets that may need coverage.

Start an Emergency Fund   Most financial planners suggest that an investment program should begin with the accumulation of an emergency fund. An *emergency fund* is a certain amount of money that can be obtained quickly in case of immediate need. This money should be deposited in a savings account at the highest available interest rate.

The amount of money that should be salted away in the emergency fund varies from person to person. However, most financial planners agree that an amount equal to three months' salary (after taxes) is reasonable.[1] For example, Debbie Martin earns $24,000 a year. Her monthly take-home pay after deductions is $1,600. Before Debbie can begin investing, she must save $4,800 ($1,600 × 3 months) in a savings account or other near-cash investment to meet any unexpected emergencies. A few financial planners suggest that the amount in an emergency fund should be based on the amount of expenses the individual must pay each month. If you adopt this guideline, an amount equal to three months' expenses is reasonable.

Have Access to Other Sources of Cash for Emergency Needs
financial planners also recommend establishing a line of credit at a commercial bank, savings and loan association, or credit union. A **line of credit** is a short-term loan that is approved before the money is actually needed. Because all of the necessary paperwork has already been completed and the loan has been preapproved, the individual can later obtain the money as soon as it is required.

The cash advance provision offered by major credit card companies can also serve as a source of emergency financing. In addition, credit cards can be used to purchase necessities in an emergency situation.

It should be mentioned, however, that both lines of credit and credit cards have a ceiling, or maximum dollar amount, that limits the amount of available credit. If

From *The Wall Street Journal*, with permission of Cartoon Features Syndicate.

you have already exhausted both of these sources of credit on everyday expenses, they will not be available in an emergency.

Getting the Money Needed to Start an Investment Program

Once you have established your investment goals and completed your personal financial checkup, it's time to start investing—assuming that you have enough money to finance your investments. Unfortunately, that is a wrong assumption in many cases because the needed financing doesn't automatically appear. In today's world, you must work to accumulate the money you need to start any type of investment program.

Priority of Investment Goals   How badly do you want to achieve your investment goals? Are you willing to sacrifice some short-term purchases in order to provide financing for your investments? The answers to both questions are extremely important. Take the case of Rita Johnson, a 32-year-old nurse in a large St. Louis hospital. As part of a divorce settlement in 1986, she received a cash payment of almost $55,000. At first, she was tempted to spend this money on a trip to Europe, a new BMW, and new furniture. But after some careful planning, she decided to invest $35,000 in a long-term certificate of deposit and the remainder in a conservative mutual fund. On December 31, 1990, these investments were valued at $84,000.

As pointed out earlier in this chapter, no one can make you save money to finance your investment program. You have to want to do it. Some suggestions that may help you obtain the money needed for a successful investment program are presented below.

You must pay yourself first. Too often, individuals save or invest what is left over after everything else has been paid. As you might guess, there is nothing left over in many cases, and your investment program is put on hold for another month. A second and much better approach is to (1) pay your monthly bills, (2) save a reasonable amount of money, and (3) use whatever money is left over for personal expenses such as entertainment. This approach allows you to make savings for an investment program a top budget priority.

You should participate in an elective savings program. Many employees can elect to have a specific amount of money withheld from their paychecks each payday. The money withheld by the employer is then deposited in an account for the employee at a bank, savings and loan association, or credit union. Employees can always withdraw their money from the savings account, but they must make a special trip to the bank, savings and loan association, or credit union to do so. Thus, it is much easier to put money into the account than it is to get money out of the account.

You can also make a special savings effort one or two months each year. Some financial planners recommend that investors really cut back to the basics for one or two months each year in order to obtain additional money for investment purposes. Every expenditure during that time is examined, and only the most essential ones are allowed. Expenditures that are not necessities are eliminated.

You should take advantage of gifts, inheritances, and windfalls. During your lifetime, you will receive unexpected sums of money. These may result from gifts, inheritances, salary increases, year-end bonuses, or federal income tax refunds. Most individuals will opt to spend this extra money on something that they could not afford under normal circumstances. An alternative approach is to use the money to fund your investment program.

The Value of Long-Term Investment Programs

Many individuals never start an investment program because they only have a small sum of money. But even small sums of money grow over a long period of time. For example, if you invest $10,000 for 20 years at a 10 percent annual interest rate, your investment will grow to $67,270 during the 20-year period. This means that if you invest $10,000 on your 30th birthday, your investment will have increased to over $67,000 by the time you are 50. The rate of return for an investment does make a difference. Exhibit 15–1 shows how an increase in the interest rate affects the return to the investor at the end of 1 year, 5 years, and 10 years.

Notice that the amount of money returned to the investor increases for each year that the initial investment is left on deposit. For example, the original $5,000 deposited at 8 percent will return $7,345 at the end of five years, which represents an increase of $2,345 over the original investment. It should be noted, however, that the interest earned on the investment illustrated in Exhibit 15–1 is taxable as ordinary income under current Internal Revenue Service guidelines. To avoid this problem, investors sometimes choose one of the tax-free investments that are described later in this chapter. Although taxes must be considered, this complication does not destroy the basic principles of future value. In fact, future value is so important for a successful investment program that you may want to review this Chapter 1 concept before you begin to invest.

A Personal Plan of Action for Investing

To be a successful investor, you must develop a plan and then implement it. The individual begins investment planning by establishing realistic goals. The next step is to perform a personal financial checkup to make sure that he or she is ready to invest. If your goals are realistic and you are ready to invest, investment opportunities will be available. Each opportunity must be evaluated, including the potential return and the risk involved. At the very least, this requires some expert advice and careful study. Then, generally through a process of comparison and elimination, particular alternatives are chosen and combined into an investment plan.

The steps required for an effective personal plan of action are presented in Exhibit 15–2. Your first step is to summarize your investment goals. Your second step is to determine the amount of money that you will obtain by a specific date.

EXHIBIT 15–1

Growth Rate for $5,000 Invested at Current Interest Rates (*Compounded Annually*)

Fixed savings: Starting balance = $5,000

	Balance at the End of Year		
Rate	**1**	**5**	**10**
6%	$5,300	$6,690	$ 8,955
7	5,350	7,015	9,835
8	5,400	7,345	10,795
9	5,450	7,695	11,835
10	5,500	8,053	12,969
11	5,550	8,425	14,197

The total amount of money specified in Step 2 should be based on the goals that you have summarized in Step 1. The amount of money that you now have available for investment purposes is specified in Step 3. For most investors, the money currently available for investment purposes has been accumulated over a period of time. For example, Shannon and Fred Rogers began saving $200 a month to finance a future investment program over three years ago. The money was deposited in an interest-bearing savings account. Now, after three years, they have accumulated over $9,000 to finance an investment program. In Step 4, specific investment alternatives are listed.

Because of the relationship between projected returns and risk factors for each investment alternative, Step 5 is divided into two components. Step 5A examines the projected return for each investment alternative. Step 5B examines the risk factor associated with each of these alternatives. In Step 6, the choice of investments is reduced to the top three alternatives. A final decision to choose the top two alternatives is made in Step 7. By choosing at least two alternatives, you are building a certain amount of diversification into your investment program and avoiding the problem of putting all your eggs in one basket.

EXHIBIT 15–2   A Personal Plan of Action for Investing

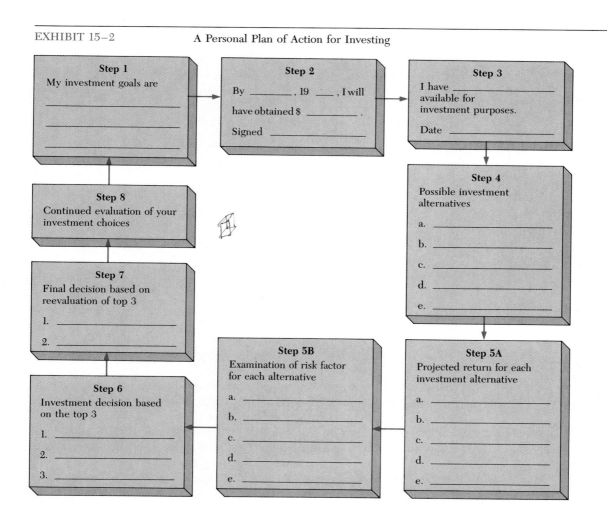

Step 8 provides for continued evaluation of your investments. The circumstances of investors often change as they go through life. As a result, investors are often forced to adapt their planning to new situations. For example, if an investor takes a new job at a substantially higher salary, changes in investment goals may make his or her present investment plan obsolete.

Also, different investment alternatives may become more or less attractive because of changes in economic and financial conditions. During the early 1980s, for example, many investors sold their holdings in common stocks and invested the money in certificates of deposit (CDs) that paid high guaranteed interest. A short time later, many of the same investors cashed in their CDs, which were now paying lower interest rates, and purchased common stocks that were rebounding from low values.

If, after careful evaluation, you feel that for any reason your financial plan or your investment goals need changing, then change them.

To illustrate, let's fill in the blanks in Exhibit 15–2, using the case of Sally Morton, who got a promising job in advertising after college graduation. After three years, Sally is earning $30,000 a year. Her take-home pay after deductions is $2,000 a month. Her living expenses come to about $1,600 a month, which leaves a surplus of $400. Sally has no family responsibilities, so she must decide what to do with the extra money. After graduating from college, she immediately began saving a portion of each month's surplus. Now she has $14,000 available for investment purposes, as illustrated in Step 3 of Exhibit 15–3. If Sally applies the model for personal financial planning presented in Exhibit 15–2 to her specific situation, she will develop a plan that establishes the goals she thinks are important. Sally's plan is illustrated in Exhibit 15–3.

Your own plan may be quite different from Sally's, but the principle is the same. Each individual has different ideas and goals. Establish your investment goals first, and then follow through.

FACTORS AFFECTING THE CHOICE OF INVESTMENTS

L.O.2
Describe how the factors of safety, risk, income, growth, and liquidity affect your investment options.

Millions of Americans have a savings account, buy stocks or bonds, purchase gold and silver, or make similar investments. And they all have reasons for investing their money. Some individuals want to supplement their retirement income when they reach age 65, while others want to become millionaires before they are 50. Although each investor may have specific, individual reasons for investing, there are a number of factors that all investors must consider.

The Safety and Risk Factors

The safety and risk factors are two sides of the same coin. You cannot evaluate any investment without assessing how the factor of safety relates to the factor of risk. Safety in an investment means minimal risk of loss. On the other hand, risk in an investment means a measure of uncertainty about the outcome. Investments range from very safe to very risky. At one end of the investment spectrum are very safe investments that attract conservative investors. Investments in this category include government bonds, savings accounts and certificates of deposit, and certain stocks and bonds. Mutual funds and real estate may also be very safe investments. Investors pick such investments because they know there is very little chance that investments of this kind will become worthless.

At the other end of the investment spectrum are very risky investments. Such investments offer the possibility of a larger dollar return, but if they are

EXHIBIT 15–3   A Personal Plan of Action for Sally Morton

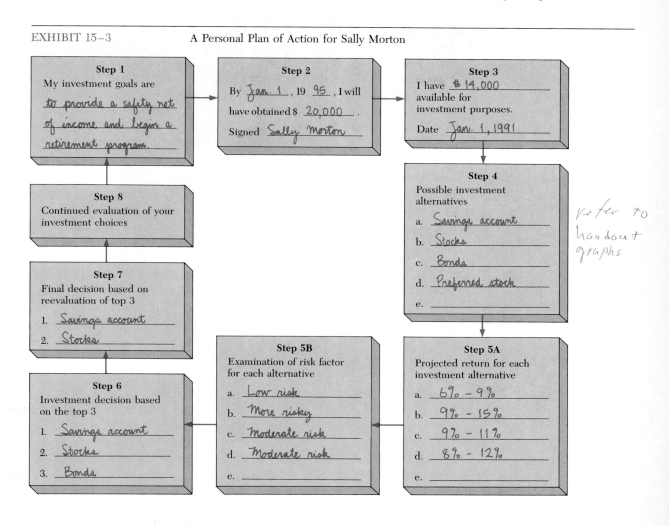

Step 1

My investment goals are

to provide a safety net of income and begin a retirement program.

Step 2

By *Jan. 1*, 19 *95*, I will have obtained $ *20,000* .

Signed *Sally Morton*

Step 3

I have $ *14,000* available for investment purposes.

Date *Jan. 1, 1991*

Step 8

Continued evaluation of your investment choices

Step 4

Possible investment alternatives

a. *Savings account*

b. *Stocks*

c. *Bonds*

d. *Preferred stock*

e. _____

refer to handout graphs

Step 7

Final decision based on reevaluation of top 3

1. *Savings account*

2. *Stocks*

Step 6

Investment decision based on the top 3

1. *Savings account*

2. *Stocks*

3. *Bonds*

Step 5B

Examination of risk factor for each alternative

a. *Low risk*

b. *More risky*

c. *Moderate risk*

d. *Moderate risk*

e. _____

Step 5A

Projected return for each investment alternative

a. *6% – 9%*

b. *9% – 15%*

c. *9% – 11%*

d. *8% – 12%*

e. _____

unsuccessful, the investor may lose most or all of the initial investment. Speculative stocks, certain bonds, certain types of real estate, commodities, options, precious metals, gemstones, and collectibles are risk-oriented investments. Such investments, discussed in detail in later chapters, are often considered too risky for the smaller, beginning investor.

From an investor's standpoint, one basic rule sums up the relationship between the factors of safety and risk:

The potential return on any investment should be directly related to the risk that the investor assumes.

For example, an investor who wants an investment with virtually no risk may choose to invest in a stock that offers an 8 percent dividend and a great degree of safety because of the financial stability of the corporation that issued it. A more risk-oriented investor (sometimes referred to as a *speculator*) may choose to invest in a more speculative stock that offers a greater potential for dollar gain in market value even though the corporation that issued it is not paying any dividends at present.

By now, you probably realize that the safety and risk factors are more complex than the two simple definitions presented above. According to John J. Curran, an editor of *Fortune* magazine, "The financial world, as any weather-worn veteran knows, is a muddle of risk and opportunity."[2] The problem of assessing safety and risk is further complicated by the large number of potential investments from which the investor may choose. Every investor must determine how much risk he or she is willing to assume. To help you determine how much risk you are willing to assume, take the test for risk tolerance presented in Exhibit 15–4.

Components of the Risk Factor

The factor of risk associated with a specific investment does change from time to time. For example, the stock of Computer-Tabulating-Recording Company was considered a risky investment. Today, the company is known as International Business Machines (IBM) and its stock is part of most conservative investment portfolios. When choosing an investment, you must carefully evaluate changes in the risk factor. In fact, the overall risk factor can be broken down into the following four components.

Inflation Risk   During inflationary times, there is a risk that the financial return on an investment will not keep pace with the rate of inflation. To see how inflation reduces the buying power of investments, let's say that you have deposited $1,000 in the bank at 7 percent interest. At the end of one year, your money would have earned $70 in interest ($1,000 × 7% = $70). Assuming an inflation rate of 9 percent, it would cost you $1,090 to purchase the same amount of goods that you could have purchased for $1,000 a year earlier. Thus, even though your bank account earned $70, you have lost $20 in purchasing power.

Interest Rate Risk   The interest rate risk associated with a fixed return investment in a preferred stock or a government or corporate bond is the result of changes in the interest rates in the economy. The value of a fixed return investment decreases when overall interest rates increase and increases when overall interest rates decrease. For example, suppose that you purchase a $1,000 corporate bond that matures in 15 years and pays 9 percent interest until maturity. This means that the corporation will pay you $90 ($1,000 × 9% = $90) each year for the next 15 years. If bond interest rates increase to 11 percent, the market value of your 9 percent bond will decrease. No one is willing to purchase your bond at the price you paid for it since at that price a comparable bond that pays 11 percent can be purchased. As a result, you would have to sell your bond for less than $1,000 or hold the bond until maturity. If you decide to sell the bond, the approximate dollar price that you could sell it for would be $818 ($90 ÷ 11% = $818). This price would provide the purchaser with an 11 percent return, and you would lose $182 ($1,000 − $818 = $182) because you owned a bond with a fixed interest rate during a period when overall interest rates in the economy increased.

Business Failure Risk   The risk of business failure is associated with investments in common stock, preferred stock, and corporate bonds. With each of these investments, you face the possibility that bad management, unsuccessful products, or a host of other reasons may cause a business to be less profitable than was originally anticipated. Lower profits usually mean lower dividends or no dividends

EXHIBIT 15–4

A Quick Test for Risk Tolerance

The following quiz, adapted from one prepared by the T. Rowe Price group of mutual funds, aims to help investors discover how comfortable they are with varying degrees of risk. Other things being equal, your risk tolerance score is a useful guide in deciding how heavily your portfolio should be weighted toward start-ups or blue chips, junk bonds or Treasury bills—while allowing you a peaceful night's sleep. A four-page primer on asset allocation that includes the quiz is available from T. Rowe Price at 100 East Pratt Street, Baltimore, MD 21202 (800-638-5660).

1. You're the winner on a TV game show. Which prize would you choose?
    ☐ $2,000 in cash (1 point).
    ☐ A 50% chance to win $4,000 (3 points).
    ☒ A 20% chance to win $10,000 (5 points).
    ☐ A 2% chance to win $100,000 (9 points).
2. You're down $500 in a poker game. How much more would you be willing to put up to win the $500 back?
    ☐ More than $500 (8 points).
    ☒ $500 (6 points).
    ☐ $250 (4 points).
    ☐ $100 (2 points).
    ☐ Nothing—you'll cut your losses now (1 point).
3. A month after you invest in a stock, it suddenly goes up 15%. With no further information, what would you do?
    ☒ Hold it, hoping for further gains (3 points).
    ☐ Sell it and take your gains (1 point).
    ☐ Buy more—it will probably go higher (4 points).
4. Your investment suddenly goes down 15% one month after you invest. Its fundamentals still look good. What would you do?
    ☐ Buy more. If it looked good at the original price, it looks even better now (4 points).
    ☒ Hold on and wait for it to come back (3 points).
    ☐ Sell it to avoid losing even more (1 point).
5. You're a key employee in a start-up company. You can choose one of two ways to take your year-end bonus. Which would you pick?
    ☐ $1,500 in cash (1 point).
    ☒ Company stock options that could bring you $15,000 next year if the company succeeds, but will be worthless if it fails (5 points).

Your total score: _23_

_2_

Scoring

5–18 points:
More Conservative Investor. You prefer to minimize financial risks. The lower your score, the more cautious you are. When you choose investments, look for high credit ratings, well-established records, and an orientation toward stability. Avoid bonds with the very highest yields; they pay those yields because they involve bigger risks. In stocks and real estate, look for a focus on income.

19–30 points:
Less Conservative Investor. You are willing to take more chances in pursuit of greater rewards. The higher your score, the bolder you are. When you invest, look for high overall returns within the appropriate time category. You may want to consider bonds with the steepest yields and lower credit ratings, the stocks of newer companies, and real estate investments that use mortgage debt.

SOURCE: T. Rowe Price Mutual Funds, 100 East Pratt Street, Baltimore, MD 21202.

at all. If the business continues to operate at a loss, even interest payments and repayment of bond indebtedness may be questionable. The business may even fail and be forced to file for bankruptcy, in which case your investment may become totally worthless. Of course, the best way to protect yourself against such losses is to evaluate carefully the investments you make.

Market Risk   The price of stocks, bonds, and other investments may fluctuate because of the behavior of investors in the marketplace. As a result, economic growth is not as systematic and predictable as most investors would like to believe. Generally, a period of rapid expansion is followed by a period of recession. During periods of recession, it may be quite difficult to sell such investments as real estate. Fluctuations in the market price for stocks and bonds may have nothing to do with the fundamental changes in the financial health of corporations. Such fluctuations may be caused by political or social conditions. For example, the price of petroleum stocks may increase or decrease as a result of political activity in the Middle East.

The Income Factor

Investors sometimes purchase certain investments because they want a predictable return or distribution of income from the investment. The safest investments—passbook savings accounts, CDs, U.S. savings bonds, and U.S. Treasury notes—are also the most predictable source of income for an investor. With these investments, the investor knows exactly what the interest rate is and how much income will be paid on a specific future date.

If income is a primary objective, most investors choose corporate bonds, preferred stock, or conservative common stock issues. When purchasing stocks or bonds for potential income, most investors are concerned about a corporation's overall profits, future earnings picture, and dividend policies. For example, some corporations are very proud of their long record of consecutive dividend payments and will maintain that policy if at all possible (see Exhibit 15–5). For some corporations, consistent dividend policies are a matter of pride. For other corporations, maintaining dividend payments is an obvious reward to stockholders who purchase their stock and an incentive to purchase more.

Other investments that provide income potential are mutual funds and real estate rental property. Although the income from mutual funds is not guaranteed, investors can choose funds whose primary objective is income. Income from real estate rental property is not guaranteed because there is always the possibility of either vacancies or unexpected repair bills. Yet one of the objectives in investing in rental property is to generate income. The more speculative investments, such as commodities, options, precious metals, gemstones, and collectibles, offer little, if any, potential for regular income.

The Growth Factor

To investors, growth means that their investment will increase in value. To some extent, all investments may grow. The chief difference among investments is how fast growth occurs. Often, the greatest opportunity for growth is an investment in common stock. During the 1980s, investors found that stocks issued by corporations in the electronics, energy, and health care industries provided the greatest growth potential. In fact, goods and services provided by companies in these industries will be in even greater demand in the next 5 to 10 years.

EXHIBIT 15–5

Corporations with Consecutive Dividend Payments for at Least 80 Years

Corporation	Dividends Since	Type of Business
Allied Corporation	1887	Chemical and petroleum products
American Telephone & Telegraph	1881	Telephone utility
Borden, Inc.	1899	Foods
Burroughs Corporation	1895	Computers
Citicorp	1903	Banking
Commonwealth Edison Company	1890	Electric utility
Continental Corporation	1854	Insurance
Du Pont (E. I.) de Nemours & Co.	1904	Chemicals
Eastman Kodak Company	1902	Photography
Exxon Corporation	1882	Chemical and petroleum products
General Electric Company	1899	Electrical equipment
Kroger Company	1902	Foods
Norfolk & Western Railway	1901	Railroad
PPG Industries, Inc.	1899	Glass
Procter & Gamble Company	1891	Soap products
Standard Oil Company (Indiana)	1894	Chemical and petroleum products
Sterling Drug, Inc.	1902	Drugs
Union Pacific Corporation	1900	Railroad

When growth stocks are purchased, investors must often sacrifice immediate cash dividends in return for greater dollar value in the future. For most growth companies, profits that would normally be paid to common stockholders in the form of dividends are reinvested in the companies in the form of *retained earnings.* The money kept by the companies can provide at least part of the capital they need for future growth and expansion. As a result, they grow at an even faster pace. Growth financed by retained earnings normally increases the dollar value of stock for the investor.

Certificates of deposit (assuming that the interest is allowed to accumulate), corporate bonds, mutual funds, and real estate may offer growth possibilities. Precious metals, gemstones, and collectibles are more speculative investments that offer less predictable growth possibilities, and investments in commodities and options are more speculative investments that usually stress immediate returns as opposed to continued growth. Generally, government bonds are not purchased for growth.

The Liquidity Factor

Liquidity is the ease with which an asset can be converted to cash without a substantial loss in dollar value. Investments range from cash or near cash to a frozen investment from which it is impossible to get your money. Cash is the most liquid asset because no conversion is necessary. Checking and savings accounts are very liquid investments because they can be quickly converted to cash. Another type of bank account, a certificate of deposit, is not quite as liquid as a checking or savings account. With a certificate of deposit, there are penalties for withdrawing money before the maturity date.

With other investments, you may be able to sell quickly, but market conditions, economic conditions, or many other reasons may prevent you from regaining the amount of money you originally invested. For example, the owner of real estate may have to lower the asking price in order to find a buyer. It may even be difficult to find a buyer for investments in such collectibles as antiques and paintings.

AN OVERVIEW OF INVESTMENT ALTERNATIVES

L.O.3
Identify the major types of investment alternatives available to investors.

When establishing an investment program, investors should begin by gathering as much information as possible about investment alternatives. Then they will be able to decide whether purchasing stocks, bonds, mutual funds, real estate, or other investment alternatives is a better use of their money than putting it in the bank. Before examining the above investment alternatives, let's review the typical financial services available at a bank, savings and loan association, or credit union.

As pointed out in Chapter 5, most Americans have a passbook savings account at some time. Savings accounts provide a safe place to store money—especially your emergency fund. A second option is a certificate of deposit (CD). A CD's chief advantage over a passbook savings account is that the CD pays a higher rate of interest. A third option is a NOW (negotiable order of withdrawal) account. A NOW account is an interest-bearing checking account.

Once you have established your emergency fund and have some money in the bank, it's time to consider other investment alternatives. The material in the remainder of this section provides a brief overview of investment alternatives. In the remaining chapters of Part V, more detailed information is provided on stocks, bonds, mutual funds, real estate, and other investment alternatives.

Stock or Equity Financing

Equity capital is money that a business obtains from its owners. If a business is a sole proprietorship or a partnership, equity capital is acquired when the owners invest their own money in the business. In the case of a corporation, equity capital is provided by stockholders who buy shares of its stock. Since all stockholders are owners, they share in the success of the corporation. This can make buying stock an attractive investment opportunity.

However, you should consider at least two factors before investing in stock. First, a corporation is not obligated to repay the money obtained from the sale of stock or to repurchase the stock at a later date. A stockholder who decides to sell his or her stock must sell it to another investor. In many cases, a stockholder sells a stock because he or she thinks its price is going to decrease in value. The purchaser, on the other hand, buys that stock because he or she thinks its price is going to increase. This creates a situation in which either the seller or the buyer is going to lose money.

Second, a corporation is under no legal obligation to pay dividends to stockholders. Dividends are paid out of earnings, but if a corporation that usually pays dividends should have a bad year, its board of directors can vote to omit the dividend payments in order to help pay necessary business expenses. Corporations may also retain earnings so that they can be used for expansion, research and development, or other business activities.

There are two types of stock—common stock and preferred stock. Both types have advantages and disadvantages that you should consider before deciding on which to use for an investment program. A share of common stock represents the most basic form of corporate ownership. Most large corporations sell common stock to satisfy a large part of their financing needs.

A corporation generally issues only one type of common stock, but it can issue many types of preferred stocks, with different features and different dividends or dividend rates. The most important priority an investor in preferred stock enjoys is receiving cash dividends before common stockholders are paid any cash dividends. This factor is especially important when a corporation is experiencing financial problems and cannot pay cash dividends to both preferred and common stockholders. Other factors that you should consider before purchasing common or preferred stock will be discussed in Chapter 16.

Corporate and Government Bonds

Debt capital is money that corporations or governments obtain by borrowing from outside sources. In many cases, the outside sources are investors like you. There are two types of bonds that an investor should consider. A **corporate bond** is a corporation's written pledge that it will repay a specified amount of money, with interest. A **government bond** is the written pledge of a government or a municipality that it will repay a specified sum of money, with interest. Regardless of who issues the bond, you need to consider two major questions before investing in bonds. First, will the bond be repaid at maturity? The maturity dates for most bonds range between 1 and 40 years. An investor who purchases a bond has two options: keep the bond until maturity and then redeem it, or sell the bond to another investor. In either case, the value of the bond is closely tied to the ability of the corporation or the government agency to repay the bond indebtedness. Second, will the corporation or government agency be able to maintain interest payments to bondholders? Bondholders normally receive interest payments every six months. Again, if a corporation or a government agency cannot pay the interest on its bonds, the value of those bonds will decrease.

Holding bonds until maturity is one method of making money on this type of investment. Investors also use two other methods that can provide more liberal returns on bond investments. Each of these methods will be discussed in Chapter 17.

Mutual Funds

A **mutual fund** is an investment alternative available to individuals who pool their money to buy stocks, bonds, certificates of deposit, and other securities based on the selections of professional managers who work for an investment company. Professional management is an especially important factor for small investors with little or no previous experience in financial matters. Another reason why investors choose this investment alternative is *diversification*. Since mutual funds invest in various types of securities, an occasional loss in one security is often offset by gains in other securities.

The goals of one investor may differ from those of another investor. The managers of mutual funds realize this and tailor programs to meet individual needs and objectives. While most investors consider mutual funds a long-term, conservative investment, some mutual funds are more speculative than others. In fact, mutual funds range from very conservative to extremely speculative investments. Although investing money in a mutual fund provides professional management, even the best managers can make errors in judgment. The responsibility for choosing the right mutual fund is still the individual investor's. More information on the different types of mutual funds, the costs that they involve, and techniques for evaluating them is presented in Chapter 18.

Real Estate

Real estate ownership represents one of the best hedges against inflation. But not all property will increase in value. Poor location, for example, can cause a piece of property to decrease in value. Many people were "taken" by unscrupulous promoters who sold inaccessible land in the Florida Everglades.

Any investment has its disadvantages, and real estate is no exception. To sell your property, you must find an interested buyer who is able to obtain enough money to complete the transaction. Finding a buyer can be difficult if loan money is scarce, if the real estate market is in a decline, or if you overpaid for a piece of property. If you are forced to hold your investment longer than you originally planned, taxes and installment payments must also be considered. As a rule, real estate increases in value and eventually sells at a profit, but there are no guarantees. Success in real estate investments depends on how well you evaluate alternatives. Questions concerning a real estate property that deserve answers include the following:

1. Is the property priced competitively with similar properties?
2. What type of financing, if any, is available?
3. How much are the taxes?
4. What is the condition of the buildings and houses in the immediate area?
5. Why are the present owners selling the property?
6. Is there a chance that the property will decrease in value?

Additional information on how to evaluate a real estate investment is presented in Chapter 19.

Other Investment Alternatives

A **speculative investment** is an investment that is made in the hope of earning a relatively large profit in a short time. By its very nature, any investment may be speculative—that is, it may be quite risky. However, a *true* speculative investment is speculative because of the methods that investors use to earn a quick profit. This section provides a brief overview of speculative investments in commodities, options, and precious metals, gemstones, and collectibles.

Commodities   The ownership of certain commodities—cattle, hogs, pork bellies, wheat, corn, soybeans, rice, oats, sugar, coffee, cocoa, cotton, and many others—is traded on a regular basis. A commodity exchange provides a place for investors and speculators to buy and sell commodity contracts. The principal commodity exchanges include the Chicago Mercantile Exchange, the Kansas City Board of Trade, and the New York Futures Exchange. While it is possible to buy commodities for immediate delivery (this is sometimes called *spot trading*), most transactions involve a future delivery date. A **futures contract** is an agreement to buy or sell a commodity at a guaranteed price on some specified future date. You should not trade in commodities unless you understand all of the procedures and risks that are explained in Chapter 19.

Options   An **option** gives an investor the right to buy or sell 100 shares of a stock at a predetermined price within a specified period of time. Investors who think that a stock's market value or price will increase during a short period of time may decide to purchase a call option. A **call option** is sold by a stockholder and gives the purchaser the right to buy 100 shares of a stock at a guaranteed price before a definite expiration date. On the other hand, some investors may feel that a stock's price will go down during the option period. To safeguard their investment, these investors may purchase a put option. A **put option** is the right to sell 100 shares of a stock at a guaranteed price before a definite expiration date.

Whether the investor purchases a call option or a put option, the expiration date must be considered. If either type of option cannot be exercised before the expiration date, the investor loses the cost of the option. Needless to say, options are risky business and not something for the inexperienced investor. The practical details needed for investing in options are presented in Chapter 16.

Precious Metals, Gemstones, and Collectibles   Investments in this category include gold, silver, and other precious metals; gemstones; and such collectibles as coins, stamps, antiques, and paintings. Without exception, investments of this kind are normally referred to as high-risk investments for one reason or another. For example, the gold market is ridden with unscrupulous dealers who sell worthless gold-plated lead coins to unsuspecting, uninformed investors. With each of the investments in this category, it is extremely important that you deal with reputable dealers and recognized investment firms. It pays to be careful. While investments in this category can lead to large dollar gains, they should not be used by anyone who does not fully understand the risks involved. Information on precious metals, gemstones, and collectibles is presented in Chapter 19.

Summary of the Factors That Affect the Choice of Investments

Earlier in this chapter, we examined how the factors of safety, risk, income, growth, and liquidity affect your investment choices. In the preceding section, we took a look at available investment alternatives. Now it is possible to compare the factors that affect the choice of investments with each of these alternatives. Exhibit 15–6 ranks the alternatives high, average, or low for the factors of safety, risk, income, growth, and liquidity.

EXHIBIT 15–6   The Risks Involved with Typical Investment Alternatives

Type of Investment	Factors to Be Evaluated				
	Safety	**Risk**	**Income**	**Growth**	**Liquidity**
Bank accounts	High	Low	Average	Low	High
Common stock	Average	Average	Average	High	Average
Preferred stock	Average	Average	High	Average	Average
Corporate bonds	Average	Average	High	Low	Average
Government bonds	High	Low	High	Low	High
Mutual funds	Average	Average	Average	Average	Average
Real estate	Average	Average	Average	Average	Low
Commodities	Low	High	N/A	Low	Average
Options	Low	High	N/A	Low	Average
Precious metals, gemstones, and collectibles	Low	High	N/A	Low	Low

N/A = Not applicable.

FINANCIAL PLANNERS AND OTHER FACTORS THAT REDUCE INVESTMENT RISK

L.O.4
Recognize the role of the professional financial planner in your investment program and the sources of financial information that can reduce investment risks.

More information is available to investors today than ever before. Sources of investment information include financial planners, newspapers, corporate reports, and investors' services. Even your own financial records should help you fine-tune your investment program. In the last section of this chapter, we will examine the factors that can spell the difference between success and failure for an investor.

The Role of a Financial Planner

Personal financial planning was defined in Chapter 1 as the process of managing your money to achieve personal economic satisfaction. In an attempt to achieve financial goals, most individuals seek professional help. In many cases, they turn to lawyers, accountants, bankers, or insurance agents. However, these professionals are specialists in one specific field and may not be qualified to provide the type of advice required to develop a thorough financial plan.

A *true* financial planner has had at least two years of training in securities, insurance, taxes, real estate, and estate planning and has passed a rigorous examination. As evidence of training and successful completion of the qualifying examination, the College of Financial Planning in Denver allows individuals who have completed the necessary courses and successfully passed the examination to use the designation Certified Financial Planner (CFP). In a similar manner, the American College in Bryn Mawr, Pennsylvania, allows individuals to use the designation Chartered Financial Consultant (ChFC) if they complete the necessary requirements.

Financial planners may be divided into one or two categories. The first category consists of the financial planners who charge a fee but have no financial interest in the investment or insurance products they recommend. Most financial planners in this first category charge consultant's fees that range between $100 and $125 an hour.

The second category consists of the financial planners who earn a commission on any insurance, stocks, mutual funds, or other investments that the client buys. These individuals are often employed by financial services companies with a nationwide network of offices. Critics contend that the financial planning assistance provided by such planners and the companies they represent is just a marketing ploy to sell their investment or insurance products.

Before choosing a financial planner, you should ask some questions to determine whether you and the financial planner are on the same wavelength with regard to investment goals and objectives. Typical questions include the following:

1. How much training and experience does the financial planner have?
2. Can you talk to clients who have used the financial planner's services?
3. What do local bankers, lawyers, and accountants say about the financial planner?
4. How much will consultation with the financial planner cost?
5. After the initial consultation, do you feel that you will be able to achieve your investment objectives with the help of the financial planner?

Don't be surprised if your financial planner wants to ask you a few questions too. To provide better service, he or she must know what type of investment program you want to establish. Often, this initial conversation will last a couple of hours. It is important that you be honest with the financial planner. Your honesty ensures that both parties understand their responsibilities. If, after a reasonable period of time, you become dissatisfied with your investment program, do not hesitate to

..

PERSONAL FINANCE JOURNAL

How to Choose a Financial Adviser

Picking a financial adviser isn't easy. The professional qualifications and personal virtues of financial advisers vary tremendously. And if you select the wrong adviser, the financial results can be disastrous.

After years of managing their own toy factory, Rudolf and Anastasia Koestner of Norwalk, Connecticut, decided it was time to retire. They sold their factory for $975,000 and invested their money with James L. Condron—an investment adviser in Wilton, Connecticut. The Koestners chose Condron because he told them that the government checked his books every two weeks. He also told them that his own father invested with him.

Condron was so convincing that he was able to raise more than $4 million over a two-year period. Most of his investors were happy because he convinced them that their investments were increasing in value. In reality, however, the value of the investments that he managed decreased to less than $1 million. In February 1985, the Securities and Exchange Commission (SEC) charged Condron and his associates with engaging in fraud, lying to investors, and misappropriating assets. Investors also initiated legal actions against Condron.*

Actually, the Koestners were like a lot of investors today. Investors, on the whole, don't ask enough questions. While the majority of financial advisers are honest, a few are not. When you choose an adviser to help you manage your investments, you ought to be curious about where the adviser's ideas come from and what factors determine his or her investment strategies.

The trick to finding the right financial adviser is to take enough time to ask the right questions. Actually, most of the reliable financial planners encourage questions because this is one way of finding out whether the investor understands the adviser's suggestions.

In addition to asking questions, try to determine whether the investment suggestions of the prospective financial adviser are based on what has succeeded in the past. Suggestions of this type represent what has happened, not what will happen. A good financial adviser should be able to justify investment suggestions based on his or her knowledge of the volatile financial world.

One last point. The number of financial advisers registered with the SEC has more than doubled since 1981.† As a result, investors have more financial advisers to choose from. If you don't feel comfortable with a prospective financial adviser, keep looking until you find one that will help you achieve your investment objectives.

---

*"SEC Files Show How Easily People Take Dubious Investment Advice," *The Wall Street Journal,* November 18, 1986, p. 39.
†Ibid. For more information, see Michael K. Farr, "Tips on Finding an Investment Advisor," *Consumers' Research,* November 1989, pp. 35–37; Andrea Rock, "Finance Advice You Can Trust," *Money,* November 1989, pp. 80–82+; Jill Rachlin, "They've Got Your Money in Their Hands," *U.S. News & World Report,* February 16, 1987, p. 59+; and "Brokerage Firms Scramble to Offer Investment Advice Tied to Tax Bill, *The Wall Street Journal,* October 6, 1986, p. 31.

..

discuss this with the financial planner. You may even find it necessary to choose another financial planner if your dissatisfaction continues. This step is not at all uncommon. But when all is said and done, it is your money and you must make the final decisions that help meet your investment goals. Further information on selecting a financial planner is presented in Appendix A.

Your Role in the Investment Process

Good investors continually assess the value of their investments. They never sit back and let their money manage itself. Obviously, different types of investments will require different methods of evaluation. Some basic elements of evaluation are described below.

Monitor the Value of Your Investment   If you invest your money in a savings account, a checking account, or a certificate of deposit, most financial institutions will provide you with a detailed statement of all activity in the accounts. If you choose to invest in stocks, bonds, mutual funds, commodities, or options, the value of your holdings can be determined by looking at the price quotations reported daily in the financial section of your local newspaper. Your real estate holdings may be compared with similar properties that are currently available for sale in the surrounding area. The value of your precious metals and gemstones may be determined by checking with reputable dealers and investment firms. Finally, the value of collectibles is usually determined by comparing your investment with the value of similar articles. Regardless of which type of investment you choose, close surveillance will keep you informed of whether your investment increases in value, remains the same, or falls in value.

Keep Accurate and Current Records   All of the information relating to a particular investment should be kept together so that it is readily available. Accurate recordkeeping is necessary for tax purposes, but it can also help you spot opportunities to maximize profits or reduce dollar losses when you sell your investments. And accurate recordkeeping can help you decide whether you want to invest additional funds in a particular investment. It will also enable you to do at least three simple calculations that help you monitor the success of an investment.

1. Calculation of Current Yield   One of the most common calculations that investors use to monitor the value of their investments is the current yield. The **current yield** is the yearly dollar amount of income generated by any investment divided by the investment's current market value. For example, let us assume that you purchase stock in General Motors Corporation. Let us also assume that General Motors pays an annual dividend of $2.75 and is currently selling for $41 a share. The current dividend yield is 6.7 percent, as calculated below:

$$\text{Current yield} = \frac{\text{Annual income amount}}{\text{Market value}}$$
$$= \frac{\$2.75}{\$41}$$
$$= 0.067, \text{ or } 6.7 \text{ percent}$$

This example involves common stock, but the same procedure will work for bonds, mutual funds, and other investments that provide annual income.

2. Calculation of Total Return   Although the current yield calculation is useful, you should also consider whether the investment is increasing or decreasing in dollar value. **Total return** is a calculation that includes not only the yearly dollar amount of income but also any increase or decrease in the original purchase price of the investment.

Total return = Current return + Future return

While this concept may be used for any investment, let us illustrate it by using the assumptions for General Motors stock presented in the preceding example. Assume, in addition, that you own 100 shares of the stock and that you hold your stock for two years before deciding to sell it at the current market price of $53 a share. Your total return for this investment would be $1,750, as calculated below:

$$\text{Total return} = \text{Current return} + \text{Future return}$$
$$\$1,750 \quad = \quad \$550 \quad + \quad \$1,200$$

In this example, the current return of $550 results from the payment of dividends for two years ($2.75 per share dividend $\times$ 100 shares $\times$ 2 years). The future return of $1,200 results from the increase in the stock price, from $41 a share to $53 a share ($12 per share increase $\times$ 100 shares $=$ $1,200). (Of course, commissions to buy and sell your stock—a topic covered in the next chapter—would reduce your total return.)

Since in this example the investment increased in value, the total return was greater than the current return. For an investment that decreases in value, the total return will be less than the current return.

3. Annualized Holding Period Yield   The **annualized holding period yield** is a yield calculation that takes into account the total return, the original investment, and the time that the investment is held. The following formula is used to calculate the annualized holding period yield:

$$\text{Annualized holding period yield} = \frac{\text{Total return}}{\text{Original investment}} \times \frac{1}{N}$$

where

N = Number of years investment is held

To illustrate this concept, let's return to your General Motors investment, for which the total return was $1,750, the original investment was $4,100, and the holding period was two years. As shown below, the annualized holding period yield for this investment is 21.3 percent for each of the two years that the investment was held.

$$\text{Annualized holding period yield} = \frac{\$1,750}{\$4,100} \times \frac{1}{2}$$
$$= 0.213, \text{ or}$$
$$= 21.3 \text{ percent}$$

Tax Considerations

With the exception of the interest paid on tax-free bonds, the dividends, interest, and profits you receive from your investments are subject to federal income tax. It is therefore every investor's responsibility to determine how taxes and current tax rulings affect his or her investments. Areas of concern include dividend and interest income, capital gains, and capital losses.

Dividend and Interest Income   A **dividend** is a distribution of money, stock, or other property that a corporation pays to stockholders. Like wages or salaries, dividend income is reported on your federal tax return as ordinary income. Generally, the payer will send you a Form 1099-DIV that states how much dividend income has been reported to the Internal Revenue Service in your name.

Interest from banks, credit unions, and savings and loan associations is subject to federal taxation. Generally, the payer will send you a Form 1099-INT that states how much interest income has been reported to the Internal Revenue Service in your name. Interest that you receive from notes, loans, bonds, and U.S. securities must also be reported as income. There is no exclusion for interest income, and the total amount of such income must be reported as ordinary income on your income tax return.

Capital Gains and Capital Losses   Under the Tax Reform Act of 1986, profits resulting from the sale of investments are taxed as ordinary income. For example, assume that Joe Coit sold 100 shares of General Motors stock for a profit of $1,000. If Joe is in the 28 percent tax bracket, his tax on the $1,000 profit is $280 ($1,000 × 28% = $280). If he had sold the stock at a loss, he could have used the dollar amount of the loss to offset or reduce ordinary income. Under the Tax Reform Act of 1986, capital losses are first used to offset capital gains. Up to $3,000 in capital losses may then be used each year to offset ordinary income. Capital losses in excess of $3,000 may be used in future tax years.

In 1990, Congress considered a bill to reduce the amount of tax that an investor would pay on capital gains resulting from the sale of long-term investments. To date, this bill is still under consideration.

Sources of Investment Information

With most investments, there is more information than an investor can read and comprehend. Therefore, an investor must be selective in the type of information he or she uses for evaluation purposes. With other investments, only a limited amount of information is available. For example, a wealth of information is available on stocks, whereas the amount of information on a metal such as cobalt or manganese may be limited to one source. Regardless of the number or the availability of sources, it is always the investor's job to determine how reliable and accurate the information is. Listed below are sources of information that an investor can use to evaluate present and future investments.

Newspapers   The most available source of information for the average investor is the financial page of a daily metropolitan newspaper or *The Wall Street Journal.* There you will find a summary of the day's trading on the two most widely quoted stock exchanges in the United States, the New York Stock Exchange and the American Stock Exchange. In addition to stock coverage, most newspapers also provide information on stocks traded in the over-the-counter markets, corporate and government bonds, commodities, options, and some metals. Detailed information on how to read price quotations for stocks, bonds, mutual funds, commodities, and options will be presented in the remaining chapters of Part V.

Business Periodicals and Government Publications   Most business periodicals are published weekly, twice a month, or monthly. *Business Week, Fortune, Forbes, Dun's Review,* and similar business periodicals provide not only general economic news about the overall economy but also detailed financial information about certain individual corporations. There are even business periodicals—for example, *Advertising Age* and *Business Insurance*—that focus on information about the firms in a specific industry. In addition to business periodicals, more general magazines such as *U.S. News & World Report, Time,* and *Newsweek* provide investment information as a regular feature. Finally, *Money, Consumer Reports, Changing Times,* and similar magazines provide information and advice designed to improve the individual's investment skills.

The U.S. government may be the world's largest disseminator of information. Much of this information is of value to investors and is either free or available at minimal cost. U.S. government publications that investors may find useful include the *Federal Reserve Bulletin, Monetary Trends,* and *National Economic Trends,* published by the Federal Reserve System, and the *Survey of Current Business, Weekly Business Statistics,* and *Business Conditions Digest,* published by the Department of Commerce. In addition, the Census Bureau also provides statistical information that may be useful to investors. Information on the types of data and reports that are available is contained in the bureau's annual *Catalog of U.S. Census Publications.*

Corporate Reports   The federal government requires corporations selling new issues of securities to disclose information about corporate earnings, assets and liabilities, products or services, and the qualifications of top management in a prospectus that they must give to investors. In addition to the prospectus, all publicly owned corporations send their stockholders an annual report and quarterly reports that contain detailed financial data. Included in both annual and quarterly corporate reports is a statement of financial position, which describes changes in assets, liabilities, and owners' equity. Also included in these reports is a profit and loss statement, which provides dollar amounts for sales, expenses, and profit or loss.

Statistical Averages   Investors often gauge the value of their investments by following one or more widely recognized statistical averages. Such an average is a statistical measure that indicates whether a broad investment category (stocks, bonds, mutual funds, etc.) is increasing or decreasing in value.

How much importance should an investor attach to statistical averages? These averages show trends and direction, but they do not pinpoint the actual value of a specific investment. Some of the more widely used statistical averages are listed in Exhibit 15–7. Many of these averages will be described in the remaining chapters of Part V.

Investor Services and Newsletters   Many stockholders and financial planners mail a free monthly newsletter to their clients. In addition, individuals can subscribe to services that provide investment information. The fees for investor services generally range from $30 to $300 a year.

There are three widely accepted services for investors who specialize in stocks and bonds:

1. *Standard & Poor's Reports.* These up-to-date reports on corporations listed on the major stock exchanges cover such topics as recommendations, sales and earnings, prospects, recent developments, profit and loss statements, and statements of financial position.
2. *Value Line.* These reports supply detailed information about major corporations—earnings, dividends, sales, liabilities, and the like.
3. *Moody's Investors Service.* Moody's reports help investors evaluate potential investments in corporate securities and provide information similar to that contained in the Standard & Poor's and Value Line reports.

Other investment services and newsletters that may help you evaluate potential investments include Dun & Bradstreet's *Key Business Ratios,* the *Dow Jones-Irwin Business and Investment Almanac,* and the Wiesenberger Services annual

EXHIBIT 15–7

Statistical Averages That Can Be Used to Evaluate Investments

Statistical Average	Type of Investment
Dow Jones Industrial Average	Stocks
Barron's Stock Index	Stocks
Standard & Poor's 500 Stock Index	Stocks
Value Line Stock Index	Stocks
Wilshire Stock Index	Stocks
New York Stock Exchange Index	Stocks on New York Stock Exchange
American Stock Exchange Market Value Index	Stocks on American Stock Exchange
NASDAQ Composite Stock Index	Over-the-counter stocks
Wiesenberger Mutual Funds Index	Mutual funds
Moody's Corporate Bond Average	Corporate bonds
Standard & Poor's Municipal Bond Index	Municipal bonds
Donoghue's Money Market Fund Index	Money market rates
New One-Family House Price Index	Real estate
Commodity Spot Market Index	Commodities
Diamond Price Index	Diamonds
Sotheby's Fine Art Index	Art/paintings
Linn's Composite Index	Stamps

issue on mutual funds. There are even investor services and newsletters for more speculative investments. The *Commodity Yearbook* is a yearly publication that can be supplemented by the *Commodity Yearbook Statistical Abstract* three times per year. The International Monetary Market publishes the *I.M.M. Weekly Report*, which discusses interest rates, foreign exchange markets, and gold. The Chicago Board of Trade publishes the *Interest Rate Futures Newsletter*. Scott Publishing Company publishes the *Stamp Market Update*, which is a quarterly report on current trends and prices of the stamp market.

The above discussion of investor services and newsletters is not exhaustive, but it does give you some idea of the amount and scope of the information that is available to serious investors. Although most small investors find that many of the services and newsletters described here are too expensive for personal subscriptions, some of these investors obtain copies from stockbrokers or financial planners. This type of information is also available at most public libraries.

SUMMARY

L.O.1

Explain why it is to your advantage to prepare for and establish an investment program.

Personal investment is the use of one's personal funds to earn a financial return. Investment goals must be specific and measurable and should be classified as short term, intermediate, and long term.

Before beginning an investment program, you must make sure your personal financial affairs are in order. Most financial planners suggest that an investment program should begin with the accumulation of an emergency fund that is equal to three months' salary after taxes.

KEY FORMULAS

A Reference Guide

Page	Topic	Formula
438	Current yield	$\text{Current yield} = \dfrac{\text{Annual income amount}}{\text{Market value}}$
438	Total return	$\text{Total return} = \text{Current return} + \text{Future return}$
439	Annualized holding period yield	$\text{Annualized holding period yield} = \dfrac{\text{Total return}}{\text{Original investment}} \times \dfrac{1}{N}$ $N = \text{Number of years investment is held}$

L.O.2
Describe how the factors of safety, risk, income, growth, and liquidity affect your investment options.

L.O.3
Identify the major types of investment alternatives available to investors.

L.O.4
Recognize the role of the professional financial planner in your investment program and the sources of financial information that can reduce investment risks.

Although each investor may have specific, individual reasons for investing, the factors of safety, risk, income, growth, and liquidity must be considered by all investors.

Investment alternatives include stocks, bonds, mutual funds, and real estate. More speculative investment alternatives include commodities, options, precious metals, gemstones, and collectibles.

A true financial planner has had at least two years of training in securities, insurance, taxes, real estate, and estate planning and has passed a rigorous examination. Financial planners can help individuals achieve their investment goals.

Since there is more information on investments than most investors can read and comprehend, investors must be selective in the type of information that they use for evaluation purposes.

GLOSSARY

Annualized holding period yield   A yield calculation that takes into account the total return, the original investment, and the time that the investment is held.

Call option   Gives the purchaser the right to buy 100 shares of a stock at a guaranteed price before a definite expiration date.

Corporate bond   A corporation's written pledge that it will repay a specified amount of money, with interest.

Current yield   The yearly dollar amount of income generated by any investment divided by the investment's current market value.

Debt capital   Money that corporations or governments obtain by borrowing from outside sources.

Dividend   A distribution of money, stock, or other property that a corporation pays to stockholders.

Equity capital   Money that a business obtains from its owners.

Futures contract   An agreement to buy or sell a commodity at a guaranteed price on some specified future date.

Government bond   The written pledge of a government or a municipality that it will repay a specified amount of money, with interest.

Line of credit   A short-term loan that is approved before the money is actually needed.

Liquidity   The ease with which an asset can be converted to cash without a substantial loss in dollar value.

Mutual fund   An investment alternative available to individuals who pool their money to buy stocks, bonds, certificates of deposit, and other securities based on the selections of professional managers who work for an investment company.

Option   The right to buy or sell 100 shares of a stock at a predetermined price within a specified period of time.

Personal financial planning   The process of managing your money to achieve personal economic satisfaction.

Personal investment   The use of one's personal funds to earn a financial return.

Put option   Gives the purchaser the right to sell 100 shares of a stock at a guaranteed price before a definite expiration date.

Speculative investment   An investment that is made in the hope of earning a relatively large profit in a short time.

Total return   A calculation that includes not only the yearly dollar amount of income but also any increase or decrease in the original purchase price of an investment.

DISCUSSION QUESTIONS

L.O.1	1. What is the overall objective of investing?
L.O.1	2. Before beginning an investment program, an individual should perform a financial checkup. What four factors should the individual evaluate before making the first investment?
L.O.1	3. What is an emergency fund? Why do individuals need to establish an emergency fund before investing money in stocks, bonds, or other investments?
L.O.1	4. What suggestions did this chapter offer to help individuals get the money they need to start an investment program?
L.O.2	5. What factors account for the increased risk that is involved in purchases of commodities, options, precious metals, gemstones, and collectibles?
L.O.2	6. How do the factors of safety, risk, income, growth, and liquidity influence an individual's investment decisions?
L.O.3	7. From an investor's standpoint, how do corporate and government bonds differ from common and preferred stock?

L.O.3   8. An individual may invest in stocks either directly or through a mutual fund. How do the two investment methods differ?

L.O.3   9. What questions should an investor ask before purchasing a piece of real estate for investment purposes?

L.O.4   10. What factors should you consider when choosing a financial planner?

L.O.4   11. What kinds of information would you like to have before you invest in a particular common stock? Where can you get that information?

Opening Case Questions

1. Why did Bob Martin become upset when he learned that one of his best friends had decided to take their firm's early retirement option?
2. Based on the information presented in the Opening Case, what type of financial plan would you recommend for Bob Martin?

PROBLEMS AND ACTIVITIES

L.O.1   1. Develop at least two short-term objectives, two intermediate objectives, and two long-term objectives that you could use in an investment program.

L.O.1   2. Assume that you are single and have graduated from college. Your monthly take-home pay is $1,750, and your monthly expenses total $1,500, which leaves you with a monthly surplus of $250. Develop a personal plan of action for investing like the one illustrated in Exhibit 15–2.

L.O.2   3. List three personal factors that might lead some investors to emphasize income rather than growth in their investment planning. List three personal factors that might lead some investors to emphasize growth rather than income in their investment planning.

L.O.3   4. Choose three of the investment alternatives presented in this chapter and then rank them from high to low on the factors of safety, risk, and liquidity. Assume that 3 is the highest score and 1 is the lowest score for each factor. Based on the results of your survey, which one of the three alternatives would you choose for your own investment program. Why?

L.O.4   5. More than 200,000 people call themselves financial planners. Prepare 10 questions that you could use to determine whether any one of them can really help you achieve your financial goals.

L.O.4   6. Assume that you purchased 100 shares of IBM common stock for $106 a share, that you received an annual dividend of $4.80 per share, and that you sold your IBM stock for $120 a share at the end of three years.
   a. Calculate the current yield for your IBM stock at the time you purchased it.
   b. Calculate the total return on your IBM investment.
   c. Calculate the annualized holding period yield of your IBM investment at the end of the three-year period.

L.O.4   7. Suppose that you have just inherited 500 shares of General Motors stock. List five sources of information that you could use to evaluate your inheritance. Beside each of these sources, briefly state how the information it contains could help you evaluate your inheritance.

LIFE SITUATION   Case 15–1

From Inheritance to Investment

Joe and Mary Garner were married nine years ago, and they have an eight-year-old child. Four years ago, they purchased a home, on which they owe about $80,000. They also owe $6,000 on their two-year-old automobile. All of their furniture is paid for, and they have no monthly credit card payments.

Joe is employed as an engineer and makes $35,000 a year. Mary works part-time and earns about $5,000 a year. Their monthly income after deductions is $2,725. Their monthly expenses are listed below:

Fixed expenses		
Home mortgage payment	$840	
Automobile loan	220	
Insurance	150	
Emergency fund	140	
Total fixed expenses		$1,350
Variable expenses		
Food	310	
Clothing	150	
Gasoline	90	
Automobile repairs	70	
Gifts and donations	100	
Electricity	95	
Gas	65	
Water	25	
Telephone	60	
Medical costs	130	
Recreation	120	
Total variable expenses		1,215
Total expenses		$2,565
Surplus for additional savings		$ 160
($2,725 − $2,565 − $160)		

About six months ago, the Garners decided that it was time to get serious about finances. Based on the above information, they decided to pay themselves first and save $160 a month. After each payday, they deposited $160 in a savings account designated as their emergency fund. Now, after six months, they have $960 in the fund. They also have about $2,000 in a separate savings account.

Last month, Joe and Mary were notified by a lawyer that Mary's uncle had died and left them $75,000. While they were saddened by the uncle's death, they certainly appreciated their newfound wealth. Now they must decide how to invest their inheritance.

Questions

1. How would you rate the financial status of the Garners before they inherited the $75,000?
2. If you were Joe or Mary Garner, what would you do with the $75,000 inheritance?

3. Which of the investment alternatives described in this chapter would you recommend for the Garners? Why?
4. Where would you gather information to support your investment recommendation?

LIFE SITUATION   Case 15–2

What Should She Do Next?

For Ann Jackson, the three years since her divorce have been a disaster. Most of her $120,000 cash settlement was soon swallowed up by hospital bills that resulted from an automobile accident. Physical therapy improved her condition, but she was unable to resume her assembly line job. As a result, she was forced to use what little cash she had left for everyday expenses.

After a lengthy court battle with the driver of the other car and his insurance company, Ms. Jackson won a $425,000 settlement, of which she paid $125,000 to her attorney. Now partially disabled and able to work only 20 hours a week, she is trying to rebuild her life with the remaining $300,000. She has talked to two financial planners. The first, whose ideas she considered too conservative, advised her to sell her house, move into an apartment, live on $45 a week, and put all of her money into certificates of deposit. The second would not handle accounts smaller than $500,000. After striking out twice with financial planners, she has decided to plan her own financial future. Although she has had no experience with stocks, bonds, or mutual funds, she thinks that such investments might provide her with both the safety and the income she needs.

Questions

1. How would you rate the advice that the first financial planner gave Ms. Jackson?
2. How do the factors of safety, risk, income, growth, and liquidity affect the investments in stocks, bonds, and mutual funds that Ms. Jackson might make?
3. If you were Ms. Jackson, what would you do with the $300,000 cash settlement?

SUPPLEMENTARY READINGS

For Additional Information on Preparing for an Investment Program

Gilder, Barbara. "What Should You Do with $1,000 Savings?" *Glamour,* January 1990, pp. 50+.

Rock, Andrea. "How to Change Your Life and Achieve Financial Security." *Money,* March 1990, pp. 77–82+.

For Additional Information on Investment Alternatives

Hardy, E. "Fixed Income Review." *Forbes,* March 5, 1990, p. 158.

McManus, Kevin. "Nine Quick Ways to Size Up a Stock." *Changing Times,* February 1990, p. 24.

Meyer et al, Marsha. "Picking the Best Funds." *Money,* February 1990, pp. 126–137 +.

"Your Best Moves for 1990." *Changing Times,* January 1990, pp. 25–46.

For Additional Information on Choosing a Financial Planner

Farr, Michael K. "Tips on Finding a Financial Advisor." *Consumers' Research,* November 1989, pp. 35–37.

Rock, Andrea. "Financial Advice You Can Trust." *Money,* November 1989, pp. 80–82 +.

16

Investing in Stocks

As you learned in Chapter 15, there are many investment alternatives that serious investors must consider. Two of these alternatives—common stock and preferred stock—are discussed in this chapter. An investment in either type of stock is based on two simple assumptions. First, a corporation sells stock to raise money. Second, investors purchase the corporation's stock because it represents a "good investment." Today, about one out of every five Americans owns shares of common or preferred stock. In this chapter, we will examine why these investment alternatives are so popular and what factors successful investors use to evaluate potential stock investments.

LEARNING OBJECTIVES
After studying this chapter, you will be able to

L.O.1　Identify the most important features of common stock and discuss why people invest in common stock.

L.O.2　Identify the most important features of preferred stock and discuss why people invest in preferred stock.

L.O.3　Explain how investors can evaluate stock investments.

L.O.4　Describe how stocks are bought and sold through brokerage firms and securities exchanges.

L.O.5　Explain the traditional trading techniques used by long-term and short-term investors.

OPENING CASE

A Long-Term Investment for the Overalls

Like many other small investors, Jack and Susan Overall didn't have a lot of money when they bought their first stock. At that time, in 1979, the Overalls had graduated from college, were expecting their first child, had just purchased their first home, and were driving a 1976 Ford with over 85,000 miles on it. Nevertheless, Susan talked Jack into buying 100 shares of Federal Express stock at $6.50 per share for a total of $690.50, including the broker's commission.

During the next six months, the Overalls received no dividends and the market value of their Federal Express stock dropped to $5.25. They were disappointed, but they decided to hold their investment a little longer. Then, in the last part of 1980, Federal Express announced a 2-for-1 stock split. A stock split is usually the division of a corporation's outstanding shares of stock into a greater number of shares. The Overalls' 100 shares were transformed into 200 shares. Although the 2-for-1 stock split caused the dollar value of a share of Federal Express stock to go down, this didn't seem to matter, because the Overalls owned twice as much stock. And besides, the price per share eventually rose even higher than their $6.50 purchase price. Now both Jack and Susan were tempted to sell their stock because they had more than doubled their original investment. However, Susan persuaded Jack that they should hold onto it.

In 1983, the stock of Federal Express again split 2-for-1. The Overalls' original 100 shares had grown to 400 shares. Again, they were tempted to sell their stock and take their profit. Instead, four years after having purchased its stock, they decided to find out something about Federal Express.

They learned that as a student at Yale in the 1960s, Frederick Smith, the founder of Federal Express, came up with the idea of an overnight delivery service for a term project that he needed in order to complete a management course. As Smith envisioned this idea, the company offering the service would fly planeloads of packages from all over the country to a central distribution point in the early evening—after business hours. Overnight, the packages would be sorted by destination, reloaded onto the same planes, and flown to the appropriate cities for delivery the next day. Smith's teacher told him the idea was impractical and gave him a C for his project. Smith liked the idea, however, and in 1971 he founded Federal Express, which was based on it. From 1974 to 1983 the firm doubled in size every two years, and from 1979 to 1983 the number of communities it served rose from 8,000 to 17,000.

Based on this information, the Overalls decided to hold onto their Federal Express stock for a time. In 1989, they sold it for $55 a share. They received nearly $22,000 for their 400 shares.

On the surface, it would seem that the Overalls were just lucky. But their investment in Federal Express was just the beginning. After this first investment, they continued to invest in stocks whenever they could afford it. As a result, their portfolio in 1989 consisted of 15 stocks valued at more than $200,000. According to Jack Overall, the secret of their success was that they concentrated on long-range investment goals and didn't try to make a big killing overnight.

For more information, see *Moody's Handbook of Common Stock, Summer 1989* (New York: Moody's Investors Service, Inc., 1989); Joani Nelson-Horchler, "The Overnight Race: Airborne's Flying Right at Federal Express," *Industry Week*, March 19, 1984, pp. 67–69; "Turbulence Hits the Air Couriers," *Fortune*, July 21, 1986, pp. 101–6; and Roy Rowan, "Business Triumphs of the Seventies," *Fortune*, December 3, 1979, p. 34.

COMMON STOCK

L.O.1
Identify the most important features of common stock, and discuss why people invest in common stock.

The term **securities** encompasses a broad range of investment instruments, including stocks and bonds, mutual funds, options, and municipal bonds. In this chapter, we examine stocks. Today, a lot of people buy stocks and share the long-term investment philosophy of the Overalls—the couple in the above case. Why? The most obvious answer to that question is quite simple: They are willing to assume the greater risks of investing in stocks in order to obtain larger returns on their investments. Stocks, as measured by Standard & Poor's 500 Stock Average, have provided an average annual return of 9.5 percent since 1926, which is as far back as complete stock market returns have been recorded.[1] In fact, the annual return on stocks has been more than double the annual return on corporate bonds (4.4 percent) and nearly triple the annual return on U.S.

Treasury bills (3.3 percent) over the same period of time.[2] Moreover, most financial experts are predicting that the annual return on stocks will be even higher in the future.

There are two types of stocks, common stock and preferred stock. Common stock is discussed in this section, and preferred stock is discussed in the next section. A common stock certificate and a preferred stock certificate are shown in Exhibit 16–1.

Since common stockholders are the actual owners of the corporation, they share in its success. However, finding a successful corporation whose stock will increase in value is more difficult than just picking a name out of the financial section of the newspaper. Successful stockholders evaluate a number of factors before they invest in any stock. The first factor they evaluate is why a corporation sells common stock.

Why Corporations Issue Common Stock

Corporations sell common stock to finance their business start-up costs and help pay for their ongoing business activities. Today, corporations are classified as either private corporations or public corporations. A *private corporation* is a corporation whose stock is owned by relatively few people and is not traded openly in stock markets. A *public corporation* is a corporation whose stock is traded openly in stock markets and may be purchased by an individual. Public corporations may have thousands, or sometimes even millions, of stockholders. American Telephone & Telegraph, for example, has about 2.6 million stockholders, while General Motors has over 1 million stockholders. Corporate managers prefer selling common stock as a method of financing for several reasons.

Common Stock: A Form of Equity   Corporations don't have to repay the money a stockholder pays for stock. Generally, a stockholder in a public corporation may sell his or her stock to another stockholder. The selling price is determined by how much a buyer is willing to pay for the stock. Stock transactions between stockholders are a practical example of the supply and demand theories presented in Chapter 1. If the demand for a particular stock increases, the price of the stock will increase. If the demand for a particular stock decreases, the price of the stock will decrease.

Occasionally, a corporation will buy its own stock, but only because this is in its best interest. For example, IBM, faced with excess profits to invest, recently decided to purchase its own stock. IBM officials believed that this was the best investment they could make at that time.

Common Stock: Dividends Not Mandatory   Dividends are paid out of profits, and dividend payments must be approved by a corporation's board of directors. Dividend policies vary among corporations, which usually distribute from 30 to 70 percent of their earnings to stockholders. However, some corporations follow a policy of smaller dividend distributions to stockholders. In general, these are rapidly growing firms that retain a large share of their earnings for research and development. On the other hand, utility companies and other financially secure enterprises may distribute 80 to 90 percent of their earnings. If a corporation has a bad year, board members may vote to omit dividend payments to stockholders.

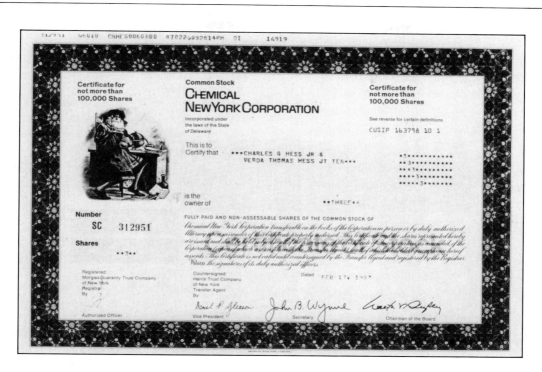

Common Stock: Voting Rights and Control of the Company   In return for the financing provided by selling common stock, management must make concessions to stockholders that may restrict or change corporate policies. For example, corporations are required by law to have an annual meeting at which stockholders have a right to vote, usually casting one vote per share of stock. Stockholders may vote in person or by proxy. A **proxy** is a legal form that lists the issues to be decided at a stockholders' meeting and requests that stockholders transfer their voting rights to some individual or individuals. The common stockholders elect the board of directors and must approve major changes in corporate policies. Typical changes of this kind include (1) any amendment of the corporate charter or bylaws, (2) the sale of certain assets, (3) possible mergers, (4) the issuance of preferred stock or corporate bonds, and (5) changes in the amount of common stock.

Most states require that a provision for preemptive rights be included in the charter of every corporation. A **preemptive right** is the right of current stockholders to purchase any new stock that the corporation issues before it is offered to the general public. By exercising their preemptive rights, stockholders are able to maintain their current proportion of corporate ownership. This may be important when the corporation is a small one and management control is a matter of concern to stockholders.

Finally, corporations are required by law to distribute annual and quarterly reports to stockholders. These reports contain detailed information about sales, earnings, profits and losses, and other vital financial matters.

Although the money that corporations acquire through the sale of common stock is essentially cost free, few investors will buy common stock if they cannot foresee some return on their investment. Now we'll examine common stock from the point of view of the investor.

Why Investors Purchase Common Stock

How do you make money by buying common stock? Basically, there are three ways that an investment in common stock can increase in value. These three ways—income from dividends, dollar appreciation of stock value, and possible increase in value from stock splits—are described below.

Income from Dividends   While the corporation's board members are under no legal obligation to pay dividends, most board members like to keep stockholders happy (and prosperous). It should be noted that few things will unite stockholders into a powerful opposition force more rapidly than omitted or lowered dividends. Therefore, board members usually declare dividends if the corporation's after-tax profits are sufficient for them to do so. Since dividends are a distribution of profits, intelligent investors must be concerned about future after-tax profits. In short, how secure is the dividend?

Corporate dividends for common stock may be in the form of cash, additional stock, or company products. However, the last type of dividend is extremely unusual. If a cash dividend is declared by the board of directors, each stockholder by law receives an equal amount per share. Although dividend policies vary, most corporations pay dividends on a quarterly basis. Some corporations, particularly those having large swings in earnings, declare special year-end or extra dividends in addition to their regular quarterly dividends.

In order to determine who actually owns stock and is entitled to receive dividends on a certain date, this simple rule is followed: dividends remain with the stock until four business days *before* the date of record. The **date of record** is the date when a stockholder must be registered on the corporation's books in order to receive dividends. On the fourth day before the date of record, the stock begins selling ex-dividend. Anyone who purchases an ex-dividend stock is not entitled to receive dividends for this quarter. In this case, the dividend is paid to the previous owner of the stock.

For example, Atlanta Gas and Light declared a quarterly dividend of 49 cents per share to stockholders owning its stock on May 18, 1990 (see Exhibit 16–2). The stock went ex-dividend on May 14, 1990, four business days before the May 18 date. A stockholder who purchased the stock on May 14 or after was not entitled to this quarterly dividend payment. The actual dividend payment was made by Atlanta Gas and Light on June 1, 1990, to stockholders who owned the stock on the date of record. Investors are generally very conscious of the date on which a stock goes ex-dividend, and the dollar value of the stock may go down by the value of the quarterly dividend on the ex-dividend date.

Dollar Appreciation of Stock Value   In most cases, a stockholder purchases a stock and then holds onto that stock for a period of time. If the market value of the stock increases, the stockholder must decide whether he or she wants to sell the stock at the higher price or continue to hold it. If the stockholder decides to sell the stock, the dollar amount of difference between the purchase price and the selling price represents profit.

EXHIBIT 16–2

Typical Information on Corporate Dividends as Presented in a Financial Publication

CORPORATE DIVIDEND NEWS

Dividends Reported May 4

Company		Period	Amt.	Payable date	Record date
REGULAR					
Allen Organ clB	Q		.10	6– 8–90	5–25
Atlanta Gas Light	Q		.49	6– 1–90	5–18
Broad Inc	Q		.05	5–18–90	5–14
Broad Inc clB	Q		.04½	5–18–90	5–14
Burnham Corp clA	Q		.45	6– 4–90	5–21
Burnham Corp clB	Q		.45	6– 4–90	5–21
Cominco Ltd	S		b.25	6–30–90	6–11
EasternAir deppf	Q		.71	5–31–90	5–15
First Finl Mgmt	S		m.05	7– 2–90	6– 1
m-Correction; this is a regular semi-annual payment. Appeared as irregular in May 4th edition.					
Flexsteel Indus	Q		.12	6– 4–90	5–23
Haverty Furniture	Q		.09	5–25–90	5–15
Haverty Furn clA	Q		.08½	5–25–90	5–15
HinghamInstSvg MA	Q		.08	5–31–90	5–18
Intl Multifoods	Q		.29½	7–15–90	6–28
Kaufman&BroadHome	Q		.07½	5–26–90	5–16
Litton Indus pfB	Q		.50	7– 1–90	6–13
MacDermid Inc	Q		.15	7– 2–90	6–15
Overseas Shiphldg	Q		.12½	5–24–90	5–14
Ryder System	Q		.15	6–20–90	5–28
Texfi Indus pf'87	Q		.27½	6– 1–90	5–15
Timken Co	Q		.23	6–11–90	5–21
Weigh-Tronix Inc	Q		.10	6–15–90	5–24

SOURCE: *The Wall Street Journal,* May 7, 1990, C8.

Let's assume that on September 8, 1990, you purchase 100 shares of Eastman Kodak at a cost of $49 a share and that your cost for the stock is $4,900 plus $80 in commission charges, for a total investment of $4,980. Let's also assume that you hold your 100 shares until September 8, 1991, and then sell them for $59 each and that during the 12 months you own Eastman Kodak the company pays quarterly dividends totaling $2 a share. Your return on investment is shown in Exhibit 16–3. In this case, you make money through a dividend paid every three months and through an increase in stock value from $49 per share to $59 per share.

Increased Value from Stock Splits   Investors can also increase earnings and potential profits through a stock split. A **stock split** is a procedure in which the shares of common stock owned by existing stockholders are divided into a larger number of shares. In 1989, for example, the Honda Motor's board of directors approved a 2-for-1 stock split. After the stock split, a stockholder who had previously owned 100 shares now owned 200 shares. The most common stock splits are 2-for-1, 3-for-1, and 4-for-1.

Why do corporations split their stock? In many cases, a firm's management has a "theoretical" ideal price range for the firm's stock. If the market price of the stock rises above the ideal price range, a stock split brings the market price back in line. In the case of Honda, the 2-for-1 stock split reduced the market price to about half of the stock's previous price. The lower market price for each share of stock was the result of dividing the dollar value of the company by a larger number of shares of common stock. Also, a decision to split a company's stock makes the stock more attractive to the investing public. *Although there are no guarantees that a stock's price will go up after a split, the investing public feels that there is a potential for an increase because the stock is offered at a lower price.*

A less common type of stock split occurs when the number of outstanding shares of common stock is reduced. This usually occurs when the market price of

EXHIBIT 16–3

Sample Stock Transaction
for Eastman Kodak

Assumptions

100 shares of common stock purchased September 8, 1990, sold September 8, 1991;
dividends of $2 per share per year

Costs when purchased		Return when sold	
100 shares @ $49 =	$4,900	100 shares @ $59 =	5,900
Plus commission	+80	Minus commission	90
Total investment	4,980	Total return	5,810

Transaction summary

Total return	$ 5,810
Minus total investment	−4,980
Profit from stock sale	$ 830
Plus dividends	+200
Total return for the transaction	$ 1,030

a corporation's stock has dropped to a point at which the directors consider it too low. In a *reverse split,* stockholders exchange their shares for a proportionately lesser number of shares. As a result, the market price is adjusted upward by a proportionate amount.

PREFERRED STOCK

L.O.2

Identify the most important features of preferred stock, and discuss why people invest in preferred stock.

In addition to purchasing common stock, investors purchase preferred stock. Certain factors must be considered before preferred stock is purchased. The most important priority that an investor in preferred stock enjoys is receiving cash dividends before common stockholders are paid any cash dividends. This factor is especially important when a corporation is experiencing financial problems and cannot pay cash dividends to both preferred and common stockholders. The dollar amount of the dividend on preferred stock is known before the stock is purchased—unlike the amount of the dividend on common stock. The dividend amount is either a stated amount of money for each share of stock or a certain percentage of the par value of the preferred stock. The **par value** is an assigned (and often arbitrary) dollar value that is printed on a stock certificate. Usually, the dollar amount of the dividend or the specific rate of the dividend is set forth in the preferred stock agreement. The dividend is paid before any dividend payments are made to common stockholders.

While preferred stock does not represent a legal debt that must be repaid, if the firm is dissolved or declares bankruptcy, preferred stockholders do have first claim to the corporation's assets after creditors (including bondholders). Generally, a preferred stock certificate contains a clause that allows the corporation to recall the preferred stock issue. **Callable preferred stock** is stock that a corporation may exchange, at its option, for a specified amount of money. To understand why a corporation would want to call in a preferred stock issue, you must first realize that interest and dividend rates in the economy increase and decrease because of changes in the overall supply and demand for money plus a number of related factors. If interest rates in the economy are decreasing and similar investments provide a smaller return than the corporation's preferred stock issue, management may decide to call in the issue and substitute a new preferred stock issue that pays a lower dividend. Management may also decide to call in the preferred stock issue and issue common stock with no specified dividend.

Corporations issue preferred stock because it is an alternative method of financing that may attract investors who do not wish to buy common stock or corporate bonds. Potential investors often regard preferred stock as a safer investment than common stock because the claim of preferred stock to both dividends and assets is prior to that of common stock. And yet preferred stock, like common stock, is equity financing. Dividends on preferred stock, as on common stock, may be omitted by action of the board of directors and do not have to be repaid at a future date. Many small investors consider preferred stock to be as safe as corporate bonds. Generally, it is less safe, however because corporate bonds are debt capital. Corporate bonds are a more conservative investment than preferred stock because bondholders are more likely to receive interest payments until maturity and eventual repayment of their initial investment than are preferred stockholders to continue receiving dividends or to recover their initial investment in the stock. To make preferred stock issues more attractive, some corporations offer the additional features described below.

The Cumulative Feature of Preferred Stock

If the corporation's board of directors believes that omitting dividends is justified, it can vote to omit not only the dividends paid to common stockholders but also the dividends paid to preferred stockholders. One way preferred stockholders can protect themselves against omitted dividends is to purchase cumulative preferred stock. **Cumulative preferred stock** is a stock issue whose unpaid dividends accumulate and must be paid before any cash dividend is paid to the common stockholders. If a corporation does not pay dividends to the cumulative preferred stockholders during one dividend period, the amount of the missed dividends is added to the following period's preferred dividends.

The Participation Feature of Preferred Stock

To make a preferred stock issue more attractive, corporations sometimes add a participation feature. This allows preferred stockholders to share in the earnings of the corporation with the common stockholders. Participating preferred stock is a rare form of investment; Moody's Investors Service lists less than 100 issues of this kind.[3]

The participation feature of preferred stock works like this: (1) the required dividend is paid to preferred stockholders; (2) a stated dividend, usually equal to the dividend amount paid to preferred stockholders, is paid to common stockholders; and (3) the remainder of the earnings available for distribution is shared by both preferred and common stockholders. If a preferred stock issue does not have the participation feature, the preferred stockholders receive only the regular dividend and the excess dividends are paid to the common stockholders.

The Conversion Feature of Preferred Stock

Convertible preferred stock is preferred stock that can be exchanged, at the stockholder's option, for a specified number of shares of common stock. The conversion feature provides the investor with the safety of preferred stock and the possibility of greater speculative gain through conversion to common stock.

All of the information relating to the number of shares of common stock that may be obtained through conversion of preferred stock is stated in the corporate records and is usually printed on the preferred stock certificate. For example, assume that the Martin & Martin Manufacturing Corporation has issued a convertible preferred stock. Each share of preferred stock in this issue is convertible into two shares of common stock. Assume that the market price of Martin & Martin's convertible preferred stock is $24 and that the stock pays an annual dividend of $3 a share. Also assume that the market price of the company's common stock is $9 and that the common stock currently pays an annual dividend of $1 a share. Under these circumstances, a preferred stockholder would keep the preferred stock. If the market price of the common stock were to increase to above $12 a share, however, the preferred stockholder would have an incentive to exercise the conversion option.

The decision to convert preferred stock to common stock is complicated by three factors. First, the dividends paid on preferred stock are more secure than the dividends paid on common stock. Second, the dividend yield for preferred stock is generally higher than the dividend yield for common stock. The dividend yield for Martin & Martin's preferred stock is $3 ÷ $24 = 12.5 percent, and the dividend yield for its common stock is $1 ÷ $9 = 11.1 percent. Third, because of the conversion option, the price of convertible preferred stock usually increases as the price of common stock increases.

There are also other factors that an investor should evaluate before purchasing either preferred stock or common stock. Additional information that will help you evaluate potential stock investments is discussed in the next section.

EVALUATION OF A STOCK ISSUE

L.O.3
Explain how investors can evaluate stock investments.

A wealth of information is available to investors in stocks. The sources of this information include newspapers and business periodicals, corporate reports, and investor services. Most local newspapers carry several pages of business news, including reports of securities transactions. *The Wall Street Journal* (which is published on weekdays) and *Barron's* (which is published once a week) are devoted almost entirely to financial and economic news. Obviously, different types of investments require different methods of evaluation, but a logical place to start the evaluation process for common and preferred stock is with the most available source of information—the daily newspaper.

How to Read the Financial Section of the Newspaper

Most daily newspapers contain information about stocks listed on the major stock exchanges and stocks of local interest. Although not all newspapers print exactly the same information, the basic information is usually provided. Stocks are listed alphabetically, so your first task is to move down the table to find the stock you're interested in. Then, to read the stock quotation, you simply read across the table. The market price for the stocks on each line of the table is quoted in dollars and fractional equivalents of one eighth. Thus, ⅛ means $0.125, or 12.5 cents, and ¾ means $0.75, or 75 cents. For General Cinema, the first stock down from the top in Exhibit 16–4, you would find the following information. (The numbers in this list refer to the column numbers that have been added to the figure.)

1. The highest price paid for a share of General Cinema during the past 52 weeks was $28½, or $28.50.

EXHIBIT 16–4

Financial Information about
Common and Preferred
Stock that Is Available in
the Daily Newspaper

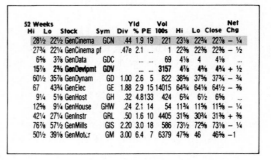

52 Weeks		Stock	Sym	Div	Yld %	P-E Rat.	Vol 100s	High	Low	Close	Net Chg.
High	Low										
1	2	3	4	5	6	7	8	9	10	11	12
28½	22½	GenCinema	GCN	.44	1.9	19	221	23⅛	22¾	22⅞	− ¼
27¾	22¼	GenCinema pf		.47e	2.1	...	1	22⅜	22⅜	22⅜	− ½
6⅝	3⅞	GenData	GDC		...	...	69	4⅛	4	4⅛	...
15⅞	2⅜	GenDevlpmt	GDV		...	...	3157	4⅞	4⅜	4¾	+ ½
60½	35⅞	GenDynam	GD	1.00	2.6	5	822	38⅝	37⅝	37¾	− ¾
67	43¾	GenElec	GE	1.88	2.9	15	14015	64¾	64⅛	64½	− ⅜
9¼	5⅛	GenHost	GH	.32	4.8	133	424	6¾	6½	6⅝	...
12⅝	9¼	GenHouse	GHW	.24	2.1	14	54	11¾	11⅝	11⅝	− ¼

1. Highest price paid for one share during the past year.
2. Lowest price paid for one share during the past year.
3. Abbreviated name of the corporation.
4. Symbol used to identify the corporation on the New York Stock Exchange.
5. Total dividends paid per share during the last 12 months; pf denotes a preferred stock.
6. Yield percentage, or the percentage of return based on the current dividend and current price of the stock.
7. Price earnings ratio: the price of a share of the stock divided by the corporation's earnings per share of stock outstanding over the last 12 months.
8. Number of shares traded during the day, expressed in hundreds of shares.
9. Highest price paid for one share during the day.
10. Lowest price paid for one share during the day.
11. Price paid in the last transaction for the day.
12. Difference between the price paid for the last share today and the price paid for the last share on the previous day.

SOURCE: *The Wall Street Journal*, March 30, 1990, p. C4.

2. The lowest price paid for a share of General Cinema during the past 52 weeks was $22½, or $22.50.
3. The name of the corporation (often abbreviated) is listed in the third column.
4. The symbol used to identify the corporation on the New York Stock Exchange is listed in this column.
5. The dividend paid to holders of General Cinema common stock over the past year was $0.44 per share.

6. The current annual yield for General Cinema is
   $0.44 ÷ $22.875 = 0.019, or 1.9 percent.
7. The current price of General Cinema common stock is 19 times the firm's per share earnings.
8. On this day, 22,100 shares of General Cinema were traded.
9. The highest price paid for a share of General Cinema on this day was 23⅛, or $23.125.
10. The lowest price paid for a share of General Cinema on this day was $22¾, or $22.75.
11. The price of the last share of General Cinema traded on this day was $22⅞, or $22.875.
12. The last price paid for a share of General Cinema on this day was $0.25 lower than the last price paid on the previous trading day. In Wall Street terms, General Cinema "closed down ¼" on this day.

If a corporation has more than one stock issue, the common stock is always listed first. Note that there are two listings of General Cinema Corporation in Exhibit 16–4. The first is for the company's common stock. The second is for its preferred stock, as indicated by the letters *pf*.

Classification of Stock Investments

When evaluating a stock investment, stockbrokers, financial planners, and investors often classify stocks into different categories. We will describe five commonly used classifications.

 A **blue-chip stock** is a very safe investment that generally attracts conservative investors. Stocks of this kind are issued by the strongest and most respected companies, such as IBM, Hewlett-Packard, and Dow Chemical. Company characteristics to watch for when evaluating this type of stock include leadership in an industrial group, a history of stable earnings, and consistency in paying dividends.

 An **income stock** is a stock that pays higher than average dividends. In order to pay above-average dividends, a corporation must have a steady, predictable source of income. Stocks issued by electric, gas, telephone, and other utility companies, are generally classified as income stocks. Investors purchase these stocks because of their income potential and not necessarily because they will increase in price.

 A **growth stock** is a stock issued by a corporation earning profits above the average profits of all the firms in the economy. Key factors to evaluate when choosing a growth stock include an expanding product line of quality merchandise and an effective research and development department. In fact, most growth companies retain a large part of their earnings to pay for their research and development efforts. As a result, such companies generally pay out less than 35 percent of their earnings in dividends to their stockholders. Therefore, most investors purchase growth stocks in the hope that the market price of these stocks will "grow" or increase.

 A **cyclical stock** is a stock that follows the business cycle of advances and declines in the economy. Typically, the increases and decreases in the price of a cyclical stock are directly related to the advances and declines in the nation's overall economic activity. When the economy expands, the market price of a cyclical stock increases. When the economy declines, the market price of a cyclical stock decreases. Most cyclical stocks are in basic industries such as automobiles, steel, paper, and heavy manufacturing. Investors try to buy cyclical stocks just before the economy expands and try to sell them just before the economy declines.

A **defensive stock** is a stock that remains stable during declines in the economy. For this reason, stocks in this classification are sometimes referred to as countercyclical. Generally, companies that issue such stocks have a history of stable earnings and are able to maintain dividend payments to stockholders during periods of economic decline. Many stocks that are classified as income stocks are also classified as countercyclical or defensive stocks because of their stable earnings and their consistent dividend policies.

Stock Advisory Services

A source of information in addition to newspapers that investors can use to evaluate potential stock investments is a stock advisory service. In choosing among the hundreds of stock advisory services that charge fees for their information, the investor must be concerned about both the quality and the quantity of the information they provide. The information provided by stock advisory services ranges from simple alphabetical listings to detailed financial reports. For example, Standard & Poor's stock rankings range from A+ (the highest) to D (in reorganization).

Standard & Poor's Reports, Value Line, and Moody's Investors Service were briefly described in the last chapter. Here we will examine a detailed report for Dow Jones & Company that is published in the *Moody's Handbook of Common Stock* (see Exhibit 16–5).

The basic report illustrated in Exhibit 16–5 is divided into six main sections. At the top of the report, information about the capitalization, earnings, and dividends of Dow Jones is provided. In the "Background" section, the company's major operations are described in detail. Dow Jones is described as a publisher with interests in business publications, community newspapers and information services. In the next section, "Recent Developments," current information about the company's net income and sales revenues is provided. The net income of Dow Jones rose 93 percent, to $200 million, and its sales revenues rose 4 percent, to $406.8 million. In the "Prospects" section, the company's outlook is described. This section states: "The Company will continue to grow as the world's leading supplier of business news. However, sharp declines in financial advertising in the Wall Street Journal and Barron's will affect results." The "Statistics" section provides important data on the company for the past 10 years. Among the topics included in this section are gross revenues, operating profit margin, return on equity, and net income. The final section of the report states, among other things, when and where the company was incorporated, where the company's principal office is located, who its transfer agent is, and who its main corporate officers are.

Other stock advisory services provide basically the same types of information that are illustrated in Exhibit 16–5. It is the investor's job to interpret such information and decide whether the company's stock is a good investment.

Factors that Influence the Price of a Stock

A *bull market* develops when investors are optimistic about the overall economy and purchase stocks. A *bear market* develops when investors are pessimistic about the overall economy and sell stocks. But how do individual investors determine whether it is the right time to buy or sell a particular stock? The price of a stock is affected by many factors. As mentioned, stocks sold on an exchange are practical

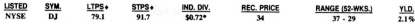

DOW JONES & COMPANY, INC.

LISTED	SYM.	LTPS♦	STPS♦	IND. DIV.	REC. PRICE	RANGE (52-WKS.)	YLD.
NYSE	DJ	79.1	91.7	$0.72•	34	37 - 29	2.1%

INVESTMENT GRADE. A LEADING FINANCIAL PUBLISHER WHOSE PRODUCTS ARE NOTED FOR HIGH QUALITY.

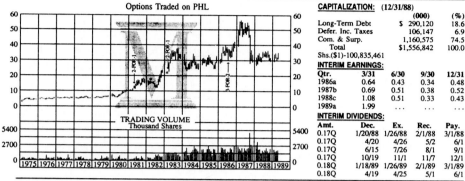

Options Traded on PHL

TRADING VOLUME
Thousand Shares

CAPITALIZATION: (12/31/88)

	(000)	(%)
Long-Term Debt	$ 290,120	18.6
Defer. Inc. Taxes	106,147	6.9
Com. & Surp.	1,160,575	74.5
Total	$1,556,842	100.0

Shs.($1)-100,835,461

INTERIM EARNINGS:

Qtr.	3/31	6/30	9/30	12/31
1986a	0.64	0.43	0.34	0.48
1987b	0.69	0.51	0.38	0.52
1988c	1.08	0.51	0.33	0.43
1989a	1.99	...	...	...

INTERIM DIVIDENDS:

Amt.	Dec.	Ex.	Rec.	Pay.
0.17Q	1/20/88	1/26/88	2/1/88	3/1/88
0.17Q	4/20	4/26	5/2	6/1
0.17Q	6/15	7/26	8/1	9/1
0.17Q	10/19	11/1	11/7	12/1
0.18Q	1/18/89	1/26/89	2/1/89	3/1/89
0.18Q	4/19	4/25	5/1	6/1

BACKGROUND:

Dow Jones publishes business publications, community newspapers, and information services. Business publications includes The Wall Street Journal and Barron's National Business and Financial Weekly. Information services include Dow Jones news services, news/retrieval service and 67%-owned Telerate, Inc. Community newspapers, published by Ottaway Newspapers, include 20 dailies. It also has interest in newsprint production, and business and financial wire services. For 1988, business publications accounted for 47% of revenues (32% of operating profit); community newspapers, 15% (12%); information services, 38% (60%); and corporate, 0% (4%).

RECENT DEVELOPMENTS:

For the quarter ended 3/31/89, net income advanced 93% to $200.0 million compared with $103.6 million in the similar period last year. Revenues improved 4% to $406.8 million from $392.5 million. The jump in earnings was primarily due to a one-time gain of $164.1 million. Operating profit fell 13%, reflecting weak financial advertising at the Wall Street Journal. Total advertising linage declined 12% at the Journal. The information services segment, which includes Telerate, Inc., reported a 15% gain in revenues. In the community newspaper segment, Ottaway Newspapers Inc. saw operating profit fall 14%.

PROSPECTS:

The Company will continue to grow as the world's leading supplier of business news. However, sharp declines in financial advertising in the Wall Street Journal and Barron's will affect results. The information services group should continue to post solid gains due to the success of Telerate, Inc. and new product initiatives to improve service. Cost containment efforts such as cuts in employment levels will help offset any advertising decline. In addition, new revenue sources such as localized Journal ad editions will be introduced.

STATISTICS:

YEAR	GROSS REVS. (SMILL)	OPER. PROFIT MARGIN %	RET. ON EQUITY %	NET INCOME (SMILL)	WORK CAP. (SMILL)	SENIOR CAPITAL (SMILL)	SHARES (000)	EARN. PER SH.$	DIV. PER SH.$	DIV. PAY %	PRICE RANGE	P/E RATIO	AVG. YIELD %
79	440.9	19.5	27.5	51.1	d	15.9	93,162	0.55	0.24	44	6⅝ - 5⅜	10.9	4.0
80	530.7	18.2	26.6	58.9	4.9	8.7	93,459	0.63	0.27	42	10½ - 5⅞	12.9	3.3
81	641.0	21.1	26.5	71.4	d	49.7	91,197	0.76	0.31	40	18⅜ - 9⅞	18.6	2.2
82	730.7	20.5	26.4	88.1	d	35.1	95,720	0.93	0.36	39	23½ - 11⅞	19.1	2.0
83	866.4	24.3	27.4	114.2	d	16.8	96,131	1.19	0.40	34	37½ - 21⅜	24.7	1.4
84	965.6	23.8	25.5	129.1	d	21.0	96,455	1.34	0.48	36	34¼ - 23½	21.5	1.7
85	1,039.3	23.4	23.1	138.6	d	248.1	96,714	1.43	0.52	36	33⅜ - 24½	20.2	1.8
86	1,134.9	23.2	25.2	a183.4	d	59.6	96,751	a1.89	0.55	29	42⅛ - 28	18.6	1.6
87	1,314.4	22.5	24.0	b203.0	d	444.2	96,305	b2.10	0.64	30	56¼ - 28	20.1	1.5
88	1,603.1	21.9	19.7	c228.2	d	290.1	100,835	c2.35	0.68	29	36½ - 26¾	13.5	2.2

♦Long-Term Price Score — Short-Term Price Score; see page 4a. STATISTICS ARE AS ORIGINALLY REPORTED Adjusted for 2-for-1 split, 4/81 & 2/83 and a 50% stock dividend payable 6/86. a-Includes a net gain of $34.1 million in 1986 and $164.1 million in 1989 on the sale of interests in Continental Cablevision, Inc. b-Includes a net gain of $29.4 million from sale of interest in South China Morning Post Ltd. c-Includes net gains of $68.0 million in 1988 and $29.4 million in 1987.

INCORPORATED:
Nov.22, 1949 — Delaware

PRINCIPAL OFFICE:
World Financial Center
200 Liberty Street
New York, N.Y. 10281
Tel.: (212) 416-2000

ANNUAL MEETING:
Third Wednesday in April

NUMBER OF STOCKHOLDERS:
21,500

TRANSFER AGENT(S):
Morgan Shareholder Services Trust Co.
New York, NY

REGISTRAR(S):
Morgan Shareholder Services Trust Co.
New York, NY

INSTITUTIONAL HOLDINGS:
No. of Institutions: 247
Shares Held: 31,674,084

OFFICERS:
Chairman & C.E.O.
  W. H. Phillips
President & C.O.O.
  R. Shaw.
V.P. & C.F.O.
  K. L. Burenga
Vice Pres., Gen. Coun. & Secretary
  K. J. Roche
Treasurer
  L. E. Doherty

SOURCE: *Moody's Handbook of Common Stock, Summer 1989* (New York: Moody's Investors Service, Inc., 1989).

examples of the supply and demand theories presented earlier, but an investor must also consider other factors when determining whether a stock is priced too high or too low. In this section, we examine numerical measures for a corporation and the fundamental, technical, and efficient market theories that investors use to determine whether a stock is priced right.

Numerical Measures for a Corporation   With a few exceptions, a corporation's book value has little direct relationship to the market price of its stock.[4] However, book value per share is such a widely reported measure of a stock's value that it deserves mention. The **book value** for a share of stock is determined by deducting all liabilities from the corporation's assets and dividing the remainder by the number of outstanding shares of common stock. For example, assume that XYZ Corporation has assets of $6 million and liabilities of $3 million and that it has issued 100,000 shares of common stock. In this situation, the book value for a share of XYZ stock is $30 per share, as illustrated below.

$$\frac{\begin{array}{cc} Assets & Liabilities \\ \$6,000,000 & - \ \$3,000,000 \end{array}}{100{,}000 \text{ shares of stock}} = \$30 \text{ per share}$$

Book value may be a useful tool for evaluating a stock issued by a company that has large amounts of capital invested in natural resources. The future profits of such a company are tied directly to the ability to utilize investments in oil, timber, copper, iron ore, and so on. It should be noted, however, that the book value a corporation's financial statements report for assets may be higher or lower than the actual market value of those assets. If the calculations in the above formula are based on inaccurate dollar amounts for assets or liabilities, they will usually result in an inaccurate estimate of the book value per share.

Earnings per share are a corporation's after-tax earnings divided by the number of outstanding shares of common stock. For example, assume that in 1990 XYZ Corporation has after-tax earnings of $800,000. As mentioned above, XYZ has 100,000 shares of common stock. This means that XYZ's earnings per share are $8 ($800,000 ÷ 100,000 = $8). Most stockholders consider the amount of earnings per share important because it is a measure of the company's profitability.

The **price-earnings ratio (P-E ratio)** is the price of a share of stock divided by the corporation's earnings per share of stock outstanding over the last 12 months. For example, assume that XYZ Corporation's common stock is selling for $112 a share. As determined above, XYZ's earnings per share are $8. XYZ's price-earnings ratio is therefore 14 ($112 ÷ $8 = 14). The price-earnings ratio is a key factor that serious investors use to evaluate stock investments. Generally, the price-earnings ratio for a corporation must be studied over a period of time. For example, if XYZ's price-earnings ratio has ranged from 12 to 30 over the past three years, then its current price-earnings ratio of 14 indicates that it may be a potentially good investment. If XYZ's current price-earnings ratio were 27, toward the high end of the range, then it might be a poor investment at this time. For most corporations, price-earnings ratios range between 5 and 20. Again, a low price-earnings ratio indicates that a stock may be a good investment and a high price-earnings ratio indicates that it may be a poor investment.

The **beta** is an index that compares the risk associated with a specific stock issue with the risk of the stock market in general. The beta for the stock market in general is 1.0. The majority of stocks have betas between 0.5 and 2.0. Generally, conservative stocks have low betas and risky stocks have high betas. For example, assume that XYZ Corporation's stock has a beta of 0.50. This means that its stock is less responsive than the market in general. When the market in general increases by 10 percent, XYZ's stock will go up 5 percent. If, on the other hand, ABC Corporation has a beta of 2.0, this means that ABC's stock is twice as responsive as the market in general. When the market in general increases by 10 percent, ABC's stock will go up 20 percent.

Investment Theories Investors often use three investment theories to determine a stock's market value. The **fundamental theory** is based on the assumption that a stock's intrinsic or real value is determined by the future earnings of the company. If the expected earnings for a corporation are higher than the present earnings, the corporation's stock should increase in value. If the expected earnings for a corporation are lower than the present earnings, the corporation's stock should decrease in value. In addition to expected earnings, fundamentalists consider (1) the financial strength of the company, (2) the type of industry the company is in, and (3) the economic growth of the overall economy. The **technical theory** is based on the assumption that a stock's market value is determined by the forces of supply and demand in the stock market as a whole. It is based, not on the expected earnings or the intrinsic value of an individual stock, but on factors found in the market as a whole. Typical technical factors are the total number of shares traded, the number of buy orders, and the number of sell orders. Technical analysts, sometimes called chartists, construct charts that plot price movements and other market index movements. By means of these charts, they can observe trends and patterns that enable them to predict whether a stock's market price will increase or decrease.

The **efficient market theory,** sometimes called the random walk theory, is based on the assumption that stock price movements are purely random. Advocates of the efficient market theory assume that the stock market is completely efficient and that buyers and sellers have considered all of the available information about an individual stock. Any news on an individual corporation, an oil embargo, or a change in the tax laws that may affect the price of a stock is quickly absorbed by all investors seeking a profit. Thus, a stock's market price reflects its true value. The efficient market theory rejects both the fundamental theory and the technical theory. According to this theory, it is impossible for an investor to outperform the average for the stock market as a whole over a long period of time.

BUYING AND SELLING STOCKS

L.O.4
Describe how stocks are bought and sold through brokerage firms and securities exchanges.

To purchase a pair of jeans, you simply walk into a store that sells jeans, choose a pair, and pay for your purchase. To purchase common or preferred stock, you generally have to work through a financial representative. In turn, your financial representative must buy the stock in either the primary or secondary market. The **primary market** is a market in which an investor purchases financial securities (via an investment bank or other representative) from the issuer of those securities. An **investment bank** is a financial firm that assists organizations in raising funds, usually by helping sell new security issues. An example of stock sold through the primary market is the new common stock issue sold by Chrysler Corporation during the early 1980s. Investors bought this stock through brokerage firms acting as agents for an investment banking firm, and the money they paid for common stock flowed to Chrysler Corporation and not to other investors. After a stock has been sold through the primary market, it is traded through the secondary market. The **secondary market** is a market for existing financial securities that are currently traded between investors. Once the Chrysler stock has been sold in the primary market, it can be sold time and again in the secondary market.

Primary Markets for Stocks

How would you sell $100 million worth of common stocks or preferred stocks? For a large corporation, the decision to sell stocks or bonds is often complicated, time consuming, and expensive. There are basically two methods.

First, a large corporation may use an investment bank to sell and distribute the new stock issue. This method is used by most large corporations that need a lot of financing. If this method is used, analysts for the investment bank examine the corporation's financial position to determine whether the new issue is financially sound and how difficult it will be to sell the issue.

If the investment bank is satisfied that the new stock is a good risk, it will buy the stock and then resell the stock to its customers—commercial banks, insurance companies, pension funds, mutual funds, and the general public. The investment bank's commission, or spread, ranges from 2.3 to 11.3 percent of the gross proceeds received by a corporation issuing common stock.[5] The size of the commission depends on the quality and financial health of the corporation issuing the new stock. The commission allows the investment bank to make a profit while guaranteeing that the corporation will receive the needed financing.

If the stock issue is too large for one investment bank, a group of investment bankers may form an underwriting syndicate. Then each member of the syndicate is responsible for selling only a part of the new issue. If the investment bank's analysts feel that the new issue will be difficult to sell, the investment bank may agree to take the stock on a best efforts basis, without guaranteeing that the stock will be sold. Because the investment bank does not guarantee the sale of the issue, most large corporations are unwilling to accept this arrangement.

The second method used by a corporation that is trying to obtain financing through the primary market is to sell directly to current stockholders. Usually, promotional materials describing the new stock issue are mailed to current stockholders. These stockholders may then purchase the stock directly from the corporation. As mentioned earlier in this chapter, most states require that a provision for preemptive rights be included in the charter of every corporation. This provision gives current stockholders the right to purchase any new stock that the corporation issues before it is offered to the general public.

You may ask, "Why would a corporation try to sell its own stock?" The most obvious reason for doing so is to avoid the investment bank's commission. Of course, a corporation's ability to sell a new stock issue without the aid of an investment bank is tied directly to the public's perception of the corporation's financial health.

Secondary Markets for Stocks

How does an individual buy or sell common or preferred stock in the secondary market? To purchase common or preferred stock, you have to work through a financial representative—your stockbroker. Then your broker must buy or sell for you in a securities marketplace, which is either a securities exchange or the over-the-counter market.

Securities Exchanges   A **securities exchange** is a marketplace where member brokers who are representing investors meet to buy and sell securities. The securities sold at a particular exchange must first be listed, or accepted for trading, at that exchange. Generally, the securities issued by nationwide corporations are traded at either the New York Stock Exchange or the American Stock Exchange. The securities of regional corporations are traded at smaller, regional exchanges. These are located in Chicago, San Francisco, Philadelphia, Boston, and several other cities. The securities of very large corporations may be traded at more than one exchange. American firms that do business abroad may also be listed on foreign securities exchanges—in Tokyo, London, or Paris, for example.

The New York Stock Exchange (NYSE) is the largest securities exchange in the United States and accounts for approximately 70 percent of all U.S. stock transactions. This exchange lists over 2,200 securities, issued by approximately 1,500 corporations with a market value of about $3 trillion.[6] The New York Stock Exchange has 1,366 members, or "seats," as they are often called. Most of these members represent brokerage firms that charge commissions on security trades made by their representatives for their customers. The cost of a seat is determined largely by sales volume and stock prices on the exchange. The lowest price in this century was $17,000, paid in 1942. In the late 1980s, a seat sold for approximately $1 million.[7]

Before a corporation's stock is approved for listing on the New York Stock Exchange, the corporation must meet five criteria:[8]

1. Its annual earnings before federal income taxes must be at least $2.5 million in the most recent year or $2 million or more in the preceding two years.
2. It must own net tangible assets valued at $18 million or more.
3. The market value of its publicly held stock must equal or exceed $9 million.
4. A total of at least 1.1 million shares of its common stock must be publicly owned.
5. At least 2,000 stockholders must each own 100 or more shares of its stock.

The American Stock Exchange and various regional exchanges also have listing requirements, but typically these are less stringent than the NYSE requirements. The stock of corporations that cannot meet the NYSE requirements, find it too expensive to be listed, or choose not to be listed on the NYSE is often traded on the American Stock Exchange or one of the regional exchanges or through the over-the-counter market.

The Over-the-Counter Market   The **over-the-counter (OTC) market** is a network of stockbrokers who buy and sell the securities of corporations that are not listed on a securities exchange. Usually, the brokers in this network specialize, or make a market, in the securities of one or more specific firms. The securities of each firm are traded through its specialist, who is generally aware of their prices and of investors who are willing to buy or sell them. Most OTC trading is conducted by telephone. Since 1971, the brokers and dealers operating in the

Pepper . . . and Salt

SUPPORT YOUR LOCAL STOCK MARKET

From *The Wall Street Journal,* with permission of Cartoon Features Syndicate.

OTC market have used an electronic quotation system called NASDAQ—the letters stand for the National Association of Securities Dealers Automated Quotation System. NASDAQ is a computerized system that displays current price quotations on a terminal in the subscriber's office.

Brokerage Firms and Account Executives

Most securities transactions are made through an account executive or stockbroker who works for a brokerage firm. An **account executive,** or stockbroker, is an individual who buys or sells securities for his or her clients. (Actually, account executive is the more descriptive title because such individuals handle all types of securities—not just stocks. Most account executives also provide securities information and advise their clients regarding investments.) Account executives are employed by such stock brokerage firms as Merrill Lynch, Prudential-Bache, and A. G. Edwards.

Before choosing an account executive, you should have already decided on what your short-term and long-term financial objectives are. Then, you must be careful to communicate those objectives to the account executive so that he or she can do a better job of advising you. Needless to say, account executives may err in their investment recommendations. To help avoid a situation in which your account executive's recommendations are automatically implemented, you should be actively involved in the decisions of your investment program and you should not allow your account executive to use his or her discretion (make decisions without your approval) in managing your account. Watch your account for signs of churning. **Churning** is excessive buying and selling of securities in order to generate commissions. From a total dollar return standpoint, this practice usually

FINANCIAL PLANNING IN ACTION

Choosing an Account Executive

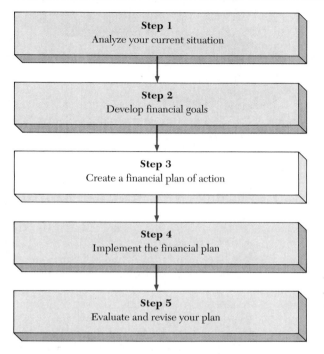

Step 1
Analyze your current situation

Step 2
Develop financial goals

Step 3
Create a financial plan of action

Step 4
Implement the financial plan

Step 5
Evaluate and revise your plan

investments. Many investors begin their search for an account executive by asking friends or business associates for recommendations. This is a logical starting point, but remember that some account executives are conservative, while others are risk oriented. It is quite common for investors to test an account executive's advice over a period of time. Then, if the account executive's track record is acceptable, his or her investment suggestions can be taken more seriously. At this point, most investors begin to rely more heavily on the account executive's advice and less on their own intuition and research.

Why You Need an Account Executive

Basically, your account executive sees that your order to buy or sell stocks or bonds is correctly executed according to exchange rules. Your account executive should also be able to provide you with current financial information about the stocks or bonds in which you are interested. There are no guarantees that the securities you buy on the basis of your account executive's recommendation will increase in value, but he or she should help in the evaluation process.

A Final Word of Caution

Before choosing an account executive, you should ask a few questions to determine whether you and the account executive are on the same wavelength with regard to investment goals and objectives. Don't be surprised if your account executive wants to ask you a few questions too. In order to provide better service, he or she must know what type of investment program you want to establish. If, after a reasonable period of time, you become dissatisfied with your investment program, do not hesitate to discuss your dissatisfaction with the account executive. You may even find it necessary to choose another account executive if your dissatisfaction continues. This is not at all uncommon. But when all is said and done, it is your money and you must make the final decisions that help you achieve your investment goals.

A good investment program should start before you choose an account executive. First of all, you must establish financial goals and objectives to meet your individual needs. Then you must accumulate enough money to get started. Most authorities suggest maintaining a cash reserve equal to at least three months' salary. Once you have accumulated funds in excess of the cash reserve amount, it's time to choose an account executive.

How Do You Find an Account Executive?

All account executives can buy or sell stock for you, but most investors expect more from their account executives. Ideally, an account executive should provide information and advice that can be used in evaluating potential

leaves the client worse off or no better off. Churning is illegal under the rules established by the Securities and Exchange Commission, but it may be difficult to prove. Finally, keep in mind that account executives are generally not liable for client losses that result from their recommendations. In fact, most brokerage firms require that new clients sign a statement in which they promise to submit any complaints to an arbitration board. This arbitration clause generally prevents a client from suing an account executive or a brokerage firm. The accompanying "Financial Planning in Action" feature presents specific suggestions that will help you in choosing an account executive.

The Typical Transaction   Once an investor and his or her account executive have decided on a particular transaction, the investor gives the account executive an order for that transaction. A **market order** is a request that a stock be bought or sold at the current market price. Since the stock exchange is an auction market, the account executive's representative will try to get the best price possible and the transaction will be completed as soon as possible. A **limit order** is a request that a stock be bought or sold at a specified price. A limit order assures you that you will pay no more than the limit price when you buy stock or that you will receive no less than the limit price when you sell stock. For example, if you place a limit order to sell Kellogg common stock for $78 a share, the stock will not be sold for less than that amount. Likewise, if your limit order is to buy Kellogg for $78 a share, the stock will not be purchased until the price drops to $78 a share or lower. Limit orders are used by stockholders to buy stocks at prices thought to be at the low end of a price range and to sell stocks at prices thought to be at the high end of a price range.

Many stockholders are certain that they want to buy or sell their stock if a specified price is reached. A limit order does not guarantee that this will be done. Orders by other investors may be placed ahead of your order. If you want to guarantee that your order is executed, you place a stop order. A **stop order** is a request that an order be executed at the next available opportunity after the market price of a stock reaches a specified price. For example, assume that you purchased Texaco common stock at $50 a share. Two weeks after your Texaco investment, Texaco is facing multiple lawsuits resulting from an industrial accident at one of its refineries. Fearing that the market value of your Texaco stock will decrease, you enter a stop order to sell your Texaco stock at $32. This means that if the price of the Texaco stock decreases to $32 or lower, the broker will sell it at the best price he or she can get for you. Both limit orders and stop orders can be day orders that expire at the end of the day if not executed, or they can be good until canceled.

Exhibit 16–6 illustrates how a market order to sell stock is actually executed. Two things should be noted. First, every stock is traded at a particular trading post, which is a desk on the trading floor. Generally, around 10 or 12 issues are traded at each trading post. Second, each transaction is recorded, and the pertinent information (stock symbol, number of shares, and price) is transmitted to interested parties through a communications network called a ticker tape. Payment for stocks is generally required within five business days of the transaction.

Commission Charges   Most brokerage firms have a minimum commission charge for buying or selling stock, usually between $20 and $35. Additional commission charges are based on the number of shares and the value of stock bought and sold. On the trading floor of a stock exchange, stocks are traded in round lots or odd lots. A **round lot** is 100 shares or multiples of 100 shares of a particular stock. Exhibit 16–7 shows typical commission charges for some round lot transactions. An **odd lot** is fewer than 100 shares of a particular stock.

EXHIBIT 16–6

The Steps Involved for a
Typical Transaction for
Stock Traded on the New
York Stock Exchange

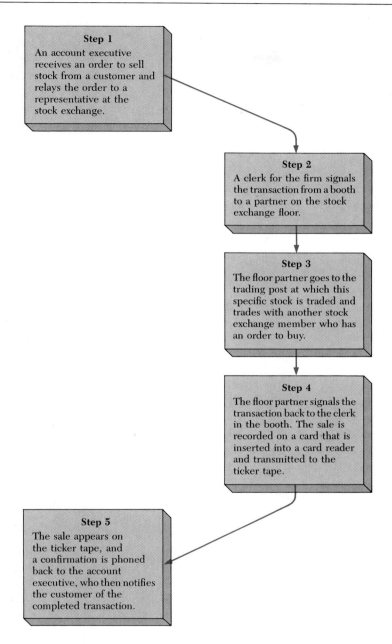

Step 1
An account executive
receives an order to sell
stock from a customer and
relays the order to a
representative at the
stock exchange.

Step 2
A clerk for the firm signals
the transaction from a booth
to a partner on the stock
exchange floor.

Step 3
The floor partner goes to the
trading post at which this
specific stock is traded and
trades with another stock
exchange member who has
an order to buy.

Step 4
The floor partner signals the
transaction back to the clerk
in the booth. The sale is
recorded on a card that is
inserted into a card reader
and transmitted to the
ticker tape.

Step 5
The sale appears on
the ticker tape, and
a confirmation is phoned
back to the account
executive, who then notifies
the customer of the
completed transaction.

Brokerage firms generally charge higher per share fees for trading in odd lots,
primarily because odd lots must be combined into round lots before they can
actually be traded.

Notice that the commission charged by full-service brokers is higher than the
commission charged by discount brokers. Full-service brokers usually spend more
time with each client. Their recommendations on specific stocks or investment
strategies are tailored to the client's individual needs. On the other hand, discount
brokers generally just buy or sell securities on behalf of the client. When investors

EXHIBIT 16–7

Typical Commission
Charges for Round Lot
Transactions through a
Full-Service Broker and
a Discount Broker

		Commission	
	Stock Dollar Cost	**Full-Service Broker**	**Discount Broker**
100 shares @ $40 per share	$ 4,000	$ 82	$35
100 shares @ $60 per share	6,000	90	35
200 shares @ $35 per share	7,000	136	70
400 shares @ $40 per share	16,000	268	140

choose a discount broker, they should understand that they are going to make their own decisions without benefit of the broker's advice. Because discount brokers spend less time with each client than do full-service brokers, they are able to handle more clients and to charge a lower commission on each security transaction. However, there are situations in which some discount brokerage firms charge higher commissions than some full-service brokerage firms. This generally occurs when the transaction is small—involving a total dollar amount of less than $1,000—and the investor is charged the minimum commission charge of the discount brokerage firm.

LONG-TERM AND SHORT TERM INVESTMENT STRATEGIES

Once stock has been purchased, it may be classified as either a long-term investment or a short-term investment. Generally, individuals who hold an investment for a long period of time are referred to as investors. Individuals who buy and then sell stocks within a short period of time are called speculators or traders.

L.O.5
Explain the traditional trading techniques used by long-term and short-term investors.

Long-Term Techniques

In this section, we will discuss the long-term techniques of buy and hold, dollar cost averaging, and dividend reinvestment programs.

The Buy and Hold Technique   Many long-term investors purchase common and preferred stock and hold on to that stock for a number of years. When this is done, there are three ways in which their investment can increase in value. First, they are entitled to dividends if the board of directors approves dividend distributions to stockholders. Second, the price of the stock may go up. Third, the stock may be split. Although there are no guarantees, stock splits usually increase the value of a stock investment over a long period of time. Jack and Susan Overall—the people in the Opening Case of this chapter—used a buy and hold technique when they purchased their Federal Express stock in 1979. As a result, they made more than $21,000 through a combination of appreciation in value and stock splits.

Dollar Cost Averaging   Dollar cost averaging is a long-term technique used by investors who purchase an equal dollar amount of the same stock at equal intervals. Assume that you invest $2,000 in XYZ Corporation's common stock each year for a period of three years. The results of your investment program are illustrated in Exhibit 16–8. Notice that when the price increased in 1991, you purchased fewer shares of stock. When the price of the stock decreased in 1992,

EXHIBIT 16–8
Dollar Cost Averaging

Year	Investment	Stock Price	Shares Purchased
1990	$2,000	$50	40.0
1991	2,000	65	30.8
1992	2,000	60	33.3
	$6,000		104.1

you purchased more shares of stock. The average cost for a share of stock, determined by dividing the total investment ($6,000) by the total number of shares (104.1), is $57.64. Another application of dollar cost averaging occurs when employees purchase shares of their company's stock through a payroll deduction plan.

Investors use dollar cost averaging to avoid the common practice of buying high and selling low. In the situation shown in Exhibit 16–8, you would lose money only if you sold your stock at less than the average cost of $57.64. Thus, with dollar cost averaging an investor can make money if the stock is sold at a price higher than the average purchase price.

Direct Investment and Dividend Reinvestment Plans   Today, a large number of corporations offer direct investment plans. A **direct investment plan** allows stockholders to purchase stock directly from a corporation without having to use an account executive or a brokerage firm. In a similar manner, a **dividend reinvestment plan** allows current stockholders the option of reinvesting their cash dividends in the stock of a corporation. For stockholders, the chief advantage of both types of plans is that through these plans they can purchase stock without paying a commission charge to a brokerage firm. As an added incentive, some corporations even offer their stock at a small discount to encourage stockholders to use their direct investment and dividend investment plans. For corporations, the chief advantage of both types of plans is that they provide an additional source of capital.

Short-Term Techniques

In addition to the long-term techniques presented in the preceding section, short-term investors sometimes use more speculative techniques. In this section, we will discuss buying stock on margin, selling short, and trading in options. The methods presented in this section are quite risky and should not be used by investors who do not fully understand the underlying risks.

Buying Stock on Margin

When buying stock on **margin** an investor borrows part of the money necessary to buy a particular stock. The margin requirement is set by the Federal Reserve Board and is subject to periodic change. The current margin requirement is 50 percent, which means that an investor may borrow up to half of the stock purchase price. Usually, the stock brokerage firm either lends the money or arranges the loan with another financial institution. Investors buy on margin because doing so offers them the potential for greater profits. Exhibit 16–9 gives an example of buying stock on margin.

EXHIBIT 16–9

A Typical Margin Transaction

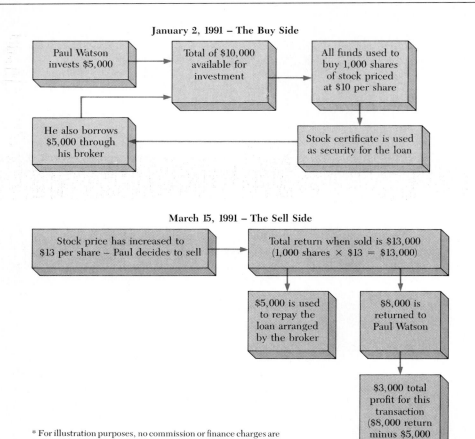

January 2, 1991 – The Buy Side

Paul Watson invests $5,000 → Total of $10,000 available for investment → All funds used to buy 1,000 shares of stock priced at $10 per share

He also borrows $5,000 through his broker

Stock certificate is used as security for the loan

March 15, 1991 – The Sell Side

Stock price has increased to $13 per share – Paul decides to sell → Total return when sold is $13,000 (1,000 shares × $13 = $13,000)

$5,000 is used to repay the loan arranged by the broker

$8,000 is returned to Paul Watson

$3,000 total profit for this transaction ($8,000 return minus $5,000 investment)*

* For illustration purposes, no commission or finance charges are included. In reality, commission would be approximately $400 and finance charges would be approximately $150.

As shown in Exhibit 16–9, it is more profitable to use margin. In effect, the financial leverage of borrowed money allowed the stockholder to purchase a larger number of shares of stock. Since the dollar value of each share increased, the stockholder obtained a much greater total profit by buying the stock on margin.

In the example illustrated in Exhibit 16–9, the investor's stock did exactly what it was supposed to do. It increased in value. Had the value of the stock gone down, buying on margin would have increased the investor's loss. In this example, Paul Watson would have lost $3,000 if the price of the stock had dropped from $10 a share (the original purchase price) to $7 a share. If the market value of a margined stock decreases to approximately one half of the original price, the investor will receive a margin call from the brokerage firm. The exact price at which the brokerage firm issues the margin call is determined by the amount of money that the investor borrowed when the stock was purchased. Generally, the more money the investor borrows, the sooner he or she will receive a margin call. After the margin call, the investor must pledge additional cash or securities to serve as collateral for the loan. If the investor doesn't have acceptable collateral, the margined stock is sold and the proceeds are used to repay the loan.

In addition to facing the possibility of larger dollar losses, the margin investor must pay interest on the money borrowed to purchase stock on margin. Most brokerage firms charge 1 to 3 percent above the prime interest rate for such loans. Normally, bankers define the prime rate as the interest rate that they charge their best business customers. Interest charges can absorb the potential profits if the value of margined stock does not increase rapidly enough.

Selling Short

An investor's ability to make money by buying and selling securities is related to how well he or she can predict whether a certain stock will increase or decrease in market value. Normally, the investor buys stocks and assumes that they will increase in value—a procedure referred to as *buying long*. But not all stocks increase in value. In fact, there are many reasons why the market value of a security may decrease. With this fact in mind, investors oriented to greater risk often use a procedure called selling short to make money when the price of a security is falling. *Selling short* is selling stock that has been borrowed from a stockbroker and must be replaced at a later date. When you sell short, you sell today, knowing that you must buy or *cover* your short transaction at a later date. To make money in a short transaction, an investor must take these steps:

1. Arrange to borrow a stock certificate for a certain number of shares of a particular stock from an account executive.
2. Sell the borrowed stock, assuming that it will drop in price in a reasonably short period of time.
3. Buy the stock at a lower price than the price that it sold for in Step 2.
4. Use the stock purchased in Step 3 to replace the stock borrowed in Step 1.

For example, Paul Watson believes that General Motors is overpriced because of lower demand for cars and numerous other factors. As a result, he decides to sell short 100 shares of General Motors (Exhibit 16–10).

As shown in Exhibit 16–10, Paul Watson's total return for this short transaction was $700 because the stock did what it was supposed to do—decrease in value. A price decrease is especially important to the investor selling short because he or she must replace the stock borrowed from the brokerage firm with stock purchased at a later date. If the stock increases in value, the investor will lose money because he or she must replace the borrowed stock with stock purchased at a higher price. If the price of the General Motors stock in Exhibit 16–10 had increased from $60 to $67, Paul Watson would have lost $700.

There is usually no brokerage charge for selling a stock short since the brokerage firm receives a commission when the stock is bought and sold. Before selling short, consider two factors. First, since the stock you borrow from your broker is actually owned by another investor, you must pay any dividends that the stock earns during your short transaction. After all, you borrowed the stock and then sold the borrowed stock. The dividends you pay can absorb the profits from your short transaction if the price of the stock does not decrease rapidly enough. Second, to make money selling short, you must be correct in predicting that a stock will decrease in value. If the value of the stock increases, you lose.

EXHIBIT 16–10

An Example of Selling
Short

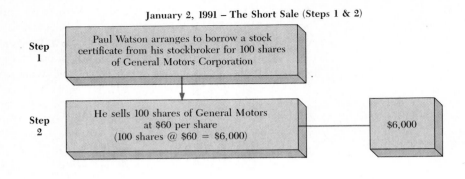

January 2, 1991 – The Short Sale (Steps 1 & 2)

Step 1 Paul Watson arranges to borrow a stock certificate from his stockbroker for 100 shares of General Motors Corporation

Step 2 He sells 100 shares of General Motors at $60 per share (100 shares @ $60 = $6,000) $6,000

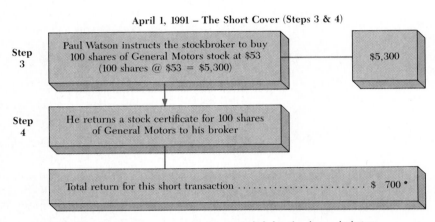

April 1, 1991 – The Short Cover (Steps 3 & 4)

Step 3 Paul Watson instructs the stockbroker to buy 100 shares of General Motors stock at $53 (100 shares @ $53 = $5,300) $5,300

Step 4 He returns a stock certificate for 100 shares of General Motors to his broker

Total return for this short transaction . . . . $ 700 *

* For illustration purposes, no commission was included in the above calculations.
In reality, commission would amount to approximately $200.

Trading in Options

An **option** gives an investor the right to buy or sell 100 shares of a stock at a predetermined price during a specified period of time. An investor who thinks that the market price of a stock will increase during a short period of time may decide to purchase a call option. A **call option** is sold by a stockholder and gives the purchaser the right to *buy* 100 shares of a stock at a guaranteed price before a definite expiration date. For instance, Bob Gray invests $150 to purchase a call option on Control Data stock. His call option enables him to buy 100 shares of Control Data before the expiration date at a guaranteed price of $45 per share. In this case, if the price of Control Data stock does increase, Bob Gray can make money in one of two ways:

1. Before the expiration date, he can sell his option to another investor. Since his option is more valuable as a result of the stock's higher price, he can sell it to another investor at a price higher than he paid for it.
2. He can exercise his option and purchase the stock at the price guaranteed by the option. Since the stock price guaranteed by the option is lower than the market price, he can make a profit by selling the stock at a higher price.

Some stock owners who believe that the price of their stock will go down during the option period will purchase a put option to safeguard their investment. A **put option** is the right to *sell* 100 shares of a stock at a guaranteed price before a definite expiration date. For example, Patsy Jones owns 100 shares of Eastman Kodak. She decides to safeguard her investment from a drop in market value by purchasing a put option for $325. Her put option enables her to sell 100 shares of Eastman Kodak before the expiration date at a guaranteed price of $75. In this case, if the price of Eastman Kodak stock does go down to less than $75, Patsy Jones can sell her Eastman Kodak shares at the higher price guaranteed by the put option.

Securities Regulation

Government regulation of securities trading began as a response to abusive and fraudulent practices in the sale of stocks. Individual states were the first to react, early in this century. Later, federal legislation was passed to regulate the interstate sale of securities.

State Regulation   In 1911, Kansas enacted the first state law regulating securities transactions. Within a few years, a number of other states had passed similar laws. Most of the state laws provide for (1) registration of securities, (2) licensing of brokers and securities salespeople, and (3) prosecution of any individual who sells fraudulent stocks and bonds. These laws are often called blue-sky laws because they were designed to stop the sale of securities that had nothing to back them up except the sky.

Federal Regulation   The Securities Act of 1933, sometimes referred to as the Truth in Securities Act, provides for full disclosure of important facts about corporations issuing new securities. Such corporations are required to file a registration statement containing specific information about the corporation's earnings, assets, and liabilities; its products or services; and the qualifications of its top management. Publication of the prospectus, which is a summary of information contained in the registration statement, is also required by this act.

The Securities Exchange Act of 1934 created the Securities and Exchange Commission (SEC), the agency that enforces federal securities regulations. The operations of the SEC are directed by five commissioners who are appointed by the president of the United States and approved by a two-thirds vote of the Senate. The 1934 act gave the SEC the power to regulate trading on the New York Stock Exchange and the American Stock Exchange. It empowered the SEC to make brokers and securities dealers pass an examination before being allowed to sell securities, and it required that registration statements be brought up-to-date periodically.

Seven other federal acts were passed primarily to protect investors:

- The Maloney Act of 1938 made the National Association of Securities Dealers (NASD) responsible for the self-regulation of the over-the-counter securities market.
- The Investment Company Act of 1940 placed investment companies that sell mutual funds under the jurisdiction of the SEC.
- The Federal Securities Act of 1964 extended the SEC's jurisdiction to companies whose stock is sold over the counter if they have total assets of at least $1 million or more than 500 stockholders of any one class of stock.

- The Securities Investor Protection Act of 1970 created the Securities Investor Protection Corporation (SIPC). This organization provides insurance of up to $500,000 for securities left on deposit with a brokerage firm that later fails. There is also an insurance limit of $100,000 on cash deposited with a brokerage firm that fails.
- The Securities Acts Amendments of 1975 amended the Securities Exchange Act of 1934. These amendments directed the SEC to work toward establishing a computerized national market system for nationwide clearance and settlement of securities transactions. The amendments also eliminated fixed commissions and allowed more competition among brokerage firms.
- The Insider Trading Sanctions Act of 1984 strengthened the penalty provisions of the 1934 Securities Exchange Act. Under this act, people are guilty of insider trading if they use information that is available only to account executives or other employees of brokerage firms. The act also expanded the SEC's power to investigate such illegal behavior.
- The Insider Trading Act of 1988 made the top management of brokerage firms responsible for reporting transactions based on inside information to the SEC. This act also enabled the SEC to levy fines of up to $1 million for failure to report such violations of the law.

SUMMARY

L.O.1
Identify the most important features of common stock, and discuss why people invest in common stock.

People invest in common stock because of dividend income, appreciation of value, and the possibility of stock splits. Dividend payments to common stockholders must be approved by a corporation's board of directors.

L.O.2
Identify the most important features of preferred stock, and discuss why people invest in preferred stock.

The most important priority that an investor in preferred stock enjoys is receiving cash dividends before any cash dividends are paid to common stockholders. To make preferred stock issues more attractive, corporations may add a cumulative feature, a participating feature, and/or a conversion feature to these issues. People invest in preferred stock because of dividend income and appreciation of value.

L.O.3
Explain how investors can evaluate stock investments.

A number of factors can make a share of stock increase or decrease in value. When evaluating a particular stock issue, most investors begin with the information contained in daily newspapers. Classification of stocks, stock advisory services, numerical measures, and the fundamental, technical, and efficient market investment theories can all be used to help evaluate a stock investment.

L.O.4
Describe how stocks are bought and sold through brokerage firms and securities exchanges.

A corporation may sell a new stock issue through an investment bank or directly to current stockholders. Once the stock has been sold in the primary market, it can be sold time and again in the secondary market. In the secondary market, investors purchase stock listed on a securities exchange or traded in the over-the-counter market. Most securities transactions are made through an account executive or stockbroker who works for a brokerage firm. Most brokerage firms charge a minimum commission for buying or selling stock. Additional commission charges are based on the number and value of the stock shares that are bought or sold.

KEY FORMULAS

A Reference Guide

Page	Topic	Formula
464	Book value	$$\text{Book value} = \frac{\text{Assets} - \text{Liabilities}}{\text{Number of outstanding shares of common stock}}$$
464	Earnings per share	$$\text{Earnings per share} = \frac{\text{After-tax earnings}}{\text{Number of outstanding shares of common stock}}$$
464	Price = earnings (P-E) ratio-	$$\text{P-E ratio} = \frac{\text{Price per share}}{\text{Earnings per share of stock outstanding over the last 12 months}}$$

L.O.5
Explain the traditional trading techniques used by long-term and short-term investors.

Purchased stock may be classified as either a long-term investment or a speculative investment. Traditional trading techniques used by long-term investors include the buy and hold technique, dollar cost averaging, direct investment plans, and dividend reinvestment plans. More speculative techniques include buying on margin, selling short, and trading in options.

GLOSSARY

Account executive   An individual who buys or sells securities for his or her clients; also called a stockbroker.

Beta   An index that compares the risk associated with a specific stock issue with the risk of the stock market in general.

Blue-chip stock   A very safe investment that generally attracts conservative investors.

Book value   Determined by deducting all liabilities from the corporation's assets and dividing the remainder by the number of outstanding shares of common stock.

Callable preferred stock   Stock that a corporation may exchange, at its option, for a specified amount of money.

Call option   The right, sold by a stockholder to a purchaser, to buy 100 shares of a stock at a guaranteed price before a definite expiration date.

Churning   The excessive buying and selling of securities in order to generate commissions.

Cumulative preferred stock   A stock issue whose unpaid dividends accumulate and must be paid before any cash dividend is paid to the common stockholders.

Cyclical stock   A stock that follows the business cycle of advances and declines in the economy.

Date of record   The date when a stockholder must be registered on the corporation's books in order to receive dividends.

Defensive stock   A stock that remains stable during declines in the economy.

Direct investment plan   A plan that allows stockholders to purchase stock directly from a corporation without having to use an account executive or a brokerage firm.

Dividend reinvestment plan   A plan that allows current stockholders the option of reinvesting their cash dividends in the stock of a corporation.

Dollar cost averaging   A long-term technique used by investors who purchase an equal dollar amount of the same stock at equal intervals.

Earnings per share   A corporation's after-tax earnings divided by the number of outstanding shares of common stock.

Efficient market theory   An investment theory that is based on the assumption that stock price movements are purely random; also called the random walk theory.

Fundamental theory   An investment theory that is based on the assumption that a stock's intrinsic or real value is determined by the future earnings of the company.

Growth stock   A stock issued by a corporation earning profits above the average profits of all the firms in the economy.

Income stock   A stock that pays higher than average dividends.

Investment bank   A financial firm that assists organizations in raising funds, usually by helping sell new security issues.

Limit order   A request that a stock be bought or sold at a specified price.

Margin   A speculative technique where an investor borrows part of the money necessary to buy a particular stock.

Market order   A request that a stock be bought or sold at the current market value.

Odd lot   Fewer than 100 shares of a particular stock.

Option   The right to buy or sell 100 shares of a stock at a predetermined price during a specified period of time.

Over-the-counter (OTC) market   A network of stockbrokers who buy and sell the securities of corporations that are not listed on a securities exchange.

Par value   An assigned (and often arbitrary) dollar value that is printed on a stock certificate.

Preemptive right   The right of current stockholders to purchase any new stock that the corporation issues before it is sold to the general public.

Price-earnings ratio (P-E ratio)   The price of a share of stock divided by the corporation's earnings per share of stock outstanding over the last 12 months.

Primary market   A market in which an investor purchases financial securities (via an investment bank or other representative) from the issuer of those securities.

Proxy   A legal form that lists the issues to be decided at a stockholders' meeting and requests that stockholders transfer their voting rights to some individual or individuals.

Put option   The right, purchased by a stock owner, to sell 100 shares of a stock at a guaranteed price before a definite expiration date.

Round lot   One hundred shares or multiples of 100 shares of a particular stock.

Secondary market   A market for existing financial securities that are currently traded between investors.

Securities   A term that encompasses a broad range of investment instruments, including stocks and bonds, mutual funds, options, and municipal bonds.

Securities exchange   A marketplace where member brokers who are representing investors meet to buy and sell securities.

Stock split   A procedure in which the shares of common stock owned by existing stockholders are divided into a larger number of shares.

Stop order   A request that an order be executed at the next available opportunity after the market price of a stock reaches a specified price.

Technical theory   An investment theory that is based on the assumption that a stock's market value is determined by the forces of supply and demand in the stock market as a whole.

DISCUSSION QUESTIONS

L.O.1   1. Why do corporations issue common stock? Why do investors purchase common stock?

L.O.1   2. What major changes in corporate policies may be decided at the stockholders' meeting of a corporation?

L.O.1   3. Why do corporations split their stock?

L.O.2   4. Why do corporations issue preferred stock? Why do investors purchase preferred stock?

L.O.2   5. What priorities do preferred stockholders enjoy as compared to common stockholders?

L.O.2   6. Preferred stock certificates may include a cumulative feature, a participation feature, and/or a conversion feature. What do these features mean to preferred stockholders?

L.O.3   7. How can the information contained in newspaper stock quotations help investors evaluate a specific stock issue?

L.O.3   8. Describe the five classifications of stock that this chapter discussed.

L.O.3   9. What types of detailed financial information do stock advisory services provide?

L.O.3 10. The fundamental theory, the technical theory, and the efficient market theory were described in this chapter. How do these theories explain the price movements of a stock traded on the NYSE?

L.O.4 11. What is the difference between the primary and secondary markets for stocks?

L.O.4 12. What steps are involved in the sale of a stock listed on the NYSE?

L.O.5 13. Describe the long-term techniques of buy and hold, dollar cost averaging, direct investment plans, and dividend reinvestment plans.

L.O.5 14. Describe the speculative techniques of buying on margin, selling short, and trading in options.

Opening Case Questions

1. In 1979, Jack and Susan Overall invested $690.50 in Federal Express. By 1989, when they sold the stock, their total return on this investment was more than $21,000. Explain how the Overalls made money on this investment.
2. In 1989, the Overalls' stock portfolio consisted of 15 stocks valued at more than $200,000. What did Jack Overall regard as the secret of their investment success? Do you agree with him? Why?

PROBLEMS AND ACTIVITIES

L.O.1   1. Prepare a list of reasons why a corporation would sell common stock. Then explain in a short paragraph the advantages of equity financing as compared to long-term financing through a commercial bank.

L.O.2   2. Assume that you have inherited $10,000 and that you want to invest it in one of the following: a certificate of deposit, a preferred stock issue, or a common stock issue. Prepare a chart that ranks each of these investments high, medium, or low on the factors of safety, risk, income, growth, and liquidity.

L.O.2   3. Tammy Jackson purchased 100 shares of All-American Manufacturing Company stock at $29½ a share. One year later, she sold the stock for $34⅜ a share. She paid her broker a $34 commission when she purchased the stock and a $42 commission when she sold it. During the 12 months that she owned the stock, she received $184 in dividends. Calculate Ms. Jackson's total return on this investment.

L.O.3   4. Divide a sheet of paper into three columns. In the first column, list sources of information that can be used to evaluate stock investments. In the second column, state where you would find each of these sources. Finally, in the third column, describe the types of information that each of these sources would provide.

L.O.3   5. Pick a stock of interest to you, and research the stock at a library by examining the information contained in Moody's Handbook of Common Stock, Standard & Poor's Reports, or Value Line. Then write a one-page summary of your findings. Based on your research, would you still want to invest in this stock? Why?

L.O.4   6. Prepare a list of questions that you could use to interview a stockbroker or an account executive.

L.O.4   7. As a stockholder of Bozo Oil Company, you receive its annual report. In the financial statements, the firm has reported assets of $9 million, liabilities of $5 million, after-tax earnings of $2 million, and 750,000 outstanding shares of common stock.
    a. Calculate the book value of a share of Bozo Oil's common stock.
    b. Calculate the earnings per share of Bozo Oil's common stock.
    c. Assuming that a share of Bozo Oil's common stock has a market value of $40, what is the firm's price-earnings ratio?

L.O.4   8. Ask friends or relatives who own or have owned stock about the process they used to buy or sell their stock.

L.O.5   9. What type of person would choose a buy and hold technique or dollar cost averaging? What type of person would buy stock on margin or purchase options?

L.O.5   10. Compile a list of the advantages and disadvantages of buying stock on margin, selling short, and purchasing a call or put option.

LIFE SITUATION   Case 16–1

One Stockholder's Dilemma

Betty Franklin, 46, is a successful engineer employed by a large electronics manufacturer. Her current salary is $52,000 a year. She owns her own town house, and she has over $30,000 in a certificate of deposit at a local savings and loan association. Her only debt obligation is a $350 monthly car payment.

Betty Franklin also owns common stock in American Telephone & Telegraph (AT&T), International Business Machines (IBM), General Mills, and USX (formerly U.S. Steel). She admits that she has no idea of what her stock investments are currently worth, because she quit monitoring them back in 1986. She used to keep monthly charts on which she recorded relevant information for each of the stocks she owned, but she stopping doing so because the information didn't seem to change very much. Now she admits that she just got lazy. The chart for October 1986 —the last chart she completed—is shown below. All of the information for this chart was taken from *The Wall Street Journal* on Wednesday, October 8, 1986.

Stock	Original Purchase Price	Number of Shares	Current Price per Share	Current Total Value	Current Dividend	Current Yield
AT&T	$ 26	50	$ 22	$1,100	$1.20	5.4%
General Mills	60	40	77	3,080	2.56	3.3
IBM	160	25	133	3,325	4.40	3.3
USX	32	75	27	2,025	1.20	4.4

Questions

1. Assume that you have been asked by Betty Franklin to evaluate her stock investments. Complete the following chart, using *current* information.
2. Based on your findings and on the information provided for 1986, what changes, if any, would you recommend to Betty Franklin?
3. What other information would you need to evaluate these corporations? Where would you get this information?

Stock	Original Purchase Price	Number of Shares	Current Price per Share	Current Total Value	Current Dividend	Current Yield
AT&T	$ 26	50				
General Mills	60	40				
IBM	160	25				
USX	32	75				

Source for the above information:_____   Date_____

LIFE SITUATION   Case 16–2

Moody's Research Information

In this chapter, we have stressed the importance of evaluating potential investments. Now it's your turn to try your skill at evaluating a potential investment in Dow Jones & Company. Assume that you could invest $10,000 in the common stock of this company. To help you evaluate this potential investment, carefully examine Exhibit 16–5, a reproduction of the research report on Dow Jones & Company that appeared in *Moody's Handbook of Common Stock, Summer 1989.*

Questions

1. Based on the Moody's research report, would you buy Dow Jones common stock? Justify your answer.
2. What other investment information would you need to evaluate Dow Jones common stock? Where would you obtain this information?

SUPPLEMENTARY READINGS

For Additional Information on Common Stock

Hirt, Geoffrey A. and Stanley B. Block. *Fundamentals of Investment Management,* 3rd. ed. Homewood, Ill.: Irwin, 1990.

Nickel, Karen. "The Best and Worst Stocks of 1989." *Fortune,* January 29, 1990, pp. 114–17.

Rowe, Frederick E. "The Dubious Art of Short-Selling." *Forbes,* January 22, 1990, p. 152.

Sheeline, William E. "Don't Be Afraid of the Big Bad Market." *Fortune,* April 9, 1990, pp. 79–82.

Widicus, Wilbur W. and Thomas E. Stitzel. *Personal Investing,* 5th ed. Homewood, Ill.: Irwin, 1989.

For additional information on Evaluation of Stock Investments

Egan, J. "How You Can Move with the Averages." *U.S. News & World Report,* January 8, 1990, p. 63.

Frailey, Fred W. "How to Decode the Financial Pages." *Changing Times,* March 1990, pp. 83–84.

Markese, John. "How P/E Ratios Can Lead You to Best Buys." *Money,* March 1990, pp. 159–60.

Rolo, Charles J. and Robert J. Klein. *Gaining on the Market.* Boston: Little, Brown and Company, 1988.

Smith, Marguerite T. and Jordan E. Goodman. "You Can Beat the Pros Again and Again with This Simple High-Yield Strategy." *Money,* January 1990, p. 57.

17

Investing in Bonds

In Chapter 16, we discussed common stock and preferred stock. Here we examine another investment alternative—bonds. To invest successfully, an investor must carefully evaluate all three of these investment alternatives. In this chapter, we discuss corporate bonds first. Then we look at bonds issued by federal, state, and local governments.

LEARNING OBJECTIVES
After studying this chapter, you will be able to

L.O.1 Understand the characteristics of corporate bonds.

L.O.2 Discuss why corporations issue bonds.

L.O.3 Explain why investors purchase bonds.

L.O.4 Discuss why bonds are issued by federal, state, and local governments.

L.O.5 Evaluate bonds when making an investment.

L.O.6 Calculate both the current yield and the yield to maturity for a bond investment.

L.O.7 Describe how bonds are bought and sold.

OPENING CASE

There Are Bonds, and Then There Are Bonds

After more than 20 years of investing in stocks and mutual funds, Joanna and Mike Nations thought they should sell some of their stocks and invest the money in something a little more conservative. Since they were both almost 50 and their only child had just graduated from college, they felt that it was time to start investing in something not quite so volatile as stocks.

After considering the traditionally safe investments (certificates of deposit, government bonds, and corporate bonds), the Nations decided to consider corporate bonds. They wanted a conservative investment but a larger return than that offered by certificates of deposit and government bonds.

Their account executive, Tom Bartlett, suggested that they evaluate two corporate bond issues—an IBM issue and a Carter Hawley Hale issue. After a 30-minute discussion with Bartlett, the Nations decided to do this.

A trip to the library yielded some interesting information about both bond issues. Bonds in the IBM issue had a maturity value of $1,000, matured in 2004, and had a current yield of 9.2 percent. Moody's Investors Service rated these bonds Aaa, which meant that Moody's judged them to be of the highest quality. Bonds in the Carter Hawley Hale issue had a maturity value of $1,000, matured in 2002, and had a current yield of 13 percent. Moody's assigned these bonds the B rating that it used for bonds generally lacking the characteristics of a desirable investment.

Although the Nations liked the higher yield offered by the Carter Hawley Hale bonds, they decided to purchase the IBM bonds. The main reason for their decision was the high rating that Moody's gave these bonds. After all, their goal was to reduce the amount of their investment risk.°

°For more information, see John Heins, "It's Not All Junk," *Forbes,* June 26, 1989, pp. 244–45; Jeffrey M. Laderman, "Does Junk Have Lasting Value? Probably," *Business Week,* May 1, 1989, pp. 118–19; Carolyn Friday and David Pauly, "A Junk Pile for Junk Bonds?" *Newsweek,* May 8, 1989, p. 42; and *Moody's Transportation Manual, 1989,* vol. 1 (A–I), p. vii.

Bonds used to be considered conservative investments for cautious investors. Traditionally, corporate and government bonds offered a steady source of income and eventual repayment of the principal amount at maturity. Today, as the Nations found out, there are important differences in corporate bonds. The IBM bond issue offered a 9.2 percent current yield, while the Carter Hawley Hale bond issue offered a 13 percent current yield. Based on just current yield, the Carter Hawley Hale bond issue would have been the better investment. But current yield is only one of the factors that must be considered when investments in corporate bonds are being made. Other factors that must be considered include the corporation's ability to repay the bonds at maturity and the corporation's ability to continue to pay interest to the bondholder until maturity.

The Nations' choice of the IBM bond issue was based on the concept of opportunity costs—a concept that we have discussed throughout this text. Simply put, the Carter Hawley Hale bond issue was too speculative to meet the goals of the Nations' current financial plan. Therefore, the Nations invested in the more conservative IBM bond issue despite its smaller return.

A particular bond issue, like any other investment, must be carefully evaluated before you decide to purchase it. The material in the next section—"Characteristics of Corporate Bonds"—will help you evaluate investments in bonds.

CHARACTERISTICS OF CORPORATE BONDS

L.O.1
Understand the characteristics of corporate bonds.

A **corporate bond** is a corporation's written pledge that it will repay a specified amount of money, with interest. Exhibit 17–1 illustrates a typical corporate bond. Note that it states the dollar amount of the bond, the interest rate, and the maturity date. The usual face value of a corporate bond is $1,000, although the face value of some corporate bonds may be as high as $50,000. The total face value of all the bonds in an issue usually runs into the millions of dollars (see Exhibit 17–2). Generally, an individual or a firm buys a corporate bond through an account executive who represents a brokerage firm. Between the time of purchase and the maturity date, the corporation pays interest to the bondholder—usually every six months—at the stated interest rate. For example, assume that you purchase a $1,000 bond issued by American Telephone & Telegraph (AT&T) and that the interest rate for this bond is 8.8 percent. In this situation, you receive interest of $88 ($1,000 × 8.8% = $88) a year from the corporation. The interest is paid every six months in $44 installments.

The **maturity date** of a corporate bond is the date on which the corporation is to repay the borrowed money. At the maturity date, the bondholder returns the bond to the corporation and receives cash equaling its face value. Maturity dates for bonds range from 1 to 40 years after the date of issue.

EXHIBIT 17–1   A Typical Corporate Bond

The actual legal conditions for a corporate bond are described in a bond indenture. A **bond indenture** is a legal document that details all of the conditions relating to a bond issue. Often comprising over 100 pages of complicated legal wording, the bond indenture remains in effect until the bonds reach maturity or are redeemed by the corporation.

Since corporate bond indentures are very difficult for the average person to read and understand, a corporation issuing bonds appoints a trustee. The **trustee** is a financially independent firm or individual that acts as the bondholders' representative. Usually, the trustee is a commercial bank or some other financial institution. The corporation must report to the trustee periodically regarding its ability to make interest payments and eventually redeem the bonds. In turn, the trustee transmits this information to the bondholders along with its own evaluation of the corporation's ability to pay. If the corporation fails to live up to all the provisions contained in the indenture agreement, the trustee may bring legal action to protect the bondholders' interests.

EXHIBIT 17–2

An Advertisement for 9 Percent Convertible Subordinated Bonds Issued by SCI Systems, Inc.

The Wall Street Journal, May 3, 1990, p. C17.

WHY
CORPORATIONS
SELL CORPORATE
BONDS

L.O.2
Discuss why corporations issue
bonds.

Corporations sell corporate bonds to help finance their ongoing business activities. They usually sell bonds when it is difficult or impossible to sell common stock or preferred stock. The sale of bonds can also improve a corporation's financial leverage—the use of borrowed funds to increase the corporation's return on investment. Finally, the interest paid on corporate bonds is a tax-deductible expense and thus can be used to reduce the taxes that a corporation must pay. While a corporation may use both bonds and stocks to finance its activities, there are important distinctions between the two. Corporate bonds are a form of debt financing, whereas stock is a form of equity financing. Bonds must be repaid at a future date; common stock and preferred stock do not have to be repaid. Interest payments on bonds are mandatory; dividends paid to stockholders are at the discretion of the board of directors. Finally, in case of bankruptcy, bondholders have a claim to the assets of the corporation prior to that of stockholders. Before issuing bonds, a corporation must decide what type of bond to issue and how the bond issue will be repaid.

Types of Bonds

Most corporate bonds are debentures. A **debenture** is a bond that is backed only by the reputation of the issuing corporation. If the corporation does not make either interest or principal payments, debenture holders become general creditors, much like the firm's suppliers. In case of bankruptcy, general creditors can claim any asset not specifically used as collateral for another financial obligation.

To make a bond issue more appealing to investors, a corporation may issue a mortgage bond. A **mortgage bond** (sometimes referred to as a secured bond) is a corporate bond that is secured by various assets of the issuing firm. A first mortgage bond may be backed up by a lien on a specific asset, usually real estate. A general mortgage bond is secured by all the fixed assets of the firm that are not pledged as collateral for other financial obligations. A mortgage bond is considered more secure than a debenture because corporate assets or collateral may be sold to repay the bondholders if the corporation defaults on interest or principal payments.

A third type of bond that a corporation may issue is called a subordinated debenture. A **subordinated debenture** is an unsecured bond that gives bondholders a claim secondary to that of other designated bondholders with respect to both income and assets. Investors who purchase subordinated debentures usually enjoy higher interest rates than other bondholders because of the increased risk associated with this type of bond.

A fourth type of bond that a corporation may issue is called a convertible bond. A **convertible bond** is a bond that can be exchanged, at the owner's option, for a specified number of shares of the corporation's common stock. The corporation gains three advantages by issuing convertible bonds. First, the interest rate of a convertible bond is often lower than that of traditional bonds. Second, the conversion feature attracts investors who are interested in the speculative gain that may be provided by conversion to common stock. And third, if the bondholder converts to common stock, the corporation no longer has to redeem the bond at maturity. We will examine convertible bonds from the investor's standpoint later in this chapter.

FINANCIAL PLANNING IN ACTION

The "How To" of Researching a Bond

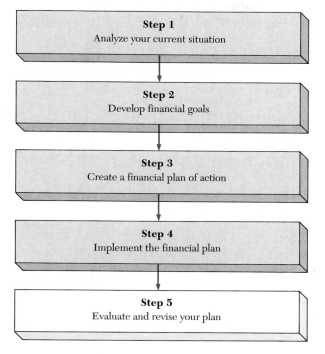

Step 1
Analyze your current situation

Step 2
Develop financial goals

Step 3
Create a financial plan of action

Step 4
Implement the financial plan

Step 5
Evaluate and revise your plan

How do you find out whether or not a corporate bond is callable? Where can you find out who the trustee for a specific bond issue is? These are two examples of the multitude of questions that concern investors who are trying to evaluate prospective bond investments. Fortunately, the answers are easy to obtain if you know where to look.

Today, the most readily available source of detailed information about a corporation, including information about its bond issues, is *Moody's Manuals.* Individual subscriptions to this series of publications are too expensive for most investors, but the series is available at both college and public libraries. It includes individual manuals on industrial companies, public utilities, banks and financial institutions, and transportation companies. Each of these manuals contains detailed information on each of the companies it covers, including information on the company's history, operations, products, and bond issues.

The following data on a corporate bond issued by Bristol-Myers Company will give you an idea of the contents of the "Long-Term Debt" section of a Moody's report.°

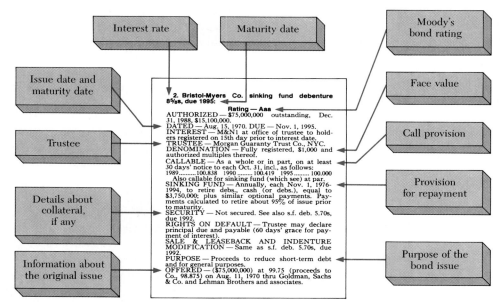

Interest rate

Maturity date

Moody's bond rating

Issue date and maturity date

Face value

Trustee

Call provision

Details about collateral, if any

Provision for repayment

Information about the original issue

Purpose of the bond issue

2. Bristol-Myers Co. sinking fund debenture 8⅝s, due 1995:

Rating — Aaa

AUTHORIZED — $75,000,000 outstanding, Dec. 31, 1988, $15,100,000.

DATED — Aug. 15, 1970. DUE — Nov. 1, 1995.

INTEREST — M&N1 at office of trustee to holders registered on 15th day prior to interest date.

TRUSTEE — Morgan Guaranty Trust Co., NYC.

DENOMINATION — Fully registered, $1,000 and authorized multiples thereof.

CALLABLE — As a whole or in part, on at least 30 days' notice to each Oct. 31, incl., as follows:
1989.........100.838 1990 ....100.419 1995 .... 100.000
Also callable for sinking fund (which see) at par.

SINKING FUND — Annually, each Nov. 1, 1976-1994, to retire debs., cash (or debs.), equal to $3,750,000; plus similar optional payments. Payments calculated to retire about 95% of issue prior to maturity.

SECURITY — Not secured. See also s.f. deb. 5.70s, due 1992.

RIGHTS ON DEFAULT — Trustee may declare principal due and payable (60 days' grace for payment of interest).

SALE & LEASEBACK AND INDENTURE MODIFICATION — Same as s.f. deb. 5.70s, due 1992.

PURPOSE — Proceeds to reduce short-term debt and for general purposes.

OFFERED — ($75,000,000) at 99.75 (proceeds to Co., 98.875) on Aug. 11, 1970 thru Goldman, Sachs & Co. and Lehman Brothers and associates.

°The information for the Bristol Myers corporate bond was taken from *Moody's Industrial Manual, 1989,* vol. 1 (A–I), p. 181+.

Provisions for Repayment

Today, most corporate bonds are callable. A **call feature** allows the corporation to call in or buy outstanding bonds from current bondholders before the maturity date. In most cases, corporations issuing callable bonds agree not to call them for the first 5 to 10 years after the bonds have been issued. When a call feature is used, the corporation generally must pay the bondholders a *premium*—an additional amount above the face value of the bond. The amount of the premium is specified in the bond indenture, but a 5 to 10 percent premium over the bond's face value is common.

A corporation may use one of two methods to ensure that it has sufficient funds available to redeem a bond issue. First, the corporation may establish a sinking fund. A **sinking fund** is a fund to which annual or semiannual deposits are made for the purpose of redeeming a bond issue. The inclusion of a sinking fund provision in the bond indenture is generally advantageous to bondholders because such a provision forces the corporation to make arrangements for bond repayment before the bond maturity date. If the terms of the provision are not met, the trustee or bondholders may take legal action against the company. Second, a corporation may issue serial bonds. **Serial bonds** are bonds of a single issue that mature on different dates. For example, Seaside Productions used a 20-year, $100 million bond issue to finance its expansion. None of the bonds matures during the first 10 years. Thereafter, 10 percent of the bonds mature each year until all the bonds are retired at the end of the 20-year period.

WHY INVESTORS PURCHASE CORPORATE BONDS

L.O.3
Explain why investors purchase bonds.

Investors purchase corporate bonds for three reasons: (1) interest income, (2) possible increase in value, and (3) repayment at maturity. First, as mentioned earlier in this chapter, bondholders normally receive interest payments every six months. The dollar amount of interest is determined by multiplying the interest rate by the face value of the bond. For example, if General Electric issues a 7½ percent bond with a face value of $1,000, the investor will receive $75 ($1,000 × 7.5% = $75) a year, paid in installments of $37.50 at the end of each six-month period.

Second, corporate bonds may increase in value. Most beginning investors think that a $1,000 bond is always worth $1,000. In reality, the price of a corporate bond may fluctuate until the maturity date. Changes in overall interest rates in the economy are the primary cause of most bond price fluctuations. Changing bond prices that result from changes in overall interest rates in the economy are an example of the concept of interest rate risk discussed in Chapter 15. When General Electric issued the bond mentioned above, the 7½ percent interest rate was competitive with the interest rate offered by other corporations issuing bonds at that time. If overall interest rates fall, then the General Electric bond will go up in value because of the bond's higher interest rate. On the other hand, if overall interest rates rise, the market value of the General Electric bond will fall. The financial condition of the corporation and the probability of its repaying the bond also affect the bond's value. This concept—business failure risk—was also discussed in Chapter 15. As a result of these factors, an investor may be able to purchase bonds at less than their face value and, if the value of the bonds increases, sell them at a higher price.

Third, corporate bonds are repaid at maturity. When you purchase a bond, you have two options: you may keep the bond until maturity and then redeem it, or you may sell the bond at any time to another investor. In either case, the value of your bond is closely tied to the corporation's ability to repay its bond indebtedness. For example, the LTV Corporation filed for reorganization under the provisions of the U.S. Bankruptcy Act. As a result, the bonds issued by the LTV Corporation immediately dropped in value because of questions concerning the prospects for repayment of the bonds at maturity.

A Typical Bond Transaction

People invest in corporate bonds for at least three reasons. First, bondholders earn interest each day that they own a bond. Second, the corporation will redeem a bond for its face value at maturity. Third, bondholders may be able to sell a bond at a price higher than the price they paid when they bought it.

Assume that on October 8, 1986, you purchased a 4¼ percent corporate bond issued by American Airlines. Your cost for the bond was $770 plus a $10 commission charge, for a total investment of $780. Also assume that you held the bond until October 8, 1990, when you sold it at its current market value of $930. The return on your investment is shown in Exhibit 17–3.

In this example, you made a total return of $310, which came from two sources. After paying commissions for buying and selling your American Airlines bond, you made $140 because the market value of the bond increased from $770 to $930. The increase in the value of the bond resulted from three factors. First, because overall interest rates in the economy declined during the four-year period in which you owned the bond, the 4¼ percent fixed interest rate of your bond became more attractive. Second, American Airlines established a reputation for efficiency and productivity during this period. Increased efficiency and productivity help ensure that American Airlines will be able to repay bondholders when the bond reaches maturity. Finally, the bond matures in 1992. As it approaches

---

EXHIBIT 17–3

Sample Corporate Bond Transaction for American Airlines

Assumptions

Interest, 4¼ percent; maturity date, 1992; purchased October 8, 1986; sold October 8, 1990

Costs when Purchased		**Return when Sold**	
1 bond @ $770 =	$770	1 bond @ $930 =	$930
Plus commission	+10	Minus commission	−10
Total investment	$780	Total return	$920

Transaction Summary

Total return	$ 920
Minus total investment	−780
Profit from bond sale	$ 140
Plus interest (4 years)	+170
Total return for the transaction	$ 310

maturity, its value moves closer to the original issue price or face value of $1,000. On the maturity date, American Airlines will pay bondholders $1,000 for each of the bonds they own.

You also made money on your American Airlines bond because of interest payments. For each of the four years you owned the bond, American Airlines paid you $42.50 ($1,000 × 4.25% = $42.50) interest. Thus, you received interest payments totaling $170.

Of course, you should remember that the price of a corporate bond can decrease and that interest payments and eventual repayment may be a problem for a corporation that encounters financial difficulties or enters bankruptcy.

Convertible Bonds

Corporations sometimes choose to issue bonds that are convertible into a specified number of shares of common stock. This conversion feature allows investors to enjoy the low risk of a corporate bond, but also to take advantage of the speculative nature of common stock by exercising their right of conversion. For example, assume that you purchase a $1,000 corporate bond that is convertible to 50 shares of the company's common stock. This means that you can convert the bond to common stock whenever the price of the company's common stock is $20 ($1,000 ÷ 50 shares = $20) or higher. Assume that at the time of your bond purchase, the company's stock is selling for $12. In this situation, there is no reason to convert because the common stock you receive would be worth only $600 ($12 × 50 shares = $600).

In reality, there is no guarantee that bondholders will convert to common stock even if the market value of the common stock does increase to $20 or higher. The reason for not exercising the conversion feature in the above example is quite simple. As the market value of the common stock increases, the price of the convertible bond also increases. By not converting to common stock, bondholders enjoy the interest income from the bond in addition to the increased bond value caused by the price movement of the stock.

Convertible bonds, like all potential investments, must be carefully evaluated. Remember, not all convertible bonds are quality investments. In fact, the interest rates paid on convertible bonds are often 1 to 2 percent lower than the interest rates paid on corporate bonds without the conversion feature.

GOVERNMENT BONDS AND DEBT SECURITIES

L.O.4
Discuss why bonds are issued by federal, state, and local governments.

In addition to corporations, the U.S. government and state and local governments issue bonds to obtain financing. In this section, we discuss bonds issued by the federal government and by state and local governments.

Treasury Bills, Notes, and Bonds

The federal government sells bonds and securities to finance both the national debt and the government's ongoing activities. The main reason why investors choose U.S. government securities is that most investors consider them risk free. In fact, some financial planners refer to them as the ultimate safe investment because their quality is considered to be higher than that of any other securities issued. They are backed by the full faith and credit of the U.S. government. Because of the decreased risk of default, they offer lower interest returns than corporate bonds. Four principal types of bonds and securities are issued by the U.S. Treasury Department: Treasury bills, Treasury notes, Treasury bonds, and savings bonds. Treasury bills, notes, and bonds can be purchased directly from the 12 Federal Reserve banks or one of their 25 branches. When U.S. government securities are purchased through the Federal Reserve System (the Fed), buyers pay no commission charge. The Federal Reserve System, acting as agent for the Treasury Department, conducts auctions to sell Treasury bills, notes, and bonds. Buyers interested in purchasing these securities at such auctions may bid competitively or noncompetitively. If they bid competitively, they must specify the price or yield that they are willing to accept. If they bid noncompetitively, they are willing to pay the average price or accept the average yield at which the securities are sold. U.S. government securities may also be purchased through banks or brokers, which charge a commission. Savings bonds can be purchased through the Federal Reserve banks and branches, commercial banks, savings and loan associations, or other financial institutions. U.S. government securities can be held until maturity or sold before maturity. Current price information on them can be found in *The Wall Street Journal* and other financial publications.

Treasury Bills   Treasury bills, sometimes called T-bills, are issued in minimum units of $10,000 with maturities that range from 91 days to one year. T-bills are discounted securities. For example, a one-year, $10,000 T-bill with a stated interest rate of 8 percent will initially cost the purchaser $9,200. In reality, the interest rate for T-bills is slightly higher than the stated interest rate. In the above example, the investor is receiving $800 ($10,000 × 8% = $800) interest on a $9,200 investment, which represents an 8.7 percent ($800 ÷ $9,200 = 8.7%) return on an annual basis. The $800 interest amount is taxable for federal income tax purposes. It is not subject to state and local taxes. At maturity, the government will repay the face value of the T-bill.

Treasury Notes   Treasury notes are issued in $1,000 or $5,000 units with maturities that range from 1 year to 10 years. Interest rates for Treasury notes are slightly higher than interest rates for Treasury bills. Interest for Treasury notes is paid every six months. Like the interest for T-bills, this interest is free from state and local taxation but not federal taxation.

Treasury Bonds   Treasury bonds are issued in minimum units of $1,000 with maturities that range from 10 to 30 years. Interest rates for Treasury bonds are generally higher than interest rates for either Treasury bills or Treasury notes. Like interest on Treasury notes, interest on Treasury bonds is paid every six months and taxable for federal income tax purposes. Treasury bonds are exempt from state and local taxation.

Savings Bonds   Generally, Series EE bonds are purchased and held until maturity. These bonds are issued with maturity values that range from $50 to $10,000. The purchase price for Series EE bonds is one half of their maturity value. Thus, a $50 bond costs $25 when purchased. A Series EE bond purchased after November 1, 1982, and held for at least five years returns a guaranteed minimum of 6 percent or 85 percent of the average yield of five-year Treasury notes during the life of the bond, whichever is higher. Therefore, if Treasury notes earn 9 percent, a Series EE savings bond will earn 7.65 percent, which is 85 percent of the Treasury bond rate. Series EE bonds held for less than five years receive interest ranging from 4.1 percent to 6 percent, depending on the holding period.

The interest on Series EE bonds, which some financial planners call dollar appreciation, is exempt from state and local taxes and accumulates free from federal taxation until the bonds are redeemed. Once these bonds are cashed in, the interest on them is subject to federal taxation unless it is used to finance a college education.

Federal taxation of the interest paid on Series EE bonds can also be postponed if they are converted to Series HH bonds. Series HH bonds pay out interest semiannually to investors who hold them for more than six months.

Federal Agency Debt Issues

In addition to the bonds and securities issued by the Treasury Department, debt securities are issued by federal agencies. New agency issues have been running at the rate of $20 billion to $30 billion per year.[1] Federal agencies that issue debt securities include the Federal National Mortgage Association (sometimes referred to as Fannie Mae), the Federal Housing Administration (FHA), and the Government National Mortgage Association (sometimes referred to as Ginnie Mae).

Although agency issues are, for practical purposes, risk free, they offer a slightly higher yield than government securities issued by the Treasury Department. Generally, their minimum denomination is $5,000. Securities issued by federal agencies have maturities that range from 1 year to 40 years, with an average life of about 15 years.

State and Local Government Securities

A municipal bond, sometimes called a muni, is a debt security issued by a state or local government. Such securities are used to finance the ongoing activities of state and local governments and major projects such as airports, schools, toll roads, and toll bridges. State and local securities are classified as either general obligation bonds or revenue bonds. A general obligation bond is a bond backed by the full faith, credit, and unlimited taxing power of the government that issued it. A revenue bond is a bond that is repaid from the income generated by the project it is designed to finance. Although both types of bonds are relatively safe, there have been defaults in recent years (see accompanying "Personal Finance Journal" feature). Over the years, the default rate on municipal securities has amounted to less than 1 percent of the face value of all municipal bonds.[2] Still, an investor must evaluate each municipal bond before investing in it. In 1983, for example, the Washington Public Power Supply could not pay off its debt on municipal bonds worth more than $2 billion and thousands of investors lost money. Several years ago, New York City was on the verge of defaulting on a bond issue that was about to mature. Strong financial measures and new loans saved the city and the bondholders, but the experience affected the market value of all New York City bonds. In addition, the city had to pay higher than usual interest rates to attract investors to new bond issues. If the risk of default worries you, you can purchase insured municipal bonds. A number of states offer to guarantee payments on selected securities. There are also two large private insurers—the

PERSONAL FINANCE JOURNAL

Is Risk Associated with Municipal Bonds?

What could be a more attractive investment than a municipal bond issued and backed by a local government and providing interest payments free of federal income tax? For those investors who bought Series 4 and 5 bonds of the Washington Public Power Supply System (WPPSS), the answer may be "almost anything." In 1983, WPPSS defaulted on these bonds. Today, WPPSS bondholders are still waiting for a settlement that is estimated to be about 40 cents on the dollar.

Revenues from the WPPSS Series 4 and 5 bonds were to be used to erect two nuclear power plants. Like most municipal bonds, those bonds seemed as safe as could be—and their 13 percent tax-free interest was extremely attractive. But that exceptionally high interest rate should have served as a warning that the bonds were far from supersafe.

The WPPSS default is the largest municipal default in U.S. history, but it is far from the only one that investors have had to endure. Since 1983, there have been more than 500 municipal defaults totaling roughly $3.6 billion, according to the Bond Investors Association.° Two factors that may help you avoid investing in questionable municipal bonds are discussed below.

Municipal Bond Ratings

Both Standard & Poor's and Moody's rate municipal bond issues. Moody's municipal bond ratings range from Aaa (the highest) to C (the lowest). Generally, the municipal bonds that Moody's rates B or lower are considered speculative investments. In addition, bonds are rated conditionally if their security depends on the completion of some act or the fulfillment of some condition.

Insurance on Municipal Bonds

Investors may purchase insured municipal bonds. Today, approximately 25 to 30 percent of all municipal bonds are insured. If insured municipal bonds are in default, the insurance company pays the interest on the bonds and redeems them at maturity. Indirectly, the bondholder pays the cost of the protection because the yield on insured municipal bonds is about ½ to 1 percent lower than the yield on comparable municipals without insurance. A slightly smaller return on your municipal bond may be a small price to pay if the government agency issuing the bond cannot pay interest as scheduled or redeem the bond at maturity.

°Laura Zinn, "Munis Are Evolving into More Dangerous Animals," *Business Week,* June 19, 1989, p. 106.

For more information, see David Zigas, "Whoops: Investors May Let Bygones Be Bygones," *Business Week,* September 4, 1989, p. 92; Ben Weberman, "Default Risk," *Forbes,* November 14, 1988, p. 361; and Walter L. Updegrave, "Riding the Wave of Long Bond Yields," *Money,* April 1989, pp. 100–101 + .

Municipal Bond Insurance Association and the American Municipal Bond Assurance Corporation. Usually, guaranteed municipal securities carry a slightly lower interest rate than uninsured bonds because of the reduced risk of default.

Like a corporate bond, a municipal bond may be callable by the government unit that issued it. Typically, there is some call protection. In most cases, the municipality that issues the bond agrees not to call it for the first 10 years. If the bond is not called, the investor has two options. First, the bond may be held until maturity, in which case the investor will be repaid its face value. Second, the bond may be sold to another investor. However, it may be difficult to find a buyer for some municipal bond issues.

One of the most important features of municipal securities is that the interest on them may be exempt from federal taxes. Whether the interest on municipal bonds is tax exempt or not depends on how the funds obtained from their sale are used. If you invest in municipal bonds, be certain that the bonds you buy are tax exempt. In other words, it is your responsibility as an investor to determine whether municipal bonds are taxable. Municipal bonds exempt from federal taxation are generally exempt from state and local taxes in the state where they are issued.

To some extent, the tax advantages associated with municipal bonds have been lessened because tax law changes in 1986 lowered the maximum federal income tax rate for individuals. (Before those changes were enacted, the maximum rate for individuals was 50 percent!) Even with the lower tax rates, municipal bonds are still very popular among wealthy investors. Because of their tax-exempt status, their interest rates are lower than those of taxable bonds. By using the following formula, you can calculate the taxable equivalent yield for a municipal security.

they are tax free

$$\text{Taxable equivalent yield} = \frac{\text{Tax-exempt yield}}{1.0 - \text{Your tax rate}}$$

For example, the taxable equivalent yield on a 7 percent tax-exempt municipal bond for a person in the 28 percent tax bracket is 9.7 percent, as illustrated below.

$$\text{Taxable equivalent yield} = \frac{.07}{1.0 - .28} = .097, \text{ or } 9.7 \text{ percent}$$

Once the taxable equivalent yield has been calculated, it is possible to compare the return on tax-exempt securities with the return on taxable securities.

THE INVESTOR'S DECISION TO BUY OR SELL BONDS

L.O.5
Evaluate bonds when making an investment.

One of the basic principles that we have stressed throughout this text is the need to evaluate any potential investment. Certainly, corporate and government bonds are no exception. Only after you have completed your evaluation should you purchase bonds. Of course, a decision to sell bonds also requires evaluation. In this section, we examine methods that you can use to evaluate an investment in bonds and we look at the mechanics of buying and selling bonds.

How to Read the Bond Section of the Newspaper

Not all local newspapers contain bond quotations, but *The Wall Street Journal* and *Barron's* publish complete and thorough information on this subject. Purchases and sales of corporate bonds are reported in tables like that shown at the top of Exhibit 17–4. In bond quotations, prices are given as a percentage of the face value, which is usually $1,000. Thus, to find the actual price paid, you must multiply the face value ($1,000) by the newspaper quote. For example, a price that is quoted as 84 means a selling price of $1,000 × 84% = $840. The first row of Exhibit 17–4 gives the following information for the Citicorp corporate bond. (The numbers in this list refer to the column numbers that have been added to the figure.)

1. The abbreviated name of the issuing firm is Citicp, which stands for Citicorp. The bond pays annual interest at the rate of 8⅛ percent of its face value, or $1,000 × 8.125% = $81.25 per year. It matures in the year 2007.
2. The current yield, or return, based on today's market price, is $81.25 ÷ $860, or 9.4 percent.
3. Eighty-six $1,000 bonds were traded on this day.
4. The last price paid for a Citicorp bond during the day was $1,000 × 86%, or $860.
5. The last price paid on this day was − 0.5% × $1,000, or $5 lower than the last price paid on the previous trading day. In Wall Street terms, the Citicorp bond "closed down ½" on this day.

EXHIBIT 17–4

Financial Information about Corporate Bonds That Is Available in *The Wall Street Journal*

1 Bonds	2 Cur Yld	3 Vol.	4 Close	5 Net Chg.
Citicp 8⅛07	9.4	86	86 −	½
Clmt zrD03	...	13	24½ +	¼
ClevEl 9.85s10	9.9	25	99¼ −	½
Coastl 11¼496	10.9	40	103¼	...
Coastl 11¾406	11.3	13	104 +	½
Coastl 8.48s91	8.6	100	98¼ −	⅛
Coastl 11⅛98	10.8	5	102⅞ +	⅞
CmwE 8¾405	9.6	10	91	...
CmwE 9⅜04	9.7	7	97	...
CmwE 8⅛07J	9.5	1	85½ −	⅜
CmwE 9⅛08	9.8	94	93⅜ −	⅝
CmwE 15⅜00	14.1	6	108⅞ +	⅞
Compq 6½13	cv	110	151 −	1½

1. Abbreviated name of the corporation, the bond's interest rate, and the year of maturity.
2. Current yield, determined by dividing the annual interest in dollars by the current price of the bond. A "cv" in this column indicates that the bond is convertible into a specified number of shares of common stock.
3. Number of bonds traded during the day.
4. Price paid for the bond in the last transaction of the day.
5. Difference between the last price paid for the bond today and the last price paid for the bond on the previous day.

Source: *The Wall Street Journal*, March 29, 1990, p. C16.

For government bonds, two price quotations are included in most financial publications. The first price quotation, or the *bid price,* is the highest price that has been offered to purchase a particular government security. The bid price represents the amount that a seller could receive for that security. The second price quotation, or the *asked price,* represents the lowest price at which the government security has been offered for sale. The asked price represents the amount for which a buyer could purchase the security. In addition to price quotations, financial publications provide information about the interest rates, maturity dates, and yields of government securities.

Bond Ratings

To determine the quality and risk associated with bond issues, investors rely on the bond ratings provided by Moody's Investors Service, Inc. and Standard & Poor's Corporation. Both companies rank thousands of corporate and municipal bonds.

As illustrated in Exhibit 17–5, bond ratings generally range from AAA (the highest) to D (the lowest). For both Moody's and Standard & Poor's, the first four individual categories represent investment-grade securities. Bonds in the next two categories are considered speculative in nature. Finally, the C and D categories are used to rank bonds that may be in default because of poor prospects of

---

EXHIBIT 17–5   Description of Bond Ratings Provided by Moody's Investors Service and
                                     Standard & Poor's

Quality	Moody's	Standard & Poor's	Description
High-grade	Aaa	AAA	Bonds that are judged to be of the best quality. They carry the smallest degree of investment risk and are generally referred to as "gilt edge." Interest payments are protected by a large or exceptionally stable margin, and principal is secure.
	Aa	AA	Bonds that are judged to be of high quality by all standards. Together with the first group, they comprise what are generally known as high-grade bonds. They are rated lower than the best bonds because their margins of protection may not be as large.
Medium-grade	A	A	Bonds that possess many favorable investment attributes and are to be considered upper medium-grade obligations. The factors giving security to principal and interest are considered adequate.
	Baa	BBB	Bonds that are considered medium-grade obligations; i.e., they are neither highly protected nor poorly secured.
Speculative	Ba	BB	Bonds that are judged to have speculative elements; their future cannot be considered well assured. Often, their protection of interest and principal payments may be very moderate.
	B	B	Bonds that generally lack characteristics of the desirable investment. Assurance of interest and principal payments or of maintenance of other terms of the contract over any long period of time may be small.
Default	Caa	CCC	Bonds that are of poor standing. Such issues may be in default, or elements of danger may be present with respect to principal or interest.
	Ca	CC	Bonds that represent obligations that are speculative to a high degree. Such issues are often in default or have other marked shortcomings.
	C		The lowest-rated class in Moody's designation. These bonds can be regarded as having extremely poor prospects of attaining any real investment standing.
		C	Rating given to income bonds on which interest is not currently being paid.
		D	Issues in default with arrears in interest and/or principal payments.

SOURCE: Sumner N. Levine, *1989 Dow Jones-Irwin Business and Investment Almanac* (Homewood, Ill.: Dow Jones-Irwin, 1989), pp. 422–26.

---

repayment or even continued payment of interest. Although bond ratings may be flawed or inaccurate, most investors regard the work of both Moody's and Standard & Poor's as highly reliable.

Generally, U.S. government securities issued by the Treasury Department and various federal agencies are not graded because they are risk free for practical purposes. The rating of long-term municipal bonds is similar to that of corporate bonds. In addition, Standard & Poor's rates shorter-term municipal bonds (sometimes referred to as municipal notes) maturing in three years or less with the following designations:

SP–1 Very strong or strong capacity to pay principal and interest. Those issues determined to possess overwhelming safety characteristics will be given a plus (+) designation.

SP–2 Satisfactory capacity to pay principal and interest.

SP–3 Speculative capacity to pay principal and interest.[3]

..

PERSONAL FINANCE JOURNAL

Are Junk Bonds Really Junk?

According to financial analysts, a junk bond is a high-yield corporate bond that Standard & Poor's rates BB or lower. The Standard & Poor's BB rating stands for "speculative." Because junk bonds are speculative, investors expect higher returns on them than on more conservative corporate bond issues. And from 1980 to 1988, junk bonds have returned an average 14 percent—well above the yield on high-grade corporate bonds or U.S. Treasury bonds. As a result, investors have bought these bonds in record numbers. And there are more junk bonds to choose from than ever before. Currently, the total face value of outstanding junk bonds is estimated to be over $200 billion. Before deciding on junk bonds, there are a number of factors to consider.

The Risks Involved

Two risks are associated with junk bonds. The first, and the ultimate fear of any investor in junk bonds, is the risk of default. Corporate bonds are supposed to be income-producing investments that are repaid at maturity. There is a greater likelihood with junk bonds than with other corporate bonds that the corporation will not be able to repay the bonds at maturity. In early 1990, for example, Allied and Federated Department stores filed for Chapter 11 bankruptcy and stopped payment on junk bonds with a total face value of $2.8 billion. Moreover, most Wall Street experts expect the approximately 2.5 percent current default rate for junk bonds to climb much higher during the 1990s. The second risk associated with junk bonds is that the corporation will be unable to make interest payments to bondholders.

A Warning from Wall Street

Today, Wall Street experts warn that there is more reason than ever to exercise caution with regard to junk bonds. According to Ben Weberman, a senior editor for *Forbes,* "the distinguishing feature about junk bond investing is that there is no such thing as average and that each issue has its own personality."° Therefore, each junk bond issue must be evaluated on its own merits. Wall Street experts also point out that junk bonds, for the most part, were introduced in the 1980s, so that the junk bond market has not yet undergone a significant economic recession. Most experts are not quite sure what will happen to that market when the economy takes a nosedive.

A Final Word of Caution

Investors should remember this basic rule of investing: *The potential return on any investment should be directly related to the risk that the investor assumes.* If you want to invest in bonds and enjoy 14 percent annual yields, you have to take some chances. With junk bonds, as with any other investment, the key requirements for successful investing may be careful evaluation and diversification. Failure to evaluate potential junk bond investments and failure to diversify junk bond investments could mean that your junk bond investments are simply that—*junk*!

°Ben Weberman, "The Real and the Junk," *Forbes,* July 28, 1986, p. 224.
For more information, see Walter L. Updegrave, "Riding the Wave of Long Bond Yields," *Money,* April 1989, pp. 100–101 + ; John Heins, "It's Not All Junk," *Forbes,* June 26, 1989, pp. 244–45; and C. David Chase, *Chase Global Investment Almanac* (Homewood, Ill.: Chase Global Data & Research, 1989), pp. 202–3.

..

Bond Yield Calculations

L.O.6
Calculate both the current yield and the yield to maturity for a bond investment.

For a bond investment, the **yield** is the rate of return earned by an investor that holds a bond for a stated period of time. Two methods are used to measure the yield on a bond investment.

The **current yield** is determined by dividing the annual interest dollar amount of a bond by its current market price. Generally, the current yield for a bond is included in most financial publications, but there are occasions when you must calculate it. The following formula may help you complete this calculation.

$$\text{Current yield} = \frac{\text{Interest amount}}{\text{Market value}}$$

For example, assume that you own a Mobil corporate bond that pays 8½ percent interest on an annual basis. This means that each year you will receive $1,000 times 8.5 percent, or $85. Also assume that the current market price of the Mobil bond is $930. The current yield is 9.1 percent, as illustrated below.

$$\text{Current yield} = \frac{\$85}{\$930}$$
$$= 0.091, \text{ or } 9.1 \text{ percent}$$

The **yield to maturity** is a yield calculation that takes into account the relationship among a bond's maturity value, the time to maturity, the current price, and the dollar amount of interest. The formula for calculating the yield to maturity is presented below.

$$\text{Yield to maturity} = \frac{\text{Interest amount} + \dfrac{\text{Face value} - \text{Market value}}{\text{Number of periods}}}{\dfrac{\text{Market value} + \text{Face value}}{2}}$$

For example, assume that on December 31, 1990, you purchase at the current market price of $850 a corporate bond with a $1,000 face value issued by Detroit Edison. The bond pays 8⅛ percent annual interest, and its maturity date is 2001. The yield to maturity is 10.3 percent, as illustrated below.

$$\text{Yield to maturity} = \frac{\$81.25 + \dfrac{\$1,000 - \$850}{11}}{\dfrac{\$850 + \$1,000}{2}}$$
$$= \frac{\$94.89}{\$925}$$
$$= .103, \text{ or } 10.3 \text{ percent}$$

In this situation, the yield to maturity takes into account two types of return on the bond. First, the bondholder will receive interest income from the purchase date until the maturity date. Second, at maturity the bondholder will receive a payment for the face value of the bond. If the bond is purchased at a price below the face value, the yield to maturity is greater than the stated interest rate. If the bond is purchased at a price above the face value, the yield to maturity is less than the stated interest rate.

The Mechanics of a Bond Transaction

L.O.7
Describe how bonds are bought and sold.

Bonds are purchased in much the same manner as stocks. Corporate bonds may be purchased in the primary market or the secondary market. (Remember, the *primary* market is a market in which an investor purchases financial securities, via an investment bank or other representative, from the issuer of those securities. The *secondary* market is a market for existing financial securities that are currently traded between investors.) In the secondary market, most corporate bonds are traded on either the New York Bond Exchange or the American Bond Exchange. As mentioned earlier, U.S. government bonds and securities may be purchased through the Federal Reserve System, commercial banks, savings and loan associations, and account executives representing brokerage firms. Municipal bonds are sold through account executives.

Generally, the commissions that brokerage firms charge on bond transactions are smaller than the commissions they charge on stock transactions. In fact, most brokerage firms charge $10 to buy or sell a $1,000 bond.

Bond Prices   All bonds are issued with a stated face value. This is the amount the bondholder will receive if the bond is held until it matures. But once the bond has been issued, its price may be higher or lower than its face value. When a bond is selling for less than its face value, it is said to be selling at a *discount*. When a bond is selling for more than its face value, it is said to be selling at a *premium*. As discussed earlier in the chapter, interest rates for comparable investments and interest rates in the economy are two factors that may cause the market value of a bond to increase or decrease. Generally, investors consult *The Wall Street Journal* or a local newspaper to determine the price of a bond. It is also possible to approximate a bond's market value by completing the following formula:

$$\text{Approximate market value} = \frac{\text{Interest amount}}{\text{Comparable interest rate}}$$

For example, assume that you purchase a Consolidated Edison bond that pays 7¾ percent based on a face value of $1,000. Also assume that new corporate bond issues of comparable quality are currently paying 10 percent. The approximate market value for the Consolidated Edison bond is therefore $775, as shown below.

$$\text{Approximate market value} = \frac{\$77.50}{0.10}$$
$$= \$775$$

The market value of a bond may be affected not only by increases or decreases in interest rates for comparable investments or in the overall interest rates of the economy, but also by the financial condition of the company or government unit issuing the bond, the proximity of the bond's maturity date, and the factors of supply and demand.

Registered Bonds, Coupon Bonds, and Zero-Coupon Bonds   The method used to pay bondholders their interest depends on whether they own registered bonds, coupon bonds, or zero-coupon bonds. A **registered bond** is a bond that is registered in the owner's name by the issuing company. Interest checks for registered bonds are mailed directly to the bondholder of record. When a registered bond is sold, it must be endorsed by the seller before ownership can be transferred on the company's books. A **coupon bond** is a bond whose ownership is not registered by the issuing company. To collect interest on a coupon bond, bondholders must clip a coupon and then redeem it by following the procedures outlined by the issuer. Coupon bonds, sometimes called bearer bonds, are more dangerous than registered bonds. If a coupon bond is lost or stolen, interest on the bond may be collected and the bond may be redeemed at maturity by anyone who finds it. For this reason, most corporate bonds are registered.

A **zero-coupon bond** is a bond that is sold at a price far below its face value, makes no annual or semiannual interest payments, and is redeemed for its face value at maturity. With a zero-coupon bond, the buyer receives a return based on the bond's dollar appreciation as its maturity date approaches. For example, assume that a Merrill Lynch zero-coupon bond is purchased for $270 in 1990 and that Merrill Lynch will pay the bondholder $1,000 when this bond matures in 2006. For holding the bond 16 years, the bondholder receives interest of $730 ($1,000 face value − $270 purchase price = $730 return) at maturity.

Before investing in zero-coupon bonds, you should consider at least two factors. First, even though all of the interest on these bonds is paid at maturity, the IRS requires zero-coupon bondholders to report interest each year—as it is earned and not when it is actually received. Second, zero-coupon bonds are more volatile than other types of bonds. Today, zero-coupon bonds are issued by corporations, the U.S. Treasury, and municipalities. In evaluating such bonds, as in evaluating any other type of bond, the most important criterion is the quality of the issuer. It pays to be careful.

SUMMARY

A corporate bond is a corporation's written pledge that it will repay a specified amount of money, with interest. All of the details about a bond (face value, interest rate, maturity, repayment, etc.) are contained in the bond indenture.

Corporations issue bonds and other securities to help finance their ongoing activities.

Investors purchase corporate bonds for three reasons: (1) interest income, (2) possible increase in value, and (3) repayment at maturity.

Bonds issued by the U.S. Treasury and federal agencies are used to finance the national debt and the ongoing activities of the federal government. State and local governments issue bonds to finance their ongoing activities and special projects such as airports, schools, toll roads, and toll bridges.

Some local newspapers and *The Wall Street Journal* and *Barron's* provide bond investors with some of the information needed to evaluate a bond issue. To determine the quality of a bond issue, most investors study the ratings provided by Standard & Poor's and Moody's. Both of these companies rate thousands of corporate and municipal bonds.

The current yield is determined by dividing the annual interest dollar amount of a bond by its current market price. The yield to maturity is a yield calculation that takes into account the relationship among a bond's maturity value, the time to maturity, the current price, and the dollar amount of interest.

Bonds can be purchased through account executives who represent brokerage firms. U.S. government bonds can also be purchased through Federal Reserve banks and branches, commercial banks, savings and loan associations, and other financial institutions.

KEY FORMULAS

A Reference Guide

Page	Topic	Formula
498	Taxable equivalent yield	$\text{Taxable equivalent yield} = \dfrac{\text{Tax-exempt yield}}{1.0 - \text{Your tax rate}}$
501	Current yield	$\text{Current yield} = \dfrac{\text{Interest amount}}{\text{Market value}}$
502	Yield to maturity	$\text{Yield to maturity} = \dfrac{\text{Interest amount} + \dfrac{\text{Face value} - \text{Market value}}{\text{Number of periods}}}{\dfrac{\text{Market value} + \text{Face value}}{2}}$
503	Approximate market value	$\text{Approximate market value} = \dfrac{\text{Interest amount}}{\text{Comparable interest rate}}$

GLOSSARY

Bond indenture   A legal document that details all of the conditions relating to a bond issue.

Call feature   A feature that allows the corporation to call in or buy outstanding bonds from current bondholders before the maturity date.

Convertible bond   A bond that can be exchanged, at the owner's option, for a specified number of shares of the corporation's common stock.

Corporate bond   A corporation's written pledge that it will repay a specified amount of money, with interest.

Coupon bond   A bond whose ownership is not registered by the issuing company.

Current yield   Determined by dividing the annual interest dollar amount of a bond by its current market price.

Debenture   A bond that is backed only by the reputation of the issuing corporation.

General obligation bond   A bond backed by the full faith, credit, and unlimited taxing power of the government that issued it.

Maturity date   For a corporate bond, this is the date on which the corporation is to repay the borrowed money.

Mortgage bond   A corporate bond that is secured by various assets of the issuing firm.

Municipal bond   A debt security issued by a state or local government.

Registered bond   A bond that is registered in the owner's name by the issuing company.

Revenue bond   A bond that is repaid from the income generated by the project it is designed to finance.

Serial bonds   Bonds of a single issue that mature on different dates.

Sinking fund   A fund to which annual or semiannual deposits are made for the purpose of redeeming a bond issue.

Subordinated debenture   An unsecured bond that gives bondholders a claim secondary to that of other designated bondholders with respect to both income and assets.

Trustee   A financially independent firm or individual that acts as the bondholders' representative.

Yield   The rate of return earned by an investor that holds a bond for a stated period of time.

Yield to maturity   A yield calculation that takes into account the relationship among a bond's maturity value, the time to maturity, the current price, and the dollar amount of interest.

Zero-coupon bond   A bond that is sold at a price far below its face value, makes no interest payments, and is redeemed for its face value at maturity.

DISCUSSION QUESTIONS

L.O.1   1. What types of information are contained in a bond indenture?

L.O.2   2. Why do corporations sell bonds?

L.O.2   3. What is a debenture? How does a debenture differ from a mortgage bond?

L.O.2   4. Why do corporations issue convertible bonds?

L.O.2   5. A corporation may use one of two methods to ensure that it has sufficient funds available to redeem a bond issue. Explain the two methods.

L.O.3   6. Why do investors purchase bonds?

L.O.3   7. Why would an investor prefer the purchase of a convertible bond to other investment alternatives?

L.O.4   8. What is the difference between a Treasury bill, a Treasury note, and a Treasury bond?

L.O.4   9. How are Treasury securities bought and sold? What is the difference between a competitive bid and a noncompetitive bid for Treasury securities?

L.O.4   10. State and local bonds are classified as either general obligation bonds or revenue bonds. How do these classifications affect repayment of the bonds?

L.O.5   11. Describe the bond rating system used by Standard & Poor's and Moody's.

L.O.6   12. What is the difference between the current yield and the yield to maturity?

L.O.7   13. How do interest rates in the economy affect the market value of a corporate or government bond?

L.O.7   14. What is the difference between a registered bond, a coupon bond, and a zero-coupon bond?

Opening Case Questions

1. When Joanna and Mike Nations thought they should sell some of their stocks and make more conservative investments, after considering the traditionally safe investments (certificates of deposit, government bonds, and corporate bonds), they decided to invest in corporate bonds. If you had been in their position, would you have made the same decision?

2. The Nations' account executive suggested two corporate bond issues—an IBM issue and a Carter Hawley Hale issue. The first was rated Aaa by Moody's and had a current yield of 9.2 percent. The second was rated B by Moody's and had a current yield of 13 percent. How do the ratings and current yields for these bond issues illustrate the concept of opportunity costs that is discussed throughout this text?

PROBLEMS AND ACTIVITIES

L.O.1   1. In your own words, define each of the following terms:

     a. Corporate bond._____

    _____

     b. Maturity date._____

    _____

     c. Bond indenture._____

    _____

L.O.2   2. List the reasons why a corporation would use bonds (debt financing) to finance its ongoing business activities.

L.O.2   3. Dorothy Martin wants to invest $5,000 in corporate bonds. Her account executive suggested that she consider debentures, mortgage bonds, and convertible bonds. Since she has never invested in bonds, she is not quite sure how these bonds differ. How would you explain their differences to her?

L.O.3   4. List the reasons why an investor would purchase corporate bonds.

L.O.4   5. Complete the following grid:

	Minimum Amount	Maturity Range	How Interest Is Paid
Treasury bills	_____	_____	_____
Treasury notes	_____	_____	_____
Treasury bonds	_____	_____	_____

L.O.4   6. Assume that you are in the 28 percent tax bracket and that you purchase an 8 percent tax-exempt municipal bond. Calculate the taxable equivalent yield for this investment.

L.O.5   7. Choose a corporate bond listed on the New York Bond Exchange and use *Moody's Industrial Manuals* (available at your college or public library) to answer the following questions on this bond issue.

  a. What is Moody's rating for the issue?
  b. What is the purpose of the issue?
  c. Does the issue have a call provision?
  d. Who is the trustee for the issue?
  e. What collateral, if any, has been pledged as security for the issue?
  f. Based on the information you have obtained, would the bond be a good investment for you? Why?

L.O.5   8. Using information from *The Wall Street Journal* or a local newspaper, answer the following questions on the bond issues listed below.

Newspaper_____   Date_____

	Current Yield	Volume	Close Price
E Kod 8⅝ 16			
Procter & Gamble 8¼ 05			
UBrnd 10½ 04			

L.O.6   9. Assume that you purchase a corporate bond at its current market price of $850 in 1990. It pays 9 percent interest, and it will mature in the year 2000, at which time the corporation will pay you the face value of $1,000.
  a. Determine the current yield on your bond investment.
  b. Determine the yield to maturity on your bond investment.

L.O.7 10. List the reasons why investors might want to buy zero-coupon bonds. Then list the reasons why investors might want to avoid zero-coupon bonds. Based on these lists, do you consider zero-coupon bonds a good alternative for your investment program? Why?

LIFE SITUATION   Case 17–1

The ABCs of Bond Ratings

Are bonds safer than common or preferred stock? The answer to that question depends on such factors as the conditions contained in the bond agreement and the likelihood of repayment at maturity. Most investors rely on two financial services, Standard & Poor's and Moody's, to provide ratings for bonds. Standard & Poor's bond ratings range from AAA (the highest) to D (the lowest). Moody's bond ratings range from Aaa (the highest) to C (the lowest). For most investors, a bond rated A or better is probably as safe as a blue-chip stock, while a C-rated bond could be as risky as the most speculative stock.

Recently, a number of corporate bond issues whose Standard & Poor's ratings are lower than A have been sold in the bond market. The reasons for the lower ratings vary. A bond may have been assigned a low rating because the corporation that issued it has long-term debt that is too high or earnings that are too low or because changing economic conditions may make payment of bond interest or repayment of the bond principal doubtful. Whatever the reasons, the corporations issuing the low-rated bonds had to increase the interest rate on them in order to attract purchasers. As a result, the bonds offer extremely attractive current yields to investors who are willing to take a chance. For example, a $1,000 corporate bond issued by Continental Airlines is paying 11 percent interest until its maturity in 1995. The current market price of this bond is $770, which means that the current yield is 14.3 percent. Moody's rates the bond B.

Questions

1. How important are the Moody's and Standard & Poor's bond ratings? What does the Moody's B rating mean?
2. A 14.3 percent current yield is at least 3 to 4 percent higher than the current yield of more conservative corporate bond issues. Is this additional interest worth the added risks involved in purchasing a bond with lower ratings such as the Continental Airlines bond?
3. As the maturity date of the Continental Airlines bond approaches, what should happen to the price of this bond? Why?
4. What other information would you need to evaluate the Continental Airlines bond? Where would you get this information?

For more information, see *Moody's Transportation Manual, 1989*, vol. 1 (A–I), p. 619; John Paul Newport, Jr., "Junk Bonds Face the Big Unknown," *Fortune*, May 22, 1989, pp. 129–30; and *The Wall Street Journal*, Friday, October 27, 1989, American Bond Exchange quotations.

LIFE SITUATION   Case 17–2

A Questionable Bond Investment

On November 20, Joan Sanders got a telephone call from an account executive in New York City who said that one of his other clients had given him her name. Then he told her that his brokerage firm was selling a new corporate bond issue for New World Explorations, a company heavily engaged in oil exploration in the western United States. The bonds in this issue paid investors 13.2 percent a year and matured on December 31, 2000, and Moody's rating for the issue was "just a little below" B. The account executive said that his firm was selling these high-yield bonds to new clients as a way of thanking them for becoming its clients.

Before you read on, put yourself in Joan Sanders' place and answer the following questions.

Questions

1. Based on what you have learned thus far, would you buy the 13.2 percent corporate bonds issued by New World Explorations if you were Joan Sanders? Why?
2. What information would you like to have before you invest in New World Explorations? Where can you get this information?

Ms. Sanders was interested in the bonds that the account executive had offered her, but she decided to check out New World Explorations before investing in them. When she visited the library, she was unable to find any mention of New World Explorations. The account executive hadn't given her a telephone number but had promised to call back in two or three days to take her order. After two days, he did call back. When Ms. Sanders told him that she had been unable to find any information about New World Explorations, he hung up!

SUPPLEMENTARY READINGS

For Additional Information on Corporate Bonds

Nichols, Donald R. *The Personal Investor's Complete Book of Bonds.* Chicago: Longman Financial Services Publishing, 1989.

Norton, Robert E. "Dividends and Interest Matter a Lot More Than You Think," *Fortune,* November 6, 1989, p. 19+.

Wasik, John F. "Your Best Investments for Under $1,000." *Consumers Digest,* May–June 1990, p. 57+.

Widicus, Wilbur W., and Thomas E. Stitzel. *Personal Investing,* 5th ed. Homewood, Ill.: Richard D. Irwin, 1989.

Zigas, David. "Blue-Chip Bonds Look Like a 'Buyer's Dream.'" *Business Week,* December 4, 1989, p. 103.

For Additional Information on Government Bonds

Barnes, Robert E. "Government Issues Remain Safe in Shaky Times." *Black Enterprise,* March 1990, pp. 31–32.

Luxenberg, Stan. "Take Another Look at Ginnie Maes," *Money,* March 1990, pp. 34–36.

Weberman, Ben. "Bonus Bonds." *Forbes,* February 5, 1990, p. 197.

For Additional Information on Evaluation of Bonds

Hubert, Mark. "Life after Drexel." *Forbes,* March 19, 1990, p. 202.

Kuhn, Susan E. "Munis, State by State: Bargains that Beat the Tax Man." *Fortune,* April 9, 1990, p. 29+.

Malkiel, Burton G. "The Case for Bonds." *Forbes,* June 26, 1989, p. 180+.

Nichols, Donald R. *Zero Coupon Investments.* Homewood, Ill.: Dow Jones-Irwin, 1989.

Serwer, Andrew E. "How to Find Gems in a Rough Bond Market." *Fortune,* January 1, 1990, p. 23+.

18 Investing in Mutual Funds and Investment Companies

In the last two chapters, we discussed three investment alternatives—common stock, preferred stock, and bonds. In this chapter, we examine another investment alternative—mutual funds. We consider the reasons for investing in mutual funds, the characteristics of mutual funds, the mechanics of mutual fund transactions, and methods for evaluating mutual funds.

LEARNING OBJECTIVES

After studying this chapter, you will be able to

L.O.1 Explain why individuals invest in mutual funds.

L.O.2 Understand the unique characteristics of investments in mutual funds.

L.O.3 Classify mutual funds by investment objective.

L.O.4 Evaluate mutual funds for investment purposes.

L.O.5 Describe how and why mutual funds are bought and sold.

• •

OPENING CASE

One Investor's Disappointment

According to Martha Blackstone, a 55-year-old widow who lives in Denver, mutual funds were one of the biggest disappointments in her life. In August 1987, she invested over $11,500 in the Fidelity Select—Electronics Mutual Fund. Two years later, this investment had a market value of $6,000. What went wrong?

For one thing, Ms. Blackstone thought that because mutual funds were professionally managed and provided diversification, they were safe investments—almost guaranteed to increase in value. After losing over $5,000, she realized that "almost guaranteed" was not the same thing as "guaranteed." When she made her investment, she thought that almost everybody must be investing in mutual funds since there were over 2,300 of them. At that time, it seemed "almost fashionable" to invest in mutual funds. And besides, the mutual funds made it "so easy"—just open an account, send the money, and let the professional managers make all the decisions.

Two years later, Ms. Blackstone admitted that she had invested her money without researching Fidelity Select's Electronics Mutual Fund. She made her investment decision because she had heard "good things" about Fidelity. In fact, she didn't even realize that Fidelity, the nation's largest mutual fund family, offered over 170 mutual funds that ranged all the way from very conservative to very speculative investments. Simply put, she chose the wrong Fidelity mutual fund. Had Ms. Blackstone chosen Fidelity Select's Broadcast/Media fund, her original investment would have been worth over $17,000.°

°Values for the Fidelity Select—Broadcast/Media Fund and the Fidelity Select—Electronics Mutual Fund were taken from Jeffrey M. Laderman, "How Mutual Funds Have Battled Back," *Business Week*, September 18, 1989, pp. 100–101.

• •

A **mutual fund** is an investment alternative chosen by individuals who pool their money to buy stocks, bonds, and other securities selected by professional managers who work for an investment company. The mutual fund investment of Ms. Blackstone, the woman in our Opening Case, was disappointing because she made two serious mistakes: she didn't evaluate her investment, and she didn't consider its risks. As a result, she lost almost $6,000 in just two years.

Any decision to invest in mutual funds, including Ms. Blackstone's, is based on the concept of opportunity costs, which we have discussed throughout this text. Simply put, you have to be willing to take some chances if you want to get a larger return on your investment. Before deciding whether mutual funds are the right investment for you, you should consider certain factors.

WHY INVESTORS PURCHASE MUTUAL FUNDS

L.O.1
Explain why individuals invest in mutual funds.

The major reasons why investors purchase mutual funds are professional management and *diversification,* or investment in a wide variety of securities. Most investment companies do everything possible to convince individual investors that they can do a better job of picking securities than individual investors can. Sometimes these claims are true, and sometimes they are just so much hot air. Still, investment companies do have professional portfolio managers with years of experience who devote large amounts of time to picking just the "right" securities for mutual funds. In addition, numerous investment companies have developed elaborate systems and procedures to help their portfolio managers make the right selections. But even the best portfolio managers make mistakes. As an investor, *you have to evaluate an investment in mutual funds just as you would evaluate any other potential investment.*

FINANCIAL PLANNING IN ACTION

Are Mutual Funds for You?

In 1988, Americans invested over $134 billion in mutual funds, or about $360 million a day. In the same year, over 40 million Americans owned shares in a mutual fund. Today, there are more mutual funds than ever before—all developed to meet the needs of investors like you. And while putting your money in a mutual fund may seem like a carefree method of investing, nothing can be further from the truth.

In evaluating a mutual fund, the first factor you should consider is the fund's investment objectives. Whether you want your money in conservative, long-term government bonds or in speculative foreign stocks, there is a mutual fund for you. The key question may be, "Do the objectives of a specific mutual fund match your objectives?"

The second factor you should consider is the fund's past performance. It is fairly easy to obtain a comparative performance ranking for periods ranging from the last 10 years to the most recent quarter. Sources of information on mutual funds that are available at most libraries include *Donoghue's Mutual Funds Almanac, The Investor's Guide to No-Load Mutual Funds, Changing Times, Money,* and *Forbes.* The most comprehensive reference sources on mutual funds are the Wiesenberger Investment Companies Service and the reports published by Lipper Analytical Services.

The third factor you should consider is the information available in newsletters on mutual funds. Thanks to the great interest in mutual funds, over 50 newsletters now specialize in this subject. Many of these newsletters have survived the test of time and provide investors with reliable advice for fees ranging from $85 to $300 a year. But some of these newsletters mislead investors by backdating the performance of their suggested investment portfolios—a practice akin to betting on a horse after the race is over.

Two inexpensive directories list mutual funds by investment goals and give details on commission charges. A guide to funds with small or no sales commissions is available for $5 from the No-Load Mutual Fund Association, P.O. Box 2004, JAF Building, New York, NY 10116. A similar guide is available for $1 from the Investment Company Institute, 1600 M Street, NW, Suite 600, Washington, DC 20036, Attention: Guide.

For more information on the evaluation of mutual funds, see the *1989 Mutual Fund Fact Book* (Washington, D.C.: Investment Company Institute, 1989), pp. 13–18; Jonathan Clements, "How to Pick a Mutual Fund," *Forbes,* September 4, 1989, p. 192; Leonard Wiener, "Choosing a Fund: A Survival Guide for Small Investors," *U.S. News & World Report,* February 16, 1987, p. 56+; and Jan Wong, "Mutual Fund Newsletters Multiply, but What Do They Offer Readers?" *The Wall Street Journal,* June 30, 1986, p. 23.

The diversification of mutual funds spells safety, because an occasional loss incurred with one investment is usually offset by gains from other investments. For example, consider the number of securities in the portfolio of The Travelers Aggressive Stock Trust shown in Exhibit 18–1. Note that nearly 200 companies are represented in this portfolio. Common stocks constitute 98.5 percent of this mutual fund's investments. The fund comprises 27 classifications of common stock, a fact of particular interest to investors who are seeking diversification.

Another reason why investors purchase mutual funds is that these funds are a convenient way to invest money. Transactions with mutual funds can be completed by mail or over the phone.

Judging from the number and size of the currently available mutual funds, a large number of people believe that these advantages are important. According to the Investment Company Institute, there are more than 2,700 mutual funds and their combined assets exceed $800 billion.[1]

EXHIBIT 18–1 There are nearly 200 different companies represented in The Travelers Aggressive Stock Trust.

AGGRESSIVE STOCK TRUST

SCHEDULE OF INVESTMENTS—*December 31, 1989*

	Number of Shares	Market Value		Number of Shares	Market Value
COMMON STOCKS (98.5%)			**Capital Goods** *(Cont.)*		
Advertising and Publishing (2.9%)			★ Kaydon Corp.	1,400	$ 44,975
★ Central Newspapers Inc. Class A ...	4,400	$100,100	Masco Industries, Inc. (b)	8,700	66,881
Comcast Corp. Class A	895	14,376	Measurex Corp.	2,300	57,788
★ TCA Cable TV, Inc.	5,600	95,900	★ Stewart & Stevenson Services, Inc.	1,400	39,200
★ Turner Broadcasting System Inc. (b)	4,600	230,000	Terex Corp.	3,300	71,362
		440,376	Thermo Electron Corp. (b)	3,500	107,188
					606,269
Aerospace (0.5%)					
★ Pacific Scientific Co. (b)	1,400	21,175	**Chemicals (1.1%)**		
Precision Castparts Corp.	1,900	58,900	★ Fuller (H.B.) Co.	1,500	33,187
		80,075	★ Schulman (A.), Inc.	2,100	73,763
			Vista Chemical Co.	1,734	67,409
Air Transportation (1.2%)					174,359
Alaska Air Group, Inc.	3,100	63,938			
Texas Air Corp. (b)	10,100	117,412	**Consumer Goods (3.5%)**		
		181,350	★ Armour All Products Corp.	4,100	84,563
			CPI Corp.	2,800	94,150
Amusements (3.6%)			★ Gibson Greetings Inc.	3,300	85,181
Atari Corporation (b)	8,000	68,000	Helene Curtis Industries, Inc.	1,500	37,312
★ Chris Craft Industries, Inc. (b)	2,500	90,938	★ Huffy Corp.	2,600	49,400
King World Productions, Inc. (b)	3,400	129,625	Neutrogena Corp.	2,925	85,191
★ Live Entertainment Inc. (b)	3,800	62,700	★ Sanford Corp.	3,500	93,187
Mattel, Inc. (b)	8,500	167,875	★ Town & Country Corp. (b)	2,000	12,500
Tonka Corp. (b)	3,000	33,375			541,484
		552,513			
			Drugs (11.3%)		
Automotive (1.1%)			★ Acuson Corp. (b)	3,500	112,000
★ Danaher Corp. (b)	4,200	64,050	ALZA Corp. Class A (b)	4,800	210,600
★ Donnelly Corp.	2,000	18,000	Amgen Inc. (b)	3,100	152,288
★ Gentex Corp. (b)	1,900	24,462	Applied Biosystems, Inc. (b)	3,500	96,687
★ J.P. Industries, Inc. (b)	5,000	62,500	Biomet Inc. (b)	4,450	121,819
		169,012	Centocor Inc. (b)	3,400	85,850
			Cetus Corp. (b)	4,200	59,587
Building (1.8%)			★ Chiron Corp. (b)	2,900	81,925
★ Apogee Enterprises, Inc.	3,200	50,000	Cordis Corp. (b)	3,000	46,875
★ Kaufman & Broad Home Corp.	3,200	43,600	★ FHP International Corp. (b)	3,600	74,250
Morgan Products Ltd. (b)	2,700	27,675	★ Forest Labs, Inc. (b)	1,900	79,563
Ryland Group (The), Inc.	2,500	47,188	Genetics Institute Inc. (b)	2,600	89,050
★ TJ International Inc.	1,900	46,075	Puritan-Bennett Corp.	3,000	72,375
★ Watts Industries, Inc.	1,700	62,475	St. Jude Medical, Inc. (b)	4,000	192,500
		277,013	Surgical Care Affiliates Inc.	2,400	45,600
			U.S. Bioscience Inc. (b)	930	11,513
Capital Goods (3.9%)			U.S. Healthcare, Inc.	6,700	92,963
Applied Power Inc. Class A	3,000	67,125	★ Westmark International Inc. (b)	1,700	77,988
★ CRSS Inc.	2,000	34,000			
Harley-Davidson Motor Co. (b)	3,000	117,750			

★ *Additions—July 1 to December 31, 1989.*

SOURCE: The Travelers, *Annual Report*, December 31, 1989, pp. 79–82.

EXHIBIT 18–1   Continued

	Number of Shares	Market Value
Drugs *(Cont.)*		
★ Xoma Corp. (b)	1,700	$ 37,400
		1,740,833
Diversified Companies (0.2%)		
Kaman Corp. Class A	3,500	32,813
Electronics (4.5%)		
Advanced Micro Devices, Inc. (b)	11,600	91,350
Anthem Electronics, Inc. (b)	2,900	50,750
Applied Materials, Inc. (b)	2,300	65,550
Cypress Semiconductor Corp. (b)	8,000	78,000
★ Dallas Semiconductor Corp. (b)	4,300	27,681
Dionex Corp. (b)	1,300	35,262
★ Genus Inc. (b)	4,800	37,500
★ Integrated Device Technology, Inc. (b)	8,600	68,800
KLA Instruments Corp. (b)	4,100	35,363
National Semiconductor Corp. (b)	11,800	85,550
Novellus Systems Inc. (b)	3,000	40,875
Teradyne, Inc. (b)	6,600	72,600
		689,281
Finance (3.1%)		
★ Cash American Investments Inc.	2,600	58,825
★ First Capital Holdings Corp. (b)	7,100	62,125
First Empire State Corp.	1,600	105,200
★ Mercury Finance Co.	3,867	70,567
★ Schwab Charles Corp. New	5,300	73,538
TCF Financial Corp.	4,000	54,000
★ Washington Mutual Savings Bank (Seattle, Wash.)	3,000	55,687
		479,942
Foods (1.6%)		
★ A & W Brands Inc. (b)	2,100	61,163
Dreyer's Grand Ice Cream, Inc. (b)	2,800	77,000
Golden Valley Microwave Foods, Inc. (b)	3,600	108,000
		246,163
Insurance (2.8%)		
Berkley W.R. Corp.	2,100	84,262
Broad Inc.	7,400	86,950
★ Harleysville Group Corp.	1,000	27,625
★ NAC Re. Corp.	2,400	84,900

	Number of Shares	Market Value
Insurance *(Cont.)*		
★ Trenwick Group Inc.	2,000	$ 48,750
★ 20th Century Industries, Inc.	4,400	100,925
		433,412
Metals & Mining (3.5%)		
★ Addington Resources, Inc. (b)	2,400	40,200
★ Amax Gold Inc.	6,400	113,600
Battle Mining Gold Co. Class A	6,850	113,881
★ Cleveland-Cliffs Inc.	1,900	55,100
★ Lukens, Inc.	1,700	65,025
★ Oregon Steel Mills Inc.	3,500	84,875
Quanex Corp.	5,000	75,000
		547,681
Natural Gas (1.1%)		
★ Kirby Exploration Co.	4,200	38,850
★ Renaissance Energy Ltd. (b)	3,300	73,392
★ Valero Energy Corp.	4,000	60,500
		172,742
Office and Business Equipment (8.9%)		
Adaptec Inc. (b)	8,000	141,500
Autodesk, Inc.	6,500	251,875
★ Cadence Design System Inc. (b)	3,100	65,487
★ Conner Peripherals Inc. (b)	4,700	61,394
★ Convex Computer Corp. (b)	4,200	64,575
Intergraph Corp. (b)	6,000	102,750
★ Intermec Corp. (b)	1,900	54,387
Mentor Graphics Corp.	9,800	162,925
★ Quantum Corp. (b)	5,700	61,988
Sequent Computer System Inc. (b)	6,600	131,175
Silcon Graphics Inc. (b)	5,000	146,875
Stratus Computer Inc. (b)	2,600	59,800
★ Teradata Corp. (b)	3,200	71,200
		1,375,931
Oil (2.4%)		
Ranger Oil Ltd. (b)	10,800	63,450
Seagull Energy Corp. (b)	3,700	84,175
Tejas Gas Corp. (b)	1,325	37,100
Tosco Corp.	2,051	46,660
★ Triton Energy Corp.	3,400	52,700
Wainoco Oil Corp. (b)	8,000	88,000
		372,085

EXHIBIT 18–1   Continued

AGGRESSIVE STOCK TRUST

SCHEDULE OF INVESTMENTS—*December 31, 1989*

	Number of Shares	Market Value		Number of Shares	Market Value
Oil Service (2.6%)			**Services (8.3%)**		
Baroid Corp.	9,200	$ 103,500	★ Allwaste Inc. (b)	7,400	$ 79,088
Daniel Industries Inc.	3,500	54,688	★ Brand Cos., Inc. (b)	1,200	38,400
★ Grace Energy Corp. (b)	2,900	71,050	CUC International (b)	8,200	118,900
Parker Drilling Co. (b)	10,600	106,000	★ Calgon Carbon Corp.	3,200	140,400
Tidewater Inc. (b)	4,500	64,687	Canonie Environmental Services		
		399,925	Corp. (b)	1,600	29,600
			★ Enstar Group Inc.	1,733	5,091
Paper & Packaging (1.2%)			Groundwater Technology, Inc. (b)	1,600	32,000
★ Mosinee Paper Corp.	1,700	30,069	International Lease Finance Corp.	4,600	115,287
★ Pope & Talbot Inc.	1,400	36,225	★ Ionics Inc. (b)	1,700	40,906
★ Sealright Inc.	1,800	45,225	★ Occupational Urgent Care (b)	3,100	56,575
★ Shorewood Packaging Corp. (b)	1,700	42,712	★ Ogden Projects Inc. (b)	4,800	121,800
★ Wausau Paper Mills Co.	1,100	37,400	★ Paychex Inc.	2,900	56,187
		191,631	Telecredit, Inc.	2,000	79,500
			★ Thermedics Inc. (b)	4,500	64,125
Restaurants (1.9%)			★ Wellman Inc.	3,800	133,475
★ Applebee's International Inc. (b)	2,400	31,500	★ Wheelabrator Corp. (b)	4,800	168,600
★ Buffets Inc. (b)	3,200	54,000			1,279,934
★ Karcher (Carl) Enterprises, Inc.	4,000	49,500			
★ Ryan's Family Steak Houses			**Software Services (6.4%)**		
Inc. (b)	9,700	73,356	Adobe Systems, Inc.	4,000	80,500
★ TCBY Enterprises Inc.	4,600	89,125	★ Aldus Corp. (b)	3,200	49,200
		297,481	★ American Software Inc.	2,700	60,750
			★ BMC Software Inc. (b)	3,000	91,125
Retail Trade (11.1%)			Computer Associates International,		
Ames Department Stores, Inc.	5,100	52,912	Inc. (b)	10,000	125,000
★ Baker J. Inc.	3,000	61,688	★ Legent Corp. (b)	4,700	123,962
★ Blockbuster Entertainment			Lotus Development Corp. (b)	7,900	243,913
Corp. (b)	9,700	164,900	National Data Corp.	1,600	53,700
★ CML Group Inc. (b)	1,800	36,900	★ OMI Corp. (b)	4,800	47,400
Charming Shoppes, Inc.	4,750	50,766	Policy Management Systems		
★ Consolidated Stores Corp. (b)	5,000	19,375	Corp. (b)	3,300	111,788
★ Costco Wholesale Corp. (b)	5,400	189,337			987,338
Dress Barn, Inc. (The) (b)	5,900	67,112			
★ Jan Bell Marketing Inc. (b)	5,200	130,650	**Telecommunications (6.4%)**		
★ Medicine Shoppe International, Inc.	3,000	64,125	Cellular Communications, Inc. (b)	4,133	165,837
★ Office Depot Inc. (b)	5,100	91,800	★ DSC Communications Corp. (b)	9,000	129,938
Reebok International Ltd.	12,800	243,200	Digital Microwave Corp. (b)	3,200	95,600
★ Ross Stores Inc. (b)	4,100	58,169	Digital Communications Associates,		
Service Merchandise Inc.	8,000	75,000	Inc. (b)	4,400	86,900
★ Sotheby's Holdings Inc.	7,700	180,950	Metro Mobile Controls, Inc.		
Stride Rite Corp.	5,200	150,150	Class B (b)	1,350	97,875
Waban Inc. (b)	6,700	80,400	Microcom, Inc. (b)	2,300	36,225
		1,717,434			

★ *Additions—July 1 to December 31, 1989.*

EXHIBIT 18–1   Concluded

	Number of Shares	Market Value			Market Value
Telecommunications *(Cont.)*			**TOTAL INVESTMENTS**		
★ Newbridge Networks Corp. (b)	4,300	$ 64,231	(Cost $14,431,968) (a)		$15,227,720
Novell Inc. (b)	3,300	101,887	**OTHER ASSETS AND LIABILITIES**		
★ Octel Communications Corp.(b)	2,500	55,312	—NET (1.5%)		228,228
★ SynOptics Communications Inc. (b) ..	2,400	60,000			
★ 3Com Corp. (b)	3,000	41,063	**NET ASSETS (100%)**		$15,455,948
★ Vitalink Communications Corp. (b) ...	3,600	56,925			
		991,793	**Notes to Schedule of Investments:**		
			(a) The cost of investments for federal income tax purposes		
Transportation (1.6%)			amounted to $14,550,016. Gross unrealized appreciation		
Builders Transport, Inc. (b)	900	9,788	and depreciation of investments, based on identified tax		
★ Expeditors International of			cost, at December 31,1989 are as follows:		
Washington, Inc. (b)	1,100	29,150	Gross unrealized appreciation		$ 1,832,379
★ Harper Group Inc.	1,600	32,400	Gross unrealized depreciation		(1,154,675)
★ Hunt (J.B.) Transport Services, Inc. ..	3,700	74,000	Net unrealized appreciation		$ 677,704
★ Stolt Tankers & Terminals					
Holdings	4,900	103,512	(b) Non-income-producing security.		
		248,850			

SOURCE: The Travelers, *Annual Report,* December 31, 1989, pp. 79–82.

Characteristics of Investment in Mutual Funds

L.O.2
Understand the unique
characteristics of investments
in mutual funds.

Barron's *Dictionary of Finance and Investment Terms* defines an **investment company** as a firm that, for a management fee, invests the pooled funds of small investors in securities appropriate to its stated investment objectives.[2] Although the investment company concept originated in Europe and then spread to the United States in the late 1800s, it wasn't until the last 20 years that investment companies gained real popularity. In 1970, there were 360 mutual funds with about 10 million shareholders. In 1988, there were 2,718 mutual funds with over 40 million shareholders. Today, investment companies, financial analysts, and most investors include *both* closed-end funds and open-end funds under the broad classification of mutual fund investments.

Closed-End Investment Companies or Open-End Mutual Funds   There are two ways to invest in the mutual funds offered by investment companies. Approximately 10 to 15 percent of all mutual funds are closed-end funds offered by investment companies. A **closed-end fund** is a mutual fund whose shares are issued by an investment company only when the fund is organized. As a result, only a certain number of shares are available to investors. After all the shares originally issued have been sold, an investor can purchase shares only from another investor who is willing to sell them. Shares of closed-end funds are traded on the floor of stock exchanges. Like the prices of stock shares, the prices of these shares are determined by the factors of supply and demand and by investor expectations.

Approximately 85 to 90 percent of all mutual funds are classified as open-end funds. An **open-end fund** is a mutual fund whose shares are issued and redeemed by the investment company at the request of investors. In an open-end fund, there is no limitation on the number of shares that the investment company can issue. Investors are free to buy and sell shares at the net asset value plus a small commission. The **net asset value (NAV)** per share is equal to the current market value of the mutual fund's portfolio minus the mutual fund's liabilities divided by the number of shares outstanding. For most mutual funds, the net asset value is calculated at least once a day. In addition to buying and selling shares on request, most open-end funds provide their investors with a wide variety of services that are not provided by the closed-end funds.

Load Funds and No-Load Funds   The investor should compare the cost of investing in a mutual fund with the cost of other investment alternatives, such as purchasing stocks or bonds. With regard to cost, mutual funds are classified as load funds, low-load funds, or no-load funds. A **load fund** is a mutual fund in which investors pay a commission every time they purchase shares. The commission charge, sometimes referred to as a sales fee or simply as the load charge, may be as high as 8½ percent of the purchase price for investments under $10,000. (Typically, this percentage declines as the amount of the investment increases.) The "stated" advantage of a load fund is that the fund's sales force will explain the mutual fund to investors and offer advice as to when shares of the fund should be bought or sold. A **low-load fund,** as the name implies, charges a lower commission than a load fund. This commission usually ranges between 1 and 3 percent of the purchase price for investments under $10,000.

A **no-load fund** is a mutual fund in which no sales charge is paid by the individual investor. No-load funds don't charge commissions when you buy shares because they have no salespeople. If you want to buy shares of a no-load fund, you must deal directly with the investment company. The usual means of contact is telephone or mail. As an investor, you must decide whether to invest in a load fund or a no-load fund. Some investment salespeople have claimed that load funds outperform no-load funds. But several major research studies indicate that there is no significant difference between mutual funds that charge commissions and those that do not.[3] *Since no-load funds offer the same investment opportunities that load funds offer, you should investigate them further before deciding which type of mutual fund is best for you.* Although the sales commission should not be the decisive factor, the possibility of saving 8½ percent is a factor that you should consider.

Management Fees and Other Charges   In evaluating a specific mutual fund, you should consider management fees and other charges. Most mutual funds charge a management fee. This fee, which is calculated yearly, usually ranges from 0.50 to 1 percent of the fund's total assets.

Some mutual funds charge a redemption fee (sometimes referred to as a back-end fee). A **redemption fee** is a 1 to 5 percent charge that shareholders pay when they withdraw their investment from a mutual fund. If all other factors are equal, a fund that doesn't charge a redemption fee is superior to a fund that does.

The investment company may levy a **12b–1 fee** to defray the costs of marketing and distributing a mutual fund. Approved by the Securities and Exchange Commission in 1980, this annual fee usually ranges from 1 to 1½ percent of a fund's assets. Many very popular funds charge this fee, though some do not. As part of your evaluation of a mutual fund, you should determine whether it charges a 12b–1 fee and, if so, how much the fee is.

The investment company's prospectus must provide all of the details regarding management fees, redemption charges, and 12b–1 fees. The fee table of the Prudential-Bache FlexiFund prospectus is reproduced in Exhibit 18–2. This mutual fund comprises a conservatively managed portfolio and an aggressively managed portfolio. Notice that the fund offers investors two alternatives: one that charges an initial sales charge and one that has a deferred sales charge. Also notice that the fund's operating expenses include management fees, 12b–1 fees, and other expenses.

Classifications of Mutual Funds

L.O.3
Classify mutual funds by investment objective.

The managers of mutual funds tailor their investment portfolios to the investment objectives of their customers. Usually, a fund's objectives are plainly disclosed in its prospectus. For example, the objectives of the Kemper Investors Fund—Equity Portfolio are described as follows:

> This portfolio seeks maximum appreciation of capital through diversification of investment securities having potential for capital appreciation. Current income will not be a significant factor. This portfolio's investments normally will consist of common stocks and securities convertible into or exchangeable for common stocks; however, it may also make private placement investments (which are normally restricted securities).[4]

The major categories of mutual funds, in terms of the types of securities they invest in, are as follows:

- *Balanced funds,* which apportion their investments among common stocks, preferred stocks, and bonds.
- *Growth funds,* which invest in the common stocks of well-managed, rapidly growing corporations.
- *Growth-income funds,* which invest in common and preferred stocks that pay good dividends and are expected to increase in market value.
- *Income funds,* which invest in stocks and bonds that pay high dividends and interest.
- *Index funds,* which invest in common stocks that react in the same way as the stock market as a whole does.
- *Industry funds,* sometimes called specialty funds, which invest in the common stocks of companies in the same industry.
- *Money market funds,* which invest in short-term corporate obligations and government securities that offer high interest.
- *Municipal bond funds,* which invest in municipal bonds that provide investors with tax-free interest income.

A **family of funds** exists when one investment company manages a group of mutual funds. Each fund within the family has a different financial objective. For instance, one of these funds may be a money market fund and another may be a growth fund. Most investment companies offer exchange privileges that enable shareholders to readily switch among the mutual funds in a fund family. For example, if you own shares in the Mutual of Omaha growth fund, you may, at your option, switch to the Mutual of Omaha income fund. The family of funds concept makes it convenient for shareholders to switch their assets among funds as different funds offer more investment potential.

EXHIBIT 18–2   To invest in the Prudential-Bache FlexiFund, investors must pay a sales charge, management fees, 12b–1 fees, and other expenses.

FEE TABLE
(for each Portfolio)

	Class A Shares (Initial Sales Charge Alternative)	Class B Shares (Deferred Sales Charge Alternative)
Shareholder Transaction Expenses		
Maximum Sales Load Imposed on Purchases (as a percentage of offering price)	4.50%	None
Maximum Sales Load or Deferred Sales Load Imposed on Reinvested Dividends	None	None
Deferred Sales Load (as a percentage of original purchase price or redemption proceeds, whichever is lower)	None	5% during the first year, decreasing by 1% annually to 1% in the fifth and sixth years and 0% the seventh year and thereafter
Redemption Fees	None	None
Exchange Fee	None	None

Annual Fund Operating Expenses* (as a percentage of average net assets)	Class A		Class B	
Management Fees:				
Aggressively Managed Portfolio	.65%		.65%	
Conservatively Managed Portfolio		.65%		.65%
12b-1 Fees:				
Aggressively Managed Portfolio	.20%†		1.00%	
Conservatively Managed Portfolio		.20%†		1.00%
Other Expenses:				
Aggressively Managed Portfolio	.79%		.79%	
Conservatively Managed Portfolio		.44%		.44%
Total Fund Operating Expenses:				
Aggressively Managed Portfolio	1.64%		2.44%	
Conservatively Managed Portfolio		1.29%		2.09%

Example (Aggressively Managed Portfolio)*

	1 year	3 years	5 years	10 years
You would pay the following expenses on a $1,000 investment, assuming (1) 5% annual return and (2) redemption at the end of each time period:				
Class A	$61	$ 94	$130	$231
Class B	$75	$106	$140	$278
You would pay the following expenses on the same investment, assuming no redemption:				
Class A	$61	$ 94	$130	$231
Class B	$25	$ 76	$130	$278

Example (Conservatively Managed Portfolio)*

	1 year	3 years	5 years	10 years
You would pay the following expenses on a $1,000 investment, assuming (1) 5% annual return and (2) redemption at the end of each time period:				
Class A	$58	$ 84	$113	$194
Class B	$71	$ 95	$122	$242
You would pay the following expenses on the same investment, assuming no redemption:				
Class A	$58	$ 84	$113	$194
Class B	$21	$ 65	$112	$242

The above examples are based on restated data for the Fund's fiscal year ended July 31, 1989. *The examples should not be considered representations of past or future expenses. Actual expenses may be greater or less than those shown.*

The purpose of this table is to assist investors in understanding the various costs and expenses that an investor in each Portfolio of the Fund will bear, whether directly or indirectly. For more complete descriptions of the various costs and expenses, see "Management of the Fund." "Other Expenses" include operating expenses of the Fund, such as Trustees' and professional fees, registration fees, reports to shareholders, shareholder servicing fees and custodian fees.

* Estimated, based on expenses expected to have been incurred if Class A shares had been in existence for the entire fiscal year ended July 31, 1989. The data has been restated to reflect a change in the most restrictive expense limitation enforced by state securities commissions.

† The Distributor has advised the Fund that it does not presently expect its distribution expenses with respect to the Class A shares of the Fund to exceed .20 of 1% of the average daily net asset value of the Class A shares for the fiscal year. See "Management of the Fund—Distributor."

SOURCE: This fee table is an excerpt from the 1990 Prudential-Bache FlexiFund prospectus. Used with permission.

••

PERSONAL FINANCE JOURNAL
Junk Bond Funds—Is the Risk Worth It?

According to Kurt Brouwer, a San Francisco–based investment adviser, "If you can't take a wild ride, don't buy a junk fund."° Today, with almost $100 billion invested in high-yield (junk) bond mutual funds, a record number of investors are taking the wild ride.

The Risks Involved

Unsuspecting investors often forget that only risky investments yield high returns. To maximize returns, some junk bond funds buy some of the "junkiest" bonds. A true junk bond fund is a mutual fund that invests in corporate bonds rated BB or lower. The Standard & Poor's BB rating stands for "speculative." Because of their higher risk, junk bonds promise interest rates that are often 4 to 5 percent higher than the interest rates paid on government bonds or investment-grade corporate securities.

Before deciding to invest in a junk bond fund, consider two risks associated with bonds in general and junk bonds in particular. The first of these risks is the risk of default. Junk bonds are less likely to be repaid than bonds with a higher rating at maturity. The second risk is that interest payments will not be made. This risk is greater for junk bonds than for bonds with a higher rating. If either of these

risks materializes, the value of a bond and of the bond fund that owns it will decrease dramatically.

A Word of Caution

When investing in a junk bond fund, you must distinguish between total return and high interest rates. Total return combines the yield from bond interest payments with increases or decreases in the value of the bonds contained in the fund's portfolio. Thus, attractive interest rates can be offset by declines in the value of the bonds in a bond fund. In 1989 and 1990, for example, the prices of junk bonds declined because of fears of recession and of the possibility that corporations would be unable to repay the bondholders. As a result, the share price of most junk bond funds declined and the total return of junk bond funds was actually quite a bit lower than the double-digit interest rates offered on most junk bond issues.

°Marsha Meyer, "Now that Interest Rates Are Down, What's Up with Fixed-Income Funds?" *Money*, September 1989, pp. 45–48.

For more information on junk bond funds, see Jane Bryant Quinn, "What Can Go Wrong," *Newsweek*, August 14, 1989, p. 39; David Zigas, "Hunting for Treasure in the Junkyard," *Business Week*, October 9, 1989, p. 172; and Jack Egan, "Not Quite Ready for the Junk Heap," *U.S. News & World Report*, October 2, 1989, p. 69.

••

If you get the feeling that there are mutual funds designed to meet just about any conceivable investment objective, you are probably right. Hundreds of mutual funds trade daily under the headings "capital appreciation," "small-company growth," and "equity-income." It is your job to determine which fund is right for you. The material in the next section will also help you decide which fund can help you achieve your investment objectives. For more information on mutual fund classifications, see Case 18–2 at the end of this chapter.

EVALUATION OF MUTUAL FUNDS

L.O.4
Evaluate mutual funds for investment purposes.

Often, the decision to buy or sell shares in mutual funds is "too easy" because investors assume that there is no need for them to evaluate their investments. Why question what the professional portfolio managers decide to do? Yet the professionals do make mistakes. The responsibility for choosing the right mutual fund rests with the individual investors. After all, they are the only ones who know how a particular mutual fund can help them achieve their financial objectives. Although investing money in a mutual fund provides professional management, individual investors should continually evaluate their mutual fund investments. Some of the basic means for doing this are described below.

EXHIBIT 18–3

Financial Information about Mutual Funds that Is Available in *The Wall Street Journal*

```
John Hancock:
  AstAll    10.58 11.08− .02
  Bond p    14.46 15.14− .03
  Globl     16.54 17.32+ .03
  Grwth     14.38 15.06− .05
  HiInc p    7.40  7.75.....
  FdlPl      9.12  9.55− .02
  PcBas p   11.04 11.56+ .02
  SpciE p    6.20  6.49+ .05
  TxEx p    10.56 11.06.....
  USGv p     8.59  8.99− .01
  GtdMt p    9.87 10.34− .03
  Kaufmn r   1.64  NL− .01
Kemper Funds:
  BluCh p   10.10 10.58− .01
  DivInc     6.85  7.17+ .04
  EnhG p     8.16  8.54− .05
  CalTx      7.04  7.37− .01
  GlbInc     9.38  9.82+ .06
  Gold p     8.38  8.77+ .03
```

John Hancock Funds

1	2 NAV	3 Offer Price	4 NAV Chg.
AstAII	10.58	11.08 −	.02
Bond p	14.46	15.14 −	.03
Globl	16.54	17.32 +	.03
Growth	14.38	15.06 −	.05
Hilac p	7.48	7.75	
FcEPI	9.12	9.53 −	.02
PcBas p	11.04	11.56 +	.02
SpciE p	6.28	6.49 +	.05
TxEx p	10.56	11.06	
USGv p	8.59	8.99 −	.01
GtdMt p	9.87	10.34 −	.03

1. The name of the mutual fund is placed in Column 1.
2. The net asset value (NAV) of one share during the day. (Col. 2)
3. The offer price for one share during the day. (Col. 3)
4. The difference between the price paid for the last share today and the price paid for the last share on the previous trading day. (Col. 4)

SOURCE: *The Wall Street Journal*, March 30, 1990, p. C18.

How to Read the Mutual Funds Section in the Newspaper

Most local newspapers, *The Wall Street Journal,* and *Barron's* provide information about mutual funds. The net asset value, offer price, and change in net asset value are reported in tables like that shown in Exhibit 18–3. The fourth row of Exhibit 18–3 gives the following information on the John Hancock Growth Fund. (The numbers in this list refer to the column numbers that have been added to the exhibit.)

1. The name of this fund is the John Hancock Growth Fund.
2. The net asset value of one share of the John Hancock Growth Fund during the day was $14.38.
3. The offer price for one share of the John Hancock Growth Fund during the day was $15.06. (The offer price is determined by adding the sales commission to the net asset value.) Therefore, you could purchase one share of the John Hancock Growth Fund for $15.06.
4. The last price paid for a share of the John Hancock Growth Fund on this day was $0.05 lower than the last price paid on the previous trading day.

The letters beside the name of a specific fund can be very informative. You can find out what they mean by looking at the footnotes that accompany the newspaper's mutual fund quotations. Generally, "NL" means no load, "p" means that a 12b–1 fee is charged, "r" means that a redemption charge may be made, and "t" means that both the p and r footnotes apply.

Other Factors and Sources to Consider

The newspaper coverage described in the last section is a good means of monitoring the value of your mutual fund investments. However, there are other factors and sources that provide a more adequate basis for evaluating mutual fund investments.

Financial Objectives—One More Time   In Chapter 15, we talked about establishing investment goals and objectives. In this chapter, we talked about the investment objectives of mutual funds. Here our aim is to get you to realize the relationship between the two. In establishing your own investment goals and objectives, you must evaluate the personal factors of age, family situation, income, and future earning power. Only then can you establish short-term, intermediate, and long-term objectives. Now your aim is to find a mutual fund whose investment objectives match your own. Once you have found a match, it is necessary to gather as much information as possible about the fund and about the investment company that sponsors it.

The Importance of Long-Term Performance   Most investors in mutual funds will tell you that the most important consideration in evaluating a mutual fund is long-term performance. What determines a fund's long-term performance is its ability to make money in an up market and to preserve money in a down market. This can be determined by comparing a fund's long-term performance with the performance of the Standard & Poor's stock index over an extended period of time.

In evaluating a mutual fund, don't forget the role of its financial manager in determining its success. One important question is how long the present fund manager has been managing the fund. If a fund has performed well under its present manager over a 5- or 10-year period, there is a strong likelihood that it will continue to perform well under that manager in the future.

Long-term performance should not be the only factor that you consider in evaluating a mutual fund. This factor is based on what has happened, but you should also consider what will happen. It is hoped that other information you obtain in the evaluation process will enable you to avoid basing your investment decision on past performance alone.

Information on a fund's long-term performance is available in its prospectus and in other sources of financial information that are described below.

The Prospectus and Annual Report   An investment company sponsoring a mutual fund must give potential investors a prospectus. Once you are a shareholder, the investment company will send you annual reports. Both the prospectus and the annual reports provide information that you can use to evaluate the fund. Take a second look at the investment portfolio contained in the Annual Report for The Travelers Aggressive Stock Trust illustrated in Exhibit 18–1. This portfolio, like those of most funds, comprises a large number of securities and thus achieves a high degree of diversification. The prospectus and annual reports also provide information about your rights as a shareholder and about the fund's investment objectives, methods of buying and selling shares, fees, and financial condition.

Financial Publications   Another source of information about mutual funds is investment-oriented magazines. *Forbes, Changing Times, Money,* and other finance- or consumer-oriented magazines provide information that may be useful to mutual fund investors. For example, *Changing Times* publishes an annual mutual funds survey. A portion of the annual survey for 1988 is illustrated in Exhibit 18–4. This survey ranks funds from 1 (the best) to 1,515 (the worst) on their one-year performance. In addition, it provides their 1-, 5-, and 10-year total returns and other valuable information. (The 1-, 5-, and 10-year total returns are equivalent to the yields discussed in Chapter 15 and can be used to keep track of how well funds are performing.)

Professional Advisory Services   A number of subscription services provide detailed information on mutual funds. Moody's Investors Service, Lipper Analytical Services, and the Wiesenberger Investment Companies are three widely used sources of such information. In addition, various mutual fund newsletters provide financial information to subscribers for a fee. All of these sources are rather expensive, but their reports may be available from brokerage firms or libraries.

For more information on the evaluation process, study the checklist provided in the accompanying "Personal Finance Journal" feature.

THE MECHANICS OF A MUTUAL FUND TRANSACTION

L.O.5
Describe how and why mutual funds are bought and sold.

In this section, we discuss three important topics. First, we examine how shareholders can make money by investing in closed-end funds or open-end funds. Next, we look at the options that can be used to purchase shares in a mutual fund. Finally, we look at the options that can be used to withdraw shares from a mutual fund.

Return on Investment

As with other investments, the purpose of investing in a closed-end fund or an open-end fund is to earn a financial return. Shareholders in such funds can receive a return in one of two ways. First, both types of funds pay income dividends, capital gain distributions, or both. **Income dividends** are the earnings that a fund pays to shareholders after it has deducted expenses from its dividend and interest income. **Capital gain distributions** are the payments made to a fund's shareholders that result from the sale of securities in the fund's portfolio.

Second, as with stock investments, it is possible to buy shares in both types of funds at a low price and then to sell them after the price has increased. For example, assume that you purchased shares in the Vanguard Asset mutual fund at $11.50 per share and that two years later you sold your shares at $14 per share. In this case, you made $2.50 ($14 selling price − $11.50 purchase price) per share. The profit that results from this type of transaction is referred to as a capital gain. Note the difference between a capital gain distribution, described above, and a capital gain, described in this paragraph. Of course, if the price of a fund's shares goes down between the time of purchase and the time of sale, the shareholder incurs a loss.

Financial gains and losses from the transactions of closed-end or open-end funds are subject to taxation. At the end of each year, investment companies are required to send each shareholder a statement specifying how much he or she

EXHIBIT 18–4

EXHIBIT 18–4 A Portion of the 1988 Annual Mutual Funds Survey of *Changing Times*

| Fund | One-Year Rank | Type | Total Return | | | | Risk Rating | Min. Inv. | Percent Maximum Load | Telephone Numbers | |
			1 Year	5 Years	10 Years					(800)	Toll
AAL Capital Growth	244	LG	18.62%	—	—	5	$ 500	4.75	553-6319	414-734-5721 (Wis.)
AAL Income	958	BQ	10.08	—	—	1	500	4.75	553-6319	414-734-5721 (Wis.)
AAL Municipal Bond	1,133	MQ	8.67	—	—	1	1,000	4.75	553-6319	414-734-5721 (Wis.)
AARP Capital Growth	27	LG	32.36	—	—	6	250	None	253-2277	617-439-4640 (Mass.)
AARP General Bond	799	BY	11.55	—	—	1	250	None	253-2277	617-439-4640 (Mass.)
AARP GNMA and U.S. Treasury	1,088	GS	9.14	—	—	1	250	None	253-2277	617-439-4640 (Mass.)
AARP Growth and Income	164	GI	20.79	—	—	4	250	None	253-2277	617-439-4640 (Mass.)
AARP Insured Tax Free General Bond	466	MQ	14.95	—	—	1	250	None	253-2277	617-439-4640 (Mass.)
AARP Insured Tax Free Short	1,366	MQ	4.66	—	—	1	250	None	253-2277	617-439-4640 (Mass.)
ABT Growth and Income Trust	949	GI	10.14	133.40%	331.34%	4	1,000	4.75	289-2281	215-834-3500 (Pa.)
ABT Investment Series—Emerging Growth	1,002	AG	9.83	96.98	—	8	1,000	4.75	289-2281	215-834-3500 (Pa.)
ABT Investment Series—Security Income	104	GI	23.72	60.88	—	3	1,000	4.75	289-2281	215-834-3500 (Pa.)
ABT Utility Income	204	GI	19.49	127.71	152.48	3	1,000	4.75	289-2281	215-834-3500 (Pa.)
Acorn	185	LG	20.17	157.15	408.88	5	4,000	None†	922-6769	312-621-0630 (Ill.)
Addison Capital Shares	434	LG	15.44	—	—	6	1,000	3.00	526-6397	215-665-6000 (Pa.)

Fund										
Advance America Corporate Bond	788	BQ	11.63	—	—	1	1,000	4.50	338-3807	312-644-3100 (Ill.)
Advance America GNMA Mortgage	1,005	GM	9.80	—	—	1	1,000	4.50	338-3807	312-644-3100 (Ill.)
Advance America Tax Free Bond	595	MY	13.40	—	—	1	1,000	4.50	338-3807	312-644-3100 (Ill.)
Advance America U.S. Government	1,121	GS	8.76	—	—	1	1,000	4.50	338-3807	312-644-3100 (Ill.)
Advantage Government Securities	1,289	GS	6.64	—	—	1	500	None†	243-8115	203-525-1421 (Conn.)
Advantage Growth	228	LG	19.01	—	—	5	500	None†	243-8115	203-525-1421 (Conn.)
Advantage Income	622	GI	13.19	—	—	2	500	None†	243-8115	203-525-1421 (Conn.)
Advantage Special	453	AG	15.10	—	—	5	500	None†	243-8115	203-525-1421 (Conn.)
Affiliated	793	GI	11.60	129.94	354.72	4	250	7.25	874-3733	212-848-1800 (N.Y.)
Afuture	990	LG	9.90	17.86	118.60	5	500	None	523-7594	215-344-7910 (Pa.)
Age High Income	1,237	BY	7.39	75.51	167.21	1	100	4.00	342-5236	415-570-3000 (Calif.)
Aim Charter	140	GI	21.80	118.43	359.80	5	1,000	5.50	231-0803	713-626-1919 (Tex.)
Aim Constellation	713	AG	12.27	142.46	441.01	8	1,000	5.50	231-0803	713-626-1919 (Tex.)
Aim Convertible Securities	1,343	GI	5.40	36.02	145.20	4	1,000	4.75	231-0803	713-626-1919 (Tex.)
Aim High Yield Securities	1,269	BY	6.96	58.07	155.59	1	1,000	4.75	231-0803	713-626-1919 (Tex.)
Aim Limited Maturity Treasury Shares	1,188	GS	8.01	—	—	1	1,000	1.75	231-0803	713-626-1919 (Tex.)
Aim Summit	504	LG	14.49	104.47	—	6	50	8.50	231-0803	713-626-1919 (Tex.)

*Closed to new investors.

†Redemption fee may apply.

Fund types: AG—aggressive growth, BQ—high-quality bond, BY—high-yield bond, GB—global bond, GE—global equity, GI—growth and income, GM—Ginnie Mae/mortgage bond, GS—government security, IB—international bond, IE—international equity, LG—long-term growth, MQ—high-quality muni, MY—high-yield muni, PM—precious metal, SF—sector.

SOURCE: Excerpted from *Changing Times*, September 1989, pp. 27–34+.

· ·

PERSONAL FINANCE JOURNAL
Evaluation of a Mutual Fund

No checklist can serve as a foolproof guide for choosing a mutual fund, but the following questions will help you evaluate a potential investment in such a fund.

Category 1: Fund Characteristics

1. What is the value of the assets of this fund?_____
    _____

2. Is this fund registered with the SEC?
    ☐ Yes ☐ No

3. Is this fund registered in your state?
    ☐ Yes ☐ No

4. What is the minimum investment?_____

5. Does the fund allow telephone exchange?
    ☐ Yes ☐ No

Category 2: Costs

6. Is there a front-end load charge? How much is it?
    _____

7. Is there a redemption fee? How much is it?
    _____

8. How much is the annual management fee?
    _____

9. Is there a 12b–1 fee? How much is it?_____

10. What is the fund's expense ratio?_____

Category 3: Diversification

11. What is the fund's objective?_____
    _____

12. What types of securities does the fund's portfolio include?_____
    _____

13. How many securities does the fund's portfolio include?_____

14. How many types of industries does the fund's portfolio include?_____

Category 4: Fund Performance

15. How long has the fund manager been with the fund?_____

16. How would you describe the fund's performance over the past 12 months?_____
    _____

17. How would you describe the fund's performance over the past five years?_____
    _____

18. How would you describe the fund's performance over the past 10 years?_____
    _____

Category 5: Conclusion

19. Based on the above information, do you think that an investment in this fund will help you achieve your investment goals?   ☐ Yes ☐ No

20. Explain your answer to Question 19._____
    _____
    _____
    _____

Special Note

When you use a checklist, there is always a danger of overlooking important relevant information. The above checklist, like most checklists, does not prevent this danger, but it does provide some very good questions that you should answer before making a mutual fund investment decision. Quite simply, it is a place to start. If other information is needed, you must assume the responsibility for obtaining it and for determining how it affects the potential investment.

· ·

received in dividends and capital gain distributions. Although investment companies may provide this information as part of their year-end statement, most funds use IRS Form 1099 DIV. Capital gains or losses that result from the sale of fund shares must also be reported as taxable income.

To ensure having all of the documentation required for tax reporting purposes, it is essential that you keep accurate records. The same records will help you monitor the value of your mutual fund investments and to make more intelligent decisions with regard to the purchase and sale of such investments.

Purchase Options

The shares of a closed-end fund are traded on various stock exchanges. The shares of an open-end fund may be purchased through a salesperson who is authorized to sell them, through an account executive of a brokerage firm, or directly from the investment company that sponsors the fund. Because of the unique nature of open-end fund transactions, we examine how investors buy and sell shares in this type of mutual fund.

To purchase shares in an open-end mutual fund, you may use these four options: regular account transactions, voluntary savings plans, contractual savings plans, and reinvestment plans. The most popular and least complicated method of purchasing shares in an open-end fund is through a regular account transaction. When a regular account is used, investors decide how much money they want to invest and simply buy as many shares as possible. Commissions, if any, are deducted from the amount of the investment, and the remainder is used to purchase shares.

Voluntary savings plans allow investors to open an account with an investment company for as little as $25. For most investment companies, the minimum amount for opening this type of account ranges between $25 and $1,000. At the time of the initial purchase, the investor declares an intent to make regular minimum purchases of the fund's shares. The chief advantage of the voluntary savings plan is that it allows investors to make smaller purchases than the minimum purchases required by the regular account method described above. For most voluntary savings plans, the minimum purchase ranges from $25 to $100 for each additional investment. Although there is no penalty for not making regular purchases, most investors feel an "obligation" to make purchases on a regular basis. Thus, the number of shares they own and their total investment increase.

Contractual savings plans require that investors make regular purchases over a specified period of time—usually 10 to 15 years. These plans are sometimes referred to as front-end load funds because almost all of the commissions are paid in the first few years of the contract period. There are penalties if the investor does not fulfill the purchase requirements. For example, if an investor drops out of a contractual savings plan before completing the purchase requirements, he or she sacrifices the prepaid commissions. Many investors and government regulatory agencies are critical of contractual savings plans. As a result, the Securities and Exchange Commission and many states have imposed new rules on investment companies offering contractual savings plans.

It is also possible to purchase shares in an open-end fund by using the fund's reinvestment plan. A **reinvestment plan** is a service that a mutual fund provides in which shareholder dividends and capital gain distributions are automatically reinvested to purchase additional shares of the fund. Most reinvestment plans allow shareholders to use reinvested money in this way without having to pay additional sales charges or commissions.

All four purchase options allow investors to buy shares over a long period of time. As a result, they can use the principle of *dollar cost averaging,* which was explained in Chapter 16. Dollar cost averaging allows the investor to average many individual purchase prices over a long period of time. Thus, the investor avoids the problem of buying high and selling low. Investors who use dollar cost averaging can make money if they sell their mutual fund shares at a price higher than their average purchase price.

Withdrawal Options

Because closed-end funds are listed on securities exchanges, it is possible to sell shares in such a fund to another investor. Shares in an open-end fund can be sold on any business day to the investment company that sponsors the fund. In this case, the shares are redeemed at their net asset value. In addition to just selling shares, the investor may use at least four options to systematically withdraw money from an open-end fund. Most funds have a provision that allows investors with a minimum net asset value of at least $5,000 to systematically withdraw money. First, the investor may withdraw a specified, fixed dollar amount each investment period until the investor's fund has been exhausted. Normally, an investment period is three months. Most funds require that an investor withdraw a minimum amount—ranging from $25 to $50—each investment period.

A second option allows the investor to liquidate or "sell off" a certain number of shares each investment period. Since the net asset value of shares in a fund varies from one period to the next, the amount of money that the investor receives will also vary. Once the specified number of shares has been sold, a check is mailed directly to the investor.

A third option allows investors to withdraw a fixed percentage of asset growth. For example, assume that you arrange to receive 60 percent of the asset growth of your investment and that the asset growth of your investment amounts to $800 in a particular investment period. For that period, you would receive a check for $480 ($800 × 60% = $480). If there is no asset growth, no payment is made to the investor. Under this option, the investor's principal remains untouched.

A final option allows the investor to withdraw all income that results from interest, dividends, and capital gains earned by the fund during an investment period. Under this option, the investor's principal also remains untouched.

SUMMARY

L.O.1
Explain why individuals invest in mutual funds.

The major reasons why investors choose mutual funds are professional management and diversification. Mutual funds are also a convenient way to invest money.

L.O.2
Understand the unique characteristics of investments in mutual funds.

There are two types of mutual funds. A closed-end fund is a mutual fund whose shares are issued only when the fund is organized. An open-end fund is a mutual fund whose shares are issued and redeemed by the investment company at the request of investors. Mutual funds are also classified as load, low-load, or no-load funds. Both load and low-load funds charge a commission every time an investor purchases shares. No commission is charged to purchase shares in a no-load fund.

L.O.3
Classify mutual funds by investment objective.

The major categories of mutual funds, in terms of the types of securities they invest in, are balanced funds, growth funds, growth-income funds, income funds, index funds, industry funds, money market funds, and municipal bond funds.

L.O.4
Evaluate mutual funds for
investment purposes.

The responsibility for choosing the "right" mutual fund rests with you—the investor. The information in newspapers, the financial objectives of the fund, the long-term performance of the fund, the information in the prospectus and annual reports, financial publications, and professional advisory services can all help you evaluate a mutual fund.

L.O.5
Describe how and why mutual
funds are bought and sold.

The shares of a closed-end fund are traded (bought and sold) on organized stock exchanges. The shares of an open-end fund may be purchased through a salesperson who is authorized to sell them, through an account executive of a brokerage firm, or from the investment company that sponsors the fund. The shares in an open-end fund can be sold to the investment company that sponsors the fund. There are a number of purchase and withdrawal options.

GLOSSARY

Capital gains distributions   The payments made to a fund's shareholders that result from the sale of securities in the fund's portfolio.

Closed-end fund   A mutual fund whose shares are issued by an investment company only when the fund is organized.

Family of funds   A group of mutual funds managed by one investment company.

Income dividends   The earnings that a fund pays to shareholders after it has deducted expenses from its dividend and interest income.

Investment company   A firm that, for a management fee, invests the pooled funds of small investors in securities appropriate to its stated investment objectives.

Load fund   A mutual fund in which investors pay a commission every time they purchase shares. (The commission charge may be as high as 8½ percent.)

Low-load fund   A mutual fund in which investors pay a lower commission than that charged by a load fund every time they purchase shares. (The commission charge usually ranges between 1 and 3 percent.)

Mutual fund   An investment alternative chosen by individuals who pool their money to buy stocks, bonds, and other securities selected by professional managers who work for an investment company.

Net asset value (NAV)   The current market value of the mutual fund's portfolio minus the mutual fund's liabilities divided by the number of shares outstanding.

No-load fund   A mutual fund in which no sales charge is paid by the individual investor.

Open-end fund   A mutual fund whose shares are issued and redeemed by the investment company at the request of investors.

Redemption fee   A 1 to 5 percent charge that shareholders pay when they withdraw their investment from a mutual fund.

Reinvestment plan   A service that a mutual fund provides in which shareholder dividends and capital gain distributions are automatically reinvested to purchase additional shares of the fund.

12b–1 fee   A fee that the investment company may levy to defray the costs of marketing and distributing a mutual fund.

DISCUSSION QUESTIONS

L.O.1 1. What are the major advantages and disadvantages of investing through mutual funds?

L.O.2 2. What is the role of investment companies with regard to investing in mutual funds?

L.O.2 3. How do closed-end funds differ from open-end funds? How do load funds differ from no-load funds?

L.O.2 4. How is a mutual fund's net asset value per share determined?

L.O.2 5. What is the usual amount of the management fees that mutual funds charge? What is a 12b–1 fee?

L.O.3 6. What major categories of mutual funds does this chapter describe?

L.O.4 7. Describe how each of the following can be used to evaluate mutual funds.
   a. Newspaper.
   b. Financial objectives.
   c. Long-term performance.
   d. The prospectus.
   e. Financial publications.
   f. Professional advisory services.

L.O.5 8. Describe the options that investors can use to purchase shares in mutual funds.

L.O.5 9. What options in addition to just selling their shares can investors use to withdraw money from a mutual fund?

Opening Case Questions

1. In 1987, Martha Blackstone invested over $11,500 in the Fidelity Select—Electronics Mutual Fund without evaluating her investment. Assume that it is 1987 and that you are Martha Blackstone. How would you evaluate this investment?

2. According to Martha Blackstone, the investment company made it "so easy" to invest in a mutual fund. All you have to do is open an account, send the money, and let the professional managers make all the decisions. What is wrong with this approach to investing in mutual funds?

PROBLEMS AND ACTIVITIES

L.O.1 1. Find out from a friend or relative who owns shares in a mutual fund why this person chose to invest in a mutual fund. How do his or her reasons compare with the factors of professional management and diversification that were discussed in this chapter?

L.O.2 2. In your own words, define each of the following concepts.
   a. Closed-end fund.
   b. Open-end fund.
   c. Net asset value.
   d. Load fund.
   e. No-load fund.

L.O.2 3. Mike Jackson invested a total of $8,500 in ABC Mutual Fund. The management fee for this particular fund is 0.70 percent of the total investment amount. Calculate the management fee that Mike must pay each year.

L.O.3 (4.) In this chapter, mutual funds were classified into eight categories based on the nature of their investments. Using the information presented below, pick a mutual fund category that you consider suitable for each of the investors described below and justify your choice.

a. A young, single investor 25 years of age with a new job that pays $30,000 a year.
Mutual fund category_____
Why?_____
_____

b. A single parent with two children who has just received a $100,000 divorce settlement, has no job, and has not worked outside the home for the past five years.
Mutual fund category_____
Why?_____
_____

L.O.4 (5.) Assume that one year ago you bought 100 shares of a mutual fund for $15 per share, that you received $0.75 per share distribution during the past 12 months, and that the market value of the fund is now $18. Calculate (a) the current yield for this investment and (b) the total return for this investment if you were to sell it now.

L.O.4 6. The following are five mutual funds that are listed in *The Wall Street Journal:*

Name of Fund	Type of Fund
American Capital Enterprise	Growth
Axe-Houghton Fund B	Balanced
Bartlett Basic Value	Growth-income
Fidelity Select—Electronics	Industry
Value Line—Income	Income

Choose one of the funds, and then evaluate your choice using the checklist in the "Personal Finance Journal" feature on the evaluation of a mutual fund. (*Hint:* You may want to examine issues of *Forbes, Changing Times,* or *Money* for ideas on how to complete the checklist.)

L.O.5 7. Explain how the concept of dollar cost averaging applies to the options that are used to purchase mutual funds?

LIFE SITUATION   Case 18–1

Fidelity's Magellan Mutual Fund

In 1963, Fidelity Distributors Corporation organized the Magellan fund. This fund's success over its first 27 years was phenomenal. For example, a $10,000 investment in the fund made in 1976 was estimated to be worth over $240,000 in 1989. With over $13 billion in assets, the Magellan fund has been the nation's largest and best-performing mutual fund over the past 15 years. Over the past five years, it has averaged a 21 percent return.

Peter Lynch, the Magellan fund's manager from 1977 until 1990, always invested in consumer-oriented companies such as Ford, General Electric, General Motors, PepsiCo, American Express, Wal-Mart, Borden, and AT&T.° In 1989, the Magellan fund owned over 1,400 stocks and had over 1 million shareholders. In early 1990, Mr. Lynch announced his retirement. At that time, financial analysts concluded that the surprise retirement decision would test the loyalty of the Magellan fund's shareholders.†

Questions

1. The minimum dollar amount required to open a Magellan account is $1,000. If you had $1,000, would you invest it in the Magellan fund?
2. The Magellan fund was extremely successful from 1963 to 1990. Why is past performance an important factor in the evaluation of a mutual fund?
3. How important has one man been to the success of the Magellan fund?
4. What other information would you need to evaluate the Magellan fund? Where would you get this information?

°Gene G. Marcial, "What Magellan's Man at the Top Is Buying," *Business Week,* October 9, 1989, p. 142.

†For more information, see Christopher J. Chipello, Michael Siconolfi, and Jonathan Clements, "Both Fidelity Investors and Firm Are at Sea as Magellan Boss Goes," *The Wall Street Journal,* March 29, 1990, p. 1; Mark Hulbert, "Lynch's Law?" *Forbes,* April 17, 1989, p. 230; Greg Anrig, Jr., "Fidelity's Newest Wunderkind Runs the Fund That May Be the Next Magellan," *Money,* April 1989, pp. 201–2; and Jon Friedman, "Johnson and Lynch: An Odd Couple with a Hit Formula," *Business Week,* April 17, 1989, p. 73.

LIFE SITUATION   Case 18–2

A Mutual Fund for Everyone

Investment companies in the mutual fund industry have always tried to tailor their funds to the needs of the investing public. Never has this statement been more true. From 1975 to 1989, the number of mutual funds increased from approximately 400 to just over 2,700. During the same period, the number of fund classifications increased from 7 to 22. Table 18–1 lists these classifications and tells how many funds each of the classifications comprises.

Questions

1. Describe how one of the fund classifications presented in Table 18–1 can help you achieve your personal investment objectives.
(*Hint:* To arrive at your answers to Question 2, you may want to examine issues of *Forbes, Changing Times,* or *Money.*)
2. At the library, find a mutual fund that is representative of the fund classification you chose in Question 1. Answer the following questions on this fund:
   a. What is the name of the mutual fund you chose?
   b. Which publication did you use to evaluate this mutual fund?
   c. After examining the information presented in *Forbes, Changing Times,* or *Money,* would you still want to invest in this mutual fund? Justify your answer with facts that you obtained in your research.

TABLE 18–1
Mutual Funds Classified by
Investment Objective

Investment Objective	Number of Funds
Aggressive growth	214
Growth	329
Growth and income	251
Precious metals	34
International	59
Global equity	45
Income—equity	66
Option/income	17
Flexible portfolio	39
Balanced	39
Income—mixed	85
Income—bond	86
U.S. government income	184
Ginnie Mae	62
Global bond	27
Corporate bond	57
High-yield bond	102
Long-term municipal bond	172
State municipal bond, long term	243
Short-term municipal bond	121
State municipal bond, short-term	54
Money market	432

SOURCE: *1989 Mutual Fund Fact Book,* Investment Company Institute, 1600 M Street, NW, Suite 600, Washington, D.C. 20036, 1989, p. 20.

SUPPLEMENTARY READINGS

For Additional Information on Mutual Funds and Investment Companies

Nickel, Karen. "Best Bets among the Bond Funds." *Fortune,* April 23, 1990, p. 32.

1989 Mutual Fund Fact Book. Washington, D.C.: Investment Company Institute, 1989. 1600 M Street, NW, Suite 600, Washington, DC 20036.

Rugg, Donald D. *New Strategies for Mutual Fund Investing.* Homewood, Ill.: Dow Jones-Irwin, 1989.

Schiffres, Manuel. "The Case for Closed-End Funds." *Changing Times,* April 1990, pp. 49–51+.

Zigas, David. "How Risky Is Your Money-Market Fund?" *Business Week,* March 26, 1990, p. 86.

For Additional Information on Evaluation of Mutual Funds and Investment Companies

"Annual Mutual Fund Guide." *U.S. News & World Report,* February 12, 1990, pp. 63–66+.

Meyer, Marsha, et al. "Picking the Best Funds." *Money,* February 1990, pp. 126–37+.

Smith, Steve. "Mutual Fund All-Stars." *Changing Times,* March 1990, pp. 25–32.

"Want a Winner? Look Here First." *Business Week,* February 19, 1990, pp. 70–72+.

Weiss, Gary. "Fixed-Income Funds: Where Safety Pays." *Business Week,* February 26, 1990, pp. 94–102.

19

Real Estate and Other Investment Alternatives

In this chapter, we will discuss tangible investments, such as real estate, gold, silver, diamonds and other precious stones, works of art, rare coins, stamps, and antiques. The advantages and disadvantages of real estate and other investment alternatives will be presented.

Traditionally, Americans have invested in real estate. It is an asset that we can see, touch, and smell, and it is generally a good hedge against inflation. But, as you will see, the choices in real estate investment are bewildering for the new investor. Furthermore, the Tax Reform Act of 1986 has lessened the appeal of investing in real estate.

LEARNING OBJECTIVES
After studying this chapter, you will be able to

L.O.1 Identify types of real estate investments.

L.O.2 Evaluate the advantages of real estate investments.

L.O.3 Assess the disadvantages of real estate investments.

L.O.4 Analyze the risks and rewards of investing in precious metals, gems, and collectibles.

. .

OPENING CASE

Homing In on Shared Down Payments°

Formerly, young couples who didn't have enough saved up for a down payment on a house would turn to their relatives for help. These days, total strangers are providing the cash by investing in shared-equity mortgages. In return for putting up some or all of the down payment for cash-strapped home buyers, the investors get a share of increases in the value of the house, and sometimes additional fees as well.

In the late 1980s, individual investors had been raking in big profits with shared-equity mortgages in parts of the country where housing prices had soared. Now brokers and mortgage companies are eagerly matching up additional investors with prospective homebuyers. Two private limited partnerships have been launched to pool investors' money.

But while some investors have done well, shared-equity mortgages also present plenty of pitfalls.

"Investors are betting on escalating home prices and the ability of their partners to make the monthly mortgage payments," says Michael Evans, chairman of Arthur Young & Co.'s national real estate advisory group. "Real estate prices don't go up for ever, and in a slowing economy some people lose their jobs and can't make the mortgage payments. You could get stuck with a house in a collapsing market."

Shared-equity mortgages were popular in 1979 and 1980, when both mortgage interest rates and housing prices were sky-high. But these mortgages disappeared in 1982, when interest rates dropped.

Today, they've reemerged as an answer to the severe affordability problem faced by hopeful homebuyers in some of the country's hottest real estate markets. In Orange County, California, for instance, the price of a no-frills entry-level home in 1989 climbed to $260,000. "It's hard even for a couple making $60,000 a year *each* to save up enough for a down payment," says Mr. Evans.

Many people who once invested in rental apartments have switched to equity-sharing mortgages. Jesse Vint, an airline pilot, who has invested in four equity-sharing mortgages in the past 11 months, says his rental apartment investment was "a nightmare." But he figures he'll get an annual return of about 24 percent on his shared-equity investments—assuming that the houses appreciate about 6 percent a year and none of the buyers default. "I can't think of a better investment for me," he says.

Whether a shared-equity mortgage actually is a good deal for an investor depends a lot on the local real estate market. "If you had a shared-equity mortgage in New Jersey in the past 18 months, you would have been killed as prices dropped 25 percent," says Stanley Zimmerman, president of the Mortgage Institute of California. "Yet in Southern California, you would have done very well, since prices went up 30 percent."

Moreover, investors cannot count on a continuing price surge just because a particular housing market has been booming. For example, Mr. Zimmerman believed that the fast inflation in California home prices was over.

In this chapter, among other things, you will learn how you can calculate your rate of return on shared-equity investments.

°Condensed from Earl C. Gottschalk, Jr., "Homing In on Shared Down Payments," *The Wall Street Journal*, July 28, 1989, p. C1.

. .

INVESTING IN REAL ESTATE

L.O.1
Identify types of real estate investments.

Real estate investments are classified as direct or indirect. In **direct investment,** the investor holds legal title to the property. Direct real estate investments include single-family dwellings, duplexes, apartments, land, and nonresidential real estate.

In **indirect investment,** the investors appoint a trustee to hold legal title on behalf of all the investors in the group. Limited partnerships and syndicates, real estate investment trusts, mortgages, and mortgage pools are examples of indirect real estate investments. Exhibit 19–1 summarizes the advantages and disadvantages of the two types of investments.

EXHIBIT 19-1

Types of Real Estate
Investments, Their
Advantages and
Disadvantages

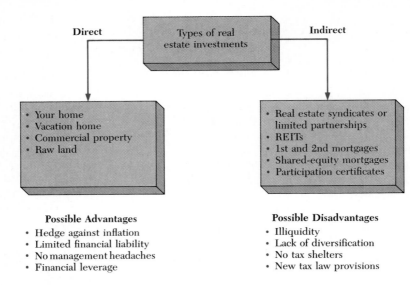

Possible Advantages
- Hedge against inflation
- Limited financial liability
- No management headaches
- Financial leverage

Possible Disadvantages
- Illiquidity
- Lack of diversification
- No tax shelters
- New tax law provisions

Direct Real Estate Investments[1]

Your Home as an Investment   The benefits of home ownership were discussed in Chapter 9 and will not be repeated here. Your home is primarily a place to live; secondarily, it is an income shelter if you have a mortgage on it; and finally, it is a possible hedge against inflation.

Until recent years, few people regarded their homes as investments. During a long period, from 1880 to 1945, the prices of single-family houses rose less than the consumer price index (CPI). Since that time, however, housing prices have risen more rapidly than the consumer price index. Therefore, the family home has become identified as an asset that can maintain its purchasing power.

Exhibit 19-2 shows percentage increases in the CPI, the Standard & Poor's 500 Stock Average, and an index of the average price of existing homes.

It is obvious from Exhibit 19-2 that from 1970 to 1987 the value of existing homes increased, on average, more rapidly than the CPI. Therefore, home ownership was protected against inflation. During the same period, the stock market averages performed poorly relative to either the housing price index or the CPI. (The average stock prices shown in Exhibit 19-2 do not include dividends received. These increased stock profits somewhat, but not greatly.)

Your Vacation Home   If you have a vacation home, the after-tax cost of owning it has risen since 1987. Just how much it has risen depends largely on whether the Internal Revenue Service views the place as your second home or as a rental property. It is deemed a second home as long as you don't rent it for more than 14 days a year, and in that case you can write off your mortgage interest and property tax. But if you rent the vacation home regularly, the size of your deductions is determined by whether you actively manage it and by the size of

EXHIBIT 19–2

Comparison of Changes in the Average Price of Existing Homes, the Consumer Price Index, and Standard & Poor's 500 Stock Average *(Base Year 1970)*

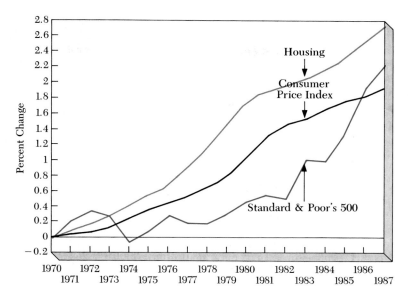

Every year since 1973, the prices of existing homes increased faster than the CPI and the S&P 500 Stock Average.

SOURCE: National Association of Realtors, Standard & Poor's, Inc., and U.S. Bureau of Labor Statistics.

your income. You are allowed to deduct your mortgage interest, property taxes, and expenses for the house as long as the total is no more than your rental income plus any passive partnership income you may have. If your expenses on the house exceed the income you derive from it, the new rules let you deduct up to $25,000 of your annual losses on the house against your salary and your investment income.

Commercial Property   The term **commercial property** refers to land and buildings that produce lease or rental income. Such property includes duplexes, apartments, hotels, office buildings, stores, and all sorts of other types of commercial establishments. Aside from a home, the real property investment most widely favored by the small investor is the duplex, four-plex, or small apartment building. Many investors have been able to acquire sizable commercial properties by first investing in a duplex and then "trading up" to larger units as equity in the original property increased.

The investment potential of commercial property, unlike that of raw land or a personal residence, can be accurately measured. There are several methods for doing this, all of which compare the expected future income from a property with the cost of the property. Exhibit 19–3 shows one method that may be used to calculate the expected profitability of commercial properties. More sophisticated analytic methods are being used, but this one covers most of the areas of investigation. Its greatest weaknesses are that the analysis covers a maximum of

EXHIBIT 19–3

Current-Year Income
Analysis for Outflow
Apartments

Property name		Outflow Apartments		Type		Ten-Plex

Location				List price	$200,000

Assessed value:	$151,500	100%	Less loans	$140,000
Land	30,000	20%	= List price equity	$60,000
Improvements	120,000	79%		
Personal property	1,500	1%		

	Year	%	Year 2	%	Year 3	%
Gross scheduled income	$ 30,000	100				
Less vacancy and credit losses	1,500	5				
= Gross operating income	28,500	95				
Less operating expenses:						
Taxes	5,700	19				
Utilities	1,200	4				
Insurance	300	1				
Management	2,400	8				
Services	200	1				
Supplies						
Maintenance	1,500	5				
Other	200	1				
Total operating expenses	11,500	39				
= Net operating income	17,000	56				
Less loan payments	16,022	—				
= Gross spendable income	978	—				
Plus principal repayment	2,868	—				
= Gross equity income	3,846	—				
Less depreciation	7,272	—				
= Taxable income	(3,426)	—				

SOURCE: Wilbur W. Widicus and Thomas E. Stitzel, *Personal Investing*, 5th ed. (Homewood, Ill.: Richard D. Irwin, 1989), p. 334. © 1989 Richard D. Irwin, Inc.

three years and that the expected market or sales price of the property plays no role in the analysis.

Exhibit 19–3 contains information about a six-year-old 10-unit apartment that is assumed to be for sale. When such a property is placed on the market, the real estate broker listing it prepares information of the type contained in this exhibit. If the property is not listed, the seller prepares this information. Typically, only current-year information is supplied.

Income and Expenses   "Gross scheduled income" is the total amount of income that would be obtained if the apartments were completely rented and all rents were paid. But commercial properties are seldom fully rented, and rents sometimes cannot be collected. "Gross operating income" is what remains after these losses.

"Operating expenses" are the nonfinancial expenses of operating the apartments. Traditionally, each expense category of this income statement is divided by gross scheduled income to provide a relative measure of each cost. Estimates of income and expenses must be made for new properties. Owners of existing properties typically provide the most recent year's income statement to prospective buyers. Taxes and utility expenses can usually be verified by examining receipts. It is much more difficult to check the accuracy of most other expense and income items.

"Net operating income" represents the income from the investment before financing payments and depreciation. A widely used measure of the gross profitability of such an investment is the ratio of net operating income (NOI) to the cost of the property. In this example, the ratio of operating income earned to the list price is

$$\frac{NOI}{List\ price} = Rate\ of\ return$$

$$\frac{\$17,000}{\$200,000} = 0.085,\ or\ 8.5\ percent$$

A similar ratio of gross operating income to market price is also calculated. Both ratios are often used by appraisers and lenders.

Financing and Depreciation Charges   Financing and depreciation are so important that even after the Tax Reform Act of 1986, they are handled separately from operating expenses. Beginning in 1987, the depreciation stretches to 27½ years for residential buildings and 31½ years for other commercial property. The Tax Reform Act of 1986 dictates straight-line depreciation: an equal percentage of the cost must be deducted each year. In Exhibit 19–3, the allowed depreciation is $200,000 divided by 27½ years, that is, $7,272 per year.

Exhibit 19–4 shows a three-year loan schedule. This schedule assumes that the purchaser can assume the balance of a 25-year, 7.5 percent loan ($89,675) and can obtain an additional loan at 13 percent, for total financing of $140,000. The original loan has 19 more years to run before it is paid off; the second loan will also have a 19-year maturity.

Returning to Exhibit 19–3, you can see how financing costs are deducted from net operating income to produce gross spendable income. Adding the yearly principal repayment on loans to gross spendable income produces gross equity income. Subtracting yearly depreciation costs from this figure gives a loss of $3,426 for the first year that this investment is held. Gross spendable income and gross equity income are often divided by the amount of the investor's equity to compare returns with the equity investment..

Outflow Apartments' gross spendable income is only $978, but depreciation reduces the owner's taxable income by $3,426. If the owner were in the new marginal 28 percent income tax bracket, his or her taxes would be lowered by

$$0.28 \times \$3,426 = \$959$$

EXHIBIT 19–4

Financing Schedule for Outflow Apartments

Existing financing	Principal Amount	Term	Annual Payment	Interest Rate
1st loan	$100,000	25 years	$8,868	7½%
Proposed financing				
1st loan	$ 89,675	19 years	$8,868	7½%
2nd loan	50,325	19 years	7,156	13

Repayment schedule, all loans

Year	Interest Paid	Principal Paid	Total Payment	Principal Remaining
1	$13,154	$2,868	$16,022	$137,132
2	12,892	3,130	16,022	134,002
3	12,604	3,418	16,022	130,584

SOURCE: Wilbur W. Widicus and Thomas E. Stitzel, *Personal Investing*, 5th ed. (Homewood, Ill.: Richard D. Irwin, 1989), p. 337. © 1989 Richard D. Irwin, Inc.

This amount is often called a *tax saving*. Deducting this amount from the book loss shown on the income analysis form results in an after-tax cost of only $2,467.

$3,426 − $959 = $2,467

The investment still produces a loss, but that loss is lowered by the investment's income tax effects.

Many real property investors are interested primarily in the yearly after-tax cash returns (or losses) from their investments. Traditionally, these returns are calculated by using the following format, in which amounts from Exhibit 19–3 have been rearranged to show the after-tax cash cost of holding Outflow Apartments.

Net operating income	$17,000
Less: Financing payments	16,022
= Gross spendable income	$ 978
Plus: Income tax benefit	959
Net spendable cash	$ 1,937

So far, Outflow Apartments appears to be a poorer investment than almost anything you could imagine. However, we have not considered market price appreciation. Practically all real property prices in many parts of the United States have risen dramatically in recent years. Many people expect these price rises to continue and look to them for profits. They are quite willing to hold real property that breaks even on a cash basis, or even runs a cash loss, hoping to take their profits in a lump sum when they sell the property.

The Outflow Apartments investment would be highly profitable if its value were to increase by 6 percent per year. The investment would then be worth $212,000 in one year, $224,720 in two, $238,203 in three, and $267,645 in five. Because the investor has never had more than $60,000 of equity in the apartments, large profits on invested equity would be created if prices rose at this rate. Continued market price increases will cause real property to be sold at what seem to be unjustifiably high prices.

Under the new tax act, such deductions as the mortgage interest, depreciation, property taxes, and other expenses of rental property are limited to the amount of rental income you receive. Any excess deductions are considered a passive loss and—with some exceptions—can be used only to offset income from a similar activity, such as another rental property. A **passive activity** is a business or trade in which you do not materially participate or rental activity. **Passive loss** is the total amount of losses from a passive activity minus the total income from the passive activity.

Raw Land   With the passage of the new tax act, popular real estate investments—the typical suburban garden apartments—have no longer been tempting real estate investors. Instead, these investors have been favoring more exotic property, such as raw land ripe for development.

If land investments have promised tremendous gains, they have also posed enormous risks, as investors with land in the oil patch could attest. With their money riding on a single parcel, investors could end up owning overpriced cropland in the event of a building slowdown or an economic downturn.

Many investors buy land with the intention of subdividing it. Purchases of this kind are speculative because of the many risks involved. You must be certain that water, sewers, and other utilities will be available. The most common and least expensive way of obtaining water and sewage service is by hooking onto existing facilities of an adjoining city or town.

Many towns and cities now refuse to annex property or provide water and sewage service without an affirmative vote of the citizens. This adds another element of uncertainty to what is usually an already risky proposition. Wells and septic tanks might serve the same purposes, but they are typically more expensive. In many parts of the country, well water is not easily found. County land zoning ordinances may rule against septic tanks or may allow them only on lots that are at least one-half acre in size. Unless the area is remote, telephone and electric service is seldom a problem because of the ease with which electric lines can be installed.

Thus far, we have focused on direct real estate investments, in which the investor holds legal title to the property. In the next section, you will learn how you can invest in real estate without the hassles of direct ownership.

Indirect Real Estate Investments

Bernice R. Hecker, a Seattle, Washington, anesthesiologist, made her first real estate investment in 1985. She joined a partnership that bought an office building in Midland, Texas. "Why real estate? Probably superstition," she said. "I wanted a tangible asset. I felt I could evaluate a piece of property much more readily" than stocks, bonds, or "a cattle ranch."[2]

Dr. Hecker used one of the three basic methods of investing in real estate. The three methods, each of which offers progressively more risk and higher potential rewards, are real estate syndicates, which are partnerships that buy properties; real estate investment trusts (REITs), which are stockholder-owned real estate companies; and direct investments, which were explained in the preceding section.

Real Estate Syndicates or Limited Partnerships   A **syndicate** is a temporary association of individuals or firms, organized to perform a specific task that requires a large amount of capital.[3] The syndicate may be organized as a corporation, as a trust, or, more commonly, as a limited partnership.

The limited partnership works as follows. It is formed by a general partner, who has unlimited liability for its liabilities. The general partner then sells participation units to the limited partners, whose liability is generally limited to the extent of their initial investment, say $5,000 or $10,000. Limited liability is particularly important in real estate syndicates because their mortgage debt obligations may exceed the net worth of the participants.

In addition to limited liability, a real estate syndicate provides professional management for its members. A syndicate that owns several properties may also provide diversification.

Traditionally, real estate syndicates have been tax shelters for the investors, but the Tax Reform Act of 1986 has limited the creativity of real estate syndicators. It hits real estate syndicates particularly hard by preventing losses from "passive" investments in partnerships from offsetting income from other sources. It also limits deductions of interest and depreciation and increases the tax on capital gains.

Under the new tax act, all real estate investors have their depreciation deductions for all commercial property spread out, from 19½ to 31½ years. And interest expense and other losses that tax-oriented partnerships generate—passive losses—can offset passive income only, that is, income from other limited partnerships. So if you have dividends, interest income, wages, and so on from other sources, you can't shelter it any more.

Real Estate Investment Trusts (REITs)   Another way for the small investor to invest in big-time real estate deals is the real estate investment trust (REIT). A **REIT** is similar to a mutual fund or an investment company, and it trades on stock exchanges or over the counter. Like mutual funds, REITs pool investor funds. These funds, along with borrowed funds, are invested in real estate or used to make construction or mortgage loans.

There are three types of REITs: equity REITs, which invest in properties; mortgage REITs, which pool money to finance construction loans and mortgages on developed properties; and hybrid REITs, combinations of mortgage and equity REITs.

Federal law requires REITs to

- Distribute at least 95 percent of their net annual earnings to shareholders.
- Not engage in speculative, short-term holding of real estate in order to sell for quick profits.
- Hire independent real estate professionals to carry out certain management activities.
- Have at least 100 shareholders. No more than half the shares may be owned by five or fewer people.

The accompanying "Personal Finance Journal" feature weighs the risks and rewards of investing in REITs.

The investor may choose among more than 200 REITs. Further information on REITs can be obtained from the National Association of Real Estate Investment Trusts, 1101 17th Street, NW, Washington, DC 20036.

Investing in First and Second Mortgages   Mortgages and other debt contracts are commonly purchased by the more well-to-do members of most communities. Often, the purchaser of a mortgage takes on some sort of risk that

---

PERSONAL FINANCE JOURNAL
Risks and Rewards of Investing in REITs

Making money in real estate has become harder in recent years because of tax overhaul, low inflation, and overbuilding. "Real estate isn't a get-rich-quick investment anymore, and never will be again," says Allen Parker, portfolio manager of the U.S. Real Estate Fund. "But you can find quality and make a lot of money, especially if you buy big, publicly traded companies like REITs."

Investing in property through REITs is a favorite strategy these days, in part because REITs are exempt from corporate taxes if they pay out 95 percent of their taxable income to shareholders. This "single tax" status is especially important in the wake of tax overhaul, which made income, not tax write-offs, the main component of return for real estate investments.

REITs also offer advantages that aren't generally available in direct real estate investing. Because REIT shares are traded on major stock exchanges, investors can get daily price quotes, liquidity, diversification, low dollar cost, and rigorous quarterly financial reporting. "For individuals, REITs offer push-button real estate investing," says Robert Frank, a real estate securities analyst with Alex, Brown & Sons.

Of course, REIT investing isn't free of pitfalls. Analysts advise investors to take special care of these points:

Target Market Exposure. Analysts like the Northwest, Midwest, mid-Atlantic, and California markets the best. They are leery about the Southwest (aside from Houston), the Boston–New York corridor, and parts of Florida.

Market Sectors. Analysts favor apartments and regional shopping centers, and they frown on hotels, raw land, and office buildings. Their verdicts on industrial properties are mixed.

Value Added. "The good REITs can increase the value of the properties they hold," says William Morrill, director of portfolio management at Alex, Brown Realty Advisors, Inc.

The Numbers. REITs should have debt no higher than 50 percent of equity and should avoid such financing gimmicks as accrual mortgages and zero-coupon bonds. As for performance, most analysts expect three to five years of steady cash flow and dividend growth.

SOURCE: Adapted from Barbara Donnelly, "Finding Real Estate Opportunities despite Hard Times on the Market," *The Wall Street Journal*, August 28, 1989, p. C1.

---

is unacceptable to the financial institutions from which mortgage financing is ordinarily obtained. Perhaps the mortgage is on a property for which there is no ready market. Perhaps the title to the property is not legally clear. Perhaps the title is not insurable. At any rate, many people purchase such mortgages. Investments of this kind may provide relatively high rates of return because of their special risk characteristics.

Most financial institutions will not make loans on second or third mortgages; these loans are left mainly to individuals. Such debt contracts are riskier than first mortgages because of their junior legal status, but they pay higher interest yields.

Shared-Equity Mortgages[4]   As you learned in the Opening Case, you can invest in shared-equity mortgages by putting up the down payment for cash-strapped home buyers. In a **shared-equity mortgage**, there are three parties—the buyer, a co-owner, and the lender. Experts advise that you carefully examine each shared-equity mortgage.

Equitymaker Partners, Ltd., Reston, Virginia, matches investors with home buyers. The investor puts up a 10 percent down payment. The buyer pays the

EXHIBIT 19–5

How Equity Sharing Works

Here's the way an investor's return would be calculated on one type of equity-sharing agreement. The example is based on the purchase of a $150,000 home in which the investor puts up a 10 percent down payment and the buyer pays the closing costs and makes the payments on the $135,000 mortgage. The example assumes that the house appreciates 7 percent a year for five years and is then sold.

Resale price of house after five years	$ 210,000
Less remaining mortgage principal	− 131,700
Less costs of sale (8% of sales price)	− 16,800
Total equity	$ 61,500
Less investor's down payment	− 15,000
Total shared equity (to be split 50–50 between investor and person selling the house)	$ 46,500
Investor's profit (compound annual average rate of return = 20.58%)	$ 23,250

SOURCE: *The Wall Street Journal,* July 28, 1989, p.C1; based on data from Equitymakers Partners, Ltd.

closing costs and other expenses, makes the monthly mortgage payments, and pays for all home maintenance. The buyer also gets all of the tax deductions from the home.

The agreement lasts for three to five years. Then either party can buy out the other, or the property will be sold to someone else. After the amount of the down payment has been returned to the investor, the mortgage has been retired, and the sales commission has been paid, the investor and the person selling the house split the appreciation equally. Exhibit 19–5 shows how equity sharing works and how an investor can calculate his or her return on such an investment.

Participation Certificates   If you want risk-proof real estate investment, participation certificates (PCs) are for you. Participation certificates are sold by such federal agencies as the Government National Mortgage Association (Ginnie Mae), the Federal Home Loan Mortgage Corporation (Freddie Mac), the Federal National Mortgage Association (Fannie Mae), and the Student Loan Marketing Association (Sallie Mae). A few states issue little siblings, such as the State of New York Mortgage Agency (Sonny Mae) and the New England Education Loan Marketing Corporation (Nellie Mae).

A **participation certificate** is an equity investment in a pool of mortgages that have been purchased by one of these government agencies. Maes and Macs are guaranteed by agencies closely tied to the federal government, making them just as secure as Uncle Sam's own bonds and notes. At one time, you needed a minimum of $25,000 to invest in PCs. Thanks to Maes and Macs mutual funds, you now need as little as $1,000 to buy shares in a unit trust or a mutual fund whose portfolio consists entirely of these securities. Either way, you assume the role of a mortgage lender. Each month, as payments are made on the mortgages, you receive interest and principal by check, or if you wish, the mutual fund will reinvest the amount for you.

The accompanying "Personal Finance Journal" describes various types of participation certificates sold by federal agencies.

PERSONAL FINANCE JOURNAL

Uncle Sam and His Family

The government securities named Maes and Macs can offer safety and relatively high yields for the right investor.

1. *Ginnie Mae*—Government National Mortgage Association (GNMA)

Introduced the first mortgage-backed securities in 1970 and still dominates this market.

The residential mortgage-backed securities are packaged in pools and then resold to investors as certificates ($25,000), or as shares by mutual funds.

Regular payments to investors are guaranteed by the GNMA—an agency of the Department of Housing and Urban Development.

Ginnie Maes are backed by the full faith and credit of the federal government.

The average life of mortgages is 12 years.

2. *Freddie Mac*—Federal Home Loan Mortgage Corporation (FHLMC)

Issues mortgage-backed securities similar to Ginnie Maes.

The pools of fixed rate home mortgages are made up of conventional home loans rather than mortgages insured by the FHA or the VA.

The timely payment of interest and the *ultimate* payment of principal are guaranteed.

3. *Fannie Mae*—Federal National Mortgage Association (FNMA)

Issues mortgage-backed securities similar to Ginnie Maes and Freddie Macs.

The pools of fixed rate home mortgages are similar to Freddie Macs, not Ginnie Maes.

Like Ginnie Maes, Fannie Maes guarantee a fair share of interest and principal *every month* even if homeowners do not meet their obligations.

As with Ginnie Maes and Freddie Macs, newly issued Fannie Mae certificates require a minimum investment of $25,000; the older certificates (whose principal has been partially paid off) require an investment of as little as $10,000.

4. *Sallie Mae*—Student Loan Marketing Association

Created by Congress in 1972 to provide a national secondary market for government-guaranteed student loans.

Issues bonds, each of which is backed by Sallie Mae as a whole, rather than specific pools of loans.

Sallie Mae bonds are considered virtually as safe as government Treasuries.

Brokers sell bonds having minimum denominations of $10,000.

Investors can also buy shares of Sallie Mae *stock:* the corporation is government chartered but publicly owned, and its shares are traded on the New York Stock Exchange.

5. *Sonny Mae*—State of New York Mortgage Agency

Issues bonds backed by fixed rate single-family home mortgages and uses proceeds to subsidize below-market-rate mortgages for first-time home buyers.

As with ordinary bonds, interest on Sonny Maes is paid only until the bonds mature.

Sonny Maes are exempt from federal income tax, and New York State residents do not pay state income tax on them.

6. *Nellie Mae*—New England Education Loan Marketing Corporation

A nonprofit corporation created by the Commonwealth of Massachusetts.

Provides a secondary market for federally guaranteed student loans issued in Massachusetts and New Hampshire.

The AAA-rated Nellie Mae bonds mature in three years.

The bonds are sold in minimum denominations of $5,000.

ADVANTAGES OF REAL ESTATE INVESTMENTS

L.O.2
Evaluate the advantages of real estate investments.

There are so many kinds of real estate investments that blanket statements about their investment advantages and disadvantages are not possible. However, certain types of real estate investments may possess some of the following advantages.

A Hedge against Inflation

Real property equity investments usually provide protection against purchasing power risk. In some areas, the prices of homes have increased dramatically. For example, in Hawaii, California, and Washington, D.C., they have increased 15 to 20 percent per year or more. It has not been uncommon for real estate investors to buy a house for $100,000 and sell it for $125,000 six months later. One woman sold her house for $160,000. Then, two days after it was put back on the market, she realized that she had sold it too cheaply and bought it back for $165,000. After painting the house inside and out, she sold it for $190,000.

Easy Entry

You can gain entry to a shopping center or a large apartment building by investing as little as $5,000 in a limited partnership. The minimum capital requirements for the total venture may be as high as $1 million or more, which is beyond the limits of a typical real estate investor.

Limited Financial Liability

If you are a limited partner, you are not liable for losses beyond your initial investment. That can be important if the venture is speculative and rewards are not assured. General partners, however, must bear all financial risks.

No Management Headaches

If you have invested in limited partnerships, REITs, mortgages, or participation certificates, you do not need to worry about paperwork and accounting, maintenance chores, and other administrative duties.

Financial Leverage

Financial leverage is the use of borrowed funds for investment purposes. It enables you to acquire a more expensive property than you could acquire on your own. This is an advantage when property values and incomes are rising. Assume that you buy a $100,000 property with no loan and then sell it for $120,000. The $20,000 gain represents a 20 percent return on your $100,000 investment. Then assume instead that you invest only $10,000 of your own money and borrow the other $90,000 (90 percent financing). Now you have made $20,000 on your $10,000 investment, or a 200 percent return.

Other traditional advantages of real estate investments, such a deductions for interest, property taxes, depreciation, deferred capital gains, and personal federal income taxes, have been restricted or eliminated under the Tax Reform Act of 1986. Previously, these were tax advantages; now they are disadvantages.

DISADVANTAGES OF REAL ESTATE INVESTMENTS

L.O.3
Assess the disadvantages of real estate investments.

Real estate investments have several disadvantages. However, these disadvantages do not affect all kinds of real estate investments to the same extent.

Declining Property Values

As discussed earlier, real property investments usually provide a hedge against inflation. But during deflationary and recessionary periods, the value of such investments may decline. For example, hundreds of developers, lenders, and investors have been victims of a deflation in commercial real estate that began sporadically in the early 1980s.

Illiquidity

Perhaps the largest drawback of direct real estate investments is the absence of large, liquid, and relatively efficient markets for them. Whereas stocks or bonds can generally be sold in a few minutes at the market price, this is not the case for real estate. It may take months to sell your commercial property or your limited partnership shares.

Lack of Diversification

Diversification in direct real estate investments is difficult because of the large size of most real estate projects. REITs, Ginnie Maes, Freddie Macs, and other syndicates, however, do provide various levels of diversification.

To these traditional disadvantages of real estate investments, the Tax Reform Act of 1986 has added the following tax-related problems.

No Tax Shelter

First and foremost, the new act limits the ability of taxpayers to use losses generated by real estate investments to offset income gained from other sources. Thus, investors cannot deduct their real estate losses from income generated by wages, salaries, dividends, and interest. In short, the tax shelter aspect of real estate syndicates is gone.

Elimination of Capital Gains Tax Benefits

Under the new tax act, the long-standing favored treatment afforded long-term capital gains is eliminated entirely. However, the new act reduces all marginal tax rates to a maximum of 15 percent for most taxpayers and to 28 percent for taxpayers with higher incomes. In the past, reduced capital gains taxes have been an important reason for investing in real estate partnerships.

Pepper . . . and Salt

"There's a man here who says he's looking for an honest tax shelter."

FROM *The Wall Street Journal,* with permission of Cartoon Features Syndicate.

Long Depreciation Period

Before the Tax Reform Act of 1986 went into effect, commercial real estate could be depreciated within 18 years. Under the accelerated cost recovery system (ACRS) adopted in 1980, an investor was allowed to use accelerated depreciation methods to recover the costs. Now you are required to use the straight-line depreciation method over 27½ years for residential real estate and over 31½ years for all other types of real estate.

Other provisions of the new act affect real estate investments, and all of them reduce the value of the tax credits for such investments. Investors are not allowed to take losses in excess of the actual amounts they invest. Furthermore, investment tax credit is eliminated entirely for all types of real estate except low-income housing projects.

If you believe that investing in real estate is too risky or too complicated, you might want to consider other tangible investments. These investments include gold and other precious metals, gems, and collectibles. But remember, risk and reward go hand in hand.

INVESTING IN PRECIOUS METALS, GEMS, AND COLLECTIBLES

L.O.4.
Analyze the risks and rewards of investing in precious metals, gems, and collectibles.

When the economy picks up, some investors predict higher inflation. Therefore, many think the precious metals, such as gold, platinum, and silver, will regain some of their glitter. In this section, we will discuss several methods for buying precious metals.

Gold

Gold prices tend to be driven up by such factors as fear of war, political instability, and inflation. On the other hand, the easing of international tensions or disinflation causes a decline in gold prices. High interest rates also depress gold prices because they make it very expensive to carry gold as an investment.

Many people have acquired the metal itself; many others have gone into gold through a number of other kinds of investment that serve a variety of purposes. Some of these investments promise quick profits at high risk; others preserve capital; and yet others provide income from dividends or interest. But none of them are exempt from daily gold price fluctuations. Exhibit 19–6 shows gold price fluctuations between 1976 and 1990.

Gold Bullion   Gold bullion includes gold bars or wafers. The basic unit of gold bullion is one kilogram (32.15 troy ounces of .995 fine gold). Coin dealers, precious metals dealers, and some banks sell gold bullion in sizes ranging from five grams (16/100 of a troy ounce) to 500 ounces or more. On small bars, dealers and banks add 5 to 8 percent premium over the pure gold bullion value; on larger bars, the premium is usually 1 to 2 percent. Gold bullion presents storage problems, and unless the gold bar or wafer remains in the custody of the bank or dealer that sells it initially, it must be reassayed before being sold.

Gold Bullion Coins   You can avoid storage and assaying problems by investing in gold bullion coins. In the early 1980s, before the intensification of South Africa's political problems, South African Krugerrands were the most popular gold bullion coins in the United States. Popular gold bullion coins today include the Canadian Gold Maple Leaf, the Mexican 50 Pesos, the Austrian 100 Koronas,

EXHIBIT 19–6

Fluctuations in the Price of
Gold since 1976

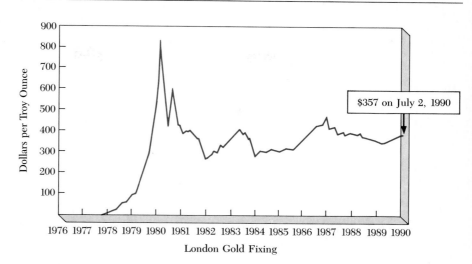

$357 on July 2, 1990

London Gold Fixing

Since 1976, the price of gold has fluctuated from $850 to $284 an ounce.

and the British Sovereign. The new American Eagle gold coin, the first gold bullion coin ever produced by the U.S. government, was issued in late 1986. The demand for it was so strong that the initial minting of 558,000 ounces was sold out within a few hours.[5]

Most brokers require a minimum order of 10 coins and charge a commission of at least 2 percent. Later, we will discuss rare gold and silver coins that are purchased for their numismatic value, not the intrinsic value of their gold or silver content.

Gold Stocks   In addition to investing in gold bullion and gold bullion coins, you may invest in gold by purchasing the common stocks of gold mining companies. Among the gold mining stocks listed on U.S. stock exchanges are those of Homestake Mining (based in the United States) and Campbell Red Lake and Dome Mines (based in Canada). Because such stocks often move in a direction opposite to that of the stock market as a whole, they may provide excellent portfolio diversification. You may also wish to examine closed-end investment companies with heavy positions in gold mining stocks (such as ARA, Ltd.).

Gold Futures Contracts   Finally, you may wish to consider trading in gold futures contracts. Gold futures are traded on five U.S. exchanges and on many foreign exchanges.

Be sure to find a reputable firm before you invest in precious metals. The accompanying "Financial Planning in Action" feature provides guidance on how to protect yourself from fraudulent precious metal schemes.

Silver, Platinum, and Palladium

Investments in silver, platinum, and palladium, like investments in gold, are used as a hedge against inflation and as a safe haven during political or economic upheavals. During the last 59 years, silver prices ranged from a historic low of

FINANCIAL PLANNING IN ACTION

Suckers Being Hooked by Precious Metal Lures

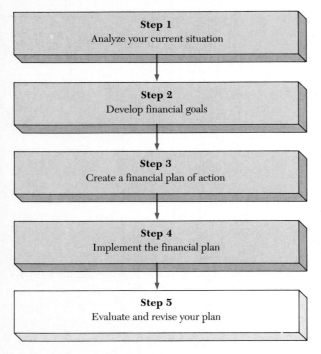

Step 1
Analyze your current situation

Step 2
Develop financial goals

Step 3
Create a financial plan of action

Step 4
Implement the financial plan

Step 5
Evaluate and revise your plan

A new siren song of promised profits in precious metals is luring another wave of gullible investors.

It has a financially fashionable name—"collateralized loan program"—and it works like this: An investor, making the mistake of responding to a telephone solicitor, says he is interested in precious metals but doesn't have a lot of money to invest. Don't worry, says the fast-talking "broker," who assures the investor that he will arrange to have a bank lend 80 percent of the cost of gold, silver, platinum, or, lately, palladium. Because the metal is collateral for the loan, the interest charged investors is temptingly attractive, often the prime rate that banks charge favored customers. The ties to banks, intended to lend credibility to the proposals, are usually real, according to Terree A. Bowers, chief of the major fraud section of the U.S. attorney's office in Los Angeles.

If the investor knows anything about leverage, he can daydream happily about rising prices pushing up the value

of his gold or whatever, for which his cash outlay was only 20 percent. Of course, if prices fall, the losses are going to be substantially higher too, but that's always the case with a leveraged investment.

So where's the hidden whammy that stacks the deck against investors? It's in the extra charges, such as commissions and other fees, that are added onto the purchase price and interest rates.

Morgan Whitney Trading Group, Inc., operating from offices in Venice, California, is one of the firms offering investors what its telephone solicitors describe as an "unbelievable opportunity" to capitalize on "rising metal prices." A salesman from Morgan Whitney recently explained in a telephone pitch that his firm adds only two charges over the cost of the metal: a commission equal to 15 percent of the value of the metal and a refining charge, which in the case of platinum, for example, is $16 an ounce.

When a sale of 100 ounces of platinum can generate commission and fees of $9,872, it isn't surprising that the salespeople are aggressive. Max Welborn of Yadkinville, North Carolina, says that he was subjected to several weeks of persistent calls from a Morgan Whitney salesman. "They called me 10 or 15 times, mostly at dinnertime," he says, "and then they got angry at me when I wouldn't buy."

The commission and fees are so heavy that unless platinum rises by more than $120 an ounce—or 22 percent—an investor will lose money on the deal. Such price moves within a six-month period occur only rarely in platinum. Six months enters into the calculation because that's the initial term of the bank loan.

But a salesman for Morgan Whitney assured a recent caller, "We project the price rising to $750 to $800 an ounce within the next six months." The salesman said that he thought platinum investors could make 30 to 80 percent in the next six months. To make those rates of return through Morgan Whitney, platinum would have to rise by at least $186 and as much as $291 an ounce—increases of 34 to 53 percent.

SOURCE: Condensed from Stanley W. Angrist, "Precious Metal Lures Are Hooking Plenty of Suckers," *The Wall Street Journal,* April 24, 1989, p. C1.

24.25 cents an ounce in 1932, to over $50 an ounce in early 1980, and then back to less than $5 an ounce in July 1990.

Two less well known precious metals, platinum and palladium, are also popular investments. Both have industrial uses as catalysts, particularly in automobile production. Some investors think that increased car sales could mean higher prices for these metals. Platinum currently sells for about $479 an ounce, palladium for about $135 an ounce.

As discussed earlier, finding storage for your precious metals can be tricky. While $20,000 in gold, for example, occupies only as much space as a thick paperback, $20,000 in silver weighs more than 200 pounds and could require a few safe-deposit boxes. Those boxes, moreover, are not insured against fire and theft.

You should remember, too, that unlike stocks, bonds, and other interest-bearing investments, precious metals sit in vaults earning nothing. And whether you profit on an eventual sale depends entirely on how well you call the market.

Precious Stones

Precious stones include diamonds, sapphires, rubies, and emeralds. Diamonds and other precious stones appeal to investors because of their small size, easy concealment, and great durability and because of their potential as a hedge against inflation. Inflation and the interest in tangible assets helped increase diamond prices 40-fold between 1970 and 1980. A lucky few made fortunes, and brokerage and diamond firms took up the investment diamond business.

Whether you are buying precious stones to store in a safe-deposit box or to wear around your neck, there are a few things to keep in mind about risks. Diamonds and other precious stones are not easily turned into cash. It is hard to know whether you are getting a good stone. Diamond prices can be affected by the whims of De Beers Consolidated Mines of South Africa, Ltd., which controls 85 percent of the world's supply of rough diamonds, and by political instability in diamond-producing countries. Moreover, the average buyer should expect to buy at retail and sell at wholesale, a difference of at least 10–15 percent—and perhaps of as much as 50 percent.

The best way to know exactly what you are getting, especially if you are planning to spend more than $1,000, is to insist that your stone be certified by an independent gemological laboratory, one not connected with a diamond-selling organization. (The acknowledged industry leader in this area is the Gemological Institute of America.) The certificate should list the stone's characteristics, including its weight, color, clarity, and quality of cut. The grading of diamonds, however, is not an exact science, and recent experiments have shown that when the same diamond is submitted twice to the same institute, it can get two different ratings.

Michael Roman, chairman of the Jewelers of America, a trade group representing 12,000 retailers, stated that his group did not recommend diamonds as an investment and scoffed at the notion that local retail jewelers were realizing huge profits on diamond sales to misguided customers. He also did not believe in certification unless the stone in question is a high-grade diamond weighing at least one carat.

Despite the present rosy scenarios for precious metals and gems, the risks in trading them are sizable. Just ask investors who in 1980 bought gold at as much as $850 an ounce, platinum at $1,040 an ounce, silver at $48 an ounce, and a one-carat diamond at $62,000.

Collectibles

Collectibles include rare coins, works of art, antiques, stamps, rare books, sports memorabilia, rugs, Chinese ceramics, paintings, and other items that appeal to collectors and investors. Each of these items offers the collector/investor both pleasure and the opportunity for profit. Many collectors have discovered only incidentally that items they bought for their own pleasure had gained greatly in value while they owned them.

Collecting can be a good investment and a satisfying hobby, but for many Americans it has recently become a financial disaster. For example, the art market is booming, but so is the billion-dollar business of art fraud.[6] Art experts and law enforcement officials say that a new generation of collectors is being victimized by forgeries more sophisticated, more expensive, and more difficult to detect than ever before. "The problem of forgeries is so enormous with the big three—Marc Chagall, Joan Miró, Pablo Picasso—we can't handle them anymore, there are so many," says Virginia Pancoast, director of authentication at the International Foundation for Art Research.[7]

Rare coin scams have increased, and many investors in rare coins have lost most of their investment as a result of fraudulent sales practices. If you are investing in coins, the Federal Trade Commission and the American Numismatic Association urge you to protect yourself by following these rules:

- Use common sense when evaluating any investment claims, and do not rush into buying.
- Make sure that you know your dealer's reputation and reliability before you send money or authorize a credit card transaction.
- Do not be taken in by promises that the dealer will buy back your coins or that grading is guaranteed unless you are confident that the dealer has the financial resources to stand behind these promises.
- Get a second opinion from another source about grade and value as soon as you receive your coins. So, before you buy, find out what remedies you will have if the second opinion differs.
- Be cautious about grading certificates, especially those furnished by coin dealers. Grading is not an exact science, and grading standards vary widely.
- Comparison shop. Visit several dealers before buying.[8]

Collecting for investment purposes is very different from collecting as a hobby. Investing in collectibles can be just as serious as investing in real estate or the stock market and should be approached with equal study and care.

Investment counselors caution that collectibles do not provide interest or dividends, that it may be difficult to sell them at the right price on short notice, and that if they become valuable enough, they must be insured against loss or theft.

Exhibits 19–7 and 19–8 compare the percentage annual rate of return on various kinds of tangible and intangible assets for the 1980s and the 1970s, respectively. If the 1980s were the decade for financial assets, such as stocks,

EXHIBIT 19–7   1980s—A Decade for Financial Assets *(Compound Annual Rate of Return, 1980–1988)*

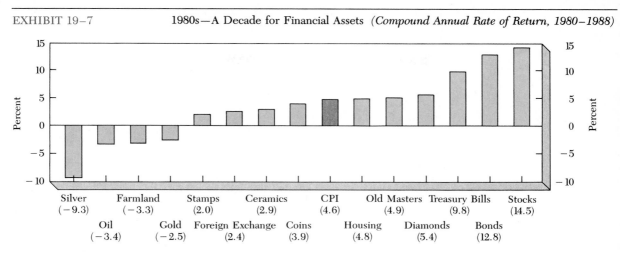

source: Adapted from Sumner N. Levine, ed., *Business and Investment Almanac, 1989* (Homewood, Ill.: Dow Jones-Irwin, 1989), p. 261.
© Sumner N. Levine, 1989.

EXHIBIT 19–8   The 1970s—A Decade for Collectibles and Commodities *(Compound Annual Rate of Return, 1970–1980)*

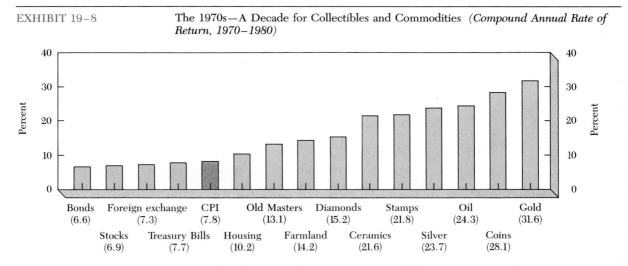

source: Adapted from Sumner N. Levine, ed., *Business and Investment Almanac, 1989* (Homewood, Ill.: Dow Jones-Irwin, 1989), p. 261.
© Sumner N. Levine, 1989.

bonds, and T-bills, then the 1970s were the decade for collectibles and tangibles, such as oil, gold, coins, silver, and stamps.

SUMMARY

L.O.1
Identify types of real estate investments.

Real estate investments are classified as direct or indirect. Direct real estate investments, in which the investor holds legal title to the property, include a home, a vacation home, commercial property, and raw land. Indirect real estate investments include real estate syndicates, REITs, mortgages, and participation certificates.

L.O.2
Evaluate the advantages of real estate investments.

Real estate investments may have these advantages: a hedge against inflation, easy entry, limited financial liability, no management headaches, and financial leverage.

L.O.3
Assess the disadvantages of real estate investments.

Real estate investments may have these disadvantages: declining values, illiquidity, lack of diversification, and the reduction or elimination of tax advantages.

L.O.4
Analyze the risks and rewards of investing in precious metals, gems, and collectibles.

Some investors prefer to invest in precious metals, such as gold, platinum, and silver; precious stones, such as diamonds; or collectibles, such as stamps, rare coins, works of art, antiques, rare books, and Chinese ceramics. Collectibles do not provide current income, and they may be difficult to sell in a hurry.

GLOSSARY

Collectibles   Rare coins, works of art, antiques, stamps, rare books, and other items that appeal to collectors and investors.

Commercial property   Land and buildings that produce lease or rental income.

Direct investment   Investment in which the investor holds legal title to property.

Indirect investment   Investment in which a trustee holds legal title to property on behalf of the investors.

Participation certificate   An equity investment in a pool of mortgages that have been purchased by a government agency, such as Ginnie Mae.

Passive activity   A business or trade in which the investor does not materially participate or rental activity.

Passive loss   The total amount of losses from a passive activity minus the total income from the passive activity.

REIT   A firm that pools investor funds and invests them in real estate or uses them to make construction or mortgage loans.

Shared-equity mortgage   A mortgage in which there are three parties—the buyer, a co-owner, and the lender.

Syndicate   A temporary association of individuals or firms, organized to perform a specific task that requires a large amount of capital.

DISCUSSION QUESTIONS

L.O.1   1. Compare and distinguish between direct and indirect real estate investments. Give an example of each.

L.O.1   2. Distinguish among gross scheduled income, gross operating income, operating expenses, net operating income, and rate of return.

L.O.1   3. What is a real estate syndicate or limited partnership? What are the responsibilities of a general partner? A limited partner?

L.O.1   4. Why are REITs compared to mutual funds?

L.O.1   5. Compare three types of REITs. What four federal requirements must REITs adhere to in their operations?

L.O.1   6. What are first and second mortgages? What are their usual investment and legal requirements?

L.O.1   7. What is a Ginnie Mae participation certificate? Evaluate the investment characteristics—financial risk, marketability, and purchasing power risk—of this form of investment.

L.O.2   8. Assess major advantages of owning real estate directly and indirectly.

L.O.3   9. What are disadvantages of real estate investments?

L.O.4   10. What are the various ways of owning gold, silver, and platinum?

L.O.4   11. Describe some advantages and disadvantages of investing your money in such collectibles as stamps, rare coins, antiques, and sports memorabilia.

Opening Case Questions

1. Would you invest in a shared-equity mortgage? Why?
2. Many people who once invested in rental apartments have been switching to equity-sharing mortgages. Why?

PROBLEMS AND ACTIVITIES

L.O.1   1. Exhibit 19–3 shows current-year income analysis for Outflow Apartments. Perform second- and third-year income analysis for Outflow Apartments. Assume that revenues and costs (except for interest payments) will increase by 3 percent each year over the next two years.

L.O.1   2. Based on the above analysis, answer the following:
   a. What is the net operating income for Year 2? Year 3?
   b. What is the gross spendable income for Year 2? Year 3?
   c. What is the gross equity income for Year 2? Year 3?
   d. What is the taxable income for Year 2? Year 3?

L.O.1   3. Why is taxable income declining in Years 2 and 3?

L.O.1   4. What is the income tax benefit for Year 2? Year 3? Why is this benefit decreasing?

L.O.1   5. Calculate net spendable cash for Years 2 and 3. Why is this figure increasing?

L.O.2   6. Why might investments in real estate serve as an inflation hedge?

L.O.2   7. In what way does real estate provide a high degree of leverage?

L.O.3   8. "Ownership of a commercial property is one of the best investments you can make." Comment on this statement, paying particular attention to the investment characteristics of the average commercial property.

L.O.3   9. Obtain the duplex mortgage rates from your local commercial bank, a savings and loan association, and a credit union. Compare these rates and such terms as the down payment, loan costs (points), loan length, and maximum amount available to determine which of the three offers the best financing.

L.O.4   10. Listen to business news on radio or television. What are the current quotes for an ounce of gold and an ounce of silver? Are the prices of precious metals going up or down? How do the latest prices compare with the prices quoted in the textbook? What might be some reasons for fluctuations in the prices of precious metals?

LIFE SITUATION   Case 19-1

Born-Again Financial Planners

More than 15,000 Americans lost a total of $450 million in the past five years in bogus moneymaking schemes promoted by religious charlatans, according to a report released by the North American Securities Administrators Association and the Council of Better Business Bureaus.

There has been an "alarming increase" in complaints about self-proclaimed born-again financial planners, con artists claiming to be endorsed by local and national church officials, and givers of "divinely inspired" investment advice, says John C. Baldwin, president of the North American Securities Administrators Association.

Victims of the scams include worshipers of all persuasions. Among the victims have been Lutheran ministers, black churchgoers, Hispanic Catholic parishioners, and members of Baptist, Jewish, Mormon, and Greek Orthodox congregations.

The report mentions a Washington State promoter who sold $56 million of real estate securities by advertising on Christian radio stations. When the promoter's company collapsed, 7,000 investors were left holding $50 million in defaulted notes.

The Idaho Department of Finance recently filed a civil lawsuit against Lawrence W. McGary and his Shama Resources Limited Partnership in Sun Valley, Idaho, charging fraud and misrepresentation in the sale of $4 million in partnership interests. McGary's prospectus describing the partnership's gold mining and oil-and-gas drilling plans is filled with biblical quotations and references to divine inspiration. "As we acquired this block, we believe we were led by the Holy Spirit," the prospectus says of one piece of property. Referring to an oil-and-gas plan, it says, "God is leading us to move ahead in this very area when no one else is interested."

Questions

1. Why has there been a surge in investment scams using religious affiliations to fleece the faithful?
2. What can the federal government and state governments do to stop such scams?
3. What can you do to protect yourself from investment swindles?

SOURCE: Condensed from Earl C. Gottschalk, Jr., "Churchgoers Are the Prey as Scams Rise," *The Wall Street Journal,* August, 7, 1989, p. C1.

LIFE SITUATION   Case 19-2

Bogus Brushstroke: Art Fraud

Richard Welch received a letter inviting him to participate in a drawing for a free original lithograph by a famous artist. He was asked to return a postcard with his name, address, and phone number. After he returned the postcard, he was telephoned for more information, including his credit card number.

At some point, the caller asked Richard to buy a print, using such glowing terms as "fabulous opportunity," "onetime offer," "limited edition," and "excellent investment" to describe the purchase. Richard was told that the print was the work of a famous artist who was near death and that its value would increase after the artist's death. He was assured that when the artist died, the company that the caller represented would gladly buy back the print at two to three times what he paid for it and that he could always resell the print elsewhere at a substantial profit. He was told that he would receive a certificate testifying to the "authenticity" of the print. And he was promised a trial examination period with a 30-day money-back guarantee.

Questions

1. Does the offer seem genuine to you? Explain your answer.
2. How can Richard protect himself against a phony offer? List at least five suggestions that you would give him.
3. If Richard bought the work of art and discovered fraud, how should he try to resolve his dispute with the company that sold it to him? Where should he complain if the dispute is not resolved?

SUPPLEMENTARY READINGS

For Additional Information on Real Estate Investments

Cymrot, Allen. *Street Smart Real Estate Investing.* Homewood, Ill.: Dow Jones-Irwin, 1988.

Greer, Gaylon. *The New Dow Jones-Irwin Guide to Real Estate Investing.* Homewood, Ill.: Dow Jones-Irwin, 1989.

Widicus, Wilbur W., and Thomas E. Stitzel. *Personal Investing,* 5th ed. Chap. 11. Homewood, Ill.: Richard D. Irwin, 1989.

For Additional Information on Coin and Gold Investments

Consumer Alert: Investing in Rare Coins. Federal Trade Commission, n.d.

A Consumer's Guide to Coin Investment. Jefferson, La.: James U. Blanchard, 1988.

Scheibla, Shirley Hobbs. "Gold Scams: They're Bilking Investors out of Hundreds of Millions." *Barron's,* September 5, 1988, pp. 56ff.

For Additional Information on Art Investment

"Art Fraud." *Facts for Consumers.* Washington, D.C.: Federal Trade Commission, August 1988.

COMPREHENSIVE CASE FOR PART V

Down, but Hopefully Not Out!

Two years ago, Gene Martin, 43, thought that everything in his life was pretty much on target. He was happily married, had two children, a good job as a chemical engineer, $10,000 in the bank, and had even invested $70,000 in conservative stocks and bonds.

Now, two years later, most of that is gone. It all started when the company he worked for was purchased by a larger corporation. Gene, along with a lot of other engineers, was "fired" because he was no longer needed. Of course, the fact that he was unemployed didn't stop the monthly bills, and his unemployment benefits didn't help much. The $10,000 bank account was quickly exhausted. Gene and his wife, Karen, began selling their stocks and bonds to make ends meet.

Then, to make matters worse, Gene and Karen started to argue about finances, career plans, the children, and just about everything else. Karen filed for divorce six months after Gene lost his job. Since Gene and Karen could not agree on a property settlement, they each got a lawyer. Their legal fees totaled $8,500. After another six months, their divorce became final. As part of the property settlement, Karen got the kids, house, and car; one half of their furniture; and one half of the remaining stocks and bonds. She was also required to pay Gene $15,000 for his portion of the equity in their home. Gene got the $15,000 payment from Karen and the other half of the furniture and of the remaining stocks and bonds. Also, Gene was required to pay VISA, MasterCard, and medical bills that totaled $3,700. Finally, he was required to pay $600 a month child support for their two children.

According to Gene, the next nine months were the "low point in his life." He could not find a job, and he was living in a one-room efficiency apartment separated from his two kids. He was existing on the cash settlement he got from Karen and the money he received for his share of the remaining stocks and bonds.

At the end of his second year of unemployment, Gene got a job as a chemical engineer with a large, well-respected company. Because of his past work experience, the company agreed to pay him $56,000 a year. His take-home pay was approximately $2,900 a month, and his problems seemed to be over. But it quickly dawned on him that he was 45 years old—20 years from retirement—and had a grand total of $4,500 in assets. He realized that he

had to do some careful financial planning unless he wanted to work forever.

He performed a financial checkup and found that his monthly expenses were $2,450. An itemized list of these expenses is shown below.

Expense	Amount
Apartment	$ 550
Child support	600
Transportation	400
Utilities	200
Food and entertainment	450
Clothing and cleaning	150
Miscellaneous	100
Total monthly expenses	$2,450

After analyzing the results of his financial checkup, Gene realizes that he has about $450 a month, or $5,400 a year, left over after all of his expenses have been paid. Now he must decide what to do with the excess.

Questions

1. How would you rank the Martins' financial condition before Gene lost his job? How could their financial condition have been improved?

2. If the divorce could not be avoided, what could Gene and Karen have done differently? Why do you think they each had to have a lawyer?

3. As a result of the divorce, Gene is a single taxpayer earning $56,000 a year. Because he lives in an apartment and doesn't have any other tax deductions, he is afraid that he will end up paying a large percentage of his income to the federal government. In what ways could Gene minimize the amount of taxes that he pays?

4. Assume that you are a financial planner and Gene is your client. Given the information in this case, develop a thorough financial plan that takes into account Gene's immediate needs and his retirement needs. Be sure to include specific investment goals.

5. What types of investments would you recommend for Gene? Explain.

VI
Controlling Your Financial Future

The final part of *Personal Finance* emphasizes planning for retirement and estate management. In Chapter 20, we discuss the importance of retirement

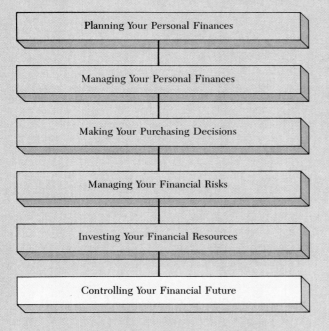

Planning Your Personal Finances

Managing Your Personal Finances

Making Your Purchasing Decisions

Managing Your Financial Risks

Investing Your Financial Resources

Controlling Your Financial Future

planning and offer a framework for analysis of your retirement resources. We examine how to invest for your retirement years and how to plan for the use of retirement income. In Chapter 21, we focus on the steps that you should take to provide financial protection for your family now and in the future. We discuss wills, trust management, and methods of property ownership. We help you determine what property is included in the valuation of your estate and how your estate is settled. Finally, we offer details regarding the calculation and payment of estate taxes and how to minimize these taxes. This part consists of

Chapter 20   Retirement Planning
Chapter 21   Estate Planning

Retirement Planning

Retirement can be a rewarding phase of your life. However, a successful, happy retirement doesn't just happen—it takes planning and continual evaluation. Thinking about retirement in advance can help you understand the retirement process and gain a sense of control over the future. Anticipating future changes can be useful.

LEARNING OBJECTIVES
After studying this chapter, you will be able to

L.O.1   Recognize the importance of retirement planning.

L.O.2   Analyze your current assets and liabilities for retirement.

L.O.3   Estimate your retirement spending needs.

L.O.4   Identify your retirement housing needs.

L.O.5   Evaluate your planned retirement income.

L.O.6   Develop a balanced budget based on your retirement income.

OPENING CASE

Why Many Retirees Soon Go Back to Work°

Many Americans delay making final plans for retirement. However, a lack of sufficient planning can place severe hardships on you and your family. Although dealing with money matters may seem dull, unpleasant, or even frightening, if you plan carefully and make the necessary decisions for your retirement, you will be in better control of your future.

A survey suggests that retirees who return to work often do so relatively quickly—and primarily for economic reasons.

Recently, Travelers Corporation and its affiliated companies canvassed 1,400 retirees—750 men and women registered with the Travelers retiree job bank and a 650-person sampling of nonregistered retirees. The idea was to find out why they did or didn't work after retirement and to figure out ways to give retirees more work options. The results indicated that about one out of four of the Travelers retirees had returned to work and that two out of three of these returned workers had returned within a year of retiring.

Although many of the returned workers said that they derived social and emotional benefits from working, the main reason they went back was to meet living expenses or pay for major special outlays. One third of the returned workers reported that their jobs underused their skills, but most of these workers said that they were satisfied to have it that way.

Not surprisingly, as compared to the nonworking retirees, the retirees who went back to work expressed greater dissatisfaction with their initial decision to retire. Many of them had retired early, and so had lower social security and pension income than they might have had.

Most of the nonworking retirees said that they didn't need the extra money they could earn from working and that they were too busy with other activities to find time for working. A significant number, however, said that they would have been working were it not for poor health, care-giving responsibilities, transportation problems, and concern over losing social security benefits if they worked too many hours.

°Adopted from "Why Many Retirees Soon Go Back to Work," *The Wall Street Journal*, June 23, 1989, p. B1.

WHY RETIREMENT PLANNING?

L.O.1
Recognize the importance of retirement planning.

It is vital to engage in basic retirement planning activities throughout your working years and to update your retirement plans periodically. While it is never too late to begin sound financial planning, you can avoid many unnecessary and serious difficulties by starting this planning early. Saving now for the future requires tackling the trade-offs between spending and saving.

Tackling the Trade-Offs

Although there are exceptions, the old adage "You can't have your cake and eat it too" is particularly true in planning for your retirement. For example, if you buy state-of-the-art home stereo systems, drive sports cars, and take expensive vacations now, don't expect to retire with plenty of money.

More than half of the young professionals who participated in a recent survey said that they would rather spend money today than save for retirement. Yet 61 percent of them were worried about not having enough money to retire comfortably. The study, conducted in New York and Chicago by Creative Research Associates, revealed that a group of prosperous, educated people wanted the good life now. They also wanted the good life to last forever but weren't sure how to make this happen.[1]

Only saving now and curtailing current spending can ensure comfortable retirement later. Yet saving money doesn't come naturally to many young people. It is ironic that—although the time to begin saving is when you are young, the people who are in the best position to save are middle-aged.

"I think our generation is more attached to impulse items," said Jeff Greenberg, aged 30, an editor at a New York publishing company. "For instance, I have a microwave oven, and I don't really know why I got it. . . . I have a VCR; do I really need it? The list goes on—it's endless."[2]

The Importance of Starting Early

For 40 years, your life, and probably the life of your family, revolves around your job. One day you retire—and practically every aspect of your life is different. There's less money, more time, and no daily structure.

You can expect to spend about 16 to 20 years in retirement—too many years to be bored, lonely, and poor. You want your retirement years to be rewarding, active, and rich in new experiences. But you have to plan—and plan early. It's never too early to begin planning for retirement; some experts even suggest starting while you are in school. Be certain you don't let your 45th birthday roll by without a comprehensive retirement plan. Remember, the longer you wait, the less influence you will have on the shape of your life in retirement.

Retirement planning is both emotional and financial. Emotional planning for retirement involves identifying your personal goals and setting out to meet them. Financial planning for retirement involves assessing your postretirement needs and income and plugging any gaps you find. Financial planning for retirement is vitally important for several reasons:

1. You can expect to live in retirement for many years. At age 65, the average life expectancy of a man is 14 years and the average life expectancy of a woman is 19 years.
2. Social security and a private pension, if you have one, may be insufficient to cover the cost of living.
3. Inflation may diminish the purchasing power of your retirement savings.

You should anticipate your retirement years by analyzing your long-range goals. What does retirement mean to you? Does it mean an opportunity to stop work and rest, or does it mean time to travel, develop a hobby, or start a second career? Where and how do you want to live during your retirement? Once you have considered your retirement goals, you are ready to evaluate the cost of your plans and whether you can afford them.

The Basics of Retirement Planning

Before you decide where you want to be financially, you have to find out where you are. Your first step, therefore, is to analyze your current assets and liabilities. Then you estimate your spending needs and adjust them for inflation. Next you evaluate your planned retirement income. Finally, you increase your income if necessary.

"Retirement plan? I wouldn't worry about that.
You'd be out of your mind to work here
that long."

FROM *The Wall Street Journal,* with permission of Cartoon Features
Syndicate.

CONDUCTING A FINANCIAL ANALYSIS

L.O.2
Analyze your current assets and
liabilities for retirement.

As you learned in Chapter 3, your current assets include everything you own that has value: cash on hand and in checking and savings accounts; the current value of your stocks, bonds, and other investments; the current value of your house, car, jewelry, and furnishings; and the current value of your life insurance and pensions. Your current liabilities are everything you owe: your mortgage, car payments, credit card balances, taxes due, and so forth. The difference between the two totals is your net worth, a figure that you should increase each year as you move toward retirement. Use Exhibit 20–1 to calculate your net worth now and at retirement.

Review Your Assets

Reviewing your assets to make sure they are suitable for retirement is a sound idea. Make necessary shifts in your investments and holdings to fit your circumstances. In reviewing your assets, consider the following factors.

Housing   If you own your house, it is probably your biggest single asset. The amount tied up in your house may be out of line, however, with your retirement income. If it is, consider selling your house and buying a less expensive one. The selection of a smaller, more easily maintained house can also decrease your maintenance costs. The difference saved can be put into a savings account or certificates or into other income-producing investments. If your mortgage is largely or completely paid off, you may be able to get an annuity that provides you with extra income during retirement. In this arrangement, a lender uses your house as collateral to buy an annuity for you from a life insurance company. Each

EXHIBIT 20–1

Review Your Assets,
Liabilities, and Net Worth

	George and May B	Your Figures
Assets—What We Own		
Cash		
Checking account	$ 800	_____
Savings account	4,500	_____
Investments		
U.S. savings bonds (current cash-in value)	5,000	_____
Stocks, mutual funds	4,500	_____
Life insurance		
Cash value, accumulated dividends	10,000	_____
Company pension rights:		
Accrued pension benefit	20,000	_____
Property		
House (resale value)	50,000	_____
Furniture and appliances	8,000	_____
Collections and jewelry	2,000	_____
Automobile	3,000	_____
Other		
Loan to brother	1,000	_____
Gross assets	$108,800	_____
Liabilities—What We Owe		
Current unpaid bills	600	_____
Home mortgage (remaining balance)	9,700	_____
Auto loan	1,200	_____
Property taxes	1,100	_____
Home improvement loan	3,700	_____
Total liabilities	$ 16,300	_____

Net worth: Assets of $108,800 minus liabilities of $16,300 equals $92,500.

month, the lender pays you (the homeowner) from the annuity, after deducting the mortgage interest payment. The mortgage principal, which was used to obtain the annuity, is repaid to the lender by probate after your death. This special annuity is known as a **reverse annuity mortgage**. Such mortgages may not be available in your area. Check with your banker or a savings institution about availability and details.

Life Insurance   You may have set up your life insurance to provide support and education for your children. Now you may want to convert some of this asset into cash or income (an annuity). Another possibility is to reduce premium payments by decreasing the face value of your insurance. Doing this will give you extra money to spend on living expenses or to invest for additional income.

U.S. Savings Bonds   Both Series EE and Series HH savings bonds are easy to obtain and redeem. The bonds are safe, and their interest is free from state and local income taxes.

Series EE bonds are issued in denominations of $50 to $15,000. You purchase them at 50 percent of their face value and redeem them for their full face value on a specified date. Interest on these bonds is paid when they are redeemed. Series HH bonds are issued in denominations of $500 to $10,000 and earn a fixed interest rate. These bonds are no longer available for purchase, but you can exchange Series EE bonds for them. You obtain them at their face value, and every six months the U.S. Treasury sends you your interest earnings. You may redeem Series EE bonds and Series HH bonds any time after six months from their issue date.

Other Investments   Evaluate any other investments you may have. When you chose them, you may have been more interested in making your money grow than in getting an early return. Has the time come to take the income from your investments? You may now want to take dividends rather than reinvest them.

After thoroughly reviewing your assets, estimate your spending needs during your retirement years.

RETIREMENT LIVING EXPENSES

L.O.3
Estimate your retirement spending needs.

The exact amount of money you will need in retirement is impossible to predict. However, you can estimate the amount of money you will need by considering the changes you plan to make in your spending patterns and in where and how you live.

Your spending patterns will probably change. A study conducted by the Bureau of Labor Statistics on how families spend money shows that retired families use a greater share for food, housing, and medical care than nonretired families. Although no two families are alike in how they adjust their spending patterns to changes in the life cycle, the Bureau of Labor Statistics tabulation in Exhibit 20–2 can guide you in anticipating your own future spending patterns.

The following expenses may be lowered or eliminated:

Work Expenses   You will no longer have to make payments into your retirement system. You will not be buying gas and oil for the drive back and forth to work or for train or bus fares. You may be buying fewer lunches away from home.

Clothing Expenses   You probably will not need as many clothes after you retire, and your dress may be more casual.

Housing Expenses   If you have paid off your house mortgage by the time you retire, your cost of housing may be reduced, although increases in property taxes may offset this gain.

Federal Income Taxes   Your federal income taxes will be lower. No federal tax has to be paid on some forms of income, such as railroad retirement benefits and certain veterans' benefits. A retirement credit is allowed for some sources of

EXHIBIT 20–2

Spending Patterns of
Retired Families—Average
Annual Expenditures of
Older (65+) Households in
the Late 1980s

Category	Amount	Percent of Total
Housing	$ 4,592	31%
Food	2,419	17
Clothing and personal care	760	5
Transportation	2,528	17
Health care°	1,635	11
Life insurance/pensions	680	5
Contributions	889	6
Entertainment, reading, and education	596	4
Miscellaneous	537	4
Total	$14,636	100%

°A recent study by the House of Representatives Select Committee on Aging found that out-of-pocket health care costs paid by the elderly rose to 18.1 percent in 1988. The study was based on data supplied by the Health Care Financing Administration.

SOURCES: Bureau of Labor Statistics and Select Committee on Aging, House of Representatives, Washington, D.C., 1989.

income, such as annuities. You will probably be paying taxes at a lower rate because your taxable income will be lower.

Under the U.S. Civil Service Retirement System, your retirement income is not taxed until you have received the amount you have invested in the retirement fund. After that, your retirement income is taxable.

You can also estimate which of the following expenses may increase:

Insurance   The loss of your employer's contribution to health and life insurance will increase your payments. Medicare, however, may offset part of this increased expense.

Medical Expenses   Although medical expenses vary from person to person, they tend to increase with age.

Expenses for Leisure Activities   With more free time, many retirees want to spend more money on leisure activities. You may want to put aside extra money for a retirement trip or other large recreational expenses.

Gifts and Contributions   Many retirees who continue to spend the same amount of money on gifts and contributions find that their spending in this area takes a larger share of their smaller income. Some retirees may want to reevaluate such spending.

Using the worksheet in Exhibit 20–3, list your present expenses and estimate what these expenses would be if you were retired.

To make a realistic comparison, list your major spending categories, starting with fixed expenses, such as rent or mortgage payments, utilities, insurance premiums, and taxes. Then list less fixed outlays—food, clothing, transportation,

EXHIBIT 20–3

Your Monthly Present
Expenses and Your
Estimated Monthly
Retirement Expenses

Item	Monthly Expenses	
	Present	**Retirement**
Fixed expenses		
Rent or mortgage payment	$_____	$_____
Taxes	_____	_____
Insurance	_____	_____
Savings	_____	_____
Debt payment	_____	_____
Other	_____	_____
Total fixed expenses	_____	_____
Variable expenses		
Food and beverages	_____	_____
Household operation and maintenance	_____	_____
Furnishings and equipment	_____	_____
Clothing	_____	_____
Personal	_____	_____
Transportation	_____	_____
Medical care	_____	_____
Recreation and education	_____	_____
Gifts and contributions	_____	_____
Other	_____	_____
Total variable expenses	_____	_____
Total expenses	_____	_____

and so on. Finally, enter miscellaneous expenditures, such as hospitals, doctors, dentists, prescriptions, entertainment, vacations, gifts, contributions, and unforeseen expenses.

However, be sure you have an emergency fund for unforeseen expenses. Even when you are living a tranquil life, the unexpected can occur.

Also be sure to build a cushion to cope with inflation. Be pessimistic in your estimates of how much the prices of goods and services will rise.

Adjust Your Expenses for Inflation

You now have a list of your probable monthly (and annual) expenses if you were to retire today. With inflation, however, those expenses will not be fixed. The possible loss of buying power due to inflation is what makes planning ahead so important. During the 1970s and the early 1980s, the cost of living increased an average of 6.1 percent a year, though the annual increase slowed to about 5 percent between 1983 and mid-1990.

To help you cope with this probable increase in your expenses, plan your retirement income needs accordingly. By using the inflation factor in the accompanying "Financial Planning Calculations" feature, you can estimate what your monthly and annual expenses will be when you retire.

• •

FINANCIAL PLANNING CALCULATIONS

Inflation Factor Table: How Much Inflation in Your Future?

Years to Retirement	Estimated Annual Rate of Inflation between Now and Retirement									
	4%	5%	6%	7%	8%	9%	10%	11%	12%	13%
5	1.2	1.3	1.3	1.4	1.5	1.5	1.6	1.7	1.8	1.8
8	1.4	1.5	1.6	1.7	1.8	2.0	2.1	2.3	2.5	2.7
10	1.5	1.6	1.8	2.0	2.2	2.4	2.6	2.8	3.1	3.4
12	1.6	1.8	2.0	2.3	2.5	2.8	3.1	3.5	3.9	4.3
15	1.8	2.1	2.4	2.8	3.2	3.6	4.2	4.8	5.5	6.3
18	2.0	2.4	2.8	3.4	4.0	4.7	5.6	6.5	7.7	9.0
20	2.2	2.7	3.2	3.9	4.7	5.6	6.7	8.1	9.6	11.5
25	2.7	3.4	4.3	5.4	6.8	8.6	10.8	13.6	17.0	21.1

First, choose from the left-hand column the approximate number of years until your retirement.

Second, choose an estimated annual rate of inflation. The rate of inflation cannot be predicted accurately and will vary from year to year. The 1990 inflation rate was about 5 percent.

Third, find the inflation factor corresponding to the number of years until your retirement and the estimated annual inflation rate. (Example: 10 years to retirement combined with a 4 percent estimated annual inflation rate yields a 1.5 inflation factor.)

Fourth, multiply the inflation factor by your estimated retirement income and your estimated retirement expenses. (Example: $6,000 × 1.6 = $9,600.)

Total annual inflated retirement income: $_____.
Total annual inflated retirement expenses: $_____.

NOTE: The above figures are from a compound interest table showing the effective yield of lump-sum investments after inflation that appeared in Charles D. Hodgman, ed., *Mathematical Tables from the Handbook of Chemistry and Physics* (Cleveland: Chemical Rubber Publishing, 1959); *Citicorp Consumer Views*, July 1985, pp. 2–3, © Citicorp, 1985.

• •

PLANNING YOUR RETIREMENT HOUSING

L.O.4
Identify your retirement housing needs.

Think about where you will want to live. If you think you will want to live in another city, it's a good idea to plan vacations in areas you might enjoy. When some area begins to appeal to you, visit it during various times of the year to experience the year-round climate. Meet the people. Check into available activities, transportation, taxes. Be honest about what you will have to give up and what you will gain.

Where you live in retirement can influence your financial needs. You must make some important decisions about whether or not to stay in your present community and about whether or not to stay in your present home. Everyone has particular needs and preferences; you are the only one who can determine the location and housing that are best for you.

Before moving, consider what this involves. Moving is expensive, and if you are not satisfied with your new location, returning to your former home may be impossible. Consider the social aspects of moving. Will you want to be near your children, other relatives, and good friends? Are you prepared for new circumstances?

Type of Housing

The housing needs of people often change as they grow older. The ease and cost of maintenance and nearness to public transportation, shopping, church, and entertainment often become more important to people when they retire.

There are many housing alternatives, and several of them were discussed in Chapter 9. Here we will examine how each of the following alternatives would meet a retiree's housing needs.

Present Home   Staying in their present home is the alternative preferred by most of the persons who are approaching retirement. A recent survey of over 5,000 men and women revealed that 92 percent of them wanted to own their home in retirement.[3]

Housesharing   You might consider sharing your home with others. Under this increasingly popular option, called housesharing or shared housing, two or more people, usually unrelated, live together in a house or a large apartment.

Accessory Apartment   An accessory apartment is a separate apartment that is built into a single-family house. Often, a basement, garage, or other extra space is converted into such an apartment. This arrangement allows you to live independently without living alone.

ECHO Unit   An elder cottage housing opportunity (ECHO) unit is a small, freestanding, home that is built on the same property as an existing residence. You might consider this alternative if you want to be near family and friends but retain the privacy of living in your own detached dwelling.

You may also want to look into some of the following alternatives. Remember to check with your local zoning board for any restrictions.

Boardinghouse/Rooming House   The accommodations in such facilities may include a bedroom, a sitting room, and a shared or private bathroom. The tenants usually eat together.

Single-Room Occupancy   Here a single room is rented at a specified price under a short-term, renewable lease. Widely varying facilities offer single-room occupancy. It is frequently found in converted hotels, schools, and factories.

Professional Companionship Arrangement   In this arrangement, you offer your services as a companion to a person who wants the help and company of another person in exchange for living accommodations.

Caretaker Arrangement   If you like caring for a home, gardening, or baby-sitting, you can reduce your costs for room and board by performing these tasks for a family whose home has an extra bedroom or apartment.

Commercial Rental   With commercial rentals, rooms are leased, usually for longer periods than the leases of single-room occupancies. Commercial rentals are found in apartment houses or auxiliary buildings of large single-family homes.

One day you may conclude that living alone in your own housing unit is becoming too difficult. You should then examine the options in supportive housing. Supportive housing refers to a variety of housing arrangements that run the gamut from board and care homes to nursing homes. Among these arrangements are the ones described below.

Board and Care Home   If you need help with food preparation and personal care but want to maintain as much independence as possible, a board and care home may be the answer.

Congregate Housing   If you are interested in living with a group that shares meals, congregate housing is an attractive option. Under this option, heavy housekeeping is provided and staff is available to organize a variety of social and recreational activities.

Continuing Care Retirement Community   This option allows you to lead an independent lifestyle in a community that offers a full range of services and activities, including health care services. A contract, which you sign upon entering the community, specifies, among other things, how much nursing care is provided.

Nursing Home   The nursing home option provides you with continuous medical care if you are frail and need nursing care services or if you have a disabling chronic condition.

Whatever your retirement housing alternative is, make sure you know what you are signing and understand what you are buying.

Caveat Emptor   Buying a piece of land for a retirement home is an exciting prospect for many people, but before you sign a contract, be sure you know what you are doing. Land fraud is a serious problem, especially in Florida, Arizona, and New Mexico. The usually high-pressure sales deal begins with a dinner invitation. You see an attractive film of the area where the parcel is supposed to be located, and then you are encouraged to close a deal with only a few dollars down and a small monthly payment. Although the interstate sale of land is regulated by laws, these laws are sometimes ignored or not adhered to strictly. The HUD Office of Interstate Land Sales Registration (OILSR), which regulates interstate land sales, receives nearly 2,500 complaints each year from people who believe they have been treated unfairly in land deals.

PLANNING YOUR RETIREMENT INCOME

L.O.5
Evaluate your planned retirement income.

Once you have determined your approximate future expenses, you must evaluate the sources and amounts of your retirement income. Possible sources of income for many retirees are social security, other public pension plans, employer pension plans, personal retirement plans, and annuities.

Social Security

Social security is the most widely used source of retirement income. Many Americans think of social security as benefiting only retired people. But it is actually a package of protection—retirement, survivors, and disability income. The package protects you and your family while you work and after you retire.

Social security should not be the only source of your retirement income, however. Jay Schabacker, president of Schabacker Investment Management, says, "Social security should be only a small part of your plan, or you won't live a very exciting retired life." And Andrew Tobias, author of *The Only Investment Guide You'll Ever Need,* adds, "Social security was never meant to be anything more than a safety net. Instead [of receiving social security as the only source of your retirement income], you should think of social security as a bonus and just keep piling up as much as you can on your own."[4] Even the Social Security Administration cautions that social security was never intended to provide 100 percent of retirement income.

When and Where to Apply   Most people can qualify for reduced social security retirement benefits at age 62; widows or widowers can begin collecting social security benefits earlier.

Three months before you retire, apply for social security benefits by telephoning the social security office at 800–2345–SSA or by visiting the nearest social security office. The payments will not start unless you apply for them. If you apply late, you risk the loss of benefits.

What Information Will You Need?   The social security office will tell you what proof you need to establish your particular case. You will generally be asked to provide the following:

- Proof of your age.
- Your social security card or your social security number.
- Your W-2 withholding forms for the past two years.
- Your marriage license if you are applying for a spouse's benefits.
- The birth certificates of your children if you are applying for their benefits.

What if You Retire at 62 instead of 65?   Your social security benefits will be reduced if you retire before age 65. Currently, there is a permanent reduction of five ninths of 1 percent for each month that you receive payments before you are 65. Thus, if you retire at 62, your monthly payments will be reduced permanently by 20 percent of what they would be if you wait until 65 to retire. If you work after 65, your benefits will be increased by one fourth of 1 percent for each month past age 65 that you delay retirement, but only up to age 70.

Estimating Your Retirement Benefits   The Social Security Administration will, upon request, provide a history of your earnings and an estimate of your future monthly benefits. To obtain this earnings and benefits statement, call 1–800–937–2000; write to Consumer Information Center, Department 55, Social Security Administration, Pueblo, CO 81009; or complete and mail Form SSA-7004, which you can obtain at any local social security office. You will receive the statement in about a month. The statement includes an estimate, in today's dollars, of how much you will get each month from social security when you retire—at age 62, 65, or 70—based on your earnings to date and your projected future earnings.

How to Become Eligible   To qualify for social security retirement benefits, you must have the required number of quarters of coverage. The number of quarters you need depends on your year of birth. Persons born after 1928 need 40 quarters to qualify for benefits.

Minimum and Maximum Benefits   Social security retirement benefits are based on earnings over the years. Currently, a worker who retired at age 65 in 1989 and always earned the maximum amount covered by Social Security receives a monthly benefit of $899, and if such a worker is married, the couple receives $1,348.

Exhibit 20–4 shows approximate monthly social security benefits for workers at age 65.

Social Security Benefits May Be Taxable   Up to one half of your social security benefits may be subject to federal income tax for any year in which your adjusted gross income plus your nontaxable interest income and one half of your social security benefits exceeds a base amount.

The base amount is $25,000 for an individual, $32,000 for a couple filing jointly, and zero for a couple filing separately if they lived together any part of the year. In addition, 13 states currently include social security benefits in income subject to their state income tax.

If You Work after You Retire   Your social security benefits may be reduced if you earn above a certain amount a year, depending on your age and on the amount you earn. You will receive all of your benefits for the year if your employment earnings do not exceed the annual exempt amount. For 1989, the annual exempt amount was $6,480 for persons under age 65 and $8,800 for persons aged 65 through 69.

Benefits Increase Automatically   Social security benefits increase automatically each January if the cost of living has increased during the preceding year. Each year, the cost of living is compared with that of the year before. If it has increased, social security benefits are increased by the same percentage.

The Future of Social Security   Some people are concerned about the future of social security. But the fact is that the social security program is on a sound financial footing. The social security taxes received in 1988 exceeded the social security benefits that were paid. Such surpluses are expected to continue until 2038, at which time a sizable reserve fund is expected to exist.

Other Public Pension Plans

Besides social security, the federal government administers several other retirement plans (for federal government and railroad employees). Employees covered under these plans are not covered by social security. The Veterans Administration provides pensions for many survivors of men and women who died while in the Armed Forces and disability pensions for eligible veterans. The Railroad Retirement System is the only retirement system administered by the federal government that covers a single private industry. Many state, county, and city governments operate retirement plans for their employees.

Employer Pension Plans

Another source of retirement income for you may be the pension plan offered by your company. With employer plans, your employer contributes to your retirement benefits—and sometimes you contribute too. Contributions and earnings on those contributions accumulate tax free until you receive them.

Since private pension plans vary, you should go to your firm's personnel office or union office to find out (1) when you become eligible for pension benefits and

EXHIBIT 20–4   Approximate Monthly Retirement Benefits If Worker Retires at Normal Retirement Age and Had Steady Lifetime Earnings

The following table shows benefits payable to the worker and spouse. To use the table, find your age and the earnings closest to your earnings in 1988. These figures will give you an estimate of the amount of your retirement benefits at various ages.

Worker's Age in 1989	Worker's Family	Retired Worker's Earnings in 1988							
		$10,000	$15,000	$20,000	$25,000	$30,000	$35,000	$40,000	$45,000 or More*
25	Retired worker only†	$ 634	$ 817	$ 999	$ 1,173	$ 1,259	$ 1,344	$ 1,430	$ 1,516
	Worker and spouse†	951	1,225	1,498	1,759	1,888	2,016	2,145	2,274
	Final year earnings‡	13,700	20,550	27,400	34,250	41,100	47,950	54,800	61,650
	Replacement rate§	56%	48%	44%	41%	37%	34%	31%	30%
35	Retired worker only†	586	755	924	1,086	1,165	1,244	1,323	1,403
	Worker and spouse†	879	1,132	1,386	1,629	1,747	1,866	1,984	2,104
	Final year earnings‡	12,700	19,050	25,400	31,750	38,100	44,450	50,800	57,150
	Replacement rate§	55%	48%	44%	41%	37%	34%	31%	29%
45	Retired worker only†	537	690	844	996	1,068	1,135	1,199	1,257
	Worker and spouse†	805	1,035	1,266	1,494	1,602	1,702	1,798	1,885
	Final year earnings‡	11,700	17,550	23,400	29,250	35,100	40,950	46,800	52,650
	Replacement rate§	55%	47%	43%	41%	37%	33%	31%	29%
55	Retired worker only†	487	626	765	897	953	994	1,030	1,063
	Worker and spouse†	730	939	1,147	1,345	1,429	1,491	1,545	1,594
	Final year earnings‡	10,700	16,050	21,400	26,750	32,100	37,450	42,800	48,150
	Replacement rate§	55%	47%	43%	40%	36%	32%	29%	26%
65	Retired worker only†	438	563	688	800	841	865	884	899
	Worker and spouse†	657	844	1,032	1,200	1,261	1,297	1,326	1,348
	Final year earnings‡	10,000	15,000	20,000	25,000	30,000	35,000	40,000	45,000
	Replacement rate§	53%	43%	41%	38%	34%	30%	27%	24%

*Earnings equal the social security wage base from age 22 through 1988.

†Spouse is assumed to be the same age as the worker. Spouse may qualify for a higher retirement benefit based on his or her own work record.

‡Worker's earnings in the year before retirement.

§Replacement rates are shown for retired worker only.

NOTE: The accuracy of these estimates depends on the pattern of the worker's actual past earnings and on his or her earnings in the future. It is assumed that there are no future benefit increases after January 1989 and no average wage increases after 1987. To reflect expected real wage gains, estimated benefits are adjusted upward by 1 percent for each year that the year of initial eligibility exceeds 1989.

SOURCE: *Retirement* (Washington, D.C.: Social Security Administration, 1989), pp. 10–11.

PERSONAL FINANCE JOURNAL
Social Security Is Not Just for the Retired or Disabled

Social Security Checks for Students

Social security checks can be paid to a young unmarried person when a parent insured under social security dies or receives disability or retirement benefits. The son or daughter is eligible if he or she is

Under 18—whether or not in school.
Under 19—and attending secondary school (high school in most cases) full-time.
Any age—if severely disabled before age 22.

Who Is a "Full-Time Student"?

You are a full-time student if you attend high school, junior high, or elementary school, provided

The school considers you in full-time attendance.
You are enrolled for at least 20 hours a week in a course of study lasting at least 13 weeks.

When Checks Can Be Paid

Social security checks can be paid for all months you attend high school (or other approved school) up to the month you reach age 19. In some cases, payment can continue longer—generally until completion of the school year or for two months after the month you are 19, whichever comes first.

You cannot get student checks if you work and your employer asked or required you to attend school and pays you for doing so. Nor can you receive checks if you are imprisoned for conviction of a felony.

If You Will Soon Be 18

If you now get social security checks as a child under 18, you will receive a notice a few months before your 18th birthday. It will explain what to do to have your benefits continue if you have not yet completed high school.

You must apply for social security if you are a high school student who first becomes eligible for benefits between 18 and 19. This may be when a parent starts receiving retirement or disability checks, or dies. Call any social security office for more information.

source: Social Security Administration, 1990.

(2) what benefits you will be entitled to. Most employer plans are defined-benefit or defined-contribution plans.

A **defined-contribution plan** has an individual account for each employee; therefore, these plans are sometimes called individual account plans. The plan document describes the amount that the employer will contribute, but it does not promise any particular benefit. When a plan participant retires or otherwise becomes eligible for benefits, the benefit is the total amount in the participant's account, including past investment earnings on amounts put into the account.

Defined-contribution plans include

1. Money-purchase pension plans, in which your employer promises to set aside a certain amount for you each year, generally a percentage of your earnings.
2. Stock bonus plans, in which your employer's contribution is used to buy stock in your company for you. The stock is usually held in trust until you retire, when you can receive your shares or sell them at their fair market value.
3. Profit sharing plans, in which your employer's contribution depends on the company's profits.
4. Salary reduction or 401(k) plans. Under a **401(k) plan,** your employer makes nontaxable contributions to the plan for your benefit and reduces your salary by

the same amounts. If your employer is a tax-exempt institution such as a hospital, university, or museum, the salary reduction plan is called a Section 403(b) plan. These plans are often referred to as tax-sheltered annuity (TSA) plans.

The Tax Reform Act of 1986 retains the $30,000 cap on annual contributions for money-purchase pension plans, stock bonus plans, and profit sharing plans. Eventually, the annual limit on such plans will increase in response to inflation.

The tax act reduced from $30,000 to $7,627 (in 1989) the maximum annual amount that an employee could defer for a 401(k) plan. The maximum annual amount that you may contribute to a 403(b) plan now ranges from $9,500 up to $12,500 if you have worked for the same employer for 15 years or more. The maximum can be higher in plans to which your employer contributes.

Under some circumstances, you are allowed to make withdrawals from a 401(k) plan before age 59½ without penalty. In addition, lump-sum distributions that you receive from your 401(k) are eligible for five-year income averaging if you have been a participant in the plan for at least five years.

An Example: How Funds Accumulate   All earnings in a TSA grow without current federal taxation. The fact that your dollars are saved on a pretax basis while your earnings grow tax deferred has a dynamic effect on the growth of your funds.

Assume that you are in the 28 percent tax bracket. In that case, on gross earnings of $100, only $72 is available for an after-tax savings account whose interest is taxable. However, the entire $100 is available for a tax-sheltered savings account. Assuming that both of these accounts pay 8 percent interest and that these amounts—$72 and $100, respectively—are deposited in them each month, here is what their value would be in future years:

Year	After Tax* $72/Month at 8% Taxable Interest	Pretax $100/Month at 8% Tax Deferred
1	$ 891	$ 1,253
3	2,836	4,081
5	5,017	7,397
10	11,703	18,417
15	20,614	34,835
20	32,492	59,295
25	48,324	95,737
30	69,424	150,030
35	97,548	230,918
		$133,370 more

*Assumes 28 percent federal tax bracket.

How does saving in a TSA compare to saving in a regular savings account? The illustration used here shows that a TSA may actually allow you to increase your spendable income. Assuming that you are saving $100 per pay period and are in the 28 percent tax bracket, here are the results of the two methods:

After-Tax Saving Method—Saving $100 per Pay

Gross Pay	Tax	Net Pay	After-Tax Savings	Spendable Income
$1,000	$280	$720	$100	$620

Saving with a Tax-Sheltered Annuity—Saving $100 per Pay

Gross Pay	TSA	Net Pay	Tax	Spendable Income
$1,000	$100	$900	$252	$648

If you are not currently saving in a 401(k) or 403(b) plan, consider the following illustration. Note that if you save $100 in a TSA, your spendable income decreases by only $72 ($720 − $648).

Not Currently Saving

Gross Pay	Tax	Net Pay	Savings	Spendable Income
$1,000	$280	$720	0	$720

Saving $100 in a Tax-Sheltered Annuity

Gross Pay	TSA	Taxable Income	Tax	Spendable Income
$1,000	$100	$900	$252	$648

The accompanying "Financial Planning in Action" feature tells how 401(k) plans have grown into an enormously popular employee benefit.

What happens to your benefits under an employer pension plan if you change jobs? One of the most important aspects of such plans is vesting. **Vesting** is your right to at least a portion of the benefits you have accrued under an employer pension plan (within certain limits) even if you leave the employer before you retire.

In a **defined-benefit plan,** the plan document specifies the benefits promised to the employee at the normal retirement age. The plan itself does not specify how much the employer must contribute annually. The plan's actuary determines the annual employer contribution required so that the plan fund will be sufficient to pay the promised benefits as each participant retires. If the fund is inadequate, the employer must make additional contributions. Because of their actuarial aspects, defined-benefit plans tend to be more complicated and more expensive to administer than defined-contribution plans.

Some pension plans allow portability. This enables you to carry earned benefits from one employer's pension plan to another employer's pension plan when you change jobs.

The Employee Retirement Income Security Act of 1974 (ERISA) sets minimum standards for pension plans in private industry and protects more than 50 million workers.

Use the checklist in Exhibit 20–5 to help you determine what your pension plan provides and requires.

FINANCIAL PLANNING IN ACTION

The 401(k) Grows Popular as a Nest for Retirement Eggs

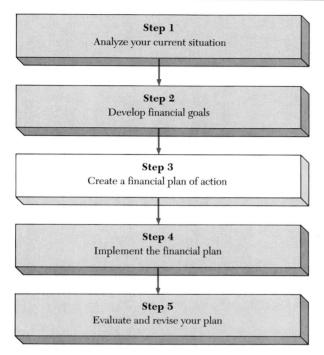

Step 1
Analyze your current situation

Step 2
Develop financial goals

Step 3
Create a financial plan of action

Step 4
Implement the financial plan

Step 5
Evaluate and revise your plan

Despite the handicap of being named after an obscure section of the Internal Revenue Code, 401(k) plans for retirement saving have grown into an enormously popular employee benefit.

Nine out of 10 Fortune 1000 companies sponsor 401(k)s or similar tax-deferral plans, often in addition to regular pensions. Many smaller companies are adopting such plans as their main pension program. The 401(k)s allow employees to defer taxes on part of their salaries, generally until retirement, when the tax bite is less.

More than $100 billion has piled up in these accounts, some of which were nearly a decade old in 1989. In 1986, active accounts held an average of almost $22,000.

"If you take a typical person who contributes regularly to a 401(k) over a long career, 35 years from now he or she will have enough money to buy an annuity that will far outshine social security and be far bigger than any pension," says John J. Mulligan, Jr., vice president of Boston's State Street Bank and Trust Company. "It's a big, big nest egg."

But with a 401(k) plan, the workers—not their bosses—bear all of the investment risk. This can be a heavy burden for inexperienced investors. Here's a rundown on how 401(k) plans work and how to get the most out of them.

What Is a 401(k)?

A 401(k) is a retirement plan that allows you to defer paying taxes on a part of your salary—as much as $7,627 in salary in 1989—if it is contributed to a special account set up by your company. Taxes aren't paid on the earnings until the money is withdrawn, usually at retirement. Companies typically set ceilings on contributions, say 6 percent of salary. In addition to the tax-deferred contributions, some 401(k) plans allow contributions of after-tax dollars, on which only earnings are sheltered.

How Do I Get My Money Out?

You can start making 401(k) withdrawals without penalty after age 59½—earlier than that if you are permanently disabled. You must start withdrawing your 401(k) money by age 70½. Employees can take a lump-sum distribution, but many 401(k) plans also provide for installment payments or the purchase of an annuity. These withdrawals are subject to regular income tax.

If you leave for another job, you can transfer your 401(k) balance to your new company if that company accepts rollovers. You can also move your balance into an IRA. In many cases, you can leave it at your old company until you are ready to collect it.

Can I Touch My 401(k) Money before Retiring?

Yes, either by withdrawals, which are taxed, or by loans, which aren't. The Internal Revenue Service recently tightened guidelines that allow the withdrawal of contributions to 401(k) plans in certain "hardship" cases. The main hardships are paying for medical emergencies, college tuition, or a principal residence for you and your dependents. Financial planners warn, however, that dipping into 401(k) funds for short-term expenses can put your retirement nest egg at risk.

SOURCE: Condensed from James A. White, "The "401(k) Grows Popular as a Nest for Retirement Eggs," *The Wall Street Journal,* June 21, 1989, p. C1.

EXHIBIT 20–5
Know Your Pension Plan
Checklist

A. Plan Type Checklist

My plan is a

Defined-benefit plan.

☐ Integrated with social security
☐ Nonintegrated

Defined-contribution plan.

☐ Integrated with social security
☐ Nonintegrated

My social security benefit

☐ Will not be deducted from my plan benefit.
☐ Will be deducted from my plan benefit to the extent of ____ percent of the social security benefit I am due to receive at retirement.

B. Contributions Checklist

My pension plan is financed by

☐ Employer contributions only.
☐ Employer and employee contributions.
☐ Union dues and assessments.

I contribute to my pension plan at the rate of $_____ per ☐ month ☐ week ☐ hour or _____ percent of my compensation.

C. Vesting Checklist

My plan provides

☐ Full and immediate vesting.
☐ Cliff vesting.
☐ Graded vesting.
☐ Rule-of-45 vesting.
☐ Other (specify).

I need ____ more years of service to be fully vested.

D. Credited Service Checklist

I will have a year of service under my pension plan

☐ If I work ____ hours in a 12-consecutive-month period.
☐ If I meet other requirements (specify).

The plan year (12-month period for which plan records are kept) ends on _____ of each year.
I will be credited for work performed

☐ Before I became a participant in the plan.
☐ After the plan's normal retirement age.

As of now, _____[date], I have earned _____ years of service toward my pension.
My plan's break-in-service rules are as follows:

E. Retirement Benefit Checklist

I may begin to receive full normal retirement benefits at age _____.
Working beyond the normal retirement age ☐ will ☐ will not increase the pension that will be paid to me when I retire.
I may retire at age ____ if I have completed _____ years of service. Apart from the age requirement,

EXHIBIT 20–5
Concluded

I need _____ more years of service to be eligible for early retirement benefits.
The amount of my normal retirement benefit is computed as follows:

The amount of my early retirement benefit is computed as follows:

My retirement benefit will be

☐ Paid monthly for life.
☐ Paid to me in a lump sum.
☐ Adjusted to the cost of living.
☐ Paid to my survivor in the event of my death (see "Survivors' Benefit Checklist" below).

F. Disability Benefit Checklist

My plan ☐ does ☐ does not provide disability benefits.
My plan defines the term *disability* as follows:

To be eligible for disability retirement benefits, I must be _____ years old and must have _____ years of service.
A determination as to whether my condition meets my plan's definition of disability is made by

☐ A doctor chosen by me.
☐ A doctor designated by the plan administrator.
☐ The Social Security Administration, in deciding that I qualify for social security disability benefits.

I must send my application for disability retirement benefits to _____
within _____ months after I stop working.
If I qualify for disability benefits, I will continue to receive benefits

☐ For life, if I remain disabled.
☐ Until I return to my former job.
☐ As long as I am eligible for social security disability benefits.

G. Survivors' Benefit Checklist

My pension plan ☐ provides ☐ does not provide a joint and survivor option or a similar provision for death benefits.
My spouse and I ☐ have ☐ have not rejected in writing the joint and survivor option.
Electing the joint and survivor option will reduce my pension benefit to _____.
My survivor will receive _____ per month for life if the following conditions are met (specify):

H. Plan Termination Checklist

My benefits ☐ are ☐ are not insured by the Pension Benefits Guaranty Corporation.

I. Benefit Application Checklist

My employer ☐ will ☐ will not automatically submit my pension application for me.
I must apply for my pension benefits ☐ on a special form that I get from _____
within _____ months ☐ before ☐ after I retire.
My application for pension benefits should be sent to _____.
I must furnish the following documents when applying for my pension benefits:

If my application for pension benefits is denied, I may appeal in writing to _____
_____ within _____ days.

J. Suspension of Benefits Checklist

☐ I am covered by a single-employer plan or by a plan involving more than one employer that does not meet ERISA's definition of a multiemployer plan.
☐ I am covered by a multiemployer plan, as that term is defined in ERISA.

source: *Know Your Pension Plan* (Washington, D.C.: U.S. Department of Labor, 1986), pp. 5–10.

In addition to the retirement plans offered by social security, other public pension plans, and employer pension plans, many individuals have set up personal retirement plans.

Personal Retirement Plans

The two most popular personal retirement plans are individual retirement accounts (IRAs) and Keogh accounts.

Individual Retirement Accounts (IRAs) The **individual retirement account (IRA),** which entails the establishment of a trust or a custodial account, was by far the most popular type of personal retirement plan until the Tax Reform Act of 1986 imposed new rules on IRA contributions.

Before the passage of that act, a working person could make a tax-deductible contribution of up to $2,000 a year to an IRA and a nonworking spouse could chip in $250. The IRA's earnings were not taxed until they were withdrawn.

The new tax act makes several important changes in the IRA rules. The rules remain unchanged for persons not covered by company pension plans. But if a pension plan at work covers you or your spouse, the IRA deduction may be reduced or eliminated for both of you. The new act does not affect your IRA deduction if you are covered by a pension plan and have adjusted gross income of less than $25,000 ($40,000 for joint filers). But you are allowed only a partial deduction if you earn between $40,000 and $50,000 on a joint return or between $25,000 and $35,000 on a single return. Beyond those income limits, the IRA deduction is completely eliminated.

However, whether or not you are covered by a pension plan, you can still make nondeductible IRA contributions and all of the income your IRA earns will compound tax deferred until you withdraw money from the IRA. Remember, the biggest benefit of an IRA lies in its tax-deferred earnings growth, and the longer the money accumulates tax deferred, the bigger the benefit.

Exhibit 20–6 shows the power of tax-deferred compounding of earnings—an important advantage offered by an IRA. Consider how compounded earnings transformed the lives of Abe and Ben.

As the exhibit shows, Abe regularly invested $2,000 a year in an IRA for 10 years—from age 25 to age 35. Then Abe sat back and let compounding work its magic. Ben started making regular $2,000 annual contributions at age 35 and contributed for 30 years, until age 65. As you can see, Abe retired with a much larger nest egg—over $192,000 more than Ben's. Moral? Get an early start on your plan for retirement.

A Comparison: 401(k) Contributions versus IRA Contributions How do 401(k) contributions compare with IRA contributions? As shown in Exhibit 20–7, almost all of the advantages are with 401(k) contributions.[5]

Simplified Employee Pension Plans–IRA (SEP–IRA) SEP plans are nothing more than individual retirement accounts funded by an employer. Each employee sets up an IRA account at a bank or a brokerage house. Then the employer makes an annual contribution of up to 15 percent of the employee's salary or $30,000, whichever is less.

EXHIBIT 20–6   Tackling the Trade-Offs—Saving Now versus Saving Later

Saver Abe				Saver Ben			
Age	**Years**	**Contributions**	**Year-End Value**	**Age**	**Years**	**Contributions**	**Year-End Value**
25	1	$2,000	$ 2,188	25	1	$ 0	$ 0
26	2	2,000	4,580	26	2	0	0
27	3	2,000	7,198	27	3	0	0
28	4	2,000	10,061	28	4	0	0
29	5	2,000	13,192	29	5	0	0
30	6	2,000	16,617	30	6	0	0
31	7	2,000	20,363	31	7	0	0
32	8	2,000	24,461	32	8	0	0
33	9	2,000	28,944	33	9	0	0
34	10	2,000	33,846	34	10	0	0
35	11	0	40,494	35	11	2,000	2,188
36	12	0	37,021	36	12	2,000	4,580
37	13	0	44,293	37	13	2,000	7,198
38	14	0	48,448	38	14	2,000	10,061
39	15	0	52,992	39	15	2,000	13,192
40	16	0	57,963	40	16	2,000	16,617
41	17	0	63,401	41	17	2,000	20,363
42	18	0	69,348	42	18	2,000	24,461
43	19	0	75,854	43	19	2,000	28,944
44	20	0	82,969	44	20	2,000	33,846
45	21	0	90,752	45	21	2,000	39,209
46	22	0	99,265	46	22	2,000	45,075
47	23	0	108,577	47	23	2,000	51,490
48	24	0	118,763	48	24	2,000	58,508
49	25	0	129,903	49	25	2,000	66,184
50	26	0	142,089	50	26	2,000	74,580
51	27	0	155,418	51	27	2,000	83,764
52	28	0	169,997	52	28	2,000	93,809
53	29	0	185,944	53	29	2,000	104,797
54	30	0	203,387	54	30	2,000	116,815
55	31	0	222,466	55	31	2,000	129,961
56	32	0	243,335	56	32	2,000	144,340
57	33	0	266,162	57	33	2,000	160,068
58	34	0	291,129	58	34	2,000	177,271
59	35	0	318,439	59	35	2,000	196,088
60	36	0	348,311	60	36	2,000	216,670
61	37	0	380,985	61	37	2,000	239,182
62	38	0	416,724	62	38	2,000	263,807
63	39	0	455,816	63	39	2,000	290,741
64	40	0	498,574	64	40	2,000	320,202
65	41	0	545,344	65	41	2,000	352,427

Value at retirement°	$545,344	
Less total contributions	$ 20,000	
Net earnings	$525,344	

Value at retirement°	$352,427	
Less total contributions	$ 62,000	
Net earnings	$290,427	

°The table assumes a 9 percent fixed rate of return, compounded monthly, and no fluctuation of the principal. Distributions from an IRA are subject to ordinary income taxes when withdrawn and may be subject to other limitations under IRA rules.

SOURCE: *Franklin Investor,* Franklin Distributors, Inc., San Mateo, CA 94404, January 1989, n.p.

EXHIBIT 20–7   401(k) or IRA—Which Is Better?

This exhibit demonstrates how 401(k) contributions by employees can be more advantageous than IRA contributions.

401(k) Plans	**IRA**
Employers usually match employee contributions, so funds accumulate rapidly.	Contributions are not matched.
Salary deferrals reduce withholding and W-2 earnings immediately.	Contributions are taxed first and then qualify for a tax deduction.
Salary deferrals are made through affordable payroll deduction.	Contributions are usually made in single deposits at tax time, limiting affordability to available funds.
$7,627 limit	$2,000 limit
Available regardless of income level or participation in other retirement programs.	May be unavailable if there is participation in other retirement programs or if income level exceeds a certain amount.
Permanent insurance protection can be provided.	Insurance not allowed.
May qualify for favorable tax treatment after age 59½.	Distributions taxed at ordinary income rates.
Withdrawals because of financial hardship allowed without penalty.	Withdrawals prior to age 59½ are subject to penalty tax.

The SEP–IRA is the simplest type of retirement plan if you are fully or partially self-employed. Your contributions, which can vary from year to year, are tax deductible, and earnings accumulate on a tax-deferred basis. A SEP–IRA has no IRS filing requirements, so there is a minimum of paperwork.

Your investment opportunities for IRA funds are not limited to savings accounts and certificates of deposit. You can put your IRA funds in many kinds of investments—mutual funds, annuities, stocks, bonds, U.S. minted gold and silver coins, real estate, and so forth. Only investments in life insurance, precious metals, collectibles, and securities bought on margin are forbidden.

IRA Withdrawals   When you retire, you will be able to withdraw your IRA in a lump sum, withdraw it in installments over your life expectancy, or place it in an annuity that guarantees payments over your lifetime. If you take the lump sum, the entire amount will be taxable as ordinary income and the only tax break you will have is standard five-year income averaging. IRA withdrawals made before age 59½ are now subject to a 10 percent tax in addition to ordinary income tax, unless the participant dies or is disabled. You can avoid this tax if you roll over your IRA.

The Rollover IRA Strategy   If you change jobs or if you retire before age 59½, one of your most attractive options for managing your retirement plan distribution will be the rollover IRA. This option enables you to avoid the early distribution penalty on pre-59½ distributions.

Keogh Plans   A **Keogh plan,** also known as an H.R.10 plan or as a self-employed retirement plan, is a qualified pension plan that has been developed for self-employed individuals and their employees. Generally, Keogh plans must not discriminate in favor of a self-employed person or any employee. Both defined-contribution and defined-benefit Keogh plans have tax-deductible contribution

EXHIBIT 20–8		Summary of Important Features of Various Retirement Savings/Investment Plans	
Type of Plan	**Annual Maximum Allowed**	**Available for**	**Tax Deductible?**
IRA	$ 2,000 $ 2,250	Everyone under age 70½ with earnings	Deductible amount depends on filing status, adjusted gross income, and current plan participation status

Rollover IRA	Eligible amounts distributed from an employer plan	Any person who is receiving a payout of retirement funds because
		  The person is retiring
		  The person is the beneficiary of a deceased spouse's retirement plan
		  The person has become disabled
		  The person's employer is terminating the retirement plan
		  The person is leaving to take a new job
			Simply continues the tax shelter of the amount rolled into the IRA

SEP plans	$30,000	Any employer, whether a corporation, a partnership, or a sole proprietorship	Yes
Keogh (profit sharing and/or money-purchase plans)	$30,000	Self-employed persons	Yes
Qualified plans (profit sharing, money-purchase, target benefit, 401(k), 403(b), and defined-benefit plans)	Varies—depends on type of plan established by the employer	Employers, small and large, incorporated or unincorporated	Yes

limits, and other restrictions also apply to Keogh plans. Therefore, you should obtain professional tax advice before using this type of retirement plan. The new tax act did not change the rules for Keogh plans.

Whether you have an employer pension plan or personal retirement plans, you must start withdrawing at age 70½ or the IRS will charge you a penalty.

Exhibit 20–8 summarizes the important features of IRA, rollover IRA, SEP, Keogh, and various qualified plans.

Annuities

In Chapter 14, you learned what an annuity is and how annuities provide lifelong security. You can outlive the proceeds of your IRA, your Keogh plan, or your investments, but an **annuity** provides guaranteed income for life.

You can buy an annuity as your individual retirement account—with the proceeds of an IRA or a company pension—or as supplemental retirement income. You can buy an annuity with a single payment or with periodic payments. You can buy an annuity that will begin payouts immediately, or, as is more common, you can buy one that will begin payouts at a later date.

To the extent that annuity payments exceed your premiums, these payments are taxed as ordinary income as you receive them, but earned interest on annuities accumulates tax free until the payments begin. Annuities may be fixed, providing a specific income for life, or they may be variable, with payouts above a guaranteed minimum level dependent on investment return. Either way, the rate of return on annuities is often pegged to market rates.

Types of Annuities   Immediate annuities are generally purchased by people of retirement age. Such annuities provide income payments at once. They are usually purchased with a lump-sum payment.

With deferred annuities, income payments start at some future date. Interest builds up on the money you deposit. Such annuities are often used by younger people to save money toward retirement.

A *deferred annuity* purchased with a lump sum is known as a single-premium deferred annuity. In recent years, such annuities have been popular because of the tax-free buildup during the accumulation period.

If you are buying a deferred annuity, you may wish to obtain a contract that permits flexible premiums. With such an annuity, your contributions may vary from year to year. An annuity of this kind can be used to provide funds for an IRA. Most of the deferred annuities sold today are either single-premium or flexible premium annuities.

The cash value of your life insurance policy may be converted to an annuity. If you are over 65 and your children have completed their education and are financially self-sufficient, you may feel that you no longer need all of your life insurance coverage. An option in your life insurance policy lets you convert its cash value to a lifetime income.

Options in Annuities

You can decide on the terms under which your annuity pays off for you and your family. The major options are as follows.

Straight Life Annuity   With a straight life annuity, also called a pure annuity, you receive an income for the rest of your life, but no payments are made to anyone after your death. This type of annuity provides the largest amount of income per dollar of purchase money. It is recommended for a person who needs as much annuity income as possible and either has no dependents or has taken care of them by other means.

Life Annuity with Installments Certain   You receive an income for the rest of your life. If you die within a certain period after you start receiving income, usually 10 or 20 years, your beneficiary receives regular payments for the balance of that period.

Installment Refund Annuity   You receive an income for the rest of your life. However, if you die before receiving as much money as you paid in, your beneficiary receives regular income until the total payments equal that amount.

Which Annuity Option Is the Best?

The straight life annuity gives more income per dollar of outlay than any other type. But its payments stop when you die, whether that's a month or many years after the payout begins.

Should you get an annuity with a guaranteed return? There are differences of opinion. Some experts argue that it is a mistake to diminish your monthly income just to make sure that your money is returned to your survivors. Some suggest that if you want to assure that your spouse or someone else continues to receive annuity income after your death, you might choose the joint and survivor annuity. Such an annuity pays its installments until the death of the last designated survivor.

There is still another choice that you must make: how your annuity premiums are to be invested.

With a fixed dollar annuity, the money you pay is invested in bonds and mortgages that have a guaranteed return. With such an annuity, you are guaranteed a fixed amount each payout period.

With a variable annuity, the money you pay is generally invested in common stocks or other equities. The income you receive will depend on the investment results.

An annuity guarantees lifetime income, but you have a choice about the form it will take. Discuss all of the possible options with your insurance agent.

The costs, fees, and other features of annuities differ from policy to policy. Ask about sales and administrative charges, purchase and withdrawal fees, and interest rate guarantees.

Will You Have Enough Money during Retirement?

Now that you have reviewed all the possible sources of your retirement income, estimate what your annual retirement income will be. Don't forget to inflate incomes or investments that increase with the cost of living (such as social security) to what they will be when you retire. (Use the inflation factor table presented earlier in this chapter.)

Now compare your total estimated retirement income with your total inflated retirement expenses, as figured earlier. If your estimated income exceeds your estimated expenses and a large portion of your planned income will automatically increase with the cost of living during your retirement, you are in good shape. (You should evaluate your plans every few years between now and retirement to be sure your planned income is still adequate to meet your planned expenses.)

If, however, your planned retirement income is less than your estimated retirement expenses, now is the time to take action that will increase your retirement income. Also, if a large portion of your retirement income is fixed and will not increase with inflation, you should make plans for a much larger retirement income to meet your inflating expenses during retirement.

Investing for Retirement

The guaranteed income part of your retirement fund consists of money paid into lower-yield, very safe forms of investment. This part of your fund may already be taken care of through social security or retirement plans, discussed earlier. If you would like to add to this part, other low-risk investments, as discussed in previous chapters, are savings accounts and certificates of deposit, U.S. savings bonds, money market securities, municipal and corporate bonds, and real estate.

LIVING ON YOUR RETIREMENT INCOME

L.O.6
Develop a balanced budget based on your retirement income.

As you planned your retirement, you estimated a budget or spending plan. Now you may find that your actual expenses at retirement are higher than you anticipated.

The first step in stretching your retirement income is to make sure you are receiving all of the income to which you are entitled. Examine the possible sources of retirement income mentioned earlier to see whether there are more programs or additional benefits that you could qualify for. What assets or valuables could you use as a cash or income source?

To stay within your income, you may also need to make some changes in your spending plans. For example, you could use your skills and time instead of your money. There are probably many things that you could do yourself instead of paying someone else to do them. Take advantage of free and low-cost recreation, such as walks, picnics, public parks, lectures, museums, libraries, art galleries, art fairs, gardening, and church and club programs.

Tax Advantages

Be sure to take advantage of all the tax savings given to retirees. You may need to file a quarterly estimated income tax return beginning with the first quarter of your first year of retirement. For more information, ask your local IRS for a free copy of *Tax Benefits for Older Americans*. If you have any questions about your taxes, get help from someone at the IRS.

Working during Retirement

You may want to work part-time or start a new part-time career after you retire. Retirement work can provide you with a greater sense of usefulness, involvement, and self-worth and may be the ideal way to add to your retirement income. You may want to pursue a personal interest or hobby, or you can contact your state or local agency on aging for information on employment opportunities for retirees.

If you decide to work part-time after you retire, you should be aware of how your earnings will affect your social security income. As long as you do not earn more than the annually exempt amount, your social security payments will not be affected. But if you earn more than the annual exempt amount, your social security payments will be reduced. Check with your local social security office for the latest information.

Dipping into Your Nest Egg

Should you draw down your savings? The answer depends on your financial circumstances, your age, and how much you want to leave to your heirs. Your savings may be large enough to allow you to live comfortably on the interest alone. Or you may need to make regular withdrawals to help finance your retirement. Dipping into savings isn't wrong, but you must do so with caution.

How long would your savings last if you invaded them for monthly income? If you have $10,000 in savings that earn 5.5 percent interest, compounded quarterly, you could take out $68 every month for 20 years before reducing this nest egg to zero. If you have $40,000, you could collect $224 every month for 30 years before exhausting your nest egg. For different possibilities, see Exhibit 20–9.

Exhibit 20–10 summarizes major sources of retirement income and their advantages and disadvantages.

EXHIBIT 20–9
Dipping into Your
Nest Egg

Starting with a nest egg of . . . ,	. . . you can reduce the nest egg to zero by withdrawing this much each month for the stated number of years . . .					. . . or you can withdraw this much each month and leave the nest egg intact.
	10 Yrs.	15 Yrs.	20 Yrs.	25 Yrs.	30 Yrs.	
$ 10,000	$ 107	$ 81	$ 68	$ 61	$ 56	$ 46
15,000	161	121	102	91	84	69
20,000	215	162	136	121	112	92
25,000	269	202	170	152	140	115
30,000	322	243	204	182	168	138
40,000	430	323	272	243	224	184
50,000	537	404	340	304	281	230
60,000	645	485	408	364	337	276
80,000	859	647	544	486	449	368
100,000	1,074	808	680	607	561	460

NOTE: Based on an interest rate of 5.5 percent per year, compounded quarterly.
SOURCE: Select Committee on Aging, House of Representatives, 1989.

EXHIBIT 20–10   Major Sources of Retirement Income: Advantages and Disadvantages

Source	Advantages	Disadvantages
Social Security		
In planning	Forced savings Portable from job to job Cost shared with employer	Increasing economic pressure on the system as U.S. population ages
At retirement	Inflation-adjusted survivorship rights	Minimum retirement age specified Earned income partially offsets benefits
Employee Pension Plans		
In planning	Forced savings Cost shared or fully covered by employer	May not be portable *not true — have control* No control over how funds are managed
At retirement	Survivorship rights	Cost-of-living increases may not be provided on a regular basis *— true of defined ben. plan.*
Individual Saving and Investing (Including Housing, IRA, and Keogh Plans)		
In planning	Current tax savings (e.g., IRAs) Easily incorporated into family (ie., housing) Portable Control management of funds	Current needs compete with future needs Penalty for early withdrawal (IRAs and Keoghs)
At retirement	Inflation resistant Can usually use as much of funds as you wish, when you wish	Some sources taxable Mandatory minimum withdrawal restrictions (IRAs and Keoghs)
Postretirement Employment		
In planning	Special earning skills can be used as they are developed	Technology and skills needed to keep up may change rapidly
At retirement	Inflation resistant	Ill health can mean loss of this income source

SUMMARY

L.O.1
Recognize the importance of retirement planning.

Retirement planning is important because you will probably spend many years in retirement; social security and a private pension may be insufficient to cover the cost of living; and inflation may erode the purchasing power of your retirement savings.

L.O.2
Analyze your current assets and liabilities for retirement.

Analyze your current assets (everything you own) and your current liabilities (everything you owe). The difference between your assets and your liabilities is your net worth. Review your assets to make sure they are suitable for retirement.

L.O.3
Estimate your retirement spending needs.

The spending patterns of retirees change, so it is impossible to predict the exact amount of money you will need in retirement. However, you can estimate your expenses. Some of those expenses will increase; others will decrease.

L.O.4
Identify your retirement housing needs.

Where you live in retirement can influence your financial needs. You are the only one who can determine the location and housing that are best for you. The types of housing available to retirees include their present homes, housesharing, accessory apartment, ECHO unit, boarding house, single-room occupancy, professional companionship agreement, caretaker arrangement, commercial rental, and supportive housing. Each of these living arrangements has its advantages and disadvantages.

L.O.5
Evaluate your planned retirement income.

Estimate your retirement expenses, and adjust those expenses for inflation, using the appropriate inflation factor.
Your possible sources of income during retirement include social security, other public pension plans, employer pension plans, personal retirement plans, and annuities.

L.O.6
Develop a balanced budget based on your retirement income.

Compare your total estimated retirement income with your total inflated retirement expenses. If your income approximates your expenses, you are in good shape; if not, determine additional income needs and sources.

GLOSSARY

Annuity   A contract that provides an income for life.

Defined-benefit plan   A plan that specifies the benefits that the employee will receive at retirement.

Defined-contribution plan   A plan—profit sharing, money purchase, Keogh, or 401(k)—in which an individual account is provided for each participant.

401(k) plan   A plan under which employees can defer current taxation on a portion of their salary.

Individual retirement account (IRA)   A special account in which you set aside a portion of your income; taxes are not paid on the principal or interest until money is withdrawn from the account.

Keogh plan   A plan in which tax-deductible contributions fund the retirement of self-employed persons and their employees.

Reverse annuity mortgage   A mortgage in which the lender uses your house as collateral to buy annuity for you from a life insurance company.

Vesting   Your right to at least a portion of the benefits you have accrued under an employer pension plan even if you leave the employer before you retire.

DISCUSSION QUESTIONS

L.O.1   1.   Give three reasons why it is important to plan for your retirement.

L.O.2   2.   What factors will you consider in reviewing your assets? What determines the suitability of those assets for retirement?

L.O.3   3.   What expenses are likely to increase and decrease during retirement? Why?

L.O.4   4.   What factors will you consider in estimating your retirement living needs? What types of housing are available to retirees? Assess the advantages and disadvantages of these housing types?

L.O.5   5.   Discuss various sources of retirement income. What is a major source of retirement income for most Americans?

L.O.5   6.   Compare defined-benefit and defined-contribution plans? What are the differences between the two?

L.O.5   7.   Evaluate the pros and cons of fixed and variable annuities for retirement? How are the payments on these annuities taxed?

L.O.5   8.   What are some possible vehicles for investing during retirement? Which of these vehicles are relatively risk free? Which are riskier?

L.O.6   9.   Outline the steps you must take in order to live on your retirement income and balance your retirement budget.

Opening Case Questions

1.   Why did about 25 percent of Travelers Corporation retirees return to work?

2.   Two thirds of the Travelers Corporation retirees who returned to work did so within a year of retiring. What was the main reason for their hasty return?

3.   What were the consequences of retiring early among the retirees canvassed by Travelers Corporation and its affiliated companies?

PROBLEMS AND ACTIVITIES

L.O.1   1.   If young professionals are worried about their retirement, why don't they do something about it? Where should they start? Where will you start? Outline your steps.

L.O.1   2.   Why are many of the young professionals who worry about the future reluctant to plan for retirement? Interview your colleagues and friends to get their views on retirement planning.

L.O.2   3.   Prepare your net worth statement using the guidelines presented in Exhibit 20–1.

L.O.3   4. How will your spending patterns change during your retirement years? Compare your spending patterns with the ones shown in Exhibit 20–2.

L.O.4   5. Which type of housing will best meet your retirement housing needs? Make a checklist of the advantages and disadvantages of your choice.

L.O.5   6. Gene and Dixie Sladek, husband and wife, are both working. They have an adjusted gross income of $40,000, and they are filing a joint income tax return. What is the maximum IRA contribution that they can make? How much of that contribution is tax deductible?

L.O.5   7. Assume that your gross pay per pay period is $2,000 and that you are in the 33 percent tax bracket. Calculate your net pay and spendable income if you save
   a. $200 per pay period after paying income tax on $2,000.
   b. $200 per pay period in a tax-sheltered annuity.

L.O.5   8. Write a letter urging your congressman or congresswoman to introduce or support legislation repealing the provisions of the present social security law that limit the earnings of Americans aged 65 to 69 who must work to provide for their needs.

L.O.5   9. After obtaining Form SSA-7004 from your local social security office, complete and mail the form so as to receive a personal earnings and benefits statement. Use the information in this statement to plan your retirement.

L.O.6   10. You have $50,000 in your retirement fund that is earning 5.5 percent per year, compounded quarterly. How many dollars in withdrawals per month would reduce this nest egg to zero in 20 years? How many dollars per month can you withdraw as long as you live and still leave this nest egg intact?

LIFE SITUATION   Case 20–1

Helen's Plans for Retirement

Helen, 66, a resident of the suburban area of a large eastern city, lives alone in the house that she and her husband bought when they were first married. She has three adult children, all of whom live in other parts of the country. Helen's income is modest—she works as a salesclerk in a department store. She took this job soon after her husband's death because she could not support herself and her teenage son, the only child who was still living at home, on the insurance and social security benefits left by her husband.

Helen has found it increasingly difficult to maintain her large house. The costs of heating and cooling it have increased, and she must pay for minor repairs and yardwork. Helen has spent most of her holidays and vacations with one of her children. However, she is quite lonely and she misses her children and grandchildren.

Helen will retire soon. She has three financial goals: (1) to maintain enough income to support herself after she retires, (2) to have enough savings to meet emergencies, and (3) to eliminate some of the expense and responsibility of maintaining a large house.

Helen's daughter, Janet, had tried for several years to get her mother to move in with her and her family. Helen resisted until recently, afraid of losing her independence and becoming a burden. Now that Janet is divorced and could use day-to-day help with her two children, Helen has reconsidered. She realizes that once she moves in with Janet, she could sell her house and use the money for savings and living expenses. However, after careful thought, Helen has decided not to sell her house in case living with her daughter does not work out. Instead, she has arranged to have a real estate company find tenants, manage the property, collect the rent, and mail it to her (minus the company's fees) each month.

Helen knows that she should review and update her will so that her property will be handled according to her wishes if she dies or becomes unable to handle her own affairs. Because of the income that she expects from rent and social security and the decreased expenses that will result from sharing her daughter's household, Helen is looking forward to retirement.

Questions

1. What are some of the housing options that might be available to Helen after her retirement? What might be some advantages and disadvantages of each of these options?
2. Do you agree with Helen's decision to move in with her daughter? Why? What might be a few disadvantages of this choice?
3. Is it a sound financial idea for Helen not to sell her house? Why?

LIFE SITUATION   Case 20–2

Retiree Health Plans

Retiree health plans have come under critical review by major employers. Faced with rising health costs and the prospect of setting aside billions of dollars for future health benefits, companies have been rethinking their offers of medical insurance to retirees. Armstrong World Industries now hands out shares that can be sold after retirement to pay for health coverage. Adolph Coors Company doesn't cover retirees over 65 but pays $31 a month toward the cost of Medicare. United Technologies Corporation has devised flexible benefits that future retirees can buy until they become eligible for Medicare at 65. "We aren't happy with the way medical cost increases are going, and retirees are obviously not happy," an official explains.

Providing medical coverage for the average early retiree cost companies $2,397 in 1988, according to A. Foster Higgins & Co., a consulting firm. That topped the $2,160 bill for active workers and the $1,372 cost for retirees on Medicare. In response, many companies cut back. The Hay Group, another consulting firm, says that the percentage of companies providing medical coverage for over-65 retirees dropped from 80 percent in 1987 to 71 percent in 1988. Only 52 percent were picking up the full cost of coverage in 1988, down from 73 percent in 1983.

Questions

1. Why are employers scrutinizing the medical insurance costs of their retirees?
2. What new arrangements are being used by companies to meet the challenge of retirees' health coverage?

SOURCE: "Labor Letter" column, *The Wall Street Journal*, July 18, 1989, p. 1.

SUPPLEMENTARY READINGS

For Additional Information on Purchasing Annuities and Other Retirement Plans

DelPrete, Dom. "Retirement Plans for Small Businesses." *Investment Vision,* September–October 1989, p. 36.

Freedman, Rick. "Annuities: Viable Investments for the Post–Tax Reform Era." *Investment Vision,* September–October 1989, pp. 38–41.

For Additional Information on Retirement Affordability

"How to Afford Retirement." *U.S. News & World Report,* August 14, 1989, pp. 55–62.

Kirkpatrick, David. "Will You Be Able to Retire?" *Fortune,* July 31, 1989, p. 56.

For Additional Information on Housing Options

Activities with Impact. Washington, D.C.: American Association of Retired Persons, 1987.

A Handbook about Care in the Home. Washington, D.C.: American Association of Retired Persons, 1989.

For Additional Information on Pension Plans

Advantages of Qualified Pension and Profit-Sharing Plans. Washington, D.C.: American Association of Retired Persons, 1988.

What You Should Know about Your Pension Law. Washington, D.C.: U.S. Department of Labor, May 1988.

Estate Planning

While you work, your objective is to accumulate funds for your future and for your dependants. However, your point of view will change. The emphasis in your financial planning will shift from accumulating assets to distributing them wisely. Your hard-earned wealth should go to those whom you wish to support and not to the various taxing agencies.

Contrary to widely held notions, estate planning, which includes wills and trusts, is not useful only to the rich and the elderly. Trusts can be used for purposes other than tax advantages. Furthermore, most persons can afford the expense of using them.

LEARNING OBJECTIVES
After studying this chapter, you will be able to

L.O.1   Analyze the personal aspects of estate planning.

L.O.2   Assess the legal aspects of estate planning.

L.O.3   Distinguish among various types and formats of wills.

L.O.4   Appraise various types of trusts and estates.

L.O.5   Evaluate the effects of federal and state taxes on estate planning.

OPENING CASE

Object Lessons in Faulty Estate Planning°

The Spanish artist Casso Aruza originally wanted to be a bullfighter. One Sunday, Casso entered the ring on horseback as a picador, an armored spear carrier who torments the bull. He was unskilled as a pic, and the bull was strong.

Casso was thrown from his horse and was helpless. Before he was rescued by members of the cuadrilla, there was blood on the sand. "That pic has got to be loco," someone muttered, and the name stuck. For the rest of his life, the great artist was known as "Crazy Pic" Casso.

Picasso then emigrated to the United States, became a citizen, married, and raised a family. He was eccentric, unpredictable, colorful, and a genius. He died in 1973 at the age of 92. He left everything to his wife, including about 1,500 paintings worth about $2 million. In his will, Picasso expressed the wish that his wife should sell the paintings only if this were necessary to support herself in the manner to which she had been accustomed. Upon her death, the remainder of the paintings were to go to his many children. There was no estate tax liability, since he left everything to his wife. But when she died, the estate tax problem was serious, primarily because of the paintings. There was a cash shortfall, and the estate had to sell some property to pay the hefty estate tax.

Consider the plight of the Wrigley family and the heirs of Adolph Coors, Jr. The Coors heirs were forced to sell stock in the Coors Brewery to raise the funds needed to satisfy Uncle Sam's claim against the estate. The Wrigley family had to sell the Chicago Cubs to pay taxes that came due upon the death of two family members.

But estate planning and estate taxes are not just for the Cassos, Coors, and Wrigleys; an estate plan is needed by everyone—rich or poor, single or married, male or female, parent or child. As a result of inflation, many middle-class Americans who own their own homes, have life insurance policies, and are enrolled in company pension plans have a net worth approaching the estate tax threshold.

The subject of estate taxes, wills, and trusts is just part of the larger area of estate planning. Estate planning entails analysis of your entire financial picture to determine the best ways to secure your financial well-being and that of your family now and in the future.

°Adapted from *Monthly Tax Report*, December 1985, Laventhol & Horwath, Certified Public Accountants, 1825 Walnut Street, Philadelphia, PA 19103; "Keeping It in the Family," *Changing Times*, January 1986, p. 66; and D. Larry Crumbley and Edward E. Milam, *Estate Planning* (Homewood, Ill.: Dow Jones-Irwin, 1986), p. 1.

WHY ESTATE PLANNING? AN INTRODUCTION

L.O.1
Analyze the personal aspects of estate planning.

This chapter discusses a subject most people would rather avoid: death—your own or that of your spouse. Many people do not give a single thought to preparing for death. Some people give only cursory attention to setting their personal and financial affairs in order.

As you learned in the previous chapter, most people now live long lives. They have ample time to think about and plan for the future. Yet a large percentage of people do little or nothing to provide for those who will survive them.

It is not always easy to plan for your family's financial security in the event of your death or the death of your spouse. Therefore, the objective of this chapter is to help you initiate discussions about questions that should be asked before that happens. Does my spouse, for instance, know what all of the family's resources and debts are? Does my family have enough insurance protection?

The question whether your family can cope financially without your or your spouse's income and support is a difficult one. This chapter can't provide all of the answers, but it does supply a basis of sound estate planning for you and your family.

"As a firm believer in reincarnation, I'm leaving everything to me."

From *The Wall Street Journal*, with permission of Cartoon Features Syndicate.

What Is Estate Planning?

Estate planning is a definite plan for the administration and disposition of one's property during one's lifetime and at one's death. Thus, it involves both handling your property while you are alive and dealing with what happens to that property after your death.

Estate planning is an essential part of retirement planning and an integral part of financial planning. It has two parts. The first consists of building your estate through savings, investments, and insurance. The second consists of transferring your estate, at your death, in the manner you have specified. As this chapter explains, an estate plan is usually implemented by a will and one or more trust agreements.

Nearly every adult is involved with financial decision making and must keep important records. Whatever your status—single or married; male or female; Ph.D. professor or U.S. marine; taxi driver, corporate executive, farmer, rancher, sports champion, or coal miner—you must make financial decisions that are important to you. Those decisions may be even more important to others in your family.

Knowledge in certain areas and good recordkeeping can simplify those decisions. There are things you should know—and do—to protect your interests and those of your heirs.

At first, planning for financial security and estate planning may seem complicated. Although many money matters require legal and technical advice, if you and your spouse learn the necessary skills, you will find yourself managing your money affairs more efficiently and wisely. Begin by answering the questionnaire in Exhibit 21–1 to see how much you and your family know about your own money affairs. You and your family should be able to answer some of these questions. Do you find the questions bewildering? They can be if the subjects are unfamiliar to you.

EXHIBIT 21–1

Estate Planning Checklist: Do You and Your Family Members Know the Answers to the Following Questions?

	Yes	No
1. Can you locate your copies of last year's income tax returns?	☐	☐
2. Where is your safe-deposit box located? Where is the key to it kept?	☐	☐
3. Do you know what kinds and amounts of life insurance protection you have?	☐	☐
4. Can you locate your insurance policies—life, health, property, casualty, and auto?	☐	☐
5. Do you know the names of the beneficiaries and contingent beneficiaries of your life insurance policies?	☐	☐
6. Do you know what type of health insurance protection you have and what the provisions of your health insurance policy are?	☐	☐
7. Do you and your spouse have current wills? Can you locate those wills, along with the name and address of the attorney who drafted them?	☐	☐
8. Do you have a separate record of the important papers you keep in your safe-deposit box? Where is this record located?	☐	☐
9. Do you have a record of your spouse's social security number?	☐	☐
10. Can you locate your marriage certificate? The birth certificates of all the members of your family?	☐	☐
11. Do you know the name and address of your life insurance agent?	☐	☐
12. Do you have a clear understanding of what the principal financial resources and liabilities of your estate are?	☐	☐
13. Are you knowledgeable about simple, daily, and compound interest rates? About retirement funds and property ownership?	☐	☐
14. Have you given any thought to funerals and burial arrangements?	☐	☐
15. Do you know what papers and records will be important in the event of your death?	☐	☐
16. Can you explain the functions of a bank trust department, the meaning of joint ownership, and so forth?	☐	☐

SOURCE: *Planning with Your Beneficiaries* (Washington, D.C.: American Council of Life Insurance, Education and Community Services, n.d.), p. 2.

If You Are Married

If you are married, your estate planning involves the interests of at least two people—more if there are children. Legal requirements and responsibilities can create problems for married persons that are entirely different from the problems of single persons. Situations become more complex. Possessions accumulate. The need for orderliness and clarity becomes greater.

Your death will mean a new lifestyle for your spouse. If there are no children or if the children have grown up and lead separate lives, your spouse will once again be single. The surviving spouse must confront problems of grief and adjustment. Daily life must continue. At the same time, the estate must be settled. If not, there may be catastrophic financial consequences.

If children survive you, making sure that your estate can be readily analyzed and distributed may be all the more critical. If relatives or friends are beneficiaries, bequests have to be made known quickly and clearly.

Your wishes and information about your estate have to be accessible, understandable, and legally proper. Otherwise, there may be problems for your beneficiaries and your intentions may not be carried out.

If You Never Married

Never having been married does not eliminate the need to organize your papers. For persons who live alone, as for married persons, it is essential that important documents and personal information be consolidated and accessible.

Remember that in the event of your death difficult questions and situations are going to confront some person at a time of severe emotional strain. That person may not be prepared to face them objectively.

Probably the single most important thing that you can do is take steps to see that your beneficiaries have the information and the knowledge they need to survive emotionally and financially if you die suddenly.

Such steps should be taken by everyone. But the need to take them is especially great if you are only 5 or 10 years away from retirement. By then, your possessions will probably be of considerable value. Your savings and checking account balances will probably be substantial. Your investment plans will have materialized. If you stop and take a look at where you are, you may be pleasantly surprised at the worth of your estate.

The Opportunity Cost of Rationalizing

Daily living gets in the way of thinking about death. You mean to organize things that need to be known in case you die, but you haven't done this yet. One of your rationalizations may be that you are not sure of what information you need to provide.

Think about the outcome of your delay. Your beneficiary will meet people who offer specific types of assistance—morticians, clergy, lawyers, insurance agents, clerks of federal government agencies, and so on. These people will probably be strangers—sympathetic, courteous, helpful, but disinterested. And your bereaved beneficiary may find it difficult to reveal confidences to them.

LEGAL ASPECTS OF ESTATE PLANNING

L.O.2
Assess the legal aspects of estate planning.

In case of death, proof of claims must be produced or the claims will not be processed. If no thought was given to gathering the necessary documents beforehand (with a sufficient number of copies), a period of financial hardship may follow until proof is obtained. If needed documentation cannot be located, there may be irretrievable loss of funds. Emotionally painful delays may be experienced until rights have been established.

Some important needed papers are

1. Birth certificates—yours, your spouse's, your children's.
2. Marriage certificates—always important, but especially important if your spouse or you were married previously.
3. Legal name changes—judgment of court documents pertaining to any legal changes in the names that appear on birth certificates (especially important to protect the adopted children of a previous marriage or children who have been adopted through adoption agencies).
4. Military service records—the standard DD–214 (Armed Forces of the United States Report of Transfer or Discharge) or any other official statement of your military service details, if appropriate.

You can obtain these papers with minimum difficulty. You simply need the determination to follow through on your plan. Exhibit 21–2 lists important documents for which proof is needed.

EXHIBIT 21–2

Important Documents for
Which Proof Will Be
Needed

Social security documents
Veteran documents
Insurance policies
Transfer records of joint bank accounts
Safe-deposit box records
Registration of automobiles
Title to stock and bond certificates

You should have several copies of certain documents because when you submit a claim, the accompanying proof often becomes a permanent part of the claim file and is not returned. Remember, too, that there are circumstances in which your children may be required to furnish proof of their parents' birth, marriage, or divorce.

One of the most vital records you should have is a will. Every adult should have a written will.

Wills

A **will** is the legal declaration of a person's mind as to the disposition of his or her property after his or her death. Thus, a will is a way to transfer your property according to your wishes after you die.

Whether you prepare a will before you die or neglect to take that sensible step, you have a will. If you fail to prepare your own will, the state in which you legally reside steps in and controls the distribution of your estate without regard for wishes that you may have had but that you failed to define in legal form. Thus, if you die **intestate**—without a valid will—the state's law of descent and distribution becomes your will, as shown in Exhibit 21–3.

Consider the opportunity cost of a husband and father who died without a will. By default, he has authorized his estate to be disposed of according to the provisions of the fictitious document shown in Exhibit 21–3. The wording in this exhibit represents a pattern of distribution that could occur unless you prepare a valid will specifying otherwise.

This need not happen to a husband only. It could happen to anyone. To avoid such consequences, make a will! Consulting an attorney for this purpose can save your heirs many troubles, especially since the passage of the Economic Recovery Tax Act of 1981. This act created estate planning opportunities and problems for many people. You may be one of them. The act also created some difficult choices as to type of wills.

TYPES AND FORMATS OF WILLS

L.O.3
Distinguish among various types and formats of wills.

A brief review of the types of wills may be helpful since the tax effects of these wills differ. The four types of wills are the simple will, the traditional marital share will, the exemption trust will, and the stated dollar amount will.

Simple Will   A **simple will,** sometimes called an "I love you" will, is one in which you leave everything to your spouse. Such a will is sufficient for most smaller estates. But if you have a large or complex estate, especially one involving business interests that you want to pass on to your children, a simple will may not meet your objectives. It might also cause a greater overall amount of taxation because everything would then be taxed in your spouse's subsequent estate.

EXHIBIT 21–3

Opportunity Cost of Not Making a Will, or What Will the State Do to Your Property if You Die Intestate?

𝕸𝖞 𝕷𝖆𝖘𝖙 𝖂𝖎𝖑𝖑 𝖆𝖓𝖉 𝕿𝖊𝖘𝖙𝖆𝖒𝖊𝖓𝖙

Being of sound mind and memory, I, _____, do hereby publish this as my last Will and Testament.

FIRST

I give my wife only one third of my possessions, and I give my children the remaining two thirds.

A. I appoint my wife as guardian of my children, but as a safeguard I require that she report to the Probate Court each year and render an accounting of how, why, and where she spent the money necessary for the proper care of my children.

B. As a further safeguard, I direct my wife to produce to the Probate Court a Performance Bond to guarantee that she exercise proper judgment in the handling, investing, and spending of the children's money.

C. As a final safeguard, my children shall have the right to demand and receive a complete accounting from their mother of all of her financial actions with their money as soon as they reach legal age.

D. When my children reach age 18, they shall have full rights to withdraw and spend their share of my estate. No one shall have any right to question my children's actions on how they decide to spend their respective shares.

SECOND

Should my wife remarry, her second husband shall be entitled to one third of everything my wife possesses. Should my children need some of this share for their support, the second husband shall not be bound to spend any part of his share on my children's behalf.

A. The second husband shall have the sole right to decide who is to get his share, even to the exclusion of my children.

THIRD

Should my wife predecease me or die while any of my children are minors, I do not wish to exercise my right to nominate the guardian of my children.

A. Rather than nominating a guardian of my preference, I direct my relatives and friends to get together and select a guardian by mutual agreement.

B. In the event that they fail to agree on a guardian, I direct the Probate Court to make the selection. If the court wishes, it may appoint a stranger acceptable to it.

FOURTH

Under existing tax law, certain legitimate avenues are open to me to lower death rates. Since I prefer to have my money used for government purposes rather than for the benefit of my wife and children, I direct that no effort be made to lower taxes.

IN WITNESS WHEREOF, I have set my hand to this, my LAST WILL AND TESTAMENT, this _____ day of _____ 19 _____

For example, if your estate is $1,200,000 and you leave it all to your spouse, there would be no tax at your death. However, there would be a tax of $235,000 at your spouse's death, assuming that the value of the estate remains constant. To avoid that, you could use a two-part marital will to split your estate into two halves, resulting in no tax at either death. If your spouse had separate property or if the value of your estate increased, the simple will would cause greater taxation.

Traditional Marital Share Will   The **traditional marital share will** leaves one half of your **adjusted gross estate** (the gross estate minus debts and costs) to your spouse outright as a marital share. The other half of your adjusted gross estate could go to your children or other heirs or be held in trust for your family. A trust could provide your spouse with a lifelong income and would not be taxed at your spouse's death.

Under this type of will, half of your estate is taxed at your death and half at your spouse's death. This results in the lowest overall amount of federal estate taxes on estates above a certain size (twice the exemption amount). However, there are other considerations. State inheritance taxes might be greater, especially at the first death, due to conflicting federal and state exemption and beneficiary classification. Also, under this type of will, unlike a simple will or an exemption trust, federal estate taxes may have to be paid up front at the first death that involves the loss of use of money. If your spouse has considerable assets in his or her own right, it might not be prudent to increase your spouse's estate by any amount. In such a situation, a will that equalizes estates might be better. Finally, the eight community property states severely limit your options as to how your money is allocated.

Exemption Trust Will   The **exemption trust will** has been gaining in popularity due to its increased exemption ($600,000 since 1987). Under this type of will, everything passes to your spouse with the exception of an amount equal to the exemption, which would pass into trust. The amount passed to your spouse could be by will, trust, or other means. The exemption trust can provide your spouse with a lifelong income.

There would be little or no tax at your death because of the combination of the exemption and the marital deduction. The exemption amount, and any appreciation on it, would not be taxed in your spouse's estate.

This type of will is not practical in small estates because under it not much would pass to the spouse. In 1990, for example, only $200,000 of an $800,000 estate would go to the spouse.

The main advantage of the exemption trust will is that it eliminates future taxation of the exemption amount and any growth on it. This may be an important factor if property values appreciate considerably.

Stated Dollar Amount Will   This type of will allows you to pass to your spouse any amount that satisfies your family objectives. These objectives may or may not include tax considerations. For example, you could pass the stated amount of $600,000. But the stated amount could be related to anticipated income needs or to the value of personal items.

State law may dictate how much you must leave your spouse. Most states require that your spouse receive a certain amount, usually one half or one third. Some states require that such interests pass outright, and others permit life interests. The stated dollar amount will might satisfy such requirements and pass the balance to others. You might, for example, decide to pass most of your estate to your children, thereby avoiding subsequent taxation of your spouse's estate. It may also make sense to pass interests in a business to children who are involved in the business.

Such plans may increase taxes at your death since not all of your property passes to your spouse. However, the taxes at your spouse's subsequent death would be less. You can also leave your spouse an outright amount equal to the exemption with a life estate in the balance, or a life estate in trust.

The stated dollar amount has one major shortcoming. The will may leave specific dollar amounts to listed heirs and the balance to the surviving spouse. Although these amounts may be fine when the will is drafted, they can soon become obsolete. What if estate values suddenly decrease because of a business setback or a drop in the stock market? Consider an individual with an extensive equities portfolio who drafted a will in September 1987. After the October 17 market crash, the value of the portfolio may have shrunk by one third. None of that decrease will be borne by those who have been left specific dollar amounts. The entire decrease will be borne by the surviving spouse. Use percentages instead of designated amounts.[1]

Which Type of Will Is Best for You?   The four types of wills discussed above are your basic choices. Which one is best for you?

Prior to the Economic Recovery Tax Act of 1981, many experts advocated the traditional marital share will. Today, many attorneys believe that the exemption trust will is best However, there is no one ideal will. Which will is best for you depends on such factors as the size of your estate, the future appreciation of your estate, inflation, the respective ages of the spouses, relative liquidity, and—most important—your objectives.

Formats of Wills

Wills may be holographic or formal. A **holographic will** is a handwritten will that you prepare. It should be written, dated, and signed entirely in your handwriting—no printed or typed information should be on its pages. It should not be witnessed. Some states may not recognize a holographic will.

A **formal will** is usually prepared with an attorney's assistance. It may be either typed or on a preprinted form. You must sign the will and acknowledge it as your will in the presence of two witnesses, neither of whom is a **beneficiary** (a person you have named to receive property under the will). The witnesses must then sign the will in your presence.

A **statutory will** is one type of formal will. It is a preprinted form that may be obtained from lawyers and stationery stores. There are serious risks in using this or any other preprinted form. One risk is that such a form usually requires you to conform to rigid provisions, some of which may not be in the best interests of your beneficiaries. And if you change the preprinted wording, you may violate the law regarding wills, which may cause the changed sections or the entire will to be declared invalid. There is also a risk that the form is out-of-date and does not reflect current law. It is always prudent to seek legal assistance in developing these documents.

Writing Your Will

The way to transfer your property according to your wishes is to write a will specifying those wishes. Joint ownership is no substitute for a will. Although jointly owned property passes directly to the joint owner and may be appropriate for some assets, such as your home, only with a will can you distribute your property as a whole exactly as you wish. Select a person who will follow your instructions (your executor or executrix). By naming your own executor, you will eliminate the need for a court-appointed administrator, prevent unnecessary delay in the distribution of your property, and minimize estate taxes and settlement costs. See the accompanying "Financial Planning in Action" feature for guidance on important aspects of making a will.

FINANCIAL PLANNING IN ACTION

The 10 Commandments of Making Your Will

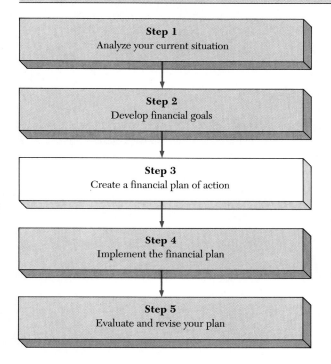

Step 1
Analyze your current situation

Step 2
Develop financial goals

Step 3
Create a financial plan of action

Step 4
Implement the financial plan

Step 5
Evaluate and revise your plan

1. Work closely with your spouse as you prepare your will. Seek professional help so that your family objectives can be met regardless of who dies first.

2. Write your will to conform with your current wishes. When your circumstances change (for example, when you retire or when you move to another state), review your will, and if appropriate, write a new one.

3. Do not choose a beneficiary as a witness. If such a person is called upon to validate your will, he or she may not be able to collect an inheritance.

4. If you are remarrying, consider signing a prenuptial agreement to protect your children. If you sign such an agreement before the wedding, you and your intended spouse can legally agree that neither of you will make any claim on the other's estate. The agreement can be revoked later, if you both agree.

5. Consider using percentages rather than dollar amounts when you divide your estate. If you leave $15,000 to a friend and the rest to your spouse, your spouse will suffer if your estate shrinks to $17,000.

6. Both you and your spouse should have a will, and those wills should be separate documents.

7. Be flexible. Don't insist that your heirs keep stock or run a cattle ranch. Should you do so, they may suffer if economic conditions change.

8. Sign the original of your will and keep it in a safe place; keep an unsigned copy at home for reference.

9. Alter your will by preparing a new will or adding a codicil. Don't change beneficiaries by writing on the will itself; this may invalidate the will.

10. Select an executor who is both willing and able to carry out the complicated tasks associated with the job.

Selecting an Executor   Select an executor who is both willing and able to carry out the complicated tasks associated with the job. These tasks are preparing an inventory of assets, collecting any money due, paying off any debts, preparing and filing all income and estate tax returns, liquidating and reinvesting other assets to pay off debts and provide income for your family while the estate is being administered, distributing the estate, and making a final accounting to your beneficiaries and to the probate court.

Your executor can be a family member, a friend, an attorney, an accountant, or the trust department of a bank. Fees for executors, whether professionals or friends, are set by state laws. Exhibit 21–4 summarizes typical duties of an executor.

EXHIBIT 21–4

Major Responsibilities of
an Executor

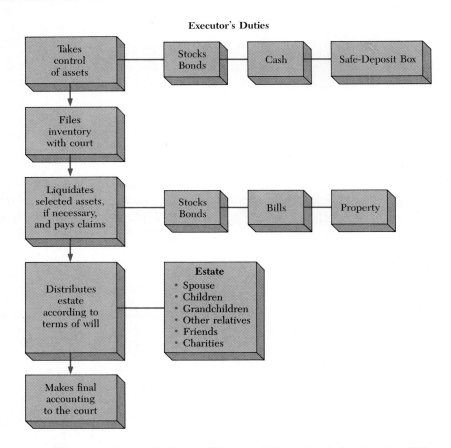

SOURCE: *Trust Services from Your Bank,* rev. ed. (Washington, D.C.: American Bankers Association, 1978), p.9, © ABA.

Selecting a Guardian   In addition to disposing of your estate, your will should name a guardian and/or trustee to care for minor children if both parents die at the same time, such as in an automobile accident or a plane crash. A **guardian** is a person who assumes the responsibilities of providing the children with personal care and of managing the estate for them. A **trustee,** on the other hand, is a person or an institution that holds or generally manages property for the benefit of someone else under a trust agreement.

You should take great care in selecting a guardian for your children. You want a guardian whose philosophy on raising children is similar to yours and who is willing to accept the responsibility.

Most states require a guardian to post a bond with the probate court. The bonding company promises to reimburse the minor's estate up to the amount of the bond if the guardian uses the property of the minor for his or her own gain. The bonding fee of several hundred dollars is paid from the estate. However, you can waive the bonding requirement in your will.

Through your will, you may want to provide funds to raise your children. You could, for instance, leave a lump sum for an addition to the guardian's house and establish monthly payments to cover your children's living expenses.

The guardian of the minor's estate manages the property you leave behind for your children. This guardian can be a person or the trust department of a financial institution, such as a bank. Property that you place in trust for your children can be managed by the trustee rather than by the guardian of the minor's estate.

Altering or Rewriting Your Will

Sometimes you will need to change provisions of your will. Consider one change involving the marital deduction. The old law limited the amount that you could pass to your spouse tax free to one half of your adjusted gross estate. But the Economic Recovery Tax Act of 1981 created an unlimited marital deduction. You can now pass any amount to your spouse tax free.

If you do have a will, you should review it. This is necessary even if you have already done some planning and your will refers to the old 50 percent marital deduction. Why? The new 100 percent marital deduction is not automatic. Congress would not alter or rewrite your will. This task was left to you. Therefore, unless you change your will or unless your state passes a law making the new definition applicable, you will have to rewrite your will to make the unlimited marital deduction apply. Because there are many choices of a personal nature, few, if any, states will get involved. For example, some people may not want to leave the entire estate to the spouse, perhaps for valid tax reasons.

You should review your will if any of these things takes place: if you move to a different state; if you have sold property mentioned in the will; if the size and composition of your estate has changed; if you have married, divorced, or remarried; if new potential heirs have died or been born.

Don't make any changes on the face of your will. Additions, deletions, or erasures on a will that has been signed and witnessed can invalidate the will.

If only a few changes are needed in your will, adding a codicil may be the best choice. A **codicil** is a document that explains, adds, or deletes provisions in your existing will. It identifies the will being amended and confirms the unchanged sections of the will. To be valid, it must conform to the legal requirements for a holographic or formal will.

If you wish to make major changes in your will or if you have already added a codicil, preparing a new will is preferable to adding a new codicil. In the new will, however, include a clause revoking all earlier wills and codicils.

If you are rewriting a will because of a remarriage, consider drafting a **prenuptial agreement.** This is a documentary agreement between spouses before marriage. In such agreements, one or both parties often waive a right to receive property under the other's will or under state law. Be sure to consult an attorney in drafting a prenuptial agreement.

Wills like some of those discussed in this section have existed for thousands of years; the oldest known will was written by the Egyptian pharaoh Uah in 2448 B.C. Recently, a new type of will, called a living will, has emerged.

A Living Will

A **living will** provides for your wishes being followed if you become so physically or mentally disabled that you are unable to act on your own behalf.

A living will is a document that a person can prepare in anticipation of death, and in that respect it resembles a traditional will. It enables an individual, while well, to express the intention that life be allowed to end if he or she becomes

EXHIBIT 21–5

A Living Will: Example 1

TO MY FAMILY, MY PHYSICIAN, MY LAWYER, MY CLERGYMAN
TO ANY MEDICAL FACILITY IN WHOSE CARE I HAPPEN TO BE
TO ANY INDIVIDUAL WHO MAY BECOME RESPONSIBLE FOR
MY HEALTH, WELFARE, OR AFFAIRS:

Death is as much a reality as birth, growth, maturity, and old age—it is the one certainty of life. If the time comes when I, _____, can no longer take part in decisions for my own future, let this statement stand as an expression of my wishes, while I am still of sound mind.

If the situation should arise in which there is no reasonable expectation of my recovery from physical or mental disability, I request that I be allowed to die and not be kept alive by artificial means or "heroic measures." I do not fear death itself as much as the indignities of deterioration, dependence, and hopeless pain. I, therefore, ask that medication be mercifully administered to me to alleviate suffering even though this may hasten the moment of death.

This request is made after careful consideration. I hope you who care for me will feel morally bound to follow its mandate. I recognize that this appears to place a heavy responsibility upon you, but it is with the intention of relieving you of such responsibility and of placing it upon myself in accordance with my strong convictions, that this statement is made.

Signed_____

Date_____

Witness_____

Witness_____

Copies of this request have been given to _____
_____
_____
_____

SOURCE: *Don't Wait until Tomorrow* (Hartford, Conn.: Aetna Life and Casualty Company, n.d.), p. 10.

terminally ill. Living wills are recognized in many states, and you may consider writing one when you draw a conventional will. Exhibits 21–5 and 21–6 are examples of typical living wills.

To ensure the effectiveness of a living will, discuss your intention of preparing such a will with the people closest to you. You should also discuss this with your family doctor. Sign and date your document before two witnesses. Witnessing shows that you signed of your own free will.

Give copies of your living will to those closest to you, and have your family doctor place a copy in your medical file. Keep the original document readily accessible, and look it over periodically, preferably once a year, to be sure that your wishes have remained unchanged. To verify your intent, redate and initial each later endorsement.

A living will can become a problem. A once-healthy person may have a change of heart and prefer to remain alive even as death seems imminent. "You can pass living wills around a roomful of young people, and 95 percent will sign them," said a geriatric internist. "But pass them around a nursing home, and you will get a different response." A psychiatrist specializing in the care of elderly people added, "People who are old, enfeebled, slowly dying, are still living existentially. They may enjoy their meals, the sunlight on their skin, sensory pleasures."[2]

EXHIBIT 21–6
A Living Will: Example 2

Living Will Declaration

Declaration made this _____ day of _____ (month, year)

I, _____, being of sound mind, willfully and voluntarily make known my desire that my dying shall not be artificially prolonged under the circumstances set forth below, do hereby declare

If at any time I should have an incurable injury, disease, or illness regarded as a terminal condition by my physician and if my physician has determined that the application of life-sustaining procedures would serve only to artificially prolong the dying process and that my death will occur whether or not life-sustaining procedures are utilized, I direct that such procedures be withheld or withdrawn and that I be permitted to die with only the administration of medication or the performance of any medical procedure deemed necessary to provide me with comfort care.

In the absence of my ability to give directions regarding the use of such life-sustaining procedures, it is my intention that this declaration shall be honored by my family and physician as the final expression of my legal right to refuse medical or surgical treatment and accept the consequences from such refusal.

I understand the full import of this declaration, and I am emotionally and mentally competent to make this declaration.

Signed_____

City, County, and State of Residence_____

The declarant has been personally known to me, and I believe him or her to be of sound mind.

Witness_____

Witness_____

SOURCE: *Don't Wait until Tomorrow* (Hartford, Conn.: Aetna Life and Casualty Company, n.d.), p. 11.

Living wills call for careful thought, but they do provide you with a choice as to the manner of your death. Related to the concept of a living will is a power of attorney.

Power of Attorney

A **power of attorney** is a legal document authorizing someone to act on your behalf. At some point in your life, you may become ill or incapacitated. You may then wish to have someone attend to your needs and your personal affairs. You can assign a power of attorney to anyone you choose.

The person you name can be given a limited power or a great deal of power. The power given can be special—to carry out certain acts or transactions; or it can be general—to act completely for you. A conventional power of attorney is automatically revoked in a case of legal incapacity.

Letter of Last Instruction

In addition to your will, you should prepare a letter of last instruction. This document, though not legally enforced, can provide your heirs with important information. It should contain the details of your funeral arrangements. It should also contain the names of the persons who are to be notified of your death and the locations of your bank accounts, safe-deposit box, and other important items listed in Exhibit 21–2.

TYPES OF TRUSTS AND ESTATES

L.O.4
Appraise various types of trusts and estates.

It is a good idea to discuss with your attorney the possibility of establishing a trust as a means of managing your estate. Basically, a **trust** is a legal arrangement through which your assets are held by a trustee for your benefit or that of your beneficiaries.

Trusts are either revocable or irrevocable. If you establish a **revocable trust,** you retain the right to end the trust or change its terms during your lifetime. You might choose a revocable trust if you think you may need its assets for your own use at a later time or if you want to monitor the performance of the trust and the trustee before the arrangement is made irrevocable by your death. If you establish an **irrevocable trust,** you cannot change its terms or end it. However, an irrevocable trust offers tax advantages not offered by a revocable trust.

Types of Trusts

You can use a trust to

- Free yourself from management of your assets while you receive a regular income from the trust.
- Provide income for a surviving spouse or other beneficiaries.
- Assure that your property serves a desired purpose after your death.

Trustee services are commonly provided by banks, and in some instances they are provided by life insurance companies. There are four types of trusts: living or inter vivos trusts, self-declaration trusts, testamentary trusts, and life insurance trusts. Each of these types has particular advantages and may be the most appropriate for your family situation.

Living or Inter Vivos Trusts   A **living trust** is a property management arrangement that you establish while you are alive. You simply transfer some property to a trustee, giving him or her instructions regarding its management and disposition while you are alive and after your death. A living trust has these advantages:

- Property held in it avoids probate at your death.
- It enables you to review your trustee's performance and to make changes if necessary.
- It can remove management responsibilities from your shoulders.
- It is less subject to attack by disappointed heirs than a will.
- It can guide your family and doctors if you should become terminally ill or incompetent.

Self-Declaration Trusts   A **self-declaration trust** is a variation of the living trust. Its unique feature is that the creator of the trust is also the trustee. The trust document usually includes a procedure for removing the creator of the trust as the trustee without going to court. Typically, one or more physicians or family members, or a combination of physicians and family members, have removal power. If the creator of the trust is removed, a named successor trustee takes over.

Many people of retirement age who are concerned about the possibility of a disabling illness don't want to set up a living trust, because they want to handle their own business as long as they are able to do so. The self-declaration trust gives them full control until they die or are disabled.

PERSONAL FINANCE JOURNAL:

Trusts with Insurance Find New Life

After rummaging the federal tax code for shelters that avoided the reformers' ax and finding new survivors, estate planners have dusted off an old standby—the life insurance trust.

Trusts that contain life insurance policies are "the best game in town right now" for people who need a federal estate tax shelter, says Stephan R. Leimberg, a professor of taxes and estate planning at American College, a specialized school for insurance agents and financial planners in Bryn Mawr, Pennsylvania.

But the trusts are complex arrangements with serious tax and legal implications that must be carefully considered. "Proper planning is extremely important," says Mr. Leimberg. The IRS "is going to make sure you toe the line."

Estate planning is an important part of personal financial management because death taxes can take such a huge bite out of the assets people struggle all their lives to accumulate. To be sure, the first $600,000 of assets escapes federal estate taxes and all property left to a spouse, regardless of value, is exempt. But when the property passes beyond husbands and wives, federal estate taxes can be steep. Marginal rates start at 18 percent and rise to 55 percent for estates valued at more than $3 million.

One common estate planning device is life insurance. People regularly buy policies, naming a spouse or child as beneficiary, to provide future income or to help pay estate taxes.

The trouble is that although death benefits from the policies generally aren't subject to income tax, the IRS considers them part of the dead person's estate. So the insurance can actually increase the federal estate tax bill. In some cases, heirs are forced to sell property from the estate to pay the levies.

That's where life insurance trusts come in handy, according to financial consultants. These trusts allow people to set aside assets that are shielded from estate taxes and made available to family members immediately after the property owner dies.

The estate tax savings of such an arrangement can be significant. Jane Ann Schiltz, an assistant marketing director at Northwestern Mutual Life Insurance Company, says that a woman with $2.5 million in assets who wants to leave her property to her husband, and then to her children after he dies, saves her heirs about $517,000 in taxes by establishing a life insurance trust that purchases a $500,000 policy.

If the woman simply leaves the entire $2.5 million to her husband, and then to her children after his death, the children will owe $833,000 on these assets when their father dies. The husband won't owe any taxes when the wife dies because of the exemption for property left to a spouse.

SOURCE: Condensed from Sonja Steptoe, "Trusts with Insurance Find New Life," *The Wall Street Journal*, March 15, 1989, p. C1.

Testamentary Trusts   A **testamentary trust** is a trust established by your will that becomes effective upon your death. Such a trust can be valuable if your beneficiaries are inexperienced in financial matters or if the potential estate tax is substantial. Like a living trust, a testamentary trust provides the benefits of asset management, financial bookkeeping, protection of the beneficiaries, and minimizing of estate taxes.

Insurance Trusts   In many families, the proceeds of life insurance policies are the largest single asset of the estate. A **life insurance trust** is established while you are living. The trust receives your life insurance benefits upon your death and administers them in an agreed-upon manner. Such trusts can be canceled if there is a change in your family or financial circumstances or if you wish to make new plans for the future. The accompanying "Personal Finance Journal" feature tells you why life insurance trusts are "the best game in town right now."

To summarize, a trust is a property arrangement in which a trustee, such as a person or a bank trust department, holds title to, takes care of, and, in most cases, manages property for the benefit of someone else. The creator of the trust is called the **trustor** or grantor. A bank, as trustee, charges a modest fee for its services, generally based on the value of the trust assets. All trust assets added together are known as an estate.

Estates

Your **estate** is everything you own. It includes all of your property—tangible and intangible, however acquired or owned, whether inside or outside the country. It may include jointly owned property, life insurance and employee benefits, and property you no longer own. Thus, an important step in estate planning is taking inventory of everything you own, such as

1. Cash, checking accounts, savings accounts, CDs, and money market funds.
2. Stocks, bonds (including municipals and U.S. savings bonds), mutual funds, commodity futures, and tax shelters.
3. Life insurance, employee benefits, and annuities.
4. Your home and any other real estate, land and buildings, furniture, and fixtures.
5. Farms, grain, livestock, machinery, and equipment.
6. Proprietorship, partnership, and close corporation interests.
7. Notes, accounts, and claims receivable.
8. Interests in trusts and powers of appointment.
9. Antiques, works of art, collections, cars, boats, planes, personal effects, and everything else.

In the community property states (Arizona, California, Idaho, Louisiana, Nevada, New Mexico, Texas, and Washington), where each spouse owns 50 percent of the property, half of the community assets are included in each spouse's estate. **Community property** is "any property that has been acquired by either of the spouses during their marriage, but not by gift, devise, bequest or inheritance, or, often, by the income therefrom."[3] In the other states (the non–community property states), property is included in the estate of the spouse who owns it. The way you own property can make a tax difference.

Joint Ownership   Joint ownership of property between spouses is very common. Joint ownership may also exist between parents and children, other relatives, or any two or more persons. While joint ownership may avoid *probate* (official proof of a will), creditor attachment, and inheritance taxes in some states, it does not avoid federal estate taxes. In fact, it may increase them.

There are three types of joint ownership, and they have different tax and estate planning consequences.

If you and your spouse own property as *joint tenants with the right of survivorship* (*JT/WROS*), the property is considered owned 50–50 for estate tax purposes and will automatically pass to your spouse at your death, and vice versa. No gift tax is paid on creating such ownership, nor, due to the unlimited marital deduction, is any estate tax paid at the first death. However, this type of joint ownership may result in more taxes overall at the surviving spouse's later death than would have been the case with a traditional marital share will, discussed earlier.

If you put property in joint ownership with a child (or anyone else other than your spouse), you have made a potentially taxable gift to the child to the extent that the child's share of ownership exceeds his or her own contribution. There are exceptions for U.S. savings bonds and savings accounts. In any event, the property is included in your gross estate except to the extent of the child's contribution.

If you and your spouse or anyone else own property as *tenants in common*, each individual is considered to own a proportionate share for tax purposes, and only your share is included in your estate. That share does not go to the other tenants in common at your death but is included in your probate estate and subject to your decision as to who gets it. While there are no gift or estate tax consequences between spouse joint owners, gifts of joint interests to children or others can cause taxation.

Joint ownership is not a good substitute for a will. It gives you less control over the disposition and taxation of your property. Your state laws govern the types and effects of joint ownership. Some states require that survivorship rights be spelled out in the deed, or at least abbreviated (for example, JT/WROS). Only your attorney can advise you on these matters.

Tenancy by the entirety, the third type of co-ownership, is limited to married couples. Under this type of co-ownership, both spouses own the property; when one spouse dies, the other gets it automatically. Neither spouse may sell the property without the consent of the other.

Life Insurance and Employee Benefits   Life insurance proceeds are free of income tax, excluded from probate, and wholly or partially exempt from most state inheritance taxes.

These proceeds are included in your estate for federal estate tax purposes if the policy contains any incidents of ownership such as the right to change beneficiaries, to surrender the policy for cash, or to make loans on the policy.

Assignment of ownership to your beneficiary or a trust could remove a life insurance policy from your estate. But if your spouse is the intended beneficiary, you do not need to assign ownership, since the proceeds would be free of estate tax due to the marital deduction.

Death benefits from qualified pension, profit sharing, or Keogh plans are excluded from your estate unless they are payable to it or unless your beneficiary elects the special provision for averaging income tax in lump-sum distributions. (Any benefits attributable to your own nondeductible contributions are included.) Benefits from IRA plans are also excluded if they are paid as an annuity or for a period of 36 months or more. Other benefits, such as deferred compensation and stock option plans, are fully included. Such benefits are also subject to income taxation. Careful planning is needed to minimize both income and estate taxes.

Lifetime Gifts and Trusts   Gifts or trusts with strings attached, such as retaining the income, use, or control of the property, are fully included at their date of death value, whether your rights are expressed or implied. For example, if you transfer title of your home to a child but continue to live in it, the home is taxed in your estate. Or if you put property in trust and retain certain control over the income or principal, the property is included in your estate even though you cannot obtain it yourself. Also, if you are the beneficiary of a trust established by someone else and you have general rights to the principal during life or the power to appoint it to anyone at death, that amount is included in your estate.

Settling Your Estate

If you have had a will drawn, you are "testate" in the eyes of the law and an executor (named in your will) will carry out your wishes in due time. If you have not named an executor, the probate court (the court that supervises the distribution of estates) will appoint an administrator to carry out the instructions in your will.

If you don't have a will, you become "intestate" at your death. In this case, what you own is put under the control of a court-appointed administrator for distribution according to laws of the state in which you reside.

FEDERAL AND STATE ESTATE TAXES

L.O.5
Evaluate the effects of federal and state taxes on estate planning.

The tax aspects of estate planning have changed considerably because of recent major changes in the federal tax structure. The maximum tax rate on estates and gifts, for example, is gradually declining.

You can reduce your taxable estate by giving away assets during your lifetime. (But don't give away assets just to reduce your estate tax liability if you may need those assets in your retirement.) No gift tax is due on gifts of up to $10,000 to any one person in any one year. (A married couple, acting together, may give up to $20,000 to one person in one year.) Thus, if at age 82 Picasso had had 20 descendents, he could have given each of them six or seven paintings a year (using his $10,000 annual exclusion from gift tax on each gift). In this way, he would have removed at least 120 paintings a year from his estate tax free (while still keeping them in the family). After 10 years, he would have given away more than 1,000 paintings, two thirds of the total on hand when he died.

Also, if Picasso had died in 1985, he could have made bequests of up to $400,000 to his children or anyone else he wished without paying any tax at all (the exemption was $600,000 in 1987 and thereafter). Then he could have left the balance of his estate to his widow. The estate would have been tax free, too, because of the unlimited marital deduction.

Types of Taxes

Federal and state governments levy various types of taxes that must be considered in planning your estate. The four major taxes of this kind are estate taxes, estate income taxes, inheritance taxes, and gift taxes.

Estate Taxes   An **estate tax** is a federal tax levied on the right of a deceased person to transmit his or her property and life insurance at death. Estate taxes have undergone extensive revision since the mid-1970s. The Economic Recovery Tax Act of 1981 makes important tax concessions—particularly the unlimited marital deduction and the increased exemption equivalent shown in Exhibit 21–7.

Under present law, with intelligent estate planning and properly drawn wills, you may leave all of your property free of federal estate taxes to your surviving spouse. The surviving spouse's estate in excess of $600,000 is faced with estate taxes of from 37 percent to 50 percent.

EXHIBIT 21–7   Unified Transfer Tax Rates

| | | Tentative Tax° for Decedents Dying and for Gifts Made in | | | | | |
| **If the Amount Is** | | **1989–1992** | | | **1993 and After** | | |
Over	**But Not Over**	**This Amount +**	**This Percent**	**Of Excess Over**	**This Amount +**	**This Percent**	**Of Excess Over**
$ —	$ 10,000	$ —	18%	$ —	$ —	18%	$ —
10,000	20,000	1,800	20	10,000	1,800	20	10,000
20,000	40,000	3,800	22	20,000	3,800	22	20,000
40,000	60,000	8,200	24	40,000	8,200	24	40,000
60,000	80,000	13,000	26	60,000	13,000	26	60,000
80,000	100,000	18,200	28	80,000	18,200	28	80,000
100,000	150,000	23,800	30	100,000	23,800	30	100,000
150,000	250,000	38,800	32	150,000	38,800	32	150,000
250,000	500,000	70,800	34	250,000	70,800	34	250,000
500,000	750,000	155,800	37	500,000	155,800	37	500,000
750,000	1,000,000	248,300	39	750,000	248,300	39	750,000
1,000,000	1,250,000	345,800	41	1,000,000	345,800	41	1,000,000
1,250,000	1,500,000	448,300	43	1,250,000	448,300	43	1,250,000
1,500,000	2,000,000	555,800	45	1,500,000	555,800	45	1,500,000
2,000,000	2,500,000	780,800	49	2,000,000	780,800	49	2,000,000
2,500,000	3,000,000	1,025,800	53	2,500,000	1,025,800	50	2,500,000
3,000,000	—	1,290,800	55[†]	3,000,000	1,275,800	50[†]	3,000,000

°The tentative tax is the tax before reduction for the unified transfer tax credit, the credit for state death taxes, the credit for gift taxes, and certain other credits.
[†]A 5 percent surtax applies to base amounts between $10 million and $21,040,000 for 1989–92 (producing a total rate of 60 percent) and between $10 million and $18,340,000 after 1992 (producing a total rate of 55 percent).

All limits have been removed from transfers between spouses during lifetime as well as at death. Whatever you give your spouse is exempt from gift and estate taxes. Gift tax returns need not be filed for interspousal gifts. There is still the possibility, however, that such gifts will be included in your estate if they have been given within three years of your death.

Estates and Trusts Federal Income Taxes   In addition to the federal estate tax, estates and certain trusts must file federal income tax returns with the Internal Revenue Service. Generally speaking, taxable income for estates and trusts is computed in very much the same manner as taxable income for individuals. Under the Tax Reform Act of 1986, trusts and estates must pay quarterly estimated taxes and new trusts must use the calendar year as the tax year.

Inheritance Taxes   An **inheritance tax** is levied on the right of an heir to receive all or part of the estate and life insurance proceeds of a deceased person. The tax payable depends on the net value of the property and insurance received. It also depends on the relationship of the heir to the deceased.
Inheritance taxes are imposed only by the state governments. Most states levy an inheritance tax, but the state laws differ widely as to exemptions, rates of taxation, and the treatment of property and life insurance. A reasonable average

for state inheritance taxes would be 4–10 percent of your estate, with the higher percentages on larger amounts.

In the past few years, many states have been phasing out their inheritance tax provisions—usually over a period of three or four years. This apparently reflects a desire to retain older and wealthy citizens as residents and to discourage them from leaving the states where they have lived most of their lives to seek tax havens in such states as Florida and Nevada. The New England states, in particular, are fearful of an exodus of the elderly, with its accompanying loss of sales and income tax revenues. Since the federal estate tax changes have raised exemptions and lowered rates, the state inheritance taxes have become more burdensome for many people. For increasing numbers, state inheritance taxes are the only taxes at death that remain. Increasingly, state legislatures have been questioning the equity of further taxes at death and are opting instead for sales and income taxes to provide state revenues.

Gift Taxes   But the federal government and state governments levy a **gift tax** on the privilege of making gifts to others. Estate and inheritance taxes can be avoided by giving property during the lifetime of the property owner. For this reason, the federal tax laws provide for taxes on gifts of property. The tax rates on gifts used to be only 75 percent of the tax rates on estates, but since 1976 the gift tax rates have been the same as the estate tax rates. Indeed, the tax rates are now called unified transfer tax rates.

Many states have gift tax laws. The state gift tax laws are similar to the federal gift tax laws, but the exemptions and the dates for filing returns vary widely among the states.

As discussed earlier, the federal gift tax allows you to give up to $10,000 each year to any person without incurring gift tax liability or having to report the gift to the IRS. Gifts from a husband or a wife to a third party are considered as having been made in equal amounts by each spouse. Consequently, a husband and wife may give as much as $20,000 per year to anyone without incurring tax liability.

Property owners sometimes make a formal gift of property to wife or children but actually retain control over the property. In such cases, the courts have often disregarded the gift and have held that the property is still part of the donor's estate. If gifts are made to avoid taxes, they should be made in good faith and the resulting change in ownership should be observed carefully.

Tax Avoidance and Tax Evasion

A poorly arranged estate may be subject to unduly large taxation. Therefore, you should study the tax laws and seek advice to avoid estate taxes larger than those the lawmakers intended you to pay. You should have a clear idea of the distinction between tax avoidance and tax evasion. Tax avoidance is the use of legal methods to reduce or escape taxes; tax evasion is the use of illegal methods to reduce or escape taxes.

Charitable Gifts and Bequests   Gifts made to certain recognized charitable or educational agencies are exempt from gift, estate, and inheritance taxes. Accordingly, such gifts or bequests (gifts through a will) represent one method of reducing or avoiding estate and inheritance taxes.

Calculation of Tax

The estate tax is applied, not to your total gross estate, but to your net taxable estate at death. As shown in Exhibit 21–8, this estate is your testamentary net worth after your debts, liabilities, probate costs, and administration costs have been subtracted. These items, all of which are taken off your estate before calculating your tax, are cash requirements to be paid by your estate.

Debts and Liabilities   In arriving at your taxable estate, the amount of your debts and other creditor obligations are subtracted. You are liable for the payment of these debts while living; your estate will be liable at your death. Your debts may include mortgages, collateralized loans, margin accounts, bank loans, notes payable, installment and charge accounts, and accrued income and property taxes. They may also include your last illness and funeral expenses.

 Probate and Administration Costs   Your estate administration costs will include fees for attorneys, accountants, appraisers, executors or administrators

EXHIBIT 21–8
Estate Tax Calculation
Worksheet

1. Gross estate values
    Personal property $_____
    Real estate   _____
    Joint ownership   _____
    Business interests   _____
    Life insurance   _____
    Employee benefits   _____
    Controlled gifts/trusts   _____
    Prior taxable gifts   _____
        Total $_____
2. Deductible debts, costs, expenses
    Mortgages and secured loans   _____
    Unsecured notes and loans   _____
    Bills and accounts payable   _____
    Funeral and medical expenses   _____
    Probate administration costs   _____
        Total   − $_____
3. Charitable bequests   − $_____
4. Marital deduction   − $_____
5. Taxable estate   = $_____
6. Gross estate tax $_____
7. Allowable credits
    Unified credit   _____
    Gift tax credit   _____
    State tax credit   _____
    Foreign tax credit   _____
    Prior tax credit   _____
        Total   − $_____
8. Net estate tax   = $_____

and trustees, court costs, bonding and surety costs, and miscellaneous other expenses. These administration costs may run 5–8 percent of your estate, depending on its size and complexity. While the percentage usually decreases as the size of the estate increases, it may be increased by additional complicating factors, such as handling a business interest.

Next deductions are made for bequests to qualified charities and for property passing to your spouse (the marital deduction). That leaves your net taxable estate, to which the rates shown in Exhibit 21–9 are applied to determine your gross estate tax.

Inheritance and estate taxes in your own state are additional costs, and these costs are not deductible in arriving at your taxable estate. In fact, you may have to pay inheritance taxes in two or more states, depending on the location of your property.

Paying the Tax

If after various estate tax reduction techniques have been employed, there is still an estate tax to pay, then consideration must be given as to how best to pay it. The federal estate tax is due and payable in cash nine months after your death. State taxes, probate costs, debts, and expenses usually also fall due within that time. These costs can, and often do, result in a real cash bind, because rarely do wealthy people keep a lot of cash on hand. Their wealth was derived from putting their money to work in businesses, real estate, or other investments. Estate liquidity— having enough cash to pay taxes and costs without forced sales of assets or heavy borrowing—is often a problem.

One way to handle the estate tax is to set aside or accumulate enough cash to pay it when it falls due. The trouble with this suggestion is that you may die before you have accumulated enough cash and that the cash you accumulate may be subject to income tax during your life and to estate tax at your death.

Another way to handle the estate tax would be for your family to sell assets to pay taxes, as did the families of Picasso, Coors, and Wrigley. The first assets that might be sold are stocks, bonds, gold or silver coins, and similar liquid assets. But these assets may be the source of your family's income after your death, and the market for them may be down. Such assets as real estate might also be sold, but prices on forced sales are usually only a fraction of the fair value.

Your family could consider borrowing, but it is unusual to find a commercial lender that will lend money to pay back taxes. And if one were found, personal

EXHIBIT 21–9
Simplified Tax Table,
1987 and Thereafter

Taxable Estate	Estate Tax°	Rate on Excess
$ 600,000	$ 0	37%
750,000	55,500	39
1,000,000	153,000	41
1,250,000	255,500	43
1,500,000	363,000	45
2,000,000	588,000	49
2,500,000	833,000	50

°After deducting the maximum allowable credit.

liability might be required. In any event, borrowing does not solve the problem; it only prolongs it, adding interest costs in the process.

Borrowing from the IRS itself in the form of deferred payments or installments may be possible for reasonable cause. Tax extension and installment payment provisions are helpful, but they still leave a tax debt to be paid by your heirs at your death. Paying that debt, even over an extended period of time, could be a real burden and severely restrict their income and flexibility.

Life insurance may be a reasonable, feasible, and economical means of paying your estate tax. Instead of forcing your family to pay off the estate tax and other debts and costs by borrowing or selling, through insurance you can provide your family with tax-free cash at a fraction of the cost of borrowing.

SUMMARY

L.O.1
Analyze the personal aspects of estate planning.

Estate planning is an essential part of retirement planning and an integral part of financial planning. The first part of estate planning consists of building your estate; the second part consists of transferring your estate, at your death, in the manner you have specified. The personal aspects of estate planning depend on whether you are single or married. If you are married, your estate planning involves the interests of at least two people—more if there are children. Never having been married does not eliminate the need to organize your papers.

L.O.2
Assess the legal aspects of estate planning.

In case of death, proof of claims must be produced, or the claims will not be processed. Among the papers needed are birth certificates, marriage certificates, legal name changes, and military service records.

L.O.3
Distinguish among various types and formats of wills.

The four types of wills are the simple will, the traditional marital share will, the exemption trust will, and the stated dollar amount will. Which type is best for you depends on your personal and financial circumstances.

L.O.4
Appraise various types of trusts and estates.

Establishing a trust can be an excellent way to manage your estate. Trusts are revocable or irrevocable. Popular forms of trusts include living trusts, testamentary trusts, and insurance trusts. An attorney's help is needed to establish a trust.

L.O.5
Evaluate the effects of federal and state taxes on estate planning.

The tax aspects of estate planning have changed considerably because of recent major changes in the federal tax structure. The four major federal and state taxes that must be considered in planning your estate are estate taxes, estate income taxes, inheritance taxes, and gift taxes.

GLOSSARY

Adjusted gross estate   The gross estate minus debts and costs.

Beneficiary   A person who has been named to receive property under a will.

Codicil   A document that modifies provisions in an existing will.

Community property   Any property that has been acquired by either of the spouses during their marriage.

Estate   Everything you own.

Estate planning   A definite plan for the administration and disposition of one's property during one's lifetime and at one's death.

Estate tax   A federal tax on the right to transfer property and life insurance at death.

Exemption trust will   A will in which everything passes to the spouse except the exemption ($600,000 since 1987).

Formal will   A will that is usually prepared with an attorney's assistance.

Gift tax   Federal and state tax on the privilege of making gifts to others.

Guardian   A person who assumes responsibility for providing your children with personal care and managing your estate for them.

Holographic will   A handwritten will.

Inheritance tax   A tax levied on the right of an heir to receive an estate.

Intestate   Without a valid will.

Irrevocable trust   A trust that cannot be altered or ended by its creator.

Life insurance trust   A trust whose assets are derived at least in part from the proceeds of life insurance.

Living trust   A trust created and providing benefits during the trustor's lifetime.

Living will   A document that enables an individual, while well, to express the intention that life be allowed to end if he or she becomes terminally ill.

Power of attorney   A legal document authorizing someone to act on your behalf.

Prenuptial agreement   A documentary agreement between spouses before marriage.

Revocable trust   A trust whose terms the trustor retains the right to change.

Self-declaration trust   A variation of the living trust in which the creator of the trust is also the trustee.

Simple will   A will that leaves everything to the spouse; also called an "I love you" will.

Statutory will   A formal will on a preprinted form.

Testamentary trust   A trust established by your will that becomes effective upon your death.

Traditional marital share will   A will in which the grantor leaves one half of the adjusted gross estate to the spouse.

Trust   A legal arrangement through which your assets are held by a trustee.

Trustee   A person or an institution that holds or manages property for the benefit of someone else under a trust agreement.

Trustor   The creator of a trust; also called the grantor.

Will   The legal declaration of a person's mind as to the disposition of his or her property after his or her death.

DISCUSSION QUESTIONS

L.O.1   1. What is estate planning? What special considerations are there in estate planning if you are married? If you are single?

L.O.2   2. What is a will? Describe the four types of wills, and list advantages and disadvantages of each type. What type of will is best for you? Why?

L.O.3 3. What differences are there among a holographic will, a formal will, and a statutory will?

L.O.3 4. Define and explain the following terms: *codicil, prenuptial agreement, guardian, executor, trustor, trustee, living will,* and *power of attorney.*

L.O.3 5. What is a letter of last instruction? Is it a substitute for a will? Why? What information is generally included in a letter of last instruction?

L.O.4 6. What is a trust? Describe a living trust, a testamentary trust, and a life insurance trust. What are advantages and disadvantages of each?

L.O.4 7. What is an estate? What property is included in it?

L.O.4 8. Discuss and distinguish among joint tenancy with the right of survivorship, tenancy in common, and tenancy by the entirety. Is one form of ownership better than the others?

L.O.5 9. How is the property of a deceased person assessed for federal estate taxes?

L.O.5 10. Describe estate, inheritance, and gift taxes? Who levies these taxes, and why?

L.O.5 11. How is estate tax calculated? When does it become due?

Opening Case Questions

1. If Casso Aruza wanted to use the marital deduction and still control who would ultimately receive his paintings, what type of trust would you have suggested to him?
2. Why were the Coors heirs forced to sell stock in the Coors Brewery?
3. Are estate planning and estate taxes just for rich people such as the Aruzas, the Coors, and the Wrigleys?
4. Why should middle-class American homeowners worry about estate planning?

PROBLEMS AND ACTIVITIES

L.O.1 1. Prepare a record of personal information that would be helpful to you and your heirs. Make sure to include the location of family records, your military service file, and other important papers; medical records; bank accounts; charge accounts; the location of your safe-deposit box; U.S. savings bonds; stocks, bonds, and other securities owned; property owned; life insurance; annuities; and social security information.

L.O.1 2. Develop a list of specific long-term estate planning goals with your family. Discuss how those goals could be achieved even if one spouse died unexpectedly.

L.O.2 3. Draft your simple will, using Exhibit 21–3 as a guideline. Whom will you appoint as a trustee or guardian for your minor children? Why?

L.O.3 4. Contact several lawyers in your area to find out how much they would charge to prepare your simple will. Are their fees about the same?

L.O.3 5. Make a list of the criteria that you will use in deciding who will be the guardian of your minor children if you and your spouse die at the same time.

L.O.3 6. Draft a living will, using Exhibits 21–5 and 21–6 as guidelines.

L.O.3 7. Prepare your own letter of last instructions.

L.O.4   8.   Discuss with your attorney the possibility of establishing a trust as a means of managing your estate.

L.O.5   9.   In 1990, you gave a $10,000 gift to a friend. What is the gift tax? What would the gift tax be if you had given $30,000?

LIFE SITUATION   Case 21–1

Retirement and Estate Planning in a High-Income Family

Rich, 48, and Mariann, 47, have a gross estate of $1,160,000 and a high family income. Last year, their combined gross income was about $175,000, most of which came from a medical clinic, in which Rich and several other physicians are partners. The remaining income came from Mariann's part-time job and from interest and dividends on various stocks, bonds, mutual funds, tax-sheltered investments, and rental property that Rich holds.

Rich and Mariann also own, in joint tenancy with right of survivorship, a home, a summer home, and an undeveloped lot in another state, and Mariann will receive $100,000 from a trust fund next year. Their net worth is about $510,000.

Since their holdings are extensive, Rich and Mariann contacted an estate planner for help in determining the most advantageous way of organizing their estate. Naturally, they wanted to be sure that the estate was set up in such a way as to minimize tax and probate shrinkage when it was passed on, first to the surviving spouse and ultimately to their four children. They also wanted to accumulate additional assets and to minimize their income taxes.

Questions

1.   Should Rich and Mariann retitle some of the assets they currently hold in joint tenancy, so as to take advantage of the unified estate and gift tax credit? Why?
2.   Should Rich and Mariann establish a gifting program to reduce their income taxes and build up education funds for their children? Why?

LIFE SITUATION   Case 21–2

Court Rules in Favor of Life Insurance Trust

Life insurance trusts got a boost when a federal district court in Oklahoma ruled that death benefits from an insurance policy in a trust are tax exempt as long as the trust, rather than the insured person, buys the policy—even if the insured person pays the premiums.

"The decision allowed tax planners to use the trusts with more certainty as to tax consequences," says Jane Ann Schiltz, an assistant marketing director at Northwestern Mutual Life Insurance Company. Although the IRS has appealed the decision, many estate planners are confident that the decision won't be reversed.

Estate planners say that it's best to work with a lawyer to establish a trust because the documents are so complex. Stephan R. Leimberg, a professor of taxes and estate planning at American College, says that the trust terms should authorize the administrator or trustee to buy the policy. The insured party should then make annual gifts to the trust, and the trustee should buy the insurance and pay the premiums from the gifts. Such a setup is less likely to be challenged by the IRS, he says, because the trust—not the insured person—owns and controls the assets.

The trusts can also be established for policies that are already in force. But the insured person risks having the proceeds swept back into the estate if he dies within three years of putting a policy in the trust.

Not surprisingly, people generally spend many hours with family members, lawyers, and insurance agents hammering out the details of a trust. So estate planners advise their clients to wait until they are older before setting one up.

"We look at trusts for people who are a little more mature," says Ms. Schiltz. "When you are between 40 and 60, you have a good idea how you feel about your children and relatives, and it's easier to [make a decision] that's irrevocable."

Questions

1. If you were a financial consultant or an estate planner, would you recommend a life insurance trust for your clients? Why?
2. If you were a client, would you consider a life insurance trust for your estate? What are the possible advantages and disadvantages of such a trust arrangement?
3. Do you agree that "when you are between 40 and 60, you have a good idea how you feel about your children and relatives, and it's easier to [make a decision] that's irrevocable"? Explain your answer.

SOURCE: Adapted from Sonja Steptoe, "Trusts with Insurance Find New Life," *The Wall Street Journal*, March 15, 1989, p. C1.

SUPPLEMENTARY READINGS

For Additional Information on Legal Matters in Estate Planning

Aging—Everybody's Doing It. Pp. 36–40. Hartford, Conn.: Aetna Life Insurance and Annuity Company, May 1988.

Estate Planning. Springfield, Ill.: Illinois Bar Association, n.d.

Iseman, Murray. "Common Estate Planning Fiascos." *Barron's,* January 2, 1989, p. 27.

For Additional Information on Estate Planning Advice

Bruss, Robert. "Tips on How to Leave More of Your Estate to Loved Ones." *Chicago Tribune,* July 30, 1989, sec. 16, p. 2E.

Hayner, Don. "Don't Leave Your Heirs with a Financial Mess." *Chicago Sun-Times,* July 30, 1989, p. 58.

For Additional Information on Estate Tax Planning

How Much of Your Business Are You Planning to Give to the IRS? Hartford, Conn.: Aetna Life and Casualty Company, n.d.

Planning with Your Beneficiaries. Washington, D.C.: American Council of Life Insurance, n.d.

Prestopino, Chris J. *Introduction to Estate Planning.* Homewood, Ill.: Richard D. Irwin, 1989.

COMPREHENSIVE CASE FOR PART VI

Retirement and Beyond!

Brett and Robin are a happily married couple in their late 60s who have two children: Neil, aged 36, and Connie, aged 34. Brett retired last year. At present, Brett and Robin have the following property interests. In community property states, assume that all tenancies in common (TIC) held by the spouses are actually held as community property.

$210,000	Home: Joint tenancy; cost, $50,000.
$500,000	Money market fund: spousal TIC.
$21,000	Autos: Brett's property.
$160,000	Face value life insurance policy (LI) on Brett's life: cash value, $31,000. Robin is owner and beneficiary. Premiums are paid with her separate property.
$90,000	Face value life insurance policy (L2) on Robin's life: cash value, $17,000. Brett is owner and beneficiary. Premiums are paid with spousal TIC property.
$130,000	(Replacement value) qualified pension, with income payable to Brett for his life, then to Robin for her life. Brett's contributions (his property) totaled 30 percent of the total contributions made. The employer contributed the rest.
Trust	Revocable trust (Trust A) was set up in 1982, funded with land owned by Brett, then worth $180,000. At present, it is worth $490,000. Upon Brett's death, the trust terminates and all property passes to Connie.
$960,000	Apartment house: Brett's property.

Brett and Robin are planning to have their first wills—"All to surviving spouse" wills—drafted next month.

In 1982, Brett made the following additional gifts: (*a*) $26,000 cash outright to Neil, (*b*) $14,500 cash outright to Connie, and (*c*) $700,000 in stock into an irrevocable trust (Trust B), with all income accumulated until Neil reaches age 41. At that time, the trust will terminate and all income and principal will be paid to Neil and Connie equally. Brett has never made any other gifts.

Questions

1. How would you evaluate the financial arrangements that Brett and Robin have made for their retirement?
2. What are the positive and negative aspects of Brett and Robin's estate planning?
3. Calculate Brett's total taxable gifts for the gift year, assuming gift splitting. This will be a single amount.
4. Assuming that Brett dies in 1990, calculate the amount of Brett's probate estate.
5. Why is retirement and estate planning important for all individuals and families?

SOURCE: Chris J. Prestopino, *Introduction to Estate Planning* (Homewood, Ill.: Richard D. Irwin, 1987), p. 190. Copyright 1987 Richard D. Irwin, Inc.

Using a Financial Planner and Other Financial Planning Information Sources

This book offers the foundation you need for successful personal financial planning. Due to changing social and economic conditions, however, you will need to continually supplement and update your knowledge. Various resources are available to assist you with your personal financial decisions. These resources include printed materials, financial institutions, courses and seminars, computer software, and financial planning specialists.

PRINTED MATERIALS

As presented in Exhibit A–1, a variety of personal finance periodicals are available to expand and update your knowledge. These periodicals, as well as an extensive number of books on various personal finance topics, can be found in your library.

In addition to these sources, there are a vast number of specialized publications. Financial planning newsletters key in on such specific topics as mutual funds, commodity investments, low-priced stocks, real estate investments, tax planning, and investments in gold and coins. You can find a newsletter on almost any financial area that is of interest to you.

As with any purchase, you should determine whether the amount you pay for a newsletter will give you a commensurate benefit. The unregulated financial newsletter industry has many participants that promise much more than they deliver. Investment advisers publish recommendations and charge clients high fees for this service. Not all investment services offer more informaiton than you can obtain from other, less expensive resources. Obtain a sample copy of any high-priced newsletter before you subscribe to it.

FINANCIAL INSTITUTIONS

Some financial advisers, such as insurance agents and investment brokers, are affiliated with companies that sell financial services and assistance. Through national marketing efforts or local promotions, banks, savings and loan associations,

629

EXHIBIT A–1

Personal Financial Planning Periodicals

The area of personal finance is constantly changing. You can keep up with this dynamic field by reading the following periodicals. You can subscribe to them or read them at your school or community library.

Bottom Line Personal
Box 1027
Millburn, NJ 07041

Business Week
1221 Avenue of the Americas
New York, NY 10020

Changing Times
1729 H Street, NW
Washington, DC 20006

Consumer Digest
5705 North Lincoln Avenue
Chicago, IL 60659

Consumer Reports
Consumers Union
256 Washington Street
Mount Vernon, NY 10553

Forbes
Subscriber Service
60 Fifth Avenue
New York, NY 10011

Fortune
Time & Life Building
Rockefeller Center
New York, NY 10020-1393

Money
Time & Life Building
Rockefeller Center
New York, NY 10020-1393

U.S. News & World Report
Subscription Department
2400 N Street, NW
Washington, DC 20037-1196

The Wall Street Journal
200 Burnett Road
Chicopee, MA 01020

credit unions, insurance companies, investment brokers, and real estate offices offer suggestions on budgeting, saving, investing, and other aspects of financial planning. These organizations also offer booklets, financial planning worksheets, and other materials.

COURSES AND SEMINARS

Colleges and universities offer courses in investment, real estate, insurance, taxation, and estate planning that will enhance your knowledge of personal financial planning. The Cooperative Extension Service, funded through the U.S. Department of Agriculture, has offices located at universities in every state (see Exhibit A–3 at the end of this appendix). The programs of these offices include community seminars and continuing education courses in the areas of family financial management, housing, consumer purchasing, health care, and food and nutrition. In addition, the Cooperative Extension Service offers a variety of publications, videos, and software to assist consumers.

Civic clubs and community business organizations schedule free and inexpensive programs featuring speakers and workshops on career planning, budgeting, life insurance, tax return preparation, and investments. Financial institutions and financial service trade associations present seminars for current and prospective customers and members.

COMPUTER SOFTWARE

As personal computers and financial planning software have become more affordable and available, their use for personal finance has increased. Experts do not recommend buying a personal computer for financial planning unless doing so will help you improve your decision-making skills. A personal computer cannot change your saving, spending, and borrowing habits; this can only be done by you. But a personal computer can provide fast and current analyses of your financial situation and progress.

Many personal financial planning software programs are on the market; these range in price from $15 to $200. Popular programs include *Andrew Tobias' Managing Your Money, Dollars and Sense,* and *Quicken.* These programs help you analyze your current financial situation and project your future financial position. Specialized computer programs are also available for conducting investment analyses, preparing tax returns, and determining the costs of financing and owning a home. For further information, see Appendix C, "Using a Personal Computer for Personal Financial Planning."

Home computers can also be used to access databases that provide business and investment news. *CompuServe* and *Dow Jones News/Retrieval* allow the use of electronic databases in the comfort of your home or office. The Dow Jones system provides more than 30 types of information, including articles in *The Wall Street Journal* and *Barron's,* stock prices, research reports, movie reviews, sports scores, and weather reports.

FINANCIAL PLANNING SPECIALISTS

Specialists from different fields can provide specific financial assistance and advice.

- *Accountants* specialize in tax matters and financial documents.
- *Bankers* assist you with financial services and trusts.
- *Credit counselors* suggest ways to reduce spending and eliminate credit problems.
- *Certified financial planners* coordinate your finances into a single plan.
- *Insurance agents* sell types of insurance coverage that will protect your wealth and property.
- *Investment brokers* provide information on stocks, bonds, and other investments and handle transactions for their purchase and sale.
- *Lawyers* help you with wills, estate planning, tax problems, and other legal matters.
- *Real estate agents* assist you in handling the details of buying and selling a home or other real estate.
- *Tax preparers* specialize in the completion of income tax returns and other tax forms.

In recent years, many of these specialists have expanded their services to include various aspects of financial planning.

Since most people spend most of their time in earning or using income, many people are unable to give their personal financial planning as much attention as it requires. Financial planners are individuals who can help you establish and accomplish financial goals by coordinating your financial decisions. These individuals operate under a variety of titles, such as financial adviser and financial counselor. Legal, competitive, and economic changes in financial services have enabled financial planners to expand their offerings of financial assistance.

Before employing the services of a financial planner, you should consider who the financial planners are, whether you need one, how to select one, how financial planners are certified, and how helpful computerized financial plans are.

Who Are the Financial Planners?

Many financial planners represent major insurance companies or investment businesses. Financial planners may also be individuals whose primary profession is tax accounting, real estate, or law. In total, over 200,000 individuals call themselves financial planners.

Financial planners may be placed in one of two categories. The first category consists of the financial planners who charge a fee but have no interest in the financial products they recommend. These individuals are commonly accountants, lawyers, credit counselors, or independent financial advisers.

The second category consists of the financial planners who earn a commission on any insurance, stocks, mutual funds, or other investments that the client buys. These individuals are often employed by financial services companies with a nationwide network of offices. Critics contend that the financial planning assistance provided by such companies is just a marketing ploy to sell other items.

A financial planner's background or the company a financial planner represents is a good gauge of the financial planner's principal area of expertise. An accountant is likely to be most knowledgeable about tax laws, while an insurance company representative will probably emphasize how you can use insurance to achieve your financial goals.

Do You Need a Financial Planner?

The two main factors that determine whether you need financial planning assistance are your income and your willingness to make independent decisions. If you earn less than $40,000 a year, you probably do not need a financial planner. Anything less does not allow for many major financial decisions once you have allocated the funds for the spending, savings, insurance, and tax elements of your personal financial planning. Exhibit A–2 offers a way to assess your need for a financial planner.

Taking a personal interest in your financial affairs can minimize your need for a financial planner. If you are willing to keep up-to-date on developments related to investments, insurance, taxes, and other personal business topics, you can probably reduce the amount of money you spend on financial advisers. This will require an ongoing investment of time and effort on your finances, but it will enable you to control your own financial direction, which many people consider necessary.

When deciding whether to use a financial planner, also consider the services that financial planners usually provide. First, the financial planner should assist you in assessing your current financial position with regard to spending, savings, insurance, taxes, and potential investments. Second, he or she should offer a clearly written plan with different courses of action for your consideration. Third, he or she should take time to discuss the components of the plan and help you monitor your financial progress. Finally, he or she should guide you to other experts and sources of financial services as needed.

You may not always receive specific advice from a financial planner. A financial planner who charges a flat fee will probably not give you specific investment recommendations. Some consider this approach more objective than that of commission-based planners who push products that increase their earnings.

EXHIBIT A-2

Do You Need a Financial Planner?

Compute the following "financial planning need index" to determine whether the use of a financial planner would be to your advantage.

Income   For each $5,000 of family income above $20,000, score one point, through $50,000. Over $50,000, score one point for each additional $10,000 up to a 15-point limit. For example, an income of $90,000 would score 10 points.

_____

Taxes   For each $1,000 paid in taxes above $5,000 up to $10,000, score one point. Score another point for each $2,000 in taxes over $10,000 up to a maximum of 15 points. For example, $20,000 in federal taxes would score 10 points.

_____

Financial Assets   In this category, you receive points as follows: one point if you own common stocks or bonds; one point for a margin account or borrowing to finance investments: one point if you own a mutual fund, variable annuity, or more than three life insurance policies; if all of the above apply, take an additional point; double your total of the above if you have more than five investments or use more than one stockbroker, banker, or insurance agent; two additional points for an investment in a venture company or family business or investment real estate; one point for a limited partnership investment, and two more points if this is a private rather than a public offering. The maximum number of points for this category is 10.

_____

Financial Planning Need Index (divide total by three)   A score of five or higher is usally an indication that you should consider formal assistance for financial planning.

_____

SOURCE: Carl E. Andersen, _Andersen on Financial Planning_ (Homewood, Ill.: Dow Jones-Irwin, 1986), pp. 20–21.

How Should You Select a Financial Planner?

You can locate financial planners by using a telephone directory, by contacting financial institutions, or by obtaining references from friends, business associates, or professionals with whom you currently deal, such as insurance agents or real estate brokers.

When evaluating a financial planner, investigate the following:

- Is financial planning the primary activity of the individual, or are other activities primary?
- What is the individual's educational background and formal training?
- What are the individual's areas of expertise?
- Are experts in other areas, such as taxes, law, or insurance, available to assist you in your financial planning?
- What professional titles and certification does the individual possess?
- Is the individual licensed as an investment broker or as a seller of life insurance?
- Are you allowed a free initial consultation?
- What method of payment is required? Will you be able to afford the service?
- Does the individual have an independent practice, or is he or she affiliated with a major financial services company?
- What are typical insurance, tax, and investment decisions that the individual makes for current clients?

- Is the individual able to communicate in a manner with which you feel comfortable?

Such an investigation takes time and effort, but remember that you are considering placing your entire financial future in the hands of one person.

How Are Financial Planners Certified?

The requirements for becoming a financial planner are not regulated. Only about 10 percent of those who call themselves financial planners have met specific training requirements for that role. Organizations that provide details on the certification of financial planners are the Institute of Certified Financial Planners, the International Association for Financial Planning, and the National Association of Personal Financial Planners.

Many financial planners use abbreviations for the titles they have earned. Some of these abbreviations are quite familiar—for example, CPA (certified public accountant, JD (doctor of law), and MBA (master of business administration); others are unknown to most people. Less well known abreviations used by financial planners include CFP (certified financial planner), ChFC (chartered financial consultant in the life insurance industry), and CFA (chartered financial analyst handling stock and bond portfolios).

While these credentials provide some assurance of expertise, not all planners are licensed. The Better Business Bureau estimated that fraudulent planners took consumers for nearly $90 million in bad investments and advice between 1983 and 1985. Such financial planning activities as insurance and investment security sales do come under regulatory control. Consumers should be wary of and investigate any financial planning operation they are considering.

How Helpful Are Computerized Financial Plans?

Computerized financial plans are an inexpensive alternative to financial planners. The low-priced advice by such plans, called *prefab planning* by some, can provide appropriate financial direction. While cost of a financial planner can range from a couple of hundred dollars to several thousand dollars, computerized assistance ranges in price from nothing at all to a few hundred dollars.

Computerized financial advice has been available for several years from many of the organizations that financial planners represent. Investment brokers, insurance companies, and other financial institutions offer computerized financial evaluations and recommendations. For companies with a financial product to sell, computerized financial plans serve to attract new customers. Clients may have the option of meeting with a company representative to interpret results. Again, beware of bias toward insurance or specific types of investments that may have been built into the computerized plan.

Despite their drawbacks, computerized financial plans can have value. Systems users are usually under no obligation to purchase additional products or services. The printed report assesses your current financial position and suggests actions that you can take. You are not likely to get a lot of detail since this type of financial plan is designed to provide general advice and accepted methods for reaching goals and to offer recommendations on savings plans, investment strategies, insurance needs, tax estimates, and financial prospects for retirement. These low-price plans will probably not recommend specific stocks or tax actions.

What Career Opportunities Are Available in Personal Finance?

As you learn to handle your personal finances, you may wish to use your money management skills in a financial planning career. For employment in this field, a basic knowledge of insurance, taxes, investments, and estate planning will be required. Also important will be such business subjects as accounting, economics, and marketing and strong public speaking and writing skills.

Employment in financial planning usually starts with experience as a stockbroker, insurance agent, bank officer, or accountant. As your practical background increases, you can get involved as a personal financial planner through your employer or you can start your own service.

The expanding field of financial services is creating a demand for individuals who desire to help others analyze and plan their finances. For further information on a career in financial planning, contact the International Association for Financial Planning, Two Concourse Parkway, Suite 800, Atlanta, GA 30328; the College for Financial Planning, 4695 South Monaco Street, Denver, CO 80237-3403; or the National Association of Personal Financial Advisors, 1130 Lake Cook Road, Suite 105, Buffalo Grove, IL 60089.

EXHIBIT A–3
Cooperative Extension
Service State Contacts

Alabama
Cooperative Extension Service
Auburn University
264 Spidle Hall
Auburn, AL 36849-5644
(205) 844-3243

Arizona
Cooperative Extension Service
University of Arizona
School of Family and Consumer
Resources
Tucson, AZ 85721
(602) 621-3347

California
Cooperative Extension Service
University of California
Cooperative Extension Annex
Riverside, CA 92521
(714) 787-5241

Connecticut
Cooperative Extension Service
University of Connecticut
Box U–117
Storrs, CT 06269-1117
(203) 486-2229

**District of
Columbia**
Cooperative Extension Service
University of the District of Columbia
901 Newton Street, NE
Washington, DC 20017
(202) 576-6951

Alaska
Cooperative Extension Service
University of Alaska
Fairbanks, AK 99701-6285
(907) 452-1530

Arkansas
Cooperative Extension Service
Box 391
Little Rock, AR 72203
(501) 373-2962

Colorado
Cooperative Extension Service
Colorado State University
160 Aylesworth, SE
Fort Collins, CO 80523
(303) 491-5772

Delaware
Cooperative Extension Service
University of Delaware
120 Townsend Hall
Newark, DE 19717-1303
(302) 451-2509

Florida
Cooperative Extension Service
University of Florida
3008 McCarty Hall
Gainesville, FL 32611-0130
(904) 392-1869

Georgia
Cooperative Extension Service
University of Georgia
Hoke Smith Annex
Athens, GA 30602
(404) 542-8884

Hawaii
Cooperative Extension Service
Miller Hall
Krauss Annex
Honolulu, HI 96822
(808) 948-6519

Illinois
Cooperative Extension Service
University of Illinois/Bevier Hall
905 South Goodwin Avenue
Urbana, IL 61801
(217) 244-2848

Iowa
Cooperative Extension Service
Iowa State University
Department of Family Environment
52N LeBaron Hall
Ames, IA 50011
(515) 294-6568

Kentucky
Cooperative Extension Service
University of Kentucky
321 Funkhouser Building
Lexington, KY 40506
(606) 257-7758

Maine
Cooperative Extension Service
University of Maine
128 College Avenue
Orono, ME 04473
(207) 581-3107

Massachusetts
Cooperative Extension Service
University of Massachusetts
Skinner Hall
Amherst, MA 01003
(413) 545-2313

Minnesota
Cooperative Extension Service
University of Minnesota/McNeal Hall
1985 Buford Avenue
St. Paul, MN 55108-1011
(612) 625-1763

Guam
Cooperative Extension Service
University of Guam
UOG Station
Mangilao, GU 96823
(671) 734-2562

Idaho
Cooperative Extension Service
University of Idaho
103A School of Home Economics
Moscow, ID 83843
(208) 885-5778

Indiana
Cooperative Extension Service
Purdue University
319 Matthews Hall
West Lafayette, IN 47907
(317) 494-8304

Kansas
Cooperative Extension Service
Kansas State University
343 Justin Hall
Manhattan, KS 66506
(913) 532-5780

Louisiana
Cooperative Extension Service
Louisiana State University
297 Knapp Hall
Baton Rouge, LA 70803
(504) 388-1425

Maryland
Cooperative Extension Service
University of Maryland
2309 CSS Building
College Park, MD 20742-2451
(301) 454-3601

Michigan
Cooperative Extension Service
Michigan State University
203 Human Ecology Building
East Lansing, MI 48824
(517) 353-3886

Mississippi
Cooperative Extension Service
Mississippi State University
Box 5446
Mississippi State, MS 39762
(601) 325-3082

Missouri
Cooperative Extension Service
University of Missouri
162 Stanley Hall
Columbia, MO 65211
(314) 882-5115

Montana
Cooperative Extension Service
Montana State University
Linfield Hall
Bozeman, MT 59717
(406) 994-3511

Nebraska
Cooperative Extension Service
University of Nebraska
113 Home Economics
Lincoln, NE 68583-0801
(402) 472-5517

Nevada
Cooperative Extension Service
University of Nevada—Reno
School of Home Economics
Reno, NV 89557-0040
(702) 784-6977

New Hampshire
Cooperative Extension Service
University of New Hampshire
327 Daniel Webster Highway
Boscawen, NH 03303
(603) 796-2151

New Jersey
Cooperative Extension Service
Cook College
Box 231
New Brunswick, NJ 08903
(201) 932-9737

New Mexico
Cooperative Extension Service
New Mexico State University
Box 3AE
Las Cruces, NM 88003
(505) 646-2009

New York
Cooperative Extension Service
Cornell University
105 MVR Hall
Ithaca, NY 14853
(607) 255-2592

North Carolina
Cooperative Extension Service
North Carolina State University
Box 7605
Raleigh, NC 27695-7605
(919) 737-2770

North Dakota
Cooperative Extension Service
North Dakota State University
Box 5016
Fargo, ND 58105
(701) 237-8593

Ohio
Cooperative Extension Service
Ohio State University
1787 Neil Avenue
Columbus, OH 43210
(614) 292-8991

Oklahoma
Cooperative Extension Service
Oklahoma State University
Home Economics West
Stillwater, OK 74078-0337
(405) 744-6282

Oregon
Cooperative Extension Service
Oregon State University
161 Milam Hall
Corvallis, OR 97331-5106
(503) 754-3211

Pennsylvania
Cooperative Extension Service
Pennsylvania State University
207 Armsby Building
University Park, PA 16802
(814) 865-5406

Puerto Rico
Cooperative Extension Service
University of Puerto Rico
Box 21120
Rio Piedras, PR 00928
(809) 765-8000 (Ext. 256)

Rhode Island
Cooperative Extension Service
University of Rhode Island
311 Lippitt Hall—REN
Kingston, RI 02881-0804
(401) 792-4587

South Carolina
Cooperative Extension Service
Clemson University
243 P&A Science Building
Clemson, SC 29634-0312
(803) 656-3090

Tennessee
Agricultural Extension Service
University of Tennessee
Box 1071
Knoxville, TN 37901-1071
(615) 974-8198

Utah
Cooperative Extension Service
Utah State University
College of Family Life
Logan, UT 84322-2949
(801) 750-1533

Virginia
Cooperative Extension Service
Virginia Polytechnic Institute
and State University
100 Human Resources Annex
Blacksburg, VA 24061-8399
(703) 231-4191

West Virginia
Cooperative Extension Service
West Virginia University
Knapp Hall, Box 6031
Morgantown, WV 26506-6031
(304) 293-2694

Wyoming
Cooperative Extension Service
University of Wyoming
University Station, Box 3354
Laramie, WY 82071
(307) 766-5689

South Dakota
Cooperative Extension Service
South Dakota State University
Box 2275A, NHE 243
Brookings, SD 57007
(605) 688-6191

Texas
Texas Extension Service
Texas A&M University
237 Special Services Building
College Station, TX 77843
(409) 845-7227

Vermont
Cooperative Extension Service
University of Vermont
207 Terrill Hall
Burlington, VT 05405
(802) 656-2097

Washington
Cooperative Extension Service
Washington State University
415 Hulbert Hall
Pullman, WA 99164-6230
(509) 335-2837

Wisconsin
Cooperative Extension Service
University of Wisconsin
235 Home Economics Building
Madison, WI 53706
(608) 262-0080

The Time Value of Money
Future Value and Present Value Computations

As introduced in Chapter 1, and used to measure financial opportunity costs in other chapters, the *time value of money*, more commonly referred to as *interest*, is the price of money that is borrowed or lent. Interest is the cost of using money; it can be compared to rent, the cost of using an apartment or other item. The time value of money is based on the fact that a dollar received today is worth more than a dollar that will be received one year from today, because the dollar received today can be saved or invested and will be worth more than a dollar a year from today. In a similar manner, a dollar that will be received one year from today is currently worth less than a dollar today.

The time value of money consists of two major aspects: future value and present value. *Future value*, also referred to as *compounding*, is the amount to which a current sum will increase based on a certain interest rate and period of time. *Present value*, also called *discounting*, is the current value of a future sum based on a certain interest rate and period of time.

In future value problems, you are given an amount to save or invest and you need to calculate the amount that will be available at some future date based on a certain interest rate. With present value problems, you are given the amount that will be available at some future date and you must calculate the current monetary value of that amount based on a certain interest rate. Both future value and present value computations are based on basic interest rate calculations.

INTEREST RATE BASICS

Simple interest is the dollar cost of borrowing or earnings from lending money. The interest is based on three elements:

- The dollar amount, called the *principal*.
- The *rate of interest*.
- The amount of *time*.

The formula for computing interest is

Interest = Principal × Rate of interest × Time

The interest rate is stated as a percentage for a year. For example, you must convert 12 percent to either 0.12 or $^{12}/_{100}$ before doing your calculations. The time element must also be converted to a decimal or fraction. For example, three months would be shown as either 0.25 or ¼ of a year. Interest over 2 ½ years would involve a time period of 2.5.

Example A Suppose $1,000 is borrowed at 5 percent and repaid in one payment at the end of one year. Using the simple interest calculation, the interest is $50, computed as follows:

$50 = $1,000 × 0.05 × 1(year)

Example B If you deposited $750 in a savings account paying 8 percent, how much interest would you earn in nine months? You would compute this amount as follows:

Interest = $750 × 0.08 × ¾(or 0.75 of a year)
        = $45

Sample Problem 1 How much interest would you earn if you deposited $300 at 6 percent for 27 months? (*Answers to sample problems are at the end of this appendix.*)

Sample Problem 2 How much interest would you pay to borrow $670 for eight months at 12 percent?

FUTURE VALUE OF A SINGLE AMOUNT

The future value of an amount consists of the original amount plus compound interest. This calculation involves the following elements:

FV = Future value
PV = Present value
 i = Interest rate
 n = Number of time periods

The formula for future value is

$$FV = PV(1 + i)^n$$

Example C The future value of $1 at 10 percent after three years is $1.33. This amount is calculated as follows:

$$\$1.33 = \$1.00(1 + 0.10)^3$$

Future value tables are available to help you determine compounded interest amounts (see Exhibit B–1). By looking at Exhibit B–1 for 10 percent and three years, you can see that $1 would be worth $1.33 at that time. For other amounts, multiply the table factor by the original amount.

Example D If your savings of $400 earns 12 percent, compounded *monthly,* over a year and a half, you would use the table factor for 1 percent for 18 time periods. The future value of this amount is $478.40, calculated as follows:

$478.40 = $400 (1.196)

Sample Problem 3   What is the future value of $800 at 8 percent after six years?

Sample Problem 4   How much would you have in savings if you kept $200 on deposit for eight years at 8 percent compounded *semiannually?*

FUTURE VALUE OF A SERIES OF EQUAL AMOUNTS

Future value may also be calculated for a situation in which regular additions are made to savings. The following formula is used:

$$FV = \frac{(1 + i)^n - 1}{i}$$

This formula assumes that each deposit is for the same amount, that the interest rate is the same for each time period, and that the deposits are made at the end of each time period.

Example E   The future value of three $1 deposits made at the end of the next three years earning 10 percent interest is $3.31. This is calculated as follows:

$$\$3.31 = \$1\,\frac{(1 + 0.10)^3 - 1}{0.10}$$

With the use of Exhibit B–2, this same amount can be found for 10 percent for three time periods. To use the table for other amounts, multiply the table factors by the annual deposit.

Example F   If you plan to deposit $40 a year for 10 years earning 8 percent compounded annually, you would use the table factor for 8 percent for 10 time periods. The future value of this amount is $579.48, calculated as follows:

$579.48 = $40(14.487)

Sample Problem 5   What is the future value of an annual deposit of $230 earning 6 percent for 15 years?

Sample Problem 6   What amount would a person have in a retirement account if annual deposits of $375 were made for 25 years earning 12 percent compounded annually?

PRESENT VALUE OF A SINGLE AMOUNT

If you want to know how much you need to deposit in the present in order to receive a certain amount in the future, the following formula is used:

$$PV = \frac{1}{(1 + i)^n}$$

Example G   The present value of $1 to be received three years from now based on a 10 percent interest rate is $0.75. This amount is calculated as follows:

$$\$0.75 = \frac{\$1}{(1 + 0.10)^3}$$

Present value tables are available to assist in this process (see Exhibit B–3). Notice that $1 at 10 percent for three years has a present value of $0.75. For amounts other than $1, multiply the table factor by the amount involved.

Example H   If you want to have $300 seven years from now and your savings earns 10 percent compounded *semiannually,* you would use the table factor for 5 percent for 14 time periods. In this situation, the present value is $151.50, calculated as follows:

$151.50 = $300(0.505)

Sample Problem 7   What is the present value of $2,200 earning 15 percent for eight years?

Sample Problem 8   In order to have $6,000 for a daughter's education in 10 years, what amount should a parent deposit in a savings account that earns 12 percent compounded *quarterly?*

PRESENT VALUE OF A SERIES OF EQUAL AMOUNTS

The final time value of money situation allows a person to receive an amount at the end of each time period for a certain number of periods. This amount would be calculated as follows:

$$PV = \frac{1 - \dfrac{1}{(1 + i)^n}}{i}$$

Example I   The present value of a $1 withdrawal at the end of the next three years would be $2.49, calculated as follows:

$$\$2.49 = \$1 \left[\frac{1 - \dfrac{1}{(1 + 0.10)^n}}{0.10} \right]$$

This same amount can be found in Exhibit B–4 for 10 percent and three time periods. To use the table for other situations, multiply the table factor by the amount to be withdrawn each year.

Example J   If you would like to withdraw $100 at the end of each year for 10 years from an account that earns 14 percent compounded annually, what amount must you deposit now? Use the table factor for 14 percent for 10 time periods. In this situation, the present value is $521.60, calculated as follows:

$521.60 = $100(5.216)

Sample Problem 9   What is the present value of a withdrawal of $200 at the end of each year for 14 years with an interest rate of 7 percent?

Sample Problem 10   How much would you have to deposit now to be able to withdraw $650 at the end of each year for 20 years from an account that earns 11 percent?

ANSWERS TO
SAMPLE
PROBLEMS

1. $300 × 0.06 × 2.25 years (27 months) = $40.50.
2. $670 × 0.12 × ⅔ (of a year) = $53.60.
3. $800(1.587) = $1,269.60. (Use Exhibit B–1, 8%, 6 periods.)
4. $200(1.873) = $374.60. (Use Exhibit B–1, 4%, 16 periods.)
5. $230(23.276) = $5,353.48. (Use Exhibit B–2, 6%, 15 periods.)
6. $375(133.33) = $49,998.75. (Use Exhibit B–2, 12%, 25 periods.)
7. $2,200(0.327) = $719.40. (Use Exhibit B–3, 15%, 8 periods.)
8. $6,000(0.307) = $1,842. (Use Exhibit B–3, 3%, 40 periods.)
9. $200(8.745) = $1,749. (Use Exhibit B–4, 7%, 14 periods.)
10. $650(7.963) = $5,175.95. (Use Exhibit B–4, 11%, 20 periods.)

EXHIBIT B–1   Future Value (Compounded Sum) of $1 after a Given Number of Time Periods

Period	1%	2%	3%	4%	5%	6%	7%	8%	9%	10%	11%
1	1.010	1.020	1.030	1.040	1.050	1.060	1.070	1.080	1.090	1.100	1.110
2	1.020	1.040	1.061	1.082	1.103	1.124	1.145	1.166	1.188	1.210	1.232
3	1.030	1.061	1.093	1.125	1.158	1.191	1.225	1.260	1.295	1.331	1.368
4	1.041	1.082	1.126	1.170	1.216	1.262	1.311	1.360	1.412	1.464	1.518
5	1.051	1.104	1.159	1.217	1.276	1.338	1.403	1.469	1.539	1.611	1.685
6	1.062	1.126	1.194	1.265	1.340	1.419	1.501	1.587	1.677	1.772	1.870
7	1.072	1.149	1.230	1.316	1.407	1.504	1.606	1.714	1.828	1.949	2.076
8	1.083	1.172	1.267	1.369	1.477	1.594	1.718	1.851	1.993	2.144	2.305
9	1.094	1.195	1.305	1.423	1.551	1.689	1.838	1.999	2.172	2.358	2.558
10	1.105	1.219	1.344	1.480	1.629	1.791	1.967	2.159	2.367	2.594	2.839
11	1.116	1.243	1.384	1.539	1.710	1.898	2.105	2.332	2.580	2.853	3.152
12	1.127	1.268	1.426	1.601	1.796	2.012	2.252	2.518	2.813	3.138	3.498
13	1.138	1.294	1.469	1.665	1.886	2.133	2.410	2.720	3.066	3.452	3.883
14	1.149	1.319	1.513	1.732	1.980	2.261	2.579	2.937	3.342	3.797	4.310
15	1.161	1.346	1.558	1.801	2.079	2.397	2.759	3.172	3.642	4.177	4.785
16	1.173	1.373	1.605	1.873	2.183	2.540	2.952	3.426	3.970	4.595	5.311
17	1.184	1.400	1.653	1.948	2.292	2.693	3.159	3.700	4.328	5.054	5.895
18	1.196	1.428	1.702	2.206	2.407	2.854	3.380	3.996	4.717	5.560	6.544
19	1.208	1.457	1.754	2.107	2.527	3.026	3.617	4.316	5.142	6.116	7.263
20	1.220	1.486	1.806	2.191	2.653	3.207	3.870	4.661	5.604	6.727	8.062
25	1.282	1.641	2.094	2.666	3.386	4.292	5.427	6.848	8.623	10.835	13.585
30	1.348	1.811	2.427	3.243	4.322	5.743	7.612	10.063	13.268	17.449	22.892
40	1.489	2.208	3.262	4.801	7.040	10.286	14.974	21.725	31.409	45.259	65.001
50	1.645	2.692	4.384	7.107	11.467	18.420	29.457	46.902	74.358	117.39	184.57

Percent

Period						Percent					
	12%	13%	14%	15%	16%	17%	18%	19%	20%	25%	30%
1	1.120	1.130	1.140	1.150	1.160	1.170	1.180	1.190	1.200	1.250	1.300
2	1.254	1.277	1.300	1.323	1.346	1.369	1.392	1.416	1.440	1.563	1.690
3	1.405	1.443	1.482	1.521	1.561	1.602	1.643	1.685	1.728	1.953	2.197
4	1.574	1.630	1.689	1.749	1.811	1.874	1.939	2.005	2.074	2.441	2.856
5	1.762	1.842	1.925	2.011	2.100	2.192	2.288	2.386	2.488	3.052	3.713
6	1.974	2.082	2.195	2.313	2.436	2.565	2.700	2.840	2.986	3.815	4.827
7	2.211	2.353	2.502	2.660	2.826	3.001	3.185	3.379	3.583	4.768	6.276
8	2.476	2.658	2.853	3.059	3.278	3.511	3.759	4.021	4.300	5.960	8.157
9	2.773	3.004	3.252	3.518	3.803	4.108	4.435	4.785	5.160	7.451	10.604
10	3.106	3.395	3.707	4.046	4.411	4.807	5.234	5.696	6.192	9.313	13.786
11	3.479	3.836	4.226	4.652	5.117	5.624	6.176	6.777	7.430	11.642	17.922
12	3.896	4.335	4.818	5.350	5.936	6.580	7.288	8.064	8.916	14.552	23.298
13	4.363	4.898	5.492	6.153	6.886	7.699	8.599	9.596	10.699	18.190	30.288
14	4.887	5.535	6.261	7.076	7.988	9.007	10.147	11.420	12.839	22.737	39.374
15	5.474	6.254	7.138	8.137	9.266	10.539	11.974	13.590	15.407	28.422	51.186
16	6.130	7.067	8.137	9.358	10.748	12.330	14.129	16.172	18.488	35.527	66.542
17	6.866	7.986	9.276	10.761	12.468	14.426	16.672	19.244	22.186	44.409	86.504
18	7.690	9.024	10.575	12.375	14.463	16.879	19.673	22.091	26.623	55.511	112.46
19	8.613	10.197	12.056	14.232	16.777	19.748	23.214	27.252	31.948	69.389	146.19
20	9.646	11.523	13.743	16.367	19.461	23.106	27.393	32.429	38.338	86.736	190.05
25	17.000	21.231	26.462	32.919	40.874	50.658	62.669	77.388	95.396	264.70	705.64
30	29.960	39.116	50.950	66.212	85.850	111.07	143.37	184.68	237.38	807.79	2,620.0
40	93.051	132.78	188.88	267.86	378.72	533.87	750.38	1,051.7	1,469.8	7,523.2	36,119.
50	289.00	450.74	700.23	1,083.7	1,670.7	2,566.2	3,927.4	5,988.9	9,100.4	70,065.	497,929.

SOURCE: Maurice Joy, *Introduction to Financial Management* (Homewood, Ill.: Richard D. Irwin).

Future Value (Compounded Sum) of $1 Paid In at the End of Each Period for a Given Number of Time Periods

					Percent						
Period	1%	2%	3%	4%	5%	6%	7%	8%	9%	10%	11%
1	1.000	1.000	1.000	1.000	1.000	1.000	1.000	1.000	1.000	1.000	1.000
2	2.010	2.020	2.030	2.040	2.050	2.060	2.070	2.080	2.090	2.100	2.110
3	3.030	3.060	3.091	3.122	3.153	3.184	3.215	3.246	3.278	3.310	3.342
4	4.060	4.122	4.184	4.246	4.310	4.375	4.440	4.506	4.573	4.641	4.710
5	5.101	5.204	5.309	5.416	5.526	5.637	5.751	5.867	5.985	6.105	6.228
6	6.152	6.308	6.468	6.633	6.802	6.975	7.153	7.336	7.523	7.716	7.913
7	7.214	7.434	7.662	7.898	8.142	8.394	8.654	8.923	9.200	9.487	9.783
8	8.286	8.583	8.892	9.214	9.549	9.897	10.260	10.637	11.028	11.436	11.859
9	9.369	9.755	10.159	10.583	11.027	11.491	11.978	12.488	13.021	13.579	14.164
10	10.462	10.950	11.464	12.006	12.578	13.181	13.816	14.487	15.193	15.937	16.722
11	11.567	12.169	12.808	13.486	14.207	14.972	15.784	16.645	17.560	18.531	19.561
12	12.683	13.412	14.192	15.026	15.917	16.870	17.888	18.977	20.141	21.384	22.713
13	13.809	14.680	15.618	16.627	17.713	18.882	20.141	21.495	22.953	24.523	26.212
14	14.947	15.974	17.086	18.292	19.599	21.015	22.550	24.215	26.019	27.975	30.095
15	16.097	17.293	18.599	20.024	21.579	23.276	25.129	27.152	29.361	31.772	34.405
16	17.258	18.639	20.157	21.825	23.657	25.673	27.888	30.324	33.003	35.950	39.190
17	18.430	20.012	21.762	23.698	25.840	20.213	30.840	33.750	36.974	40.545	44.301
18	19.615	21.412	23.414	25.645	28.132	30.906	33.999	37.450	41.301	45.599	50.396
19	20.811	22.841	25.117	27.671	30.539	33.760	37.379	41.446	46.018	51.159	56.939
20	22.019	24.297	26.870	29.778	33.066	36.786	40.995	45.762	51.160	57.275	64.203
25	28.243	32.030	36.459	41.646	47.727	54.865	63.249	73.106	84.701	98.347	114.41
30	34.785	40.588	47.575	56.085	66.439	79.058	94.461	113.28	136.31	164.49	199.02
40	48.886	60.402	75.401	95.026	120.80	154.76	199.64	259.06	337.89	442.59	581.83
50	64.463	84.579	112.80	152.67	209.35	290.34	406.53	573.77	815.08	1,163.9	1,668.8

EXHIBIT B–2   (concluded)

| | | | | | | Percent | | | | | |
Period	12%	13%	14%	15%	16%	17%	18%	19%	20%	25%	30%
1	1.000	1.000	1.000	1.000	1.000	1.000	1.000	1.000	1.000	1.000	1.000
2	2.120	2.130	2.140	2.150	2.160	2.170	2.180	2.190	2.200	2.250	2.300
3	3.374	3.407	3.440	3.473	3.506	3.539	3.572	3.606	3.640	3.813	3.990
4	4.779	4.850	4.921	4.993	5.066	5.141	5.215	5.291	5.368	5.766	6.187
5	6.353	6.480	6.610	6.742	6.877	7.014	7.154	7.297	7.442	8.207	9.043
6	8.115	8.323	8.536	8.754	8.977	9.207	9.442	0.683	9.930	11.259	12.756
7	10.089	10.405	10.730	11.067	11.414	11.772	12.142	12.523	12.916	15.073	17.583
8	12.300	12.757	13.233	13.727	14.240	14.773	15.327	15.902	16.499	19.842	23.858
9	14.776	15.416	16.085	16.786	17.519	18.285	19.086	19.923	20.799	25.802	32.015
10	17.549	18.420	19.337	20.304	21.321	22.393	23.521	24.701	25.959	33.253	42.619
11	20.655	21.814	23.045	24.349	25.733	27.200	28.755	30.404	32.150	42.566	56.405
12	24.133	25.650	27.271	29.002	30.850	32.824	34.931	37.180	39.581	54.208	74.327
13	28.029	29.985	32.089	34.352	36.786	39.404	42.219	45.244	48.497	68.760	97.625
14	32.393	34.883	37.581	40.505	43.672	47.103	50.818	54.841	59.196	86.949	127.91
15	37.280	40.417	43.842	47.580	51.660	56.110	60.965	66.261	72.035	109.69	167.29
16	42.753	46.672	50.980	55.717	60.925	66.649	72.939	79.850	87.442	138.11	218.47
17	48.884	53.739	59.118	65.075	71.673	78.979	87.068	96.022	105.93	173.64	285.01
18	55.750	61.725	68.394	75.836	84.141	93.406	103.74	115.27	128.12	218.05	371.52
19	63.440	70.749	78.969	88.212	98.603	110.29	123.41	138.17	154.74	273.56	483.97
20	72.052	80.947	91.025	102.44	115.38	130.03	146.63	165.42	186.69	342.95	630.17
25	133.33	155.62	181.87	212.79	249.21	292.11	342.60	402.04	471.98	1,054.8	2,348.80
30	241.33	293.20	356.79	434.75	530.31	647.44	790.95	966.7	1,181.9	3,227.2	8,730.0
40	767.09	1,013.7	1,342.0	1,779.1	2,360.8	3,134.5	4,163.21	5,529.8	7,343.9	30,089.	120,393.
50	2,400.0	3,459.5	4,994.5	7,217.7	10,436.	15,090.	21,813.	31,515.	45,497.	280,256.	165,976.

SOURCE: Maurice Joy, *Introduction to Financial Management* (Homewood, Ill.: Richard D. Irwin).

EXHIBIT B–3   Present Value of $1 to Be Received at the End of a Given Number of Time Periods

Percent

Period	1%	2%	3%	4%	5%	6%	7%	8%	9%	10%	11%	12%
1	0.990	0.980	0.971	0.962	0.952	0.943	0.935	0.926	0.917	0.909	0.901	0.893
2	0.980	0.961	0.943	0.925	0.907	0.890	0.873	0.857	0.842	0.826	0.812	0.797
3	0.971	0.942	0.915	0.889	0.864	0.840	0.816	0.794	0.772	0.751	0.731	0.712
4	0.961	0.924	0.885	0.855	0.823	0.792	0.763	0.735	0.708	0.683	0.659	0.636
5	0.951	0.906	0.863	0.822	0.784	0.747	0.713	0.681	0.650	0.621	0.593	0.567
6	0.942	0.888	0.837	0.790	0.746	0.705	0.666	0.630	0.596	0.564	0.535	0.507
7	0.933	0.871	0.813	0.760	0.711	0.665	0.623	0.583	0.547	0.513	0.482	0.452
8	0.923	0.853	0.789	0.731	0.677	0.627	0.582	0.540	0.502	0.467	0.434	0.404
9	0.914	0.837	0.766	0.703	0.645	0.592	0.544	0.500	0.460	0.424	0.391	0.361
10	0.905	0.820	0.744	0.676	0.614	0.558	0.508	0.463	0.422	0.386	0.352	0.322
11	0.896	0.804	0.722	0.650	0.585	0.527	0.475	0.429	0.388	0.350	0.317	0.287
12	0.887	0.788	0.701	0.625	0.557	0.497	0.444	0.397	0.356	0.319	0.286	0.257
13	0.879	0.773	0.681	0.601	0.530	0.469	0.415	0.368	0.326	0.290	0.258	0.229
14	0.870	0.758	0.661	0.577	0.505	0.442	0.388	0.340	0.299	0.263	0.232	0.205
15	0.861	0.743	0.642	0.555	0.481	0.417	0.362	0.315	0.275	0.239	0.209	0.183
16	0.853	0.728	0.623	0.534	0.458	0.394	0.339	0.292	0.252	0.218	0.188	0.163
17	0.844	0.714	0.605	0.513	0.436	0.371	0.317	0.270	0.231	0.198	0.170	0.146
18	0.836	0.700	0.587	0.494	0.416	0.350	0.296	0.250	0.212	0.180	0.153	0.130
19	0.828	0.686	0.570	0.475	0.396	0.331	0.277	0.232	0.194	0.164	0.138	0.116
20	0.820	0.673	0.554	0.456	0.377	0.312	0.258	0.215	0.178	0.149	0.124	0.104
25	0.780	0.610	0.478	0.375	0.295	0.233	0.184	0.146	0.116	0.092	0.074	0.059
30	0.742	0.552	0.412	0.308	0.231	0.174	0.131	0.099	0.075	0.057	0.044	0.033
40	0.672	0.453	0.307	0.208	0.142	0.097	0.067	0.046	0.032	0.022	0.015	0.011
50	0.608	0.372	0.228	0.141	0.087	0.054	0.034	0.021	0.013	0.009	0.005	0.003

EXHIBIT B–3 *(concluded)*

Period	13%	14%	15%	16%	17%	18%	19%	20%	25%	30%	35%	40%	50%
1	0.885	0.877	0.870	0.862	0.855	0.847	0.840	0.833	0.800	0.769	0.741	0.714	0.667
2	0.783	0.769	0.756	0.743	0.731	0.718	0.706	0.694	0.640	0.592	0.549	0.510	0.444
3	0.693	0.675	0.658	0.641	0.624	0.609	0.593	0.579	0.512	0.455	0.406	0.364	0.296
4	0.613	0.592	0.572	0.552	0.534	0.515	0.499	0.482	0.410	0.350	0.301	0.260	0.198
5	0.543	0.519	0.497	0.476	0.456	0.437	0.419	0.402	0.320	0.269	0.223	0.186	0.132
6	0.480	0.456	0.432	0.410	0.390	0.370	0.352	0.335	0.262	0.207	0.165	0.133	0.088
7	0.425	0.400	0.376	0.354	0.333	0.314	0.296	0.279	0.210	0.159	0.122	0.095	0.059
8	0.376	0.351	0.327	0.305	0.285	0.266	0.249	0.233	0.168	0.123	0.091	0.068	0.039
9	0.333	0.300	0.284	0.263	0.243	0.225	0.209	0.194	0.134	0.094	0.067	0.048	0.026
10	0.295	0.270	0.247	0.227	0.208	0.191	0.176	0.162	0.107	0.073	0.050	0.035	0.017
11	0.261	0.237	0.215	0.195	0.178	0.162	0.148	0.135	0.086	0.056	0.037	0.025	0.012
12	0.231	0.208	0.187	0.168	0.152	0.137	0.124	0.112	0.069	0.043	0.027	0.018	0.008
13	0.204	0.182	0.163	0.145	0.130	0.116	0.104	0.093	0.055	0.033	0.020	0.013	0.005
14	0.181	0.160	0.141	0.125	0.111	0.099	0.088	0.078	0.044	0.025	0.015	0.009	0.003
15	0.160	0.140	0.123	0.108	0.095	0.084	0.074	0.065	0.035	0.020	0.011	0.006	0.002
16	0.141	0.123	0.107	0.093	0.081	0.071	0.062	0.054	0.028	0.015	0.008	0.005	0.002
17	0.125	0.108	0.093	0.080	0.069	0.060	0.052	0.045	0.023	0.012	0.006	0.003	0.001
18	0.111	0.095	0.081	0.069	0.059	0.051	0.044	0.038	0.018	0.009	0.005	0.002	0.001
19	0.098	0.083	0.070	0.060	0.051	0.043	0.037	0.031	0.014	0.007	0.003	0.002	0
20	0.087	0.073	0.061	0.051	0.043	0.037	0.031	0.026	0.012	0.005	0.002	0.001	0
25	0.047	0.038	0.030	0.024	0.020	0.016	0.013	0.010	0.004	0.001	0.001	0	0
30	0.026	0.020	0.015	0.012	0.009	0.007	0.005	0.004	0.001	0	0	0	0
40	0.008	0.005	0.004	0.003	0.002	0.001	0.001	0.001	0	0	0	0	0
50	0.002	0.001	0.001	0.001	0	0	0	0	0	0	0	0	0

Percent

SOURCE: Maurice Joy, *Introduction to Financial Management* (Homewood, Ill.: Richard D. Irwin).

EXHIBIT B–4   Present Value of $1 Received at the End of Each Period for a Given Number of Time Periods

Period	1%	2%	3%	4%	5%	6%	7%	8%	9%	10%	11%	12%
1	0.990	0.980	0.971	0.962	0.952	0.943	0.935	0.926	0.917	0.909	0.901	0.893
2	1.970	1.942	1.913	1.886	1.859	1.833	1.808	1.783	1.759	1.736	1.713	1.690
3	2.941	2.884	2.829	2.775	2.723	2.673	2.624	2.577	2.531	2.487	2.444	2.402
4	3.902	3.808	3.717	3.630	3.546	3.465	3.387	3.312	3.240	3.170	3.102	3.037
5	4.853	4.713	4.580	4.452	4.329	4.212	4.100	3.993	3.890	3.791	3.696	3.605
6	5.795	5.601	5.417	5.242	5.076	4.917	4.767	4.623	4.486	4.355	4.231	4.111
7	6.728	6.472	6.230	6.002	5.786	5.582	5.389	5.206	5.033	4.868	4.712	4.564
8	7.652	7.325	7.020	6.733	6.463	6.210	5.971	5.747	5.535	5.335	5.146	4.968
9	8.566	8.162	7.786	7.435	7.108	6.802	6.515	6.247	5.995	5.759	5.537	5.328
10	9.471	8.983	8.530	8.111	7.722	7.360	7.024	6.710	6.418	6.145	5.889	5.650
11	10.368	9.787	9.253	8.760	8.306	7.887	7.499	7.139	6.805	6.495	6.207	5.938
12	11.255	10.575	9.954	9.385	8.863	8.384	7.943	7.536	7.161	6.814	6.492	6.194
13	12.134	11.348	10.635	9.986	9.394	8.853	8.358	7.904	7.487	7.103	6.750	6.424
14	13.004	12.106	11.296	10.563	9.899	9.295	8.745	8.244	7.786	7.367	6.982	6.628
15	13.865	12.849	11.939	11.118	10.380	9.712	9.108	8.559	8.061	7.606	7.191	6.811
16	14.718	13.578	12.561	11.652	10.838	10.106	9.447	8.851	8.313	7.824	7.379	6.974
17	15.562	14.292	13.166	12.166	11.274	10.477	9.763	9.122	8.544	8.022	7.549	7.102
18	16.398	14.992	13.754	12.659	11.690	10.828	10.059	9.372	8.756	8.201	7.702	7.250
19	17.226	15.678	14.324	13.134	12.085	11.158	10.336	9.604	8.950	8.365	7.839	7.366
20	18.046	16.351	14.877	13.590	12.462	11.470	10.594	9.818	9.129	8.514	7.963	7.469
25	22.023	19.523	17.413	15.622	14.094	12.783	11.654	10.675	9.823	9.077	8.422	7.843
30	25.808	22.396	19.600	17.292	15.372	13.765	12.409	11.258	10.274	9.427	8.694	8.055
40	32.835	27.355	23.115	19.793	17.159	15.046	13.332	11.925	10.757	9.779	8.951	8.244
50	39.196	31.424	25.730	21.482	18.256	15.762	13.801	12.233	10.962	9.915	9.042	8.304

EXHIBIT B–4   (concluded)

Percent

Period	13%	14%	15%	16%	17%	18%	19%	20%	25%	30%	35%	40%	50%
1	0.885	0.877	0.870	0.862	0.855	0.847	0.840	0.833	0.800	0.769	0.741	0.714	0.667
2	1.668	1.647	1.626	1.605	1.585	1.566	1.547	1.528	1.440	1.361	1.289	1.224	1.111
3	2.361	2.322	2.283	2.246	2.210	2.174	2.140	2.106	1.952	1.816	1.696	1.589	1.407
4	2.974	2.914	2.855	2.798	2.743	2.690	2.639	2.589	2.362	2.166	1.997	1.849	1.605
5	3.517	3.433	3.352	3.274	3.199	3.127	3.058	2.991	2.689	2.436	2.220	2.035	1.737
6	3.998	3.889	3.784	3.685	3.589	3.498	3.410	3.326	2.951	2.643	2.385	2.168	1.824
7	4.423	4.288	4.160	4.039	3.922	3.812	3.706	3.605	3.161	2.802	2.508	2.263	1.883
8	4.799	4.639	4.487	4.344	4.207	4.078	3.954	3.837	3.329	2.925	2.598	2.331	1.922
9	5.132	4.946	4.772	4.607	4.451	4.303	4.163	4.031	3.463	3.019	2.665	2.379	1.948
10	5.426	5.216	5.019	4.833	4.659	4.494	4.339	4.192	3.571	3.092	2.715	2.414	1.965
11	5.687	5.453	5.234	5.029	4.836	4.656	4.486	4.327	3.656	3.147	2.752	2.438	1.977
12	5.918	5.660	5.421	5.197	4.988	4.793	4.611	4.439	3.725	3.190	2.779	2.456	1.985
13	6.122	5.842	5.583	5.342	5.118	4.910	4.715	4.533	3.780	3.223	2.799	2.469	1.990
14	6.302	6.002	5.724	5.468	5.229	5.008	4.802	4.611	3.824	3.249	2.814	2.478	1.993
15	6.462	6.142	5.847	5.575	5.324	5.092	4.876	4.675	3.859	3.268	2.825	2.484	1.995
16	6.604	6.265	5.954	5.668	5.405	5.162	4.938	4.730	3.887	3.283	2.834	2.489	1.997
17	6.729	6.373	6.047	5.749	5.475	5.222	4.988	4.775	3.910	3.295	2.840	2.492	1.998
18	6.840	6.467	6.128	5.818	5.534	5.273	5.033	4.812	3.928	3.304	2.844	2.494	1.999
19	6.938	6.550	6.198	5.877	5.584	5.316	5.070	4.843	3.942	3.311	2.848	2.496	1.999
20	7.025	6.623	6.259	5.929	5.628	5.353	5.101	4.870	3.954	3.316	2.850	2.497	1.999
25	7.330	6.873	6.464	6.097	5.766	5.467	5.195	4.948	3.985	3.329	2.856	2.499	2.000
30	7.496	7.003	6.566	6.177	5.829	5.517	5.235	4.979	3.995	3.332	2.857	2.500	2.000
40	7.634	7.105	6.642	6.233	5.871	5.548	5.258	4.997	3.999	3.333	2.857	2.500	2.000
50	7.675	7.133	6.661	6.246	5.880	5.554	5.262	4.999	4.000	3.333	2.857	2.500	2.000

SOURCE: Maurice Joy, *Introduction to Financial Management* (Homewood, Ill.: Richard D. Irwin).

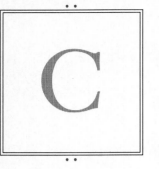

Using a Personal Computer for Personal Financial Planning

Personal computers can make handling personal financial matters easier and faster. Reduced computer costs and increased availability of programs are allowing individuals to budget, plan investments, and prepare their taxes with assistance from an automated information system.

SOURCES OF COMPUTER PURCHASING INFORMATION

Choosing a personal computer will require considering a number of factors and gathering information from various sources. The make, model, and size of the computer you choose will be influenced by the intended uses and your financial constraints. The most popular personal computers are the Apple Macintosh and the IBM PC and compatibles. A wide range of capabilities and prices exist in the marketplace.

Obtaining product and price information will help you purchase a personal computer that will serve your needs. Personal computer buying guides and magazines are available in bookstores and libraries. Among the publications that can be helpful are *Home-Office Computing, Compute!, PC Magazine, PC World,* and *PC Computing. Consumer Reports, Changing Times,* and other personal finance periodicals offer computer buying assistance. People who own and work with computers can also offer valuable insights.

The retailers that sell personal computers are another source of information. Stores that specialize in computer equipment and accessories can be found in most areas. These full-service computer stores, which may be locally owned or part of a national chain, will usually demonstrate the computers, printers, software, and other items that they sell.

Many department stores and discount stores sell computers for home and business use. These retailers may not provide the same level of expertise and service as that provided by stores specializing in computers. Advertisements in computer magazines are a helpful source of purchasing information. Mail-order businesses sell all the ingredients of personal computer systems at reasonable prices. But, of course, assistance is not available from out-of-town firms.

Local newspaper advertisements, computer periodicals, and computer stores provide information on used computers. As owners upgrade their systems, trade-ins become available to people who want a low-cost personal computer. As with used cars, be sure to "test-drive" the used computer by running the software you plan to use.

USING A SPREADSHEET FOR PERSONAL FINANCIAL PLANNING ACTIVITIES

A spreadsheet program such as *Lotus 1–2–3*, *V-P Planner*, or *Quattro* can be used to handle various financial planning tasks. With spreadsheet software, data can be stored, manipulated, used for future projections, and reported for such activities as

- Creating budget categories and recording spending patterns.
- Maintaining tax records for various types of expenses, including mileage, travel-related costs, materials and supplies, and business-related items.
- Calculating the growth of savings and investment accounts.
- Monitoring changes in the market value of investments.
- Keeping records of the value of items in a home inventory.
- Projecting needed amounts of life insurance and retirement income.

SOURCES OF PERSONAL FINANCE SOFTWARE

A variety of specialized software packages are available for various aspects of personal financial planning. Since over 2,000 microcomputer programs related to *finance* and *investing* are available, the ones mentioned here are only a sampling of those from which you can choose. The prices of such programs range from under $20 to several hundred dollars.

Budgeting and Financial Planning Programs

Some personal finance software packages are designed to maintain records on various spending categories. They may also prepare personal financial statements, write checks, and maintain your checkbook balance. More extensive financial planning programs will also maintain tax records, estimate tax payments, and analyze investments. Popular programs available in this category include

Byte Size Personal Finance, Publishing International, 333 West El Camino Real, Suite 222, Sunnyvale, CA 94087 (408-738-4311)

Dac Easy Light, DacEasy, Inc., 17950 Preston Road, Suite 800, Dallas, TX 75252 (800-887-8088)

Dollars and Sense, Monogram Software, Inc., 21821 Plummer Street, Chatsworth, CA 91311 (818-700-6200)

Financial Navigator, MoneyCare, Inc., 253 Martens Avenue, Mountain View, CA 94094 (800-824-9827 or 415-962-0333)

Managing Your Money, Meca Ventures, Inc., 355 Riverside Avenue, Westport, CT 06880 (203-222-9150)

Money Counts, Parsons Technology, 375 Collins Road, NE, Cedar Rapids, IA 52402 (800-779-6000 or 319-395-7300)

Money Matters, Great American Software, Inc., 615 Amherst Street, Nashua, NH 03060 (603-889-5400)

On Balance, Broderbund Software, Inc., 17 Paul Drive, San Rafael, CA 94903-2101 (800-527-6263 or 415-492-3200)

Quicken, Intuit, Inc., 66 Willow Place, Menlo Park, CA 94025 (800-624-8742)

Investment Programs

Personal computer programs are available to monitor and plan your investments. These software packages can provide you with data on the current value of your portfolio and on individual stocks, bonds, mutual funds, commodities, and futures. Investment software includes

Business Week Mutual Fund Scoreboard, 185 Bridge Plaza North, Suite 302, Fort Lee, NJ 07024 (800-553-3575)

Captool!, Techserve, Inc., Box 70056, Bellevue, WA 98007 (800-826-8082)

Personal Portfolio Manager, Abacus Software, 5370 52nd Street, SE, Grand Rapids, MI 49512 (800-451-4319)

Wealth Builder, Reality Technologies, 3624 Market Street, Philadelphia, PA 19104 (800-346-2024)

Tax Programs

A wide variety of software is available to plan, maintain, and prepare income tax forms. Each year, more and more taxpayers are using personal computers to prepare their tax returns and file electronically. The programs usually require annual updates to provide for changes in the tax laws. You may wish to consider the following:

Andrew Tobias' Tax Cut, Meca Ventures, 355 Riverside Avenue, Westport, CT 06880 (203-226-2400)

J. K. Lasser's Your Income Tax, Simon & Schuster, One Gulf and Western Plaza, New York, NY 10023 (212-698-7000)

Personal Tax Preparer, Parsons Technology, 375 Collins Road, NE, Cedar Rapids, IA 52402 (800-779-6000)

Rapid Tax, DacEasy, Inc., 17950 Preston Road, Suite 800, Dallas, TX 75252 (800-877-8088)

Swifttax, Timeworks, Inc., 444 Lake Cook Road, Deerfield, IL 60015 (708-948-9200 or 800-535-9497)

TurboTax, ChipSoft, Inc., 5045 Shoreham Place, San Diego, CA 92122 (800-782-1120 or 619-543-8722)

Before purchasing any software, make sure that it is compatible with your computer system. You should also obtain information regarding its functions, ease of operation, and current cost. Most important, you should make sure that the software serves your specific financial planning needs.

SUPPLEMENTARY READINGS

Antonoff, Michael. "What's New in Personal Finance Software." *Personal Computing,* January 1989, pp. 129–34.

Bryan, Marvin. "Many Happy Returns: Software That Helps You through the Tax Jungle." *Personal Computing,* March 20, 1990, pp. 103–5, 107, 109–10.

————. "Twelve for the Money." *Personal Computing,* May 25, 1990, pp. 117–19, 121–22.

Churbuck, David. "Five Portfolio Managers." *PC/Computing,* December 1989, pp. 137–41.

Cullen, Robert. "Is Check-Writing Software Useful?" *Home-Office Computing,* April 1990, pp. 34–35.

————. "Pathway to Computer Power." *Personal Investor,* March 1990, pp. 14–20.

Kleinholz, Lisa. "Which Is the Best Financial Software for You?" *Home-Office Computing,* October 1989, pp. 49–55.

Lockwood, Russ. "On-Line Finds." *Personal Computing,* December 1989, pp. 79–81, 83–84.

Maffei, Nick. "Software Shortcuts for Buying the Right Mutual Fund or Company Stock." *Home-Office Computing,* February 1990, p. 32.

Stern, Linda. "How I Organized My Tax Records with a Spreadsheet." *Home-Office Computing,* March 1990, pp. 34, 36.

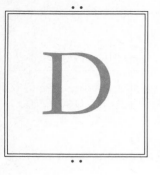

Consumer Agencies and Organizations

The following government agencies and private organizations can offer information and assistance on various financial planning and consumer purchasing areas. These groups can serve your needs when you want to

- Research a financial or consumer topic area.
- Gather information for planning a purchase decision.
- Obtain assistance to resolve a consumer problem.

Section 1 provides an overview of federal, state, and local agencies and other organizations that may be contacted for information related to various financial planning and consumer topic areas. Section 2 lists a central consumer protection office for each state that may be contacted to assist you in local matters.

SECTION 1

Topic Area	Federal Agency	State, Local Agency; Other Organizations
Advertising False advertising Product labeling Deceptive sales practices Warranties	Federal Trade Commission Sixth and Pennsylvania Avenue, NW Washington, DC 20580 (202) 523-1670	State Consumer Protection Office c/o State Attorney General or Governor's Office (see Section 2) Council of Better Business Bureaus 1515 Wilson Boulevard Arlington, VA 22209 (703) 276-0100

Topic Area	Federal Agency	State, Local Agency; Other Organizations
Air Travel Air safety Airport regulation Airline route	Federal Aviation Administration 800 Independence Avenue Washington, DC 20591 (800) FAA-SURE	International Airline Passengers Association Box 660074 Dallas, TX 75266 (800) 527-5888

Appliances/Product Safety
Potentially dangerous products
Complaints against retailers,
  manufacturers
	Consumer Product Safety
	  Commission
	Washington, DC 20207
	(800) 638-CPSC
		Major Appliance Consumer Action
		  Panel (MACAP)
		20 North Wacker Drive
		Chicago, IL 60606
		(800) 621-0477

Automobiles
New cars
Used cars
Automobile repairs
Auto safety
	Federal Trade Commission
	  (see above)
	National Highway Traffic Safety
	  Administration
	400 Seventh Street, SW
	Washington, DC 20590
	(800) 424-9393
		AUTOCAP/National Automobile
		  Dealers Association
		8400 Westpark Drive
		McLean, VA 22102
		(703) 821-7144
		Center for Auto Safety
		2001 S Street, NW
		Washington, DC 20009
		(202) 328-7700

Banking, Financial Institutions
Checking accounts
Savings accounts
Deposit insurance
Financial services
	Federal Deposit Insurance
	  Corporation
	550 17th Street, NW
	Washington, DC 20429
	(800) 424-5488
	Comptroller of the Currency
	15th St. and Pennsylvania Ave., NW
	Washington, DC 20219
	(202) 447-1600
	Federal Reserve Board
	Washington, DC 20551
	(202) 452-3946
	National Credit Union Administration
	1776 G Street, NW
	Washington, DC 20456
	(202) 682-9600
		State Banking Authority (in your state
		  capital city)
		Credit Union National Association
		Box 431
		Madison, WI 53701
		(608) 231-4000
		American Bankers Association
		1120 Connecticut Avenue, NW
		Washington, DC 20036
		(202) 663-5000
		United States League of Savings
		  Institutions
		111 East Wacker Drive
		Chicago, IL 60601
		(312) 644-3100

Career Planning Job training Employment information	Bureau of Labor Statistics Department of Labor 441 G Street, NW Washington, DC 20212 (202) 523-1913	State Department of Labor or State Employment Service

Topic Area	Federal Agency	State, Local Agency; Other Organizations
Consumer Credit Credit cards Deceptive credit advertising Truth-in-Lending Act Credit rights of women, minorities	Federal Trade Commission (see above)	Bankcard Holders of America 560 Herndon Parkway, Suite 120 Herndon, VA 22070 (703) 481-1110; (800) 638-6407 National Foundation for Consumer Credit 8701 Georgia Avenue, 507 Silver Spring, MD 20910 (301) 589-5600
Environment Air, water pollution Toxic substances	Environmental Protection Agency Washington, DC 20460 (202) 382-2080 (800) 426-4791 (drinking water safety)	Clean Water Action Project 317 Pennsylvania Avenue, SE Washington, DC 20003 (202) 547-1196
Food Food grades Food additives Nutritional information	U.S. Department of Agriculture Washington, DC 20250 (202) 382-9681 Food and Drug Administration 5600 Fishers Lane Rockville, MD 20857 (301) 443-3170	Center for Science in the Public Interest 1501 16th Street, NW Washington, DC 20036 (202) 332-9110
Funerals Cost disclosure Deceptive business practices	Federal Trade Commission (see above)	Funeral Service Consumer Arbitration Program 11121 West Oklahoma Avenue Milwaukee, WI 53227 (414) 541-2500
Housing, Real Estate Fair housing practices Mortgages Community development	Department of Housing and Urban Development 451 Seventh Street, SW Washington, DC 20410 (800) 424-8590	National Association of Realtors 430 North Michigan Avenue Chicago, IL 60611 (312) 329-8200 National Association of Home Builders 15th and M Streets, NW Washington, DC 20005 (800) 822-0409

Topic Area	Federal Agency	State, Local Agency; Other Organizations
Insurance Policy conditions Premiums Types of coverage Consumer complaints	Federal Trade Commission (see above) National Flood Insurance Program 64 Rockledge Drive Bethesda, MD 20034 (800) 638-6620	State Insurance Commissioners (in your state capital city) American Council of Life Insurance 1001 Pennsylvania Avenue, NW Washington, DC 20004 (800) 423-8000 Insurance Information Institute 110 William Street New York, NY 10038 (800) 221-4954
Investments Stocks, bonds Mutual funds Commodities Investment brokers	Securities and Exchange Commission 450 Fifth Street, NW Washington, DC 20549 (202) 272-5624 Commodity Futures Trading Commission 2033 K Street, NW Washington, DC 20581 (202) 254-8630	Investment Company Institute 1600 M Street, NW Washington, DC 20036 (202) 293-7700 National Association of Securities Dealers 1735 K Street, NW Washington, DC 20006 (202) 728-8000 National Futures Association 200 West Madison Street Chicago, IL 60606 (800) 621-3570 Securities Investor Protection Corp. 805 15th Street, NW, Suite 800 Washington, DC 20003 (202) 371-8300
Legal Matters Consumer complaints Arbitration	U.S. Office of Consumer Affairs 1009 Premier Building Washington, DC 20201 (202) 634-4140 Department of Justice Office of Consumer Litigation Washington, DC 20530 (202) 724-6786	American Arbitration Association 140 West 51st Street New York, NY 10020 (212) 484-4000 American Bar Association 750 North Lake Shore Drive Chicago, IL 60611 (312) 988-5000
Mail Order Damaged products Deceptive business practices Illegal use of U.S. mail	U.S. Postal Service Washington, DC 20260-2100 (202) 268-4267	Direct Marketing Association 6 East 43rd Street New York, NY 10017 (212) 689-4977

SECTION 1   (*concluded*)

Topic Area	Federal Agency	State, Local Agency; Other Organizations
Medical Concerns		

Prescription medications
Over-the-counter medications
Medical devices
Health care
	Food and Drug Administration
	  (see above)
	Public Health Service
	200 Independence Avenue, SW
	Washington, DC 20201
	(202) 245-7694
		American Medical Association
		535 North Dearborn
		Chicago, IL 60610
		(312) 645-5000
		Public Citizen Health Research
		  Group
		2000 P Street
		Washington, DC 20036
		(202) 872-0320

Retirement		
Old-age benefits Pension information Medicare	Social Security Administration 6401 Security Boulevard Baltimore, MD 21235 (800) 2345-SSA	American Association of Retired Persons 1909 K Street, NW Washington, DC 20049 (202) 872-4700
Taxes		
Tax information Audit procedures	Internal Revenue Service 1111 Constitution Avenue, NW Washington, DC 20204 (800) 424-1040	Department of Revenue (in your state capital city) The Tax Foundation One Thomas Circle Washington, DC 20005 (202) 822-9050
Utilities		
Cable television Utility rates	Federal Communications Commission 1919 M Street, NW Washington, DC 20554 (202) 632-7000	State Utility Commission (in your state capital city)

Information on additional government agencies and private organizations may be obtained from these publications:

- *Consumer's Resource Handbook,* U.S. Office of Consumer Affairs, Washington, DC 20201 (copies available at no charge)
- *Consumer Sourcebook,* Gale Research, Inc., Book Tower, Detroit, MI 48226 (available in many school and public libraries)

State Consumer Protection Offices

Alabama
Consumer Protection Division
Office of Attorney General
11 South Union Street
Montgomery, AL 36130
(205) 261-7334
(800) 392-5658 (toll free in Alabama)

Alaska
Consumer Protection Section
Office of Attorney General
1031 West Fourth Street
Anchorage, AK 99501
(907) 279-0428

Arizona
Consumer Fraud Division
Office of Attorney General
1275 West Washington Street
Phoenix, AZ 85007
(602) 542-3702
(800) 352-8431 (toll free in Arizona)

Arkansas
Consumer Protection Division
Office of Attorney General
200 Tower Building
Fourth and Center Streets
Little Rock, AR 72201
(501) 682-2007
(800) 482-8982 (toll free in Arkansas)

California
California Department of Consumer
  Affairs
1020 N Street
Sacramento, CA 95814
(916) 445-0660

Colorado
Consumer Protection Unit
Office of Attorney General
1525 Sherman Street, Third Floor
Denver, CO 80203
(303) 866-5167

Connecticut
Department of Consumer Protection
State Office Building
165 Capitol Avenue
Hartford, CT 06106
(203) 566-4999
(800) 842-2649 (toll free in Connecticut)

Delaware
Division of Consumer Affairs
Department of Community Affairs
820 North French St., Fourth Fl.
Wilmington, DE 19801
(302) 571-3250

District of Columbia
Department of Consumer and Regulatory
  Affairs
614 H Street, NW
Washington, DC 20001
(202) 727-7000

Florida
Department of Agriculture and Consumer
  Services
Division of Consumer Services
218 Mayo Building
Tallahassee, FL 32399
(904) 488-2226
(800) 327-3382 (toll free in Florida)

Georgia
Governor's Office of Consumer Affairs
Two M. L. King, Jr., Drive, SE
Plaza Level—East Tower
Atlanta, GA 30334
(404) 656-7000
(800) 282-5808 (toll free in Georgia)

Hawaii
Office of Consumer Protection
Department of Commerce and Consumer
  Affairs
828 Fort Street Mall
Box 3767
Honolulu, HI 96812-3767
(808) 548-2560

Idaho
Consumer Protection Unit
Office of Attorney General
Statehouse, Room 210
Boise, ID 83720
(208) 334-2424

Illinois
Consumer Protection Division
Office of Attorney General
500 South Second Street
Springfield, IL 62706
(217) 782-9011
(800) 252-8666 (toll free in Illinois)

(continued)

Indiana
Consumer Protection Division
Office of Attorney General
219 State House
Indianapolis, IN 46204
(317) 232-6330
(800) 382-5516 (toll free in Indiana)

Iowa
Consumer Protection Division
Office of Attorney General
1300 East Walnut St., Second Fl.
Des Moines, IA 50319
(515) 281-5926
(800) 358-5510

Kansas
Consumer Protection Division
Office of Attorney General
Kansas Judicial Center
Topeka, KS 66612
(913) 296-3751
(800) 432-2310 (toll free in Kansas)

Kentucky
Consumer Protection Division
Office of Attorney General
209 Saint Clair Street
Frankfort, KY 40601
(502) 562-2200
(800) 432-9257 (toll free in Kentucky)

Louisiana
Consumer Protection Section
Office of Attorney General
State Capitol Building
Box 94005
Baton Rouge, LA 70804
(504) 342-7013

Maine
Consumer and Antitrust Division
Office of Attorney General
State House Station No. 6
Augusta, ME 04333
(207) 289-3716

Maryland
Consumer Protection Division
Office of Attorney General
Seven North Calvert Street
Baltimore, MD 21202
(301) 528-8662
(800) 492-2114 (toll free in Maryland)

Massachusetts
Consumer Protection Division
Department of Attorney General
131 Tremont Street
Boston, MA 02111
(617) 727-8400

Michigan
Consumer Protection Division
Office of Attorney General
670 Law Building
Lansing, MI 48913
(517) 373-1140

Minnesota
Office of Consumer Services
Office of Attorney General
117 University Avenue
St. Paul, MN 55155
(612) 296-2331

Mississippi
Consumer Protection Division
Office of Attorney General
Box 220
Jackson, MS 39205
(601) 354-6018

Missouri
Office of Attorney General
Box 899
Jefferson City, MO 65102
(314) 751-2616
(800) 392-8222

Montana
Consumer Affairs Unit
Department of Commerce
1424 Ninth Avenue
Helena, MT 59620
(406) 444-4312

Nebraska
Consumer Protection Division
Department of Justice
2115 State Capitol
Box 98920
Lincoln, NE 68509
(402) 471-4713

(continued)

Nevada
Consumer Affairs Division
Department of Commerce
201 Nye Building
Capitol Complex
Carson City, NV 86710
(702) 885-4340

New Jersey
Division of Consumer Affairs
Department of the Public Advocate
CN 850, Justice Complex
Trenton, NJ 08625
(609) 292-7987
(800) 792-8600 (toll free in New Jersey)

New York
Consumer Protection Board
99 Washington Avenue
Albany, NY 12210
(518) 474-8583
(212) 587-4908 (New York City)

North Dakota
Office of Attorney General
600 East Boulevard
Bismarck, ND 58505
(701) 224-2210
(800) 472-2600 (toll free in North Dakota)

Oklahoma
Assistant Attorney General for Consumer
Affairs
Office of Attorney General
112 State Capitol Building
Oklahoma City, OK 73105
(405) 521-3921

Pennsylvania
Bureau of Consumer Protection
Office of Attorney General
Strawberry Square, 14th Floor
Harrisburg, PA 17120
(717) 787-9707
(800) 441-2555 (toll free in Pennsylvania)

New Hampshire
Consumer Protection and Antitrust
Division
Office of Attorney General
State House Annex
Concord, NH 03301
(603) 271-3641

New Mexico
Consumer and Economic Crime Division
Office of Attorney General
P.O. Drawer 1508
Santa Fe, NM 87504
(505) 872-6910
(800) 432-2070 (toll free in New Mexico)

North Carolina
Consumer Protection Section
Office of Attorney General
Department of Justice Building
Box 629
Raleigh, NC 27602
(919) 733-7741

Ohio
Consumer Frauds and Crimes Section
Office of Attorney General
30 East Broad Street
State Office Tower, 25th Floor
Columbus, OH 43266-0410
(614) 466-4986
(800) 282-0515 (toll free in Ohio)

Oregon
Financial Fraud Section
Department of Justice
Justice Building
Salem, OR 97310
(503) 378-4320

Puerto Rico
Department of Consumer Affairs
Minillas Station, Box 41059
Santurce, PR 00940
(809) 722-7555

(concluded)

Rhode Island
Consumer Protection Division
Department of Attorney General
72 Pine Street
Providence, RI 02903
(401) 277-2104
(800) 852-7776 (toll free in Rhode Island)

South Dakota
Division of Consumer Affairs
Office of Attorney General
State Capitol Building
Pierre, SD 57501
(605) 773-4400

Texas
Consumer Protection Division
Office of Attorney General
Capitol Station, Box 12548
Austin, TX 78711
(512) 463-2070

Vermont
Assistant Attorney General
Public Protection Division
Office of Attorney General
109 State Street
Montpelier, VT 05602
(802) 828-3171

Washington
Consumer and Business Fair Practices
  Division
Office of Attorney General
North 122 Capitol Way
Olympia, WA 98501
(206) 753-6210
(800) 551-4636 (toll free in Washington)

Wisonsin
Office of Consumer Protection and
  Citizen Advocacy
Department of Justice
Box 7856
Madison, WI 53707
(608) 266-1852
(800) 362-8189 (toll free in Wisconsin)

South Carolina
Department of Consumer Affairs
Box 5757
Columbia, SC 29250
(803) 734-9452
(800) 922-1594 (toll free in South
  Carolina)

Tennessee
Antitrust and Consumer Protection
  Division
Office of Attorney General
450 James Robertson Parkway
Nashville, TN 37219
(615) 741-2672

Utah
Division of Consumer Protection
Department of Commerce
160 East Third South, Box 45802
Salt Lake City, UT 84145
(801) 530-6601

Virginia
Antitrust and Consumer Litigation Section
Office of Attorney General
Supreme Court Building
101 North Eighth Street
Richmond, VA 23219
(804) 786-2116
(800) 451-1525 (toll free in Virginia)

West Virginia
Consumer Protection Division
Office of Attorney General
812 Quarrier Street, Sixth Floor
Charleston, WV 25301
(304) 348-8986
(800) 368-8808 (toll free in West Virginia)

Wyoming
Office of Attorney General
123 State Capitol Building
Cheyenne, WY 82002
(307) 777-7841

Notes

CHAPTER 3

1. Americans and Their Money/2: The Second National Survey from *MONEY* magazine (1984), p. 67.
2. Pamela Sebastian, "Baby Boomers Find It Hard to Save Money; Will They Do It Later?" *The Wall Street Journal,* February 13, 1989, pp. A1, A4.

CHAPTER 4

1. Jean Davidson, "Fortune's Smile Has Game Whiz Indebted," *Chicago Tribune,* December 12, 1986, sec. 2, p. 3.

CHAPTER 5

1. Andrew Tobias, "Here's How to Make Money," *Parade,* March 12, 1989, p. 4.

CHAPTER 6

1. *Facts for Consumers* (Washington, D.C.: Federal Trade Commission, Bureau of Consumer Protection, January 1988), p. 1.

CHAPTER 7

1. Adapted from *Financing Matters* (Dearborn, Mich.: Ford Motor Company, 1987), pp. 4–5.
2. *Debt Counseling,* rev. ed., AFL–CIO Publication #140, March 1981.
3. Rodolfo G. Ledesma, *How to Use Credit Wisely* (Great Barrington, Mass.: American Institute for Economic Research, April 1989), p. 3.
4. "Creditors Fume over Rise in Bankruptcies," Wheaton, Ill.: *Daily Herald,* October 13, 1989, sec. 2, p. 3.

5. *Some General Information concerning Chapter 7 of the Bankruptcy Code* (Washington, D.C.: Division of Bankruptcy, Administrative Office of the U.S. Courts, n.d.).

CHAPTER 8

1. "Overspenders Beware: That Debt Is Piling Up," *Cleveland Plain Dealer,* December 25, 1988, p. 3F.
2. Brenda J. Cude, *Shop Smart to Buy More for Less* (Urbana, Ill.: Cooperative Extension Service, University of Illinois, April 1989), pp. 3–4.
3. Ibid., p. 9.

CHAPTER 10

1. *Your Driving Costs* (Falls Church, Va.: American Automobile Association, 1989), p. 1.

CHAPTER 11

1. Adapted from William M. Pride, Robert J. Hughes, and Jack R. Kapoor, *Business,* 2nd ed. (Boston: Houghton Mifflin, 1988), pp. 538–41. © 1988 Houghton Mifflin Company.
2. *Life and Health Insurance: A Teaching Manual* (Washington, D.C.: American Council of Life Insurance, Health Insurance Association of America, 1986), p. 11/16. Copyright 1986 ACLI.

CHAPTER 12

1. Frank E. James, "Say It Isn't So: Insurance Has a Funny Side, *The Wall Steeet Journal,* July 9, 1986, p. 23.
2. "Homeowners Insurance," *Consumer Reports,* August 1985, p. 473.

CHAPTER 13

1. Joseph Pereira, "Firms Cut Drug-Treament Benefits," *The Wall Street Journal*, September 5, 1989, p. B1.
2. Labor Letter, *The Wall Street Journal*, January 30, 1990, p. 1.
3. Albert R. Karr and Mary Lu Carnevale, "Facing Off over Health-Care Benefits," *The Wall Street Journal*, August 11, 1989, p. B1.
4. Ibid.
5. Ed Bean, "Latest Survey Shows Hospital Charges Increasing Far More Quickly Than CPE," *The Wall Street Journal*, January 6, 1988, p. 19.
6. James R. Schiffman, *Health Costs* column, *The Wall Street Journal*, June 30, 1989, p. B1.
7. Sue Shellenbarger, "As HMO Premiums Soar, Employers Sour on the Plans and Check Out Alternatives," *The Wall Street Journal*, February 27, 1990, p. B1.
8. *The Blue Cross and Blue Shield Association Background Paper*, Chicago, December 1989.
9. *Insurance Handbook for Reporters*, 2nd ed. (Northbrook, Ill.: Allstate Insurance Group, 1985), p. 130.
10. *Disability Income Insurance* (Rockville, Md.: December 1988), p. 10.
11. "Paying for Long-Term Care," *U.S. News & World Report*, January 23, 1989, p. 56.
12. Esther Peterson, *Choice Time: Thinking Ahead of Long Term Care* (Hartford, Conn.: Aetna Life Insurance and Annuity Company, 1989), p. 9.
13. *U.S. Industrial Outlook, 1989* (Washington D.C.: U.S. Government Printing Office), pp. 51–54.
14. Sue Shellenbarger, "As HMO Premiums Soar, Employers Sour on the Plans and Check Out Alternatives," *The Wall Street Journal*, February 27, 1990, p. B1.
15. Andrew Leckey, "HMOs No Longer a Picture of Health," *Chicago Tribune*, May 11, 1989, sec. 3, p. 3.
16. Sue Shellenbarger, "As HMO Premiums Soar, Employers Sour on the Plans and Check Out Alternatives," *The Wall Street Journal*, February 27, 1990, p. B1.
17. *U.S. Industrial Outlook, 1989* (Washington, D.C.: U.S. Government Printing Office), pp. 51–55.
18. Ibid., pp. 51–54.
19. *James R. Schiffman, Health Costs* column, *The Wall Street Journal*, June 30, 1989, p. B1.

CHAPTER 14

1. *How Much Life Insurance Do You Need?* (Newark, N.J.: National Education Association Special Services and the Prudential Insurance Company of America, n.d.).
2. *The Wall Street Journal*, June 22, 1989, p. C1.
3. *U.S. Industrial Outlook, 1989*, pp. 48–52.

CHAPTER 15

1. Robert H. Runde, "What to Do when It's Time to Invest," *Money*, October 1982, p. 83.
2. John J. Curran, "Why Investors Misjudge the Odds," *Fortune: The 1989 Investor's Guide*, p. 85.

CHAPTER 16

1. John J. Curran, "Finding a Path between Fear and Greed," *Fortune: The 1986 Investor's Guide*, p. 10.
2. Ibid

3. Wilbur W. Widicus and Thomas E. Stitzel, *Personal Investing*, 5th ed. (Homewood, Ill.: Richard D. Irwin, 1989), p. 220.
4. Ibid. p. 200.
5. Stanley B. Block and Geoffrey A. Hirt, *Foundations of Financial Management*, 5th ed. (Homewood, Ill.: Richard D. Irwin, 1988), p. 449.
6. C. David Chase, *Chase Global Investment Almanac* (Homewood, Ill.: Chase Global Data and Research and Dow Jones-Irwin, 1989), p. 94.
7. Ibid.
8. Ibid.

CHAPTER 17

1. Geoffrey A. Hirt, and Stanley B. Block, *Fundamentals of Investment Management*, 2nd ed. (Homewood, Ill.: Richard D. Irwin, 1986), p. 274.
2. Edward Boyer, "Buying Bonds for Income, Not Safety," *Fortune: The 1986 Investor's Guide*, p. 52.
3. Sumner N. Levine, *The 1989 Dow Jones-Irwin Business and Investment Almanac* (Homewood, Ill.: Dow Jones-Irwin, 1989), p. 424.

CHAPTER 18

1. *1989 Mutual Fund Fact Book* (Washington, D.C.: Investment Company Institute, 1989), pp. 14–15.
2. John Downes and Jordan Elliot Goodman, *Dictionary of Finance and Investment Terms* (New York: Barron's, 1985), p. 192.
3. Donald D. Rugg, *New Strategies for Mutual Fund Investing* (Homewood, Ill.: Dow Jones-Irwin, 1989), p. 32.
4. This statement appeared on page 9 of the prospectus, issued on November 6, 1989, by Kemper Investors Life Insurance Company, 120 South LaSalle Street, Chicago, IL 60603.

CHAPTER 19

1. This section is based on Wilbur W. Widicus and Thomas E. Stitzel, *Personal Investing*, 5th ed. (Homewood, Ill.: Richard D. Irwin, 1989), pp. 321–23. © 1989 Richard D. Irwin, Inc.
2. Joanne Lipman, "Land and Opportunity," *The Wall Street Journal*, December 2, 1985, p. D22.
3. William M. Pride, Robert J. Hughes, and Jack R. Kapoor, *Business*, 2nd ed. (Boston: Houghton Mifflin, 1988), p. 90. © 1988 Houghton Mifflin Company.
4. Earl C. Gottschalk, Jr., "Homing In on Shared Down Payments," *The Wall Street Journal*, July 28, 1989, p. C1.
5. Michael Siconolfi, "Eagle's Success Fuels Anger of Coin Dealers," *The Wall Street Journal*, October 22, 1986, p. 31.
6. Alexandra Peers, "Bogus Brushstroke: Is It Really a Matisse, or a Forgery?" *The Wall Street Journal*, May 22, 1989, p. C1.
7. Ibid.
8. *Consumer Alert: Investing in Rare Coins* (Washington, D.C.: Federal Trade Commission, n.d.).

CHAPTER 20

1. Edwin A. Finn, Jr., "Instead of Planning for Retirement, Young Professionals Fret about It," *The Wall Street Journal*, December 9, 1985, p. 23.
2. Ibid.

3. Jeanette A. Brandt, "Housing and Community Preferences: Will They Change in Retirement?" *Family Economics Review,* U.S. Department of Agriculture, May 1989, p. 7.

4. "Retirement Planning Strategies," *Investment Vision,* March–April 1989, p. 8.

CHAPTER 21

1. Murray Iseman, "Common Estate Planning Fiascos," *Barron's,* January 2, 1989, p. 27.

2. *Don't Wait until Tomorrow* (Hartford, Conn.: Aetna Life and Casualty Company, n.d.), pp. 10–11.

3. Chris J. Prestopino, *Introduction to Estate Planning* (Homewood, Ill.: Richard D. Irwin, 1989), p. 33.

5. *Newsletter,* Wolf & Company, Certified Public Accountants, Oakbrook, Illinois, July–August 1989, p. 1.

Index

PERSONAL FINANCE ANSWERS YOUR FINANCIAL PLANNING QUESTIONS

Financial Planning (Chapter 1)

How fast can I reach my financial goals?   (pages 9–12, 22, Appendix B)

How can changing economic conditions affect personal financial planning?   (Exhibit 1–10, page 16)

What are the characteristics of clearly stated financial goals?   (pages 18–20)

What financial activities are associated with different life situations?   (Exhibit 1–12, page 19)

What are some common financial strategies for achieving financial goals?   (Exhibit 1–17, page 27)

Career Planning (Chapter 2)

What factors affect career opportunities in our society? (pages 39–41)

How do I prepare a résumé?   (pages 45–47)

What are some commonly asked interview questions? (Exhibit 2–7, page 50)

What methods can be used to compare the value of employee benefits?   (pages 52–54)

Financial Statements and Budgeting (Chapter 3)

How can I organize my personal financial records? (pages 66–69)

How do I determine my current financial position? (pages 69–73)

How can a cash flow statement assist with financial planning?   (pages 73–77)

How is a budget prepared and used?   (pages 77–85)

Tax Planning (Chapter 4)

How is a taxable income determined? (Exhibit 4–1, page 98)

How is a federal income tax return prepared? (pages 108–11)

What type of tax assistance is available? (pages 111–14)

What if my tax return is audited?   (pages 114–15)

Financial Services (Chapter 5)

How do changing interest rates affect financial service decisions?   (Exhibit 5–2, page 133)

What are the main types of financial institutions?(pages 136–38)

How can I compare savings accounts and savings plans? (pages 143–46)

How do I reconcile my checking account? (Exhibit 5–12, page 152)

Consumer Credit (Chapters 6, 7)

How much credit can I afford to use?   (pages 166–67)

Should I cosign a loan for a friend or a relative? (page 168)

What information is in a person's credit file? (page 169)

How is credit application evaluated by a lender? (Exhibit 6–7, page 176)

What federal laws exist to protect the rights of borrowers?   (Exhibit 6–9, page 181)

What is the best way to compare different credit plans? (pages 194–97)

How is the cost of credit determined? (pages 198–200)

What are some of the signs of credit overuse? (Exhibit 7–4, page 206)

Where can I seek assistance in case of credit problems? (pages 206–7)

Consumer Purchasing/Legal Protection (Chapter 8)

What are the main sources of consumer information? (pages 226–27)

What techniques can be used to get the most for your money?   (pages 231–36)

What action should a person take to solve a consumer problem?   (Exhibit 8–10, page 238)